The Poems of Jonathan Swift

The Poems of Jonathan Swift

Jonathan Swift

MINT EDITIONS

The Poems of Jonathan Swift was first published in 1726.

This edition published by Mint Editions 2020.

ISBN 9781513270289 | E-ISBN 9781513275284

Published by Mint Editions®

MINT
EDITIONS

minteditionbooks.com

Publishing Director: Jennifer Newens
Design & Production: Rachel Lopez Metzger
Project Manager: Micaela Clark
Typesetting: Westchester Publishing Services

Contents

Introduction

Dr. Johnson, in his "Life of Swift," after citing with approval Delany's character of him, as he describes him to Lord Orrery, proceeds to say: "In the poetical works there is not much upon which the critic can exercise his powers. They are often humorous, almost always light, and have the qualities which recommend such compositions, easiness and gaiety. They are, for the most part, what their author intended. The diction is correct, the numbers are smooth, and the rhymes exact. There seldom occurs a hard laboured expression or a redundant epithet; all his verses exemplify his own definition of a good style—they consist of 'proper words in proper places.'"

Of his earliest poems it is needless to say more than that if nothing better had been written by him than those Pindaric Pieces, after the manner of Cowley—then so much in vogue—the remark of Dryden, "Cousin Swift, you will never be a Poet," would have been fully justified. But conventional praise and compliments were foreign to his nature, for his strongest characteristic was his intense sincerity. He says of himself that about that time he had writ and burnt and writ again upon all manner of subjects more than perhaps any man in England; and it is certainly remarkable that in so doing his true genius was not sooner developed, for it was not till he became chaplain in Lord Berkeley's household that his satirical humour was first displayed—at least in verse—in "Mrs. Frances Harris' Petition."—His great prose satires, "The Tale of a Tub," and "Gulliver's Travels," though planned, were reserved to a later time.—In other forms of poetry he soon afterwards greatly excelled, and the title of poet cannot be refused to the author of "Baucis and Philemon"; the verses on "The Death of Dr. Swift"; the "Rhapsody on Poetry"; "Cadenus and Vanessa"; "The Legion Club"; and most of the poems addressed to Stella, all of which pieces exhibit harmony, invention, and imagination.

Swift has been unduly censured for the coarseness of his language upon Certain topics; but very little of this appears in his earlier poems, and what there is, was in accordance with the taste of the period, which never hesitated to call a spade a spade, due in part to the reaction fromthe Puritanism of the preceding age, and in part to the outspeakingfrankness which disdained hypocrisy. It is shown in Dryden, Pope, Prior, of the last of whom Johnson said that no lady objected to have his poems in her library; still more in the dramatists of that time, whom Charles Lamb has so humorously defended, and in the plays of Mrs. Aphra Behn, who, as Pope says, "fairly puts all characters to bed." But whatever coarseness there may be in some of Swift's poems, such as "The Lady's Dressing Room," and a few other pieces, there is nothing licentious, nothing which excites to lewdness; on the contrary, such pieces create simply a feeling of repulsion. No one, after reading the "Beautiful young Nymph going to bed," or "Strephon and Chloe," would desire any personal acquaintance with the ladies, but there is a moral in these pieces, and the latter poem concludes with excellent matrimonial advice. The coarseness of some of his later writings must be ascribed to his misanthropical hatred of the "animal called man," as expressed in his famous letter to Pope of September 1725, aggravated as it was by his exile from the friends he loved to a land he hated, and by the reception he met with there, about which he speaks very freely in his notes to the "Verses on his own Death."

On the morning of Swift's installation as Dean, the following scurrilous lines by Smedley, Dean of Clogher, were affixed to the doors of St. Patrick's Cathedral:

To-day this Temple gets a Dean
Of parts and fame uncommon,
Us'd both to pray and to prophane,
To serve both God and mammon.
When Wharton reign'd a Whig he was;
When Pembroke—that's dispute, Sir;
In Oxford's time, what Oxford pleased,
Non-con, or Jack, or Neuter.
This place he got by wit and rhime,
And many ways most odd,
And might a Bishop be in time,
Did he believe in God.
Look down, St. Patrick, look, we pray,
On thine own church and steeple;
Convert thy Dean on this great day,
Or else God help the people.
And now, whene'er his Deanship dies,
Upon his stone be graven,

A man of God here buried lies,
Who never thought of heaven.

It was by these lines that Smedley earned for himself a niche in "The Dunciad." For Swift's retaliation, see the poems relating to Smedley at the end of the first volume, and in volume ii, at p. 124, note.

This bitterness of spirit reached its height in "Gulliver's Travels," surely the severest of all satires upon humanity, and writ, as he tells us, not to divert, but to vex the world; and ultimately, in the fierce attack upon the Irish Parliament in the poem entitled "The Legion Club," dictated by his hatred of tyranny and oppression, and his consequent passion for exhibiting human nature in its most degraded aspect.

But, notwithstanding his misanthropical feelings towards mankind in general, and his "scorn of fools by fools mistook for pride," there never existed a warmer or sincerer friend to those whom he loved—witness the regard in which he was held by Oxford, Bolingbroke, Pope, Gay, Arbuthnot, and Congreve, and his readiness to assist those who needed his help, without thought of party or politics. Although, in some of his poems, Swift rather severely exposed the follies and frailties of the fair sex, as in "The Furniture of a Woman's Mind," and "The Journal of a Modern Lady," he loved the companionship of beautiful and accomplished women, amongst whom he could count some of his dearest and truest friends; but

He loved to be bitter at
A lady illiterate;

and therefore delighted in giving them literary instruction, most notablyin the cases of Stella and Vanessa, whose relations with him arose entirely from the tuition in letters which they received from him. Again, when on a visit at Sir Arthur Acheson's, he insisted upon making Lady Acheson read such books as he thought fit to advise, and in the doggerel verses entitled "My Lady's Lamentation," she is supposed to resent his "very imperious" manner of instruction:

No book for delight
Must come in my sight;
But instead of new plays,
Dull Bacon's Essays,

And pore every day on
That nasty Pantheon.

As a contrast to his imperiousness, there is an affectionate simplicity in the fancy names he used to bestow upon his female friends. Sir William Temple's wife, Dorothea, became Dorinda; Esther Johnson, Stella; Hester Vanhomrigh, Vanessa; Lady Winchelsea, Ardelia; while to Lady Acheson he gave the nicknames of Skinnybonia, Snipe, and Lean. But all was taken by them in good part; for his rather dictatorial ways were softened by the fascinating geniality and humour which he knew so well how to employ when he used to "deafen them with puns and rhyme."

Into the vexed question of the relations between Swift and Stella I do not purpose to enter further than to record my conviction that she was never more to him than "the dearest friend that ever man had." The suggestion of a concealed marriage is so inconsistent with their whole conduct to each other from first to last, that if there had been such a marriage, instead of Swift having been, as he was, a man of *intense sincerity*, he must be held to have been a most consummate hypocrite. In my opinion, Churton Collins settled this question in his essays on Swift, first published in the "Quarterly Review," 1881 and 1882. Swift's relation with Vanessa is the saddest episode in his life. The story is amply told in his poem, "Cadenus and Vanessa," and in the letters which passed between them: how the pupil became infatuated with her tutor; how the tutor endeavoured to dispel her passion, but in vain, by reason; and how, at last, she died from love for the man who was unable to give love in return. That Swift ought, as soon as Hester disclosed her passion for him, at once to have broken off the intimacy, must be conceded; but how many men possessed of his kindness of heart would have had the courage to have acted otherwise than he did? Swift seems, in fact, to have been constitutionally incapable of the *passion* of love, for he says, himself, that he had never met the woman he wished to marry. His annual tributes to Stella on her birthdays express the strongest regard and esteem, but he "ne'er admitted love a guest," and he had been so long used to this Platonic affection, that he had come to regard women as friends, but never as lovers. Stella, on her part, had the same feeling, for she never expressed the least discontent at her position, or ever regarded Swift otherwise than as her tutor, her counsellor, her friend. In her verses to him on his birthday, 1721, she says:

Long be the day that gave you birth
Sacred to friendship, wit, and mirth;
Late dying may you cast a shred
Of your rich mantle o'er my head;
To bear with dignity my sorrow
One day alone, then die tomorrow.

Stella naturally expected to survive Swift, but it was not to be. She died in the evening of the 28th January 1727–8; and on the same night he began the affecting piece, "On the Death of Mrs. Johnson." (See "Prose Works," vol. xi.)

With the death of Stella, Swift's real happiness ended, and he became more and more possessed by the melancholy which too often accompanies the broadest humour, and which, in his case, was constitutional. It was, no doubt, to relieve it, that he resorted to the composition of the doggerel verses, epigrams, riddles, and trifles exchanged betwixt himself and Sheridan, which induced Orrery's remark that "Swift composing Riddles is Titian painting draught-boards;" on which Delany observes that "a Riddle may be as fine painting as any other in the world. It requires as strong an imagination, as fine colouring, and as exact a proportion and keeping as any other historical painting"; and he instances "Pethox the Great," and should also have alluded to the more learned example—"Louisa to Strephon."

On Orrery's seventh Letter, Delany says that if some of the "coin is base," it is the fine impression and polish which adds value to it, and cites the saying of another nobleman, that "there is indeed some stuff in it, but it is Swift's stuff." It has been said that Swift has never taken a thought from any writer ancient or modern. This is not literally true, but the instances are not many, and in my notes I have pointed out the lines snatched from Milton, Denham, Butler—the last evidently a great favourite.

It seems necessary to state shortly the causes of Swift not having obtained higher preferment. Besides that Queen Anne would never be reconciled to the author of the "Tale of a Tub"—the true purport of which was so ill-understood by her—he made an irreconcilable enemy of her friend, the Duchess of Somerset, by his lampoon entitled "The Windsor Prophecy." But Swift seldom allowed prudence to restrain his wit and humour, and admits of himself that he "had too much satire in his vein"; and that "a genius in the reverend gown must ever keep its owner down"; and says further:

Humour and mirth had place in all he writ;
He reconciled divinity and wit.

But that was what his enemies could not do.

Whatever the excellences and defects of the poems, Swift has erected, not only by his works, but by his benevolence and his charities, a *monumentum aere perennius,* and his writings in prose and verse will continue to afford instruction and delight when the malevolence of Jeffrey, the misrepresentations of Macaulay, and the sneers and false statements of Thackeray shall have been forgotten.

Ode to Doctor William Sancroft Late Lord Bishop of Canterbury

Written in May, 1689, At the Desire of the Late Lord Bishop of Ely

I

Truth is eternal, and the Son of Heaven,
Bright effluence of th'immortal ray,
Chief cherub, and chief lamp, of that high sacred Seven,
Which guard the throne by night, and are its light by day;
First of God's darling attributes,
Thou daily seest him face to face,
Nor does thy essence fix'd depend on giddy circumstance
Of time or place,
Two foolish guides in every sublunary dance;
How shall we find Thee then in dark disputes?
How shall we search Thee in a battle gain'd,
Or a weak argument by force maintain'd?
In dagger contests, and th'artillery of words,
(For swords are madmen's tongues, and tongues are madmen's swords,)
Contrived to tire all patience out,
And not to satisfy the doubt?

II

But where is even thy Image on our earth?
For of the person much I fear,
Since Heaven will claim its residence, as well as birth,
And God himself has said, He shall not find it here.
For this inferior world is but Heaven's dusky shade,
By dark reverted rays from its reflection made;
Whence the weak shapes wild and imperfect pass,
Like sunbeams shot at too far distance from a glass;
Which all the mimic forms express,
Though in strange uncouth postures, and uncomely dress;

So when Cartesian artists try
To solve appearances of sight
In its reception to the eye,
And catch the living landscape through a scanty light,
The figures all inverted show,
And colours of a faded hue;
Here a pale shape with upward footstep treads,
And men seem walking on their heads;
There whole herds suspended lie,
Ready to tumble down into the sky;
Such are the ways ill-guided mortals go
To judge of things above by things below.
Disjointing shapes as in the fairy land of dreams,
Or images that sink in streams;
No wonder, then, we talk amiss
Of truth, and what, or where it is;
Say, Muse, for thou, if any, know'st,
Since the bright essence fled, where haunts the reverend ghost?

III

If all that our weak knowledge titles virtue, be
(High Truth) the best resemblance of exalted Thee,
If a mind fix'd to combat fate
With those two powerful swords, submission and humility,
Sounds truly good, or truly great;
Ill may I live, if the good Sancroft, in his holy rest,
In the divinity of retreat,
Be not the brightest pattern earth can show
Of heaven-born Truth below;
But foolish man still judges what is best
In his own balance, false and light,
Following opinion, dark and blind,
That vagrant leader of the mind,
Till honesty and conscience are clear out of sight.

IV

And some, to be large ciphers in a state,
Pleased with an empty swelling to be counted great,
Make their minds travel o'er infinity of space,
    Rapt through the wide expanse of thought,
    And oft in contradiction's vortex caught,
To keep that worthless clod, the body, in one place;
Errors like this did old astronomers misguide,
Led blindly on by gross philosophy and pride,
        Who, like hard masters, taught the sun
        Through many a heedless sphere to run,
Many an eccentric and unthrifty motion make,
    And thousand incoherent journeys take,
        Whilst all th'advantage by it got,
        Was but to light earth's inconsiderable spot.
The herd beneath, who see the weathercock of state
    Hung loosely on the church's pinnacle,
Believe it firm, because perhaps the day is mild and still;
But when they find it turn with the first blast of fate,
        By gazing upward giddy grow,
        And think the church itself does so;
    Thus fools, for being strong and num'rous known,
    Suppose the truth, like all the world, their own;
And holy Sancroft's motion quite irregular appears,
        Because 'tis opposite to theirs.

V

In vain then would the Muse the multitude advise,
    Whose peevish knowledge thus perversely lies
        In gath'ring follies from the wise;
    Rather put on thy anger and thy spite,
        And some kind power for once dispense
    Through the dark mass, the dawn of so much sense,
To make them understand, and feel me when I write;
    The muse and I no more revenge desire,
Each line shall stab, shall blast, like daggers and like fire;
    Ah, Britain, land of angels! which of all thy sins,

(Say, hapless isle, although
It is a bloody list we know,)
Has given thee up a dwelling-place to fiends?
Sin and the plague ever abound
In governments too easy, and too fruitful ground;
Evils which a too gentle king,
Too flourishing a spring,
And too warm summers bring:
Our British soil is over rank, and breeds
Among the noblest flowers a thousand pois'nous weeds,
And every stinking weed so lofty grows,
As if 'twould overshade the Royal Rose;
The Royal Rose, the glory of our morn,
But, ah! too much without a thorn.

VI

Forgive (original mildness) this ill-govern'd zeal,
'Tis all the angry slighted Muse can do
In the pollution of these days;
No province now is left her but to rail,
And poetry has lost the art to praise,
Alas, the occasions are so few:
None e'er but you,
And your Almighty Master, knew
With heavenly peace of mind to bear
(Free from our tyrant passions, anger, scorn, or fear)
The giddy turns of popular rage,
And all the contradictions of a poison'd age;
The Son of God pronounced by the same breath
Which straight pronounced his death;
And though I should but ill be understood,
In wholly equalling our sin and theirs,
And measuring by the scanty thread of wit
What we call holy, and great, and just, and good,
(Methods in talk whereof our pride and ignorance make use,)
And which our wild ambition foolishly compares
With endless and with infinite;
Yet pardon, native Albion, when I say,

Among thy stubborn sons there haunts that spirit of the Jews,
That those forsaken wretches who to-day
Revile his great ambassador,
Seem to discover what they would have done
(Were his humanity on earth once more)
To his undoubted Master, Heaven's Almighty Son.

VII

But zeal is weak and ignorant, though wondrous proud,
Though very turbulent and very loud;
The crazy composition shows,
Like that fantastic medley in the idol's toes,
Made up of iron mixt with clay,
This crumbles into dust,
That moulders into rust,
Or melts by the first shower away.
Nothing is fix'd that mortals see or know,
Unless, perhaps, some stars above be so;
And those, alas, do show,
Like all transcendent excellence below;
In both, false mediums cheat our sight,
And far exalted objects lessen by their height:
Thus primitive Sancroft moves too high
To be observed by vulgar eye,
And rolls the silent year
On his own secret regular sphere,
And sheds, though all unseen, his sacred influence here.

VIII

Kind star, still may'st thou shed thy sacred influence here,
Or from thy private peaceful orb appear;
For, sure, we want some guide from Heaven, to show
The way which every wand'ring fool below
Pretends so perfectly to know;
And which, for aught I see, and much I fear,
The world has wholly miss'd;
I mean the way which leads to Christ:

Mistaken idiots! see how giddily they run,
Led blindly on by avarice and pride,
What mighty numbers follow them;
Each fond of erring with his guide:
Some whom ambition drives, seek Heaven's high Son
In Caesar's court, or in Jerusalem:
Others, ignorantly wise,
Among proud doctors and disputing Pharisees:
What could the sages gain but unbelieving scorn;
Their faith was so uncourtly, when they said
That Heaven's high Son was in a village born;
That the world's Saviour had been
In a vile manger laid,
And foster'd in a wretched inn?

IX

Necessity, thou tyrant conscience of the great,
Say, why the church is still led blindfold by the state;
Why should the first be ruin'd and laid waste,
To mend dilapidations in the last?
And yet the world, whose eyes are on our mighty Prince,
Thinks Heaven has cancell'd all our sins,
And that his subjects share his happy influence;
Follow the model close, for so I'm sure they should,
But wicked kings draw more examples than the good:
And divine Sancroft, weary with the weight
Of a declining church, by faction, her worst foe, oppress'd,
Finding the mitre almost grown
A load as heavy as the crown,
Wisely retreated to his heavenly rest.

X

Ah! may no unkind earthquake of the state,
Nor hurricano from the crown,
Disturb the present mitre, as that fearful storm of late,
Which, in its dusky march along the plain,
Swept up whole churches as it list,

Wrapp'd in a whirlwind and a mist;
Like that prophetic tempest in the virgin reign,
And swallow'd them at last, or flung them down.
Such were the storms good Sancroft long has borne;
The mitre, which his sacred head has worn,
Was, like his Master's Crown, inwreath'd with thorn.
Death's sting is swallow'd up in victory at last,
The bitter cup is from him past:
Fortune in both extremes
Though blasts from contrariety of winds,
Yet to firm heavenly minds,
Is but one thing under two different names;
And even the sharpest eye that has the prospect seen,
Confesses ignorance to judge between;
And must to human reasoning opposite conclude,
To point out which is moderation, which is fortitude.

XI

Thus Sancroft, in the exaltation of retreat,
Shows lustre that was shaded in his seat;
Short glimm'rings of the prelate glorified;
Which the disguise of greatness only served to hide.
Why should the Sun, alas! be proud
To lodge behind a golden cloud?
Though fringed with evening gold the cloud appears so gay,
'Tis but a low-born vapour kindled by a ray:
At length 'tis overblown and past,
Puff'd by the people's spiteful blast,
The dazzling glory dims their prostituted sight,
No deflower'd eye can face the naked light:
Yet does this high perfection well proceed
From strength of its own native seed,
This wilderness, the world, like that poetic wood of old,
Bears one, and but one branch of gold,
Where the bless'd spirit lodges like the dove,
And which (to heavenly soil transplanted) will improve,
To be, as 'twas below, the brightest plant above;
For, whate'er theologic levellers dream,

There are degrees above, I know,
As well as here below,
(The goddess Muse herself has told me so),
Where high patrician souls, dress'd heavenly gay,
Sit clad in lawn of purer woven day.
There some high-spirited throne to Sancroft shall be given,
In the metropolis of Heaven;
Chief of the mitred saints, and from archprelate here,
Translated to archangel there.

XII

Since, happy saint, since it has been of late
Either our blindness or our fate,
To lose the providence of thy cares
Pity a miserable church's tears,
That begs the powerful blessing of thy prayers.
Some angel, say, what were the nation's crimes,
That sent these wild reformers to our times:
Say what their senseless malice meant,
To tear religion's lovely face:
Strip her of every ornament and grace;
In striving to wash off th'imaginary paint?
Religion now does on her death-bed lie,
Heart-sick of a high fever and consuming atrophy;
How the physicians swarm to show their mortal skill,
And by their college arts methodically kill:
Reformers and physicians differ but in name,
One end in both, and the design the same;
Cordials are in their talk, while all they mean
Is but the patient's death, and gain—
Check in thy satire, angry Muse,
Or a more worthy subject choose:
Let not the outcasts of an outcast age
Provoke the honour of my Muse's rage,
Nor be thy mighty spirit rais'd,
Since Heaven and Cato both are pleas'd—

(The rest of the poem is lost.)

Ode to the Hon. Sir William Temple

Written at Moor-Park in June 1689

I

Virtue, the greatest of all monarchies!
Till its first emperor, rebellious man,
Deposed from off his seat,
It fell, and broke with its own weight
Into small states and principalities,
By many a petty lord possess'd,
But ne'er since seated in one single breast.
'Tis you who must this land subdue,
The mighty conquest's left for you,
The conquest and discovery too:
Search out this Utopian ground,
Virtue's Terra Incognita,
Where none ever led the way,
Nor ever since but in descriptions found;
Like the philosopher's stone,
With rules to search it, yet obtain'd by none.

II

We have too long been led astray;
Too long have our misguided souls been taught
With rules from musty morals brought,
'Tis you must put us in the way;
Let us (for shame!) no more be fed
With antique relics of the dead,
The gleanings of philosophy;
Philosophy, the lumber of the schools,
The roguery of alchymy;
And we, the bubbled fools,
Spend all our present life, in hopes of golden rules.

III

But what does our proud ignorance Learning call?
We oddly Plato's paradox make good,
Our knowledge is but mere remembrance all;
Remembrance is our treasure and our food;
Nature's fair table-book, our tender souls,
We scrawl all o'er with old and empty rules,
Stale memorandums of the schools:
For learning's mighty treasures look
Into that deep grave, a book;
Think that she there does all her treasures hide,
And that her troubled ghost still haunts there since she died;
Confine her walks to colleges and schools;
Her priests, her train, and followers, show
As if they all were spectres too!
They purchase knowledge at th'expense
Of common breeding, common sense,
And grow at once scholars and fools;
Affect ill-manner'd pedantry,
Rudeness, ill-nature, incivility,
And, sick with dregs and knowledge grown,
Which greedily they swallow down,
Still cast it up, and nauseate company.

IV

Curst be the wretch! nay, doubly curst!
(If it may lawful be
To curse our greatest enemy,)
Who learn'd himself that heresy first,
(Which since has seized on all the rest,)
That knowledge forfeits all humanity;
Taught us, like Spaniards, to be proud and poor,
And fling our scraps before our door!
Thrice happy you have 'scaped this general pest;
Those mighty epithets, learned, good, and great,
Which we ne'er join'd before, but in romances meet,
We find in you at last united grown.

You cannot be compared to one:
I must, like him that painted Venus' face,
Borrow from every one a grace;
Virgil and Epicurus will not do,
Their courting a retreat like you,
Unless I put in Caesar's learning too:
Your happy frame at once controls
This great triumvirate of souls.

V

Let not old Rome boast Fabius' fate;
He sav'd his country by delays,
But you by peace.
You bought it at a cheaper rate;
Nor has it left the usual bloody scar,
To show it cost its price in war;
War, that mad game the world so loves to play,
And for it does so dearly pay;
For, though with loss, or victory, a while
Fortune the gamesters does beguile,
Yet at the last the box sweeps all away.

VI

Only the laurel got by peace
No thunder e'er can blast:
Th'artillery of the skies
Shoots to the earth and dies:
And ever green and flourishing 'twill last,
Nor dipt in blood, nor widows' tears, nor orphans' cries.
About the head crown'd with these bays,
Like lambent fire, the lightning plays;
Nor, its triumphal cavalcade to grace,
Makes up its solemn train with death;
It melts the sword of war, yet keeps it in the sheath.

VII

The wily shafts of state, those jugglers' tricks,
Which we call deep designs and politics,
(As in a theatre the ignorant fry,
Because the cords escape their eye,
Wonder to see the motions fly,)
Methinks, when you expose the scene,
Down the ill-organ'd engines fall;
Off fly the vizards, and discover all:
How plain I see through the deceit!
How shallow, and how gross, the cheat!
Look where the pulley's tied above!
Great God! (said I) what have I seen!
On what poor engines move
The thoughts of monarchs and designs of states!
What petty motives rule their fates!
How the mouse makes the mighty mountains shake!
The mighty mountain labours with its birth,
Away the frighten'd peasants fly,
Scared at the unheard-of prodigy,
Expect some great gigantic son of earth;
Lo! it appears!
See how they tremble! how they quake!
Out starts the little beast, and mocks their idle fears.

VIII

Then tell, dear favourite Muse!
What serpent's that which still resorts,
Still lurks in palaces and courts?
Take thy unwonted flight,
And on the terrace light.
See where she lies!
See how she rears her head,
And rolls about her dreadful eyes,
To drive all virtue out, or look it dead!
'Twas sure this basilisk sent Temple thence,
And though as some ('tis said) for their defence

Have worn a casement o'er their skin,
So wore he his within,
Made up of virtue and transparent innocence;
And though he oft renew'd the fight,
And almost got priority of sight,
He ne'er could overcome her quite,
In pieces cut, the viper still did reunite;
Till, at last, tired with loss of time and ease,
Resolved to give himself, as well as country, peace.

IX

Sing, beloved Muse! the pleasures of retreat,
And in some untouch'd virgin strain,
Show the delights thy sister Nature yields;
Sing of thy vales, sing of thy woods, sing of thy fields;
Go, publish o'er the plain
How mighty a proselyte you gain!
How noble a reprisal on the great!
How is the Muse luxuriant grown!
Whene'er she takes this flight,
She soars clear out of sight.
These are the paradises of her own:
Thy Pegasus, like an unruly horse,
Though ne'er so gently led,
To the loved pastures where he used to feed,
Runs violent o'er his usual course.
Wake from thy wanton dreams,
Come from thy dear-loved streams,
The crooked paths of wandering Thames.
Fain the fair nymph would stay,
Oft she looks back in vain,
Oft 'gainst her fountain does complain,
And softly steals in many windings down,
As loth to see the hated court and town;
And murmurs as she glides away.

X

In this new happy scene
Are nobler subjects for your learned pen;
Here we expect from you
More than your predecessor Adam knew;
Whatever moves our wonder, or our sport,
Whatever serves for innocent emblems of the court;
How that which we a kernel see,
(Whose well-compacted forms escape the light,
Unpierced by the blunt rays of sight,)
Shall ere long grow into a tree;
Whence takes it its increase, and whence its birth,
Or from the sun, or from the air, or from the earth,
Where all the fruitful atoms lie;
How some go downward to the root,
Some more ambitious upwards fly,
And form the leaves, the branches, and the fruit.
You strove to cultivate a barren court in vain,
Your garden's better worth your nobler pain,
Here mankind fell, and hence must rise again.

XI

Shall I believe a spirit so divine
Was cast in the same mould with mine?
Why then does Nature so unjustly share
Among her elder sons the whole estate,
And all her jewels and her plate?
Poor we! cadets of Heaven, not worth her care,
Take up at best with lumber and the leavings of a fare:
Some she binds 'prentice to the spade,
Some to the drudgery of a trade:
Some she does to Egyptian bondage draw,
Bids us make bricks, yet sends us to look out for straw:
Some she condemns for life to try
To dig the leaden mines of deep philosophy:
Me she has to the Muse's galleys tied:
In vain I strive to cross the spacious main,

In vain I tug and pull the oar;
And when I almost reach the shore,
Straight the Muse turns the helm, and I launch out again:
And yet, to feed my pride,
Whene'er I mourn, stops my complaining breath,
With promise of a mad reversion after death.

XII

Then, Sir, accept this worthless verse,
The tribute of an humble Muse,
'Tis all the portion of my niggard stars;
Nature the hidden spark did at my birth infuse,
And kindled first with indolence and ease;
And since too oft debauch'd by praise,
'Tis now grown an incurable disease:
In vain to quench this foolish fire I try
In wisdom and philosophy:
In vain all wholesome herbs I sow,
Where nought but weeds will grow
Whate'er I plant (like corn on barren earth)
By an equivocal birth,
Seeds, and runs up to poetry.

Ode to King William

On his Successes in Ireland

To purchase kingdoms and to buy renown,
    Are arts peculiar to dissembling France;
You, mighty monarch, nobler actions crown,
    And solid virtue does your name advance.

Your matchless courage with your prudence joins,
    The glorious structure of your fame to raise;
With its own light your dazzling glory shines,
    And into adoration turns our praise.

Had you by dull succession gain'd your crown,
    (Cowards are monarchs by that title made,)
Part of your merit Chance would call her own,
    And half your virtues had been lost in shade.

But now your worth its just reward shall have:
    What trophies and what triumphs are your due!
Who could so well a dying nation save,
    At once deserve a crown, and gain it too.

You saw how near we were to ruin brought,
    You saw th'impetuous torrent rolling on;
And timely on the coming danger thought,
    Which we could neither obviate nor shun.

Britannia stripp'd of her sole guard, the laws,
    Ready to fall Rome's bloody sacrifice;
You straight stepp'd in, and from the monster's jaws
    Did bravely snatch the lovely, helpless prize.

Nor this is all; as glorious is the care
    To preserve conquests, as at first to gain:
In this your virtue claims a double share,
    Which, what it bravely won, does well maintain.

Your arm has now your rightful title show'd,
    An arm on which all Europe's hopes depend,
To which they look as to some guardian God,
    That must their doubtful liberty defend.

Amazed, thy action at the Boyne we see!
    When Schomberg started at the vast design:
The boundless glory all redounds to thee,
    The impulse, the fight, th'event, were wholly thine.

The brave attempt does all our foes disarm;
    You need but now give orders and command,
Your name shall the remaining work perform,
    And spare the labour of your conquering hand.

France does in vain her feeble arts apply,
    To interrupt the fortune of your course:
Your influence does the vain attacks defy
    Of secret malice, or of open force.

Boldly we hence the brave commencement date
    Of glorious deeds, that must all tongues employ;
William's the pledge and earnest given by fate,
    Of England's glory, and her lasting joy.

Ode to the Athenian Society

Moor Park, Feb. 14, 1691

I

As when the deluge first began to fall,
    That mighty ebb never to flow again,
When this huge body's moisture was so great,
    It quite o'ercame the vital heat;
That mountain which was highest, first of all
Appear'd above the universal main,
To bless the primitive sailor's weary sight;
And 'twas perhaps Parnassus, if in height
    It be as great as 'tis in fame,
    And nigh to Heaven as is its name;
So, after the inundation of a war,
When learning's little household did embark,
With her world's fruitful system, in her sacred ark,
    At the first ebb of noise and fears,
Philosophy's exalted head appears;
And the Dove-Muse will now no longer stay,
But plumes her silver wings, and flies away;
    And now a laurel wreath she brings from far,
    To crown the happy conqueror,
    To show the flood begins to cease,
And brings the dear reward of victory and peace.

II

The eager Muse took wing upon the waves' decline,
    When war her cloudy aspect just withdrew,
    When the bright sun of peace began to shine,
And for a while in heavenly contemplation sat,
    On the high top of peaceful Ararat;
And pluck'd a laurel branch, (for laurel was the first that grew,
The first of plants after the thunder, storm and rain,)
    And thence, with joyful, nimble wing,

Flew dutifully back again,
And made an humble chaplet for the king.
And the Dove-Muse is fled once more,
(Glad of the victory, yet frighten'd at the war,)
And now discovers from afar
A peaceful and a flourishing shore:
No sooner did she land
On the delightful strand,
Than straight she sees the country all around,
Where fatal Neptune ruled erewhile,
Scatter'd with flowery vales, with fruitful gardens crown'd,
And many a pleasant wood;
As if the universal Nile
Had rather water'd it than drown'd:
It seems some floating piece of Paradise,
Preserved by wonder from the flood,
Long wandering through the deep, as we are told
Famed Delos did of old;
And the transported Muse imagined it
To be a fitter birth-place for the God of wit,
Or the much-talk'd-of oracular grove;
When, with amazing joy, she hears
An unknown music all around,
Charming her greedy ears
With many a heavenly song
Of nature and of art, of deep philosophy and love;
While angels tune the voice, and God inspires the tongue.
In vain she catches at the empty sound,
In vain pursues the music with her longing eye,
And courts the wanton echoes as they fly.

III

Pardon, ye great unknown, and far-exalted men,
The wild excursions of a youthful pen;
Forgive a young and (almost) virgin Muse,
Whom blind and eager curiosity
(Yet curiosity, they say,
Is in her sex a crime needs no excuse)

Has forced to grope her uncouth way,
After a mighty light that leads her wandering eye:
No wonder then she quits the narrow path of sense
For a dear ramble through impertinence;
Impertinence! the scurvy of mankind.
And all we fools, who are the greater part of it,
Though we be of two different factions still,
Both the good-natured and the ill,
Yet wheresoe'er you look, you'll always find
We join, like flies and wasps, in buzzing about wit.
In me, who am of the first sect of these,
All merit, that transcends the humble rules
Of my own dazzled scanty sense,
Begets a kinder folly and impertinence
Of admiration and of praise.
And our good brethren of the surly sect,
Must e'en all herd us with their kindred fools:
For though possess'd of present vogue, they've made
Railing a rule of wit, and obloquy a trade;
Yet the same want of brains produces each effect.
And you, whom Pluto's helm does wisely shroud
From us, the blind and thoughtless crowd,
Like the famed hero in his mother's cloud,
Who both our follies and impertinences see,
Do laugh perhaps at theirs, and pity mine and me.

IV

But censure's to be understood
Th'authentic mark of the elect,
The public stamp Heaven sets on all that's great and good,
Our shallow search and judgment to direct.
The war, methinks, has made
Our wit and learning narrow as our trade;
Instead of boldly sailing far, to buy
A stock of wisdom and philosophy,
We fondly stay at home, in fear
Of every censuring privateer;
Forcing a wretched trade by beating down the sale,

And selling basely by retail.
The wits, I mean the atheists of the age,
Who fain would rule the pulpit, as they do the stage,
Wondrous refiners of philosophy,
Of morals and divinity,
By the new modish system of reducing all to sense,
Against all logic, and concluding laws,
Do own th'effects of Providence,
And yet deny the cause.

V

This hopeful sect, now it begins to see
How little, very little, do prevail
Their first and chiefest force
To censure, to cry down, and rail,
Not knowing what, or where, or who you be,
Will quickly take another course:
And, by their never-failing ways
Of solving all appearances they please,
We soon shall see them to their ancient methods fall,
And straight deny you to be men, or anything at all.
I laugh at the grave answer they will make,
Which they have always ready, general, and cheap:
'Tis but to say, that what we daily meet,
And by a fond mistake
Perhaps imagine to be wondrous wit,
And think, alas! to be by mortals writ,
Is but a crowd of atoms justling in a heap:
Which, from eternal seeds begun,
Justling some thousand years, till ripen'd by the sun:
They're now, just now, as naturally born,
As from the womb of earth a field of corn.

VI

But as for poor contented me,
Who must my weakness and my ignorance confess,
That I believe in much I ne'er can hope to see;

Methinks I'm satisfied to guess,
That this new, noble, and delightful scene,
Is wonderfully moved by some exalted men,
Who have well studied in the world's disease,
(That epidemic error and depravity,
Or in our judgment or our eye,)
That what surprises us can only please.
We often search contentedly the whole world round,
To make some great discovery,
And scorn it when 'tis found.
Just so the mighty Nile has suffer'd in its fame,
Because 'tis said (and perhaps only said)
We've found a little inconsiderable head,
That feeds the huge unequal stream.
Consider human folly, and you'll quickly own,
That all the praises it can give,
By which some fondly boast they shall for ever live,
Won't pay th'impertinence of being known:
Else why should the famed Lydian king,
(Whom all the charms of an usurped wife and state,
With all that power unfelt, courts mankind to be great,
Did with new unexperienced glories wait,)
Still wear, still dote on his invisible ring?

VII

Were I to form a regular thought of Fame,
Which is, perhaps, as hard t'imagine right,
As to paint Echo to the sight,
I would not draw the idea from an empty name;
Because, alas! when we all die,
Careless and ignorant posterity,
Although they praise the learning and the wit,
And though the title seems to show
The name and man by whom the book was writ,
Yet how shall they be brought to know,
Whether that very name was he, or you, or I?
Less should I daub it o'er with transitory praise,
And water-colours of these days:

These days! where e'en th'extravagance of poetry
Is at a loss for figures to express
Men's folly, whimseys, and inconstancy,
And by a faint description makes them less.
Then tell us what is Fame, where shall we search for it?
Look where exalted Virtue and Religion sit,
Enthroned with heavenly Wit!
Look where you see
The greatest scorn of learned vanity!
(And then how much a nothing is mankind!
Whose reason is weigh'd down by popular air,
Who, by that, vainly talks of baffling death;
And hopes to lengthen life by a transfusion of breath,
Which yet whoe'er examines right will find
To be an art as vain as bottling up of wind!)
And when you find out these, believe true Fame is there,
Far above all reward, yet to which all is due:
And this, ye great unknown! is only known in you.

VIII

The juggling sea-god, when by chance trepann'd
By some instructed querist sleeping on the sand,
Impatient of all answers, straight became
A stealing brook, and strove to creep away
Into his native sea,
Vex'd at their follies, murmur'd in his stream;
But disappointed of his fond desire,
Would vanish in a pyramid of fire.
This surly, slippery God, when he design'd
To furnish his escapes,
Ne'er borrow'd more variety of shapes
Than you, to please and satisfy mankind,
And seem (almost) transform'd to water, flame, and air,
So well you answer all phenomena there:
Though madmen and the wits, philosophers and fools,
With all that factious or enthusiastic dotards dream,
And all the incoherent jargon of the schools;
Though all the fumes of fear, hope, love, and shame,

Contrive to shock your minds with many a senseless doubt;
Doubts where the Delphic God would grope in ignorance and
night,
The God of learning and of light
Would want a God himself to help him out.

IX

Philosophy, as it before us lies,
Seems to have borrow'd some ungrateful taste
Of doubts, impertinence, and niceties,
From every age through which it pass'd,
But always with a stronger relish of the last.
This beauteous queen, by Heaven design'd
To be the great original
For man to dress and polish his uncourtly mind,
In what mock habits have they put her since the fall!
More oft in fools' and madmen's hands than sages',
She seems a medley of all ages,
With a huge farthingale to swell her fustian stuff,
A new commode, a topknot, and a ruff,
Her face patch'd o'er with modern pedantry,
With a long sweeping train
Of comments and disputes, ridiculous and vain,
All of old cut with a new dye:
How soon have you restored her charms,
And rid her of her lumber and her books,
Drest her again genteel and neat,
And rather tight than great!
How fond we are to court her to our arms!
How much of heaven is in her naked looks!

X

Thus the deluding Muse oft blinds me to her ways,
And ev'n my very thoughts transfers
And changes all to beauty and the praise
Of that proud tyrant sex of hers.
The rebel Muse, alas! takes part,

But with my own rebellious heart,
And you with fatal and immortal wit conspire
To fan th'unhappy fire.
Cruel unknown! what is it you intend?
Ah! could you, could you hope a poet for your friend!
Rather forgive what my first transport said:
May all the blood, which shall by woman's scorn be shed,
Lie upon you and on your children's head!
For you (ah! did I think I e'er should live to see
The fatal time when that could be!)
Have even increased their pride and cruelty.
Woman seems now above all vanity grown,
Still boasting of her great unknown
Platonic champions, gain'd without one female wile,
Or the vast charges of a smile;
Which 'tis a shame to see how much of late
You've taught the covetous wretches to o'errate,
And which they've now the consciences to weigh
In the same balance with our tears,
And with such scanty wages pay
The bondage and the slavery of years.
Let the vain sex dream on; the empire comes from us;
And had they common generosity,
They would not use us thus.
Well—though you've raised her to this high degree,
Ourselves are raised as well as she;
And, spite of all that they or you can do,
'Tis pride and happiness enough to me,
Still to be of the same exalted sex with you.

XI

Alas, how fleeting and how vain
Is even the nobler man, our learning and our wit!
I sigh whene'er I think of it:
As at the closing an unhappy scene
Of some great king and conqueror's death,
When the sad melancholy Muse
Stays but to catch his utmost breath.

I grieve, this nobler work, most happily begun,
So quickly and so wonderfully carried on,
May fall at last to interest, folly, and abuse.
There is a noontide in our lives,
Which still the sooner it arrives,
Although we boast our winter sun looks bright,
And foolishly are glad to see it at its height,
Yet so much sooner comes the long and gloomy night.
No conquest ever yet begun,
And by one mighty hero carried to its height,
E'er flourished under a successor or a son;
It lost some mighty pieces through all hands it pass'd,
And vanish'd to an empty title in the last.
For, when the animating mind is fled,
(Which nature never can retain,
Nor e'er call back again,)
The body, though gigantic, lies all cold and dead.

XII

And thus undoubtedly 'twill fare
With what unhappy men shall dare
To be successors to these great unknown,
On learning's high-establish'd throne.
Censure, and Pedantry, and Pride,
Numberless nations, stretching far and wide,
Shall (I foresee it) soon with Gothic swarms come forth
From Ignorance's universal North,
And with blind rage break all this peaceful government:
Yet shall the traces of your wit remain,
Like a just map, to tell the vast extent
Of conquest in your short and happy reign:
And to all future mankind shew
How strange a paradox is true,
That men who lived and died without a name
Are the chief heroes in the sacred lists of fame.

To Mr. Congreve

Written in November, 1693

Thrice, with a prophet's voice, and prophet's power,
    The Muse was called in a poetic hour,
And insolently thrice the slighted maid
Dared to suspend her unregarded aid;
Then with that grief we form in spirits divine,
Pleads for her own neglect, and thus reproaches mine.
    Once highly honoured! false is the pretence
You make to truth, retreat, and innocence!
Who, to pollute my shades, bring'st with thee down
The most ungenerous vices of the town;
Ne'er sprung a youth from out this isle before
I once esteem'd, and loved, and favour'd more,
Nor ever maid endured such courtlike scorn,
So much in mode, so very city-born;
'Tis with a foul design the Muse you send,
Like a cast mistress, to your wicked friend;
But find some new address, some fresh deceit,
Nor practise such an antiquated cheat;
These are the beaten methods of the stews,
Stale forms, of course, all mean deceivers use,
Who barbarously think to 'scape reproach,
By prostituting her they first debauch.
    Thus did the Muse severe unkindly blame
This offering long design'd to Congreve's fame;
First chid the zeal as unpoetic fire,
Which soon his merit forced her to inspire;
Then call this verse, that speaks her largest aid,
The greatest compliment she ever made,
And wisely judge, no power beneath divine
Could leap the bounds which part your world and mine;
For, youth, believe, to you unseen, is fix'd
A mighty gulf, unpassable betwixt.
    Nor tax the goddess of a mean design
To praise your parts by publishing of mine;

That be my thought when some large bulky writ
Shows in the front the ambition of my wit;
There to surmount what bears me up, and sing
Like the victorious wren perch'd on the eagle's wing.
This could I do, and proudly o'er him tower,
Were my desires but heighten'd to my power.
    Godlike the force of my young Congreve's bays,
Softening the Muse's thunder into praise;
Sent to assist an old unvanquish'd pride
That looks with scorn on half mankind beside;
A pride that well suspends poor mortals' fate,
Gets between them and my resentment's weight,
Stands in the gap 'twixt me and wretched men,
T'avert th'impending judgments of my pen.
    Thus I look down with mercy on the age,
By hopes my Congreve will reform the stage:
For never did poetic mind before
Produce a richer vein, or cleaner ore;
The bullion stamp'd in your refining mind
Serves by retail to furnish half mankind.
With indignation I behold your wit
Forced on me, crack'd, and clipp'd, and counterfeit,
By vile pretenders, who a stock maintain
From broken scraps and filings of your brain.
Through native dross your share is hardly known,
And by short views mistook for all their own;
So small the gains those from your wit do reap,
Who blend it into folly's larger heap,
Like the sun's scatter'd beams which loosely pass,
When some rough hand breaks the assembling glass.
    Yet want your critics no just cause to rail,
Since knaves are ne'er obliged for what they steal.
These pad on wit's high road, and suits maintain
With those they rob, by what their trade does gain.
Thus censure seems that fiery froth which breeds
O'er the sun's face, and from his heat proceeds,
Crusts o'er the day, shadowing its partent beam,
As ancient nature's modern masters dream;
This bids some curious praters here below

Call Titan sick, because their sight is so;
And well, methinks, does this allusion fit
To scribblers, and the god of light and wit;
Those who by wild delusions entertain
A lust of rhyming for a poet's vein,
Raise envy's clouds to leave themselves in night,
But can no more obscure my Congreve's light,
Than swarms of gnats, that wanton in a ray
Which gave them birth, can rob the world of day.
    What northern hive pour'd out these foes to wit?
Whence came these Goths to overrun the pit?
How would you blush the shameful birth to hear
Of those you so ignobly stoop to fear;
For, ill to them, long have I travell'd since,
Round all the circles of impertinence,
Search'd in the nest where every worm did lie
Before it grew a city butterfly;
I'm sure I found them other kind of things
Than those with backs of silk and golden wings;
A search, no doubt, as curious and as wise
As virtuosoes' in dissecting flies:
For, could you think? the fiercest foes you dread,
And court in prologues, all are country bred;
Bred in my scene, and for the poet's sins
Adjourn'd from tops and grammar to the inns;
Those beds of dung, where schoolboys sprout up beaux
Far sooner than the nobler mushroom grows:
These are the lords of the poetic schools,
Who preach the saucy pedantry of rules;
Those powers the critics, who may boast the odds
O'er Nile, with all its wilderness of gods;
Nor could the nations kneel to viler shapes,
Which worshipp'd cats, and sacrificed to apes;
And can you think the wise forbear to laugh
At the warm zeal that breeds this golden calf?
    Haply you judge these lines severely writ
Against the proud usurpers of the pit;
Stay while I tell my story, short, and true;
To draw conclusions shall be left to you;

Nor need I ramble far to force a rule,
But lay the scene just here at Farnham school.
Last year, a lad hence by his parents sent
With other cattle to the city went;
Where having cast his coat, and well pursued
The methods most in fashion to be lewd,
Return'd a finish'd spark this summer down,
Stock'd with the freshest gibberish of the town;
A jargon form'd from the lost language, wit,
Confounded in that Babel of the pit;
Form'd by diseased conceptions, weak and wild,
Sick lust of souls, and an abortive child;
Born between whores and fops, by lewd compacts,
Before the play, or else between the acts;
Nor wonder, if from such polluted minds
Should spring such short and transitory kinds,
Or crazy rules to make us wits by rote,
Last just as long as every cuckoo's note:
What bungling, rusty tools are used by fate!
'Twas in an evil hour to urge my hate,
My hate, whose lash just Heaven has long decreed
Shall on a day make sin and folly bleed:
When man's ill genius to my presence sent
This wretch, to rouse my wrath, for ruin meant;
Who in his idiom vile, with Gray's-Inn grace,
Squander'd his noisy talents to my face;
Named every player on his fingers' ends,
Swore all the wits were his peculiar friends;
Talk'd with that saucy and familiar ease
Of Wycherly, and you, and Mr. Bayes:
Said, how a late report your friends had vex'd,
Who heard you meant to write heroics next;
For, tragedy, he knew, would lose you quite,
And told you so at Will's but t'other night.
Thus are the lives of fools a sort of dreams,
Rendering shades things, and substances of names;
Such high companions may delusion keep,
Lords are a footboy's cronies in his sleep.
As a fresh miss, by fancy, face, and gown,

Render'd the topping beauty of the town,
Draws every rhyming, prating, dressing sot,
To boast of favours that he never got;
Of which, whoe'er lacks confidence to prate,
Brings his good parts and breeding in debate;
And not the meanest coxcomb you can find,
But thanks his stars, that Phillis has been kind;
Thus prostitute my Congreve's name is grown
To every lewd pretender of the town.
Troth, I could pity you; but this is it,
You find, to be the fashionable wit;
These are the slaves whom reputation chains,
Whose maintenance requires no help from brains.
For, should the vilest scribbler to the pit,
Whom sin and want e'er furnish'd out a wit;
Whose name must not within my lines be shown,
Lest here it live, when perish'd with his own;
Should such a wretch usurp my Congreve's place,
And choose out wits who ne'er have seen his face;
I'll bet my life but the dull cheat would pass,
Nor need the lion's skin conceal the ass;
Yes, that beau's look, that vice, those critic ears,
Must needs be right, so well resembling theirs.
    Perish the Muse's hour thus vainly spent
In satire, to my Congreve's praises meant;
In how ill season her resentments rule,
What's that to her if mankind be a fool?
Happy beyond a private Muse's fate,
In pleasing all that's good among the great,
Where though her elder sisters crowding throng,
She still is welcome with her innocent song;
Whom were my Congreve blest to see and know,
What poor regards would merit all below!
How proudly would he haste the joy to meet,
And drop his laurel at Apollo's feet!
    Here by a mountain's side, a reverend cave
Gives murmuring passage to a lasting wave:
'Tis the world's watery hour-glass streaming fast,
Time is no more when th'utmost drop is past;

Here, on a better day, some druid dwelt,
And the young Muse's early favour felt;
Druid, a name she does with pride repeat,
Confessing Albion once her darling seat;
Far in this primitive cell might we pursue
Our predecessors' footsteps still in view;
Here would we sing—But, ah! you think I dream,
And the bad world may well believe the same;
Yes: you are all malicious slanders by,
While two fond lovers prate, the Muse and I.
    Since thus I wander from my first intent,
Nor am that grave adviser which I meant,
Take this short lesson from the god of bays,
And let my friend apply it as he please:
Beat not the dirty paths where vulgar feet have trod,
            But give the vigorous fancy room.
    For when, like stupid alchymists, you try
            To fix this nimble god,
                This volatile mercury,
    The subtile spirit all flies up in fume;
    Nor shall the bubbled virtuoso find
More than *fade* insipid mixture left behind.
    While thus I write, vast shoals of critics come,
And on my verse pronounce their saucy doom;
The Muse like some bright country virgin shows
Fallen by mishap among a knot of beaux;
They, in their lewd and fashionable prate,
Rally her dress, her language, and her gait;
Spend their base coin before the bashful maid,
Current like copper, and as often paid:
She, who on shady banks has joy'd to sleep
Near better animals, her father's sheep,
Shamed and amazed, beholds the chattering throng,
To think what cattle she is got among;
But with the odious smell and sight annoy'd,
In haste she does th'offensive herd avoid.
    'Tis time to bid my friend a long farewell,
The muse retreats far in yon crystal cell;
Faint inspiration sickens as she flies,

Like distant echo spent, the spirit dies.
    In this descending sheet you'll haply find
Some short refreshment for your weary mind,
Nought it contains is common or unclean,
And once drawn up, is ne'er let down again.

Occasioned by Sir William Temple's late illness and recovery

Written in December, 1693

Strange to conceive, how the same objects strike
At distant hours the mind with forms so like!
Whether in time, Deduction's broken chain
Meets, and salutes her sister link again;
Or haunted Fancy, by a circling flight,
Comes back with joy to its own seat at night;
Or whether dead Imagination's ghost
Oft hovers where alive it haunted most;
Or if Thought's rolling globe, her circle run,
Turns up old objects to the soul her sun;
Or loves the Muse to walk with conscious pride
O'er the glad scene whence first she rose a bride:
Be what it will; late near yon whispering stream,
Where her own Temple was her darling theme;
There first the visionary sound was heard,
When to poetic view the Muse appear'd.
Such seem'd her eyes, as when an evening ray
Gives glad farewell to a tempestuous day;
Weak is the beam to dry up Nature's tears,
Still every tree the pendent sorrow wears;
Such are the smiles where drops of crystal show
Approaching joy at strife with parting woe.
As when, to scare th'ungrateful or the proud,
Tempests long frown, and thunder threatens loud,
Till the blest sun, to give kind dawn of grace,
Darts weeping beams across Heaven's watery face;
When soon the peaceful bow unstring'd is shown,
A sign God's dart is shot, and wrath o'erblown:
Such to unhallow'd sight the Muse divine
Might seem, when first she raised her eyes to mine.
What mortal change does in thy face appear,
Lost youth, she cried, since first I met thee here!
With how undecent clouds are overcast

Thy looks, when every cause of grief is past!
Unworthy the glad tidings which I bring,
Listen while the Muse thus teaches thee to sing:
As parent earth, burst by imprison'd winds,
Scatters strange agues o'er men's sickly minds,
And shakes the atheist's knees; such ghastly fear
Late I beheld on every face appear;
Mild Dorothea, peaceful, wise, and great,
Trembling beheld the doubtful hand of fate;
Mild Dorothea, whom we both have long
Not dared to injure with our lowly song;
Sprung from a better world, and chosen then
The best companion for the best of men:
As some fair pile, yet spared by zeal and rage,
Lives pious witness of a better age;
So men may see what once was womankind,
In the fair shrine of Dorothea's mind.
You that would grief describe, come here and trace
Its watery footsteps in Dorinda's face:
Grief from Dorinda's face does ne'er depart
Farther than its own palace in her heart:
Ah, since our fears are fled, this insolent expel,
At least confine the tyrant to his cell.
And if so black the cloud that Heaven's bright queen
Shrouds her still beams; how should the stars be seen?
Thus when Dorinda wept, joy every face forsook,
And grief flung sables on each menial look;
The humble tribe mourn'd for the quick'ning soul,
That furnish'd spirit and motion through the whole;
So would earth's face turn pale, and life decay,
Should Heaven suspend to act but for a day;
So nature's crazed convulsions make us dread
That time is sick, or the world's mind is dead.—
Take, youth, these thoughts, large matter to employ
The fancy furnish'd by returning joy;
And to mistaken man these truths rehearse,
Who dare revile the integrity of verse:
Ah, favourite youth, how happy is thy lot!—
But I'm deceived, or thou regard'st me not;

Speak, for I wait thy answer, and expect
Thy just submission for this bold neglect.
    Unknown the forms we the high-priesthood use
At the divine appearance of the Muse,
Which to divulge might shake profane belief,
And tell the irreligion of my grief;
Grief that excused the tribute of my knees,
And shaped my passion in such words as these!
    Malignant goddess! bane to my repose,
Thou universal cause of all my woes;
Say whence it comes that thou art grown of late
A poor amusement for my scorn and hate;
The malice thou inspirest I never fail
On thee to wreak the tribute when I rail;
Fool's commonplace thou art, their weak ensconcing fort,
Th'appeal of dulness in the last resort:
Heaven, with a parent's eye regarding earth,
Deals out to man the planet of his birth:
But sees thy meteor blaze about me shine,
And passing o'er, mistakes thee still for mine:
Ah, should I tell a secret yet unknown,
That thou ne'er hadst a being of thy own,
But a wild form dependent on the brain,
Scattering loose features o'er the optic vein;
Troubling the crystal fountain of the sight,
Which darts on poets' eyes a trembling light;
Kindled while reason sleeps, but quickly flies,
Like antic shapes in dreams, from waking eyes:
In sum, a glitt'ring voice, a painted name,
A walking vapour, like thy sister fame.
But if thou be'st what thy mad votaries prate,
A female power, loose govern'd thoughts create;
Why near the dregs of youth perversely wilt thou stay,
So highly courted by the brisk and gay?
Wert thou right woman, thou should'st scorn to look
On an abandon'd wretch by hopes forsook;
Forsook by hopes, ill fortune's last relief,
Assign'd for life to unremitting grief;
For, let Heaven's wrath enlarge these weary days,

If hope e'er dawns the smallest of its rays.
Time o'er the happy takes so swift a flight,
And treads so soft, so easy, and so light,
That we the wretched, creeping far behind,
Can scarce th'impression of his footsteps find;
Smooth as that airy nymph so subtly born
With inoffensive feet o'er standing corn;
Which bow'd by evening breeze with bending stalks,
Salutes the weary traveller as he walks;
But o'er the afflicted with a heavy pace
Sweeps the broad scythe, and tramples on his face.
Down falls the summer's pride, and sadly shows
Nature's bare visage furrow'd as he mows:
See, Muse, what havoc in these looks appear,
These are the tyrant's trophies of a year;
Since hope his last and greatest foe is fled,
Despair and he lodge ever in its stead;
March o'er the ruin'd plain with motion slow,
Still scattering desolation where they go.
To thee I owe that fatal bent of mind,
Still to unhappy restless thoughts inclined;
To thee, what oft I vainly strive to hide,
That scorn of fools, by fools mistook for pride;
From thee whatever virtue takes its rise,
Grows a misfortune, or becomes a vice;
Such were thy rules to be poetically great:
"Stoop not to interest, flattery, or deceit;
Nor with hired thoughts be thy devotion paid;
Learn to disdain their mercenary aid;
Be this thy sure defence, thy brazen wall,
Know no base action, at no guilt turn pale;
And since unhappy distance thus denies
T'expose thy soul, clad in this poor disguise;
Since thy few ill-presented graces seem
To breed contempt where thou hast hoped esteem—"
Madness like this no fancy ever seized,
Still to be cheated, never to be pleased;
Since one false beam of joy in sickly minds
Is all the poor content delusion finds.—

There thy enchantment broke, and from this hour
I here renounce thy visionary power;
And since thy essence on my breath depends
Thus with a puff the whole delusion ends.

Written in a Lady's Ivory Table-Book, 1698

Peruse my leaves thro' ev'ry part,
And think thou seest my owner's heart,
Scrawl'd o'er with trifles thus, and quite
As hard, as senseless, and as light;
Expos'd to ev'ry coxcomb's eyes,
But hid with caution from the wise.
Here you may read, "Dear charming saint;"
Beneath, "A new receipt for paint:"
Here, in beau-spelling, "Tru tel deth;"
There, in her own, "For an el breth:"
Here, "Lovely nymph, pronounce my doom!"
There, "A safe way to use perfume:"
Here, a page fill'd with billets-doux;
On t'other side, "Laid out for shoes"—
"Madam, I die without your grace"—
"Item, for half a yard of lace."
Who that had wit would place it here,
For ev'ry peeping fop to jeer?
To think that your brains' issue is
Exposed to th'excrement of his,
In pow'r of spittle and a clout,
Whene'er he please, to blot it out;
And then, to heighten the disgrace,
Clap his own nonsense in the place.
Whoe'er expects to hold his part
In such a book, and such a heart,
If he be wealthy, and a fool,
Is in all points the fittest tool;
Of whom it may be justly said,
He's a gold pencil tipp'd with lead.

Mrs. Frances Harris's Petition, 1699

This, the most humorous example of vers de société *in the English language, well illustrates the position of a parson in a family of distinction at that period.*

—W. E. B.

To their Excellencies the Lords Justices of Ireland,
The humble petition of Frances Harris,
Who must starve and die a maid if it miscarries;
Humbly sheweth, that I went to warm myself in Lady Betty's chamber, because I was cold;
And I had in a purse seven pounds, four shillings, and sixpence, (besides farthings) in money and gold;
So because I had been buying things for my lady last night,
I was resolved to tell my money, to see if it was right.
Now, you must know, because my trunk has a very bad lock,
Therefore all the money I have, which, God knows, is a very small stock,
I keep in my pocket, ty'd about my middle, next my smock.
So when I went to put up my purse, as God would have it, my smock was unript,
And instead of putting it into my pocket, down it slipt;
Then the bell rung, and I went down to put my lady to bed;
And, God knows, I thought my money was as safe as my maidenhead.
So, when I came up again, I found my pocket feel very light;
But when I search'd, and miss'd my purse, Lord! I thought I should have sunk outright.
"Lord! madam," says Mary, "how d'ye do?"—"Indeed," says I, "never worse:
But pray, Mary, can you tell what I have done with my purse?"
"Lord help me!" says Mary, "I never stirr'd out of this place!"
"Nay," said I, "I had it in Lady Betty's chamber, that's a plain case."
So Mary got me to bed, and cover'd me up warm:
However, she stole away my garters, that I might do myself no harm.
So I tumbled and toss'd all night, as you may very well think,

But hardly ever set my eyes together, or slept a wink.
So I was a-dream'd, methought, that I went and search'd the folks round,
And in a corner of Mrs. Duke's box, ty'd in a rag, the money was found.
So next morning we told Whittle, and he fell a swearing:
Then my dame Wadgar came, and she, you know, is thick of hearing.
"Dame," said I, as loud as I could bawl, "do you know what a loss I have had?"
"Nay," says she, "my Lord Colway's folks are all very sad:
For my Lord Dromedary comes a Tuesday without fail."
"Pugh!" said I, "but that's not the business that I ail."
Says Cary, says he, "I have been a servant this five and twenty years come spring,
And in all the places I lived I never heard of such a thing."
"Yes," says the steward, "I remember when I was at my Lord Shrewsbury's,
Such a thing as this happen'd, just about the time of *gooseberries*."
So I went to the party suspected, and I found her full of grief:
(Now, you must know, of all things in the world I hate a thief:)
However, I was resolved to bring the discourse slily about:
"Mrs. Duke," said I, "here's an ugly accident has happened out:
'Tis not that I value the money three skips of a louse:
But the thing I stand upon is the credit of the house.
'Tis true, seven pounds, four shillings, and sixpence makes a great hole in my wages:
Besides, as they say, service is no inheritance in these ages.
Now, Mrs. Duke, you know, and everybody understands,
That though 'tis hard to judge, yet money can't go without hands."
"The *devil* take me!" said she, (blessing herself,) "if ever I saw't!"
So she roar'd like a bedlam, as thof I had call'd her all to naught.
So, you know, what could I say to her any more?
I e'en left her, and came away as wise as I was before.
Well; but then they would have had me gone to the cunning man:
"No," said I, "'tis the same thing, the CHAPLAIN will be here anon."
So the Chaplain came in. Now the servants say he is my sweetheart,
Because he's always in my chamber, and I always take his part.

So, as the *devil* would have it, before I was aware, out I blunder'd,
"*Parson*" said I, "can you cast a *nativity*, when a body's plunder'd?"
(Now you must know, he hates to be called *Parson*, like the *devil!*)
"Truly," says he, "Mrs. Nab, it might become you to be more civil;
If your money be gone, as a learned *Divine* says, d'ye see,
You are no *text* for my handling; so take that from me:
I was never taken for a *Conjurer* before, I'd have you to know."
"Lord!" said I, "don't be angry, I am sure I never thought you so;
You know I honour the cloth; I design to be a Parson's wife;
I never took one in *your coat* for a conjurer in all my life."
With that he twisted his girdle at me like a rope, as who should say,
"Now you may go hang yourself for me!" and so went away.
Well: I thought I should have swoon'd. "Lord!" said I, "what shall I do?
I have lost my money, and shall lose my true love too!"
Then my lord call'd me: "Harry," said my lord, "don't cry;
I'll give you something toward thy loss." "And," says my lady, "so will I."
Oh! but, said I, what if, after all, the Chaplain won't come to?
For that, he said (an't please your Excellencies), I must petition you.
The premisses tenderly consider'd, I desire your Excellencies' protection,
And that I may have a share in next Sunday's collection;
And, over and above, that I may have your Excellencies' letter,
With an order for the Chaplain aforesaid, or, instead of him, a better:
And then your poor petitioner, both night and day,
Or the Chaplain (for 'tis his *trade*,) as in duty bound, shall ever *pray*.

A Ballad on the game of Traffic

Written at the Castle of Dublin, 1699

My Lord, to find out who must deal,
Delivers cards about,
But the first knave does seldom fail
To find the doctor out.

But then his honour cried, Gadzooks!
And seem'd to knit his brow:
For on a knave he never looks
But he thinks upon Jack How.

My lady, though she is no player,
Some bungling partner takes,
And, wedged in corner of a chair,
Takes snuff, and holds the stakes.

Dame Floyd looks out in grave suspense
For pair royals and sequents;
But, wisely cautious of her pence,
The castle seldom frequents.

Quoth Herries, fairly putting cases,
I'd won it, on my word,
If I had but a pair of aces,
And could pick up a third.

But Weston has a new-cast gown
On Sundays to be fine in,
And, if she can but win a crown,
'Twill just new dye the lining.

"With these is Parson Swift,
Not knowing how to spend his time,
Does make a wretched shift,
To deafen them with puns and rhyme."

A Ballad to the tune of the Cut-purse

Written in August, 1702

I

Once on a time, as old stories rehearse,
A friar would need show his talent in Latin;
But was sorely put to 't in the midst of a verse,
Because he could find no word to come pat in;
Then all in the place
He left a void space,
And so went to bed in a desperate case:
When behold the next morning a wonderful riddle!
He found it was strangely fill'd up in the middle.
Cho. Let censuring critics then think what they list on't;
Who would not write verses with such an assistant?

II

This put me the friar into an amazement;
For he wisely consider'd it must be a sprite;
That he came through the keyhole, or in at the casement;
And it needs must be one that could both read and write;
Yet he did not know,
If it were friend or foe,
Or whether it came from above or below;
Howe'er, it was civil, in angel or elf,
For he ne'er could have fill'd it so well of himself.
Cho. Let censuring, &c.

III

Even so Master Doctor had puzzled his brains
In making a ballad, but was at a stand;
He had mixt little wit with a great deal of pains,
When he found a new help from invisible hand.
Then, good Doctor Swift

Pay thanks for the gift,
For you freely must own you were at a dead lift;
And, though some malicious young spirit did do't,
You may know by the hand it had no cloven foot.
Cho. Let censuring, &c.

The Discovery

When wise Lord Berkeley first came here,
Statesmen and mob expected wonders,
Nor thought to find so great a peer
Ere a week past committing blunders.
Till on a day cut out by fate,
When folks came thick to make their court,
Out slipt a mystery of state
To give the town and country sport.
Now enters Bush with new state airs,
His lordship's premier minister;
And who in all profound affairs,
Is held as needful as his clyster.
With head reclining on his shoulder,
He deals and hears mysterious chat,
While every ignorant beholder
Asks of his neighbour, who is that?
With this he put up to my lord,
The courtiers kept their distance due,
He twitch'd his sleeve, and stole a word;
Then to a corner both withdrew.
Imagine now my lord and Bush
Whispering in junto most profound,
Like good King Phys and good King Ush,
While all the rest stood gaping round.
At length a spark, not too well bred,
Of forward face and ear acute,
Advanced on tiptoe, lean'd his head,
To overhear the grand dispute;
To learn what Northern kings design,
Or from Whitehall some new express,
Papists disarm'd, or fall of coin;
For sure (thought he) it can't be less.
My lord, said Bush, a friend and I,
Disguised in two old threadbare coats,
Ere morning's dawn, stole out to spy
How markets went for hay and oats.

With that he draws two handfuls out,
    The one was oats, the other hay;
Puts this to's excellency's snout,
    And begs he would the other weigh.
My lord seems pleased, but still directs
    By all means to bring down the rates;
Then, with a congee circumflex,
    Bush, smiling round on all, retreats.
Our listener stood awhile confused,
    But gathering spirits, wisely ran for't,
Enraged to see the world abused,
    By two such whispering kings of Brentford.

The Problem

"That my Lord Berkeley Stinks when he is in Love"

Did ever problem thus perplex,
Or more employ the female sex?
So sweet a passion who would think,
Jove ever form'd to make a stink?
The ladies vow and swear, they'll try,
Whether it be a truth or lie.
Love's fire, it seems, like inward heat,
Works in my lord by stool and sweat,
Which brings a stink from every pore,
And from behind and from before;
Yet what is wonderful to tell it,
None but the favourite nymph can smell it.
But now, to solve the natural cause
By sober philosophic laws;
Whether all passions, when in ferment,
Work out as anger does in vermin;
So, when a weasel you torment,
You find his passion by his scent.
We read of kings, who, in a fright,
Though on a throne, would fall to sh—.
Beside all this, deep scholars know,
That the main string of Cupid's bow,
Once on a time was an a—gut;
Now to a nobler office put,
By favour or desert preferr'd
From giving passage to a t—;
But still, though fix'd among the stars,
Does sympathize with human a—.
Thus, when you feel a hard-bound breech,
Conclude love's bow-string at full stretch,
Till the kind looseness comes, and then,
Conclude the bow relax'd again.
    And now, the ladies all are bent,
To try the great experiment,

Ambitious of a regent's heart,
Spread all their charms to catch a f—
Watching the first unsavoury wind,
Some ply before, and some behind.
My lord, on fire amid the dames,
F—ts like a laurel in the flames.
The fair approach the speaking part,
To try the back-way to his heart.
For, as when we a gun discharge,
Although the bore be none so large,
Before the flame from muzzle burst,
Just at the breech it flashes first;
So from my lord his passion broke,
He f—d first and then he spoke.
The ladies vanish in the smother,
To confer notes with one another;
And now they all agreed to name
Whom each one thought the happy dame.
Quoth Neal, whate'er the rest may think,
I'm sure 'twas I that smelt the stink.
You smell the stink! by G—d, you lie,
Quoth Ross, for I'll be sworn 'twas I.
Ladies, quoth Levens, pray forbear;
Let's not fall out; we all had share;
And, by the most I can discover,
My lord's a universal lover.

The Description of a Salamander, 1705

From Pliny, "Hist. Nat.," lib. x, 67; lib. xxix.

As mastiff dogs, in modern phrase, are
Call'd *Pompey, Scipio*, and *Caesar;*
As pies and daws are often styl'd
With Christian nicknames, like a child;
As we say *Monsieur* to an ape,
Without offence to human shape;
So men have got, from bird and brute,
Names that would best their nature suit.
The *Lion, Eagle, Fox*, and *Boar*,
Were heroes' titles heretofore,
Bestow'd as hi'roglyphics fit
To show their valour, strength, or wit:
For what is understood by *fame*,
Besides the getting of a *name?*
But, e'er since men invented guns,
A diff'rent way their fancy runs:
To paint a hero, we inquire
For something that will conquer *fire.*
Would you describe *Turenne* or *Trump?*
Think of a *bucket* or a *pump.*
Are these too low?—then find out grander,
Call my Lord Cutts a *Salamander.*
'Tis well;—but since we live among
Detractors with an evil tongue,
Who may object against the term,
Pliny shall prove what we affirm:
Pliny shall prove, and we'll apply,
And I'll be judg'd by standers by.
First, then, our author has defined
This reptile of the serpent kind,
With gaudy coat, and shining train;
But loathsome spots his body stain:
Out from some hole obscure he flies,
When rains descend, and tempests rise,

Till the sun clears the air; and then
Crawls back neglected to his den.
    So, when the war has raised a storm,
I've seen a snake in human form,
All stain'd with infamy and vice,
Leap from the dunghill in a trice,
Burnish and make a gaudy show,
Become a general, peer, and beau,
Till peace has made the sky serene,
Then shrink into its hole again.
"All this we grant—why then, look yonder,
Sure that must be a Salamander!"
    Further, we are by Pliny told,
This serpent is extremely cold;
So cold, that, put it in the fire,
'Twill make the very flames expire:
Besides, it spues a filthy froth
(Whether thro' rage or lust or both)
Of matter purulent and white,
Which, happening on the skin to light,
And there corrupting to a wound,
Spreads leprosy and baldness round.
    So have I seen a batter'd beau,
By age and claps grown cold as snow,
Whose breath or touch, where'er he came,
Blew out love's torch, or chill'd the flame:
And should some nymph, who ne'er was cruel,
Like Carleton cheap, or famed Du-Ruel,
Receive the filth which he ejects,
She soon would find the same effects
Her tainted carcass to pursue,
As from the Salamander's spue;
A dismal shedding of her locks,
And, if no leprosy, a pox.
"Then I'll appeal to each bystander,
If this be not a Salamander?"

To Charles Mordaunt, Earl of Peterborough

Mordanto fills the trump of fame,
The Christian world his deeds proclaim,
And prints are crowded with his name.

In journeys he outrides the post,
Sits up till midnight with his host,
Talks politics, and gives the toast.

Knows every prince in Europe's face,
Flies like a squib from place to place,
And travels not, but runs a race.

From Paris gazette à-la-main,
This day arriv'd, without his train,
Mordanto in a week from Spain.

A messenger comes all a-reek
Mordanto at Madrid to seek;
He left the town above a week.

Next day the post-boy winds his horn,
And rides through Dover in the morn:
Mordanto's landed from Leghorn.

Mordanto gallops on alone,
The roads are with his followers strewn,
This breaks a girth, and that a bone;

His body active as his mind,
Returning sound in limb and wind,
Except some leather lost behind.

A skeleton in outward figure,
His meagre corps, though full of vigour,
Would halt behind him, were it bigger.

So wonderful his expedition,
When you have not the least suspicion,
He's with you like an apparition.

Shines in all climates like a star;
In senates bold, and fierce in war;
A land commander, and a tar:

Heroic actions early bred in,
Ne'er to be match'd in modern reading,
But by his namesake, Charles of Sweden.

On the Union

The queen has lately lost a part
Of her Entirely-English heart,
For want of which, by way of botch,
She pieced it up again with Scotch.
Blest revolution! which creates
Divided hearts, united states!
See how the double nation lies,
Like a rich coat with skirts of frize:
As if a man, in making posies,
Should bundle thistles up with roses.
Who ever yet a union saw
Of kingdoms without faith or law?
Henceforward let no statesman dare
A kingdom to a ship compare;
Lest he should call our commonweal
A vessel with a double keel:
Which, just like ours, new rigg'd and mann'd,
And got about a league from land,
By change of wind to leeward side,
The pilot knew not how to guide.
So tossing faction will o'erwhelm
Our crazy double-bottom'd realm.

On Mrs. Biddy Floyd

Or, the Receipt to Form a Beauty. 1707

When Cupid did his grandsire Jove entreat
To form some Beauty by a new receipt, Jove sent, and found, far in
a country scene,
Truth, innocence, good nature, look serene:
From which ingredients first the dext'rous boy
Pick'd the demure, the awkward, and the coy.
The Graces from the court did next provide
Breeding, and wit, and air, and decent pride:
These Venus cleans'd from ev'ry spurious grain
Of nice coquet, affected, pert, and vain.
Jove mix'd up all, and the best clay employ'd;
Then call'd the happy composition Floyd.

The Reverse

(To Swift's verses on Biddy Floyd); or, Mrs. Cludd

Venus one day, as story goes,
But for what reason no man knows,
In sullen mood and grave deport,
Trudged it away to Jove's high court;
And there his Godship did entreat
To look out for his best receipt:
And make a monster strange and odd,
Abhorr'd by man and every god.
Jove, ever kind to all the fair,
Nor e'er refused a lady's prayer,
Straight oped 'scrutoire, and forth he took
A neatly bound and well-gilt book;
Sure sign that nothing enter'd there,
But what was very choice and rare.
Scarce had he turn'd a page or two,—
It might be more, for aught I knew;
But, be the matter more or less,
'Mong friends 'twill break no squares, I guess.
Then, smiling, to the dame quoth he,
Here's one will fit you to a T.
But, as the writing doth prescribe,
'Tis fit the ingredients we provide.
Away he went, and search'd the stews,
And every street about the Mews;
Diseases, impudence, and lies,
Are found and brought him in a trice.
From Hackney then he did provide,
A clumsy air and awkward pride;
From lady's toilet next he brought
Noise, scandal, and malicious thought.
These Jove put in an old close-stool,
And with them mix'd the vain, the fool.
    But now came on his greatest care,
Of what he should his paste prepare;

For common clay or finer mould
Was much too good, such stuff to hold.
At last he wisely thought on mud;
So raised it up, and call'd it—*Cludd.*
With this, the lady well content,
Low curtsey'd, and away she went.

Apollo Outwitted

To the Honourable Mrs. Finch, under her Name of Ardelia

Phoebus, now short'ning every shade,
    Up to the northern *tropic* came,
And thence beheld a lovely maid,
    Attending on a royal dame.

The god laid down his feeble rays,
    Then lighted from his glitt'ring coach;
But fenc'd his head with his own bays,
    Before he durst the nymph approach.

Under those sacred leaves, secure
    From common lightning of the skies,
He fondly thought he might endure
    The flashes of Ardelia's eyes.

The nymph, who oft had read in books
    Of that bright god whom bards invoke,
Soon knew Apollo by his looks,
    And guess'd his business ere he spoke.

He, in the old celestial cant,
    Confess'd his flame, and swore by Styx,
Whate'er she would desire, to grant—
    But wise Ardelia knew his tricks.

Ovid had warn'd her to beware
    Of strolling gods, whose usual trade is,
Under pretence of taking air,
    To pick up sublunary ladies.

Howe'er, she gave no flat denial,
    As having malice in her heart;
And was resolv'd upon a trial,
    To cheat the god in his own art.

"Hear my request," the virgin said;
    "Let which I please of all the Nine
Attend, whene'er I want their aid,
    Obey my call, and only mine."

By vow oblig'd, by passion led,
    The god could not refuse her prayer:
He way'd his wreath thrice o'er her head,
    Thrice mutter'd something to the air.

And now he thought to seize his due;
    But she the charm already try'd:
Thalia heard the call, and flew
    To wait at bright Ardelia's side.

On sight of this celestial *prude*,
    Apollo thought it vain to stay;
Nor in her presence durst be rude,
    But made his leg and went away.

He hop'd to find some lucky hour,
    When on their queen the Muses wait;
But Pallas owns Ardelia's power:
    For vows divine are kept by Fate.

Then, full of rage, Apollo spoke:
    "Deceitful nymph! I see thy art;
And, though I can't my gift revoke,
    I'll disappoint its nobler part.

"Let stubborn pride possess thee long,
    And be thou negligent of fame;
With ev'ry Muse to grace thy song,
    May'st thou despise a poet's name!

"Of modest poets be thou first;
    To silent shades repeat thy verse,
Till Fame and Echo almost burst,
    Yet hardly dare one line rehearse.

"And last, my vengeance to compleat,
    May you descend to take renown,
Prevail'd on by the thing you hate,
    A Whig! and one that wears a gown!"

Answer to Lines from May Fair

Now First Published

I

In pity to the empty'ng Town,
Some God May Fair invented,
When Nature would invite us down,
To be by Art prevented.

II

What a corrupted taste is ours
When milk maids in mock state
Instead of garlands made of Flowers
Adorn their pails with plate.

III

So are the joys which Nature yields
Inverted in May Fair,
In painted cloth we look for fields,
And step in Booths for air.

IV

Here a Dog dancing on his hams
And puppets mov'd by wire,
Do far exceed your frisking lambs,
Or song of feather'd quire.

V

Howe'er, such verse as yours I grant
Would be but too inviting:
Were fair Ardelia not my Aunt,
Or were it Worsley's writing.

Vanbrugh's House

Built from the Ruins of Whitehall that was Burnt, 1703

In times of old, when Time was young,
And poets their own verses sung,
A verse would draw a stone or beam,
That now would overload a team;
Lead 'em a dance of many a mile,
Then rear 'em to a goodly pile.
Each number had its diff'rent power;
Heroic strains could build a tower;
Sonnets and elegies to Chloris,
Might raise a house about two stories;
A lyric ode would slate; a catch
Would tile; an epigram would thatch.
  Now Poets feel this art is lost,
Both to their own and landlord's cost.
Not one of all the tuneful throng
Can hire a lodging for a song.
For Jove consider'd well the case,
That poets were a numerous race;
And if they all had power to build,
The earth would very soon be fill'd:
Materials would be quickly spent,
And houses would not give a rent.
The God of Wealth was therefore made
Sole patron of the building trade;
Leaving to wits the spacious air,
With license to build castles there:
In right whereof their old pretence
To lodge in garrets comes from thence.
There is a worm by Phoebus bred,
By leaves of mulberry is fed,
Which unprovided where to dwell,
Conforms itself to weave a cell;
Then curious hands this texture take,
And for themselves fine garments make.

Meantime a pair of awkward things
Grow to his back instead of wings;
He flutters when he thinks he flies,
Then sheds about his spawn and dies.
Just such an insect of the age
Is he that scribbles for the stage;
His birth he does from Phoebus raise,
And feeds upon imagin'd bays;
Throws all his wit and hours away
In twisting up an ill spun Play:
This gives him lodging and provides
A stock of tawdry shift besides.
With the unravell'd shreds of which
The under wits adorn their speech:
And now he spreads his little fans,
(For all the Muses Geese are Swans)
And borne on Fancy's pinions, thinks
He soars sublimest when he sinks:
But scatt'ring round his fly-blows, dies;
Whence broods of insect-poets rise.
    Premising thus, in modern way,
The greater part I have to say;
Sing, Muse, the house of Poet Van,
In higher strain than we began.
    Van (for 'tis fit the reader know it)
Is both a Herald and a Poet;
No wonder then if nicely skill'd
In each capacity to build.
As Herald, he can in a day
Repair a house gone to decay;
Or by achievements, arms, device,
Erect a new one in a trice;
And poets, if they had their due,
By ancient right are builders too:
This made him to Apollo pray
For leave to build—the poets way.
His prayer was granted, for the God
Consented with the usual nod.
    After hard throes of many a day

Van was delivered of a play,
Which in due time brought forth a house,
Just as the mountain did the mouse.
One story high, one postern door,
And one small chamber on a floor,
Born like a phoenix from the flame:
But neither bulk nor shape the same;
As animals of largest size
Corrupt to maggots, worms, and flies;
A type of modern wit and style,
The rubbish of an ancient pile;
So chemists boast they have a power,
From the dead ashes of a flower
Some faint resemblance to produce,
But not the virtue, taste, nor juice.
So modern rhymers strive to blast
The poetry of ages past;
Which, having wisely overthrown,
They from its ruins build their own.

Vanbrugh's House

Built from the Ruins of Whitehall that was Burnt, 1703

In times of old, when Time was young,
And poets their own verses sung,
A verse would draw a stone or beam,
That now would overload a team;
Lead 'em a dance of many a mile,
Then rear 'em to a goodly pile.
Each number had its diff'rent power;
Heroic strains could build a tower;
Sonnets, or elegies to Chloris,
Might raise a house about two stories;
A lyric ode would slate; a catch
Would tile; an epigram would thatch.
    But, to their own or landlord's cost,
Now Poets feel this art is lost.
Not one of all our tuneful throng
Can raise a lodging for a song.
For Jove consider'd well the case,
Observed they grew a numerous race;
And should they build as fast as write,
'Twould ruin undertakers quite.
This evil, therefore, to prevent,
He wisely changed their element:
On earth the God of Wealth was made
Sole patron of the building trade;
Leaving the Wits the spacious air,
With license to build castles there:
And 'tis conceived their old pretence
To lodge in garrets comes from thence.
    Premising thus, in modern way,
The better half we have to say;
Sing, Muse, the house of Poet Van,
In higher strains than we began.
    Van (for 'tis fit the reader know it)
Is both a Herald and a Poet;

No wonder then if nicely skill'd
In both capacities to build.
As Herald, he can in a day
Repair a house gone to decay;
Or, by achievements, arms, device,
Erect a new one in a trice;
And as a poet, he has skill
To build in speculation still.
"Great Jove!" he cried, "the art restore
To build by verse as heretofore,
And make my Muse the architect;
What palaces shall we erect!
No longer shall forsaken Thames
Lament his old Whitehall in flames;
A pile shall from its ashes rise,
Fit to invade or prop the skies."
Jove smiled, and, like a gentle god,
Consenting with the usual nod,
Told Van, he knew his talent best,
And left the choice to his own breast.
So Van resolved to write a farce;
But, well perceiving wit was scarce,
With cunning that defect supplies:
Takes a French play as lawful prize;
Steals thence his plot and ev'ry joke,
Not once suspecting Jove would smoke;
And (like a wag set down to write)
Would whisper to himself, "a *bite*."
Then, from this motley mingled style,
Proceeded to erect his pile.
So men of old, to gain renown, did
Build Babel with their tongues confounded.
Jove saw the cheat, but thought it best
To turn the matter to a jest;
Down from Olympus' top he slides,
Laughing as if he'd burst his sides:
Ay, thought the god, are these your tricks,
Why then old plays deserve old bricks;
And since you're sparing of your stuff,

Your building shall be small enough.
He spake, and grudging, lent his aid;
Th'experienced bricks, that knew their trade,
(As being bricks at second hand,)
Now move, and now in order stand.
The building, as the Poet writ,
Rose in proportion to his wit—
And first the prologue built a wall;
So wide as to encompass all.
The scene, a wood, produc'd no more
Than a few scrubby trees before.
The plot as yet lay deep; and so
A cellar next was dug below;
But this a work so hard was found,
Two acts it cost him under ground.
Two other acts, we may presume,
Were spent in building each a room.
Thus far advanc'd, he made a shift
To raise a roof with act the fift.
The epilogue behind did frame
A place, not decent here to name.
Now, Poets from all quarters ran,
To see the house of brother Van;
Looked high and low, walk'd often round;
But no such house was to be found.
One asks the watermen hard by,
"Where may the Poet's palace lie?"
Another of the Thames inquires,
If he has seen its gilded spires?
At length they in the rubbish spy
A thing resembling a goose-pie.
Thither in haste the Poets throng,
And gaze in silent wonder long,
Till one in raptures thus began
To praise the pile and builder Van:
"Thrice happy Poet! who may'st trail
Thy house about thee like a snail:
Or harness'd to a nag, at ease
Take journeys in it like a chaise;

Or in a boat whene'er thou wilt,
Can'st make it serve thee for a tilt!
Capacious house! 'tis own'd by all
Thou'rt well contrived, tho' thou art small:
For ev'ry Wit in Britain's isle
May lodge within thy spacious pile.
Like Bacchus thou, as Poets feign,
Thy mother burnt, art born again,
Born like a phoenix from the flame:
But neither bulk nor shape the same;
As animals of largest size
Corrupt to maggots, worms, and flies;
A type of modern wit and style,
The rubbish of an ancient pile;
So chemists boast they have a power,
From the dead ashes of a flower
Some faint resemblance to produce,
But not the virtue, taste, or juice.
So modern rhymers wisely blast
The poetry of ages past;
Which, after they have overthrown,
They from its ruins build their own."

Baucis and Philemon

On the Ever-Lamented Loss of the Two Yew-Trees
in the Parish of Chilthorne, Somerset. 1706.
Imitated from the Eighth Book of Ovid

In ancient time, as story tells,
The saints would often leave their cells,
And stroll about, but hide their quality,
To try good people's hospitality.
  It happen'd on a winter's night,
As authors of the legend write,
Two brother hermits, saints by trade,
Taking their tour in masquerade,
Came to a village hard by Rixham,
Ragged and not a groat betwixt 'em.
It rain'd as hard as it could pour,
Yet they were forced to walk an hour
From house to house, wet to the skin,
Before one soul would let 'em in.
They call'd at every door: "Good people,
My comrade's blind, and I'm a creeple!
Here we lie starving in the street,
'Twould grieve a body's heart to see't,
No Christian would turn out a beast,
In such a dreadful night at least;
Give us but straw and let us lie
In yonder barn to keep us dry."
Thus in the stroller's usual cant,
They begg'd relief, which none would grant.
No creature valued what they said,
One family was gone to bed:
The master bawled out half asleep,
"You fellows, what a noise you keep!
So many beggars pass this way,
We can't be quiet, night nor day;
We cannot serve you every one;
Pray take your answer, and be gone."

One swore he'd send 'em to the stocks;
A third could not forbear his mocks;
But bawl'd as loud as he could roar
"You're on the wrong side of the door!"
One surly clown look't out and said,
"I'll fling the p—pot on your head:
You sha'nt come here, nor get a sous!
You look like rogues would rob a house.
Can't you go work, or serve the King?
You blind and lame! 'Tis no such thing.
That's but a counterfeit sore leg!
For shame! two sturdy rascals beg!
If I come down, *I'll* spoil your trick,
And cure you both with a good stick."
    Our wand'ring saints, in woful state,
Treated at this ungodly rate,
Having thro' all the village past,
To a small cottage came at last
Where dwelt a good old honest ye'man,
Call'd thereabout good man Philemon;
Who kindly did the saints invite
In his poor house to pass the night;
And then the hospitable sire
Bid Goody Baucis mend the fire;
Whilst he from out the chimney took
A flitch of bacon off the hook,
And freely from the fattest side
Cut out large slices to be fry'd;
Which tost up in a pan with batter,
And served up in an earthen platter,
Quoth Baucis, "This is wholesome fare,
Eat, honest friends, and never spare,
And if we find our victuals fail,
We can but make it out in ale."
    To a small kilderkin of beer,
Brew'd for the good time of the year,
Philemon, by his wife's consent,
Stept with a jug, and made a vent,
And having fill'd it to the brink,

Invited both the saints to drink.
When they had took a second draught,
Behold, a miracle was wrought;
For, Baucis with amazement found,
Although the jug had twice gone round,
It still was full up to the top,
As they ne'er had drunk a drop.
You may be sure so strange a sight,
Put the old people in a fright:
Philemon whisper'd to his wife,
"These men are—Saints—I'll lay my life!"
The strangers overheard, and said,
"You're in the right—but be'nt afraid:
No hurt shall come to you or yours:
But for that pack of churlish boors,
Not fit to live on Christian ground,
They and their village shall be drown'd;
Whilst you shall see your cottage rise,
And grow a church before your eyes."
Scarce had they spoke, when fair and soft,
The roof began to mount aloft;
Aloft rose ev'ry beam and rafter;
The heavy wall went clambering after.
The chimney widen'd, and grew higher,
Became a steeple with a spire.
The kettle to the top was hoist,
And there stood fastened to a joist,
But with the upside down, to show
Its inclination for below:
In vain; for a superior force
Applied at bottom stops its course:
Doom'd ever in suspense to dwell,
'Tis now no kettle, but a bell.
The wooden jack, which had almost
Lost by disuse the art to roast,
A sudden alteration feels,
Increas'd by new intestine wheels;
But what adds to the wonder more,
The number made the motion slower.

The flyer, altho't had leaden feet,
Would turn so quick you scarce could see't;
But, now stopt by some hidden powers,
Moves round but twice in twice twelve hours,
While in the station of a jack,
'Twas never known to turn its back,
A friend in turns and windings tried,
Nor ever left the chimney's side.
The chimney to a steeple grown,
The jack would not be left alone;
But, up against the steeple rear'd,
Became a clock, and still adher'd;
And still its love to household cares,
By a shrill voice at noon declares,
Warning the cookmaid not to burn
That roast meat, which it cannot turn.
    The groaning-chair began to crawl,
Like a huge insect, up the wall;
There stuck, and to a pulpit grew,
But kept its matter and its hue,
And mindful of its ancient state,
Still groans while tattling gossips prate.
The mortar only chang'd its name,
In its old shape a font became.
    The porringers, that in a row,
Hung high, and made a glitt'ring show,
To a less noble substance chang'd,
Were now but leathern buckets rang'd.
    The ballads, pasted on the wall,
Of Chevy Chase, and English Mall,
Fair Rosamond, and Robin Hood,
The little Children in the Wood,
Enlarged in picture, size, and letter,
And painted, lookt abundance better,
And now the heraldry describe
Of a churchwarden, or a tribe.
A bedstead of the antique mode,
Composed of timber many a load,
Such as our grandfathers did use,

Was metamorphos'd into pews;
Which yet their former virtue keep
By lodging folk disposed to sleep.
    The cottage, with such feats as these,
Grown to a church by just degrees,
The holy men desired their host
To ask for what he fancied most.
Philemon, having paused a while,
Replied in complimental style:
"Your goodness, more than my desert,
Makes you take all things in good part:
You've raised a church here in a minute,
And I would fain continue in it;
I'm good for little at my days,
Make me the parson if you please."
    He spoke, and presently he feels
His grazier's coat reach down his heels;
The sleeves new border'd with a list,
Widen'd and gather'd at his wrist,
But, being old, continued just
As threadbare, and as full of dust.
A shambling awkward gait he took,
With a demure dejected look,
Talk't of his offerings, tythes, and dues,
Could smoke and drink and read the news,
Or sell a goose at the next town,
Decently hid beneath his gown.
Contriv'd to preach old sermons next,
Chang'd in the preface and the text.
At christ'nings well could act his part,
And had the service all by heart;
Wish'd women might have children fast,
And thought whose sow had farrow'd last;
Against dissenters would repine.
And stood up firm for "right divine;"
Carried it to his equals higher,
But most obedient to the squire.
Found his head fill'd with many a system;
But classic authors,—he ne'er mist 'em.

Thus having furbish'd up a parson,
Dame Baucis next they play'd their farce on.
Instead of homespun coifs, were seen
Good pinners edg'd with colberteen;
Her petticoat, transform'd apace,
Became black satin, flounced with lace.
"Plain Goody" would no longer down,
'Twas "Madam," in her grogram gown.
Philemon was in great surprise,
And hardly could believe his eyes.
Amaz'd to see her look so prim,
And she admir'd as much at him.
Thus happy in their change of life,
Were several years this man and wife:
When on a day, which prov'd their last,
Discoursing o'er old stories past,
They went by chance, amidst their talk,
To the churchyard, to take a walk;
When Baucis hastily cry'd out,
"My dear, I see your forehead sprout!"—
"Sprout;" quoth the man; "what's this you tell us?
I hope you don't believe me jealous!
But yet, methinks, I feel it true,
And really yours is budding too—
Nay,—now I cannot stir my foot;
It feels as if 'twere taking root."
Description would but tire my Muse,
In short, they both were turn'd to yews.
Old Goodman Dobson of the Green
Remembers he the trees has seen;
He'll talk of them from noon till night,
And goes with folk to show the sight;
On Sundays, after evening prayer,
He gathers all the parish there;
Points out the place of either yew,
Here Baucis, there Philemon, grew:
Till once a parson of our town,
To mend his barn, cut Baucis down;

At which, 'tis hard to be believ'd
How much the other tree was griev'd,
Grew scrubby, dy'd a-top, was stunted,
So the next parson stubb'd and burnt it.

Baucis and Philemon

On the Ever-Lamented Loss of the Two Yew-Trees in the Parish of Chilthorne, Somerset. 1706.
Imitated from the Eighth Book Of Ovid

In ancient times, as story tells,
The saints would often leave their cells,
And stroll about, but hide their quality,
To try good people's hospitality.
It happen'd on a winter night,
As authors of the legend write,
Two brother hermits, saints by trade,
Taking their tour in masquerade,
Disguis'd in tatter'd habits, went
To a small village down in Kent;
Where, in the strollers' canting strain,
They begg'd from door to door in vain,
Try'd ev'ry tone might pity win;
But not a soul would let them in.
Our wand'ring saints, in woful state,
Treated at this ungodly rate,
Having thro' all the village past,
To a small cottage came at last
Where dwelt a good old honest ye'man,
Call'd in the neighbourhood Philemon;
Who kindly did these saints invite
In his poor hut to pass the night;
And then the hospitable sire
Bid Goody Baucis mend the fire;
While he from out the chimney took
A flitch of bacon off the hook,
And freely from the fattest side
Cut out large slices to be fry'd;
Then stepp'd aside to fetch 'em drink,
Fill'd a large jug up to the brink,
And saw it fairly twice go round;
Yet (what was wonderful) they found

’Twas still replenished to the top,
As if they ne’er had touch’d a drop.
The good old couple were amaz’d,
And often on each other gaz’d;
For both were frighten’d to the heart,
And just began to cry, “What *art*!”
Then softly turn’d aside, to view
Whether the lights were burning blue.
The gentle pilgrims, soon aware on’t,
Told them their calling and their errand:
“Good folk, you need not be afraid,
We are but saints,” the hermits said;
“No hurt shall come to you or yours:
But for that pack of churlish boors,
Not fit to live on Christian ground,
They and their houses shall be drown’d;
While you shall see your cottage rise,
And grow a church before your eyes.”
    They scarce had spoke, when fair and soft,
The roof began to mount aloft;
Aloft rose ev’ry beam and rafter;
The heavy wall climb’d slowly after.
    The chimney widen’d, and grew higher
Became a steeple with a spire.
    The kettle to the top was hoist,
And there stood fasten’d to a joist,
But with the upside down, to show
Its inclination for below:
In vain; for a superior force
Applied at bottom stops its course:
Doom’d ever in suspense to dwell,
’Tis now no kettle, but a bell.
    A wooden jack, which had almost
Lost by disuse the art to roast,
A sudden alteration feels,
Increas’d by new intestine wheels;
And, what exalts the wonder more,
The number made the motion slower.
The flyer, though it had leaden feet,

Turn'd round so quick you scarce could see't;
But, slacken'd by some secret power,
Now hardly moves an inch an hour.
The jack and chimney, near ally'd,
Had never left each other's side;
The chimney to a steeple grown,
The jack would not be left alone;
But, up against the steeple rear'd,
Became a clock, and still adher'd;
And still its love to household cares,
By a shrill voice at noon, declares,
Warning the cookmaid not to burn
That roast meat, which it cannot turn.
The groaning-chair began to crawl,
Like an huge snail, half up the wall;
There stuck aloft in public view,
And with small change, a pulpit grew.
    The porringers, that in a row
Hung high, and made a glitt'ring show,
To a less noble substance chang'd,
Were now but leathern buckets rang'd.
    The ballads, pasted on the wall,
Of Joan of France, and English Mall,
Fair Rosamond, and Robin Hood,
The little Children in the Wood,
Now seem'd to look abundance better,
Improved in picture, size, and letter:
And, high in order plac'd, describe
The heraldry of ev'ry tribe.
    A bedstead of the antique mode,
Compact of timber many a load,
Such as our ancestors did use,
Was metamorphos'd into pews;
Which still their ancient nature keep
By lodging folk disposed to sleep.
    The cottage, by such feats as these,
Grown to a church by just degrees,
The hermits then desired their host
To ask for what he fancy'd most.

Philemon, having paused a while,
Return'd them thanks in homely style;
Then said, "My house is grown so fine,
Methinks, I still would call it mine.
I'm old, and fain would live at ease;
Make me the parson if you please."
He spoke, and presently he feels
His grazier's coat fall down his heels:
He sees, yet hardly can believe,
About each arm a pudding sleeve;
His waistcoat to a cassock grew,
And both assumed a sable hue;
But, being old, continued just
As threadbare, and as full of dust.
His talk was now of tithes and dues:
Could smoke his pipe, and read the news;
Knew how to preach old sermons next,
Vamp'd in the preface and the text;
At christ'nings well could act his part,
And had the service all by heart;
Wish'd women might have children fast,
And thought whose sow had farrow'd last;
Against dissenters would repine,
And stood up firm for "right divine;"
Found his head fill'd with many a system;
But classic authors,—he ne'er mist 'em.
Thus having furbish'd up a parson,
Dame Baucis next they play'd their farce on.
Instead of homespun coifs, were seen
Good pinners edg'd with colberteen;
Her petticoat, transform'd apace,
Became black satin, flounced with lace.
"Plain Goody" would no longer down,
'Twas "Madam," in her grogram gown.
Philemon was in great surprise,
And hardly could believe his eyes.
Amaz'd to see her look so prim,
And she admir'd as much at him.
Thus happy in their change of life,

Were several years this man and wife:
When on a day, which prov'd their last,
Discoursing o'er old stories past,
They went by chance, amidst their talk,
To the churchyard to take a walk;
When Baucis hastily cry'd out,
"My dear, I see your forehead sprout!"—
"Sprout;" quoth the man; "what's this you tell us?
I hope you don't believe me jealous!
But yet, methinks, I feel it true,
And really yours is budding too—Nay,—now
I cannot stir my foot;
It feels as if 'twere taking root."
Description would but tire my Muse,
In short, they both were turn'd to yews.
Old Goodman Dobson of the Green
Remembers he the trees has seen;
He'll talk of them from noon till night,
And goes with folk to show the sight;
On Sundays, after evening prayer,
He gathers all the parish there;
Points out the place of either yew,
Here Baucis, there Philemon, grew:
Till once a parson of our town,
To mend his barn, cut Baucis down;
At which, 'tis hard to be believ'd
How much the other tree was griev'd,
Grew scrubby, dy'd a-top, was stunted,
So the next parson stubb'd and burnt it.

The History of Vanbrugh's House
1708

When Mother Cludd had rose from play,
And call'd to take the cards away,
Van saw, but seem'd not to regard,
How Miss pick'd every painted card,
And, busy both with hand and eye,
Soon rear'd a house two stories high.
Van's genius, without thought or lecture
Is hugely turn'd to architecture:
He view'd the edifice, and smiled,
Vow'd it was pretty for a child:
It was so perfect in its kind,
He kept the model in his mind.
    But, when he found the boys at play
And saw them dabbling in their clay,
He stood behind a stall to lurk,
And mark the progress of their work;
With true delight observed them all
Raking up mud to build a wall.
The plan he much admired, and took
The model in his table-book:
Thought himself now exactly skill'd,
And so resolved a house to build:
A real house, with rooms and stairs,
Five times at least as big as theirs;
Taller than Miss's by two yards;
Not a sham thing of play or cards:
And so he did; for, in a while,
He built up such a monstrous pile,
That no two chairmen could be found
Able to lift it from the ground.
Still at Whitehall it stands in view,
Just in the place where first it grew;
There all the little schoolboys run,
Envying to see themselves outdone.
    From such deep rudiments as these,

Van is become, by due degrees,
For building famed, and justly reckon'd,
At court, Vitruvius the Second:
No wonder, since wise authors show,
That best foundations must be low:
And now the duke has wisely ta'en him
To be his architect at Blenheim.
    But raillery at once apart,
If this rule holds in every art;
Or if his grace were no more skill'd in
The art of battering walls than building,
We might expect to see next year
A mouse-trap man chief engineer.

A Grub-Street Elegy

On the Supposed Death of Partridge the Almanack Maker. 1708

Well; 'tis as Bickerstaff has guest,
Though we all took it for a jest:
Partridge is dead; nay more, he dy'd,
Ere he could prove the good 'squire ly'd.
Strange, an astrologer should die
Without one wonder in the sky;
Not one of all his crony stars
To pay their duty at his hearse!
No meteor, no eclipse appear'd!
No comet with a flaming beard!
The sun hath rose and gone to bed,
Just as if Partridge were not dead;
Nor hid himself behind the moon
To make a dreadful night at noon.
He at fit periods walks through Aries,
Howe'er our earthly motion varies;
And twice a-year he'll cut th' Equator,
As if there had been no such matter.
Some wits have wonder'd what analogy
There is 'twixt cobbling and astrology;
How Partridge made his optics rise
From a shoe-sole to reach the skies.
A list the cobbler's temples ties,
To keep the hair out of his eyes;
From whence 'tis plain the diadem
That princes wear derives from them;
And therefore crowns are now-a-days
Adorn'd with golden stars and rays;
Which plainly shows the near alliance
'Twixt cobbling and the planet's science.
Besides, that slow-paced sign Böötes,
As 'tis miscall'd, we know not who 'tis;
But Partridge ended all disputes;

He knew his trade, and call'd it *boots*.
The horned moon, which heretofore
Upon their shoes the Romans wore,
Whose wideness kept their toes from corns,
And whence we claim our shoeing-horns,
Shows how the art of cobbling bears
A near resemblance to the spheres.
A scrap of parchment hung by geometry,
(A great refiner in barometry,)
Can, like the stars, foretell the weather;
And what is parchment else but leather?
Which an astrologer might use
Either for almanacks or shoes.
Thus Partridge, by his wit and parts,
At once did practise both these arts:
And as the boding owl (or rather
The bat, because her wings are leather)
Steals from her private cell by night,
And flies about the candle-light;
So learned Partridge could as well
Creep in the dark from leathern cell,
And in his fancy fly as far
To peep upon a twinkling star.
Besides, he could confound the spheres,
And set the planets by the ears;
To show his skill, he Mars could join
To Venus in aspect malign;
Then call in Mercury for aid,
And cure the wounds that Venus made.
Great scholars have in Lucian read,
When Philip King of Greece was dead
His soul and spirit did divide,
And each part took a different side;
One rose a star; the other fell
Beneath, and mended shoes in Hell.
Thus Partridge still shines in each art,
The cobbling and star-gazing part,
And is install'd as good a star
As any of the Caesars are.

Triumphant star! some pity show
On cobblers militant below,
Whom roguish boys, in stormy nights,
Torment by pissing out their lights,
Or through a chink convey their smoke,
Enclosed artificers to choke.
Thou, high exalted in thy sphere,
May'st follow still thy calling there.
To thee the Bull will lend his hide,
By Phoebus newly tann'd and dry'd;
For thee they Argo's hulk will tax,
And scrape her pitchy sides for wax:
Then Ariadne kindly lends
Her braided hair to make thee ends;
The points of Sagittarius' dart
Turns to an awl by heavenly art;
And Vulcan, wheedled by his wife,
Will forge for thee a paring-knife.
For want of room by Virgo's side,
She'll strain a point, and sit astride,
To take thee kindly in between;
And then the Signs will be Thirteen.

The Epitaph

Here, five feet deep, lies on his back
A cobbler, starmonger, and quack;
Who to the stars, in pure good will,
Does to his best look upward still.
Weep, all you customers that use
His pills, his almanacks, or shoes;
And you that did your fortunes seek,
Step to his grave but once a-week;
This earth, which bears his body's print,
You'll find has so much virtue in't,
That I durst pawn my ears, 'twill tell
Whate'er concerns you full as well,
In physic, stolen goods, or love,
As he himself could, when above.

A Description of the Morning

Written in April 1709, and First Printed in "The Tatler"

Now hardly here and there an hackney-coach
Appearing, show'd the ruddy morn's approach.
Now Betty from her master's bed had flown,
And softly stole to discompose her own;
The slip-shod 'prentice from his master's door
Had pared the dirt, and sprinkled round the floor.
Now Moll had whirl'd her mop with dext'rous airs,
Prepared to scrub the entry and the stairs.
The youth with broomy stumps began to trace
The kennel's edge, where wheels had worn the place.
The small-coal man was heard with cadence deep,
Till drown'd in shriller notes of chimney-sweep:
Duns at his lordship's gate began to meet;
And brickdust Moll had scream'd through half the street.
The turnkey now his flock returning sees,
Duly let out a-nights to steal for fees:
The watchful bailiffs take their silent stands,
And schoolboys lag with satchels in their hands.

A Description of a City Shower

Written in Oct., 1710; and First Printed in "The Tatler," No. 238

Careful observers may foretell the hour,
(By sure prognostics,) when to dread a shower.
While rain depends, the pensive cat gives o'er
Her frolics, and pursues her tail no more.
Returning home at night, you'll find the sink
Strike your offended sense with double stink.
If you be wise, then, go not far to dine:
You'll spend in coach-hire more than save in wine.
A coming shower your shooting corns presage,
Old a-ches throb, your hollow tooth will rage;
Sauntering in coffeehouse is Dulman seen;
He damns the climate, and complains of spleen.
Meanwhile the South, rising with dabbled wings,
A sable cloud athwart the welkin flings,
That swill'd more liquor than it could contain,
And, like a drunkard, gives it up again.
Brisk Susan whips her linen from the rope,
While the first drizzling shower is borne aslope;
Such is that sprinkling which some careless quean
Flirts on you from her mop, but not so clean:
You fly, invoke the gods; then, turning, stop
To rail; she singing, still whirls on her mop.
Not yet the dust had shunn'd the unequal strife,
But, aided by the wind, fought still for life,
And wafted with its foe by violent gust,
'Twas doubtful which was rain, and which was dust.
Ah! where must needy poet seek for aid,
When dust and rain at once his coat invade?
Sole coat! where dust, cemented by the rain,
Erects the nap, and leaves a cloudy stain!
Now in contiguous drops the flood comes down,
Threatening with deluge this *devoted* town.
To shops in crowds the daggled females fly,

Pretend to cheapen goods, but nothing buy.
The Templar spruce, while every spout's abroach,
Stays till 'tis fair, yet seems to call a coach.
The tuck'd-up sempstress walks with hasty strides,
While streams run down her oil'd umbrella's sides.
Here various kinds, by various fortunes led,
Commence acquaintance underneath a shed.
Triumphant Tories, and desponding Whigs,
Forget their feuds, and join to save their wigs.
Box'd in a chair the beau impatient sits,
While spouts run clattering o'er the roof by fits,
And ever and anon with frightful din
The leather sounds; he trembles from within.
So when Troy chairmen bore the wooden steed,
Pregnant with Greeks impatient to be freed,
(Those bully Greeks, who, as the moderns do,
Instead of paying chairmen, ran them through,)
Laocoon struck the outside with his spear,
And each imprison'd hero quaked for fear.
Now from all parts the swelling kennels flow,
And bear their trophies with them as they go:
Filth of all hues and odour, seem to tell
What street they sail'd from, by their sight and smell.
They, as each torrent drives with rapid force,
From Smithfield to St. Pulchre's shape their course,
And in huge confluence join'd at Snowhill ridge,
Fall from the conduit prone to Holborn bridge.
Sweeping from butchers' stalls, dung, guts, and blood,
Drown'd puppies, stinking sprats, all drench'd in mud,
Dead cats, and turnip-tops, come tumbling down the flood.

On the Little House by the Churchyard of Castlenock
1710

Whoever pleases to inquire
Why yonder steeple wants a spire,
The grey old fellow, Poet Joe,
The philosophic cause will show.
Once on a time a western blast,
At least twelve inches overcast,
Reckoning roof, weathercock, and all,
Which came with a prodigious fall;
And, tumbling topsy-turvy round,
Lit with its bottom on the ground:
For, by the laws of gravitation,
It fell into its proper station.
    This is the little strutting pile
You see just by the churchyard stile;
The walls in tumbling gave a knock,
And thus the steeple got a shock;
From whence the neighbouring farmer calls
The steeple, Knock; the vicar, Walls.
    The vicar once a-week creeps in,
Sits with his knees up to his chin;
Here cons his notes, and takes a whet,
Till the small ragged flock is met.
    A traveller, who by did pass,
Observed the roof behind the grass;
On tiptoe stood, and rear'd his snout,
And saw the parson creeping out:
Was much surprised to see a crow
Venture to build his nest so low.
    A schoolboy ran unto't, and thought
The crib was down, the blackbird caught.
A third, who lost his way by night,
Was forced for safety to alight,
And, stepping o'er the fabric roof,
His horse had like to spoil his hoof.

Warburton took it in his noddle,
This building was design'd a model;
Or of a pigeon-house or oven,
To bake one loaf, or keep one dove in.
Then Mrs. Johnson gave her verdict,
And every one was pleased that heard it;
All that you make this stir about
Is but a still which wants a spout.
The reverend Dr. Raymond guess'd
More probably than all the rest;
He said, but that it wanted room,
It might have been a pigmy's tomb.
The doctor's family came by,
And little miss began to cry,
Give me that house in my own hand!
Then madam bade the chariot stand,
Call'd to the clerk, in manner mild,
Pray, reach that thing here to the child:
That thing, I mean, among the kale;
And here's to buy a pot of ale.
The clerk said to her in a heat,
What! sell my master's country seat,
Where he comes every week from town!
He would not sell it for a crown.
Poh! fellow, keep not such a pother;
In half an hour thou'lt make another.
Says Nancy, I can make for miss
A finer house ten times than this;
The dean will give me willow sticks,
And Joe my apron-full of bricks.

A Town Eclogue. 1710

Scene, the Royal Exchange

Corydon: Now the keen rigour of the winter's o'er,
No hail descends, and frost can pinch no more,
While other girls confess the genial spring,
And laugh aloud, or amorous ditties sing,
Secure from cold, their lovely necks display,
And throw each useless chafing-dish away;
Why sits my Phillis discontented here,
Nor feels the turn of the revolving year?
Why on that brow dwell sorrow and dismay,
Where Loves were wont to sport, and Smiles to play?
Phillis: Ah, Corydon! survey the 'Change around,
Through all the 'Change no wretch like me is found:
Alas! the day, when I, poor heedless maid,
Was to your rooms in Lincoln's Inn betray'd;
Then how you swore, how many vows you made!
Ye listening Zephyrs, that o'erheard his love,
Waft the soft accents to the gods above.
Alas! the day; for (O, eternal shame!)
I sold you handkerchiefs, and lost my fame.
Corydon: When I forget the favour you bestow'd,
Red herrings shall be spawn'd in Tyburn Road:
Fleet Street, transform'd, become a flowery green,
And mass be sung where operas are seen.
The wealthy cit, and the St. James's beau,
Shall change their quarters, and their joys forego;
Stock-jobbing, this to Jonathan's shall come,
At the Groom Porter's, that play off his plum.
Phillis: But what to me does all that love avail,
If, while I doze at home o'er porter's ale,
Each night with wine and wenches you regale?
My livelong hours in anxious cares are past,
And raging hunger lays my beauty waste.
On templars spruce in vain I glances throw,
And with shrill voice invite them as they go.

Exposed in vain my glossy ribbons shine,
And unregarded wave upon the twine.
The week flies round, and when my profit's known,
I hardly clear enough to change a crown.
CORYDON: Hard fate of virtue, thus to be distrest,
Thou fairest of thy trade, and far the best;
As fruitmen's stalls the summer market grace,
And ruddy peaches them; as first in place
Plumcake is seen o'er smaller pastry ware,
And ice on that: so Phillis does appear
In playhouse and in Park, above the rest
Of belles mechanic, elegantly drest.
PHILLIS: And yet Crepundia, that conceited fair,
Amid her toys, affects a saucy air,
And views me hourly with a scornful eye.
CORYDON: She might as well with bright Cleora vie.
PHILLIS: With this large petticoat I strive in vain
To hide my folly past, and coming pain;
'Tis now no secret; she, and fifty more,
Observe the symptoms I had once before:
A second babe at Wapping must be placed,
When I scarce bear the charges of the last.
CORYDON: What I could raise I sent; a pound of plums,
Five shillings, and a coral for his gums;
To-morrow I intend him something more.
PHILLIS: I sent a frock and pair of shoes before.
CORYDON: However, you shall home with me to-night,
Forget your cares, and revel in delight,
I have in store a pint or two of wine,
Some cracknels, and the remnant of a chine.

And now on either side, and all around,
The weighty shop-boards fall, and bars resound;
Each ready sempstress slips her pattens on,
And ties her hood, preparing to be gone.

L. B. W. H. J. S. S. T.

A Conference

Between Sir Harry Pierce's Chariot, and Mrs. D. Stopford's Chair

Chariot: My pretty dear Cuz, tho' I've roved the town o'er,
To dispatch in an hour some visits a score;
Though, since first on the wheels, I've been every day
At the 'Change, at a raffling, at church, or a play;
And the fops of the town are pleased with the notion
Of calling your slave the perpetual motion;—
Though oft at your door I have whined (out) my love
As my Knight does grin his at your Lady above;
Yet, ne'er before this, though I used all my care,
I e'er was so happy to meet my dear Chair;
And since we're so near, like birds of a feather,
Let's e'en, as they say, set our horses together.
Chair: By your awkward address, you're that thing which should carry,
With one footman behind, our lover Sir Harry.
By your language, I judge, you think me a wench;
He that makes love to me, must make it in French.
Thou that's drawn by two beasts, and carry'st a brute,
Canst thou vainly e'er hope, I'll answer thy suit?
Though sometimes you pretend to appear with your six,
No regard to their colour, their sexes you mix:
Then on the grand-paw you'd look very great,
With your new-fashion'd glasses, and nasty old seat.
Thus a beau I have seen strut with a cock'd hat,
And newly rigg'd out, with a dirty cravat.
You may think that you make a figure most shining,
But it's plain that you have an old cloak for a lining.
Are those double-gilt nails? Where's the lustre of Kerry,
To set off the Knight, and to finish the Jerry?
If you hope I'll be kind, you must tell me what's due
In George's-lane for you, ere I'll buckle to.
Chariot: Why, how now, Doll Diamond, you're very alert;
Is it your French breeding has made you so pert?
Because I was civil, here's a stir with a pox:

Who is it that values your —— or your fox?
Sure 'tis to her honour, he ever should bed
His bloody red hand to her bloody red head.
You're proud of your gilding; but I tell you each nail
Is only just tinged with a rub at her tail;
And although it may pass for gold on a ninny,
Sure we know a Bath shilling soon from a guinea.
Nay, her foretop's a cheat; each morn she does black it,
Yet, ere it be night, it's the same with her placket.
I'll ne'er be run down any more with your cant;
Your velvet was wore before in a mant,
On the back of her mother; but now 'tis much duller,—
The fire she carries hath changed its colour.
Those creatures that draw me you never would mind,
If you'd but look on your own Pharaoh's lean kine;
They're taken for spectres, they're so meagre and spare,
Drawn damnably low by your sorrel mare.
We know how your lady was on you befriended;
You're not to be paid for 'till the lawsuit is ended:
But her bond it is good, he need not to doubt;
She is two or three years above being out.
Could my Knight be advised, he should ne'er spend his vigour
On one he can't hope of e'er making *bigger*.

To Lord Harley, on his Marriage October 31, 1713

Among the numbers who employ
Their tongues and pens to give you joy,
Dear Harley! generous youth, admit
What friendship dictates more than wit.
Forgive me, when I fondly thought
(By frequent observations taught)
A spirit so inform'd as yours
Could never prosper in amours.
The God of Wit, and Light, and Arts,
With all acquired and natural parts,
Whose harp could savage beasts enchant,
Was an unfortunate gallant.
Had Bacchus after Daphne reel'd,
The nymph had soon been brought to yield;
Or, had embroider'd Mars pursued,
The nymph would ne'er have been a prude.
Ten thousand footsteps, full in view,
Mark out the way where Daphne flew;
For such is all the sex's flight,
They fly from learning, wit, and light;
They fly, and none can overtake
But some gay coxcomb, or a rake.
How then, dear Harley, could I guess
That you should meet, in love, success?
For, if those ancient tales be true,
Phoebus was beautiful as you;
Yet Daphne never slack'd her pace,
For wit and learning spoil'd his face.
And since the same resemblance held
In gifts wherein you both excell'd,
I fancied every nymph would run
From you, as from Latona's son.
Then where, said I, shall Harley find
A virgin of superior mind,
With wit and virtue to discover,

And pay the merit of her lover?
This character shall Ca'endish claim,
Born to retrieve her sex's fame.
The chief among the glittering crowd,
Of titles, birth, and fortune proud,
(As fools are insolent and vain)
Madly aspired to wear her chain;
But Pallas, guardian of the maid,
Descending to her charge's aid,
Held out Medusa's snaky locks,
Which stupified them all to stocks.
The nymph with indignation view'd
The dull, the noisy, and the lewd;
For Pallas, with celestial light,
Had purified her mortal sight;
Show'd her the virtues all combined,
Fresh blooming, in young Harley's mind.
    Terrestrial nymphs, by formal arts,
Display their various nets for hearts:
Their looks are all by method set,
When to be prude, and when coquette;
Yet, wanting skill and power to chuse,
Their only pride is to refuse.
But, when a goddess would bestow
Her love on some bright youth below,
Round all the earth she casts her eyes;
And then, descending from the skies,
Makes choice of him she fancies best,
And bids the ravish'd youth be bless'd.
Thus the bright empress of the morn
Chose for her spouse a mortal born:
The goddess made advances first;
Else what aspiring hero durst?
Though, like a virgin of fifteen,
She blushes when by mortals seen;
Still blushes, and with speed retires,
When Sol pursues her with his fires.
    Diana thus, Heaven's chastest queen
Struck with Endymion's graceful mien

Down from her silver chariot came,
And to the shepherd own'd her flame.
    Thus Ca'endish, as Aurora bright,
And chaster than the Queen of Night
Descended from her sphere to find
A mortal of superior kind.

Phyllis; or, the Progress of Love, 1716

Desponding Phyllis was endu'd
With ev'ry talent of a prude:
She trembled when a man drew near;
Salute her, and she turn'd her ear:
If o'er against her you were placed,
She durst not look above your waist:
She'd rather take you to her bed,
Than let you see her dress her head;
In church you hear her, thro' the crowd,
Repeat the absolution loud:
In church, secure behind her fan,
She durst behold that monster man:
There practis'd how to place her head,
And bite her lips to make them red;
Or, on the mat devoutly kneeling,
Would lift her eyes up to the ceiling.
And heave her bosom unaware,
For neighb'ring beaux to see it bare.
At length a lucky lover came,
And found admittance to the dame,
Suppose all parties now agreed,
The writings drawn, the lawyer feed,
The vicar and the ring bespoke:
Guess, how could such a match be broke?
See then what mortals place their bliss in!
Next morn betimes the bride was missing:
The mother scream'd, the father chid;
Where can this idle wench be hid?
No news of Phyl! the bridegroom came,
And thought his bride had skulk'd for shame;
Because her father used to say,
The girl had such a bashful way!
Now John the butler must be sent
To learn the road that Phyllis went:
The groom was wish'd to saddle Crop;
For John must neither light nor stop,

But find her, wheresoe'er she fled,
And bring her back alive or dead.
    See here again the devil to do!
For truly John was missing too:
The horse and pillion both were gone!
Phyllis, it seems, was fled with John.
    Old Madam, who went up to find
What papers Phyl had left behind,
A letter on the toilet sees,
"To my much honour'd father—these—"
('Tis always done, romances tell us,
When daughters run away with fellows,)
Fill'd with the choicest common-places,
By others used in the like cases.
"That long ago a fortune-teller
Exactly said what now befell her;
And in a glass had made her see
A serving-man of low degree.
It was her fate, must be forgiven;
For marriages were made in Heaven:
His pardon begg'd: but, to be plain,
She'd do't if 'twere to do again:
Thank'd God, 'twas neither shame nor sin;
For John was come of honest kin.
Love never thinks of rich and poor;
She'd beg with John from door to door.
Forgive her, if it be a crime;
She'll never do't another time.
She ne'er before in all her life
Once disobey'd him, maid nor wife."
One argument she summ'd up all in,
"The thing was done and past recalling;
And therefore hoped she should recover
His favour when his passion's over.
She valued not what others thought her,
And was—his most obedient daughter."
Fair maidens all, attend the Muse,
Who now the wand'ring pair pursues:
Away they rode in homely sort,

Their journey long, their money short;
The loving couple well bemir'd;
The horse and both the riders tir'd:
Their victuals bad, their lodgings worse;
Phyl cried! and John began to curse:
Phyl wish'd that she had strain'd a limb,
When first she ventured out with him;
John wish'd that he had broke a leg,
When first for her he quitted Peg.
    But what adventures more befell 'em,
The Muse hath now no time to tell 'em;
How Johnny wheedled, threaten'd, fawn'd,
Till Phyllis all her trinkets pawn'd:
How oft she broke her marriage vows,
In kindness to maintain her spouse,
Till swains unwholesome spoil'd the trade;
For now the surgeon must be paid,
To whom those perquisites are gone,
In Christian justice due to John.
    When food and raiment now grew scarce,
Fate put a period to the farce,
And with exact poetic justice;
For John was landlord, Phyllis hostess;
They keep, at Stains, the Old Blue Boar,
Are cat and dog, and rogue and whore.

Horace, Book IV, Ode IX
Addressed to Archbishop King, 1718

Virtue conceal'd within our breast
Is inactivity at best:
But never shall the Muse endure
To let your virtues lie obscure;
Or suffer Envy to conceal
Your labours for the public weal.
Within your breast all wisdom lies,
Either to govern or advise;
Your steady soul preserves her frame,
In good and evil times, the same.
Pale Avarice and lurking Fraud,
Stand in your sacred presence awed;
Your hand alone from gold abstains,
Which drags the slavish world in chains.
    Him for a happy man I own,
Whose fortune is not overgrown;
And happy he who wisely knows
To use the gifts that Heaven bestows;
Or, if it please the powers divine,
Can suffer want and not repine.
The man who infamy to shun
Into the arms of death would run;
That man is ready to defend,
With life, his country or his friend.

To Mr. Delany

Oct. 10, 1718 Nine in the Morning

To you whose virtues, I must own
With shame, I have too lately known;
To you, by art and nature taught
To be the man I long have sought,
Had not ill Fate, perverse and blind,
Placed you in life too far behind:
Or, what I should repine at more,
Placed me in life too far before:
To you the Muse this verse bestows,
Which might as well have been in prose;
No thought, no fancy, no sublime,
But simple topics told in rhyme.
    Three gifts for conversation fit
Are humour, raillery, and wit:
The last, as boundless as the wind,
Is well conceived, though not defined;
For, sure by wit is only meant
Applying what we first invent.
What humour is, not all the tribe
Of logic-mongers can describe;
Here only nature acts her part,
Unhelp'd by practice, books, or art:
For wit and humour differ quite;
That gives surprise, and this delight,
Humour is odd, grotesque, and wild,
Only by affectation spoil'd;
'Tis never by invention got,
Men have it when they know it not.
    Our conversation to refine,
True humour must with wit combine:
From both we learn to rally well,
Wherein French writers most excel;
Voiture, in various lights, displays
That irony which turns to praise:

His genius first found out the rule
For an obliging ridicule:
He flatters with peculiar air
The brave, the witty, and the fair:
And fools would fancy he intends
A satire where he most commends.
    But as a poor pretending beau,
Because he fain would make a show,
Nor can afford to buy gold lace,
Takes up with copper in the place:
So the pert dunces of mankind,
Whene'er they would be thought refined,
Because the diff'rence lies abstruse
'Twixt raillery and gross abuse,
To show their parts will scold and rail,
Like porters o'er a pot of ale.
    Such is that clan of boisterous bears,
Always together by the ears;
Shrewd fellows and arch wags, a tribe
That meet for nothing but to gibe;
Who first run one another down,
And then fall foul on all the town;
Skill'd in the horse-laugh and dry rub,
And call'd by excellence The Club.
I mean your butler, Dawson, Car,
All special friends, and always jar.
    The mettled and the vicious steed
Do not more differ in their breed,
Nay, Voiture is as like Tom Leigh,
As rudeness is to repartee.
    If what you said I wish unspoke,
'Twill not suffice it was a joke:
Reproach not, though in jest, a friend
For those defects he cannot mend;
His lineage, calling, shape, or sense,
If named with scorn, gives just offence.
    What use in life to make men fret,
Part in worse humour than they met?
Thus all society is lost,

Men laugh at one another's cost:
And half the company is teazed
That came together to be pleased:
For all buffoons have most in view
To please themselves by vexing you.
When jests are carried on too far,
And the loud laugh begins the war,
You keep your countenance for shame,
Yet still you think your friend to blame;
For though men cry they love a jest,
'Tis but when others stand the test;
And (would you have their meaning known)
They love a jest when 'tis their own.
You wonder now to see me write
So gravely where the subject's light;
Some part of what I here design
Regards a friend of yours and mine;
Who full of humour, fire, and wit,
Not always judges what is fit,
But loves to take prodigious rounds,
And sometimes walks beyond his bounds,
You must, although the point be nice,
Venture to give him some advice;
Few hints from you will set him right,
And teach him how to be polite.
Bid him like you, observe with care,
Whom to be hard on, whom to spare;
Nor indiscreetly to suppose
All subjects like Dan Jackson's nose.
To study the obliging jest,
By reading those who teach it best;
For prose I recommend Voiture's,
For verse (I speak my judgment) yours.
He'll find the secret out from thence,
To rhyme all day without offence;
And I no more shall then accuse
The flirts of his ill-manner'd Muse.
If he be guilty, you must mend him;
If he be innocent, defend him.

An Elegy

On the Death of Demar, the Usurer; who Died on the 6th of July, 1720

Know all men by these presents, Death, the tamer,
By mortgage has secured the corpse of Demar;
Nor can four hundred thousand sterling pound
Redeem him from his prison underground.
His heirs might well, of all his wealth possesst
Bestow, to bury him, one iron chest.
Plutus, the god of wealth, will joy to know
His faithful steward in the shades below.
He walk'd the streets, and wore a threadbare cloak;
He din'd and supp'd at charge of other folk:
And by his looks, had he held out his palms,
He might be thought an object fit for alms.
So, to the poor if he refus'd his pelf,
He us'd 'em full as kindly as himself.
Where'er he went, he never saw his betters;
Lords, knights, and squires, were all his humble debtors;
And under hand and seal, the Irish nation
Were forc'd to own to him their obligation.
He that cou'd once have half a kingdom bought,
In half a minute is not worth a groat.
His coffers from the coffin could not save,
Nor all his int'rest keep him from the grave.
A golden monument would not be right,
Because we wish the earth upon him light.
Oh London Tavern! thou hast lost a friend,
Tho' in thy walls he ne'er did farthing spend;
He touch'd the pence when others touch'd the pot;
The hand that sign'd the mortgage paid the shot.
Old as he was, no vulgar known disease
On him could ever boast a pow'r to seize;
"But as the gold he weigh'd, grim death in spight
Cast in his dart, which made three moidores light;
And, as he saw his darling money fail,

Blew his last breath to sink the lighter scale."
He who so long was current, 'twould be strange
If he should now be cry'd down since his change.
    The sexton shall green sods on thee bestow;
Alas, the sexton is thy banker now!
A dismal banker must that banker be,
Who gives no bills but of mortality!

Epitaph on the Same

Beneath this verdant hillock lies
Demar, the wealthy and the wise,
His heirs, that he might safely rest,
Have put his carcass in a chest;
The very chest in which, they say,
His other self, his money, lay.
And, if his heirs continue kind
To that dear self he left behind,
I dare believe, that four in five
Will think his better self alive.

To Mrs. Houghton of Bourmont, On Praising her Husband to Dr. Swift

You always are making a god of your spouse;
But this neither Reason nor Conscience allows;
Perhaps you will say, 'tis in gratitude due,
And you adore him, because he adores you.
Your argument's weak, and so you will find;
For you, by this rule, must adore all mankind.

Verses Written on a Window, at the Deanery House, St. Patrick's

Are the guests of this house still doom'd to be cheated?
Sure the Fates have decreed they by halves should be treated.
In the days of good John if you came here to dine,
You had choice of good meat, but no choice of good wine.
In Jonathan's reign, if you come here to eat,
You have choice of good wine, but no choice of good meat.
O Jove! then how fully might all sides be blest,
Wouldst thou but agree to this humble request!
Put both deans in one; or, if that's too much trouble,
Instead of the deans, make the deanery double.

On Another Window

A bard, on whom Phoebus his spirit bestow'd,
Resolving t'acknowledge the bounty he owed,
Found out a new method at once of confessing,
And making the most of so mighty a blessing:
To the God he'd be grateful; but mortals he'd chouse,
By making his patron preside in his house;
And wisely foresaw this advantage from thence,
That the God would in honour bear most of th'expense;
So the bard he finds drink, and leaves Phoebus to treat
With the thoughts he inspires, regardless of meat.
Hence they that come hither expecting to dine,
Are always fobb'd off with sheer wit and sheer wine.

Apollo to the Dean. 1720

Right Trusty, and so forth—we let you know
We are very ill used by you mortals below.
For, first, I have often by chemists been told,
(Though I know nothing on't,) it is I that make gold;
Which when you have got, you so carefully hide it,
That, since I was born, I hardly have spied it.
Then it must be allow'd, that, whenever I shine,
I forward the grass, and I ripen the vine;
To me the good fellows apply for relief,
Without whom they could get neither claret nor beef:
Yet their wine and their victuals, those curmudgeon lubbards
Lock up from my sight in cellars and cupboards.
That I have an ill eye, they wickedly think,
And taint all their meat, and sour all their drink.
But, thirdly and lastly, it must be allow'd,
I alone can inspire the poetical crowd:
This is gratefully own'd by each boy in the College,
Whom, if I inspire, it is not to my knowledge.
This every pretender in rhyme will admit,
Without troubling his head about judgment or wit.
These gentlemen use me with kindness and freedom,
And as for their works, when I please I may read 'em.
They lie open on purpose on counters and stalls,
And the titles I view, when I shine on the walls.
    But a comrade of yours, that traitor Delany,
Whom I for your sake have used better than any,
And, of my mere motion, and special good grace,
Intended in time to succeed in your place,
On Tuesday the tenth, seditiously came,
With a certain false trait'ress, one Stella by name,
To the Deanery-house, and on the North glass,
Where for fear of the cold I never can pass,
Then and there, vi et armis, with a certain utensil,
Of value five shillings, in English a pencil,
Did maliciously, falsely, and trait'rously write,
While Stella, aforesaid, stood by with a light.

My sister hath lately deposed upon oath,
That she stopt in her course to look at them both;
That Stella was helping, abetting, and aiding;
And still as he writ, stood smiling and reading:
That her eyes were as bright as myself at noon-day,
But her graceful black locks were all mingled with grey:
And by the description, I certainly know,
'Tis the nymph that I courted some ten years ago;
Whom when I with the best of my talents endued,
On her promise of yielding, she acted the prude:
That some verses were writ with felonious intent,
Direct to the North, where I never once went:
That the letters appear'd reversed through the pane,
But in Stella's bright eyes were placed right again;
Wherein she distinctly could read ev'ry line,
And presently guessed the fancy was mine.
She can swear to the Parson whom oft she has seen
At night between Cavan Street and College Green.
    Now you see why his verses so seldom are shown,
The reason is plain, they are none of his own;
And observe while you live that no man is shy
To discover the goods he came honestly by.
If I light on a thought, he will certainly steal it,
And when he has got it, find ways to conceal it.
Of all the fine things he keeps in the dark,
There's scarce one in ten but what has my mark;
And let them be seen by the world if he dare,
I'll make it appear they are all stolen ware.
But as for the poem he writ on your sash,
I think I have now got him under my lash;
My sister transcribed it last night to his sorrow,
And the public shall see't, if I live till to-morrow.
Thro' the zodiac around, it shall quickly be spread
In all parts of the globe where your language is read.
    He knows very well, I ne'er gave a refusal,
When he ask'd for my aid in the forms that are usual:
But the secret is this; I did lately intend
To write a few verses on you as my friend:
I studied a fortnight, before I could find,

As I rode in my chariot, a thought to my mind,
And resolved the next winter (for that is my time,
When the days are at shortest) to get it in rhyme;
Till then it was lock'd in my box at Parnassus;
When that subtle companion, in hopes to surpass us,
Conveys out my paper of hints by a trick
(For I think in my conscience he deals with old Nick,)
And from my own stock provided with topics,
He gets to a window beyond both the tropics,
There out of my sight, just against the north zone,
Writes down my conceits, and then calls them his own;
And you, like a cully, the bubble can swallow:
Now who but Delany that writes like Apollo?
High treason by statute! yet here you object,
He only stole hints, but the verse is correct;
Though the thought be Apollo's, 'tis finely express'd;
So a thief steals my horse, and has him well dress'd.
Now whereas the said criminal seems past repentance,
We Phoebus think fit to proceed to his sentence.
Since Delany hath dared, like Prometheus his sire,
To climb to our region, and thence to steal fire;
We order a vulture in shape of the Spleen,
To prey on his liver, but not to be seen.
And we order our subjects of every degree
To believe all his verses were written by me:
And under the pain of our highest displeasure,
To call nothing his but the rhyme and the measure.
And, lastly, for Stella, just out of her prime,
I'm too much revenged already by Time,
In return of her scorn, I sent her diseases,
But will now be her friend whenever she pleases.
And the gifts I bestow'd her will find her a lover
Though she lives till she's grey as a badger all over.

News from Parnassus By Dr. Delany

Occasioned by "Apollo to the Dean" 1720

Parnassus, February the twenty-seventh.
The poets assembled here on the eleventh,
Convened by Apollo, who gave them to know
He'd have a vicegerent in his empire below;
But declared that no bard should this honour inherit,
Till the rest had agreed he surpass'd them in merit:
Now this, you'll allow, was a difficult case,
For each bard believed he'd a right to the place;
So, finding the assembly grow warm in debate,
He put them in mind of his Phaethon's fate:
'Twas urged to no purpose; disputes higher rose,
Scarce Phoebus himself could their quarrels compose;
Till at length he determined that every bard
Should (each in his turn) be patiently heard.
    First, one who believed he excell'd in translation,
Founds his claim on the doctrine of man's transmigration:
"Since the soul of great Milton was given to me,
I hope the convention will quickly agree."—
"Agree;" quoth Apollo: "from whence is this fool?
Is he just come from reading Pythagoras at school?
Begone, sir, you've got your subscriptions in time,
And given in return neither reason nor rhyme."
To the next says the God, "Though now I won't chuse you,
I'll tell you the reason for which I refuse you:
Love's Goddess has oft to her parents complain'd,
Of my favouring a bard who her empire disdain'd;
That at my instigation, a poem you writ,
Which to beauty and youth preferr'd judgment and wit;
That, to make you a Laureate, I gave the first voice,
Inspiring the Britons t'approve of my choice.
Jove sent her to me, her power to try;
The Goddess of Beauty what God can deny?

She forbids your preferment; I grant her desire.
Appease the fair Goddess: you then may rise higher."
  The next that appear'd had good hopes of succeeding,
For he merited much for his wit and his breeding.
'Twas wise in the Britons no favour to show him,
He else might expect they should pay what they owe him.
And therefore they prudently chose to discard
The Patriot, whose merits they would not reward:
The God, with a smile, bade his favourite advance,
"You were sent by Astraea her envoy to France:
You bend your ambition to rise in the state;
I refuse you, because you could stoop to be great."
  Then a bard who had been a successful translator,
"The convention allows me a versificator."
Says Apollo, "You mention the least of your merit;
By your works, it appears you have much of my spirit.
I esteem you so well, that, to tell you the truth,
The greatest objection against you's your youth;
Then be not concern'd you are now laid aside;
If you live you shall certainly one day preside."
  Another, low bending, Apollo thus greets,
"'Twas I taught your subjects to walk through the streets."
  You taught them to walk! why, they knew it before;
But give me the bard that can teach them to soar.
Whenever he claims, 'tis his right, I'll confess,
Who lately attempted my style with success;
Who writes like Apollo has most of his spirit,
And therefore 'tis just I distinguish his merit:
Who makes it appear, by all he has writ,
His judgment alone can set bounds to his wit;
Like Virgil correct, with his own native ease,
But excels even Virgil in elegant praise:
Who admires the ancients, and knows 'tis their due
Yet writes in a manner entirely new;
Though none with more ease their depths can explore,
Yet whatever he wants he takes from my store;
Though I'm fond of his virtues, his pride I can see,
In scorning to borrow from any but me:

It is owing to this, that, like Cynthia, his lays
Enlighten the world by reflecting my rays.
This said, the whole audience soon found out his drift:
The convention was summon'd in favour of Swift.

Apollo's Edict
Occasioned by "News from Parnassus"

Ireland is now our royal care,
We lately fix'd our viceroy there.
How near was she to be undone,
Till pious love inspired her son!
What cannot our vicegerent do,
As poet and as patriot too?
Let his success our subjects sway,
Our inspirations to obey,
And follow where he leads the way:
Then study to correct your taste;
Nor beaten paths be longer traced.
    No simile shall be begun,
With rising or with setting sun;
And let the secret head of Nile
Be ever banish'd from your isle.
    When wretched lovers live on air,
I beg you'll the chameleon spare;
And when you'd make a hero grander,
Forget he's like a salamander.
    No son of mine shall dare to say,
Aurora usher'd in the day,
Or ever name the milky-way.
You all agree, I make no doubt,
Elijah's mantle is worn out.
    The bird of Jove shall toil no more
To teach the humble wren to soar.
Your tragic heroes shall not rant,
Nor shepherds use poetic cant.
Simplicity alone can grace
The manners of the rural race.
Theocritus and Philips be
Your guides to true simplicity.
    When Damon's soul shall take its flight,
Though poets have the second-sight,
They shall not see a trail of light.
Nor shall the vapours upwards rise,

Nor a new star adorn the skies:
For who can hope to place one there,
As glorious as Belinda's hair?
Yet, if his name you'd eternize,
And must exalt him to the skies;
Without a star this may be done:
So Tickell mourn'd his Addison.
    If Anna's happy reign you praise,
Pray, not a word of halcyon days:
Nor let my votaries show their skill
In aping lines from Cooper's Hill;
For know I cannot bear to hear
The mimicry of "deep, yet clear."
    Whene'er my viceroy is address'd,
Against the phoenix I protest.
When poets soar in youthful strains,
No Phaethon to hold the reins.
    When you describe a lovely girl,
No lips of coral, teeth of pearl.
    Cupid shall ne'er mistake another,
However beauteous, for his mother;
Nor shall his darts at random fly
From magazine in Celia's eye.
With woman compounds I am cloy'd,
Which only pleased in Biddy Floyd.
For foreign aid what need they roam,
Whom fate has amply blest at home?
    Unerring Heaven, with bounteous hand,
Has form'd a model for your land,
Whom Jove endued with every grace;
The glory of the Granard race;
Now destined by the powers divine
The blessing of another line.
Then, would you paint a matchless dame,
Whom you'd consign to endless fame?
Invoke not Cytherea's aid,
Nor borrow from the blue-eyed maid;
Nor need you on the Graces call;
Take qualities from Donegal.

The Description of an Irish Feast

Given by O'Rourke, a powerful chieftain of Ulster in the reign of Queen Elizabeth, previously to his making a visit to her court. A song was composed upon the tradition of the feast, the fame of which having reached Swift, he was supplied with a literal version, from which he executed the following very spirited translation.

—W. E. B.

Translated Almost Literally out of the Original Irish. 1720

O'Rourke's noble fare
Will ne'er be forgot,
By those who were there,
Or those who were not.

His revels to keep,
We sup and we dine
On seven score sheep,
Fat bullocks, and swine.

Usquebaugh to our feast
In pails was brought up,
A hundred at least,
And a madder our cup.

O there is the sport!
We rise with the light
In disorderly sort,
From snoring all night.

O how was I trick'd!
My pipe it was broke,
My pocket was pick'd,
I lost my new cloak.

I'm rifled, quoth Nell,
    Of mantle and kercher,
Why then fare them well,
    The de'el take the searcher.

Come, harper, strike up;
    But, first, by your favour,
Boy, give us a cup:
    Ah! this hath some savour.

O'Rourke's jolly boys
    Ne'er dreamt of the matter,
Till, roused by the noise,
    And musical clatter,

They bounce from their nest,
    No longer will tarry,
They rise ready drest,
    Without one Ave-Mary.

They dance in a round,
    Cutting capers and ramping;
A mercy the ground
    Did not burst with their stamping.

The floor is all wet
    With leaps and with jumps,
While the water and sweat
    Splish-splash in their pumps.

Bless you late and early,
    Laughlin O'Enagin!
But, my hand, you dance rarely.
    Margery Grinagin.

Bring straw for our bed,
    Shake it down to the feet,
Then over us spread
    The winnowing sheet.

To show I don't flinch,
    Fill the bowl up again:
Then give us a pinch
    Of your sneezing, a Yean.

Good lord! what a sight,
    After all their good cheer,
For people to fight
    In the midst of their beer!

They rise from their feast,
    And hot are their brains,
A cubit at least
    The length of their skeans.

What stabs and what cuts,
    What clattering of sticks;
What strokes on the guts,
    What bastings and kicks!

With cudgels of oak,
    Well harden'd in flame,
A hundred heads broke,
    A hundred struck lame.

You churl, I'll maintain
    My father built Lusk,
The castle of Slane,
    And Carrick Drumrusk:

The Earl of Kildare,
    And Moynalta his brother,
As great as they are,
    I was nurst by their mother.

Ask that of old madam:
    She'll tell you who's who,
As far up as Adam,
    She knows it is true.

Come down with that beam,
    If cudgels are scarce,
A blow on the weam,
    Or a kick on the a——se.

The Progress of Beauty. 1719

When first Diana leaves her bed,
    Vapours and steams her looks disgrace,
A frowzy dirty-colour'd red
    Sits on her cloudy wrinkled face:

But by degrees, when mounted high,
    Her artificial face appears
Down from her window in the sky,
    Her spots are gone, her visage clears.

'Twixt earthly females and the moon,
    All parallels exactly run;
If Celia should appear too soon,
    Alas, the nymph would be undone!

To see her from her pillow rise,
    All reeking in a cloudy steam,
Crack'd lips, foul teeth, and gummy eyes,
    Poor Strephon! how would he blaspheme!

The soot or powder which was wont
    To make her hair look black as jet,
Falls from her tresses on her front,
    A mingled mass of dirt and sweat.

Three colours, black, and red, and white
    So graceful in their proper place,
Remove them to a different light,
    They form a frightful hideous face:

For instance, when the lily slips
    Into the precincts of the rose,
And takes possession of the lips,
    Leaving the purple to the nose:

So Celia went entire to bed,
All her complexion safe and sound;
But, when she rose, the black and red,
Though still in sight, had changed their ground.

The black, which would not be confined,
A more inferior station seeks,
Leaving the fiery red behind,
And mingles in her muddy cheeks.

The paint by perspiration cracks,
And falls in rivulets of sweat,
On either side you see the tracks
While at her chin the conflu'nts meet.

A skilful housewife thus her thumb,
With spittle while she spins anoints;
And thus the brown meanders come
In trickling streams betwixt her joints.

But Celia can with ease reduce,
By help of pencil, paint, and brush,
Each colour to its place and use,
And teach her cheeks again to blush.

She knows her early self no more,
But fill'd with admiration stands;
As other painters oft adore
The workmanship of their own hands.

Thus, after four important hours,
Celia's the wonder of her sex;
Say, which among the heavenly powers
Could cause such wonderful effects?

Venus, indulgent to her kind,
Gave women all their hearts could wish,
When first she taught them where to find
White lead, and Lusitanian dish.

Love with white lead cements his wings;
    White lead was sent us to repair
Two brightest, brittlest, earthly things,
    A lady's face, and China-ware.

She ventures now to lift the sash;
    The window is her proper sphere;
Ah, lovely nymph! be not too rash,
    Nor let the beaux approach too near.

Take pattern by your sister star;
    Delude at once and bless our sight;
When you are seen, be seen from far,
    And chiefly choose to shine by night.

In the Pall Mall when passing by,
    Keep up the glasses of your chair,
Then each transported fop will cry,
    "G——d d——n me, Jack, she's wondrous fair!"

But art no longer can prevail,
    When the materials all are gone;
The best mechanic hand must fail,
    Where nothing's left to work upon.

Matter, as wise logicians say,
    Cannot without a form subsist;
And form, say I, as well as they,
    Must fail if matter brings no grist.

And this is fair Diana's case;
    For, all astrologers maintain,
Each night a bit drops off her face,
    When mortals say she's in her wane:

While Partridge wisely shows the cause
    Efficient of the moon's decay,
That Cancer with his pois'nous claws
    Attacks her in the milky way:

But Gadbury, in art profound,
    From her pale cheeks pretends to show
That swain Endymion is not sound,
    Or else that Mercury's her foe.

But let the cause be what it will,
    In half a month she looks so thin,
That Flamsteed can, with all his skill,
    See but her forehead and her chin.

Yet, as she wastes, she grows discreet,
    Till midnight never shows her head;
So rotting Celia strolls the street,
    When sober folks are all a-bed:

For sure, if this be Luna's fate,
    Poor Celia, but of mortal race,
In vain expects a longer date
    To the materials of her face.

When Mercury her tresses mows,
    To think of oil and soot is vain:
No painting can restore a nose,
    Nor will her teeth return again.

Two balls of glass may serve for eyes,
    White lead can plaister up a cleft;
But these, alas, are poor supplies
    If neither cheeks nor lips be left.

Ye powers who over love preside!
    Since mortal beauties drop so soon,
If ye would have us well supplied,
    Send us new nymphs with each new moon!

The Progress of Marriage

Aetatis Suae fifty-two,
A reverend Dean began to woo
A handsome, young, imperious girl,
Nearly related to an earl.
Her parents and her friends consent;
The couple to the temple went:
They first invite the Cyprian queen;
'Twas answer'd, "She would not be seen;"
But Cupid in disdain could scarce
Forbear to bid them kiss his—
The Graces next, and all the Muses,
Were bid in form, but sent excuses.
Juno attended at the porch,
With farthing candle for a torch;
While mistress Iris held her train,
The faded bow bedropt with rain.
Then Hebe came, and took her place,
But show'd no more than half her face.
  Whate'er these dire forebodings meant,
In joy the marriage-day was spent;
The marriage-*day*, you take me right,
I promise nothing for the night.
The bridegroom, drest to make a figure,
Assumes an artificial vigour;
A flourish'd nightcap on, to grace
His ruddy, wrinkled, smirking face;
Like the faint red upon a pippin,
Half wither'd by a winter's keeping.
  And thus set out this happy pair,
The swain is rich, the nymph is fair;
But, what I gladly would forget,
The swain is old, the nymph coquette.
Both from the goal together start;
Scarce run a step before they part;
No common ligament that binds
The various textures of their minds;

Their thoughts and actions, hopes and fears,
Less corresponding than their years.
The Dean desires his coffee soon,
She rises to her tea at noon.
While the Dean goes out to cheapen books,
She at the glass consults her looks;
While Betty's buzzing at her ear,
Lord, what a dress these parsons wear!
So odd a choice how could she make!
Wish'd him a colonel for her sake.
Then, on her finger ends she counts,
Exact, to what his age amounts.
The Dean, she heard her uncle say,
Is sixty, if he be a day;
His ruddy cheeks are no disguise;
You see the crow's feet round his eyes.
    At one she rambles to the shops,
To cheapen tea, and talk with fops;
Or calls a council of her maids,
And tradesmen, to compare brocades.
Her weighty morning business o'er,
Sits down to dinner just at four;
Minds nothing that is done or said,
Her evening work so fills her head.
The Dean, who used to dine at one,
Is mawkish, and his stomach's gone;
In threadbare gown, would scarce a louse hold,
Looks like the chaplain of the household;
Beholds her, from the chaplain's place,
In French brocades, and Flanders lace;
He wonders what employs her brain,
But never asks, or asks in vain;
His mind is full of other cares,
And, in the sneaking parson's airs,
Computes, that half a parish dues
Will hardly find his wife in shoes.
    Canst thou imagine, dull divine,
'Twill gain her love, to make her fine?
Hath she no other wants beside?

You feed her lust as well as pride,
Enticing coxcombs to adore,
And teach her to despise thee more.
    If in her coach she'll condescend
To place him at the hinder end,
Her hoop is hoist above his nose,
His odious gown would soil her clothes.
She drops him at the church, to pray,
While she drives on to see the play.
He like an orderly divine,
Comes home a quarter after nine,
And meets her hasting to the ball:
Her chairmen push him from the wall.
The Dean gets in and walks up stairs,
And calls the family to prayers;
Then goes alone to take his rest
In bed, where he can spare her best.
At five the footmen make a din,
Her ladyship is just come in;
The masquerade began at two,
She stole away with much ado;
And shall be chid this afternoon,
For leaving company so soon:
She'll say, and she may truly say't,
She can't abide to stay out late.
    But now, though scarce a twelvemonth married,
Poor Lady Jane has thrice miscarried:
The cause, alas! is quickly guest;
The town has whisper'd round the jest.
Think on some remedy in time,
The Dean you see, is past his prime,
Already dwindled to a lath:
No other way but try the Bath.
    For Venus, rising from the ocean,
Infused a strong prolific potion,
That mix'd with Acheloüs spring,
The horned flood, as poets sing,
Who, with an English beauty smitten,
Ran under ground from Greece to Britain;

The genial virtue with him brought,
And gave the nymph a plenteous draught;
Then fled, and left his horn behind,
For husbands past their youth to find;
The nymph, who still with passion burn'd,
Was to a boiling fountain turn'd,
Where childless wives crowd every morn,
To drink in Acheloüs horn;
Or bathe beneath the Cross their limbs
Where fruitful matter chiefly swims.
And here the father often gains
That title by another's pains.
    Hither, though much against his grain
The Dean has carried Lady Jane.
He, for a while, would not consent,
But vow'd his money all was spent:
Was ever such a clownish reason!
And must my lady slip her season?
The doctor, with a double fee,
Was bribed to make the Dean agree.
    Here, all diversions of the place
Are proper in my lady's case:
With which she patiently complies,
Merely because her friends advise;
His money and her time employs
In music, raffling-rooms, and toys;
Or in the Cross-bath seeks an heir,
Since others oft have found one there;
Where if the Dean by chance appears,
It shames his cassock and his years.
He keeps his distance in the gallery,
Till banish'd by some coxcomb's raillery;
For 'twould his character expose,
To bathe among the belles and beaux.
    So have I seen, within a pen,
Young ducklings foster'd by a hen;
But, when let out, they run and muddle,
As instinct leads them, in a puddle;
The sober hen, not born to swim,

With mournful note clucks round the brim.
    The Dean, with all his best endeavour,
Gets not an heir, but gets a fever.
A victim to the last essays
Of vigour in declining days,
He dies, and leaves his mourning mate
(What could he less?) his whole estate.
    The widow goes through all her forms:
New lovers now will come in swarms.
O, may I see her soon dispensing
Her favours to some broken ensign!
Him let her marry for his face,
And only coat of tarnish'd lace;
To turn her naked out of doors,
And spend her jointure on his whores;
But, for a parting present, leave her
A rooted pox to last for ever!

The Progress of Poetry

The farmer's goose, who in the stubble
Has fed without restraint or trouble,
Grown fat with corn and sitting still,
Can scarce get o'er the barn-door sill;
And hardly waddles forth to cool
Her belly in the neighbouring pool!
Nor loudly cackles at the door;
For cackling shows the goose is poor.
    But, when she must be turn'd to graze,
And round the barren common strays,
Hard exercise, and harder fare,
Soon make my dame grow lank and spare;
Her body light, she tries her wings,
And scorns the ground, and upward springs;
While all the parish, as she flies,
Hear sounds harmonious from the skies.
    Such is the poet fresh in pay,
The third night's profits of his play;
His morning draughts till noon can swill,
Among his brethren of the quill:
With good roast beef his belly full,
Grown lazy, foggy, fat, and dull,
Deep sunk in plenty and delight,
What poet e'er could take his flight?
Or, stuff'd with phlegm up to the throat,
What poet e'er could sing a note?
Nor Pegasus could bear the load
Along the high celestial road;
The steed, oppress'd, would break his girth,
To raise the lumber from the earth.
    But view him in another scene,
When all his drink is Hippocrene,
His money spent, his patrons fail,
His credit out for cheese and ale;
His two-years coat so smooth and bare,
Through every thread it lets in air;

With hungry meals his body pined,
His guts and belly full of wind;
And, like a jockey for a race,
His flesh brought down to flying case:
Now his exalted spirit loathes
Encumbrances of food and clothes;
And up he rises like a vapour,
Supported high on wings of paper.
He singing flies, and flying sings,
While from below all Grub-Street rings.

The South-Sea Project. 1721

Apparent rari nantes in gurgite vasto,
Arma virûm, tabulaeque, et Troïa gaza per undas.

—Virg.

For particulars of this famous scheme for reducing the National Debt, projected by Sir John Blunt, who became one of the Directors of it, and ultimately one of the greatest sufferers by it, when the Bubble burst, see Smollett's "History of England," vol. ii; Pope's "Moral Essays," Epist. iii, and notes; and Gibbon's "Memoirs," for the violent and arbitrary proceedings against the Directors, one of whom was his grandfather.

—W. E. B.

Ye wise philosophers, explain
    What magic makes our money rise,
When dropt into the Southern main;
    Or do these jugglers cheat our eyes?

Put in your money fairly told;
    Presto! be gone—'Tis here again:
Ladies and gentlemen, behold,
    Here's every piece as big as ten.

Thus in a basin drop a shilling,
    Then fill the vessel to the brim,
You shall observe, as you are filling,
    The pond'rous metal seems to swim:

It rises both in bulk and height,
    Behold it swelling like a sop;
The liquid medium cheats your sight:
    Behold it mounted to the top!

In stock three hundred thousand pounds,
    I have in view a lord's estate;
My manors all contiguous round!
    A coach-and-six, and served in plate!

Thus the deluded bankrupt raves,
    Puts all upon a desperate bet;
Then plunges in the Southern waves,
    Dipt over head and ears—in debt.

So, by a calenture misled,
    The mariner with rapture sees,
On the smooth ocean's azure bed,
    Enamell'd fields and verdant trees:

With eager haste he longs to rove
    In that fantastic scene, and thinks
It must be some enchanted grove;
    And in he leaps, and down he sinks.

Five hundred chariots just bespoke,
    Are sunk in these devouring waves,
The horses drown'd, the harness broke,
    And here the owners find their graves.

Like Pharaoh, by directors led,
    They with their spoils went safe before;
His chariots, tumbling out the dead,
    Lay shatter'd on the Red Sea shore.

Raised up on Hope's aspiring plumes,
    The young adventurer o'er the deep
An eagle's flight and state assumes,
    And scorns the middle way to keep.

On paper wings he takes his flight,
    With wax the father bound them fast;
The wax is melted by the height,
    And down the towering boy is cast.

A moralist might here explain
    The rashness of the Cretan youth;
Describe his fall into the main,
    And from a fable form a truth.

His wings are his paternal rent,
He melts the wax at every flame;
His credit sunk, his money spent,
In Southern Seas he leaves his name.

Inform us, you that best can tell,
Why in that dangerous gulf profound,
Where hundreds and where thousands fell,
Fools chiefly float, the wise are drown'd?

So have I seen from Severn's brink
A flock of geese jump down together;
Swim where the bird of Jove would sink,
And, swimming, never wet a feather.

But, I affirm, 'tis false in fact,
Directors better knew their tools;
We see the nation's credit crack'd,
Each knave has made a thousand fools.

One fool may from another win,
And then get off with money stored;
But, if a sharper once comes in,
He throws it all, and sweeps the board.

As fishes on each other prey,
The great ones swallowing up the small,
So fares it in the Southern Sea;
The whale directors eat up all.

When stock is high, they come between,
Making by second-hand their offers;
Then cunningly retire unseen,
With each a million in his coffers.

So, when upon a moonshine night,
An ass was drinking at a stream,
A cloud arose, and stopt the light,
By intercepting every beam:

The day of judgment will be soon,
    Cries out a sage among the crowd;
An ass has swallow'd up the moon!
    The moon lay safe behind the cloud.

Each poor subscriber to the sea
    Sinks down at once, and there he lies;
Directors fall as well as they,
    Their fall is but a trick to rise.

So fishes, rising from the main,
    Can soar with moisten'd wings on high;
The moisture dried, they sink again,
    And dip their fins again to fly.

Undone at play, the female troops
    Come here their losses to retrieve;
Ride o'er the waves in spacious hoops,
    Like Lapland witches in a sieve.

Thus Venus to the sea descends,
    As poets feign; but where's the moral?
It shows the Queen of Love intends
    To search the deep for pearl and coral.

The sea is richer than the land,
    I heard it from my grannam's mouth,
Which now I clearly understand;
    For by the sea she meant the South.

Thus, by directors we are told,
    "Pray, gentlemen, believe your eyes;
Our ocean's cover'd o'er with gold,
    Look round, and see how thick it lies:

"We, gentlemen, are your assisters,
    We'll come, and hold you by the chin."—
Alas! all is not gold that glisters,
    Ten thousand sink by leaping in.

O! would those patriots be so kind,
Here in the deep to wash their hands,
Then, like Pactolus, we should find
The sea indeed had golden sands.

A shilling in the bath you fling,
The silver takes a nobler hue,
By magic virtue in the spring,
And seems a guinea to your view.

But, as a guinea will not pass
At market for a farthing more,
Shown through a multiplying glass,
Than what it always did before:

So cast it in the Southern seas,
Or view it through a jobber's bill;
Put on what spectacles you please,
Your guinea's but a guinea still.

One night a fool into a brook
Thus from a hillock looking down,
The golden stars for guineas took,
And silver Cynthia for a crown.

The point he could no longer doubt;
He ran, he leapt into the flood;
There sprawl'd a while, and scarce got out,
All cover'd o'er with slime and mud.

"Upon the water cast thy bread,
And after many days thou'lt find it;"
But gold, upon this ocean spread,
Shall sink, and leave no mark behind it:

There is a gulf, where thousands fell,
Here all the bold adventurers came,
A narrow sound, though deep as Hell—
'Change Alley is the dreadful name.

Nine times a-day it ebbs and flows,
Yet he that on the surface lies,
Without a pilot seldom knows
The time it falls, or when 'twill rise.

Subscribers here by thousands float,
And jostle one another down;
Each paddling in his leaky boat,
And here they fish for gold, and drown.

"Now buried in the depth below,
Now mounted up to Heaven again,
They reel and stagger to and fro,
At their wits' end, like drunken men."

Meantime, secure on Garway cliffs,
A savage race, by shipwrecks fed,
Lie waiting for the founder'd skiffs,
And strip the bodies of the dead.

But these, you say, are factious lies,
From some malicious Tory's brain;
For, where directors get a prize,
The Swiss and Dutch whole millions drain.

Thus, when by rooks a lord is plied,
Some cully often wins a bet,
By venturing on the cheating side,
Though not into the secret let.

While some build castles in the air,
Directors build them in the seas;
Subscribers plainly see them there,
For fools will see as wise men please.

Thus oft by mariners are shown
(Unless the men of Kent are liars)
Earl Godwin's castles overflown,
And palace roofs, and steeple spires.

Mark where the sly directors creep,
    Nor to the shore approach too nigh!
The monsters nestle in the deep,
    To seize you in your passing by.

Then, like the dogs of Nile, be wise,
    Who, taught by instinct how to shun
The crocodile, that lurking lies,
    Run as they drink, and drink and run.

Antæus could, by magic charms,
    Recover strength whene'er he fell;
Alcides held him in his arms,
    And sent him up in air to Hell.

Directors, thrown into the sea,
    Recover strength and vigour there;
But may be tamed another way,
    Suspended for a while in air.

Directors! for 'tis you I warn,
    By long experience we have found
What planet ruled when you were born;
    We see you never can be drown'd.

Beware, nor overbulky grow,
    Nor come within your cully's reach;
For, if the sea should sink so low
    To leave you dry upon the beach,

You'll owe your ruin to your bulk:
    Your foes already waiting stand,
To tear you like a founder'd hulk,
    While you lie helpless on the sand.

Thus, when a whale has lost the tide,
    The coasters crowd to seize the spoil:
The monster into parts divide,
    And strip the bones, and melt the oil.

Oh! may some western tempest sweep
These locusts whom our fruits have fed,
That plague, directors, to the deep,
Driven from the South Sea to the Red!

May he, whom Nature's laws obey,
Who lifts the poor, and sinks the proud,
"Quiet the raging of the sea,
And still the madness of the crowd!"

But never shall our isle have rest,
Till those devouring swine run down,
(The devils leaving the possest)
And headlong in the waters drown.

The nation then too late will find,
Computing all their cost and trouble,
Directors' promises but wind,
South Sea, at best, a mighty bubble.

Fabula Canis et Umbrae

Ore cibum portans catulus dum spectat in undis,
Apparet liquido praedae melioris imago:
Dum speciosa diu damna admiratur, et altè
Ad latices inhiat, cadit imo vortice praeceps
Ore cibus, nee non simulacrum corripit una.
Occupat ille avidus deceptis faucibus umbram;
Illudit species, ac dentibus aëra mordet.

A Prologue

Billet to a Company of Players sent with the Prologue

The enclosed prologue is formed upon the story of the secretary's not allowing you to act, unless you would pay him £300 per annum; upon which you got a license from the Lord Mayor to act as strollers.

The prologue supposes, that upon your being forbidden to act, a company of country strollers came and hired the playhouse, and your clothes, etc. to act in.

Our set of strollers, wandering up and down,
Hearing the house was empty, came to town;
And, with a license from our good lord mayor,
Went to one Griffith, formerly a player:
Him we persuaded, with a moderate bribe,
To speak to Elrington and all the tribe,
To let our company supply their places,
And hire us out their scenes, and clothes, and faces.
Is not the truth the truth? Look full on me;
I am not Elrington, nor Griffith he.
When we perform, look sharp among our crew,
There's not a creature here you ever knew.
The former folks were servants to the king;
We, humble strollers, always on the wing.
Now, for my part, I think, upon the whole,
Rather than starve, a better man would stroll.
Stay! let me see—Three hundred pounds a-year,
For leave to act in town!—'Tis plaguy dear.
Now, here's a warrant; gallants, please to mark,
For three thirteens, and sixpence to the clerk.
Three hundred pounds! Were I the price to fix,
The public should bestow the actors six;
A score of guineas given underhand,
For a good word or so, we understand.
To help an honest lad that's out of place,
May cost a crown or so; a common case:
And, in a crew, 'tis no injustice thought

To ship a rogue, and pay him not a groat.
But, in the chronicles of former ages,
Who ever heard of servants paying wages?
    I pity Elrington with all my heart;
Would he were here this night to act my part!
I told him what it was to be a stroller;
How free we acted, and had no comptroller:
In every town we wait on Mr. Mayor,
First get a license, then produce our ware;
We sound a trumpet, or we beat a drum:
Huzza! (the schoolboys roar) the players are come;
And then we cry, to spur the bumpkins on,
Gallants, by Tuesday next we must be gone.
I told him in the smoothest way I could,
All this, and more, yet it would do no good.
But Elrington, tears falling from his cheeks,
He that has shone with Betterton and Wilks,
To whom our country has been always dear,
Who chose to leave his dearest pledges here,
Owns all your favours, here intends to stay,
And, as a stroller, act in every play:
And the whole crew this resolution takes,
To live and die all strollers, for your sakes;
Not frighted with an ignominious name,
For your displeasure is their only shame.
    A pox on Elrington's majestic tone!
Now to a word of business in our own.
    Gallants, next Thursday night will be our last:
Then without fail we pack up for Belfast.
Lose not your time, nor our diversion miss,
The next we act shall be as good as this.

Epilogue

To Mr. Hoppy's Benefit-Night, at Smock-Alley

Hold! hold, my good friends; for one moment, pray stop ye,
I return ye my thanks, in the name of poor Hoppy.
He's not the first person who never did write,
And yet has been fed by a benefit-night.
The custom is frequent, on my word I assure ye,
In our famed elder house, of the Hundreds of Drury.
But then you must know, those players still act on
Some very good reasons, for such benefaction.
    A deceased poet's widow, if pretty, can't fail;
From Cibber she holds, as a tenant in tail.
Your emerited actors, and actresses too,
For what they have done (though no more they can do)
And sitters, and songsters, and Chetwood and G——,
And sometimes a poor sufferer in the South Sea;
A machine-man, a tire-woman, a mute, and a spright,
Have been all kept from starving by a benefit-night.
    Thus, for Hoppy's bright merits, at length we have found
That he must have of us ninety-nine and one pound,
Paid to him clear money once every year:
And however some think it a little too dear,
Yet, for reasons of state, this sum we'll allow,
Though we pay the good man with the sweat of our brow.
    First, because by the King to us he was sent,
To guide the whole session of this parliament.
To preside in our councils, both public and private,
And so learn, by the by, what both houses do drive at.
When bold B—— roars, and meek M—— raves,
When Ash prates by wholesale, or Be——h by halves,
When Whigs become Whims, or join with the Tories;
And to himself constant when a member no more is,
But changes his sides, and votes and unvotes;
As S——t is dull, and with S——d, who dotes;
Then up must get Hoppy, and with voice very low,
And with eloquent bow, the house he must show,

That that worthy member who spoke last must give
The freedom to him, humbly most, to conceive,
That his sentiment on this affair isn't right;
That he mightily wonders which way he came by't:
That, for his part, God knows, he does such things disown;
And so, having convinced him, he most humbly sits down.
  For these, and more reasons, which perhaps you may hear,
Pounds hundred this night, and one hundred this year,
And so on we are forced, though we sweat out our blood,
To make these walls pay for poor Hoppy's good;
To supply with rare diet his pot and his spit;
And with richest Margoux to wash down a tit-bit.
To wash oft his fine linen, so clean and so neat,
And to buy him much linen, to fence against sweat:
All which he deserves; for although all the day
He ofttimes is heavy, yet all night he's gay;
And if he rise early to watch for the state,
To keep up his spirits he'll sit up as late.
Thus, for these and more reasons, as before I did say
Hop has got all the money for our acting this play,
Which makes us poor actors look *je ne sçai quoy*.

Prologue

To a Play for the Benefit of the Distressed Weavers.
By Dr. Sheridan. Spoken by Mr. Elrington. 1721

Great cry, and little wool—is now become
The plague and proverb of the weaver's loom;
No wool to work on, neither weft nor warp;
Their pockets empty, and their stomachs sharp.
Provoked, in loud complaints to you they cry;
Ladies, relieve the weavers; or they die!
Forsake your silks for stuff's; nor think it strange
To shift your clothes, since you delight in change.
One thing with freedom I'll presume to tell—
The men will like you every bit as well.
    See I am dress'd from top to toe in stuff,
And, by my troth, I think I'm fine enough;
My wife admires me more, and swears she never,
In any dress, beheld me look so clever.
And if a man be better in such ware,
What great advantage must it give the fair!
Our wool from lambs of innocence proceeds;
Silks come from maggots, calicoes from weeds;
Hence 'tis by sad experience that we find
Ladies in silks to vapours much inclined—
And what are they but maggots in the mind?
For which I think it reason to conclude,
That clothes may change our temper like our food.
Chintzes are gawdy, and engage our eyes
Too much about the party-colour'd dyes;
Although the lustre is from you begun,
We see the rainbow, and neglect the sun.
    How sweet and innocent's the country maid,
With small expense in native wool array'd;
Who copies from the fields her homely green,
While by her shepherd with delight she's seen!
Should our fair ladies dress like her, in wool
How much more lovely, and how beautiful,

Without their Indian drapery, they'd prove!
While wool would help to warm us into love!
Then, like the famous Argonauts of Greece,
We'll all contend to gain the Golden Fleece!

Epilogue

To a Benefit Play, Given in Behalf of the Distressed Weavers. By the Dean. Spoken by Mr. Griffith

Who dares affirm this is no pious age,
When charity begins to tread the stage?
When actors, who at best are hardly savers,
Will give a night of benefit to weavers?
Stay—let me see, how finely will it sound!
Imprimis, From his grace a hundred pound.
Peers, clergy, gentry, all are benefactors;
And then comes in the *item* of the actors.
Item, The actors freely give a day—
The poet had no more who made the play.
    But whence this wondrous charity in players?
They learn it not at sermons, or at prayers:
Under the rose, since here are none but friends,
(To own the truth) we have some private ends.
Since waiting-women, like exacting jades,
Hold up the prices of their old brocades;
We'll dress in manufactures made at home;
Equip our kings and generals at the Comb.
We'll rig from Meath Street Egypt's haughty queen
And Antony shall court her in ratteen.
In blue shalloon shall Hannibal be clad,
And Scipio trail an Irish purple plaid,
In drugget drest, of thirteen pence a-yard,
See Philip's son amidst his Persian guard;
And proud Roxana, fired with jealous rage,
With fifty yards of crape shall sweep the stage.
In short, our kings and princesses within
Are all resolved this project to begin;
And you, our subjects, when you here resort,
Must imitate the fashion of the court.
    O! could I see this audience clad in stuff,
Though money's scarce, we should have trade enough:
But chintz, brocades, and lace, take all away,

And scarce a crown is left to see the play.
Perhaps you wonder whence this friendship springs
Between the weavers and us playhouse kings;
But wit and weaving had the same beginning;
Pallas first taught us poetry and spinning:
And, next, observe how this alliance fits,
For weavers now are just as poor as wits:
Their brother quillmen, workers for the stage,
For sorry stuff can get a crown a page;
But weavers will be kinder to the players,
And sell for twenty pence a yard of theirs.
And to your knowledge, there is often less in
The poet's wit, than in the player's dressing.

Answer

To Dr. Sheridan's Prologue, and to Dr. Swift's Epilogue. In Behalf of the Distressed Weavers. By Dr. Delany.

Femineo generi tribuantur.

The Muses, whom the richest silks array,
Refuse to fling their shining gowns away;
The pencil clothes the nine in bright brocades,
And gives each colour to the pictured maids;
Far above mortal dress the sisters shine,
Pride in their Indian Robes, and must be fine.
And shall two bards in concert rhyme, and huff
And fret these Muses with their playhouse stuff?
    The player in mimic piety may storm,
Deplore the Comb, and bid her heroes arm:
The arbitrary mob, in paltry rage,
May curse the belles and chintzes of the age:
Yet still the artist worm her silk shall share,
And spin her thread of life in service of the fair.
    The cotton plant, whom satire cannot blast,
Shall bloom the favourite of these realms, and last;
Like yours, ye fair, her fame from censure grows,
Prevails in charms, and glares above her foes:
Your injured plant shall meet a loud defence,
And be the emblem of your innocence.
    Some bard, perhaps, whose landlord was a weaver,
Penn'd the low prologue to return a favour:
Some neighbour wit, that would be in the vogue,
Work'd with his friend, and wove the epilogue.
Who weaves the chaplet, or provides the bays,
For such wool-gathering sonnetteers as these?
Hence, then, ye homespun witlings, that persuade
Miss Chloe to the fashion of her maid.
Shall the wide hoop, that standard of the town,
Thus act subservient to a poplin gown?
Who'd smell of wool all over? 'Tis enough

The under petticoat be made of stuff.
Lord! to be wrapt in flannel just in May,
When the fields dress'd in flowers appear so gay!
And shall not miss be flower'd as well as they?
 In what weak colours would the plaid appear,
Work'd to a quilt, or studded in a chair!
The skin, that vies with silk, would fret with stuff;
Or who could bear in bed a thing so rough?
Ye knowing fair, how eminent that bed,
Where the chintz diamonds with the silken thread,
Where rustling curtains call the curious eye,
And boast the streaks and paintings of the sky!
Of flocks they'd have your milky ticking full:
And all this for the benefit of wool!
 "But where," say they, "shall we bestow these weavers,
That spread our streets, and are such piteous cravers?"
The silk-worms (brittle beings!) prone to fate,
Demand their care, to make their webs complete:
These may they tend, their promises receive;
We cannot pay too much for what they give!

On Gaulstown House

The Seat of George Rochfort, Esq.
By Dr. Delany

'Tis so old and so ugly, and yet so convenient,
You're sometimes in pleasure, though often in pain in't;
'Tis so large, you may lodge a few friends with ease in't,
You may turn and stretch at your length if you please in't;
'Tis so little, the family live in a press in't,
And poor Lady Betty has scarce room to dress in't;
'Tis so cold in the winter, you can't bear to lie in't,
And so hot in the summer, you're ready to fry in't;
'Tis so brittle, 'twould scarce bear the weight of a tun,
Yet so staunch, that it keeps out a great deal of sun;
'Tis so crazy, the weather with ease beats quite through it,
And you're forced every year in some part to renew it;
'Tis so ugly, so useful, so big, and so little,
'Tis so staunch and so crazy, so strong and so brittle,
'Tis at one time so hot, and another so cold,
It is part of the new, and part of the old;
It is just half a blessing, and just half a curse—
wish then, dear George, it were better or worse.

The Country Life

Part of a Summer Spent at Gaulstown House, The Seat of George Rochfort, Esq.

Dramatis Personae

The Baron, Lord Chief Baron Rochfort.
George, his eldest son.
Nim, his second son, John, so called from his love of hunting.
Dan, Mr. Jackson, a parson.
Gaulstown, the Baron's seat.
Sheridan, a pedant and pedagogue.
Delany, chaplain to Sir Constantine Phipps, when Lord Chancellor of Ireland.
Dragon, the name of the boat on the canal.
Dean Percival and his wife, friends of the Baron and his lady.

Thalia, tell, in sober lays,
How George, Nim, Dan, Dean, pass their days;
And, should our Gaulstown's wit grow fallow,
Yet *Neget quis carmina Gallo?*
Here (by the way) by Gallus mean I
Not Sheridan, but friend Delany.
Begin, my Muse! First from our bowers
We sally forth at different hours;
At seven the Dean, in night-gown drest,
Goes round the house to wake the rest;
At nine, grave Nim and George facetious,
Go to the Dean, to read Lucretius;
At ten my lady comes and hectors
And kisses George, and ends our lectures;
And when she has him by the neck fast,
Hauls him, and scolds us, down to breakfast.
We squander there an hour or more,
And then all hands, boys, to the oar;
All, heteroclite Dan except,
Who never time nor order kept,

But by peculiar whimseys drawn,
Peeps in the ponds to look for spawn:
O'ersees the work, or Dragon rows,
Or mars a text, or mends his hose;
Or—but proceed we in our journal—
At two, or after, we return all:
From the four elements assembling,
Warn'd by the bell, all folks come trembling,
From airy garrets some descend,
Some from the lake's remotest end;
My lord and Dean the fire forsake,
Dan leaves the earthy spade and rake;
The loiterers quake, no corner hides them
And Lady Betty soundly chides them.
Now water brought, and dinner done;
With "Church and King" the ladies gone.
Not reckoning half an hour we pass
In talking o'er a moderate glass.
Dan, growing drowsy, like a thief
Steals off to doze away his beef;
And this must pass for reading Hammond—
While George and Dean go to backgammon.
George, Nim, and Dean, set out at four,
And then, again, boys, to the oar.
But when the sun goes to the deep,
(Not to disturb him in his sleep,
Or make a rumbling o'er his head,
His candle out, and he a-bed,)
We watch his motions to a minute,
And leave the flood when he goes in it.
Now stinted in the shortening day,
We go to prayers and then to play,
Till supper comes; and after that
We sit an hour to drink and chat.
'Tis late—the old and younger pairs,
By Adam lighted, walk up stairs.
The weary Dean goes to his chamber;
And Nim and Dan to garret clamber,
So when the circle we have run,

The curtain falls and all is done.
    I might have mention'd several facts,
Like episodes between the acts;
And tell who loses and who wins,
Who gets a cold, who breaks his shins;
How Dan caught nothing in his net,
And how the boat was overset.
For brevity I have retrench'd
How in the lake the Dean was drench'd:
It would be an exploit to brag on,
How valiant George rode o'er the Dragon;
How steady in the storm he sat,
And saved his oar, but lost his hat:
How Nim (no hunter e'er could match him)
Still brings us hares, when he can catch 'em;
How skilfully Dan mends his nets;
How fortune fails him when he sets;
Or how the Dean delights to vex
The ladies, and lampoon their sex:
I might have told how oft Dean Perceval
Displays his pedantry unmerciful,
How haughtily he cocks his nose,
To tell what every schoolboy knows:
And with his finger and his thumb,
Explaining, strikes opposers dumb:
But now there needs no more be said on't,
Nor how his wife, that female pedant,
Shews all her secrets of housekeeping:
For candles how she trucks her dripping;
Was forced to send three miles for yeast,
To brew her ale, and raise her paste;
Tells everything that you can think of,
How she cured Charley of the chincough;
What gave her brats and pigs the measles,
And how her doves were killed by weasels;
How Jowler howl'd, and what a fright
She had with dreams the other night.
    But now, since I have gone so far on,
A word or two of Lord Chief Baron;

And tell how little weight he sets
On all Whig papers and gazettes;
But for the politics of Pue,
Thinks every syllable is true:
And since he owns the King of Sweden
Is dead at last, without evading,
Now all his hopes are in the czar;
"Why, Muscovy is not so far;
Down the Black Sea, and up the Straits,
And in a month he's at your gates;
Perhaps from what the packet brings,
By Christmas we shall see strange things."
Why should I tell of ponds and drains,
What carps we met with for our pains;
Of sparrows tamed, and nuts innumerable
To choke the girls, and to consume a rabble?
But you, who are a scholar, know
How transient all things are below,
How prone to change is human life!
Last night arrived Clem and his wife—
This grand event has broke our measures;
Their reign began with cruel seizures;
The Dean must with his quilt supply
The bed in which those tyrants lie;
Nim lost his wig-block, Dan his Jordan,
(My lady says, she can't afford one,)
George is half scared out of his wits,
For Clem gets all the dainty bits.
Henceforth expect a different survey,
This house will soon turn topsyturvy;
They talk of farther alterations,
Which causes many speculations.

Dr. Delany's Villa

Would you that Delville I describe?
Believe me, Sir, I will not gibe:
For who would be satirical
Upon a thing so very small?
You scarce upon the borders enter,
Before you're at the very centre.
A single crow can make it night,
When o'er your farm she takes her flight:
Yet, in this narrow compass, we
Observe a vast variety;
Both walks, walls, meadows, and parterres,
Windows and doors, and rooms and stairs,
And hills and dales, and woods and fields,
And hay, and grass, and corn, it yields:
All to your haggard brought so cheap in,
Without the mowing or the reaping:
A razor, though to say't I'm loth,
Would shave you and your meadows both.
Though small's the farm, yet here's a house
Full large to entertain a mouse;
But where a rat is dreaded more
Than savage Caledonian boar;
For, if it's enter'd by a rat,
There is no room to bring a cat.
A little rivulet seems to steal
Down through a thing you call a vale,
Like tears adown a wrinkled cheek,
Like rain along a blade of leek:
And this you call your sweet meander,
Which might be suck'd up by a gander,
Could he but force his nether bill
To scoop the channel of the rill.
For sure you'd make a mighty clutter,
Were it as big as city gutter.
Next come I to your kitchen garden,
Where one poor mouse would fare but hard in;

And round this garden is a walk
No longer than a tailor's chalk;
Thus I compare what space is in it,
A snail creeps round it in a minute.
One lettuce makes a shift to squeeze
Up through a tuft you call your trees:
And, once a year, a single rose
Peeps from the bud, but never blows;
In vain then you expect its bloom!
It cannot blow for want of room.
  In short, in all your boasted seat,
There's nothing but yourself that's Great.

On one of the Windows at Delville

A bard, grown desirous of saving his pelf,
Built a house he was sure would hold none but himself.
This enraged god Apollo, who Mercury sent,
And bid him go ask what his votary meant?
"Some foe to my empire has been his adviser:
'Tis of dreadful portent when a poet turns miser!
Tell him, Hermes, from me, tell that subject of mine,
I have sworn by the Styx, to defeat his design;
For wherever he lives, the Muses shall reign;
And the Muses, he knows, have a numerous train."

Carberiae Rupes

In Comitatu Corgagensi. Scripsit Jun. Ann. Dom. 1723

Ecce ingens fragmen scopuli, quod vertice summo
Desuper impendet, nullo fundamine nixum,
Decidit in fluctus: maria undique et undique saxa
Horrisono stridore tenant, et ad aethera murmur
Erigitur; trepidatque suis Neptunus in undis.
Nam, longâ venti rabie, atque aspergine crebrâ
Aequorei laticis, specus imâ rupe cavatur:
Jam fultura ruit, jam summa cacumina nutant;
Jam cadit in praeceps moles, et verberat undas.
Attonitus credas, hinc dejecisse Tonantem
Montibus impositos montes, et Pelion altum
In capita anguipedum coelo jaculâsse gigantum.
    Saepe etiam spelunca immani aperitur hiatu
Exesa è scopulis, et utrinque foramina pandit,
Hinc atque hinc a ponto ad pontum pervia Phoebo
Cautibus enormè junctis laquearia tecti
Formantur; moles olim ruitura supernè.
Fornice sublimi nidos posuere palumbes,
Inque imo stagni posuere cubilia phocae.
    Sed, cum saevit hyems, et venti, carcere rupto,
Immensos volvunt fluctus ad culmina montis;
Non obsessae arces, non fulmina vindice dextrâ
Missa Jovis, quoties inimicus saevit in urbes,
Exaequant sonitum undarum, veniente procellâ:
Littora littoribus reboant; vicinia latè,
Gens assueta mari, et pedibus percurrere rupes,
Terretur tamen, et longè fugit, arva relinquens.
    Gramina dum carpunt pendentes rupe capellae,
Vi salientis aquae de summo praecipitantur,
Et dulces animas imo sub gurgite linquunt.
    Piscator terrâ non audet vellere funem;
Sed latet in portu tremebundus, et aëra sudum
Haud sperans, Nereum precibus votisque fatigat.

Carbery Rocks

Translated by Dr. Dunkin

Lo! from the top of yonder cliff, that shrouds
Its airy head amid the azure clouds,
Hangs a huge fragment; destitute of props,
Prone on the wave the rocky ruin drops;
With hoarse rebuff the swelling seas rebound,
From shore to shore the rocks return the sound:
The dreadful murmur Heaven's high convex cleaves,
And Neptune shrinks beneath his subject waves:
For, long the whirling winds and beating tides
Had scoop'd a vault into its nether sides.
Now yields the base, the summits nod, now urge
Their headlong course, and lash the sounding surge.
Not louder noise could shake the guilty world,
When Jove heap'd mountains upon mountains hurl'd;
Retorting Pelion from his dread abode,
To crush Earth's rebel sons beneath the load.
    Oft too with hideous yawn the cavern wide
Presents an orifice on either side.
A dismal orifice, from sea to sea
Extended, pervious to the God of Day:
Uncouthly join'd, the rocks stupendous form
An arch, the ruin of a future storm:
High on the cliff their nests the woodquests make,
And sea-calves stable in the oozy lake.
    But when bleak Winter with his sullen train
Awakes the winds to vex the watery plain;
When o'er the craggy steep without control,
Big with the blast, the raging billows roll;
Not towns beleaguer'd, not the flaming brand,
Darted from Heaven by Jove's avenging hand,
Oft as on impious men his wrath he pours,
Humbles their pride and blasts their gilded towers,
Equal the tumult of this wild uproar:
Waves rush o'er waves, rebellows shore to shore.

The neighbouring race, though wont to brave the shocks
Of angry seas, and run along the rocks,
Now, pale with terror, while the ocean foams,
Fly far and wide, nor trust their native homes.
    The goats, while, pendent from the mountain top,
The wither'd herb improvident they crop,
Wash'd down the precipice with sudden sweep,
Leave their sweet lives beneath th'unfathom'd deep.
    The frighted fisher, with desponding eyes,
Though safe, yet trembling in the harbour lies,
Nor hoping to behold the skies serene,
Wearies with vows the monarch of the main.

Copy of the Birth-day Verses

On Mr. Ford

Come, be content, since out it must,
For Stella has betray'd her trust;
And, whispering, charged me not to say
That Mr. Ford was born to-day;
Or, if at last I needs must blab it,
According to my usual habit,
She bid me, with a serious face,
Be sure conceal the time and place;
And not my compliment to spoil,
By calling this your native soil;
Or vex the ladies, when they knew
That you are turning forty-two:
But, if these topics shall appear
Strong arguments to keep you here,
I think, though you judge hardly of it,
Good manners must give place to profit.
  The nymphs, with whom you first began,
Are each become a harridan;
And Montague so far decay'd,
Her lovers now must all be paid;
And every belle that since arose,
Has her contemporary beaux.
Your former comrades, once so bright,
With whom you toasted half the night,
Of rheumatism and pox complain,
And bid adieu to dear champaign.
Your great protectors, once in power,
Are now in exile or the Tower.
Your foes triumphant o'er the laws,
Who hate your person and your cause,
If once they get you on the spot,
You must be guilty of the plot;
For, true or false, they'll ne'er inquire,
But use you ten times worse than Prior.

In London! what would you do there?
Can you, my friend, with patience bear
(Nay, would it not your passion raise
Worse than a pun, or Irish phrase)
To see a scoundrel strut and hector,
A foot-boy to some rogue director,
To look on vice triumphant round,
And virtue trampled on the ground?
Observe where bloody **** stands
With torturing engines in his hands,
Hear him blaspheme, and swear, and rail,
Threatening the pillory and jail:
If this you think a pleasing scene,
To London straight return again;
Where, you have told us from experience,
Are swarms of bugs and presbyterians.
I thought my very spleen would burst,
When fortune hither drove me first;
Was full as hard to please as you,
Nor persons' names nor places knew:
But now I act as other folk,
Like prisoners when their gaol is broke.
If you have London still at heart,
We'll make a small one here by art;
The difference is not much between
St. James's Park and Stephen's Green;
And Dawson Street will serve as well
To lead you thither as Pall Mall.
Nor want a passage through the palace,
To choke your sight, and raise your malice.
The Deanery-house may well be match'd,
Under correction, with the Thatch'd.
Nor shall I, when you hither come,
Demand a crown a-quart for stum.
Then for a middle-aged charmer,
Stella may vie with your Mounthermer;
She's now as handsome every bit,
And has a thousand times her wit

The Dean and Sheridan, I hope,
Will half supply a Gay and Pope.
Corbet, though yet I know his worth not,
No doubt, will prove a good Arbuthnot.
I throw into the bargain Tim;
In London can you equal him?
What think you of my favourite clan,
Robin and Jack, and Jack and Dan;
Fellows of modest worth and parts,
With cheerful looks and honest hearts?
    Can you on Dublin look with scorn?
Yet here were you and Ormond born.
    O! were but you and I so wise,
To see with Robert Grattan's eyes!
Robin adores that spot of earth,
That literal spot which gave him birth;
And swears, "Belcamp is, to his taste,
As fine as Hampton-court at least."
When to your friends you would enhance
The praise of Italy or France,
For grandeur, elegance, and wit,
We gladly hear you, and submit;
But then, to come and keep a clutter,
For this or that side of a gutter,
To live in this or t'other isle,
We cannot think it worth your while;
For, take it kindly or amiss,
The difference but amounts to this,
We bury on our side the channel
In linen; and on yours in flannel.
You for the news are ne'er to seek;
While we, perhaps, may wait a week;
You happy folks are sure to meet
A hundred whores in every street;
While we may trace all Dublin o'er
Before we find out half a score.
    You see my arguments are strong,
I wonder you held out so long;

But, since you are convinced at last,
We'll pardon you for what has past.
So—let us now for whist prepare;
Twelve pence a corner, if you dare.

On Dreams

An Imitation of Petronius

Petronii Fragmenta, xxx.

Those dreams, that on the silent night intrude,
And with false flitting shades our minds delude
Jove never sends us downward from the skies;
Nor can they from infernal mansions rise;
But are all mere productions of the brain,
And fools consult interpreters in vain.

For when in bed we rest our weary limbs,
The mind unburden'd sports in various whims;
The busy head with mimic art runs o'er
The scenes and actions of the day before.

The drowsy tyrant, by his minions led,
To regal rage devotes some patriot's head.
With equal terrors, not with equal guilt,
The murderer dreams of all the blood he spilt.

The soldier smiling hears the widow's cries,
And stabs the son before the mother's eyes.
With like remorse his brother of the trade,
The butcher, fells the lamb beneath his blade.

The statesman rakes the town to find a plot,
And dreams of forfeitures by treason got.
Nor less Tom-t—d-man, of true statesman mould,
Collects the city filth in search of gold.

Orphans around his bed the lawyer sees,
And takes the plaintiff's and defendant's fees.
His fellow pick-purse, watching for a job,
Fancies his fingers in the cully's fob.

The kind physician grants the husband's prayers,
Or gives relief to long-expecting heirs.
The sleeping hangman ties the fatal noose,
Nor unsuccessful waits for dead men's shoes.

The grave divine, with knotty points perplext,
As if he were awake, nods o'er his text:
While the sly mountebank attends his trade,
Harangues the rabble, and is better paid.

The hireling senator of modern days
Bedaubs the guilty great with nauseous praise:
And Dick, the scavenger, with equal grace
Flirts from his cart the mud in Walpole's face.

Sent by Dr. Delany to Dr. Swift, In Order to be Admitted to Speak to him when he was Deaf. 1724

Dear Sir, I think, 'tis doubly hard,
Your ears and doors should both be barr'd.
Can anything be more unkind?
Must I not see, 'cause you are blind?
Methinks a friend at night should cheer you,—
A friend that loves to see and hear you.
Why am I robb'd of that delight,
When you can be no loser by't
Nay, when 'tis plain (for what is plainer?)
That if you heard you'd be no gainer?
For sure you are not yet to learn,
That hearing is not your concern.
Then be your doors no longer barr'd:
Your business, sir, is to be heard.

The Answer

The wise pretend to make it clear,
'Tis no great loss to lose an ear.
Why are we then so fond of two,
When by experience one would do?
'Tis true, say they, cut off the head,
And there's an end; the man is dead;
Because, among all human race,
None e'er was known to have a brace:
But confidently they maintain,
That where we find the members twain,
The loss of one is no such trouble,
Since t'other will in strength be double.
The limb surviving, you may swear,
Becomes his brother's lawful heir:
Thus, for a trial, let me beg of
Your reverence but to cut one leg off,
And you shall find, by this device,
The other will be stronger twice;
For every day you shall be gaining
New vigour to the leg remaining.
So, when an eye has lost its brother,
You see the better with the other,
Cut off your hand, and you may do
With t'other hand the work of two:
Because the soul her power contracts,
And on the brother limb reacts.
But yet the point is not so clear in
Another case, the sense of hearing:
For, though the place of either ear
Be distant, as one head can bear,
Yet Galen most acutely shows you,
(Consult his book *de partium usu*)
That from each ear, as he observes,
There creep two auditory nerves,
Not to be seen without a glass,
Which near the *os petrosum* pass;

Thence to the neck; and moving thorough there,
One goes to this, and one to t'other ear;
Which made my grandam always stuff her ears
Both right and left, as fellow-sufferers.
You see my learning; but, to shorten it,
When my left ear was deaf a fortnight,
To t'other ear I felt it coming on:
And thus I solve this hard phenomenon.

'Tis true, a glass will bring supplies
To weak, or old, or clouded eyes:
Your arms, though both your eyes were lost,
Would guard your nose against a post:
Without your legs, two legs of wood
Are stronger, and almost as good:
And as for hands, there have been those
Who, wanting both, have used their toes.
But no contrivance yet appears
To furnish artificial ears.

A Quiet Life and a Good Name
To a Friend who Married a Shrew. 1724

Nell scolded in so loud a din,
That Will durst hardly venture in:
He mark'd the conjugal dispute;
Nell roar'd incessant, Dick sat mute;
But, when he saw his friend appear,
Cried bravely, "Patience, good my dear!"
At sight of Will she bawl'd no more,
But hurried out and clapt the door.
  Why, Dick! the devil's in thy Nell,
(Quoth Will,) thy house is worse than Hell.
Why what a peal the jade has rung!
D—n her, why don't you slit her tongue?
For nothing else will make it cease.
Dear Will, I suffer this for peace:
I never quarrel with my wife;
I bear it for a quiet life.
Scripture, you know, exhorts us to it;
Bids us to seek peace, and ensue it.
  Will went again to visit Dick;
And entering in the very nick,
He saw virago Nell belabour,
With Dick's own staff, his peaceful neighbour.
Poor Will, who needs must interpose,
Received a brace or two of blows.
But now, to make my story short,
Will drew out Dick to take a quart.
Why, Dick, thy wife has devilish whims;
Ods-buds! why don't you break her limbs?
If she were mine, and had such tricks,
I'd teach her how to handle sticks:
Z—ds! I would ship her to Jamaica,
Or truck the carrion for tobacco:
I'd send her far enough away——
Dear Will; but what would people say?
Lord! I should get so ill a name,

The neighbours round would cry out shame.
    Dick suffer'd for his peace and credit;
But who believed him when he said it?
Can he, who makes himself a slave,
Consult his peace, or credit save?
Dick found it by his ill success,
His quiet small, his credit less.
She served him at the usual rate;
She stunn'd, and then she broke his pate:
And what he thought the hardest case,
The parish jeer'd him to his face;
Those men who wore the breeches least,
Call'd him a cuckold, fool, and beast.
At home he was pursued with noise;
Abroad was pester'd by the boys:
Within, his wife would break his bones:
Without, they pelted him with stones;
The 'prentices procured a riding,
To act his patience and her chiding.
False patience and mistaken pride!
There are ten thousand Dicks beside;
Slaves to their quiet and good name,
Are used like Dick, and bear the blame.

Advice to the Grub-Street Verse-Writers
1726

Ye poets ragged and forlorn,
    Down from your garrets haste;
Ye rhymers, dead as soon as born,
    Not yet consign'd to paste;

I know a trick to make you thrive;
    O, 'tis a quaint device:
Your still-born poems shall revive,
    And scorn to wrap up spice.

Get all your verses printed fair,
    Then let them well be dried;
And Curll must have a special care
    To leave the margin wide.

Lend these to paper-sparing Pope;
    And when he sets to write,
No letter with an envelope
    Could give him more delight.

When Pope has fill'd the margins round,
    Why then recall your loan;
Sell them to Curll for fifty pound,
    And swear they are your own.

A Pastoral Dialogue

Written June, 1727, Just after the News of the Death of George I, Who Died the 12th of that Month in Germany

This poem was written when George II succeeded his father, and bore the following explanatory introduction:

Richmond Lodge is a house with a small park belonging to the crown. It was usually granted by the crown for a lease of years. The Duke of Ormond was the last who had it. After his exile, it was given to the Prince of Wales by the king. The prince and princess usually passed their summer there. It is within a mile of Richmond.

> *"Marble Hill is a house built by Mrs. Howard, then of the bedchamber, now Countess of Suffolk, and groom of the stole to the queen. It is on the Middlesex side, near Twickenham, where Pope lives, and about two miles from Richmond Lodge. Pope was the contriver of the gardens, Lord Herbert the architect, the Dean of St. Patrick's chief butler, and keeper of the ice-house. Upon King George's death, these two houses met, and had the above dialogue."*
>
> —Dublin Edition, 1734

In spight of Pope, in spight of Gay,
And all that he or they can say;
Sing on I must, and sing I will,
Of Richmond Lodge and Marble Hill.
Last Friday night, as neighbours use,
This couple met to talk of news:
For, by old proverbs, it appears,
That walls have tongues, and hedges ears.

Marble Hill: Quoth Marble Hill, right well I ween,
Your mistress now is grown a queen;
You'll find it soon by woful proof,
She'll come no more beneath your roof.
Richmond Lodge: The kingly prophet well evinces,
That we should put no trust in princes:

My royal master promised me
To raise me to a high degree:
But now he's grown a king, God wot,
I fear I shall be soon forgot.
You see, when folks have got their ends,
How quickly they neglect their friends;
Yet I may say, 'twixt me and you,
Pray God, they now may find as true!

Marble Hill: My house was built but for a show,
My lady's empty pockets know;
And now she will not have a shilling,
To raise the stairs, or build the ceiling;
For all the courtly madams round
Now pay four shillings in the pound;
'Tis come to what I always thought:
My dame is hardly worth a groat.
Had you and I been courtiers born,
We should not thus have lain forlorn;
For those we dext'rous courtiers call,
Can rise upon their masters' fall:
But we, unlucky and unwise,
Must fall because our masters rise.

Richmond Lodge: My master, scarce a fortnight since,
Was grown as wealthy as a prince;
But now it will be no such thing,
For he'll be poor as any king;
And by his crown will nothing get,
But like a king to run in debt.

Marble Hill: No more the Dean, that grave divine,
Shall keep the key of my (no) wine;
My ice-house rob, as heretofore,
And steal my artichokes no more;
Poor Patty Blount no more be seen
Bedraggled in my walks so green:
Plump Johnny Gay will now elope;
And here no more will dangle Pope.

Richmond Lodge: Here wont the Dean, when he's to seek,
To spunge a breakfast once a-week;
To cry the bread was stale, and mutter

Complaints against the royal butter.
But now I fear it will be said,
No butter sticks upon his bread.
We soon shall find him full of spleen,
For want of tattling to the queen;
Stunning her royal ears with talking;
His reverence and her highness walking:
While Lady Charlotte, like a stroller,
Sits mounted on the garden-roller.
A goodly sight to see her ride,
With ancient Mirmont at her side.
In velvet cap his head lies warm,
His hat, for show, beneath his arm.
Marble Hill: Some South-Sea broker from the city
Will purchase me, the more's the pity;
Lay all my fine plantations waste,
To fit them to his vulgar taste:
Chang'd for the worse in ev'ry part,
My master Pope will break his heart.
Richmond Lodge: In my own Thames may I be drownded,
If e'er I stoop beneath a crown'd head:
Except her majesty prevails
To place me with the Prince of Wales;
And then I shall be free from fears,
For he'll be prince these fifty years.
I then will turn a courtier too,
And serve the times as others do.
Plain loyalty, not built on hope,
I leave to your contriver, Pope;
None loves his king and country better,
Yet none was ever less their debtor.
Marble Hill: Then let him come and take a nap
In summer on my verdant lap;
Prefer our villas, where the Thames is,
To Kensington, or hot St. James's;
Nor shall I dull in silence sit;
For 'tis to me he owes his wit;
My groves, my echoes, and my birds,
Have taught him his poetic words.

We gardens, and you wildernesses,
Assist all poets in distresses.
Him twice a-week I here expect,
To rattle Moody for neglect;
An idle rogue, who spends his quartridge
In tippling at the Dog and Partridge;
And I can hardly get him down
Three times a-week to brush my gown.

RICHMOND LODGE: I pity you, dear Marble Hill;
But hope to see you flourish still.
All happiness—and so adieu.

MARBLE HILL: Kind Richmond Lodge, the same to you.

Desire and Possession 1727

'Tis strange what different thoughts inspire
In men, Possession and Desire!
Think what they wish so great a blessing;
So disappointed when possessing!
A moralist profoundly sage
(I know not in what book or page,
Or whether o'er a pot of ale)
Related thus the following tale.
Possession, and Desire, his brother,
But still at variance with each other,
Were seen contending in a race;
And kept at first an equal pace;
'Tis said, their course continued long,
For this was active, that was strong:
Till Envy, Slander, Sloth, and Doubt,
Misled them many a league about;
Seduced by some deceiving light,
They take the wrong way for the right;
Through slippery by-roads, dark and deep,
They often climb, and often creep.
Desire, the swifter of the two,
Along the plain like lightning flew:
Till, entering on a broad highway,
Where power and titles scatter'd lay,
He strove to pick up all he found,
And by excursions lost his ground:
No sooner got, than with disdain
He threw them on the ground again;
And hasted forward to pursue
Fresh objects, fairer to his view,
In hope to spring some nobler game;
But all he took was just the same:
Too scornful now to stop his pace,
He spurn'd them in his rival's face.
Possession kept the beaten road,
And gather'd all his brother strew'd;

But overcharged, and out of wind,
Though strong in limbs, he lagg'd behind.
    Desire had now the goal in sight;
It was a tower of monstrous height;
Where on the summit Fortune stands,
A crown and sceptre in her hands;
Beneath, a chasm as deep as Hell,
Where many a bold adventurer fell.
Desire, in rapture, gazed awhile,
And saw the treacherous goddess smile;
But as he climb'd to grasp the crown,
She knock'd him with the sceptre down!
He tumbled in the gulf profound;
There doom'd to whirl an endless round.
    Possession's load was grown so great,
He sunk beneath the cumbrous weight;
And, as he now expiring lay,
Flocks every ominous bird of prey;
The raven, vulture, owl, and kite,
At once upon his carcass light,
And strip his hide, and pick his bones,
Regardless of his dying groans.

On Censure
1727

Ye wise, instruct me to endure
An evil, which admits no cure;
Or, how this evil can be borne,
Which breeds at once both hate and scorn.
Bare innocence is no support,
When you are tried in Scandal's court.
Stand high in honour, wealth, or wit;
All others, who inferior sit,
Conceive themselves in conscience bound
To join, and drag you to the ground.
Your altitude offends the eyes
Of those who want the power to rise.
The world, a willing stander-by,
Inclines to aid a specious lie:
Alas! they would not do you wrong;
But all appearances are strong.
    Yet whence proceeds this weight we lay
On what detracting people say!
For let mankind discharge their tongues
In venom, till they burst their lungs,
Their utmost malice cannot make
Your head, or tooth, or finger ache;
Nor spoil your shape, distort your face,
Or put one feature out of place;
Nor will you find your fortune sink
By what they speak or what they think;
Nor can ten hundred thousand lies
Make you less virtuous, learn'd, or wise.
    The most effectual way to balk
Their malice, is—to let them talk.

The Furniture of a Woman's Mind
1727

A set of phrases learn'd by rote;
A passion for a scarlet coat;
When at a play, to laugh or cry,
Yet cannot tell the reason why;
Never to hold her tongue a minute,
While all she prates has nothing in it;
Whole hours can with a coxcomb sit,
And take his nonsense all for wit;
Her learning mounts to read a song,
But half the words pronouncing wrong;
Has every repartee in store
She spoke ten thousand times before;
Can ready compliments supply
On all occasions cut and dry;
Such hatred to a parson's gown,
The sight would put her in a swoon;
For conversation well endued,
She calls it witty to be rude;
And, placing raillery in railing,
Will tell aloud your greatest failing;
Nor make a scruple to expose
Your bandy leg, or crooked nose;
Can at her morning tea run o'er
The scandal of the day before;
Improving hourly in her skill,
To cheat and wrangle at quadrille.
    In choosing lace, a critic nice,
Knows to a groat the lowest price;
Can in her female clubs dispute,
What linen best the silk will suit,
What colours each complexion match,
And where with art to place a patch.
    If chance a mouse creeps in her sight,
Can finely counterfeit a fright;
So sweetly screams, if it comes near her,

She ravishes all hearts to hear her.
Can dext'rously her husband teaze,
By taking fits whene'er she please;
By frequent practice learns the trick
At proper seasons to be sick;
Thinks nothing gives one airs so pretty,
At once creating love and pity;
If Molly happens to be careless,
And but neglects to warm her hair-lace,
She gets a cold as sure as death,
And vows she scarce can fetch her breath;
Admires how modest women can
Be so robustious like a man.

In party, furious to her power;
A bitter Whig, or Tory sour;
Her arguments directly tend
Against the side she would defend;
Will prove herself a Tory plain,
From principles the Whigs maintain;
And, to defend the Whiggish cause,
Her topics from the Tories draws.

O yes! if any man can find
More virtues in a woman's mind,
Let them be sent to Mrs. Harding;
She'll pay the charges to a farthing;
Take notice, she has my commission
To add them in the next edition;
They may outsell a better thing:
So, holla, boys; God save the King!

Clever Tom Clinch Going to be Hanged. 1727

As clever Tom Clinch, while the rabble was bawling,
Rode stately through Holborn to die in his calling,
He stopt at the George for a bottle of sack,
And promised to pay for it when he came back.
His waistcoat, and stockings, and breeches, were white;
His cap had a new cherry ribbon to tie't.
The maids to the doors and the balconies ran,
And said, "Lack-a-day, he's a proper young man!"
But, as from the windows the ladies he spied,
Like a beau in the box, he bow'd low on each side!
And when his last speech the loud hawkers did cry,
He swore from his cart, "It was all a damn'd lie!"
The hangman for pardon fell down on his knee;
Tom gave him a kick in the guts for his fee:
Then said, I must speak to the people a little;
But I'll see you all damn'd before I will whittle.
My honest friend Wild (may he long hold his place)
He lengthen'd my life with a whole year of grace.
Take courage, dear comrades, and be not afraid,
Nor slip this occasion to follow your trade;
My conscience is clear, and my spirits are calm,
And thus I go off, without prayer-book or psalm;
Then follow the practice of clever Tom Clinch,
Who hung like a hero, and never would flinch.

Dr. Swift to Mr. Pope, while he was Writing the "Dunciad"

1727

Pope has the talent well to speak,
But not to reach the ear;
His loudest voice is low and weak,
The Dean too deaf to hear.

Awhile they on each other look,
Then different studies choose;
The Dean sits plodding on a book;
Pope walks, and courts the Muse.

Now backs of letters, though design'd
For those who more will need 'em,
Are fill'd with hints, and interlined,
Himself can hardly read 'em.

Each atom by some other struck,
All turns and motions tries;
Till in a lump together stuck,
Behold a poem rise:

Yet to the Dean his share allot;
He claims it by a canon;
That without which a thing is not,
Is *causa sine quâ non*.

Thus, Pope, in vain you boast your wit;
For, had our deaf divine
Been for your conversation fit,
You had not writ a line.

Of Sherlock, thus, for preaching framed
The sexton reason'd well;
And justly half the merit claim'd,
Because he rang the bell.

A Love Poem from a Physician to his Mistress

Written at London

By poets we are well assured
That love, alas! can ne'er be cured;
A complicated heap of ills,
Despising boluses and pills.
Ah! Chloe, this I find is true,
Since first I gave my heart to you.
Now, by your cruelty hard bound,
I strain my guts, my colon wound.
Now jealousy my grumbling tripes
Assaults with grating, grinding gripes.
When pity in those eyes I view,
My bowels wambling make me spew.
When I an amorous kiss design'd,
I belch'd a hurricane of wind.
Once you a gentle sigh let fall;
Remember how I suck'd it all;
What colic pangs from thence I felt,
Had you but known, your heart would melt,
Like ruffling winds in cavern pent,
Till Nature pointed out a vent.
How have you torn my heart to pieces
With maggots, humours, and caprices!
By which I got the hemorrhoids;
And loathsome worms my *anus* voids.
Whene'er I hear a rival named,
I feel my body all inflamed;
Which, breaking out in boils and blains,
With yellow filth my linen stains;
Or, parch'd with unextinguish'd thirst,
Small-beer I guzzle till I burst;
And then I drag a bloated *corpus*,

Swell'd with a dropsy, like a porpus;
When, if I cannot purge or stale,
I must be tapp'd to fill a pail.

Bouts Rimez

On Signora Domitilla

Our schoolmaster may roar i' th' fit,
 Of classic beauty, *haec et illa*;
Not all his birch inspires such wit
 As th'ogling beams of Domitilla.

Let nobles toast, in bright champaign,
 Nymphs higher born than Domitilla;
I'll drink her health, again, again,
 In Berkeley's tar, or sars'parilla.

At Goodman's Fields I've much admired
 The postures strange of Monsieur Brilla;
But what are they to the soft step,
 The gliding air of Domitilla?

Virgil has eternized in song
 The flying footsteps of Camilla;
Sure, as a prophet, he was wrong;
 He might have dream'd of Domitilla.

Great Theodose condemn'd a town
 For thinking ill of his Placilla:
And deuce take London! if some knight
 O' th' city wed not Domitilla.

Wheeler, Sir George, in travels wise,
 Gives us a medal of Plantilla;
But O! the empress has not eyes,
 Nor lips, nor breast, like Domitilla.

Not all the wealth of plunder'd Italy,
 Piled on the mules of king At-tila,
Is worth one glove (I'll not tell a bit a lie)
 Or garter, snatch'd from Domitilla.

Five years a nymph at certain hamlet,
Y-cleped Harrow of the Hill, a-
—bused much my heart, and was a damn'd let
To verse—but now for Domitilla.

Dan Pope consigns Belinda's watch
To the fair sylphid Momentilla,
And thus I offer up my catch
To the snow-white hands of Domitilla.

Helter Skelter; or, the Hue and Cry after the Attorneys Upon their Riding the Circuit

Now the active young attorneys
Briskly travel on their journeys,
Looking big as any giants,
On the horses of their clients;
Like so many little Marses
With their tilters at their a—s,
Brazen-hilted, lately burnish'd,
And with harness-buckles furnish'd,
And with whips and spurs so neat,
And with jockey-coats complete,
And with boots so very greasy,
And with saddles eke so easy,
And with bridles fine and gay,
Bridles borrow'd for a day,
Bridles destined far to roam,
Ah! never, never to come home.
And with hats so very big, sir,
And with powder'd caps and wigs, sir,
And with ruffles to be shown,
Cambric ruffles not their own;
And with Holland shirts so white,
Shirts becoming to the sight,
Shirts bewrought with different letters,
As belonging to their betters.
With their pretty tinsel'd boxes,
Gotten from their dainty doxies,
And with rings so very trim,
Lately taken out of lim—
And with very little pence,
And as very little sense;
With some law, but little justice,
Having stolen from my hostess,
From the barber and the cutler,
Like the soldier from the sutler;

From the vintner and the tailor,
Like the felon from the jailor;
Into this and t'other county,
Living on the public bounty;
Thorough town and thorough village,
All to plunder, all to pillage:
Thorough mountains, thorough valleys,
Thorough stinking lanes and alleys,
Some to—kiss with farmers' spouses,
And make merry in their houses;
Some to tumble country wenches
On their rushy beds and benches;
And if they begin a fray,
Draw their swords, and—run away;
All to murder equity,
And to take a double fee;
Till the people are all quiet,
And forget to broil and riot,
Low in pocket, cow'd in courage,
Safely glad to sup their porridge,
And vacation's over—then,
Hey, for London town again.

The Puppet-Show

The life of man to represent,
And turn it all to ridicule,
Wit did a puppet-show invent,
Where the chief actor is a fool.

The gods of old were logs of wood,
And worship was to puppets paid;
In antic dress the idol stood,
And priest and people bow'd the head.

No wonder then, if art began
The simple votaries to frame,
To shape in timber foolish man,
And consecrate the block to fame.

From hence poetic fancy learn'd
That trees might rise from human forms;
The body to a trunk be turn'd,
And branches issue from the arms.

Thus Dædalus and Ovid too,
That man's a blockhead, have confest:
Powel and Stretch the hint pursue;
Life is a farce, the world a jest.

The same great truth South Sea has proved
On that famed theatre, the alley;
Where thousands, by directors moved
Are now sad monuments of folly.

What Momus was of old to Jove,
The same a Harlequin is now;
The former was buffoon above,
The latter is a Punch below.

This fleeting scene is but a stage,
    Where various images appear;
In different parts of youth and age,
    Alike the prince and peasant share.

Some draw our eyes by being great,
    False pomp conceals mere wood within;
And legislators ranged in state
    Are oft but wisdom in machine.

A stock may chance to wear a crown,
    And timber as a lord take place;
A statue may put on a frown,
    And cheat us with a thinking face.

Others are blindly led away,
    And made to act for ends unknown;
By the mere spring of wires they play,
    And speak in language not their own.

Too oft, alas! a scolding wife
    Usurps a jolly fellow's throne;
And many drink the cup of life,
    Mix'd and embitter'd by a Joan.

In short, whatever men pursue,
    Of pleasure, folly, war, or love:
This mimic race brings all to view:
    Alike they dress, they talk, they move.

Go on, great Stretch, with artful hand,
    Mortals to please and to deride;
And, when death breaks thy vital band,
    Thou shalt put on a puppet's pride.

Thou shalt in puny wood be shown,
    Thy image shall preserve thy fame;
Ages to come thy worth shall own,
    Point at thy limbs, and tell thy name.

Tell Tom, he draws a farce in vain,
    Before he looks in nature's glass;
Puns cannot form a witty scene,
    Nor pedantry for humour pass.

To make men act as senseless wood,
    And chatter in a mystic strain,
Is a mere force on flesh and blood,
    And shows some error in the brain.

He that would thus refine on thee,
    And turn thy stage into a school,
The jest of Punch will ever be,
    And stand confest the greater fool.

The Journal of a Modern Lady

In a Letter to a Person of Quality. 1728

Sir, 'twas a most unfriendly part
In you, who ought to know my heart,
Are well acquainted with my zeal
For all the female commonweal—
How could it come into your mind
To pitch on me, of all mankind,
Against the sex to write a satire,
And brand me for a woman-hater?
On me, who think them all so fair,
They rival Venus to a hair;
Their virtues never ceased to sing,
Since first I learn'd to tune a string?
Methinks I hear the ladies cry,
Will he his character belie?
Must never our misfortunes end?
And have we lost our only friend?
Ah, lovely nymphs! remove your fears,
No more let fall those precious tears.
Sooner shall, etc.

(Here several verses are omitted.)

The hound be hunted by the hare,
Than I turn rebel to the fair.
  'Twas you engaged me first to write,
Then gave the subject out of spite:
The journal of a modern dame,
Is, by my promise, what you claim.
My word is past, I must submit;
And yet perhaps you may be bit.
I but transcribe; for not a line
Of all the satire shall be mine.
Compell'd by you to tag in rhymes
The common slanders of the times,

Of modern times, the guilt is yours,
And me my innocence secures.
Unwilling Muse, begin thy lay,
The annals of a female day.
   By nature turn'd to play the rake well,
(As we shall show you in the sequel,)
The modern dame is waked by noon,
(Some authors say not quite so soon,)
Because, though sore against her will,
She sat all night up at quadrille.
She stretches, gapes, unglues her eyes,
And asks if it be time to rise;
Of headache and the spleen complains;
And then, to cool her heated brains,
Her night-gown and her slippers brought her,
Takes a large dram of citron water.
Then to her glass; and, "Betty, pray,
Don't I look frightfully to-day?
But was it not confounded hard?
Well, if I ever touch a card!
Four matadores, and lose codille!
Depend upon't, I never will.
But run to Tom, and bid him fix
The ladies here to-night by six."
"Madam, the goldsmith waits below;
He says, his business is to know
If you'll redeem the silver cup
He keeps in pawn?"—"Why, show him up."
"Your dressing-plate he'll be content
To take, for interest *cent. per cent.*
And, madam, there's my Lady Spade
Has sent this letter by her maid."
"Well, I remember what she won;
And has she sent so soon to dun?
Here, carry down these ten pistoles
My husband left to pay for coals:
I thank my stars they all are light,
And I may have revenge to-night."
Now, loitering o'er her tea and cream,

She enters on her usual theme;
Her last night's ill success repeats,
Calls Lady Spade a hundred cheats:
"She slipt spadillo in her breast,
Then thought to turn it to a jest:
There's Mrs. Cut and she combine,
And to each other give the sign."
Through every game pursues her tale,
Like hunters o'er their evening ale.
Now to another scene give place:
Enter the folks with silks and lace:
Fresh matter for a world of chat,
Right Indian this, right Mechlin that:
"Observe this pattern—there's a stuff;
I can have customers enough.
Dear madam, you are grown so hard—
This lace is worth twelve pounds a-yard:
Madam, if there be truth in man,
I never sold so cheap a fan."
This business of importance o'er,
And madam almost dress'd by four;
The footman, in his usual phrase,
Comes up with, "Madam, dinner stays."
She answers, in her usual style,
"The cook must keep it back a while;
I never can have time to dress,
No woman breathing takes up less;
I'm hurried so, it makes me sick;
I wish the dinner at Old Nick."
At table now she acts her part,
Has all the dinner cant by heart:
"I thought we were to dine alone,
My dear; for sure, if I had known
This company would come to-day—
But really 'tis my spouse's way!
He's so unkind, he never sends
To tell when he invites his friends:
I wish ye may but have enough!"
And while with all this paltry stuff

She sits tormenting every guest,
Nor gives her tongue one moment's rest,
In phrases batter'd, stale, and trite,
Which modern ladies call polite;
You see the booby husband sit
In admiration at her wit!
    But let me now a while survey
Our madam o'er her evening tea;
Surrounded with her noisy clans
Of prudes, coquettes, and harridans,
When, frighted at the clamorous crew,
Away the God of Silence flew,
And fair Discretion left the place,
And modesty with blushing face;
Now enters overweening Pride,
And Scandal, ever gaping wide,
Hypocrisy with frown severe,
Scurrility with gibing air;
Rude laughter seeming like to burst,
And Malice always judging worst;
And Vanity with pocket glass,
And Impudence with front of brass;
And studied Affectation came,
Each limb and feature out of frame;
While Ignorance, with brain of lead,
Flew hovering o'er each female head.
    Why should I ask of thee, my Muse,
A hundred tongues, as poets use,
When, to give every dame her due,
A hundred thousand were too few?
Or how should I, alas! relate
The sum of all their senseless prate,
Their innuendoes, hints, and slanders,
Their meanings lewd, and double entendres?
Now comes the general scandal charge;
What some invent, the rest enlarge;
And, "Madam, if it be a lie,
You have the tale as cheap as I;
I must conceal my author's name:

But now 'tis known to common fame."
    Say, foolish females, bold and blind,
Say, by what fatal turn of mind,
Are you on vices most severe,
Wherein yourselves have greatest share?
Thus every fool herself deludes;
The prude condemns the absent prudes:
Mopsa, who stinks her spouse to death,
Accuses Chloe's tainted breath;
Hircina, rank with sweat, presumes
To censure Phyllis for perfumes;
While crooked Cynthia, sneering, says,
That Florimel wears iron stays;
Chloe, of every coxcomb jealous,
Admires how girls can talk with fellows;
And, full of indignation, frets,
That women should be such coquettes:
Iris, for scandal most notorious,
Cries, "Lord, the world is so censorious!"
And Rufa, with her combs of lead,
Whispers that Sappho's hair is red:
Aura, whose tongue you hear a mile hence,
Talks half a day in praise of silence;
And Sylvia, full of inward guilt,
Calls Amoret an arrant jilt.
    Now voices over voices rise,
While each to be the loudest vies:
They contradict, affirm, dispute,
No single tongue one moment mute;
All mad to speak, and none to hearken,
They set the very lap-dog barking;
Their chattering makes a louder din
Than fishwives o'er a cup of gin;
Not schoolboys at a barring out
Raised ever such incessant rout;
The jumbling particles of matter
In chaos made not such a clatter;
Far less the rabble roar and rail,
When drunk with sour election ale.

Nor do they trust their tongues alone,
But speak a language of their own;
Can read a nod, a shrug, a look,
Far better than a printed book;
Convey a libel in a frown,
And wink a reputation down;
Or by the tossing of the fan,
Describe the lady and the man.
But see, the female club disbands,
Each twenty visits on her hands.
Now all alone poor madam sits
In vapours and hysteric fits;
"And was not Tom this morning sent?
I'd lay my life he never went;
Past six, and not a living soul!
I might by this have won a vole."
A dreadful interval of spleen!
How shall we pass the time between?
"Here, Betty, let me take my drops;
And feel my pulse, I know it stops;
This head of mine, lord, how it swims!
And such a pain in all my limbs!"
"Dear madam, try to take a nap"—
But now they hear a footman's rap:
"Go, run, and light the ladies up:
It must be one before we sup."
The table, cards, and counters, set,
And all the gamester ladies met,
Her spleen and fits recover'd quite,
Our madam can sit up all night;
"Whoever comes, I'm not within."
Quadrille's the word, and so begin.
How can the Muse her aid impart,
Unskill'd in all the terms of art?
Or in harmonious numbers put
The deal, the shuffle, and the cut?
The superstitious whims relate,
That fill a female gamester's pate?
What agony of soul she feels

To see a knave's inverted heels!
She draws up card by card, to find
Good fortune peeping from behind;
With panting heart, and earnest eyes,
In hope to see spadillo rise;
In vain, alas! her hope is fed;
She draws an ace, and sees it red;
In ready counters never pays,
But pawns her snuff-box, rings, and keys;
Ever with some new fancy struck,
Tries twenty charms to mend her luck.
"This morning, when the parson came,
I said I should not win a game.
This odious chair, how came I stuck in't?
I think I never had good luck in't.
I'm so uneasy in my stays:
Your fan, a moment, if you please.
Stand farther, girl, or get you gone;
I always lose when you look on."
"Lord! madam, you have lost codille:
I never saw you play so ill."
"Nay, madam, give me leave to say,
'Twas you that threw the game away:
When Lady Tricksey play'd a four,
You took it with a matadore;
I saw you touch your wedding ring
Before my lady call'd a king;
You spoke a word began with H,
And I know whom you meant to teach,
Because you held the king of hearts;
Fie, madam, leave these little arts."
"That's not so bad as one that rubs
Her chair to call the king of clubs;
And makes her partner understand
A matadore is in her hand."
"Madam, you have no cause to flounce,
I swear I saw you thrice renounce."
"And truly, madam, I know when
Instead of five you scored me ten.

Spadillo here has got a mark;
A child may know it in the dark:
I guess'd the hand: it seldom fails:
I wish some folks would pare their nails."
While thus they rail, and scold, and storm,
It passes but for common form:
But, conscious that they all speak true,
And give each other but their due,
It never interrupts the game,
Or makes them sensible of shame.
The time too precious now to waste,
The supper gobbled up in haste;
Again afresh to cards they run,
As if they had but just begun.
But I shall not again repeat,
How oft they squabble, snarl, and cheat.
At last they hear the watchman knock,
"A frosty morn—past four o'clock."
The chairmen are not to be found,
"Come, let us play the other round."
Now all in haste they huddle on
Their hoods, their cloaks, and get them gone;
But, first, the winner must invite
The company to-morrow night.
Unlucky madam, left in tears,
(Who now again quadrille forswears,)
With empty purse, and aching head,
Steals to her sleeping spouse to bed.

The Logicians Refuted

Logicians have but ill defined
As rational, the human kind;
Reason, they say, belongs to man,
But let them prove it if they can.
Wise Aristotle and Smiglesius,
By ratiocinations specious,
Have strove to prove, with great precision,
With definition and division,
Homo est ratione praeditum;
But for my soul I cannot credit 'em,
And must, in spite of them, maintain,
That man and all his ways are vain;
And that this boasted lord of nature
Is both a weak and erring creature;
That instinct is a surer guide
Than reason, boasting mortals' pride;
And that brute beasts are far before 'em.
Deus est anima brutorum.
Whoever knew an honest brute
At law his neighbour prosecute,
Bring action for assault or battery,
Or friend beguile with lies and flattery?
O'er plains they ramble unconfined,
No politics disturb their mind;
They eat their meals, and take their sport
Nor know who's in or out at court.
They never to the levee go
To treat, as dearest friend, a foe:
They never importune his grace,
Nor ever cringe to men in place:
Nor undertake a dirty job,
Nor draw the quill to write for Bob.
Fraught with invective, they ne'er go
To folks at Paternoster Row.
No judges, fiddlers, dancing-masters,
No pickpockets, or poetasters,

Are known to honest quadrupeds;
No single brute his fellow leads.
Brutes never meet in bloody fray,
Nor cut each other's throats for pay.
Of beasts, it is confess'd, the ape
Comes nearest us in human shape;
Like man, he imitates each fashion,
And malice is his lurking passion:
But, both in malice and grimaces,
A courtier any ape surpasses.
Behold him, humbly cringing, wait
Upon the minister of state;
View him soon after to inferiors
Aping the conduct of superiors;
He promises with equal air,
And to perform takes equal care.
He in his turn finds imitators,
At court, the porters, lacqueys, waiters,
Their masters' manner still contract,
And footmen, lords and dukes can act.
Thus, at the court, both great and small
Behave alike, for all ape all.

The Elephant; or, the Parliament Man

Written many Years Since;
And taken from Coke's Fourth Institute
The High Court of Parliament, Cap. I

Sir E. Coke says: "Every member of the house being a counselor should have three properties of the elephant; first that he hath no gall; secondly, that he is inflexible and cannot bow; thirdly, that he is of a most ripe and perfect memory. . . first, to be without gall, that is, without malice, rancor, heat, and envy: . . . secondly, that he be constant, inflexible, and not be bowed, or turned from the right either for fear, reward, or favour, nor in judgement respect any person: . . . thirdly, of a ripe memory, that they remembering perils past, might prevent dangers to come."

—W. E. B.

Ere bribes convince you whom to choose,
The precepts of Lord Coke peruse.
Observe an elephant, says he,
And let him like your member be:
First take a man that's free from *Gaul*,
For elephants have none at all;
In flocks or parties he must keep;
For elephants live just like sheep.
Stubborn in honour he must be;
For elephants ne'er bend the knee.
Last, let his memory be sound,
In which your elephant's profound;
That old examples from the wise
May prompt him in his noes and ayes.
    Thus the Lord Coke hath gravely writ,
In all the form of lawyer's wit:
And then, with Latin and all that,
Shows the comparison is pat.
Yet in some points my lord is wrong,
One's teeth are sold, and t'other's tongue:

Now, men of parliament, God knows,
Are more like elephants of shows;
Whose docile memory and sense
Are turn'd to trick, to gather pence;
To get their master half-a-crown,
They spread the flag, or lay it down:
Those who bore bulwarks on their backs,
And guarded nations from attacks,
Now practise every pliant gesture,
Opening their trunk for every tester.
Siam, for elephants so famed,
Is not with England to be named:
Their elephants by men are sold;
Ours sell themselves, and take the gold.

Paulus: an Epigram

By Mr. Lindsay

Dublin, Sept. 7, 1728

"A Slave to crowds, scorch'd with the summer's heats,
In courts the wretched lawyer toils and sweats;
While smiling Nature, in her best attire,
Regales each sense, and vernal joys inspire.
Can he, who knows that real good should please,
Barter for gold his liberty and ease?"—
This Paulus preach'd:—When, entering at the door,
Upon his board the client pours the ore:
He grasps the shining gift, pores o'er the cause,
Forgets the sun, and dozes on the laws.

The Answer. By Dr. Swift

Lindsay mistakes the matter quite,
And honest Paulus judges right.
Then, why these quarrels to the sun,
Without whose aid you're all undone?
Did Paulus e'er complain of sweat?
Did Paulus e'er the sun forget;
The influence of whose golden beams
Soon licks up all unsavoury steams?
The sun, you say, his face has kiss'd:
It has; but then it greased his fist.
True lawyers, for the wisest ends,
Have always been Apollo's friends.
Not for his superficial powers
Of ripening fruits, and gilding flowers;
Not for inspiring poets' brains
With penniless and starveling strains;
Not for his boasted healing art;
Not for his skill to shoot the dart;
Nor yet because he sweetly fiddles;
Nor for his prophecies in riddles:
But for a more substantial cause—
Apollo's patron of the laws;
Whom Paulus ever must adore,
As parent of the golden ore,
By Phoebus, an incestuous birth,
Begot upon his grandam Earth;
By Phoebus first produced to light;
By Vulcan form'd so round and bright:
Then offer'd at the shrine of Justice,
By clients to her priests and trustees.
Nor, when we see Astraea stand
With even balance in her hand,
Must we suppose she has in view,
How to give every man his due;
Her scales you see her only hold,
To weigh her priests' the lawyers' gold.

Now, should I own your case was grievous,
Poor sweaty Paulus, who'd believe us?
'Tis very true, and none denies,
At least, that such complaints are wise:
'Tis wise, no doubt, as clients fat you more,
To cry, like statesmen, *Quanta patimur!*
But, since the truth must needs be stretched
To prove that lawyers are so wretched,
This paradox I'll undertake,
For Paulus' and for Lindsay's sake;
By topics, which, though I abomine 'em,
May serve as arguments *ad hominem*:
Yet I disdain to offer those
Made use of by detracting foes.
I own the curses of mankind
Sit light upon a lawyer's mind:
The clamours of ten thousand tongues
Break not his rest, nor hurt his lungs;
I own, his conscience always free,
(Provided he has got his fee,)
Secure of constant peace within,
He knows no guilt, who knows no sin.
Yet well they merit to be pitied,
By clients always overwitted.
And though the gospel seems to say,
What heavy burdens lawyers lay
Upon the shoulders of their neighbour,
Nor lend a finger to their labour,
Always for saving their own bacon;
No doubt, the text is here mistaken:
The copy's false, the sense is rack'd:
To prove it, I appeal to fact;
And thus by demonstration show
What burdens lawyers undergo.
With early clients at his door,
Though he was drunk the night before,
And crop-sick, with unclubb'd-for wine,
The wretch must be at court by nine;
Half sunk beneath his briefs and bag,

As ridden by a midnight hag;
Then, from the bar, harangues the bench,
In English vile, and viler French,
And Latin, vilest of the three;
And all for poor ten moidores fee!
Of paper how is he profuse,
With periods long, in terms abstruse!
What pains he takes to be prolix!
A thousand lines to stand for six!
Of common sense without a word in!
And is not this a grievous burden?
    The lawyer is a common drudge,
To fight our cause before the judge:
And, what is yet a greater curse,
Condemn'd to bear his client's purse:
While he at ease, secure and light,
Walks boldly home at dead of night;
When term is ended, leaves the town,
Trots to his country mansion down;
And, disencumber'd of his load,
No danger dreads upon the road;
Despises rapparees, and rides
Safe through the Newry mountains' sides.
    Lindsay, 'tis you have set me on,
To state this question *pro* and *con*.
My satire may offend, 'tis true;
However, it concerns not you.
I own, there may, in every clan,
Perhaps, be found one honest man;
Yet link them close, in this they jump,
To be but rascals in the lump.
Imagine Lindsay at the bar,
He's much the same his brethren are;
Well taught by practice to imbibe
The fundamentals of his tribe:
And in his client's just defence,
Must deviate oft from common sense;
And make his ignorance discern'd,
To get the name of counsel-learn'd,

(As *lucus* comes *a non lucendo*,)
And wisely do as other men do:
But shift him to a better scene,
Among his crew of rogues in grain;
Surrounded with companions fit,
To taste his humour, sense, and wit;
You'd swear he never took a fee,
Nor knew in law his A, B, C.
'Tis hard, where dulness overrules,
To keep good sense in crowds of fools.
And we admire the man, who saves
His honesty in crowds of knaves;
Nor yields up virtue at discretion,
To villains of his own profession.
Lindsay, you know what pains you take
In both, yet hardly save your stake;
And will you venture both anew,
To sit among that venal crew,
That pack of mimic legislators,
Abandon'd, stupid, slavish praters?
For as the rabble daub and rifle
The fool who scrambles for a trifle;
Who for his pains is cuff'd and kick'd,
Drawn through the dirt, his pockets pick'd;
You must expect the like disgrace,
Scrambling with rogues to get a place;
Must lose the honour you have gain'd,
Your numerous virtues foully stain'd:
Disclaim for ever all pretence
To common honesty and sense;
And join in friendship with a strict tie,
To M—l, C—y, and Dick Tighe.

A Dialogue

Written by Mr. Lindsay, in 1729

Between an Eminent Lawyer and Dr. Jonathan Swift, D.S.P.D. in Allusion to Horace, Book II, Satire I

"Sunt quibus in Satirâ," etc.

Dr. Swift: Since there are persons who complain
There's too much satire in my vein;
That I am often found exceeding
The rules of raillery and breeding;
With too much freedom treat my betters,
Not sparing even men of letters:
You, who are skill'd in lawyers' lore,
What's your advice? Shall I give o'er?
Nor ever fools or knaves expose,
Either in verse or humorous prose:
And to avoid all future ill,
In my scrutoire lock up my quill?
Lawyer: Since you are pleased to condescend
To ask the judgment of a friend,
Your case consider'd, I must think
You should withdraw from pen and ink,
Forbear your poetry and jokes,
And live like other Christian folks;
Or if the Muses must inspire
Your fancy with their pleasing fire,
Take subjects safer for your wit
Than those on which you lately writ.
Commend the times, your thoughts correct,
And follow the prevailing sect;
Assert that Hyde, in writing story,
Shows all the malice of a Tory;
While Burnet, in his deathless page,
Discovers freedom without rage.
To Woolston recommend our youth,

For learning, probity, and truth;
That noble genius, who unbinds
The chains which fetter freeborn minds;
Redeems us from the slavish fears
Which lasted near two thousand years;
He can alone the priesthood humble,
Make gilded spires and altars tumble.
DR. SWIFT: Must I commend against my conscience,
Such stupid blasphemy and nonsense;
To such a subject tune my lyre,
And sing like one of Milton's choir,
Where devils to a vale retreat,
And call the laws of Wisdom, Fate;
Lament upon their hapless fall,
That Force free Virtue should enthrall?
Or shall the charms of Wealth and Power
Make me pollute the Muses' bower?
LAWYER: As from the tripod of Apollo,
Hear from my desk the words that follow:
"Some, by philosophers misled,
Must honour you alive and dead;
And such as know what Greece has writ,
Must taste your irony and wit;
While most that are, or would be great,
Must dread your pen, your person hate;
And you on Drapier's hill must lie,
And there without a mitre die."

On Burning a Dull Poem

1729

An ass's hoof alone can hold
That poisonous juice, which kills by cold.
Methought, when I this poem read,
No vessel but an ass's head
Such frigid fustian could contain;
I mean, the head without the brain.
The cold conceits, the chilling thoughts,
Went down like stupifying draughts;
I found my head begin to swim,
A numbness crept through every limb.
In haste, with imprecations dire,
I threw the volume in the fire;
When, (who could think?) though cold as ice,
It burnt to ashes in a trice.
    How could I more enhance its fame?
Though born in snow, it died in flame.

An excellent new Ballad Or, the True English Dean to be Hanged for a Rape. 1730

Our brethren of England, who love us so dear,
    And in all they do for us so kindly do mean,
(A blessing upon them!) have sent us this year,
    For the good of our church, a true English dean.
A holier priest ne'er was wrapt up in crape,
The worst you can say, he committed a rape.

In his journey to Dublin, he lighted at Chester,
    And there he grew fond of another man's wife;
Burst into her chamber and would have caress'd her;
    But she valued her honour much more than her life.
She bustled, and struggled, and made her escape
To a room full of guests, for fear of a rape.

The dean he pursued, to recover his game;
    And now to attack her again he prepares:
But the company stood in defence of the dame,
    They cudgell'd, and cuff'd him, and kick'd him down stairs.
His deanship was now in a damnable scrape,
And this was no time for committing a rape.

To Dublin he comes, to the bagnio he goes,
    And orders the landlord to bring him a whore;
No scruple came on him his gown to expose,
    'Twas what all his life he had practised before.
He made himself drunk with the juice of the grape,
And got a good clap, but committed no rape.

The dean, and his landlord, a jolly comrade,
    Resolved for a fortnight to swim in delight;
For why, they had both been brought up to the trade
    Of drinking all day, and of whoring all night.
His landlord was ready his deanship to ape
In every debauch but committing a rape.

This Protestant zealot, this English divine,
    In church and in state was of principles sound;
Was truer than Steele to the Hanover line,
    And grieved that a Tory should live above ground.
Shall a subject so loyal be hang'd by the nape,
For no other crime but committing a rape?

By old Popish canons, as wise men have penn'd 'em,
    Each priest had a concubine *jure ecclesiae*;
Who'd be Dean of Fernes without a *commendam*?
    And precedents we can produce, if it please ye:
Then why should the dean, when whores are so cheap,
Be put to the peril and toil of a rape?

If fortune should please but to take such a crotchet,
    (To thee I apply, great Smedley's successor,)
To give thee lawn sleeves, a mitre, and rochet,
    Whom wouldst thou resemble? I leave thee a guesser.
But I only behold thee in Atherton's shape,
For sodomy hang'd; as thou for a rape.

Ah! dost thou not envy the brave Colonel Chartres,
    Condemn'd for thy crime at threescore and ten?
To hang him, all England would lend him their garters,
    Yet he lives, and is ready to ravish again.
Then throttle thyself with an ell of strong tape,
For thou hast not a groat to atone for a rape.

The dean he was vex'd that his whores were so willing;
    He long'd for a girl that would struggle and squall;
He ravish'd her fairly, and saved a good shilling;
    But here was to pay the devil and all.
His troubles and sorrows now come in a heap,
And hang'd he must be for committing a rape.

If maidens are ravish'd, it is their own choice:
    Why are they so wilful to struggle with men?
If they would but lie quiet, and stifle their voice,
    No devil nor dean could ravish them then.

Nor would there be need of a strong hempen cape
Tied round the dean's neck for committing a rape.

Our church and our state dear England maintains,
  For which all true Protestant hearts should be glad:
She sends us our bishops, our judges, and deans,
  And better would give us, if better she had.
But, lord! how the rabble will stare and will gape,
When the good English dean is hang'd up for a rape!

On Stephen Duck
The Thresher, and Favourite Poet

A Quibbling Epigram. 1730

The thresher Duck could o'er the queen prevail,
The proverb says, "no fence against a flail."
From threshing corn he turns to thresh his brains;
For which her majesty allows him grains:
Though 'tis confest, that those, who ever saw
His poems, think them all not worth a straw!
    Thrice happy Duck, employ'd in threshing stubble,
Thy toil is lessen'd, and thy profits double.

The Lady's Dressing-Room. 1730

Five hours (and who can do it less in?)
By haughty Celia spent in dressing;
The goddess from her chamber issues,
Array'd in lace, brocades, and tissues.
    Strephon, who found the room was void,
And Betty otherwise employ'd,
Stole in, and took a strict survey
Of all the litter as it lay:
Whereof, to make the matter clear,
An inventory follows here.
    And, first, a dirty smock appear'd,
Beneath the arm-pits well besmear'd;
Strephon, the rogue, display'd it wide,
And turn'd it round on ev'ry side:
On such a point, few words are best,
And Strephon bids us guess the rest;
But swears, how damnably the men lie
In calling Celia sweet and cleanly.
    Now listen, while he next produces
The various combs for various uses;
Fill'd up with dirt so closely fixt,
No brush could force a way betwixt;
A paste of composition rare,
Sweat, dandriff, powder, lead, and hair:
A fore-head cloth with oil upon't,
To smooth the wrinkles on her front:
Here alum-flour, to stop the steams
Exhaled from sour unsavoury streams:
There night-gloves made of Tripsey's hide,
Bequeath'd by Tripsey when she died;
With puppy-water, beauty's help,
Distil'd from Tripsey's darling whelp.
Here gallipots and vials placed,
Some fill'd with washes, some with paste;
Some with pomatums, paints, and slops,
And ointments good for scabby chops.

Hard by a filthy bason stands,
Foul'd with the scouring of her hands:
The bason takes whatever comes,
The scrapings from her teeth and gums,
A nasty compound of all hues,
For here she spits, and here she spues.
    But, oh! it turn'd poor Strephon's bowels
When he beheld and smelt the towels,
Begumm'd, bematter'd, and beslim'd,
With dirt, and sweat, and ear-wax grim'd;
No object Strephon's eye escapes;
Here petticoats in frouzy heaps;
Nor be the handkerchiefs forgot,
All varnish'd o'er with snuff and snot.
The stockings why should I expose,
Stain'd with the moisture of her toes,
Or greasy coifs, and pinners reeking,
Which Celia slept at least a week in?
A pair of tweezers next he found,
To pluck her brows in arches round;
Or hairs that sink the forehead low,
Or on her chin like bristles grow.
    The virtues we must not let pass
Of Celia's magnifying glass;
When frighted Strephon cast his eye on't,
It shew'd the visage of a giant:
A glass that can to sight disclose
The smallest worm in Celia's nose,
And faithfully direct her nail
To squeeze it out from head to tail;
For, catch it nicely by the head,
It must come out, alive or dead.
    Why, Strephon, will you tell the rest?
And must you needs describe the chest?
That careless wench! no creature warn her
To move it out from yonder corner!
But leave it standing full in sight,
For you to exercise your spight?
In vain the workman shew'd his wit,

With rings and hinges counterfeit,
To make it seem in this disguise
A cabinet to vulgar eyes:
Which Strephon ventur'd to look in,
Resolved to go thro' thick and thin.
He lifts the lid: there needs no more,
He smelt it all the time before.
As, from within Pandora's box,
When Epimetheus op'd the locks,
A sudden universal crew
Of human evils upward flew;
He still was comforted to find
That hope at last remain'd behind:
So Strephon, lifting up the lid,
To view what in the chest was hid,
The vapours flew from up the vent;
But Strephon, cautious, never meant
The bottom of the pan to grope,
And foul his hands in search of hope.
O! ne'er may such a vile machine
Be once in Celia's chamber seen!
O! may she better learn to keep
Those "secrets of the hoary deep."
As mutton-cutlets, prime of meat,
Which, tho' with art you salt and beat,
As laws of cookery require,
And toast them at the clearest fire;
If from upon the hopeful chops
The fat upon a cinder drops,
To stinking smoke it turns the flame,
Pois'ning the flesh from whence it came,
And up exhales a greasy stench,
For which you curse the careless wench:
So things which must not be exprest,
When drop'd into the reeking chest,
Send up an excremental smell
To taint the part from whence they fell:
The petticoats and gown perfume,
And waft a stink round ev'ry room.

Thus finishing his grand survey,
Disgusted Strephon slunk away;
Repeating in his amorous fits,
"Oh! Celia, Celia, Celia sh—!"
But Vengeance, goddess never sleeping,
Soon punish'd Strephon for his peeping:
His foul imagination links
Each dame he sees with all her stinks;
And, if unsavoury odours fly,
Conceives a lady standing by.
All women his description fits,
And both ideas jump like wits;
By vicious fancy coupled fast,
And still appearing in contrast.
I pity wretched Strephon, blind
To all the charms of woman kind.
Should I the Queen of Love refuse,
Because she rose from stinking ooze?
To him that looks behind the scene,
Statira's but some pocky quean.
When Celia in her glory shews,
If Strephon would but stop his nose,
(Who now so impiously blasphemes
Her ointments, daubs, and paints, and creams,
Her washes, slops, and every clout,
With which he makes so foul a rout;)
He soon would learn to think like me,
And bless his ravish'd sight to see
Such order from confusion sprung,
Such gaudy tulips raised from dung.

The Power of Time. 1730

If neither brass nor marble can withstand
The mortal force of Time's destructive hand;
If mountains sink to vales, if cities die,
And lessening rivers mourn their fountains dry;
When my old cassock (said a Welsh divine)
Is out at elbows, why should I repine?

Cassinus and Peter

A Tragical Elegy
1731

Two college sophs of Cambridge growth,
Both special wits and lovers both,
Conferring, as they used to meet,
On love, and books, in rapture sweet;
(Muse, find me names to fit my metre,
Cassinus this, and t'other Peter.)
Friend Peter to Cassinus goes,
To chat a while, and warm his nose:
But such a sight was never seen,
The lad lay swallow'd up in spleen.
He seem'd as just crept out of bed;
One greasy stocking round his head,
The other he sat down to darn,
With threads of different colour'd yarn;
His breeches torn, exposing wide
A ragged shirt and tawny hide.
Scorch'd were his shins, his legs were bare,
But well embrown'd with dirt and hair
A rug was o'er his shoulders thrown,
(A rug, for nightgown he had none,)
His jordan stood in manner fitting
Between his legs, to spew or spit in;
His ancient pipe, in sable dyed,
And half unsmoked, lay by his side.
    Him thus accoutred Peter found,
With eyes in smoke and weeping drown'd;
The leavings of his last night's pot
On embers placed, to drink it hot.
    Why, Cassy, thou wilt dose thy pate:
What makes thee lie a-bed so late?
The finch, the linnet, and the thrush,
Their matins chant in every bush;
And I have heard thee oft salute

Aurora with thy early flute.
Heaven send thou hast not got the hyps!
How! not a word come from thy lips?
    Then gave him some familiar thumps,
A college joke to cure the dumps.
    The swain at last, with grief opprest,
Cried, Celia! thrice, and sigh'd the rest.
    Dear Cassy, though to ask I dread,
Yet ask I must—is Celia dead?
    How happy I, were that the worst!
But I was fated to be curst!
    Come, tell us, has she play'd the whore?
    O Peter, would it were no more!
    Why, plague confound her sandy locks!
Say, has the small or greater pox
Sunk down her nose, or seam'd her face?
Be easy, 'tis a common case.
    O Peter! beauty's but a varnish,
Which time and accidents will tarnish:
But Celia has contrived to blast
Those beauties that might ever last.
Nor can imagination guess,
Nor eloquence divine express,
How that ungrateful charming maid
My purest passion has betray'd:
Conceive the most envenom'd dart
To pierce an injured lover's heart.
    Why, hang her; though she seem'd so coy,
I know she loves the barber's boy.
    Friend Peter, this I could excuse,
For every nymph has leave to choose;
Nor have I reason to complain,
She loves a more deserving swain.
But, oh! how ill hast thou divined
A crime, that shocks all human kind;
A deed unknown to female race,
At which the sun should hide his face:
Advice in vain you would apply—
Then leave me to despair and die.

Ye kind Arcadians, on my urn
These elegies and sonnets burn;
And on the marble grave these rhymes,
A monument to after-times—
"Here Cassy lies, by Celia slain,
And dying, never told his pain."
    Vain empty world, farewell. But hark,
The loud Cerberian triple bark;
And there—behold Alecto stand,
A whip of scorpions in her hand:
Lo, Charon from his leaky wherry
Beckoning to waft me o'er the ferry:
I come! I come! Medusa see,
Her serpents hiss direct at me.
Begone; unhand me, hellish fry:
"Avaunt—ye cannot say 'twas I."
    Dear Cassy, thou must purge and bleed;
I fear thou wilt be mad indeed.
But now, by friendship's sacred laws,
I here conjure thee, tell the cause;
And Celia's horrid fact relate:
Thy friend would gladly share thy fate.
    To force it out, my heart must rend;
Yet when conjured by such a friend—
Think, Peter, how my soul is rack'd!
These eyes, these eyes, beheld the fact.
Now bend thine ear, since out it must;
But, when thou seest me laid in dust,
The secret thou shalt ne'er impart,
Not to the nymph that keeps thy heart;
(How would her virgin soul bemoan
A crime to all her sex unknown!)
Nor whisper to the tattling reeds
The blackest of all female deeds;
Nor blab it on the lonely rocks,
Where Echo sits, and listening mocks;
Nor let the Zephyr's treacherous gale
Through Cambridge waft the direful tale;
Nor to the chattering feather'd race

Discover Celia's foul disgrace.
But, if you fail, my spectre dread,
Attending nightly round your bed—
And yet I dare confide in you;
So take my secret, and adieu:
Nor wonder how I lost my wits:
Oh! Celia, Celia, Celia sh—!

A Beautiful young Nymph going to Bed

Written for the Honour of the Fair Sex. 1731

Corinna, pride of Drury-Lane,
For whom no shepherd sighs in vain;
Never did Covent-Garden boast
So bright a batter'd strolling toast!
No drunken rake to pick her up,
No cellar where on tick to sup;
Returning at the midnight hour,
Four stories climbing to her bower;
Then, seated on a three-legg'd chair,
Takes off her artificial hair;
Now picking out a crystal eye,
She wipes it clean, and lays it by.
Her eyebrows from a mouse's hide
Stuck on with art on either side,
Pulls off with care, and first displays 'em,
Then in a play-book smoothly lays 'em.
Now dext'rously her plumpers draws,
That serve to fill her hollow jaws,
Untwists a wire, and from her gums
A set of teeth completely comes;
Pulls out the rags contrived to prop
Her flabby dugs, and down they drop.
Proceeding on, the lovely goddess
Unlaces next her steel-ribb'd bodice,
Which, by the operator's skill,
Press down the lumps, the hollows fill.
Up goes her hand, and off she slips
The bolsters that supply her hips;
With gentlest touch she next explores
Her chancres, issues, running sores;
Effects of many a sad disaster,
And then to each applies a plaster:
But must, before she goes to bed,

Rub off the daubs of white and red,
And smooth the furrows in her front
With greasy paper stuck upon't.
She takes a bolus ere she sleeps;
And then between two blankets creeps.
With pains of love tormented lies;
Or, if she chance to close her eyes,
Of Bridewell and the Compter dreams,
And feels the lash, and faintly screams;
Or, by a faithless bully drawn,
At some hedge-tavern lies in pawn;
Or to Jamaica seems transported
Alone, and by no planter courted;
Or, near Fleet-ditch's oozy brinks,
Surrounded with a hundred stinks,
Belated, seems on watch to lie,
And snap some cully passing by;
Or, struck with fear, her fancy runs
On watchmen, constables, and duns,
From whom she meets with frequent rubs;
But never from religious clubs;
Whose favour she is sure to find,
Because she pays them all in kind.
    Corinna wakes. A dreadful sight!
Behold the ruins of the night!
A wicked rat her plaster stole,
Half eat, and dragg'd it to his hole.
The crystal eye, alas! was miss'd;
And puss had on her plumpers p—st,
A pigeon pick'd her issue-pease:
And Shock her tresses fill'd with fleas.
    The nymph, though in this mangled plight
Must ev'ry morn her limbs unite.
But how shall I describe her arts
To re-collect the scatter'd parts?
Or show the anguish, toil, and pain,
Of gath'ring up herself again?
The bashful Muse will never bear

In such a scene to interfere.
Corinna, in the morning dizen'd,
Who sees, will spew; who smells, be poison'd.

Strephon and Chloe
1731

Of Chloe all the town has rung,
By ev'ry size of poets sung:
So beautiful a nymph appears
But once in twenty thousand years;
By Nature form'd with nicest care,
And faultless to a single hair.
Her graceful mien, her shape, and face,
Confess'd her of no mortal race:
And then so nice, and so genteel;
Such cleanliness from head to heel;
No humours gross, or frouzy steams,
No noisome whiffs, or sweaty streams,
Before, behind, above, below,
Could from her taintless body flow:
Would so discreetly things dispose,
None ever saw her pluck a rose.
Her dearest comrades never caught her
Squat on her hams to make maid's water:
You'd swear that so divine a creature
Felt no necessities of nature.
In summer had she walk'd the town,
Her armpits would not stain her gown:
At country dances, not a nose
Could in the dog-days smell her toes.
Her milk-white hands, both palms and backs,
Like ivory dry, and soft as wax.
Her hands, the softest ever felt,
Though cold would burn, though dry would melt.
    Dear Venus, hide this wond'rous maid,
Nor let her loose to spoil your trade.
While she engrosses ev'ry swain,
You but o'er half the world can reign.
Think what a case all men are now in,
What ogling, sighing, toasting, vowing!
What powder'd wigs! what flames and darts!

What hampers full of bleeding hearts!
What sword-knots! what poetic strains!
What billets-doux, and clouded canes!
    But Strephon sigh'd so loud and strong,
He blew a settlement along;
And bravely drove his rivals down,
With coach and six, and house in town.
The bashful nymph no more withstands,
Because her dear papa commands.
The charming couple now unites:
Proceed we to the marriage rites.
    Imprimis, at the Temple porch
Stood Hymen with a flaming torch:
The smiling Cyprian Goddess brings
Her infant loves with purple wings:
And pigeons billing, sparrows treading,
Fair emblems of a fruitful wedding.
The Muses next in order follow,
Conducted by their squire, Apollo:
Then Mercury with silver tongue;
And Hebe, goddess ever young.
Behold, the bridegroom and his bride
Walk hand in hand, and side by side;
She, by the tender Graces drest,
But he, by Mars, in scarlet vest.
The nymph was cover'd with her *flammeum* ,
And Phoebus sung th'epithalamium.
And last, to make the matter sure,
Dame Juno brought a priest demure.
Luna was absent, on pretence
Her time was not till nine months hence.
The rites perform'd, the parson paid,
In state return'd the grand parade;
With loud huzzas from all the boys,
That now the pair must crown their joys.
    But still the hardest part remains:
Strephon had long perplex'd his brains,
How with so high a nymph he might
Demean himself the wedding-night:

For, as he view'd his person round,
Mere mortal flesh was all he found:
His hand, his neck, his mouth, and feet,
Were duly wash'd, to keep them sweet;
With other parts, that shall be nameless,
The ladies else might think me shameless.
The weather and his love were hot;
And, should he struggle, I know what—
Why, let it go, if I must tell it—
He'll sweat, and then the nymph may smell it;
While she, a goddess dyed in grain,
Was unsusceptible of stain,
And, Venus-like, her fragrant skin
Exhaled ambrosia from within.
Can such a deity endure
A mortal human touch impure?
How did the humbled swain detest
His prickly beard, and hairy breast!
His night-cap, border'd round with lace,
Could give no softness to his face.
    Yet, if the goddess could be kind,
What endless raptures must he find!
And goddesses have now and then
Come down to visit mortal men;
To visit and to court them too:
A certain goddess, God knows who,
(As in a book he heard it read,)
Took Col'nel Peleus to her bed.
But what if he should lose his life
By vent'ring on his heavenly wife!
(For Strephon could remember well,
That once he heard a school-boy tell,
How Semele, of mortal race,
By thunder died in Jove's embrace.)
And what if daring Strephon dies
By lightning shot from Chloe's eyes!
    While these reflections fill'd his head,
The bride was put in form to bed:
He follow'd, stript, and in he crept,

But awfully his distance kept.
    Now, "ponder well, ye parents dear;"
Forbid your daughters guzzling beer;
And make them ev'ry afternoon
Forbear their tea, or drink it soon;
That, ere to bed they venture up,
They may discharge it ev'ry sup;
If not, they must in evil plight
Be often forc'd to rise at night.
Keep them to wholesome food confin'd,
Nor let them taste what causes wind:
'Tis this the sage of Samos means,
Forbidding his disciples beans.
O! think what evils must ensue;
Miss Moll, the jade, will burn it blue;
And, when she once has got the art,
She cannot help it for her heart;
But out it flies, even when she meets
Her bridegroom in the wedding-sheets.
Carminative and *diuretic*
Will damp all passion sympathetic;
And Love such nicety requires,
One blast will put out all his fires.
Since husbands get behind the scene,
The wife should study to be clean;
Nor give the smallest room to guess
The time when wants of nature press;
But after marriage practise more
Decorum than she did before;
To keep her spouse deluded still,
And make him fancy what she will.
    In bed we left the married pair;
'Tis time to show how things went there.
Strephon, who had been often told
That fortune still assists the bold,
Resolved to make the first attack;
But Chloe drove him fiercely back.
How could a nymph so chaste as Chloe,
With constitution cold and snowy,

Permit a brutish man to touch her?
Ev'n lambs by instinct fly the butcher.
Resistance on the wedding-night
Is what our maidens claim by right;
And Chloe, 'tis by all agreed,
Was maid in thought, in word, and deed.
Yet some assign a different reason;
That Strephon chose no proper season.
    Say, fair ones, must I make a pause,
Or freely tell the secret cause?
    Twelve cups of tea (with grief I speak)
Had now constrain'd the nymph to leak.
This point must needs be settled first:
The bride must either void or burst.
Then see the dire effects of pease;
Think what can give the colic ease.
The nymph oppress'd before, behind,
As ships are toss'd by waves and wind,
Steals out her hand, by nature led,
And brings a vessel into bed;
Fair utensil, as smooth and white
As Chloe's skin, almost as bright.
    Strephon, who heard the fuming rill
As from a mossy cliff distil,
Cried out, Ye Gods! what sound is this?
Can Chloe, heavenly Chloe,——?
But when he smelt a noisome steam
Which oft attends that lukewarm stream;
(Salerno both together joins,
As sov'reign med'cines for the loins:)
And though contriv'd, we may suppose,
To slip his ears, yet struck his nose;
He found her while the scent increast,
As mortal as himself at least.
But soon, with like occasions prest
He boldly sent his hand in quest
(Inspired with courage from his bride)
To reach the pot on t'other side;
And, as he fill'd the reeking vase;

Let fly a rouser in her face.
    The little Cupids hov'ring round,
(As pictures prove) with garlands crown'd,
Abash'd at what they saw and heard,
Flew off, nor ever more appear'd.
    Adieu to ravishing delights,
High raptures, and romantic flights;
To goddesses so heav'nly sweet,
Expiring shepherds at their feet;
To silver meads and shady bowers,
Dress'd up with amaranthine flowers.
    How great a change! how quickly made!
They learn to call a spade a spade.
They soon from all constraint are freed;
Can see each other do their need.
On box of cedar sits the wife,
And makes it warm for dearest life;
And, by the beastly way of thinking,
Find great society in stinking.
Now Strephon daily entertains
His Chloe in the homeliest strains;
And Chloe, more experienc'd grown,
With int'rest pays him back his own.
No maid at court is less asham'd,
Howe'er for selling bargains fam'd,
Than she to name her parts behind,
Or when a-bed to let out wind.
    Fair Decency, celestial maid!
Descend from Heaven to Beauty's aid!
Though Beauty may beget desire,
'Tis thou must fan the Lover's fire;
For Beauty, like supreme dominion,
Is best supported by Opinion:
If Decency bring no supplies,
Opinion falls, and Beauty dies.
    To see some radiant nymph appear
In all her glitt'ring birth-day gear,
You think some goddess from the sky
Descended, ready cut and dry:

But ere you sell yourself to laughter,
Consider well what may come after;
For fine ideas vanish fast,
While all the gross and filthy last.
    O Strephon, ere that fatal day
When Chloe stole your heart away,
Had you but through a cranny spy'd
On house of ease your future bride,
In all the postures of her face,
Which nature gives in such a case;
Distortions, groanings, strainings, heavings,
'Twere better you had lick'd her leavings,
Than from experience find too late
Your goddess grown a filthy mate.
Your fancy then had always dwelt
On what you saw and what you smelt;
Would still the same ideas give ye,
As when you spy'd her on the privy;
And, spite of Chloe's charms divine,
Your heart had been as whole as mine.
    Authorities, both old and recent,
Direct that women must be decent;
And from the spouse each blemish hide,
More than from all the world beside.
    Unjustly all our nymphs complain
Their empire holds so short a reign;
Is, after marriage, lost so soon,
It hardly lasts the honey-moon:
For, if they keep not what they caught,
It is entirely their own fault.
They take possession of the crown,
And then throw all their weapons down:
Though, by the politician's scheme,
Whoe'er arrives at power supreme,
Those arts, by which at first they gain it,
They still must practise to maintain it.
    What various ways our females take
To pass for wits before a rake!
And in the fruitless search pursue

All other methods but the true!
    Some try to learn polite behaviour
By reading books against their Saviour;
Some call it witty to reflect
On ev'ry natural defect;
Some shew they never want explaining
To comprehend a double meaning.
But sure a tell-tale out of school
Is of all wits the greatest fool;
Whose rank imagination fills
Her heart, and from her lips distils;
You'd think she utter'd from behind,
Or at her mouth was breaking wind.
    Why is a handsome wife ador'd
By every coxcomb but her lord?
From yonder puppet-man inquire,
Who wisely hides his wood and wire;
Shows Sheba's queen completely drest,
And Solomon in royal vest:
But view them litter'd on the floor,
Or strung on pegs behind the door;
Punch is exactly of a piece
With Lorrain's duke, and prince of Greece.
    A prudent builder should forecast
How long the stuff is like to last;
And carefully observe the ground,
To build on some foundation sound.
What house, when its materials crumble,
Must not inevitably tumble?
What edifice can long endure
Raised on a basis unsecure?
Rash mortals, ere you take a wife,
Contrive your pile to last for life:
Since beauty scarce endures a day,
And youth so swiftly glides away;
Why will you make yourself a bubble,
To build on sand with hay and stubble?
    On sense and wit your passion found,
By decency cemented round;

Let prudence with good-nature strive,
To keep esteem and love alive.
Then come old age whene'er it will,
Your friendship shall continue still:
And thus a mutual gentle fire
Shall never but with life expire.

Apollo; or, a Problem Solved
1731

Apollo, god of light and wit,
Could verse inspire, but seldom writ,
Refined all metals with his looks,
As well as chemists by their books;
As handsome as my lady's page;
Sweet five-and-twenty was his age.
His wig was made of sunny rays,
He crown'd his youthful head with bays;
Not all the court of Heaven could show
So nice and so complete a beau.
No heir upon his first appearance,
With twenty thousand pounds a-year rents,
E'er drove, before he sold his land,
So fine a coach along the Strand;
The spokes, we are by Ovid told,
Were silver, and the axle gold:
I own, 'twas but a coach-and-four,
For Jupiter allows no more.
    Yet, with his beauty, wealth, and parts,
Enough to win ten thousand hearts,
No vulgar deity above
Was so unfortunate in love.
    Three weighty causes were assign'd,
That moved the nymphs to be unkind.
Nine Muses always waiting round him,
He left them virgins as he found them.
His singing was another fault;
For he could reach to B in *alt*:
And, by the sentiments of Pliny,
Such singers are like Nicolini.
At last, the point was fully clear'd;
In short, Apollo had no beard.

The Place of the Damned
1731

All folks who pretend to religion and grace,
Allow there's a Hell, but dispute of the place:
But, if Hell may by logical rules be defined
The place of the damn'd—I'll tell you my mind.
Wherever the damn'd do chiefly abound,
Most certainly there is Hell to be found:
Damn'd poets, damn'd critics, damn'd blockheads, damn'd knaves,
Damn'd senators bribed, damn'd prostitute slaves;
Damn'd lawyers and judges, damn'd lords and damn'd squires;
Damn'd spies and informers, damn'd friends and damn'd liars;
Damn'd villains, corrupted in every station;
Damn'd time-serving priests all over the nation;
And into the bargain I'll readily give you
Damn'd ignorant prelates, and counsellors privy.
Then let us no longer by parsons be flamm'd,
For we know by these marks the place of the damn'd:
And Hell to be sure is at Paris or Rome.
How happy for us that it is not at home!

The Day of Judgment

With a whirl of thought oppress'd,
I sunk from reverie to rest.
An horrid vision seized my head;
I saw the graves give up their dead!
Jove, arm'd with terrors, bursts the skies,
And thunder roars and lightning flies!
Amaz'd, confus'd, its fate unknown,
The world stands trembling at his throne!
While each pale sinner hung his head,
Jove, nodding, shook the heavens, and said:
"Offending race of human kind,
By nature, reason, *learning*, blind;
You who, through frailty, stepp'd aside;
And you, who never fell—*through pride*:
You who in different sects were shamm'd,
And come to see each other damn'd;
(So some folk told you, but they knew
No more of Jove's designs than you;)
—The world's mad business now is o'er,
And I resent these pranks no more.
—I to such blockheads set my wit!
I damn such fools!—Go, go, you're *bit*."

Judas. 1731

By the just vengeance of incensed skies,
Poor Bishop Judas late repenting dies.
The Jews engaged him with a paltry bribe,
Amounting hardly to a crown a-tribe;
Which though his conscience forced him to restore,
(And parsons tell us, no man can do more,)
Yet, through despair, of God and man accurst,
He lost his bishopric, and hang'd or burst.
Those former ages differ'd much from this;
Judas betray'd his master with a kiss:
But some have kiss'd the gospel fifty times,
Whose perjury's the least of all their crimes;
Some who can perjure through a two inch-board,
Yet keep their bishoprics, and 'scape the cord:
Like hemp, which, by a skilful spinster drawn
To slender threads, may sometimes pass for lawn.
    As ancient Judas by transgression fell,
And burst asunder ere he went to hell;
So could we see a set of new Iscariots
Come headlong tumbling from their mitred chariots;
Each modern Judas perish like the first,
Drop from the tree with all his bowels burst;
Who could forbear, that view'd each guilty face,
To cry, "Lo! Judas gone to his own place,
His habitation let all men forsake,
And let his bishopric another take!"

An Epistle to Mr. Gay
1731

How could you, Gay, disgrace the Muse's train,
To serve a tasteless court twelve years in vain!
Fain would I think our female friend sincere,
Till Bob, the poet's foe, possess'd her ear.
Did female virtue e'er so high ascend,
To lose an inch of favour for a friend?
    Say, had the court no better place to choose
For triee, than make a dry-nurse of thy Muse?
How cheaply had thy liberty been sold,
To squire a royal girl of two years old:
In leading strings her infant steps to guide,
Or with her go-cart amble side by side!
    But princely Douglas, and his glorious dame,
Advanced thy fortune, and preserved thy fame.
Nor will your nobler gifts be misapplied,
When o'er your patron's treasure you preside:
The world shall own, his choice was wise and just,
For sons of Phoebus never break their trust.
    Not love of beauty less the heart inflames
Of guardian eunuchs to the sultan's dames,
Their passions not more impotent and cold,
Than those of poets to the lust of gold.
With Pæan's purest fire his favourites glow,
The dregs will serve to ripen ore below:
His meanest work: for, had he thought it fit
That wealth should be the appanage of wit,
The god of light could ne'er have been so blind
To deal it to the worst of human kind.
    But let me now, for I can do it well,
Your conduct in this new employ foretell.
    And first: to make my observation right,
I place a statesman full before my sight,
A bloated minister in all his gear,
With shameless visage and perfidious leer:
Two rows of teeth arm each devouring jaw,

And ostrich-like his all-digesting maw.
My fancy drags this monster to my view,
To shew the world his chief reverse in you.
Of loud unmeaning sounds, a rapid flood
Rolls from his mouth in plenteous streams of mud;
With these the court and senate-house he plies,
Made up of noise, and impudence, and lies.
    Now let me show how Bob and you agree:
You serve a potent prince, as well as he.
The ducal coffers trusted to your charge,
Your honest care may fill, perhaps enlarge:
His vassals easy, and the owner blest;
They pay a trifle, and enjoy the rest.
Not so a nation's revenues are paid;
The servant's faults are on the master laid.
The people with a sigh their taxes bring,
And, cursing Bob, forget to bless the king.
    Next hearken, Gay, to what thy charge requires,
With servants, tenants, and the neighbouring squires,
Let all domestics feel your gentle sway;
Nor bribe, insult, nor flatter, nor betray.
Let due reward to merit be allow'd;
Nor with your kindred half the palace crowd;
Nor think yourself secure in doing wrong,
By telling noses with a party strong.
    Be rich; but of your wealth make no parade;
At least, before your master's debts are paid;
Nor in a palace, built with charge immense,
Presume to treat him at his own expense.
Each farmer in the neighbourhood can count
To what your lawful perquisites amount.
The tenants poor, the hardness of the times,
Are ill excuses for a servant's crimes.
With interest, and a premium paid beside,
The master's pressing wants must be supplied;
With hasty zeal behold the steward come
By his own credit to advance the sum;
Who, while th'unrighteous Mammon is his friend,
May well conclude his power will never end.

A faithful treasurer! what could he do more?
He lends my lord what was my lord's before.
    The law so strictly guards the monarch's health,
That no physician dares prescribe by stealth:
The council sit; approve the doctor's skill;
And give advice before he gives the pill.
But the state empiric acts a safer part;
And, while he poisons, wins the royal heart.
    But how can I describe the ravenous breed?
Then let me now by negatives proceed.
    Suppose your lord a trusty servant send
On weighty business to some neighbouring friend:
Presume not, Gay, unless you serve a drone,
To countermand his orders by your own.
Should some imperious neighbour sink the boats,
And drain the fish-ponds, while your master dotes;
Shall he upon the ducal rights intrench,
Because he bribed you with a brace of tench?
    Nor from your lord his bad condition hide,
To feed his luxury, or soothe his pride.
Nor at an under rate his timber sell,
And with an oath assure him, all is well;
Or swear it rotten, and with humble airs
Request it of him, to complete your stairs;
Nor, when a mortgage lies on half his lands,
Come with a purse of guineas in your hands.
    Have Peter Waters always in your mind;
That rogue, of genuine ministerial kind,
Can half the peerage by his arts bewitch,
Starve twenty lords to make one scoundrel rich:
And, when he gravely has undone a score,
Is humbly pray'd to ruin twenty more.
    A dext'rous steward, when his tricks are found,
Hush-money sends to all the neighbours round;
His master, unsuspicious of his pranks,
Pays all the cost, and gives the villain thanks.
And, should a friend attempt to set him right,
His lordship would impute it all to spite;
Would love his favourite better than before,

And trust his honesty just so much more.
Thus families, like realms, with equal fate,
Are sunk by premier ministers of state.
    Some, when an heir succeeds, go bodily on,
And, as they robb'd the father, rob the son.
A knave, who deep embroils his lord's affairs,
Will soon grow necessary to his heirs.
His policy consists in setting traps,
In finding ways and means, and stopping gaps;
He knows a thousand tricks whene'er he please,
Though not to cure, yet palliate each disease.
In either case, an equal chance is run;
For, keep or turn him out, my lord's undone.
You want a hand to clear a filthy sink;
No cleanly workman can endure the stink.
A strong dilemma in a desperate case!
To act with infamy, or quit the place.
    A bungler thus, who scarce the nail can hit,
With driving wrong will make the panel split:
Nor dares an abler workman undertake
To drive a second, lest the whole should break.
    In every court the parallel will hold;
And kings, like private folks, are bought and sold.
The ruling rogue, who dreads to be cashler'd,
Contrives, as he is hated, to be fear'd;
Confounds accounts, perplexes all affairs:
For vengeance more embroils, than skill repairs.
So robbers, (and their ends are just the same,)
To 'scape inquiries, leave the house in flame.
    I knew a brazen minister of state,
Who bore for twice ten years the public hate.
In every mouth the question most in vogue
Was, when will they turn out this odious rogue?
A juncture happen'd in his highest pride:
While he went robbing on, his master died.
We thought there now remain'd no room to doubt;
The work is done, the minister must out.
The court invited more than one or two:
Will you, Sir Spencer? or will you, or you?

But not a soul his office durst accept;
The subtle knave had all the plunder swept:
And, such was then the temper of the times,
He owed his preservation to his crimes.
The candidates observed his dirty paws;
Nor found it difficult to guess the cause:
But, when they smelt such foul corruptions round him,
Away they fled, and left him as they found him.
  Thus, when a greedy sloven once has thrown
His snot into the mess, 'tis all his own.

To a Lady Who Desired the Author to Write some verses upon her In the Heroic Style

After venting all my spite,
Tell me, what have I to write?
Every error I could find
Through the mazes of your mind,
Have my busy Muse employ'd,
Till the company was cloy'd.
Are you positive and fretful,
Heedless, ignorant, forgetful?
Those, and twenty follies more,
I have often told before.
    Hearken what my lady says:
Have I nothing then to praise?
Ill it fits you to be witty,
Where a fault should move your pity.
If you think me too conceited,
Or to passion quickly heated;
If my wandering head be less
Set on reading than on dress;
If I always seem too dull t'ye;
I can solve the diffi—culty.
    You would teach me to be wise:
Truth and honour how to prize;
How to shine in conversation,
And with credit fill my station;
How to relish notions high;
How to live, and how to die.
    But it was decreed by Fate—
Mr. Dean, you come too late.
Well I know, you can discern,
I am now too old to learn:
Follies, from my youth instill'd,
Have my soul entirely fill'd;

In my head and heart they centre,
Nor will let your lessons enter.
    Bred a fondling and an heiress;
Drest like any lady mayoress:
Cocker'd by the servants round,
Was too good to touch the ground;
Thought the life of every lady
Should be one continued play-day—
Balls, and masquerades, and shows,
Visits, plays, and powder'd beaux.
    Thus you have my case at large,
And may now perform your charge.
Those materials I have furnish'd,
When by you refined and burnish'd,
Must, that all the world may know 'em,
Be reduced into a poem.
    But, I beg, suspend a while
That same paltry, burlesque style;
Drop for once your constant rule,
Turning all to ridicule;
Teaching others how to ape you;
Court nor parliament can 'scape you;
Treat the public and your friends
Both alike, while neither mends.
    Sing my praise in strain sublime:
Treat me not with dogg'rel rhyme.
'Tis but just, you should produce,
With each fault, each fault's excuse;
Not to publish every trifle,
And my few perfections stifle.
With some gifts at least endow me,
Which my very foes allow me.
Am I spiteful, proud, unjust?
Did I ever break my trust?
Which of all our modern dames
Censures less, or less defames?
In good manners am I faulty?
Can you call me rude or haughty?
Did I e'er my mite withhold

From the impotent and old?
When did ever I omit
Due regard for men of wit?
When have I esteem express'd
For a coxcomb gaily dress'd?
Do I, like the female tribe,
Think it wit to fleer and gibe?
Who with less designing ends
Kindlier entertains her friends;
With good words and countenance sprightly,
Strives to treat them more politely?
    Think not cards my chief diversion:
'Tis a wrong, unjust aspersion:
Never knew I any good in 'em,
But to dose my head like laudanum.
We, by play, as men, by drinking,
Pass our nights to drive out thinking.
From my ailments give me leisure,
I shall read and think with pleasure;
Conversation learn to relish,
And with books my mind embellish.
    Now, methinks, I hear you cry,
Mr. Dean, you must reply.
    Madam, I allow 'tis true:
All these praises are your due.
You, like some acute philosopher,
Every fault have drawn a gloss over;
Placing in the strongest light
All your virtues to my sight.
    Though you lead a blameless life,
Are an humble prudent wife,
Answer all domestic ends:
What is this to us your friends?
Though your children by a nod
Stand in awe without a rod;
Though, by your obliging sway,
Servants love you, and obey;
Though you treat us with a smile;
Clear your looks, and smooth your style;

Load our plates from every dish;
This is not the thing we wish.
Colonel ***** may be your debtor;
We expect employment better.
You must learn, if you would gain us,
With good sense to entertain us.
    Scholars, when good sense describing,
Call it tasting and imbibing;
Metaphoric meat and drink
Is to understand and think;
We may carve for others thus;
And let others carve for us;
To discourse, and to attend,
Is, to help yourself and friend.
Conversation is but carving;
Carve for all, yourself is starving:
Give no more to every guest,
Than he's able to digest;
Give him always of the prime;
And but little at a time.
Carve to all but just enough:
Let them neither starve nor stuff:
And, that you may have your due,
Let your neighbours carve for you.
This comparison will hold,
Could it well in rhyme be told,
How conversing, listening, thinking,
Justly may resemble drinking;
For a friend a glass you fill,
What is this but to instil?
    To conclude this long essay;
Pardon if I disobey,
Nor against my natural vein,
Treat you in heroic strain.
I, as all the parish knows,
Hardly can be grave in prose:
Still to lash, and lashing smile,
Ill befits a lofty style.
From the planet of my birth

I encounter vice with mirth.
Wicked ministers of state
I can easier scorn than hate;
And I find it answers right:
Scorn torments them more than spight.
All the vices of a court
Do but serve to make me sport.
Were I in some foreign realm,
Which all vices overwhelm;
Should a monkey wear a crown,
Must I tremble at his frown?
Could I not, through all his ermine,
'Spy the strutting chattering vermin;
Safely write a smart lampoon,
To expose the brisk baboon?
    When my Muse officious ventures
On the nation's representers:
Teaching by what golden rules
Into knaves they turn their fools;
How the helm is ruled by Walpole,
At whose oars, like slaves, they all pull;
Let the vessel split on shelves;
With the freight enrich themselves:
Safe within my little wherry,
All their madness makes me merry:
Like the waterman of Thames,
I row by, and call them names;
Like the ever-laughing sage,
In a jest I spend my rage:
(Though it must be understood,
I would hang them if I could;)
If I can but fill my niche,
I attempt no higher pitch;
Leave to d'Anvers and his mate
Maxims wise to rule the state.
Pulteney deep, accomplish'd St. Johns,
Scourge the villains with a vengeance;
Let me, though the smell be noisome,
Strip their bums; let Caleb hoise 'em;

Then apply Alecto's whip
Till they wriggle, howl, and skip.
    Deuce is in you, Mr. Dean:
What can all this passion mean?
Mention courts! you'll ne'er be quiet
On corruptions running riot.
End as it befits your station;
Come to use and application;
Nor with senates keep a fuss.
I submit; and answer thus:
    If the machinations brewing,
To complete the public ruin,
Never once could have the power
To affect me half an hour;
Sooner would I write in buskins,
Mournful elegies on Blueskins.
If I laugh at Whig and Tory;
I conclude *à fortiori*,
All your eloquence will scarce
Drive me from my favourite farce.
This I must insist on; for, as
It is well observed by Horace,
Ridicule has greater power
To reform the world than sour.
Horses thus, let jockeys judge else,
Switches better guide than cudgels.
Bastings heavy, dry, obtuse,
Only dulness can produce;
While a little gentle jerking
Sets the spirits all a-working.
    Thus, I find it by experiment,
Scolding moves you less than merriment.
I may storm and rage in vain;
It but stupifies your brain.
But with raillery to nettle,
Sets your thoughts upon their mettle;
Gives imagination scope;
Never lets your mind elope;
Drives out brangling and contention.

Brings in reason and invention.
For your sake as well as mine,
I the lofty style decline.
I should make a figure scurvy,
And your head turn topsy-turvy.
    I who love to have a fling
Both at senate-house and king:
That they might some better way tread,
To avoid the public hatred;
Thought no method more commodious,
Than to show their vices odious;
Which I chose to make appear,
Not by anger, but by sneer.
As my method of reforming,
Is by laughing, not by storming,
(For my friends have always thought
Tenderness my greatest fault,)
Would you have me change my style?
On your faults no longer smile;
But, to patch up all our quarrels,
Quote you texts from Plutarch's Morals,
Or from Solomon produce
Maxims teaching Wisdom's use?
    If I treat you like a crown'd head,
You have cheap enough compounded;
Can you put in higher claims,
Than the owners of St. James?
You are not so great a grievance,
As the hirelings of St. Stephen's.
You are of a lower class
Than my friend Sir Robert Brass.
None of these have mercy found:
I have laugh'd, and lash'd them round.
    Have you seen a rocket fly?
You would swear it pierced the sky:
It but reach'd the middle air,
Bursting into pieces there;
Thousand sparkles falling down
Light on many a coxcomb's crown.

See what mirth the sport creates!
Singes hair, but breaks no pates.
Thus, should I attempt to climb,
Treat you in a style sublime,
Such a rocket is my Muse:
Should I lofty numbers choose,
Ere I reach'd Parnassus' top,
I should burst, and bursting drop;
All my fire would fall in scraps,
Give your head some gentle raps;
Only make it smart a while;
Then could I forbear to smile,
When I found the tingling pain
Entering warm your frigid brain;
Make you able upon sight
To decide of wrong and right;
Talk with sense whate'er you please on;
Learn to relish truth and reason!
    Thus we both shall gain our prize;
I to laugh, and you grow wise.

Epigram on the Busts in Richmond Hermitage. 1732

"Sic siti laetantur docti."

With honour thus by Carolina placed,
How are these venerable bustoes graced!
O queen, with more than regal title crown'd,
For love of arts and piety renown'd!
How do the friends of virtue joy to see
Her darling sons exalted thus by thee!
Nought to their fame can now be added more,
Revered by her whom all mankind adore.

Another

Louis the living learned fed,
And raised the scientific head;
Our frugal queen, to save her meat,
Exalts the heads that cannot eat.

A Conclusion

Drawn from the Above Epigrams, and Sent to the Drapier

Since Anna, whose bounty thy merits had fed,
Ere her own was laid low, had exalted thy head:
And since our good queen to the wise is so just,
To raise heads for such as are humbled in dust,
I wonder, good man, that you are not envaulted;
Prithee go, and be dead, and be doubly exalted.

Dr. Swift's Answer

Her majesty never shall be my exalter;
And yet she would raise me, I know, by a halter!

To the Reverend Dr. Swift

With a Present of a Paper-Book, Finely Bound, On his Birth-Day, Nov. 30, 1732. By John, Earl of Orrery

To thee, dear Swift, these spotless leaves I send;
Small is the present, but sincere the friend.
Think not so poor a book below thy care;
Who knows the price that thou canst make it bear?
Tho' tawdry now, and, like Tyrilla's face,
The specious front shines out with borrow'd grace;
Tho' pasteboards, glitt'ring like a tinsell'd coat,
A *rasa tabula* within denote:
Yet, if a venal and corrupted age,
And modern vices should provoke thy rage;
If, warn'd once more by their impending fate,
A sinking country and an injur'd state,
Thy great assistance should again demand,
And call forth reason to defend the land;
Then shall we view these sheets with glad surprise,
Inspir'd with thought, and speaking to our eyes;
Each vacant space shall then, enrich'd, dispense
True force of eloquence, and nervous sense;
Inform the judgment, animate the heart,
And sacred rules of policy impart.
The spangled cov'ring, bright with splendid ore,
Shall cheat the sight with empty show no more;
But lead us inward to those golden mines,
Where all thy soul in native lustre shines.
So when the eye surveys some lovely fair,
With bloom of beauty graced, with shape and air;
How is the rapture heighten'd, when we find
Her form excell'd by her celestial mind!

Verses left with a Silver Standish on the Dean of St. Patrick's Desk, On his Birth-Day. By Dr. Delany

Hither from Mexico I came,
To serve a proud Iernian dame:
Was long submitted to her will;
At length she lost me at quadrille.
Through various shapes I often pass'd,
Still hoping to have rest at last;
And still ambitious to obtain
Admittance to the patriot Dean;
And sometimes got within his door,
But soon turn'd out to serve the poor:
Not strolling Idleness to aid,
But honest Industry decay'd.
At length an artist purchased me,
And wrought me to the shape you see.
    This done, to Hermes I applied:
"O Hermes! gratify my pride;
Be it my fate to serve a sage,
The greatest genius of his age;
That matchless pen let me supply,
Whose living lines will never die!"
    "I grant your suit," the God replied,
And here he left me to reside.

Verses occasioned by the foregoing Presents

A paper book is sent by Boyle,
Too neatly gilt for me to soil.
Delany sends a silver standish,
When I no more a pen can brandish.
Let both around my tomb be placed:
As trophies of a Muse deceased;
And let the friendly lines they writ,
In praise of long-departed wit,
Be graved on either side in columns,
More to my praise than all my volumes,
To burst with envy, spite, and rage,
The Vandals of the present age.

Verses Sent to the Dean with an Eagle Quill, On Hearing of the Presents by the Earl of Orrery and Dr. Delany. By Mrs. Pilkington

Shall then my kindred all my glory claim,
And boldly rob me of eternal fame?
To every art my gen'rous aid I lend,
To music, painting, poetry, a friend.
'Tis I celestial harmony inspire,
When fix'd to strike the sweetly warbling wire.
I to the faithful canvas have consign'd
Each bright idea of the painter's mind;
Behold from Raphael's sky-dipt pencils rise
Such heavenly scenes as charm the gazer's eyes.
O let me now aspire to higher praise!
Ambitious to transcribe your deathless lays:
Nor thou, immortal bard, my aid refuse,
Accept me as the servant of your Muse;
Then shall the world my wondrous worth declare,
And all mankind your matchless pen revere.

An Invitation, by Dr. Delany, in the Name of Dr. Swift

Mighty Thomas, a solemn senatus I call,
To consult for Sapphira; so come one and all;
Quit books, and quit business, your cure and your care,
For a long winding walk, and a short bill of fare.
I've mutton for you, sir; and as for the ladies,
As friend Virgil has it, I've *aliud mercedis*;
For Letty, one filbert, whereon to regale;
And a peach for pale Constance, to make a full meal;
And for your cruel part, who take pleasure in blood,
I have that of the grape, which is ten times as good:
Flow wit to her honour, flow wine to her health:
High raised be her worth above titles or wealth.

The Beasts' Confession to the Priest, On Observing how most Men Mistake their Own Talents. 1732

Preface

I have been long of opinion, that there is not a more general and greater mistake, or of worse consequences through the commerce of mankind, than the wrong judgments they are apt to entertain of their own talents. I knew a stuttering alderman in London, a great frequenter of coffeehouses, who, when a fresh newspaper was brought in, constantly seized it first, and read it aloud to his brother citizens; but in a manner as little intelligible to the standers-by as to himself. How many pretenders to learning expose themselves, by choosing to discourse on those very parts of science wherewith they are least acquainted! It is the same case in every other qualification. By the multitude of those who deal in rhymes, from half a sheet to twenty, which come out every minute, there must be at least five hundred poets in the city and suburbs of London: half as many coffeehouse orators, exclusive of the clergy, forty thousand politicians, and four thousand five hundred profound scholars; not to mention the wits, the railers, the smart fellows, and critics; all as illiterate and impudent as a suburb whore. What are we to think of the fine-dressed sparks, proud of their own personal deformities, which appear the more hideous by the contrast of wearing scarlet and gold, with what they call toupees on their heads, and all the frippery of a modern beau, to make a figure before women; some of them with hump-backs, others hardly five feet high, and every feature of their faces distorted: I have seen many of these insipid pretenders entering into conversation with persons of learning, constantly making the grossest blunders in every sentence, without conveying one single idea fit for a rational creature to spend a thought on; perpetually confounding all chronology, and geography, even of present times. I compute, that London hath eleven native fools of the beau and puppy kind, for one among us in Dublin; besides two-thirds of ours transplanted thither, who are now naturalized: whereby that overgrown capital exceeds ours in the articles of dunces by forty to one; and what is more to our farther mortification, there is no one distinguished fool of Irish birth or education, who makes any noise in that famous metropolis, unless the London prints be very partial or defective; whereas London is seldom without a dozen of their own educating, who engross the vogue for half a winter together, and are never heard of more, but give place to a new set. This has been the constant progress for at least thirty years past, only allowing for the change of breed and fashion.

The poem is grounded upon the universal folly in mankind of mistaking their talents; by which the author does a great honour to his own species, almost equalling them with certain brutes; wherein, indeed, he is too partial, as he freely confesses: and yet he has gone as low as he well could, by specifying four animals; the wolf, the ass, the swine, and the ape; all equally mischievous, except the last, who outdoes them in the article of cunning: so great is the pride of man!

When beasts could speak, (the learned say
They still can do so every day,)
It seems, they had religion then,
As much as now we find in men.
It happen'd, when a plague broke out,
(Which therefore made them more devout,)
The king of brutes (to make it plain,
Of quadrupeds I only mean)
By proclamation gave command,
That every subject in the land
Should to the priest confess their sins;
And thus the pious Wolf begins:
Good father, I must own with shame,
That often I have been to blame:
I must confess, on Friday last,
Wretch that I was! I broke my fast:
But I defy the basest tongue
To prove I did my neighbour wrong;
Or ever went to seek my food,
By rapine, theft, or thirst of blood.
    The Ass approaching next, confess'd,
That in his heart he loved a jest:
A wag he was, he needs must own,
And could not let a dunce alone:
Sometimes his friend he would not spare,

And might perhaps be too severe:
But yet the worst that could be said,
He was a wit both born and bred;
And, if it be a sin and shame,
Nature alone must bear the blame:
One fault he has, is sorry for't,
His ears are half a foot too short;
Which could he to the standard bring,
He'd show his face before the king:
Then for his voice, there's none disputes
That he's the nightingale of brutes.
The Swine with contrite heart allow'd,
His shape and beauty made him proud:
In diet was perhaps too nice,
But gluttony was ne'er his vice:
In every turn of life content,
And meekly took what fortune sent:
Inquire through all the parish round,
A better neighbour ne'er was found;
His vigilance might some displease;
'Tis true, he hated sloth like pease.
The mimic Ape began his chatter,
How evil tongues his life bespatter;
Much of the censuring world complain'd,
Who said, his gravity was feign'd:
Indeed, the strictness of his morals
Engaged him in a hundred quarrels:
He saw, and he was grieved to see't,
His zeal was sometimes indiscreet:
He found his virtues too severe
For our corrupted times to bear;
Yet such a lewd licentious age
Might well excuse a stoic's rage.
The Goat advanced with decent pace,
And first excused his youthful face;
Forgiveness begg'd that he appear'd
('Twas Nature's fault) without a beard.
'Tis true, he was not much inclined
To fondness for the female kind:

Not, as his enemies object,
From chance, or natural defect;
Not by his frigid constitution;
But through a pious resolution:
For he had made a holy vow
Of Chastity, as monks do now:
Which he resolved to keep for ever hence
And strictly too, as doth his reverence.
    Apply the tale, and you shall find,
How just it suits with human kind.
Some faults we own; but can you guess?
—Why, virtue's carried to excess,
Wherewith our vanity endows us,
Though neither foe nor friend allows us.
    The Lawyer swears (you may rely on't)
He never squeezed a needy client;
And this he makes his constant rule,
For which his brethren call him fool;
His conscience always was so nice,
He freely gave the poor advice;
By which he lost, he may affirm,
A hundred fees last Easter term;
While others of the learned robe,
Would break the patience of a Job.
No pleader at the bar could match
His diligence and quick dispatch;
Ne'er kept a cause, he well may boast,
Above a term or two at most.
    The cringing knave, who seeks a place
Without success, thus tells his case:
Why should he longer mince the matter?
He fail'd, because he could not flatter;
He had not learn'd to turn his coat,
Nor for a party give his vote:
His crime he quickly understood;
Too zealous for the nation's good:
He found the ministers resent it,
Yet could not for his heart repent it.
    The Chaplain vows, he cannot fawn,

Though it would raise him to the lawn:
He pass'd his hours among his books;
You find it in his meagre looks:
He might, if he were worldly wise,
Preferment get, and spare his eyes;
But owns he had a stubborn spirit.
That made him trust alone to merit;
Would rise by merit to promotion;
Alas! a mere chimeric notion.

The Doctor, if you will believe him,
Confess'd a sin; (and God forgive him!)
Call'd up at midnight, ran to save
A blind old beggar from the grave:
But see how Satan spreads his snares;
He quite forgot to say his prayers.
He cannot help it, for his heart,
Sometimes to act the parson's part:
Quotes from the Bible many a sentence,
That moves his patients to repentance;
And, when his medicines do no good,
Supports their minds with heavenly food:
At which, however well intended,
He hears the clergy are offended;
And grown so bold behind his back,
To call him hypocrite and quack.
In his own church he keeps a seat;
Says grace before and after meat;
And calls, without affecting airs,
His household twice a-day to prayers.
He shuns apothecaries' shops,
And hates to cram the sick with slops:
He scorns to make his art a trade;
Nor bribes my lady's favourite maid.
Old nurse-keepers would never hire,
To recommend him to the squire;
Which others, whom he will not name,
Have often practised to their shame.

The Statesman tells you, with a sneer,
His fault is to be too sincere;

And having no sinister ends,
Is apt to disoblige his friends.
The nation's good, his master's glory,
Without regard to Whig or Tory,
Were all the schemes he had in view,
Yet he was seconded by few:
Though some had spread a thousand lies,
'Twas he defeated the excise.
'Twas known, though he had borne aspersion,
That standing troops were his aversion:
His practice was, in every station:
To serve the king, and please the nation.
Though hard to find in every case
The fittest man to fill a place:
His promises he ne'er forgot,
But took memorials on the spot;
His enemies, for want of charity,
Said, he affected popularity:
'Tis true, the people understood,
That all he did was for their good;
Their kind affections he has tried;
No love is lost on either side.
He came to court with fortune clear,
Which now he runs out every year;
Must, at the rate that he goes on,
Inevitably be undone:
O! if his majesty would please
To give him but a writ of ease,
Would grant him license to retire,
As it has long been his desire,
By fair accounts it would be found,
He's poorer by ten thousand pound.
He owns, and hopes it is no sin,
He ne'er was partial to his kin;
He thought it base for men in stations,
To crowd the court with their relations:
His country was his dearest mother,
And every virtuous man his brother;
Through modesty or awkward shame,

(For which he owns himself to blame,)
He found the wisest man he could,
Without respect to friends or blood;
Nor ever acts on private views,
When he has liberty to choose.
    The Sharper swore he hated play,
Except to pass an hour away:
And well he might; for, to his cost,
By want of skill, he always lost;
He heard there was a club of cheats,
Who had contrived a thousand feats;
Could change the stock, or cog a die,
And thus deceive the sharpest eye:
Nor wonder how his fortune sunk,
His brothers fleece him when he's drunk.
    I own the moral not exact,
Besides, the tale is false, in fact;
And so absurd, that could I raise up,
From fields Elysian, fabling Æsop,
I would accuse him to his face,
For libelling the four-foot race.
Creatures of every kind but ours
Well comprehend their natural powers,
While we, whom reason ought to sway,
Mistake our talents every day.
The Ass was never known so stupid,
To act the part of Tray or Cupid;
Nor leaps upon his master's lap,
There to be stroked, and fed with pap,
As Æsop would the world persuade;
He better understands his trade:
Nor comes whene'er his lady whistles,
But carries loads, and feeds on thistles.
Our author's meaning, I presume, is
A creature *bipes et implumis;*
Wherein the moralist design'd
A compliment on human kind;
For here he owns, that now and then
Beasts may degenerate into men.

The Parson's Case

That you, friend Marcus, like a stoic,
Can wish to die in strains heroic,
No real fortitude implies:
Yet, all must own, thy wish is wise.
Thy curate's place, thy fruitful wife,
Thy busy, drudging scene of life,
Thy insolent, illiterate vicar,
Thy want of all-consoling liquor,
Thy threadbare gown, thy cassock rent,
Thy credit sunk, thy money spent,
Thy week made up of fasting-days,
Thy grate unconscious of a blaze,
And to complete thy other curses,
The quarterly demands of nurses,
Are ills you wisely wish to leave,
And fly for refuge to the grave;
And, O, what virtue you express,
In wishing such afflictions less!
    But, now, should Fortune shift the scene,
And make thy curateship a dean:
Or some rich benefice provide,
To pamper luxury and pride;
With labour small, and income great;
With chariot less for use than state;
With swelling scarf, and glossy gown,
And license to reside in town:
To shine where all the gay resort,
At concerts, coffee-house, or court:
And weekly persecute his grace
With visits, or to beg a place:
With underlings thy flock to teach,
With no desire to pray or preach;
With haughty spouse in vesture fine,
With plenteous meals and generous wine;
Wouldst thou not wish, in so much ease,
Thy years as numerous as thy days?

The hardship upon the Ladies
1733

Poor ladies! though their business be to play,
'Tis hard they must be busy night and day:
Why should they want the privilege of men,
Nor take some small diversions now and then?
Had women been the makers of our laws,
(And why they were not, I can see no cause,)
The men should slave at cards from morn to night
And female pleasures be to read and write.

A Love Song in the Modern Taste. 1733

Fluttering spread thy purple pinions,
Gentle Cupid, o'er my heart:
I a slave in thy dominions;
Nature must give way to art.

Mild Arcadians, ever blooming
Nightly nodding o'er your flocks,
See my weary days consuming
All beneath yon flowery rocks.

Thus the Cyprian goddess weeping
Mourn'd Adonis, darling youth;
Him the boar, in silence creeping,
Gored with unrelenting tooth.

Cynthia, tune harmonious numbers;
Fair Discretion, string the lyre;
Sooth my ever-waking slumbers:
Bright Apollo, lend thy choir.

Gloomy Pluto, king of terrors,
Arm'd in adamantine chains,
Lead me to the crystal mirrors,
Watering soft Elysian plains.

Mournful cypress, verdant willow,
Gilding my Aurelia's brows,
Morpheus, hovering o'er my pillow,
Hear me pay my dying vows.

Melancholy smooth Meander,
Swiftly purling in a round,
On thy margin lovers wander,
With thy flowery chaplets crown'd.

Thus when Philomela drooping
    Softly seeks her silent mate,
See the bird of Juno stooping;
    Melody resigns to fate.

The Storm

Minerva's Petition

Pallas, a goddess chaste and wise
Descending lately from the skies,
To Neptune went, and begg'd in form
He'd give his orders for a storm;
A storm, to drown that rascal Hort,
And she would kindly thank him for't:
A wretch! whom English rogues, to spite her,
Had lately honour'd with a mitre.
    The god, who favour'd her request,
Assured her he would do his best:
But Venus had been there before,
Pleaded the bishop loved a whore,
And had enlarged her empire wide;
He own'd no deity beside.
At sea or land, if e'er you found him
Without a mistress, hang or drown him.
Since Burnet's death, the bishops' bench,
Till Hort arrived, ne'er kept a wench;
If Hort must sink, she grieves to tell it,
She'll not have left one single prelate:
For, to say truth, she did intend him,
Elect of Cyprus *in commendam.*
And, since her birth the ocean gave her,
She could not doubt her uncle's favour.
    Then Proteus urged the same request,
But half in earnest, half in jest;
Said he—"Great sovereign of the main,
To drown him all attempts are vain.
Hort can assume more forms than I,
A rake, a bully, pimp, or spy;
Can creep, or run, or fly, or swim;
All motions are alike to him:
Turn him adrift, and you shall find
He knows to sail with every wind;

Or, throw him overboard, he'll ride
As well against as with the tide.
But, Pallas, you've applied too late;
For, 'tis decreed by Jove and Fate,
That Ireland must be soon destroy'd,
And who but Hort can be employ'd?
You need not then have been so pert,
In sending Bolton to Clonfert.
I found you did it, by your grinning;
Your business is to mind your spinning.
But how you came to interpose
In making bishops, no one knows;
Or who regarded your report;
For never were you seen at court.
And if you must have your petition,
There's Berkeley in the same condition;
Look, there he stands, and 'tis but just,
If one must drown, the other must;
But, if you'll leave us Bishop Judas,
We'll give you Berkeley for Bermudas.
Now, if 'twill gratify your spight,
To put him in a plaguy fright,
Although 'tis hardly worth the cost,
You soon shall see him soundly tost.
You'll find him swear, blaspheme, and damn
(And every moment take a dram)
His ghastly visage with an air
Of reprobation and despair;
Or else some hiding-hole he seeks,
For fear the rest should say he squeaks;
Or, as Fitzpatrick did before,
Resolve to perish with his whore;
Or else he raves, and roars, and swears,
And, but for shame, would say his prayers.
Or, would you see his spirits sink?
Relaxing downwards in a stink?
If such a sight as this can please ye,
Good madam Pallas, pray be easy.
To Neptune speak, and he'll consent;

But he'll come back the knave he went."
The goddess, who conceived a hope
That Hort was destined to a rope,
Believed it best to condescend
To spare a foe, to save a friend;
But, fearing Berkeley might be scared,
She left him virtue for a guard.

Ode on Science

O, heavenly born! in deepest dells
If fairest science ever dwells
    Beneath the mossy cave;
Indulge the verdure of the woods,
With azure beauty gild the floods,
    And flowery carpets lave.

For, Melancholy ever reigns
Delighted in the sylvan scenes
    With scientific light;
While Dian, huntress of the vales,
Seeks lulling sounds and fanning gales,
    Though wrapt from mortal sight.

Yet, goddess, yet the way explore
With magic rites and heathen lore
    Obstructed and depress'd;
Till Wisdom give the sacred Nine,
Untaught, not uninspired, to shine,
    By Reason's power redress'd.

When Solon and Lycurgus taught
To moralize the human thought
    Of mad opinion's maze,
To erring zeal they gave new laws,
Thy charms, O Liberty, the cause
    That blends congenial rays.

Bid bright Astræa gild the morn,
Or bid a hundred suns be born,
    To hecatomb the year;
Without thy aid, in vain the poles,
In vain the zodiac system rolls,
    In vain the lunar sphere.

Come, fairest princess of the throng,
Bring sweet philosophy along,
    In metaphysic dreams;
While raptured bards no more behold
A vernal age of purer gold,
    In Heliconian streams.

Drive Thraldom with malignant hand,
To curse some other destined land,
    By Folly led astray:
Iërne bear on azure wing;
Energic let her soar, and sing
    Thy universal sway.

So when Amphion bade the lyre
To more majestic sound aspire,
    Behold the madding throng,
In wonder and oblivion drown'd,
To sculpture turn'd by magic sound
    And petrifying song.

A Young Lady's Complaint For the Stay of the Dean in England

Blow, ye zephyrs, gentle gales;
Gently fill the swelling sails.
Neptune, with thy trident long,
Trident three-fork'd, trident strong:
And ye Nereids fair and gay,
Fairer than the rose in May,
Nereids living in deep caves,
Gently wash'd with gentle waves;
Nereids, Neptune, lull asleep
Ruffling storms, and ruffled deep;
All around, in pompous state,
On this richer Argo wait:
Argo, bring my golden fleece,
Argo, bring him to his Greece.
Will Cadenus longer stay?
Come, Cadenus, come away;
Come with all the haste of love,
Come unto thy turtle-dove.
The ripen'd cherry on the tree
Hangs, and only hangs for thee,
Luscious peaches, mellow pears,
Ceres, with her yellow ears,
And the grape, both red and white,
Grape inspiring just delight;
All are ripe, and courting sue,
To be pluck'd and press'd by you.
Pinks have lost their blooming red,
Mourning hang their drooping head,
Every flower languid seems,
Wants the colour of thy beams,
Beams of wondrous force and power,
Beams reviving every flower.
Come, Cadenus, bless once more,
Bless again thy native shore,
Bless again this drooping isle,

Make its weeping beauties smile,
Beauties that thine absence mourn,
Beauties wishing thy return:
Come, Cadenus, come with haste,
Come before the winter's blast;
Swifter than the lightning fly,
Or I, like Vanessa, die.

On the Death of Dr. Swift

Written in November, 1731

Occasioned by reading the following maxim in Rochefoucauld, "Dans l'adversité de nos meilleurs amis, nous trouvons toujours quelque chose, qui ne nous déplait pas."

This maxim was No. 99 in the edition of 1665, and was one of those suppressed by the author in his later editions. In the edition published by Didot Freres, 1864, it is No. 15 in the first supplement. See it commented upon by Lord Chesterfield in a letter to his son, Sept. 5, 1748, where he takes a similar view to that expressed by Swift.

—W. E. B.

As Rochefoucauld his maxims drew
From nature, I believe 'em true:
They argue no corrupted mind
In him; the fault is in mankind.
This maxim more than all the rest
Is thought too base for human breast:
"In all distresses of our friends,
We first consult our private ends;
While nature, kindly bent to ease us,
Points out some circumstance to please us."
If this perhaps your patience move,
Let reason and experience prove.
We all behold with envious eyes
Our *equal* raised above our *size.*
Who would not at a crowded show
Stand high himself, keep others low?
I love my friend as well as you:
But why should he obstruct my view?
Then let me have the higher post:
Suppose it but an inch at most.
If in battle you should find
One whom you love of all mankind,
Had some heroic action done,

A champion kill'd, or trophy won;
Rather than thus be overtopt,
Would you not wish his laurels cropt?
Dear honest Ned is in the gout,
Lies rackt with pain, and you without:
How patiently you hear him groan!
How glad the case is not your own!
    What poet would not grieve to see
His breth'ren write as well as he?
But rather than they should excel,
He'd wish his rivals all in hell.
    Her end when Emulation misses,
She turns to Envy, stings and hisses:
The strongest friendship yields to pride,
Unless the odds be on our side.
Vain human kind! fantastic race!
Thy various follies who can trace?
Self-love, ambition, envy, pride,
Their empire in our hearts divide.
Give others riches, power, and station,
'Tis all on me an usurpation.
I have no title to aspire;
Yet, when you sink, I seem the higher.
In Pope I cannot read a line,
But with a sigh I wish it mine;
When he can in one couplet fix
More sense than I can do in six;
It gives me such a jealous fit,
I cry, "Pox take him and his wit!"
I grieve to be outdone by Gay
In my own hum'rous biting way.
Arbuthnot is no more my friend,
Who dares to irony pretend,
Which I was born to introduce,
Refin'd it first, and shew'd its use.
St. John, as well as Pultney, knows
That I had some repute for prose;
And, till they drove me out of date
Could maul a minister of state.

If they have mortify'd my pride,
And made me throw my pen aside;
If with such talents Heav'n has blest 'em,
Have I not reason to detest 'em?
    To all my foes, dear Fortune, send
Thy gifts; but never to my friend:
I tamely can endure the first;
But this with envy makes me burst.
    Thus much may serve by way of proem:
Proceed we therefore to our poem.
    The time is not remote, when I
Must by the course of nature die;
When, I foresee, my special friends
Will try to find their private ends:
Tho' it is hardly understood
Which way my death can do them good,
Yet thus, methinks, I hear 'em speak:
"See, how the Dean begins to break!
Poor gentleman, he droops apace!
You plainly find it in his face.
That old vertigo in his head
Will never leave him till he's dead.
Besides, his memory decays:
He recollects not what he says;
He cannot call his friends to mind:
Forgets the place where last he din'd;
Plyes you with stories o'er and o'er;
He told them fifty times before.
How does he fancy we can sit
To hear his out-of-fashion'd wit?
But he takes up with younger folks,
Who for his wine will bear his jokes.
Faith! he must make his stories shorter,
Or change his comrades once a quarter:
In half the time he talks them round,
There must another set be found.
    "For poetry he's past his prime:
He takes an hour to find a rhyme;
His fire is out, his wit decay'd,

His fancy sunk, his Muse a jade.
I'd have him throw away his pen;—
But there's no talking to some men!"
And then their tenderness appears,
By adding largely to my years;
"He's older than he would be reckon'd,
And well remembers Charles the Second.
He hardly drinks a pint of wine;
And that, I doubt, is no good sign.
His stomach too begins to fail:
Last year we thought him strong and hale;
But now he's quite another thing:
I wish he may hold out till spring!"
Then hug themselves, and reason thus:
"It is not yet so bad with us!"
In such a case, they talk in tropes,
And by their fears express their hopes:
Some great misfortune to portend,
No enemy can match a friend.
With all the kindness they profess,
The merit of a lucky guess
(When daily how d'ye's come of course,
And servants answer, "*Worse and worse!*")
Wou'd please 'em better, than to tell,
That, "God be prais'd, the Dean is well."
Then he, who prophecy'd the best,
Approves his foresight to the rest:
"You know I always fear'd the worst,
And often told you so at first."
He'd rather chuse that I should die,
Than his prediction prove a lie.
Not one foretells I shall recover;
But all agree to give me over.
Yet, shou'd some neighbour feel a pain
Just in the parts where I complain;
How many a message would he send!
What hearty prayers that I should mend!
Inquire what regimen I kept;
What gave me ease, and how I slept?

And more lament when I was dead,
Than all the sniv'llers round my bed.
    My good companions, never fear;
For though you may mistake a year,
Though your prognostics run too fast,
They must be verify'd at last.
    Behold the fatal day arrive!
"How is the Dean?"—"He's just alive."
Now the departing prayer is read;
"He hardly breathes."—"The Dean is dead."
    Before the Passing-bell begun,
The news thro' half the town has run.
"O! may we all for death prepare!
What has he left? and who's his heir?"—
"I know no more than what the news is;
'Tis all bequeath'd to public uses."—
"To public use! a perfect whim!
What had the public done for him?
Mere envy, avarice, and pride:
He gave it all—but first he died.
And had the Dean, in all the nation,
No worthy friend, no poor relation?
So ready to do strangers good,
Forgetting his own flesh and blood!"
    Now, Grub-Street wits are all employ'd;
With elegies the town is cloy'd:
Some paragraph in ev'ry paper
To curse the Dean, or bless the Drapier.
    The doctors, tender of their fame,
Wisely on me lay all the blame:
"We must confess, his case was nice;
But he would never take advice.
Had he been ruled, for aught appears,
He might have lived these twenty years;
For, when we open'd him, we found,
That all his vital parts were sound."
    From Dublin soon to London spread,
'Tis told at court, "the Dean is dead."
Kind Lady Suffolk, in the spleen,

Runs laughing up to tell the queen.
The queen, so gracious, mild, and good,
Cries, "Is he gone! 'tis time he shou'd.
He's dead, you say; why, let him rot:
I'm glad the medals were forgot.
I promised him, I own; but when?
I only was a princess then;
But now, as consort of a king,
You know, 'tis quite a different thing."
Now Chartres, at Sir Robert's levee,
Tells with a sneer the tidings heavy:
"Why, is he dead without his shoes,"
Cries Bob, "I'm sorry for the news:
O, were the wretch but living still,
And in his place my good friend Will!
Or had a mitre on his head,
Provided Bolingbroke were dead!"
Now Curll his shop from rubbish drains:
Three genuine tomes of Swift's remains!
And then, to make them pass the glibber,
Revised by Tibbalds, Moore, and Cibber.
He'll treat me as he does my betters,
Publish my will, my life, my letters:
Revive the libels born to die;
Which Pope must bear, as well as I.
    Here shift the scene, to represent
How those I love my death lament.
Poor Pope will grieve a month, and Gay
A week, and Arbuthnot a day.
    St. John himself will scarce forbear
To bite his pen, and drop a tear.
The rest will give a shrug, and cry,
"I'm sorry—but we all must die!"
    Indifference, clad in Wisdom's guise,
All fortitude of mind supplies:
For how can stony bowels melt
In those who never pity felt!
When *we* are lash'd, *they* kiss the rod,
Resigning to the will of God.

The fools, my juniors by a year,
Are tortur'd with suspense and fear;
Who wisely thought my age a screen,
When death approach'd, to stand between:
The screen removed, their hearts are trembling;
They mourn for me without dissembling.
My female friends, whose tender hearts
Have better learn'd to act their parts,
Receive the news in doleful dumps:
"The Dean is dead: (and what is trumps?)
Then, Lord have mercy on his soul!
(Ladies, I'll venture for the vole.)
Six deans, they say, must bear the pall:
(I wish I knew what king to call.)
Madam, your husband will attend
The funeral of so good a friend.
No, madam, 'tis a shocking sight:
And he's engaged to-morrow night:
My Lady Club wou'd take it ill,
If he shou'd fail her at quadrille.
He loved the Dean—(I lead a heart,)
But dearest friends, they say, must part.
His time was come: he ran his race;
We hope he's in a better place."
Why do we grieve that friends should die?
No loss more easy to supply.
One year is past; a different scene!
No further mention of the Dean;
Who now, alas! no more is miss'd,
Than if he never did exist.
Where's now this fav'rite of Apollo!
Departed:—and his works must follow;
Must undergo the common fate;
His kind of wit is out of date.
Some country squire to Lintot goes,
Inquires for "Swift in Verse and Prose."
Says Lintot, "I have heard the name;
He died a year ago."—"The same."
He searches all the shop in vain.

"Sir, you may find them in Duck-lane;
I sent them with a load of books,
Last Monday to the pastry-cook's.
To fancy they could live a year!
I find you're but a stranger here.
The Dean was famous in his time,
And had a kind of knack at rhyme.
His way of writing now is past;
The town has got a better taste;
I keep no antiquated stuff,
But spick and span I have enough.
Pray do but give me leave to show 'em;
Here's Colley Cibber's birth-day poem.
This ode you never yet have seen,
By Stephen Duck, upon the queen.
Then here's a letter finely penned
Against the Craftsman and his friend:
It clearly shows that all reflection
On ministers is disaffection.
Next, here's Sir Robert's vindication,
And Mr. Henley's last oration.
The hawkers have not got them yet:
Your honour please to buy a set?
"Here's Woolston's tracts, the twelfth edition;
'Tis read by every politician:
The country members, when in town,
To all their boroughs send them down;
You never met a thing so smart;
The courtiers have them all by heart:
Those maids of honour (who can read),
Are taught to use them for their creed.
The rev'rend author's good intention
Has been rewarded with a pension.
He does an honour to his gown,
By bravely running priestcraft down:
He shows, as sure as God's in Gloucester,
That Moses was a grand impostor;
That all his miracles were cheats,
Perform'd as jugglers do their feats:

The church had never such a writer;
A shame he has not got a mitre!"
    Suppose me dead; and then suppose
A club assembled at the Rose;
Where, from discourse of this and that,
I grow the subject of their chat.
And while they toss my name about,
With favour some, and some without,
One, quite indiff'rent in the cause,
My character impartial draws:
    The Dean, if we believe report,
Was never ill receiv'd at court.
As for his works in verse and prose
I own myself no judge of those;
Nor can I tell what critics thought 'em:
But this I know, all people bought 'em.
As with a moral view design'd
To cure the vices of mankind:
And, if he often miss'd his aim,
The world must own it, to their shame,
The praise is his, and theirs the blame.
"Sir, I have heard another story:
He was a most confounded Tory,
And grew, or he is much belied,
Extremely dull, before he died."
    Can we the Drapier then forget?
Is not our nation in his debt?
'Twas he that writ the Drapier's letters!—
    "He should have left them for his betters,
We had a hundred abler men,
Nor need depend upon his pen.—
Say what you will about his reading,
You never can defend his breeding;
Who in his satires running riot,
Could never leave the world in quiet;
Attacking, when he took the whim,
Court, city, camp—all one to him.—
    "But why should he, except he slobber't,
Offend our patriot, great Sir Robert,

Whose counsels aid the sov'reign power
To save the nation every hour?
What scenes of evil he unravels
In satires, libels, lying travels!
Not sparing his own clergy-cloth,
But eats into it, like a moth!"
His vein, ironically grave,
Exposed the fool, and lash'd the knave.
To steal a hint was never known,
But what he writ was all his own.
    "He never thought an honour done him,
Because a duke was proud to own him,
Would rather slip aside and chuse
To talk with wits in dirty shoes;
Despised the fools with stars and garters,
So often seen caressing Chartres.
He never courted men in station,
Nor persons held in admiration;
Of no man's greatness was afraid,
Because he sought for no man's aid.
Though trusted long in great affairs
He gave himself no haughty airs:
Without regarding private ends,
Spent all his credit for his friends;
And only chose the wise and good;
No flatterers; no allies in blood:
But succour'd virtue in distress,
And seldom fail'd of good success;
As numbers in their hearts must own,
Who, but for him, had been unknown.
    "With princes kept a due decorum,
But never stood in awe before 'em.
He follow'd David's lesson just;
In princes never put thy trust:
And would you make him truly sour,
Provoke him with a slave in power.
The Irish senate if you named,
With what impatience he declaim'd!
Fair LIBERTY was all his cry,

For her he stood prepared to die;
For her he boldly stood alone;
For her he oft exposed his own.
Two kingdoms, just as faction led,
Had set a price upon his head;
But not a traitor could be found,
To sell him for six hundred pound.
"Had he but spared his tongue and pen
He might have rose like other men:
But power was never in his thought,
And wealth he valued not a groat:
Ingratitude he often found,
And pitied those who meant the wound:
But kept the tenor of his mind,
To merit well of human kind:
Nor made a sacrifice of those
Who still were true, to please his foes.
He labour'd many a fruitless hour,
To reconcile his friends in power;
Saw mischief by a faction brewing,
While they pursued each other's ruin.
But finding vain was all his care,
He left the court in mere despair.
"And, oh! how short are human schemes!
Here ended all our golden dreams.
What St. John's skill in state affairs,
What Ormond's valour, Oxford's cares,
To save their sinking country lent,
Was all destroy'd by one event.
Too soon that precious life was ended,
On which alone our weal depended.
When up a dangerous faction starts,
With wrath and vengeance in their hearts;
By solemn League and Cov'nant bound,
To ruin, slaughter, and confound;
To turn religion to a fable,
And make the government a Babel;
Pervert the laws, disgrace the gown,
Corrupt the senate, rob the crown;

To sacrifice old England's glory,
And make her infamous in story:
When such a tempest shook the land,
How could unguarded Virtue stand!
With horror, grief, despair, the Dean
Beheld the dire destructive scene:
His friends in exile, or the tower,
Himself within the frown of power,
Pursued by base envenom'd pens,
Far to the land of slaves and fens;
A servile race in folly nursed,
Who truckle most, when treated worst.
"By innocence and resolution,
He bore continual persecution;
While numbers to preferment rose,
Whose merits were, to be his foes;
When *ev'n his own familiar friends*,
Intent upon their private ends,
Like renegadoes now he feels,
Against him lifting up their heels.

"The Dean did, by his pen, defeat
An infamous destructive cheat;
Taught fools their int'rest how to know,
And gave them arms to ward the blow.
Envy has own'd it was his doing,
To save that hapless land from ruin;
While they who at the steerage stood,
And reap'd the profit, sought his blood.

"To save them from their evil fate,
In him was held a crime of state,
A wicked monster on the bench,
Whose fury blood could never quench;
As vile and profligate a villain,
As modern Scroggs, or old Tresilian:
Who long all justice had discarded,
Nor fear'd he God, nor man regarded;
Vow'd on the Dean his rage to vent,
And make him of his zeal repent:
But Heaven his innocence defends,

The grateful people stand his friends;
Not strains of law, nor judge's frown,
Nor topics brought to please the crown,
Nor witness hired, nor jury pick'd,
Prevail to bring him in convict.
    "In exile, with a steady heart,
He spent his life's declining part;
Where folly, pride, and faction sway,
Remote from St. John, Pope, and Gay.
Alas, poor Dean! his only scope
Was to be held a misanthrope.
This into gen'ral odium drew him,
Which if he liked, much good may't do him.
His zeal was not to lash our crimes,
But discontent against the times:
For had we made him timely offers
To raise his post, or fill his coffers,
Perhaps he might have truckled down,
Like other brethren of his gown.
For party he would scarce have bled:
I say no more—because he's dead.
What writings has he left behind?
I hear, they're of a different kind;
A few in verse; but most in prose—
Some high-flown pamphlets, I suppose;—
All scribbled in the worst of times,
To palliate his friend Oxford's crimes,
To praise Queen Anne, nay more, defend her,
As never fav'ring the Pretender;
Or libels yet conceal'd from sight,
Against the court to show his spite;
Perhaps his travels, part the third;
A lie at every second word—
Offensive to a loyal ear:
But not one sermon, you may swear."
His friendships there, to few confined
Were always of the middling kind;
No fools of rank, a mongrel breed,
Who fain would pass for lords indeed:

Where titles give no right or power,
And peerage is a wither'd flower;
He would have held it a disgrace,
If such a wretch had known his face.
On rural squires, that kingdom's bane,
He vented oft his wrath in vain;
(Biennial) squires to market brought;
Who sell their souls and (votes) for nought;
The (nation stripped,) go joyful back,
To *** the church, their tenants rack,
Go snacks with (rogues and rapparees,)
And keep the peace to pick up fees;
In every job to have a share,
A gaol or barrack to repair;
And turn the tax for public roads,
Commodious to their own abodes.
"Perhaps I may allow the Dean,
Had too much satire in his vein;
And seem'd determined not to starve it,
Because no age could more deserve it.
Yet malice never was his aim;
He lash'd the vice, but spared the name;
No individual could resent,
Where thousands equally were meant;
His satire points at no defect,
But what all mortals may correct;
For he abhorr'd that senseless tribe
Who call it humour when they gibe:
He spared a hump, or crooked nose,
Whose owners set not up for beaux.
True genuine dulness moved his pity,
Unless it offer'd to be witty.
Those who their ignorance confest,
He ne'er offended with a jest;
But laugh'd to hear an idiot quote
A verse from Horace learn'd by rote.
"Vice, if it e'er can be abash'd,
Must be or ridiculed or lash'd.
If you resent it, who's to blame?

He neither knew you nor your name.
Should vice expect to 'scape rebuke,
Because its owner is a duke?
"He knew an hundred pleasant stories,
With all the turns of Whigs and Tories:
Was cheerful to his dying day;
And friends would let him have his way.
"He gave the little wealth he had
To build a house for fools and mad;
And show'd by one satiric touch,
No nation wanted it so much.
That kingdom he hath left his debtor,
I wish it soon may have a better."
And, since you dread no farther lashes
Methinks you may forgive his ashes.

On Poetry
A Rhapsody. 1733

All human race would fain be wits,
And millions miss for one that hits.
Young's universal passion, pride,
Was never known to spread so wide.
Say, Britain, could you ever boast
Three poets in an age at most?
Our chilling climate hardly bears
A sprig of bays in fifty years;
While every fool his claim alleges,
As if it grew in common hedges.
What reason can there be assign'd
For this perverseness in the mind?
Brutes find out where their talents lie:
A bear will not attempt to fly;
A founder'd horse will oft debate,
Before he tries a five-barr'd gate;
A dog by instinct turns aside,
Who sees the ditch too deep and wide.
But man we find the only creature
Who, led by Folly, combats Nature;
Who, when she loudly cries, Forbear,
With obstinacy fixes there;
And, where his genius least inclines,
Absurdly bends his whole designs.
    Not empire to the rising sun
By valour, conduct, fortune won;
Not highest wisdom in debates,
For framing laws to govern states;
Not skill in sciences profound
So large to grasp the circle round,
Such heavenly influence require,
As how to strike the Muse's lyre.
    Not beggar's brat on bulk begot;
Not bastard of a pedler Scot;
Not boy brought up to cleaning shoes,

The spawn of Bridewell or the stews;
Not infants dropp'd, the spurious pledges
Of gipsies litter'd under hedges;
Are so disqualified by fate
To rise in church, or law, or state,
As he whom Phoebus in his ire
Has blasted with poetic fire.
What hope of custom in the fair,
While not a soul demands your ware?
Where you have nothing to produce
For private life, or public use?
Court, city, country, want you not;
You cannot bribe, betray, or plot.
For poets, law makes no provision;
The wealthy have you in derision:
Of state affairs you cannot smatter;
Are awkward when you try to flatter;
Your portion, taking Britain round,
Was just one annual hundred pound;
Now not so much as in remainder,
Since Cibber brought in an attainder;
For ever fix'd by right divine
(A monarch's right) on Grub Street line.
    Poor starv'ling bard, how small thy gains!
How unproportion'd to thy pains!
And here a simile comes pat in:
Though chickens take a month to fatten,
The guests in less than half an hour
Will more than half a score devour.
So, after toiling twenty days
To earn a stock of pence and praise,
Thy labours, grown the critic's prey,
Are swallow'd o'er a dish of tea;
Gone to be never heard of more,
Gone where the chickens went before.
How shall a new attempter learn
Of different spirits to discern,
And how distinguish which is which,
The poet's vein, or scribbling itch?

Then hear an old experienced sinner,
Instructing thus a young beginner.
    Consult yourself; and if you find
A powerful impulse urge your mind,
Impartial judge within your breast
What subject you can manage best;
Whether your genius most inclines
To satire, praise, or humorous lines,
To elegies in mournful tone,
Or prologue sent from hand unknown.
Then, rising with Aurora's light,
The Muse invoked, sit down to write;
Blot out, correct, insert, refine,
Enlarge, diminish, interline;
Be mindful, when invention fails,
To scratch your head, and bite your nails.
    Your poem finish'd, next your care
Is needful to transcribe it fair.
In modern wit all printed trash is
Set off with numerous breaks and dashes.
    To statesmen would you give a wipe,
You print it in *Italic* type.
When letters are in vulgar shapes,
'Tis ten to one the wit escapes:
But, when in capitals express'd,
The dullest reader smokes the jest:
Or else perhaps he may invent
A better than the poet meant;
As learned commentators view
In Homer more than Homer knew.
    Your poem in its modish dress,
Correctly fitted for the press,
Convey by penny-post to Lintot,
But let no friend alive look into't.
If Lintot thinks 'twill quit the cost,
You need not fear your labour lost:
And how agreeably surprised
Are you to see it advertised!
The hawker shows you one in print,

As fresh as farthings from the mint:
The product of your toil and sweating;
A bastard of your own begetting.
　　Be sure at Will's, the following day,
Lie snug, and hear what critics say;
And, if you find the general vogue
Pronounces you a stupid rogue,
Damns all your thoughts as low and little,
Sit still, and swallow down your spittle;
Be silent as a politician,
For talking may beget suspicion;
Or praise the judgment of the town,
And help yourself to run it down.
Give up your fond paternal pride,
Nor argue on the weaker side:
For, poems read without a name
We justly praise, or justly blame;
And critics have no partial views,
Except they know whom they abuse:
And since you ne'er provoke their spite,
Depend upon't their judgment's right.
But if you blab, you are undone:
Consider what a risk you run:
You lose your credit all at once;
The town will mark you for a dunce;
The vilest dogg'rel Grub Street sends,
Will pass for yours with foes and friends;
And you must bear the whole disgrace,
Till some fresh blockhead takes your place.
　　Your secret kept, your poem sunk,
And sent in quires to line a trunk,
If still you be disposed to rhyme,
Go try your hand a second time.
Again you fail: yet Safe's the word;
Take courage and attempt a third.
But first with care employ your thoughts
Where critics mark'd your former faults;
The trivial turns, the borrow'd wit,
The similes that nothing fit;

The cant which every fool repeats,
Town jests and coffeehouse conceits,
Descriptions tedious, flat, and dry,
And introduced the Lord knows why:
Or where we find your fury set
Against the harmless alphabet;
On A's and B's your malice vent,
While readers wonder whom you meant:
A public or a private robber,
A statesman, or a South Sea jobber;
A prelate, who no God believes;
A parliament, or den of thieves;
A pickpurse at the bar or bench,
A duchess, or a suburb wench:
Or oft, when epithets you link,
In gaping lines to fill a chink;
Like stepping-stones, to save a stride,
In streets where kennels are too wide;
Or like a heel-piece, to support
A cripple with one foot too short;
Or like a bridge, that joins a marish
To moorlands of a different parish.
So have I seen ill-coupled hounds
Drag different ways in miry grounds.
So geographers, in Afric maps,
With savage pictures fill their gaps,
And o'er unhabitable downs
Place elephants for want of towns.
    But, though you miss your third essay,
You need not throw your pen away.
Lay now aside all thoughts of fame,
To spring more profitable game.
From party merit seek support;
The vilest verse thrives best at court.
And may you ever have the luck
To rhyme almost as ill as Duck;
And, though you never learn'd to scan verse
Come out with some lampoon on D'Anvers.
A pamphlet in Sir Bob's defence

Will never fail to bring in pence:
Nor be concern'd about the sale,
He pays his workmen on the nail.
Display the blessings of the nation,
And praise the whole administration.
Extol the bench of bishops round,
Who at them rail, bid—confound;
To bishop-haters answer thus:
(The only logic used by us)
What though they don't believe in—
Deny them Protestants—thou lyest.
A prince, the moment he is crown'd,
Inherits every virtue round,
As emblems of the sovereign power,
Like other baubles in the Tower;
Is generous, valiant, just, and wise,
And so continues till he dies:
His humble senate this professes,
In all their speeches, votes, addresses.
But once you fix him in a tomb,
His virtues fade, his vices bloom;
And each perfection, wrong imputed,
Is fully at his death confuted.
The loads of poems in his praise,
Ascending, make one funeral blaze:
His panegyrics then are ceased,
He grows a tyrant, dunce, or beast.
As soon as you can hear his knell,
This god on earth turns devil in hell:
And lo! his ministers of state,
Transform'd to imps, his levee wait;
Where in the scenes of endless woe,
They ply their former arts below;
And as they sail in Charon's boat,
Contrive to bribe the judge's vote;
To Cerberus they give a sop,
His triple barking mouth to stop;
Or, in the ivory gate of dreams,
Project excise and South-Sea schemes;

Or hire their party pamphleteers
To set Elysium by the ears.
    Then, poet, if you mean to thrive,
Employ your muse on kings alive;
With prudence gathering up a cluster
Of all the virtues you can muster,
Which, form'd into a garland sweet,
Lay humbly at your monarch's feet:
Who, as the odours reach his throne,
Will smile, and think them all his own;
For law and gospel both determine
All virtues lodge in royal ermine:
I mean the oracles of both,
Who shall depose it upon oath.
Your garland, in the following reign,
Change but the names, will do again.
    But, if you think this trade too base,
(Which seldom is the dunce's case)
Put on the critic's brow, and sit
At Will's, the puny judge of wit.
A nod, a shrug, a scornful smile,
With caution used, may serve a while.
Proceed no further in your part,
Before you learn the terms of art;
For you can never be too far gone
In all our modern critics' jargon:
Then talk with more authentic face
Of unities, in time and place:
Get scraps of Horace from your friends,
And have them at your fingers' ends;
Learn Aristotle's rules by rote,
And at all hazards boldly quote;
Judicious Rymer oft review,
Wise Dennis, and profound Bossu.
Read all the prefaces of Dryden,
For these our critics much confide in;
Though merely writ at first for filling,
To raise the volume's price a shilling.
    A forward critic often dupes us

With sham quotations *peri hupsous*:
And if we have not read Longinus,
Will magisterially outshine us.
Then, lest with Greek he overrun ye,
Procure the book for love or money,
Translated from Boileau's translation,
And quote quotation on quotation.
At Will's you hear a poem read,
Where Battus from the table head,
Reclining on his elbow-chair,
Gives judgment with decisive air;
To whom the tribe of circling wits
As to an oracle submits.
He gives directions to the town,
To cry it up, or run it down;
Like courtiers, when they send a note,
Instructing members how to vote.
He sets the stamp of bad and good,
Though not a word be understood.
Your lesson learn'd, you'll be secure
To get the name of connoisseur:
And, when your merits once are known,
Procure disciples of your own.
For poets (you can never want 'em)
Spread through Augusta Trinobantum,
Computing by their pecks of coals,
Amount to just nine thousand souls:
These o'er their proper districts govern,
Of wit and humour judges sovereign.
In every street a city bard
Rules, like an alderman, his ward;
His undisputed rights extend
Through all the lane, from end to end;
The neighbours round admire his shrewdness
For songs of loyalty and lewdness;
Outdone by none in rhyming well,
Although he never learn'd to spell.
Two bordering wits contend for glory;
And one is Whig, and one is Tory:

And this, for epics claims the bays,
And that, for elegiac lays:
Some famed for numbers soft and smooth,
By lovers spoke in Punch's booth;
And some as justly fame extols
For lofty lines in Smithfield drolls.
Bavius in Wapping gains renown,
And Mævius reigns o'er Kentish town:
Tigellius placed in Phooebus' car
From Ludgate shines to Temple-bar:
Harmonious Cibber entertains
The court with annual birth-day strains;
Whence Gay was banish'd in disgrace;
Where Pope will never show his face;
Where Young must torture his invention
To flatter knaves or lose his pension.
But these are not a thousandth part
Of jobbers in the poet's art,
Attending each his proper station,
And all in due subordination,
Through every alley to be found,
In garrets high, or under ground;
And when they join their pericranies,
Out skips a book of miscellanies.
Hobbes clearly proves, that every creature
Lives in a state of war by nature.
The greater for the smaller watch,
But meddle seldom with their match.
A whale of moderate size will draw
A shoal of herrings down his maw;
A fox with geese his belly crams;
A wolf destroys a thousand lambs;
But search among the rhyming race,
The brave are worried by the base.
If on Parnassus' top you sit,
You rarely bite, are always bit:
Each poet of inferior size
On you shall rail and criticise,
And strive to tear you limb from limb;

While others do as much for him.
    The vermin only teaze and pinch
Their foes superior by an inch.
So, naturalists observe, a flea
Has smaller fleas that on him prey;
And these have smaller still to bite 'em,
And so proceed *ad infinitum*.
Thus every poet, in his kind,
Is bit by him that comes behind:
Who, though too little to be seen,
Can teaze, and gall, and give the spleen;
Call dunces, fools, and sons of whores,
Lay Grub Street at each other's doors;
Extol the Greek and Roman masters,
And curse our modern poetasters;
Complain, as many an ancient bard did,
How genius is no more rewarded;
How wrong a taste prevails among us;
How much our ancestors outsung us:
Can personate an awkward scorn
For those who are not poets born;
And all their brother dunces lash,
Who crowd the press with hourly trash.
    O Grub Street! how do I bemoan thee,
Whose graceless children scorn to own thee!
Their filial piety forgot,
Deny their country, like a Scot;
Though by their idiom and grimace,
They soon betray their native place:
Yet thou hast greater cause to be
Ashamed of them, than they of thee,
Degenerate from their ancient brood
Since first the court allow'd them food.
    Remains a difficulty still,
To purchase fame by writing ill.
From Flecknoe down to Howard's time,
How few have reach'd the low sublime!
For when our high-born Howard died,
Blackmore alone his place supplied:

And lest a chasm should intervene,
When death had finish'd Blackmore's reign,
The leaden crown devolved to thee,
Great poet of the "Hollow Tree."
But ah! how unsecure thy throne!
A thousand bards thy right disown:
They plot to turn, in factious zeal,
Duncenia to a common weal;
And with rebellious arms pretend
An equal privilege to descend.
    In bulk there are not more degrees
From elephants to mites in cheese,
Than what a curious eye may trace
In creatures of the rhyming race.
From bad to worse, and worse they fall;
But who can reach the worst of all?
For though, in nature, depth and height
Are equally held infinite:
In poetry, the height we know;
'Tis only infinite below.
For instance: when you rashly think,
No rhymer can like Welsted sink,
His merits balanced, you shall find
The Laureate leaves him far behind.
Concanen, more aspiring bard,
Soars downward deeper by a yard.
Smart Jemmy Moore with vigour drops;
The rest pursue as thick as hops:
With heads to point the gulf they enter,
Link'd perpendicular to the centre;
And as their heels elated rise,
Their heads attempt the nether skies.
    O, what indignity and shame,
To prostitute the Muses' name!
By flattering kings, whom Heaven design'd
The plagues and scourges of mankind;
Bred up in ignorance and sloth,
And every vice that nurses both.
    Perhaps you say, Augustus shines,

Immortal made in Virgil's lines,
And Horace brought the tuneful quire,
To sing his virtues on the lyre;
Without reproach for flattery, true,
Because their praises were his due.
For in those ages kings, we find,
Were animals of human kind.
But now, go search all *Europe* round
Among the *savage monsters*—
With vice polluting every *throne*,
(I mean all thrones except our own;)
In vain you make the strictest view
To find a—in all the crew,
With whom a footman out of place
Would not conceive a high disgrace,
A burning shame, a crying sin,
To take his morning's cup of gin.
    Thus all are destined to obey
Some beast of burthen or of prey.
    'Tis sung, Prometheus, forming man,
Through all the brutal species ran,
Each proper quality to find
Adapted to a human mind;
A mingled mass of good and bad,
The best and worst that could be had;
Then from a clay of mixture base
He shaped a—to rule the race,
Endow'd with gifts from every brute
That best the * * nature suit.
Thus think on—s: the name denotes
Hogs, asses, wolves, baboons, and goats.
To represent in figure just,
Sloth, folly, rapine, mischief, lust;
Oh! were they all but Neb-cadnezers,
What herds of—s would turn to grazers!
    Fair Britain, in thy monarch blest,
Whose virtues bear the strictest test;
Whom never faction could bespatter,
Nor minister nor poet flatter;

What justice in rewarding merit!
What magnanimity of spirit!
What lineaments divine we trace
Through all his figure, mien, and face!
Though peace with olive binds his hands,
Confess'd the conquering hero stands.
Hydaspes, Indus, and the Ganges,
Dread from his hand impending changes.
From him the Tartar and Chinese,
Short by the knees, entreat for peace.
The consort of his throne and bed,
A perfect goddess born and bred,
Appointed sovereign judge to sit
On learning, eloquence, and wit.
Our eldest hope, divine Iülus,
(Late, very late, O may he rule us!)
What early manhood has he shown,
Before his downy beard was grown,
Then think, what wonders will be done
By going on as he begun,
An heir for Britain to secure
As long as sun and moon endure.
The remnant of the royal blood
Comes pouring on me like a flood.
Bright goddesses, in number five;
Duke William, sweetest prince alive.
Now sing the minister of state,
Who shines alone without a mate.
Observe with what majestic port
This Atlas stands to prop the court:
Intent the public debts to pay,
Like prudent Fabius, by delay.
Thou great vicegerent of the king,
Thy praises every Muse shall sing!
In all affairs thou sole director;
Of wit and learning chief protector,
Though small the time thou hast to spare,
The church is thy peculiar care.
Of pious prelates what a stock

You choose to rule the sable flock!
You raise the honour of the peerage,
Proud to attend you at the steerage.
You dignify the noble race,
Content yourself with humbler place.
Now learning, valour, virtue, sense,
To titles give the sole pretence.
St. George beheld thee with delight,
Vouchsafe to be an azure knight,
When on thy breast and sides Herculean,
He fix'd the star and string cerulean.
    Say, poet, in what other nation
Shone ever such a constellation!
Attend, ye Popes, and Youngs, and Gays,
And tune your harps, and strew your bays:
Your panegyrics here provide;
You cannot err on flattery's side.
Above the stars exalt your style,
You still are low ten thousand mile.
On Lewis all his bards bestow'd
Of incense many a thousand load;
But Europe mortified his pride,
And swore the fawning rascals lied.
Yet what the world refused to Lewis,
Applied to George, exactly true is.
Exactly true! invidious poet!
'Tis fifty thousand times below it.
    Translate me now some lines, if you can,
From Virgil, Martial, Ovid, Lucan.
They could all power in Heaven divide,
And do no wrong on either side;
They teach you how to split a hair,
Give George and Jove an equal share.
Yet why should we be laced so strait?
I'll give my monarch butter-weight.
And reason good; for many a year
Jove never intermeddled here:
Nor, though his priests be duly paid,

Did ever we desire his aid:
We now can better do without him,
Since Woolston gave us arms to rout him.
Caetera desiderantur.

Verses sent to the Dean On his Birth-Day, with Pine's Horace, Finely Bound By Dr. J. Sican

(*Horace speaking*)
You've read, sir, in poetic strain,
How Varus and the Mantuan swain
Have on my birth-day been invited,
(But I was forced in verse to write it,)
Upon a plain repast to dine,
And taste my old Campanian wine;
But I, who all punctilios hate,
Though long familiar with the great,
Nor glory in my reputation,
Am come without an invitation;
And, though I'm used to right Falernian,
I'll deign for once to taste Iërnian;
But fearing that you might dispute
(Had I put on my common suit)
My breeding and my politesse,
I visit in my birth-day dress:
My coat of purest Turkey red,
With gold embroidery richly spread;
To which I've sure as good pretensions,
As Irish lords who starve on pensions.
What though proud ministers of state
Did at your antichamber wait;
What though your Oxfords and your St. Johns,
Have at your levee paid attendance,
And Peterborough and great Ormond,
With many chiefs who now are dormant,
Have laid aside the general's staff,
And public cares, with you to laugh;
Yet I some friends as good can name,
Nor less the darling sons of fame;
For sure my Pollio and Mæcenas

Were as good statesmen, Mr. Dean, as
Either your Bolingbroke or Harley,
Though they made Lewis beg a parley;
And as for Mordaunt, your loved hero,
I'll match him with my Drusus Nero.
You'll boast, perhaps, your favourite Pope;
But Virgil is as good, I hope.
I own indeed I can't get any
To equal Helsham and Delany;
Since Athens brought forth Socrates,
A Grecian isle, Hippocrates;
Since Tully lived before my time,
And Galen bless'd another clime.
    You'll plead, perhaps, at my request,
To be admitted as a guest,
"Your hearing's bad!"—But why such fears?
I speak to eyes, and not to ears;
And for that reason wisely took
The form you see me in, a book.
Attack'd by slow devouring moths,
By rage of barbarous Huns and Goths;
By Bentley's notes, my deadliest foes,
By Creech's rhymes, and Dunster's prose;
I found my boasted wit and fire
In their rude hands almost expire:
Yet still they but in vain assail'd;
For, had their violence prevail'd,
And in a blast destroy'd my frame,
They would have partly miss'd their aim;
Since all my spirit in thy page
Defies the Vandals of this age.
'Tis yours to save these small remains
From future pedant's muddy brains,
And fix my long uncertain fate,
You best know how—"which way?"—Translate.

Epigram by Mr. Bowyer Intended to be Placed under the Head of Gulliver. 1733

“Here learn from moral truth and wit refined,
How vice and folly have debased mankind;
Strong sense and humour arm in virtue’s cause;
Thus her great votary vindicates her laws:
While bold and free the glowing colours strike;
Blame not the picture, if the picture’s like.”

On Psyche

At two afternoon for our Psyche inquire,
Her tea-kettle's on, and her smock at the fire:
So loitering, so active; so busy, so idle;
Which has she most need of, a spur or a bridle?
Thus a greyhound outruns the whole pack in a race,
Yet would rather be hang'd than he'd leave a warm place.
She gives you such plenty, it puts you in pain;
But ever with prudence takes care of the main.
To please you, she knows how to choose a nice bit;
For her taste is almost as refined as her wit.
To oblige a good friend, she will trace every market,
It would do your heart good, to see how she will cark it.
Yet beware of her arts; for, it plainly appears,
She saves half her victuals, by feeding your ears.

The Dean and Duke
1734

James Brydges and the Dean had long been friends;
James is beduked; of course their friendship ends:
But sure the Dean deserves a sharp rebuke,
For knowing James, to boast he knows the duke.
Yet, since just Heaven the duke's ambition mocks,
Since all he got by fraud is lost by stocks,
His wings are clipp'd: he tries no more in vain
With bands of fiddlers to extend his train.
Since he no more can build, and plant, and revel,
The duke and dean seem near upon a level.
O! wert thou not a duke, my good Duke Humphry,
From bailiffs claws thou scarce couldst keep thy bum free.
A duke to know a dean! go, smooth thy crown:
Thy brother (far thy better) wore a gown.
Well, but a duke thou art; so please the king:
O! would his majesty but add a string!

Written by Dr. Swift on his own Deafness, in September, 1734

Vertiginosus, inops, surdus, male gratus amicis;
Non campana sonans, tonitru non ab Jove missum,
Quod mage mirandum, saltem si credere fas est,
Non clamosa meas mulier jam percutit aures.

The Dean's Complaint, Translated and Answered

Doctor: Deaf, giddy, helpless, left alone.
Answer: Except the first, the fault's your own.
Doctor: To all my friends a burden grown.
Answer: Because to few you will be shewn.
  Give them good wine, and meat to stuff,
  You may have company enough.
Doctor: No more I hear my church's bell,
  Than if it rang out for my knell.
Answer: Then write and read, 'twill do as well.
Doctor: At thunder now no more I start,
  Than at the rumbling of a cart.
Answer: Think then of thunder when you f—t.
Doctor: Nay, what's incredible, alack!
  No more I hear a woman's clack.
Answer: A woman's clack, if I have skill,
  Sounds somewhat like a throwster's mill;
  But louder than a bell, or thunder:
  That does, I own, increase my wonder.

The Dean's manner of Living

On rainy days alone I dine
Upon a chick and pint of wine.
On rainy days I dine alone,
And pick my chicken to the bone;
But this my servants much enrages,
No scraps remain to save board-wages.
In weather fine I nothing spend,
But often spunge upon a friend;
Yet, where he's not so rich as I,
I pay my club, and so good b'ye.

Epigram by Mr. Bowyer

"In Syllabam Longam in Voce Vertiginosus A. D. Swift Correptam"

Musarum antistes, Phoebi numerosus alumnus,
  Vix omnes numeros Vertiginosus habet.
Intentat charo capiti vertigo ruinam:
  Oh! servet cerebro nata Minerva caput.
Vertigo nimium longa est, divina poeta;
  Dent tibi Pierides, donet Apollo, brevem.

Verses made for Fruit-Women

Apples

Come buy my fine wares,
Plums, apples, and pears.
A hundred a penny,
In conscience too many:
Come, will you have any?
My children are seven,
I wish them in Heaven;
My husband a sot,
With his pipe and his pot,
Not a farthing will gain them,
And I must maintain them.

Asparagus

Ripe 'sparagrass
Fit for lad or lass,
To make their water pass:
O, 'tis pretty picking
With a tender chicken!

Onions

Come, follow me by the smell,
Here are delicate onions to sell;
I promise to use you well.
They make the blood warmer,
You'll feed like a farmer;
For this is every cook's opinion,
No savoury dish without an onion;
But, lest your kissing should be spoil'd,
Your onions must be thoroughly boil'd:
Or else you may spare
Your mistress a share,
The secret will never be known:

She cannot discover
The breath of her lover,
But think it as sweet as her own.

Oysters

Charming oysters I cry:
My masters, come buy,
So plump and so fresh,
So sweet is their flesh,
No Colchester oyster
Is sweeter and moister:
Your stomach they settle,
And rouse up your mettle:
They'll make you a dad
Of a lass or a lad;
And madam your wife
They'll please to the life;
Be she barren, be she old,
Be she slut, or be she scold,
Eat my oysters, and lie near her,
She'll be fruitful, never fear her.

Herrings

Be not sparing,
Leave off swearing.
Buy my herring
Fresh from Malahide,
Better never was tried.
Come, eat them with pure fresh butter and mustard,
Their bellies are soft, and as white as a custard.
Come, sixpence a-dozen, to get me some bread,
Or, like my own herrings, I soon shall be dead.

Oranges

Come buy my fine oranges, sauce for your veal,
And charming, when squeezed in a pot of brown ale;
Well roasted, with sugar and wine in a cup,
They'll make a sweet bishop when gentlefolks sup.

On Rover, A Lady's Spaniel

Instructions to a Painter

Happiest of the spaniel race,
Painter, with thy colours grace:
Draw his forehead large and high,
Draw his blue and humid eye;
Draw his neck so smooth and round,
Little neck with ribbons bound!
And the muscly swelling breast,
Where the Loves and Graces rest;
And the spreading even back,
Soft, and sleek, and glossy black;
And the tail that gently twines,
Like the tendrils of the vines;
And the silky twisted hair,
Shadowing thick the velvet ear;
Velvet ears, which, hanging low,
O'er the veiny temples flow.
    With a proper light and shade,
Let the winding hoop be laid;
And within that arching bower,
(Secret circle, mystic power,)
In a downy slumber place
Happiest of the spaniel race;
While the soft respiring dame,
Glowing with the softest flame,
On the ravish'd favourite pours
Balmy dews, ambrosial showers.
    With thy utmost skill express
Nature in her richest dress,
Limpid rivers smoothly flowing,
Orchards by those rivers blowing;
Curling woodbine, myrtle shade,
And the gay enamell'd mead;
Where the linnets sit and sing,
Little sportlings of the spring;

Where the breathing field and grove
Soothe the heart and kindle love.
Here for me, and for the Muse,
Colours of resemblance choose,
Make of lineaments divine,
Daply female spaniels shine,
Pretty fondlings of the fair,
Gentle damsels' gentle care;
But to one alone impart
All the flattery of thy art.
Crowd each feature, crowd each grace,
Which complete the desperate face;
Let the spotted wanton dame
Feel a new resistless flame!
Let the happiest of his race
Win the fair to his embrace.
But in shade the rest conceal,
Nor to sight their joys reveal,
Lest the pencil and the Muse
Loose desires and thoughts infuse.

Epigrams on Windows

Several of them Written in 1726

I. On a Window at an Inn

We fly from luxury and wealth,
To hardships, in pursuit of health;
From generous wines, and costly fare,
And dozing in an easy-chair;
Pursue the goddess Health in vain,
To find her in a country scene,
And every where her footsteps trace,
And see her marks in every face;
And still her favourites we meet,
Crowding the roads with naked feet.
But, oh! so faintly we pursue,
We ne'er can have her full in view.

II. At an Inn in England

The glass, by lovers' nonsense blurr'd,
    Dims and obscures our sight;
So, when our passions Love has stirr'd,
    It darkens Reason's light.

III. On a Window at the Four Crosses In the Watling-Street Road, Warwickshire

Fool, to put up four crosses at your door,
Put up your wife, she's Crosser than all four.

IV. Another, at Chester

The church and clergy here, no doubt,
    Are very near a-kin;
Both weather-beaten are without,
    And empty both within.

V. Another, at Chester

My landlord is civil,
But dear as the d—l:
Your pockets grow empty
With nothing to tempt ye;
The wine is so sour,
'Twill give you a scour,
The beer and the ale
Are mingled with stale.
The veal is such carrion,
A dog would be weary on.
All this I have felt,
For I live on a smelt.

VI. Another, at Chester

The walls of this town
Are full of renown,
And strangers delight to walk round 'em:
But as for the dwellers,
Both buyers and sellers,
For me, you may hang 'em, or drown 'em.

VII. Another
Written upon a Window where there was no Writing Before

Thanks to my stars, I once can see
A window here from scribbling free!
Here no conceited coxcombs pass,
To scratch their paltry drabs on glass;
Nor party fool is calling names,
Or dealing crowns to George and James.

VIII. On Seeing verses Written upon Windows at Inns

The sage, who said he should be proud
Of windows in his breast,
Because he ne'er a thought allow'd

That might not be confest;
His window scrawl'd by every rake,
His breast again would cover,
And fairly bid the devil take
The diamond and the lover.

IX. Another

By Satan taught, all conjurors know
Your mistress in a glass to show,
And you can do as much:
In this the devil and you agree;
None e'er made verses worse than he,
And thine, I swear, are such.

X. Another

That love is the devil, I'll prove when required;
Those rhymers abundantly show it:
They swear that they all by love are inspired,
And the devil's a damnable poet.

XI. Another, at Holyhead

O Neptune! Neptune! must I still
Be here detain'd against my will?
Is this your justice, when I'm come
Above two hundred miles from home;
O'er mountains steep, o'er dusty plains,
Half choked with dust, half drown'd with rains,
Only your godship to implore,
To let me kiss your other shore?
A boon so small! but I may weep,
While you're like Baal, fast asleep.

To Janus, on New Year's Day, 1726

Two-faced Janus, god of Time!
Be my Phoebus while I rhyme;
To oblige your crony Swift,
Bring our dame a new year's gift;
She has got but half a face;
Janus, since thou hast a brace,
To my lady once be kind;
Give her half thy face behind.
    God of Time, if you be wise,
Look not with your future eyes;
What imports thy forward sight?
Well, if you could lose it quite.
Can you take delight in viewing
This poor Isle's approaching ruin,
When thy retrospection vast
Sees the glorious ages past?
Happy nation, were we blind,
Or had only eyes behind!
    Drown your morals, madam cries,
I'll have none but forward eyes;
Prudes decay'd about may tack,
Strain their necks with looking back.
Give me time when coming on;
Who regards him when he's gone?
By the Dean though gravely told,
New-years help to make me old;
Yet I find a new-year's lace
Burnishes an old-year's face.
Give me velvet and quadrille,
I'll have youth and beauty still.

A Motto for Mr. Jason Hasard

Woollen-Draper in Dublin, Whose Sign was the Golden Fleece

Jason, the valiant prince of Greece,
From Colchis brought the Golden Fleece;
We comb the wool, refine the stuff,
For modern Jasons, that's enough.
Oh! could we tame yon watchful dragon,
Old Jason would have less to brag on.

To a Friend
Who had been much Abused in many Inveterate Libels

The greatest monarch may be stabb'd by night
And fortune help the murderer in his flight;
The vilest ruffian may commit a rape,
Yet safe from injured innocence escape;
And calumny, by working under ground,
Can, unrevenged, the greatest merit wound.
    What's to be done? Shall wit and learning choose
To live obscure, and have no fame to lose?
By Censure frighted out of Honour's road,
Nor dare to use the gifts by Heaven bestow'd?
Or fearless enter in through Virtue's gate,
And buy distinction at the dearest rate.

Catullus de Lesbia

Lesbia for ever on me rails,
To talk of me she never fails.
Now, hang me, but for all her art,
I find that I have gain'd her heart.
My proof is this: I plainly see,
The case is just the same with me;
I curse her every hour sincerely,
Yet, hang me but I love her dearly.

On a Curate's Complaint of hard duty

I marched three miles through scorching sand,
With zeal in heart, and notes in hand;
I rode four more to Great St. Mary,
Using four legs, when two were weary:
To three fair virgins I did tie men,
In the close bands of pleasing Hymen;
I dipp'd two babes in holy water,
And purified their mother after.
Within an hour and eke a half,
I preach'd three congregations deaf;
Where, thundering out, with lungs long-winded,
I chopp'd so fast, that few there minded.
My emblem, the laborious sun,
Saw all these mighty labours done
Before one race of his was run.
All this perform'd by Robert Hewit:
What mortal else could e'er go through it!

To Betty, the Grisette

Queen of wit and beauty, Betty,
Never may the Muse forget ye,
How thy face charms every shepherd,
Spotted over like a leopard!
And thy freckled neck, display'd,
Envy breeds in every maid;
Like a fly-blown cake of tallow,
Or on parchment ink turn'd yellow;
Or a tawny speckled pippin,
Shrivell'd with a winter's keeping.
    And, thy beauty thus dispatch'd,
Let me praise thy wit unmatch'd.
    Sets of phrases, cut and dry,
Evermore thy tongue supply;
And thy memory is loaded
With old scraps from plays exploded;
Stock'd with repartees and jokes,
Suited to all Christian folks:
Shreds of wit, and senseless rhymes,
Blunder'd out a thousand times;
Nor wilt thou of gifts be sparing,
Which can ne'er be worse for wearing.
Picking wit among collegians,
In the playhouse upper regions;
Where, in the eighteen-penny gallery,
Irish nymphs learn Irish raillery.
But thy merit is thy failing,
And thy raillery is railing.
    Thus with talents well endued
To be scurrilous and rude;
When you pertly raise your snout,
Fleer and gibe, and laugh and flout;
This among Hibernian asses
For sheer wit and humour passes.
Thus indulgent Chloe, bit,
Swears you have a world of wit.

Epigram from the French

Who can believe with common sense,
A bacon slice gives God offence;
Or, how a herring has a charm
Almighty vengeance to disarm?
Wrapp'd up in majesty divine,
Does he regard on what we dine?

Epigram

As Thomas was cudgell'd one day by his wife,
He took to the street, and fled for his life:
Tom's three dearest friends came by in the squabble,
And saved him at once from the shrew and the rabble;
Then ventured to give him some sober advice—
But Tom is a person of honour so nice,
Too wise to take counsel, too proud to take warning,
That he sent to all three a challenge next morning.
Three duels he fought, thrice ventur'd his life;
Went home, and was cudgell'd again by his wife.

Epigram added by Stella

When Margery chastises Ned,
She calls it combing of his head;
A kinder wife was never born:
She combs his head, and finds him horn.

Joan cudgels Ned

Joan cudgels Ned, yet Ned's a bully;
Will cudgels Bess, yet Will's a cully.
Die Ned and Bess; give Will to Joan,
She dares not say her life's her own.
Die Joan and Will; give Bess to Ned,
And every day she combs his head.

Verses on two Celebrated modern Poets

Behold, those monarch oaks, that rise
With lofty branches to the skies,
Have large proportion'd roots that grow
With equal longitude below:
Two bards that now in fashion reign,
Most aptly this device explain:
If this to clouds and stars will venture,
That creeps as far to reach the centre;
Or, more to show the thing I mean,
Have you not o'er a saw-pit seen
A skill'd mechanic, that has stood
High on a length of prostrate wood,
Who hired a subterraneous friend
To take his iron by the end;
But which excell'd was never found,
The man above or under ground.
    The moral is so plain to hit,
That, had I been the god of wit,
Then, in a saw-pit and wet weather,
Should Young and Philips drudge together.

Epitaph on General Gorges, and Lady Meath

Under this stone lies Dick and Dolly.
Doll dying first, Dick grew melancholy;
For Dick without Doll thought living a folly.

Dick lost in Doll a wife tender and dear:
But Dick lost by Doll twelve hundred a-year;
A loss that Dick thought no mortal could bear.

Dick sigh'd for his Doll, and his mournful arms cross'd;
Thought much of his Doll, and the jointure he lost;
The first vex'd him much, the other vex'd most.

Thus loaded with grief, Dick sigh'd and he cried:
To live without both full three days he tried;
But liked neither loss, and so quietly died.

Dick left a pattern few will copy after:
Then, reader, pray shed some tears of salt water;
For so sad a tale is no subject of laughter.
Meath smiles for the jointure, though gotten so late;
The son laughs, that got the hard-gotten estate;
And Cuffe grins, for getting the Alicant plate.

Here quiet they lie, in hopes to rise one day,
Both solemnly put in this hole on a Sunday,
And here rest—*sic transit gloria mundi*!

Verses on I know not what

My latest tribute here I send,
With this let your collection end.
Thus I consign you down to fame
A character to praise or blame:
And if the whole may pass for true,
Contented rest, you have your due.
Give future time the satisfaction,
To leave one handle for detraction.

Dr. Swift to himself on St. Cecilia's Day

Grave Dean of St. Patrick's, how comes it to pass,
That you, who know music no more than an ass,
That you who so lately were writing of drapiers,
Should lend your cathedral to players and scrapers?
To act such an opera once in a year,
So offensive to every true Protestant ear,
With trumpets, and fiddles, and organs, and singing,
Will sure the Pretender and Popery bring in,
No Protestant Prelate, his lordship or grace,
Durst there show his right, or most reverend face:
How would it pollute their crosiers and rochets,
To listen to minims, and quavers, and crochets!

(The rest is wanting.)

An Answer to a Friend's Question

The furniture that best doth please
St. Patrick's Dean, good Sir, are these:
The knife and fork with which I eat;
And next the pot that boils the meat;
The next to be preferr'd, I think,
Is the glass in which I drink;
The shelves on which my books I keep
And the bed on which I sleep;
An antique elbow-chair between,
Big enough to hold the Dean;
And the stove that gives delight
In the cold bleak wintry night:
To these we add a thing below,
More for use reserved than show:
These are what the Dean do please;
All superfluous are but these.

Epitaph
Inscribed on a Marble Tablet, in Berkeley Church, Gloucestershire

H. S. E.

Carolus Comes de Berkeley, Vicecomes Dursley,
Baro Berkeley, de Berkeley Cast., Mowbray, Segrave,
Et Bruce, è nobilissimo Ordine Balnei Eques,
Vir ad genus quod spectat et proavos usquequaque nobilis
Et longo si quis alius procerum stemmate editus;
Muniis etiam tarn illustri stirpi dignis insignitus.
Siquidem a Gulielmo III° ad ordines foederati Belgii
Ablegatus et Plenipotentiarius Extraordinarius
Rebus, non Britanniae tantùm, sed totius fere Europae
(Tunc temporis praesertim arduis) per annos V. incubuit,
Quam felici diligentia, fide quam intemerata,
Ex illo discas, Lector, quod, superstite patre,
In magnatum ordinem adscisci meruerit.
Fuit à sanctioribus consiliis et Regi Guliel. et Annae Reginae
E proregibus Hiberniae secundus,
Comitatum civitatumque Glocest. et Brist. Dominus
    Locumtenens,
Surriae et Glocest. Gustos Rot., Urbis Glocest. magnus
Senescallus, Arcis sancti de Briavell Castellanus, Guardianus
Forestae de Dean.
Denique ad Turcarum primum, deinde ad Romam Imperatorem
Cum Legatus Extraordinarius designatus esset,
Quo minus has etiam ornaret provincias
Obstitit adversa corporis valetudo.
Sed restat adhuc, prae quo sordescunt caetera,
Honos verus, stabilis, et vel morti cedere nescius
Quòd veritatem evangelicam seriò amplexus;
Erga Deum pius, erga pauperes munificus,
Adversùs omnes aequus et benevolus,
In Christo jam placidè obdormit

Cum eodem olim regnaturus unà.
Natus VIII° April. MDCXLIX. denatus
XXIV° Septem. MDCCX. aetat. suae LXII.

Epitaph

On Frederick, Duke of Schomberg

Hic infra situm est corpus
Frederici Ducis De Schomberg.
ad Budindam occisi, a.d. 1690.
Decanus et Capitulum maximopere etiam
atque etiam petierunt,
Ut Haeredes Ducis monumentum
In memoriam Parentis erigendum curarent:
Sed postquam per epistolas, per amicos,
diu ac saepè orando nil profecêre;
Hunc demum lapidem ipsi statuerunt,
Saltem ut scias, hospes,
Ubinam terrarum Sconbergensis cineres
delitescunt
"Plus potuit fama virtutis apud alienos,
Quam sanguinis proximitas apud suos."
a.d. 1731.

Verses written during Lord Carteret's administration of Ireland

As Lord Carteret's residence in Ireland as Viceroy was a series of cabals against the authority of the Prime Minister, he failed not, as well from his love of literature as from his hatred to Walpole, to attach to himself as much as possible the distinguished author of the Drapier Letters. By the interest which Swift soon gained with the Lord-Lieutenant, he was enabled to recommend several friends, whose High Church or Tory principles had hitherto obstructed their preferment. The task of forwarding the views of Delany, in particular, led to several of Swift's liveliest poetical effusions, while, on the other hand, he was equally active in galling, by his satire, Smedley, and other Whig beaux esprits, who, during this amphibious administration, sought the favour of a literary Lord-Lieutenant, by literary offerings and poetical adulation. These pieces, with one or two connected with the same subject, are here thrown together, as they seem to reflect light upon each other.

—Scott

An Apology to Lady Carteret

A lady, wise as well as fair,
Whose conscience always was her care,
Thoughtful upon a point of moment,
Would have the text as well as comment:
So hearing of a grave divine,
She sent to bid him come to dine.
But, you must know he was not quite
So grave as to be unpolite:
Thought human learning would not lessen
The dignity of his profession:
And if you'd heard the man discourse,
Or preach, you'd like him scarce the worse.
He long had bid the court farewell,
Retreating silent to his cell;
Suspected for the love he bore
To one who sway'd some time before;
Which made it more surprising how
He should be sent for thither now.
    The message told, he gapes, and stares,
And scarce believes his eyes or ears:
Could not conceive what it should mean,
And fain would hear it told again.
But then the squire so trim and nice,
'Twere rude to make him tell it twice;
So bow'd, was thankful for the honour;
And would not fail to wait upon her.
His beaver brush'd, his shoes, and gown,
Away he trudges into town;
Passes the lower castle yard,
And now advancing to the guard,
He trembles at the thoughts of state;
For, conscious of his sheepish gait,
His spirits of a sudden fail'd him;
He stopp'd, and could not tell what ail'd him.
    What was the message I received?
Why certainly the captain raved?

To dine with her! and come at three!
Impossible! it can't be me.
Or maybe I mistook the word;
My lady—it must be my lord.
    My lord 's abroad; my lady too:
What must the unhappy doctor do?
"Is Captain Cracherode here, pray?"—"No."
"Nay, then 'tis time for me to go."
Am I awake, or do I dream?
I'm sure he call'd me by my name;
Named me as plain as he could speak;
And yet there must be some mistake.
Why, what a jest should I have been,
Had now my lady been within!
What could I've said? I'm mighty glad
She went abroad—she'd thought me mad.
The hour of dining now is past:
Well then, I'll e'en go home and fast:
And, since I 'scaped being made a scoff,
I think I'm very fairly off.
My lady now returning home,
Calls "Cracherode, is the Doctor come?"
He had not heard of him—"Pray see,
'Tis now a quarter after three."
The captain walks about, and searches
Through all the rooms, and courts, and arches;
Examines all the servants round,
In vain—no doctor's to be found.
My lady could not choose but wonder;
"Captain, I fear you've made some blunder;
But, pray, to-morrow go at ten;
I'll try his manners once again;
If rudeness be th' effect of knowledge,
My son shall never see a college."
    The captain was a man of reading,
And much good sense, as well as breeding;
Who, loath to blame, or to incense,
Said little in his own defence.
Next day another message brought;

The Doctor, frighten'd at his fault,
Is dress'd, and stealing through the crowd,
Now pale as death, then blush'd and bow'd,
Panting—and faltering—humm'd and ha'd,
"Her ladyship was gone abroad:
The captain too—he did not know
Whether he ought to stay or go;"
Begg'd she'd forgive him. In conclusion,
My lady, pitying his confusion,
Call'd her good nature to relieve him;
Told him, she thought she might believe him;
And would not only grant his suit,
But visit him, and eat some fruit,
Provided, at a proper time,
He told the real truth in rhyme;
'Twas to no purpose to oppose,
She'd hear of no excuse in prose.
The Doctor stood not to debate,
Glad to compound at any rate;
So, bowing, seemingly complied;
Though, if he durst, he had denied.
But first, resolved to show his taste,
Was too refined to give a feast;
He'd treat with nothing that was rare,
But winding walks and purer air;
Would entertain without expense,
Or pride or vain magnificence:
For well he knew, to such a guest
The plainest meals must be the best.
To stomachs clogg'd with costly fare
Simplicity alone is rare;
While high, and nice, and curious meats
Are really but vulgar treats.
Instead of spoils of Persian looms,
The costly boast of regal rooms,
Thought it more courtly and discreet
To scatter roses at her feet;
Roses of richest dye, that shone
With native lustre, like her own;

Beauty that needs no aid of art
Through every sense to reach the heart.
The gracious dame, though well she knew
All this was much beneath her due,
Liked everything—at least thought fit
To praise it *par manière d'acquit*.
Yet she, though seeming pleased, can't bear
The scorching sun, or chilling air;
Disturb'd alike at both extremes,
Whether he shows or hides his beams:
Though seeming pleased at all she sees,
Starts at the ruffling of the trees,
And scarce can speak for want of breath,
In half a walk fatigued to death.
The Doctor takes his hint from hence,
T' apologize his late offence:
"Madam, the mighty power of use
Now strangely pleads in my excuse;
If you unused have scarcely strength
To gain this walk's untoward length;
If, frighten'd at a scene so rude,
Through long disuse of solitude;
If, long confined to fires and screens,
You dread the waving of these greens;
If you, who long have breathed the fumes
Of city fogs and crowded rooms,
Do now solicitously shun
The cooler air and dazzling sun;
If his majestic eye you flee,
Learn hence t' excuse and pity me.
Consider what it is to bear
The powder'd courtier's witty sneer;
To see th' important man of dress
Scoffing my college awkwardness;
To be the strutting cornet's sport,
To run the gauntlet of the court,
Winning my way by slow approaches,
Through crowds of coxcombs and of coaches,
From the first fierce cockaded sentry,

Quite through the tribe of waiting gentry;
To pass so many crowded stages,
And stand the staring of your pages:
And after all, to crown my spleen,
Be told—'You are not to be seen:'
Or, if you are, be forced to bear
The awe of your majestic air.
And can I then be faulty found,
In dreading this vexatious round?
Can it be strange, if I eschew
A scene so glorious and so new?
Or is he criminal that flies
The living lustre of your eyes?"

The Birth of Manly Virtue

Inscribed to Lord Carteret
1724

Gratior et pulcro veniens in corpore virtus.

—Virg., *Aen.*, v, 344

Once on a time, a righteous sage,
Grieved with the vices of the age,
Applied to Jove with fervent prayer—
"O Jove, if Virtue be so fair
As it was deem'd in former days,
By Plato and by Socrates,
Whose beauties mortal eyes escape,
Only for want of outward shape;
Make then its real excellence,
For once the theme of human sense;
So shall the eye, by form confined,
Direct and fix the wandering mind,
And long-deluded mortals see,
With rapture, what they used to flee!"
    Jove grants the prayer, gives Virtue birth,
And bids him bless and mend the earth.
Behold him blooming fresh and fair,
Now made—ye gods—a son and heir;
An heir: and, stranger yet to hear,
An heir, an orphan of a peer;
But prodigies are wrought to prove
Nothing impossible to Jove.
    Virtue was for this sex design'd,
In mild reproof to womankind;
In manly form to let them see
The loveliness of modesty,
The thousand decencies that shone
With lessen'd lustre in their own;
Which few had learn'd enough to prize,

And some thought modish to despise.
    To make his merit more discern'd,
He goes to school—he reads—is learn'd;
Raised high above his birth, by knowledge,
He shines distinguish'd in a college;
Resolved nor honour, nor estate,
Himself alone should make him great.
Here soon for every art renown'd,
His influence is diffused around;
The inferior youth to learning led,
Less to be famed than to be fed,
Behold the glory he has won,
And blush to see themselves outdone;
And now, inflamed with rival rage,
In scientific strife engage,
Engage; and, in the glorious strife
The arts new kindle into life.
    Here would our hero ever dwell,
Fix'd in a lonely learned cell:
Contented to be truly great,
In Virtue's best beloved retreat;
Contented he—but Fate ordains,
He now shall shine in nobler scenes,
Raised high, like some celestial fire,
To shine the more, still rising higher;
Completely form'd in every part,
To win the soul, and glad the heart.
The powerful voice, the graceful mien,
Lovely alike, or heard, or seen;
The outward form and inward vie,
His soul bright beaming from his eye,
Ennobling every act and air,
With just, and generous, and sincere.
    Accomplish'd thus, his next resort
Is to the council and the court,
Where Virtue is in least repute,
And interest the one pursuit;
Where right and wrong are bought and sold,
Barter'd for beauty, and for gold;

Here Manly Virtue, even here,
Pleased in the person of a peer,
A peer; a scarcely bearded youth,
Who talk'd of justice and of truth,
Of innocence the surest guard,
Tales here forgot, or yet unheard;
That he alone deserved esteem,
Who was the man he wish'd to seem;
Call'd it unmanly and unwise,
To lurk behind a mean disguise;
(Give fraudful Vice the mask and screen,
'Tis Virtue's interest to be seen;)
Call'd want of shame a want of sense,
And found, in blushes, eloquence.
    Thus acting what he taught so well,
He drew dumb merit from her cell,
Led with amazing art along
The bashful dame, and loosed her tongue;
And, while he made her value known,
Yet more display'd and raised his own.
    Thus young, thus proof to all temptations,
He rises to the highest stations;
For where high honour is the prize,
True Virtue has a right to rise:
Let courtly slaves low bend the knee
To Wealth and Vice in high degree:
Exalted Worth disdains to owe
Its grandeur to its greatest foe.
    Now raised on high, see Virtue shows
The godlike ends for which he rose;
For him, let proud Ambition know
The height of glory here below,
Grandeur, by goodness made complete!
To bless, is truly to be great!
He taught how men to honour rise,
Like gilded vapours to the skies,
Which, howsoever they display
Their glory from the god of day,
Their noblest use is to abate

His dangerous excess of heat,
To shield the infant fruits and flowers,
And bless the earth with genial showers.
Now change the scene; a nobler care
Demands him in a higher sphere:
Distress of nations calls him hence,
Permitted so by Providence;
For models, made to mend our kind,
To no one clime should be confined;
And Manly Virtue, like the sun,
His course of glorious toils should run:
Alike diffusing in his flight
Congenial joy, and life, and light.
Pale Envy sickens, Error flies,
And Discord in his presence dies;
Oppression hides with guilty dread,
And Merit rears her drooping head;
The arts revive, the valleys sing,
And winter softens into spring:
The wondering world, where'er he moves,
With new delight looks up, and loves;
One sex consenting to admire,
Nor less the other to desire;
While he, though seated on a throne,
Confines his love to one alone;
The rest condemn'd with rival voice
Repining, do applaud his choice.
Fame now reports, the Western isle
Is made his mansion for a while,
Whose anxious natives, night and day,
(Happy beneath his righteous sway,)
Weary the gods with ceaseless prayer,
To bless him, and to keep him there;
And claim it as a debt from Fate,
Too lately found, to lose him late.

On Paddy's Character of the "Intelligencer." 1729

As a thorn bush, or oaken bough,
Stuck in an Irish cabin's brow,
Above the door, at country fair,
Betokens entertainment there;
So bays on poets' brows have been
Set, for a sign of wit within.
And as ill neighbours in the night
Pull down an alehouse bush for spite;
The laurel so, by poets worn,
Is by the teeth of Envy torn;
Envy, a canker-worm, which tears
Those sacred leaves that lightning spares.
    And now, t'exemplify this moral:
Tom having earn'd a twig of laurel,
(Which, measured on his head, was found
Not long enough to reach half round,
But, like a girl's cockade, was tied,
A trophy, on his temple-side,)
Paddy repined to see him wear
This badge of honour in his hair;
And, thinking this cockade of wit
Would his own temples better fit,
Forming his Muse by Smedley's model,
Lets drive at Tom's devoted noddle,
Pelts him by turns with verse and prose
Hums like a hornet at his nose.
At length presumes to vent his satire on
The Dean, Tom's honour'd friend and patron.
The eagle in the tale, ye know,
Teazed by a buzzing wasp below,
Took wing to Jove, and hoped to rest
Securely in the thunderer's breast:
In vain; even there, to spoil his nod,
The spiteful insect stung the god.

An Epistle to his Excellency John, Lord Carteret
By Dr. Delany. 1729

Credis ob haec me, Pastor, opes fortasse rogare,
Propter quae vulgus crassaque turba rogat.

Mart., *Epig.*, lib. ix, 22.

Thou wise and learned ruler of our isle,
Whose guardian care can all her griefs beguile;
When next your generous soul shall condescend
T' instruct or entertain your humble friend;
Whether, retiring from your weighty charge,
On some high theme you learnedly enlarge;
Of all the ways of wisdom reason well,
How Richelieu rose, and how Sejanus fell:
Or, when your brow less thoughtfully unbends,
Circled with Swift and some delighted friends;
When, mixing mirth and wisdom with your wine,
Like that your wit shall flow, your genius shine:
Nor with less praise the conversation guide,
Than in the public councils you decide:
Or when the Dean, long privileged to rail,
Asserts his friend with more impetuous zeal;
You hear (whilst I sit by abash'd and mute)
With soft concessions shortening the dispute;
Then close with kind inquiries of my state,
"How are your tithes, and have they rose of late?
Why, Christ-Church is a pretty situation,
There are not many better in the nation!
This, with your other things, must yield you clear
Some six—at least five hundred pounds a-year."
    Suppose, at such a time, I took the freedom
To speak these truths as plainly as you read 'em;
You shall rejoin, my lord, when I've replied,
And, if you please, my lady shall decide.
    "My lord, I'm satisfied you meant me well,

And that I'm thankful, all the world can tell;
But you'll forgive me, if I own the event
Is short, is very short, of your intent:
At least, I feel some ills unfelt before,
My income less, and my expenses more."
"How, doctor! double vicar! double rector!
A dignitary! with a city lecture!
What glebes—what dues—what tithes—what fines—what rent!
Why, doctor!—will you never be content?"
"Would my good Lord but cast up the account,
And see to what my revenues amount;
My titles ample; but my gain so small,
That one good vicarage is worth them all:
And very wretched, sure, is he that's double
In nothing but his titles and his trouble.
And to this crying grievance, if you please,
My horses founder'd on Fermanagh ways;
Ways of well-polish'd and well-pointed stone,
Where every step endangers every bone;
And, more to raise your pity and your wonder,
Two churches—twelve Hibernian miles asunder:
With complicated cures, I labour hard in,
Beside whole summers absent from—my garden!
But that the world would think I play'd the fool,
I'd change with Charley Grattan for his school.
What fine cascades, what vistoes, might I make,
Fixt in the centre of th' Iërnian lake!
There might I sail delighted, smooth and safe,
Beneath the conduct of my good Sir Ralph:
There's not a better steerer in the realm;
I hope, my lord, you'll call him to the helm."—
"Doctor—a glorious scheme to ease your grief!
When cures are cross, a school's a sure relief.
You cannot fail of being happy there,
The lake will be the Lethe of your care:
The scheme is for your honour and your ease:
And, doctor, I'll promote it when you please.
Meanwhile, allowing things below your merit,
Yet, doctor, you've a philosophic spirit;

Your wants are few, and, like your income, small,
And you've enough to gratify them all:
You've trees, and fruits, and roots, enough in store:
And what would a philosopher have more?
You cannot wish for coaches, kitchens, cooks—"
"My lord, I've not enough to buy me books—
Or pray, suppose my wants were all supplied,
Are there no wants I should regard beside?
Whose breast is so unmann'd, as not to grieve,
Compass'd with miseries he can't relieve?
Who can be happy—who should wish to live,
And want the godlike happiness to give?
That I'm a judge of this, you must allow:
I had it once—and I'm debarr'd it now.
Ask your own heart, my lord; if this be true,
Then how unblest am I! how blest are you!"
"'Tis true—but, doctor, let us wave all that—
Say, if you had your wish, what you'd be at?"
"Excuse me, good my lord—I won't be sounded,
Nor shall your favour by my wants be bounded.
My lord, I challenge nothing as my due,
Nor is it fit I should prescribe to you.
Yet this might Symmachus himself avow,
(Whose rigid rules are antiquated now)—
My lord; I'd wish to pay the debts I owe—
I'd wish besides—to build and to bestow."

An Epistle upon an Epistle

From a Certain Doctor to a certain Great Lord.
Being a Christmas-Box for Dr. Delany

As Jove will not attend on less,
When things of more importance press:
You can't, grave sir, believe it hard,
That you, a low Hibernian bard,
Should cool your heels a while, and wait
Unanswer'd at your patron's gate;
And would my lord vouchsafe to grant
This one poor humble boon I want,
Free leave to play his secretary,
As Falstaff acted old king Harry;
I'd tell of yours in rhyme and print,
Folks shrug, and cry, "There's nothing in't."
And, after several readings over,
It shines most in the marble cover.
    How could so fine a taste dispense
With mean degrees of wit and sense?
Nor will my lord so far beguile
The wise and learned of our isle;
To make it pass upon the nation,
By dint of his sole approbation.
The task is arduous, patrons find,
To warp the sense of all mankind:
Who think your Muse must first aspire,
Ere he advance the doctor higher.
    You've cause to say he meant you well:
That you are thankful, who can tell?
For still you're short (which grieves your spirit)
Of his intent: you mean your merit.
    Ah! *quanto rectius, tu adepte,*
Qui nil moliris tarn inepte?
Smedley, thou Jonathan of Clogher,
"When thou thy humble lay dost offer
To Grafton's grace, with grateful heart,

Thy thanks and verse devoid of art:
Content with what his bounty gave,
No larger income dost thou crave."
    But you must have cascades, and all
Iërne's lake, for your canal,
Your vistoes, barges, and (a pox on
All pride!) our speaker for your coxon:
It's pity that he can't bestow you
Twelve commoners in caps to row you.
Thus Edgar proud, in days of yore,
Held monarchs labouring at the oar;
And, as he pass'd, so swell'd the Dee,
Enraged, as Ern would do at thee.
    How different is this from Smedley!
(His name is up, he may in bed lie)
"Who only asks some pretty cure,
In wholesome soil and ether pure:
The garden stored with artless flowers,
In either angle shady bowers:
No gay parterre with costly green
Must in the ambient hedge be seen;
But Nature freely takes her course,
Nor fears from him ungrateful force:
No shears to check her sprouting vigour,
Or shape the yews to antic figure."
    But you, forsooth, your all must squander
On that poor spot, call'd Dell-ville, yonder;
And when you've been at vast expenses
In whims, parterres, canals, and fences,
Your assets fail, and cash is wanting;
Nor farther buildings, farther planting:
No wonder, when you raise and level,
Think this wall low, and that wall bevel.
Here a convenient box you found,
Which you demolish'd to the ground:
Then built, then took up with your arbour,
And set the house to Rupert Barber.
You sprang an arch which, in a scurvy
Humour, you tumbled topsy-turvy.

You change a circle to a square,
Then to a circle as you were:
Who can imagine whence the fund is,
That you *quadrata* change *rotundis*?
To Fame a temple you erect,
A Flora does the dome protect;
Mounts, walks, on high; and in a hollow
You place the Muses and Apollo;
There shining 'midst his train, to grace
Your whimsical poetic place.
These stories were of old design'd
As fables: but you have refined
The poets mythologic dreams,
To real Muses, gods, and streams.
Who would not swear, when you contrive thus,
That you're Don Quixote redivivus?
Beneath, a dry canal there lies,
Which only Winter's rain supplies.
O! couldst thou, by some magic spell,
Hither convey St. Patrick's well!
Here may it reassume its stream,
And take a greater Patrick's name!
If your expenses rise so high;
What income can your wants supply?
Yet still you fancy you inherit
A fund of such superior merit,
That you can't fail of more provision,
All by my lady's kind decision.
For, the more livings you can fish up,
You think you'll sooner be a bishop:
That could not be my lord's intent,
Nor can it answer the event.
Most think what has been heap'd on you
To other sort of folk was due:
Rewards too great for your flim-flams,
Epistles, riddles, epigrams.
Though now your depth must not be sounded,
The time was, when you'd have compounded
For less than Charley Grattan's school!

Five hundred pound a-year's no fool!
Take this advice then from your friend,
To your ambition put an end,
Be frugal, Pat: pay what you owe,
Before you build and you bestow.
Be modest, nor address your betters
With begging, vain, familiar letters.
A passage may be found, I've heard,
In some old Greek or Latian bard,
Which says, "Would crows in silence eat
Their offals, or their better meat,
Their generous feeders not provoking
By loud and inharmonious croaking,
They might, unhurt by Envy's claws,
Live on, and stuff to boot their maws."

A Libel On the Reverend Dr. Delany, and his Excellency John, Lord Carteret 1729

Deluded mortals, whom the great
Choose for companions *tête-à-tête*;
Who at their dinners, *en famille*,
Get leave to sit whene'er you will;
Then boasting tell us where you dined,
And how his lordship was so kind;
How many pleasant things he spoke;
And how you laugh'd at every joke:
Swear he's a most facetious man;
That you and he are cup and can;
You travel with a heavy load,
And quite mistake preferment's road.
    Suppose my lord and you alone;
Hint the least interest of your own,
His visage drops, he knits his brow,
He cannot talk of business now:
Or, mention but a vacant post,
He'll turn it off with "Name your toast:"
Nor could the nicest artist paint
A countenance with more constraint.
    For, as their appetites to quench,
Lords keep a pimp to bring a wench;
So men of wit are but a kind
Of panders to a vicious mind
Who proper objects must provide
To gratify their lust of pride,
When, wearied with intrigues of state,
They find an idle hour to prate.
Then, shall you dare to ask a place,
You forfeit all your patron's grace,
And disappoint the sole design,
For which he summon'd you to dine.

Thus Congreve spent in writing plays,
And one poor office, half his days:
While Montague, who claim'd the station
To be Mæcenas of the nation,
For poets open table kept,
But ne'er consider'd where they slept:
Himself as rich as fifty Jews,
Was easy, though they wanted shoes;
And crazy Congreve scarce could spare
A shilling to discharge his chair:
Till prudence taught him to appeal
From Pæan's fire to party zeal;
Not owing to his happy vein
The fortunes of his later scene,
Took proper principles to thrive:
And so might every dunce alive.
Thus Steele, who own'd what others writ,
And flourish'd by imputed wit,
From perils of a hundred jails,
Withdrew to starve, and die in Wales.
Thus Gay, the hare with many friends,
Twice seven long years the court attends:
Who, under tales conveying truth,
To virtue form'd a princely youth:
Who paid his courtship with the crowd,
As far as modest pride allow'd;
Rejects a servile usher's place,
And leaves St. James's in disgrace.
Thus Addison, by lords carest,
Was left in foreign lands distrest;
Forgot at home, became for hire
A travelling tutor to a squire:
But wisely left the Muses' hill,
To business shaped the poet's quill,
Let all his barren laurels fade,
Took up himself the courtier's trade,
And, grown a minister of state,
Saw poets at his levee wait.
Hail, happy Pope! whose generous mind

Detesting all the statesman kind,
Contemning courts, at courts unseen,
Refused the visits of a queen.
A soul with every virtue fraught,
By sages, priests, or poets taught;
Whose filial piety excels
Whatever Grecian story tells;
A genius for all stations fit,
Whose meanest talent is his wit:
His heart too great, though fortune little,
To lick a rascal statesman's spittle:
Appealing to the nation's taste,
Above the reach of want is placed:
By Homer dead was taught to thrive,
Which Homer never could alive;
And sits aloft on Pindus' head,
Despising slaves that cringe for bread.
    True politicians only pay
For solid work, but not for play:
Nor ever choose to work with tools
Forged up in colleges and schools,
Consider how much more is due
To all their journeymen than you:
At table you can Horace quote;
They at a pinch can bribe a vote:
You show your skill in Grecian story;
But they can manage Whig and Tory;
You, as a critic, are so curious
To find a verse in Virgil spurious;
But they can smoke the deep designs,
When Bolingbroke with Pulteney dines.
    Besides, your patron may upbraid ye,
That you have got a place already;
An office for your talents fit,
To flatter, carve, and show your wit;
To snuff the lights and stir the fire,
And get a dinner for your hire.
What claim have you to place or pension?
He overpays in condescension.

But, reverend doctor, you we know
Could never condescend so low;
The viceroy, whom you now attend,
Would, if he durst, be more your friend;
Nor will in you those gifts despise,
By which himself was taught to rise:
When he has virtue to retire,
He'll grieve he did not raise you higher,
And place you in a better station,
Although it might have pleased the nation.
This may be true—submitting still
To Walpole's more than royal will;
And what condition can be worse?
He comes to drain a beggar's purse;
He comes to tie our chains on faster,
And show us England is our master:
Caressing knaves, and dunces wooing,
To make them work their own undoing.
What has he else to bait his traps,
Or bring his vermin in, but scraps?
The offals of a church distrest;
A hungry vicarage at best;
Or some remote inferior post,
With forty pounds a-year at most?
But here again you interpose—
Your favourite lord is none of those
Who owe their virtues to their stations,
And characters to dedications:
For, keep him in, or turn him out,
His learning none will call in doubt;
His learning, though a poet said it
Before a play, would lose no credit;
Nor Pope would dare deny him wit,
Although to praise it Philips writ.
I own he hates an action base,
His virtues battling with his place:
Nor wants a nice discerning spirit
Betwixt a true and spurious merit;
Can sometimes drop a voter's claim,

And give up party to his fame.
I do the most that friendship can;
I hate the viceroy, love the man.
    But you, who, till your fortune's made,
Must be a sweetener by your trade,
Should swear he never meant us ill;
We suffer sore against his will;
That, if we could but see his heart,
He would have chose a milder part:
We rather should lament his case,
Who must obey, or lose his place.
    Since this reflection slipt your pen,
Insert it when you write again;
And, to illustrate it, produce
This simile for his excuse:
    "So, to destroy a guilty land
An angel sent by Heaven's command,
While he obeys Almighty will,
Perhaps may feel compassion still;
And wish the task had been assign'd
To spirits of less gentle kind."
    But I, in politics grown old,
Whose thoughts are of a different mould,
Who from my soul sincerely hate
Both kings and ministers of state;
Who look on courts with stricter eyes
To see the seeds of vice arise;
Can lend you an allusion fitter,
Though flattering knaves may call it bitter;
Which, if you durst but give it place,
Would show you many a statesman's face:
Fresh from the tripod of Apollo,
I had it in the words that follow:
Take notice to avoid offence,
I here except his excellence:
    "So, to effect his monarch's ends,
From hell a viceroy devil ascends;
His budget with corruptions cramm'd,
The contributions of the damn'd;

Which with unsparing hand he strews
Through courts and senates as he goes;
And then at Beelzebub's black hall,
Complains his budget was too small."
    Your simile may better shine
In verse, but there is truth in mine.
For no imaginable things
Can differ more than gods and kings:
And statesmen, by ten thousand odds,
Are angels just as kings are gods.

To Dr. Delany
On the Libels Written against him. 1729

—Tanti tibi non sit opaci
Omnis arena Tagi quodque in mare volvitur aurum.

—Juv. iii, 54

As some raw youth in country bred,
To arms by thirst of honour led,
When at a skirmish first he hears
The bullets whistling round his ears,
Will duck his head aside, will start,
And feel a trembling at his heart,
Till 'scaping oft without a wound
Lessens the terror of the sound;
Fly bullets now as thick as hops,
He runs into a cannon's chops.
An author thus, who pants for fame,
Begins the world with fear and shame;
When first in print you see him dread
Each pop-gun levell'd at his head:
The lead yon critic's quill contains,
Is destined to beat out his brains:
As if he heard loud thunders roll,
Cries, Lord have mercy on his soul!
Concluding that another shot
Will strike him dead upon the spot.
But, when with squibbing, flashing, popping,
He cannot see one creature dropping;
That, missing fire, or missing aim,
His life is safe, I mean his fame;
The danger past, takes heart of grace,
And looks a critic in the face.
    Though splendour gives the fairest mark
To poison'd arrows in the dark,
Yet, in yourself when smooth and round,
They glance aside without a wound.

’Tis said, the gods tried all their art,
How pain they might from pleasure part:
But little could their strength avail;
Both still are fasten’d by the tail;
Thus fame and censure with a tether
By fate are always link’d together.
Why will you aim to be preferr’d
In wit before the common herd;
And yet grow mortified and vex’d,
To pay the penalty annex’d?
’Tis eminence makes envy rise;
As fairest fruits attract the flies.
Should stupid libels grieve your mind,
You soon a remedy may find;
Lie down obscure like other folks
Below the lash of snarlers’ jokes.
Their faction is five hundred odds,
For every coxcomb lends them rods,
And sneers as learnedly as they,
Like females o’er their morning tea.
You say the Muse will not contain
And write you must, or break a vein.
Then, if you find the terms too hard,
No longer my advice regard:
But raise your fancy on the wing;
The Irish senate’s praises sing;
How jealous of the nation’s freedom,
And for corruptions how they weed ’em;
How each the public good pursues,
How far their hearts from private views;
Make all true patriots, up to shoe-boys,
Huzza their brethren at the Blue-boys;
Thus grown a member of the club,
No longer dread the rage of Grub.
How oft am I for rhyme to seek!
To dress a thought I toil a week:
And then how thankful to the town,
If all my pains will earn a crown!
While every critic can devour

My work and me in half an hour.
Would men of genius cease to write,
The rogues must die for want and spite;
Must die for want of food and raiment,
If scandal did not find them payment.
How cheerfully the hawkers cry
A satire, and the gentry buy!
While my hard-labour'd poem pines
Unsold upon the printer's lines.
A genius in the reverend gown
Must ever keep its owner down;
'Tis an unnatural conjunction,
And spoils the credit of the function.
Round all your brethren cast your eyes,
Point out the surest men to rise;
That club of candidates in black,
The least deserving of the pack,
Aspiring, factious, fierce, and loud,
With grace and learning unendow'd,
Can turn their hands to every job,
The fittest tools to work for Bob;
Will sooner coin a thousand lies,
Than suffer men of parts to rise;
They crowd about preferment's gate,
And press you down with all their weight;
For as of old mathematicians
Were by the vulgar thought magicians;
So academic dull ale-drinkers
Pronounce all men of wit free-thinkers.
Wit, as the chief of virtue's friends,
Disdains to serve ignoble ends.
Observe what loads of stupid rhymes
Oppress us in corrupted times;
What pamphlets in a court's defence
Show reason, grammar, truth, or sense?
For though the Muse delights in fiction,
She ne'er inspires against conviction.
Then keep your virtue still unmixt,
And let not faction come betwixt:

By party-steps no grandeur climb at,
Though it would make you England's primate;
First learn the science to be dull,
You then may soon your conscience lull;
If not, however seated high,
Your genius in your face will fly.
    When Jove was from his teeming head
Of Wit's fair goddess brought to bed,
There follow'd at his lying-in
For after-birth a sooterkin;
Which, as the nurse pursued to kill,
Attain'd by flight the Muses' hill,
There in the soil began to root,
And litter'd at Parnassus' foot.
From hence the critic vermin sprung,
With harpy claws and poisonous tongue:
Who fatten on poetic scraps,
Too cunning to be caught in traps.
Dame Nature, as the learned show,
Provides each animal its foe:
Hounds hunt the hare, the wily fox
Devours your geese, the wolf your flocks
Thus Envy pleads a natural claim
To persecute the Muse's fame;
On poets in all times abusive,
From Homer down to Pope inclusive.
    Yet what avails it to complain?
You try to take revenge in vain.
A rat your utmost rage defies,
That safe behind the wainscot lies.
Say, did you ever know by sight
In cheese an individual mite!
Show me the same numeric flea,
That bit your neck but yesterday:
You then may boldly go in quest
To find the Grub Street poet's nest;
What spunging-house, in dread of jail,
Receives them, while they wait for bail;
What alley are they nestled in,

To flourish o'er a cup of gin;
Find the last garret where they lay,
Or cellar where they starve to-day.
Suppose you have them all trepann'd,
With each a libel in his hand,
What punishment would you inflict?
Or call them rogues, or get them kickt?
These they have often tried before;
You but oblige them so much more:
Themselves would be the first to tell,
To make their trash the better sell.
    You have been libell'd—Let us know,
What fool officious told you so?
Will you regard the hawker's cries,
Who in his titles always lies?
Whate'er the noisy scoundrel says,
It might be something in your praise;
And praise bestow'd in Grub Street rhymes,
Would vex one more a thousand times.
Till critics blame, and judges praise,
The poet cannot claim his bays.
On me when dunces are satiric,
I take it for a panegyric.
Hated by fools, and fools to hate,
Be that my motto, and my fate.

Directions for Making a Birth-Day Song. 1729

To form a just and finish'd piece,
Take twenty gods of Rome or Greece,
Whose godships are in chief request,
And fit your present subject best;
And, should it be your hero's case,
To have both male and female race,
Your business must be to provide
A score of goddesses beside.
    Some call their monarchs sons of Saturn,
For which they bring a modern pattern;
Because they might have heard of one,
Who often long'd to eat his son;
But this I think will not go down,
For here the father kept his crown.
    Why, then, appoint him son of Jove,
Who met his mother in a grove;
To this we freely shall consent,
Well knowing what the poets meant;
And in their sense, 'twixt me and you,
It may be literally true.
    Next, as the laws of verse require,
He must be greater than his sire;
For Jove, as every schoolboy knows,
Was able Saturn to depose;
And sure no Christian poet breathing
Would be more scrupulous than a Heathen;
Or, if to blasphemy it tends.
That's but a trifle among friends.
    Your hero now another Mars is,
Makes mighty armies turn their a—s:
Behold his glittering falchion mow
Whole squadrons at a single blow;
While Victory, with wings outspread,
Flies, like an eagle, o'er his head;
His milk-white steed upon its haunches,

Or pawing into dead men's paunches;
As Overton has drawn his sire,
Still seen o'er many an alehouse fire.
Then from his arm hoarse thunder rolls,
As loud as fifty mustard bowls;
For thunder still his arm supplies,
And lightning always in his eyes.
They both are cheap enough in conscience,
And serve to echo rattling nonsense.
The rumbling words march fierce along,
Made trebly dreadful in your song.
Sweet poet, hired for birth-day rhymes,
To sing of wars, choose peaceful times.
What though, for fifteen years and more,
Janus has lock'd his temple-door;
Though not a coffeehouse we read in
Has mention'd arms on this side Sweden;
Nor London Journals, nor the Postmen,
Though fond of warlike lies as most men;
Thou still with battles stuff thy head full:
For, must thy hero not be dreadful?
Dismissing Mars, it next must follow
Your conqueror is become Apollo:
That he's Apollo is as plain as
That Robin Walpole is Mæcenas;
But that he struts, and that he squints,
You'd know him by Apollo's prints.
Old Phoebus is but half as bright,
For yours can shine both day and night.
The first, perhaps, may once an age
Inspire you with poetic rage;
Your Phoebus Royal, every day,
Not only can inspire, but pay.
Then make this new Apollo sit
Sole patron, judge, and god of wit.
"How from his altitude he stoops
To raise up Virtue when she droops;
On Learning how his bounty flows,
And with what justice he bestows;

Fair Isis, and ye banks of Cam!
Be witness if I tell a flam,
What prodigies in arts we drain,
From both your streams, in George's reign.
As from the flowery bed of Nile"—
But here's enough to show your style.
Broad innuendoes, such as this,
If well applied, can hardly miss:
For, when you bring your song in print,
He'll get it read, and take the hint;
(It must be read before 'tis warbled,
The paper gilt and cover marbled.)
And will be so much more your debtor,
Because he never knew a letter.
And, as he hears his wit and sense
(To which he never made pretence)
Set out in hyperbolic strains,
A guinea shall reward your pains;
For patrons never pay so well,
As when they scarce have learn'd to spell.
Next call him Neptune: with his trident
He rules the sea: you see him ride in't;
And, if provoked, he soundly firks his
Rebellious waves with rods, like Xerxes.
He would have seized the Spanish plate,
Had not the fleet gone out too late;
And in their very ports besiege them,
But that he would not disoblige them;
And make the rascals pay him dearly
For those affronts they give him yearly.
'Tis not denied, that, when we write,
Our ink is black, our paper white:
And, when we scrawl our paper o'er,
We blacken what was white before:
I think this practice only fit
For dealers in satiric wit.
But you some white-lead ink must get
And write on paper black as jet;
Your interest lies to learn the knack

Of whitening what before was black.
    Thus your encomium, to be strong,
Must be applied directly wrong.
A tyrant for his mercy praise,
And crown a royal dunce with bays:
A squinting monkey load with charms,
And paint a coward fierce in arms.
Is he to avarice inclined?
Extol him for his generous mind:
And, when we starve for want of corn,
Come out with Amalthea's horn:
For all experience this evinces
The only art of pleasing princes:
For princes' love you should descant
On virtues which they know they want.
One compliment I had forgot,
But songsters must omit it not;
I freely grant the thought is old:
Why, then, your hero must be told,
In him such virtues lie inherent,
To qualify him God's vicegerent;
That with no title to inherit,
He must have been a king by merit.
Yet, be the fancy old or new,
Tis partly false, and partly true:
And, take it right, it means no more
Than George and William claim'd before.
    Should some obscure inferior fellow,
Like Julius, or the youth of Pella,
When all your list of Gods is out,
Presume to show his mortal snout,
And as a Deity intrude,
Because he had the world subdued;
O, let him not debase your thoughts,
Or name him but to tell his faults.—
    Of Gods I only quote the best,
But you may hook in all the rest.
    Now, birth-day bard, with joy proceed
To praise your empress and her breed;

First of the first, to vouch your lies,
Bring all the females of the skies;
The Graces, and their mistress, Venus,
Must venture down to entertain us:
With bended knees when they adore her,
What dowdies they appear before her!
Nor shall we think you talk at random,
For Venus might be her great-grandam:
Six thousand years has lived the Goddess,
Your heroine hardly fifty odd is;
Besides, your songsters oft have shown
That she has Graces of her own:
Three Graces by Lucina brought her,
Just three, and every Grace a daughter;
Here many a king his heart and crown
Shall at their snowy feet lay down:
In royal robes, they come by dozens
To court their English German cousins:
Beside a pair of princely babies,
That, five years hence, will both be Hebes.
    Now see her seated in her throne
With genuine lustre, all her own:
Poor Cynthia never shone so bright,
Her splendour is but borrow'd light;
And only with her brother linkt
Can shine, without him is extinct.
But Carolina shines the clearer
With neither spouse nor brother near her:
And darts her beams o'er both our isles,
Though George is gone a thousand miles.
Thus Berecynthia takes her place,
Attended by her heavenly race;
And sees a son in every God,
Unawed by Jove's all-shaking nod.
    Now sing his little highness Freddy
Who struts like any king already:
With so much beauty, show me any maid
That could resist this charming Ganymede!
Where majesty with sweetness vies,

And, like his father, early wise.
Then cut him out a world of work,
To conquer Spain, and quell the Turk:
Foretel his empire crown'd with bays,
And golden times, and halcyon days;
And swear his line shall rule the nation
For ever—till the conflagration.

But, now it comes into my mind,
We left a little duke behind;
A Cupid in his face and size,
And only wants, to want his eyes.
Make some provision for the younker,
Find him a kingdom out to conquer;
Prepare a fleet to waft him o'er,
Make Gulliver his commodore;
Into whose pocket valiant Willy put,
Will soon subdue the realm of Lilliput.

A skilful critic justly blames
Hard, tough, crank, guttural, harsh, stiff names
The sense can ne'er be too jejune,
But smooth your words to fit the tune.
Hanover may do well enough,
But George and Brunswick are too rough;
Hesse-Darmstadt makes a rugged sound,
And Guelp the strongest ear will wound.
In vain are all attempts from Germany
To find out proper words for harmony:
And yet I must except the Rhine,
Because it clinks to Caroline.
Hail, queen of Britain, queen of rhymes!
Be sung ten hundred thousand times;
Too happy were the poets' crew,
If their own happiness they knew:
Three syllables did never meet
So soft, so sliding, and so sweet:
Nine other tuneful words like that
Would prove even Homer's numbers flat.
Behold three beauteous vowels stand,
With bridegroom liquids hand in hand;

In concord here for ever fix'd,
No jarring consonant betwixt.
    May Caroline continue long,
For ever fair and young!—in song.
What though the royal carcass must,
Squeezed in a coffin, turn to dust?
Those elements her name compose,
Like atoms, are exempt from blows.
    Though Caroline may fill your gaps,
Yet still you must consult your maps;
Find rivers with harmonious names,
Sabrina, Medway, and the Thames,
Britannia long will wear like steel,
But Albion's cliffs are out at heel;
And Patience can endure no more
To hear the Belgic lion roar.
Give up the phrase of haughty Gaul,
But proud Iberia soundly maul:
Restore the ships by Philip taken,
And make him crouch to save his bacon.
Nassau, who got the name of Glorious,
Because he never was victorious,
A hanger-on has always been;
For old acquaintance bring him in.
    To Walpole you might lend a line,
But much I fear he's in decline;
And if you chance to come too late,
When he goes out, you share his fate,
And bear the new successor's frown;
Or, whom you once sang up, sing down.
Reject with scorn that stupid notion,
To praise your hero for devotion;
Nor entertain a thought so odd,
That princes should believe in God;
But follow the securest rule,
And turn it all to ridicule:
'Tis grown the choicest wit at court,
And gives the maids of honour sport;
For, since they talk'd with Dr. Clarke,

They now can venture in the dark:
That sound divine the truth has spoke all,
And pawn'd his word, Hell is not local.
This will not give them half the trouble
Of bargains sold, or meanings double.
    Supposing now your song is done,
To Mynheer Handel next you run,
Who artfully will pare and prune
Your words to some Italian tune:
Then print it in the largest letter,
With capitals, the more the better.
Present it boldly on your knee,
And take a guinea for your fee.

The Pheasant and the Lark
A Fable by Dr. Delany
1730

—quis iniquae
Tam patiens urbis, tam ferreus, ut teneat se?

—*Juv.* i, 30

In ancient times, as bards indite,
(If clerks have conn'd the records right.)
A peacock reign'd, whose glorious sway
His subjects with delight obey:
His tail was beauteous to behold,
Replete with goodly eyes and gold;
Fair emblem of that monarch's guise,
Whose train at once is rich and wise;
And princely ruled he many regions,
And statesmen wise, and valiant legions.
    A pheasant lord, above the rest,
With every grace and talent blest,
Was sent to sway, with all his skill,
The sceptre of a neighbouring hill.
No science was to him unknown,
For all the arts were all his own:
In all the living learned read,
Though more delighted with the dead:
For birds, if ancient tales say true,
Had then their Popes and Homers too;
Could read and write in prose and verse,
And speak like ***, and build like Pearce.
He knew their voices, and their wings,
Who smoothest soars, who sweetest sings;
Who toils with ill-fledged pens to climb,
And who attain'd the true sublime.
Their merits he could well descry,
He had so exquisite an eye;
And when that fail'd to show them clear,

He had as exquisite an ear;
It chanced as on a day he stray'd
Beneath an academic shade,
He liked, amidst a thousand throats,
The wildness of a Woodlark's notes,
And search'd, and spied, and seized his game,
And took him home, and made him tame;
Found him on trial true and able,
So cheer'd and fed him at his table.
    Here some shrewd critic finds I'm caught,
And cries out, "Better fed than taught"—Then
jests on game and tame, and reads,
And jests, and so my tale proceeds.
    Long had he studied in the wood,
Conversing with the wise and good:
His soul with harmony inspired,
With love of truth and virtue fired:
His brethren's good and Maker's praise
Were all the study of his lays;
Were all his study in retreat,
And now employ'd him with the great.
His friendship was the sure resort
Of all the wretched at the court;
But chiefly merit in distress
His greatest blessing was to bless.—
    This fix'd him in his patron's breast,
But fired with envy all the rest:
I mean that noisy, craving crew,
Who round the court incessant flew,
And prey'd like rooks, by pairs and dozens,
To fill the maws of sons and cousins:
"Unmoved their heart, and chill'd their blood
To every thought of common good,
Confining every hope and care,
To their own low, contracted sphere."
These ran him down with ceaseless cry,
But found it hard to tell you why,
Till his own worth and wit supplied
Sufficient matter to deride:

"'Tis envy's safest, surest rule,
To hide her rage in ridicule:
The vulgar eye she best beguiles,
When all her snakes are deck'd with smiles:
Sardonic smiles, by rancour raised!
Tormented most when seeming pleased!"
Their spite had more than half expired,
Had he not wrote what all admired;
What morsels had their malice wanted,
But that he built, and plann'd, and planted!
How had his sense and learning grieved them,
But that his charity relieved them!
    "At highest worth dull malice reaches,
As slugs pollute the fairest peaches:
Envy defames, as harpies vile
Devour the food they first defile."
    Now ask the fruit of all his favour—
"He was not hitherto a saver."—
What then could make their rage run mad?
"Why, what he hoped, not what he had."
    "What tyrant e'er invented ropes,
Or racks, or rods, to punish hopes?
Th' inheritance of hope and fame
Is seldom Earthly Wisdom's aim;
Or, if it were, is not so small,
But there is room enough for all."
    If he but chance to breathe a song,
(He seldom sang, and never long,)
The noisy, rude, malignant crowd,
Where it was high, pronounced it loud:
Plain Truth was Pride; and, what was sillier,
Easy and Friendly was Familiar.
    Or, if he tuned his lofty lays,
With solemn air to Virtue's praise,
Alike abusive and erroneous,
They call'd it hoarse and inharmonious.
Yet so it was to souls like theirs,
Tuneless as Abel to the bears!
    A Rook with harsh malignant caw

Began, was follow'd by a Daw;
(Though some, who would be thought to know,
Are positive it was a crow:)
Jack Daw was seconded by Tit,
Tom Tit could write, and so he writ;
A tribe of tuneless praters follow,
The Jay, the Magpie, and the Swallow;
And twenty more their throats let loose,
Down to the witless, waddling Goose.
Some peck'd at him, some flew, some flutter'd,
Some hiss'd, some scream'd, and others mutter'd:
The Crow, on carrion wont to feast,
The Carrion Crow, condemn'd his taste:
The Rook, in earnest too, not joking,
Swore all his singing was but croaking.
Some thought they meant to show their wit,
Might think so still—"but that they writ"—
Could it be spite or envy?—"No—
Who did no ill could have no foe."—
So wise Simplicity esteem'd;
Quite otherwise True Wisdom deem'd;
This question rightly understood,
"What more provokes than doing good?
A soul ennobled and refined
Reproaches every baser mind:
As strains exalted and melodious
Make every meaner music odious."—
At length the Nightingale was heard,
For voice and wisdom long revered,
Esteem'd of all the wise and good,
The Guardian Genius of the wood:
He long in discontent retired,
Yet not obscured, but more admired:
His brethren's servile souls disdaining,
He lived indignant and complaining:
They now afresh provoke his choler,
(It seems the Lark had been his scholar,
A favourite scholar always near him,
And oft had waked whole nights to hear him.)

Enraged he canvasses the matter,
Exposes all their senseless chatter,
Shows him and them in such a light,
As more inflames, yet quells their spite.
They hear his voice, and frighted fly,
For rage had raised it very high:
Shamed by the wisdom of his notes,
They hide their heads, and hush their throats.

Answer to Dr. Delany's Fable of the Pheasant and Lark
1730

In ancient times, the wise were able
In proper terms to write a fable:
Their tales would always justly suit
The characters of every brute.
The ass was dull, the lion brave,
The stag was swift, the fox a knave;
The daw a thief, the ape a droll,
The hound would scent, the wolf would prowl:
A pigeon would, if shown by Æsop,
Fly from the hawk, or pick his pease up.
Far otherwise a great divine
Has learnt his fables to refine;
He jumbles men and birds together,
As if they all were of a feather:
You see him first the Peacock bring,
Against all rules, to be a king;
That in his tail he wore his eyes,
By which he grew both rich and wise.
Now, pray, observe the doctor's choice,
A Peacock chose for flight and voice;
Did ever mortal see a peacock
Attempt a flight above a haycock?
And for his singing, doctor, you know
Himself complain'd of it to Juno.
He squalls in such a hellish noise,
He frightens all the village boys.
This Peacock kept a standing force,
In regiments of foot and horse:
Had statesmen too of every kind,
Who waited on his eyes behind;
And this was thought the highest post;
For, rule the rump, you rule the roast.
The doctor names but one at present,
And he of all birds was a Pheasant.

This Pheasant was a man of wit,
Could read all books were ever writ;
And, when among companions privy,
Could quote you Cicero and Livy.
Birds, as he says, and I allow,
Were scholars then, as we are now;
Could read all volumes up to folios,
And feed on fricassees and olios:
This Pheasant, by the Peacock's will,
Was viceroy of a neighbouring hill;
And, as he wander'd in his park,
He chanced to spy a clergy Lark;
Was taken with his person outward,
So prettily he pick'd a cow-t—d:
Then in a net the Pheasant caught him,
And in his palace fed and taught him.
The moral of the tale is pleasant,
Himself the Lark, my lord the Pheasant:
A lark he is, and such a lark
As never came from Noah's ark:
And though he had no other notion,
But building, planning, and devotion;
Though 'tis a maxim you must know,
"Who does no ill can have no foe;"
Yet how can I express in words
The strange stupidity of birds?
This Lark was hated in the wood,
Because he did his brethren good.
At last the Nightingale comes in,
To hold the doctor by the chin:
We all can find out what he means,
The worst of disaffected deans:
Whose wit at best was next to none,
And now that little next is gone;
Against the court is always blabbing,
And calls the senate-house a cabin;
So dull, that but for spleen and spite,
We ne'er should know that he could write
Who thinks the nation always err'd,

Because himself is not preferr'd;
His heart is through his libel seen,
Nor could his malice spare the queen;
Who, had she known his vile behaviour,
Would ne'er have shown him so much favour.
A noble lord has told his pranks,
And well deserves the nation's thanks.
O! would the senate deign to show
Resentment on this public foe,
Our Nightingale might fit a cage;
There let him starve, and vent his rage:
Or would they but in fetters bind
This enemy of human kind!
Harmonious Coffee, show thy zeal,
Thou champion for the commonweal:
Nor on a theme like this repine,
For once to wet thy pen divine:
Bestow that libeller a lash,
Who daily vends seditious trash:
Who dares revile the nation's wisdom,
But in the praise of virtue is dumb:
That scribbler lash, who neither knows
The turn of verse, nor style of prose;
Whose malice, for the worst of ends,
Would have us lose our English friends:
Who never had one public thought,
Nor ever gave the poor a groat.
One clincher more, and I have done,
I end my labours with a pun.
Jove send this Nightingale may fall,
Who spends his day and night in gall!
So, Nightingale and Lark, adieu;
I see the greatest owls in you
That ever screech'd, or ever flew.

Dean Smedley's Petition to the Duke of Grafton

Non domus et fundus, non aeris acervus et auri.

—Hor. *Epist.*, I, ii, 47

It was, my lord, the dexterous shift
Of t'other Jonathan, viz. Swift,
But now St. Patrick's saucy dean,
With silver verge, and surplice clean,
Of Oxford, or of Ormond's grace,
In looser rhyme to beg a place.
A place he got, yclept a stall,
And eke a thousand pounds withal;
And were he less a witty writer,
He might as well have got a mitre.
  Thus I, the Jonathan of Clogher,
In humble lays my thanks to offer,
Approach your grace with grateful heart,
My thanks and verse both void of art,
Content with what your bounty gave,
No larger income do I crave:
Rejoicing that, in better times,
Grafton requires my loyal lines.
Proud! while my patron is polite,
I likewise to the patriot write!
Proud! that at once I can commend
King George's and the Muses' friend!
Endear'd to Britain; and to thee
(Disjoin'd, Hibernia, by the sea)
Endear'd by twice three anxious years,
Employ'd in guardian toils and cares;
By love, by wisdom, and by skill;
For he has saved thee 'gainst thy will.
  But where shall Smedley make his nest,
And lay his wandering head to rest?
Where shall he find a decent house,

To treat his friends and cheer his spouse?
O! tack, my lord, some pretty cure,
In wholesome soil, and ether pure;
The garden stored with artless flowers,
In either angle shady bowers.
No gay parterre, with costly green,
Within the ambient hedge be seen:
Let Nature freely take her course,
Nor fear from me ungrateful force;
No shears shall check her sprouting vigour,
Nor shape the yews to antic figure:
A limpid brook shall trout supply,
In May, to take the mimic fly;
Round a small orchard may it run,
Whose apples redden to the sun.
Let all be snug, and warm, and neat;
For fifty turn'd a safe retreat,
A little Euston may it be,
Euston I'll carve on every tree.
But then, to keep it in repair,
My lord—twice fifty pounds a-year
Will barely do; but if your grace
Could make them hundreds—charming place!
Thou then wouldst show another face.
    Clogher! far north, my lord, it lies,
'Midst snowy hills, inclement skies:
One shivers with the arctic wind,
One hears the polar axis grind.
Good John indeed, with beef and claret,
Makes the place warm, that one may bear it.
He has a purse to keep a table,
And eke a soul as hospitable.
My heart is good; but assets fail,
To fight with storms of snow and hail.
Besides, the country's thin of people,
Who seldom meet but at the steeple:
The strapping dean, that's gone to Down,
Ne'er named the thing without a frown,
When, much fatigued with sermon study,

He felt his brain grow dull and muddy;
No fit companion could be found,
To push the lazy bottle round:
Sure then, for want of better folks
To pledge, his clerk was orthodox.
    Ah! how unlike to Gerard Street,
Where beaux and belles in parties meet;
Where gilded chairs and coaches throng,
And jostle as they troll along;
Where tea and coffee hourly flow,
And gape-seed does in plenty grow;
And Griz (no clock more certain) cries,
Exact at seven, "Hot mutton-pies!"
There Lady Luna in her sphere
Once shone, when Paunceforth was not near;
But now she wanes, and, as 'tis said,
Keeps sober hours, and goes to bed.
There—but 'tis endless to write down
All the amusements of the town;
And spouse will think herself quite undone,
To trudge to Connor from sweet London;
And care we must our wives to please,
Or else—we shall be ill at ease.
    You see, my lord, what 'tis I lack,
'Tis only some convenient tack,
Some parsonage-house with garden sweet,
To be my late, my last retreat;
A decent church, close by its side,
There, preaching, praying, to reside;
And as my time securely rolls,
To save my own and other souls.

The Duke's Answer
By Dr. Swift

Dear Smed, I read thy brilliant lines,
Where wit in all its glory shines;
Where compliments, with all their pride,
Are by their numbers dignified:
I hope to make you yet as clean
As that same Viz, St. Patrick's dean.
I'll give thee surplice, verge, and stall,
And may be something else withal;
And, were you not so good a writer,
I should present you with a mitre.
Write worse, then, if you can—be wise-
Believe me, 'tis the way to rise.
Talk not of making of thy nest:
Ah! never lay thy head to rest!
That head so well with wisdom fraught,
That writes without the toil of thought!
While others rack their busy brains,
You are not in the least at pains.
Down to your dean'ry now repair,
And build a castle in the air.
I'm sure a man of your fine sense
Can do it with a small expense.
There your dear spouse and you together
May breathe your bellies full of ether,
When Lady Luna is your neighbour,
She'll help your wife when she's in labour,
Well skill'd in midwife artifices,
For she herself oft falls in pieces.
There you shall see a raree show
Will make you scorn this world below,
When you behold the milky-way,
As white as snow, as bright as day;
The glittering constellations roll
About the grinding arctic pole;
The lovely tingling in your ears,

Wrought by the music of the spheres—
Your spouse shall then no longer hector,
You need not fear a curtain-lecture;
Nor shall she think that she is undone
For quitting her beloved London.
When she's exalted in the skies,
She'll never think of mutton-pies;
When you're advanced above Dean Viz,
You'll never think of Goody Griz;
But ever, ever live at ease,
And strive, and strive your wife to please;
In her you'll centre all your joys,
And get ten thousand girls and boys;
Ten thousand girls and boys you'll get,
And they like stars shall rise and set.
While you and spouse, transform'd, shall soon
Be a new sun and a new moon:
Nor shall you strive your horns to hide,
For then your horns shall be your pride.

Parody on a Character of Dean Smedley, Written in Latin by Himself

The very reverend Dean Smedley,
Of dulness, pride, conceit, a medley,
Was equally allow'd to shine
As poet, scholar, and divine;
With godliness could well dispense,
Would be a rake, but wanted sense;
Would strictly after Truth inquire,
Because he dreaded to come nigh her.
For Liberty no champion bolder,
He hated bailiffs at his shoulder.
To half the world a standing jest,
A perfect nuisance to the rest;
From many (and we may believe him)
Had the best wishes they could give him.
To all mankind a constant friend,
Provided they had cash to lend.
One thing he did before he went hence,
He left us a laconic sentence,
By cutting of his phrase, and trimming
To prove that bishops were old women.
Poor Envy durst not show her phiz,
She was so terrified at his.
He waded, without any shame,
Through thick and thin to get a name,
Tried every sharping trick for bread,
And after all he seldom sped.
When Fortune favour'd, he was nice;
He never once would cog the dice;
But, if she turn'd against his play,
He knew to stop *à quatre trois*.
Now sound in mind, and sound in *corpus*,
(Says he) though swell'd like any porpoise,
He hies from hence at forty-four
(But by his leave he sinks a score)
To the East Indies, there to cheat,

Till he can purchase an estate;
Where, after he has fill'd his chest,
He'll mount his tub, and preach his best,
And plainly prove, by dint of text,
This world is his, and theirs the next.
Lest that the reader should not know
The bank where last he set his toe,
'Twas Greenwich. There he took a ship,
And gave his creditors the slip.
But lest chronology should vary,
Upon the ides of February,
In seventeen hundred eight-and-twenty,
To Fort St. George, a pedler went he.
Ye Fates, when all he gets is spent,
RETURN HIM BEGGAR AS HE WENT!

Cadenus and Vanessa
1713

The shepherds and the nymphs were seen
Pleading before the Cyprian queen.
The counsel for the fair began,
Accusing the false creature Man.
The brief with weighty crimes was charged
On which the pleader much enlarged;
That Cupid now has lost his art,
Or blunts the point of every dart;—
His altar now no longer smokes,
His mother's aid no youth invokes:
This tempts freethinkers to refine,
And bring in doubt their powers divine;
Now love is dwindled to intrigue,
And marriage grown a money league;
Which crimes aforesaid (with her leave)
Were (as he humbly did conceive)
Against our sovereign lady's peace,
Against the statute in that case,
Against her dignity and crown:
Then pray'd an answer, and sat down.
    The nymphs with scorn beheld their foes;
When the defendant's counsel rose,
And, what no lawyer ever lack'd,
With impudence own'd all the fact;
But, what the gentlest heart would vex,
Laid all the fault on t'other sex.
That modern love is no such thing
As what those ancient poets sing:
A fire celestial, chaste, refined,
Conceived and kindled in the mind;
Which, having found an equal flame,
Unites, and both become the same,
In different breasts together burn,
Together both to ashes turn.
But women now feel no such fire,

And only know the gross desire.
Their passions move in lower spheres,
Where'er caprice or folly steers,
A dog, a parrot, or an ape,
Or some worse brute in human shape,
Engross the fancies of the fair,
The few soft moments they can spare,
From visits to receive and pay,
From scandal, politics, and play;
From fans, and flounces, and brocades,
From equipage and park parades,
From all the thousand female toys,
From every trifle that employs
The out or inside of their heads,
Between their toilets and their beds.
    In a dull stream, which moving slow,
You hardly see the current flow;
If a small breeze obstruct the course,
It whirls about, for want of force,
And in its narrow circle gathers
Nothing but chaff, and straws, and feathers.
The current of a female mind
Stops thus, and turns with every wind:
Thus whirling round together draws
Fools, fops, and rakes, for chaff and straws.
Hence we conclude, no women's hearts
Are won by virtue, wit, and parts:
Nor are the men of sense to blame,
For breasts incapable of flame;
The faults must on the nymphs be placed
Grown so corrupted in their taste.
    The pleader having spoke his best,
Had witness ready to attest,
Who fairly could on oath depose,
When questions on the fact arose,
That every article was true;
Nor further those deponents knew:
Therefore he humbly would insist,
The bill might be with costs dismiss'd.

The cause appear'd of so much weight,
That Venus, from her judgment seat,
Desired them not to talk so loud,
Else she must interpose a cloud:
For if the heavenly folks should know
These pleadings in the courts below,
That mortals here disdain to love,
She ne'er could show her face above;
For gods, their betters, are too wise
To value that which men despise.
And then, said she, my son and I
Must stroll in air, 'twixt land and sky;
Or else, shut out from heaven and earth,
Fly to the sea, my place of birth:
There live with daggled mermaids pent,
And keep on fish perpetual Lent.
    But since the case appear'd so nice,
She thought it best to take advice.
The Muses, by the king's permission,
Though foes to love, attend the session,
And on the right hand took their places
In order; on the left, the Graces:
To whom she might her doubts propose
On all emergencies that rose.
The Muses oft were seen to frown;
The Graces half ashamed look'd down;
And 'twas observed, there were but few
Of either sex among the crew,
Whom she or her assessors knew.
The goddess soon began to see,
Things were not ripe for a decree;
And said, she must consult her books,
The lovers' Fletas, Bractons, Cokes.
First to a dapper clerk she beckon'd
To turn to Ovid, book the second:
She then referr'd them to a place
In Virgil, *vide* Dido's case:
As for Tibullus's reports,
They never pass'd for law in courts:

For Cowley's briefs, and pleas of Waller,
Still their authority was smaller.
　There was on both sides much to say:
She'd hear the cause another day;
And so she did; and then a third;
She heard it—there she kept her word:
But, with rejoinders or replies,
Long bills, and answers stuff'd with lies,
Demur, imparlance, and essoign,
The parties ne'er could issue join:
For sixteen years the cause was spun,
And then stood where it first begun.
　Now, gentle Clio, sing, or say
What Venus meant by this delay?
The goddess much perplex'd in mind
To see her empire thus declined,
When first this grand debate arose,
Above her wisdom to compose,
Conceived a project in her head
To work her ends; which, if it sped,
Would show the merits of the cause
Far better than consulting laws.
　In a glad hour Lucina's aid
Produced on earth a wondrous maid,
On whom the Queen of Love was bent
To try a new experiment.
She threw her law-books on the shelf,
And thus debated with herself.
　Since men allege, they ne'er can find
Those beauties in a female mind,
Which raise a flame that will endure
For ever uncorrupt and pure;
If 'tis with reason they complain,
This infant shall restore my reign.
I'll search where every virtue dwells,
From courts inclusive down to cells:
What preachers talk, or sages write;
These will I gather and unite,
And represent them to mankind

Collected in that infant's mind.
    This said, she plucks in Heaven's high bowers
A sprig of amaranthine flowers.
In nectar thrice infuses bays,
Three times refined in Titan's rays;
Then calls the Graces to her aid,
And sprinkles thrice the newborn maid:
From whence the tender skin assumes
A sweetness above all perfumes:
From whence a cleanliness remains,
Incapable of outward stains:
From whence that decency of mind,
So lovely in the female kind,
Where not one careless thought intrudes;
Less modest than the speech of prudes;
Where never blush was call'd in aid,
That spurious virtue in a maid,
A virtue but at second-hand;
They blush because they understand.
    The Graces next would act their part,
And show'd but little of their art;
Their work was half already done,
The child with native beauty shone;
The outward form no help required:
Each, breathing on her thrice, inspired
That gentle, soft, engaging air,
Which in old times adorn'd the fair:
And said, "Vanessa be the name
By which thou shall be known to fame:
Vanessa, by the gods enroll'd:
Her name on earth shall not be told."
    But still the work was not complete;
When Venus thought on a deceit.
Drawn by her doves, away she flies,
And finds out Pallas in the skies.
Dear Pallas, I have been this morn
To see a lovely infant born:
A boy in yonder isle below,
So like my own without his bow,

By beauty could your heart be won,
You'd swear it is Apollo's son;
But it shall ne'er be said, a child
So hopeful, has by me been spoil'd:
I have enough besides to spare,
And give him wholly to your care.
    Wisdom's above suspecting wiles;
The Queen of Learning gravely smiles,
Down from Olympus comes with joy,
Mistakes Vanessa for a boy;
Then sows within her tender mind
Seeds long unknown to womankind:
For manly bosoms chiefly fit,
The seeds of knowledge, judgment, wit.
Her soul was suddenly endued
With justice, truth, and fortitude;
With honour, which no breath can stain,
Which malice must attack in vain;
With open heart and bounteous hand.
But Pallas here was at a stand;
She knew, in our degenerate days,
Bare virtue could not live on praise;
That meat must be with money bought:
She therefore, upon second thought,
Infused, yet as it were by stealth,
Some small regard for state and wealth;
Of which, as she grew up, there staid
A tincture in the prudent maid:
She managed her estate with care,
Yet liked three footmen to her chair.
But, lest he should neglect his studies
Like a young heir, the thrifty goddess
(For fear young master should be spoil'd)
Would use him like a younger child;
And, after long computing, found
'Twould come to just five thousand pound.
    The Queen of Love was pleased, and proud,
To see Vanessa thus endow'd:
She doubted not but such a dame

Through every breast would dart a flame,
That every rich and lordly swain
With pride would drag about her chain;
That scholars would forsake their books,
To study bright Vanessa's looks;
As she advanced, that womankind
Would by her model form their mind,
And all their conduct would be tried
By her, as an unerring guide;
Offending daughters oft would hear
Vanessa's praise rung in their ear:
Miss Betty, when she does a fault,
Lets fall her knife, or spills the salt,
Will thus be by her mother chid,
"'Tis what Vanessa never did!"
Thus by the nymphs and swains adored,
My power shall be again restored,
And happy lovers bless my reign—
So Venus hoped, but hoped in vain.
    For when in time the Martial Maid
Found out the trick that Venus play'd,
She shakes her helm, she knits her brows,
And, fired with indignation, vows,
To-morrow, ere the setting sun,
She'd all undo that she had done.
    But in the poets we may find
A wholesome law, time out of mind,
Had been confirm'd by Fate's decree,
That gods, of whatsoe'er degree,
Resume not what themselves have given,
Or any brother god in Heaven:
Which keeps the peace among the gods,
Or they must always be at odds:
And Pallas, if she broke the laws,
Must yield her foe the stronger cause;
A shame to one so much adored
For wisdom at Jove's council-board.
Besides, she fear'd the Queen of Love
Would meet with better friends above.

And though she must with grief reflect,
To see a mortal virgin deck'd
With graces hitherto unknown
To female breasts, except her own:
Yet she would act as best became
A goddess of unspotted fame.
She knew, by augury divine,
Venus would fail in her design:
She studied well the point, and found
Her foe's conclusions were not sound,
From premises erroneous brought,
And therefore the deduction's naught,
And must have contrary effects,
To what her treacherous foe expects.
　　In proper season Pallas meets
The Queen of Love, whom thus she greets,
(For gods, we are by Homer told,
Can in celestial language scold:)—
Perfidious goddess! but in vain
You form'd this project in your brain;
A project for your talents fit,
With much deceit and little wit.
Thou hast, as thou shall quickly see,
Deceived thyself, instead of me;
For how can heavenly wisdom prove
An instrument to earthly love?
Know'st thou not yet, that men commence
Thy votaries for want of sense?
Nor shall Vanessa be the theme
To manage thy abortive scheme:
She'll prove the greatest of thy foes;
And yet I scorn to interpose,
But, using neither skill nor force,
Leave all things to their natural course.
　　The goddess thus pronounced her doom:
When, lo! Vanessa in her bloom
Advanced, like Atalanta's star,
But rarely seen, and seen from far:
In a new world with caution slept,

Watch'd all the company she kept,
Well knowing, from the books she read,
What dangerous paths young virgins tread:
Would seldom at the Park appear,
Nor saw the play-house twice a year;
Yet, not incurious, was inclined
To know the converse of mankind.
    First issued from perfumers' shops,
A crowd of fashionable fops:
They ask'd her how she liked the play;
Then told the tattle of the day;
A duel fought last night at two,
About a lady—you know who;
Mention'd a new Italian, come
Either from Muscovy or Rome;
Gave hints of who and who's together;
Then fell to talking of the weather;
Last night was so extremely fine,
The ladies walk'd till after nine:
Then, in soft voice and speech absurd,
With nonsense every second word,
With fustian from exploded plays,
They celebrate her beauty's praise;
Run o'er their cant of stupid lies,
And tell the murders of her eyes.
    With silent scorn Vanessa sat,
Scarce listening to their idle chat;
Farther than sometimes by a frown,
When they grew pert, to pull them down.
At last she spitefully was bent
To try their wisdom's full extent;
And said, she valued nothing less
Than titles, figure, shape, and dress;
That merit should be chiefly placed
In judgment, knowledge, wit, and taste;
And these, she offer'd to dispute,
Alone distinguish'd man from brute:
That present times have no pretence
To virtue, in the noble sense

By Greeks and Romans understood,
To perish for our country's good.
She named the ancient heroes round,
Explain'd for what they were renown'd;
Then spoke with censure or applause
Of foreign customs, rites, and laws;
Through nature and through art she ranged
And gracefully her subject changed;
In vain! her hearers had no share
In all she spoke, except to stare.
Their judgment was, upon the whole,
—That lady is the dullest soul!—
Then tapt their forehead in a jeer,
As who should say—She wants it here!
She may be handsome, young, and rich,
But none will burn her for a witch!
    A party next of glittering dames,
From round the purlieus of St. James,
Came early, out of pure good will,
To see the girl in dishabille.
Their clamour, 'lighting from their chairs
Grew louder all the way up stairs;
At entrance loudest, where they found
The room with volumes litter'd round.
Vanessa held Montaigne, and read,
While Mrs. Susan comb'd her head.
They call'd for tea and chocolate,
And fell into their usual chat,
Discoursing with important face,
On ribbons, fans, and gloves, and lace;
Show'd patterns just from India brought,
And gravely ask'd her what she thought,
Whether the red or green were best,
And what they cost? Vanessa guess'd
As came into her fancy first;
Named half the rates, and liked the worst.
To scandal next—What awkward thing
Was that last Sunday in the ring?
I'm sorry Mopsa breaks so fast:

I said her face would never last.
Corinna, with that youthful air,
Is thirty, and a bit to spare:
Her fondness for a certain earl
Began when I was but a girl!
Phillis, who but a month ago
Was married to the Tunbridge beau,
I saw coquetting t'other night
In public with that odious knight!
They rallied next Vanessa's dress:
That gown was made for old Queen Bess.
Dear madam, let me see your head:
Don't you intend to put on red?
A petticoat without a hoop!
Sure, you are not ashamed to stoop!
With handsome garters at your knees,
No matter what a fellow sees.
Filled with disdain, with rage inflamed
Both of herself and sex ashamed,
The nymph stood silent out of spite,
Nor would vouchsafe to set them right.
Away the fair detractors went,
And gave by turns their censures vent.
She's not so handsome in my eyes:
For wit, I wonder where it lies!
She's fair and clean, and that's the most:
But why proclaim her for a toast?
A baby face; no life, no airs,
But what she learn'd at country fairs;
Scarce knows what difference is between
Rich Flanders lace and Colberteen.
I'll undertake, my little Nancy
In flounces has a better fancy;
With all her wit, I would not ask
Her judgment how to buy a mask.
We begg'd her but to patch her face,
She never hit one proper place;
Which every girl at five years old
Can do as soon as she is told.

I own, that out-of-fashion stuff
Becomes the creature well enough.
The girl might pass, if we could get her
To know the world a little better.
(To know the world! a modern phrase
For visits, ombre, balls, and plays.)
    Thus, to the world's perpetual shame,
The Queen of Beauty lost her aim;
Too late with grief she understood
Pallas had done more harm than good;
For great examples are but vain,
Where ignorance begets disdain.
Both sexes, arm'd with guilt and spite,
Against Vanessa's power unite:
To copy her few nymphs aspired;
Her virtues fewer swains admired.
So stars, beyond a certain height,
Give mortals neither heat nor light.
Yet some of either sex, endow'd
With gifts superior to the crowd,
With virtue, knowledge, taste, and wit
She condescended to admit:
With pleasing arts she could reduce
Men's talents to their proper use;
And with address each genius held
To that wherein it most excell'd;
Thus, making others' wisdom known,
Could please them, and improve her own.
A modest youth said something new;
She placed it in the strongest view.
All humble worth she strove to raise,
Would not be praised, yet loved to praise.
The learned met with free approach,
Although they came not in a coach:
Some clergy too she would allow,
Nor quarrell'd at their awkward bow;
But this was for Cadenus' sake,
A gownman of a different make;
Whom Pallas once, Vanessa's tutor,

Had fix'd on for her coadjutor.
    But Cupid, full of mischief, longs
To vindicate his mother's wrongs.
On Pallas all attempts are vain:
One way he knows to give her pain;
Vows on Vanessa's heart to take
Due vengeance, for her patron's sake;
Those early seeds by Venus sown,
In spite of Pallas now were grown;
And Cupid hoped they would improve
By time, and ripen into love.
The boy made use of all his craft,
In vain discharging many a shaft,
Pointed at colonels, lords, and beaux:
Cadenus warded off the blows;
For, placing still some book betwixt,
The darts were in the cover fix'd,
Or, often blunted and recoil'd,
On Plutarch's Moral struck, were spoil'd.
    The Queen of Wisdom could foresee,
But not prevent, the Fates' decree:
And human caution tries in vain
To break that adamantine chain.
Vanessa, though by Pallas taught,
By Love invulnerable thought,
Searching in books for wisdom's aid,
Was, in the very search, betray'd.
    Cupid, though all his darts were lost,
Yet still resolved to spare no cost:
He could not answer to his fame
The triumphs of that stubborn dame,
A nymph so hard to be subdued,
Who neither was coquette nor prude.
I find, said he, she wants a doctor,
Both to adore her, and instruct her:
I'll give her what she most admires
Among those venerable sires.
Cadenus is a subject fit,
Grown old in politics and wit,

Caress'd by ministers of state,
Of half mankind the dread and hate.
Whate'er vexations love attend,
She needs no rivals apprehend.
Her sex, with universal voice,
Must laugh at her capricious choice.
    Cadenus many things had writ:
Vanessa much esteem'd his wit,
And call'd for his poetic works:
Meantime the boy in secret lurks;
And, while the book was in her hand,
The urchin from his private stand
Took aim, and shot with all his strength
A dart of such prodigious length,
It pierced the feeble volume through,
And deep transfix'd her bosom too.
Some lines, more moving than the rest,
Stuck to the point that pierced her breast,
And, borne directly to the heart,
With pains unknown increased her smart.
    Vanessa, not in years a score,
Dreams of a gown of forty-four;
Imaginary charms can find
In eyes with reading almost blind:
Cadenus now no more appears
Declined in health, advanced in years.
She fancies music in his tongue;
Nor farther looks, but thinks him young.
What mariner is not afraid
To venture in a ship decay'd?
What planter will attempt to yoke
A sapling with a falling oak?
As years increase, she brighter shines;
Cadenus with each day declines:
And he must fall a prey to time,
While she continues in her prime.
Cadenus, common forms apart,
In every scene had kept his heart;
Had sigh'd and languish'd, vow'd and writ,

For pastime, or to show his wit,
But books, and time, and state affairs,
Had spoil'd his fashionable airs:
He now could praise, esteem, approve,
But understood not what was love.
His conduct might have made him styled
A father, and the nymph his child.
That innocent delight he took
To see the virgin mind her book,
Was but the master's secret joy
In school to hear the finest boy.
Her knowledge with her fancy grew;
She hourly press'd for something new;
Ideas came into her mind
So fast, his lessons lagg'd behind;
She reason'd, without plodding long,
Nor ever gave her judgment wrong.
But now a sudden change was wrought;
She minds no longer what he taught.
Cadenus was amazed to find
Such marks of a distracted mind:
For, though she seem'd to listen more
To all he spoke, than e'er before,
He found her thoughts would absent range,
Yet guess'd not whence could spring the change.
And first he modestly conjectures
His pupil might be tired with lectures;
Which help'd to mortify his pride,
Yet gave him not the heart to chide:
But, in a mild dejected strain,
At last he ventured to complain:
Said, she should be no longer teazed,
Might have her freedom when she pleased;
Was now convinced he acted wrong
To hide her from the world so long,
And in dull studies to engage
One of her tender sex and age;
That every nymph with envy own'd,
How she might shine in the *grand monde*:

And every shepherd was undone
To see her cloister'd like a nun.
This was a visionary scheme:
He waked, and found it but a dream;
A project far above his skill:
For nature must be nature still.
If he were bolder than became
A scholar to a courtly dame,
She might excuse a man of letters;
Thus tutors often treat their better;
And, since his talk offensive grew,
He came to take his last adieu.
    Vanessa, fill'd with just disdain,
Would still her dignity maintain,
Instructed from her early years
To scorn the art of female tears.
    Had he employ'd his time so long
To teach her what was right and wrong;
Yet could such notions entertain
That all his lectures were in vain?
She own'd the wandering of her thoughts;
But he must answer for her faults.
She well remember'd to her cost,
That all his lessons were not lost.
Two maxims she could still produce,
And sad experience taught their use;
That virtue, pleased by being shown,
Knows nothing which it dares not own;
Can make us without fear disclose
Our inmost secrets to our foes;
That common forms were not design'd
Directors to a noble mind.
Now, said the nymph, to let you see
My actions with your rules agree;
That I can vulgar forms despise,
And have no secrets to disguise;
I knew, by what you said and writ,
How dangerous things were men of wit;
You caution'd me against their charms,

But never gave me equal arms;
Your lessons found the weakest part,
Aim'd at the head, but reach'd the heart.
    Cadenus felt within him rise
Shame, disappointment, guilt, surprise.
He knew not how to reconcile
Such language with her usual style:
And yet her words were so exprest,
He could not hope she spoke in jest.
His thoughts had wholly been confined
To form and cultivate her mind.
He hardly knew, till he was told,
Whether the nymph were young or old;
Had met her in a public place,
Without distinguishing her face;
Much less could his declining age
Vanessa's earliest thoughts engage;
And, if her youth indifference met,
His person must contempt beget;
Or grant her passion be sincere,
How shall his innocence be clear?
Appearances were all so strong,
The world must think him in the wrong;
Would say, he made a treacherous use
Of wit, to flatter and seduce;
The town would swear, he had betray'd
By magic spells the harmless maid:
And every beau would have his joke,
That scholars were like other folk;
And, when Platonic flights were over,
The tutor turn'd a mortal lover!
So tender of the young and fair!
It show'd a true paternal care—
Five thousand guineas in her purse!
The doctor might have fancied worse.—
    Hardly at length he silence broke,
And falter'd every word he spoke;
Interpreting her complaisance,
Just as a man *sans* consequence.

She rallied well, he always knew:
Her manner now was something new;
And what she spoke was in an air
As serious as a tragic player.
But those who aim at ridicule
Should fix upon some certain rule,
Which fairly hints they are in jest,
Else he must enter his protest:
For let a man be ne'er so wise,
He may be caught with sober lies;
A science which he never taught,
And, to be free, was dearly bought;
For, take it in its proper light,
'Tis just what coxcombs call a bite.
But, not to dwell on things minute,
Vanessa finish'd the dispute;
Brought weighty arguments to prove
That reason was her guide in love.
She thought he had himself described,
His doctrines when she first imbibed;
What he had planted, now was grown;
His virtues she might call her own;
As he approves, as he dislikes,
Love or contempt her fancy strikes.
Self-love, in nature rooted fast,
Attends us first, and leaves us last;
Why she likes him, admire not at her;
She loves herself, and that's the matter.
How was her tutor wont to praise
The geniuses of ancient days!
(Those authors he so oft had named,
For learning, wit, and wisdom, famed;)
Was struck with love, esteem, and awe,
For persons whom he never saw.
Suppose Cadenus flourish'd then,
He must adore such godlike men.
If one short volume could comprise
All that was witty, learn'd, and wise,
How would it be esteem'd and read,

Although the writer long were dead!
If such an author were alive,
How all would for his friendship strive,
And come in crowds to see his face!
And this she takes to be her case.
Cadenus answers every end,
The book, the author, and the friend;
The utmost her desires will reach,
Is but to learn what he can teach:
His converse is a system fit
Alone to fill up all her wit;
While every passion of her mind
In him is centred and confined.
    Love can with speech inspire a mute,
And taught Vanessa to dispute.
This topic, never touch'd before,
Display'd her eloquence the more:
Her knowledge, with such pains acquired,
By this new passion grew inspired;
Through this she made all objects pass,
Which gave a tincture o'er the mass;
As rivers, though they bend and twine,
Still to the sea their course incline:
Or, as philosophers, who find
Some favourite system to their mind;
In every point to make it fit,
Will force all nature to submit.
    Cadenus, who could ne'er suspect
His lessons would have such effect,
Or be so artfully applied,
Insensibly came on her side.
It was an unforeseen event;
Things took a turn he never meant.
Whoe'er excels in what we prize,
Appears a hero in our eyes;
Each girl, when pleased with what is taught,
Will have the teacher in her thought.
When miss delights in her spinet,
A fiddler may a fortune get;

A blockhead, with melodious voice,
In boarding-schools may have his choice:
And oft the dancing-master's art
Climbs from the toe to touch the heart.
In learning let a nymph delight,
The pedant gets a mistress by't.
Cadenus, to his grief and shame,
Could scarce oppose Vanessa's flame;
And, though her arguments were strong,
At least could hardly wish them wrong.
Howe'er it came, he could not tell,
But sure she never talk'd so well.
His pride began to interpose;
Preferr'd before a crowd of beaux!
So bright a nymph to come unsought!
Such wonder by his merit wrought!
'Tis merit must with her prevail!
He never knew her judgment fail!
She noted all she ever read!
And had a most discerning head!
    'Tis an old maxim in the schools,
That flattery's the food of fools;
Yet now and then your men of wit
Will condescend to take a bit.
    So when Cadenus could not hide,
He chose to justify his pride;
Construing the passion she had shown,
Much to her praise, more to his own.
Nature in him had merit placed,
In her a most judicious taste.
Love, hitherto a transient guest,
Ne'er held possession of his breast;
So long attending at the gate,
Disdain'd to enter in so late.
Love why do we one passion call,
When 'tis a compound of them all?
Where hot and cold, where sharp and sweet,
In all their equipages meet;
Where pleasures mix'd with pains appear,

Sorrow with joy, and hope with fear;
Wherein his dignity and age
Forbid Cadenus to engage.
But friendship, in its greatest height,
A constant, rational delight,
On virtue's basis fix'd to last,
When love allurements long are past,
Which gently warms, but cannot burn,
He gladly offers in return;
His want of passion will redeem
With gratitude, respect, esteem:
With what devotion we bestow,
When goddesses appear below.
    While thus Cadenus entertains
Vanessa in exalted strains,
The nymph in sober words entreats
A truce with all sublime conceits;
For why such raptures, flights, and fancies,
To her who durst not read romances?
In lofty style to make replies,
Which he had taught her to despise?
But when her tutor will affect
Devotion, duty, and respect,
He fairly abdicates the throne:
The government is now her own;
He has a forfeiture incurr'd;
She vows to take him at his word,
And hopes he will not think it strange
If both should now their stations change,
The nymph will have her turn to be
The tutor; and the pupil, he;
Though she already can discern
Her scholar is not apt to learn;
Or wants capacity to reach
The science she designs to teach;
Wherein his genius was below
The skill of every common beau,
Who, though he cannot spell, is wise
Enough to read a lady's eyes,

And will each accidental glance
Interpret for a kind advance.
    But what success Vanessa met,
Is to the world a secret yet.
Whether the nymph, to please her swain,
Talks in a high romantic strain;
Or whether he at last descends
To act with less seraphic ends;
Or to compound the business, whether
They temper love and books together;
Must never to mankind be told,
Nor shall the conscious Muse unfold.
    Meantime the mournful Queen of Love
Led but a weary life above.
She ventures now to leave the skies,
Grown by Vanessa's conduct wise:
For though by one perverse event
Pallas had cross'd her first intent;
Though her design was not obtain'd:
Yet had she much experience gain'd,
And, by the project vainly tried,
Could better now the cause decide.
She gave due notice, that both parties,
Coram Regina, prox' die Martis,
Should at their peril, without fail,
Come and appear, and save their bail.
All met; and, silence thrice proclaimed,
One lawyer to each side was named.
The judge discover'd in her face
Resentments for her late disgrace;
And full of anger, shame, and grief,
Directed them to mind their brief;
Nor spend their time to show their reading:
She'd have a summary proceeding.
She gather'd under every head
The sum of what each lawyer said,
Gave her own reasons last, and then
Decreed the cause against the men.
    But in a weighty case like this,

To show she did not judge amiss,
Which evil tongues might else report,
She made a speech in open court;
Wherein she grievously complains,
"How she was cheated by the swains;
On whose petition (humbly showing,
That women were not worth the wooing,
And that, unless the sex would mend,
The race of lovers soon must end)—
She was at Lord knows what expense
To form a nymph of wit and sense,
A model for her sex design'd,
Who never could one lover find.
She saw her favour was misplaced;
The fellows had a wretched taste;
She needs must tell them to their face,
They were a stupid, senseless race;
And, were she to begin again,
She'd study to reform the men;
Or add some grains of folly more
To women, than they had before,
To put them on an equal foot;
And this, or nothing else, would do't.
This might their mutual fancy strike;
Since every being loves its like.

"But now, repenting what was done,
She left all business to her son;
She put the world in his possession,
And let him use it at discretion."

The crier was order'd to dismiss
The court, who made his last "O yes!"
The goddess would no longer wait;
But, rising from her chair of state,
Left all below at six and seven,
Harness'd her doves, and flew to Heaven.

To Love

In all I wish, how happy should I be,
Thou grand Deluder, were it not for thee!
So weak thou art, that fools thy power despise;
And yet so strong, thou triumph'st o'er the wise.
Thy traps are laid with such peculiar art,
They catch the cautious, let the rash depart.
Most nets are fill'd by want of thought and care
But too much thinking brings us to thy snare;
Where, held by thee, in slavery we stay,
And throw the pleasing part of life away.
But, what does most my indignation move,
Discretion! thou wert ne'er a friend to Love:
Thy chief delight is to defeat those arts,
By which he kindles mutual flames in hearts;
While the blind loitering God is at his play,
Thou steal'st his golden pointed darts away:
Those darts which never fail; and in their stead
Convey'st malignant arrows tipt with lead:
The heedless God, suspecting no deceits,
Shoots on, and thinks he has done wondrous feats;
But the poor nymph, who feels her vitals burn,
And from her shepherd can find no return,
Laments, and rages at the power divine,
When, curst Discretion! all the fault was thine:
Cupid and Hymen thou hast set at odds,
And bred such feuds between those kindred gods,
That Venus cannot reconcile her sons;
When one appears, away the other runs.
The former scales, wherein he used to poise
Love against love, and equal joys with joys,
Are now fill'd up with avarice and pride,
Where titles, power, and riches, still subside.
Then, gentle Venus, to thy father run,
And tell him, how thy children are undone:
Prepare his bolts to give one fatal blow,
And strike Discretion to the shades below.

A Rebus. By Vanessa

Cut the name of the man who his mistress denied,
And let the first of it be only applied
To join with the prophet who David did chide;
Then say what a horse is that runs very fast;
And that which deserves to be first put the last;
Spell all then, and put them together, to find
The name and the virtues of him I design'd.
Like the patriarch in Egypt, he's versed in the state;
Like the prophet in Jewry, he's free with the great;
Like a racer he flies, to succour with speed,
When his friends want his aid, or desert is in need.

The Dean's Answer

The nymph who wrote this in an amorous fit,
I cannot but envy the pride of her wit,
Which thus she will venture profusely to throw
On so mean a design, and a subject so low.
For mean's her design, and her subject as mean,
The first but a rebus, the last but a dean.
A dean's but a parson: and what is a rebus?
A thing never known to the Muses or Phoebus.
The corruption of verse; for, when all is done,
It is but a paraphrase made on a pun.
But a genius like hers no subject can stifle,
It shows and discovers itself through a trifle.
By reading this trifle, I quickly began
To find her a great wit, but the dean a small man.
Rich ladies will furnish their garrets with stuff,
Which others for mantuas would think fine enough:
So the wit that is lavishly thrown away here,
Might furnish a second-rate poet a year.
Thus much for the verse, we proceed to the next,
Where the nymph has entirely forsaken her text:
Her fine panegyrics are quite out of season:
And what she describes to be merit, is treason:
The changes which faction has made in the state,
Have put the dean's politics quite out of date:
Now no one regards what he utters with freedom,
And, should he write pamphlets, no great man would read 'em;
And, should want or desert stand in need of his aid,
This racer would prove but a dull founder'd jade.

Stella's Birth-Day March 13, 1718–19

Stella this day is thirty-four,
(We shan't dispute a year or more:)
However, Stella, be not troubled,
Although thy size and years are doubled
Since first I saw thee at sixteen,
The brightest virgin on the green;
So little is thy form declined;
Made up so largely in thy mind.
O, would it please the gods to split
Thy beauty, size, and years, and wit!
No age could furnish out a pair
Of nymphs so graceful, wise, and fair;
With half the lustre of your eyes,
With half your wit, your years, and size.
And then, before it grew too late,
How should I beg of gentle fate,
(That either nymph might have her swain,)
To split my worship too in twain.

Stella's Birth-Day. 1719–20

Written A.D. 1720–21.—Stella

All travellers at first incline
Where'er they see the fairest sign
And if they find the chambers neat,
And like the liquor and the meat,
Will call again, and recommend
The Angel Inn to every friend.
And though the painting grows decay'd,
The house will never lose its trade:
Nay, though the treach'rous tapster, Thomas,
Hangs a new Angel two doors from us,
As fine as daubers' hands can make it,
In hopes that strangers may mistake it,
We think it both a shame and sin
To quit the true old Angel Inn.
    Now this is Stella's case in fact,
An angel's face a little crack'd.
(Could poets or could painters fix
How angels look at thirty-six:)
This drew us in at first to find
In such a form an angel's mind;
And every virtue now supplies
The fainting rays of Stella's eyes.
See, at her levee crowding swains,
Whom Stella freely entertains
With breeding, humour, wit, and sense,
And puts them to so small expense;
Their minds so plentifully fills,
And makes such reasonable bills,
So little gets for what she gives,
We really wonder how she lives!
And had her stock been less, no doubt
She must have long ago run out.
    Then, who can think we'll quit the place,

When Doll hangs out a newer face?
Nail'd to her window full in sight
All Christian people to invite.
Or stop and light at Chloe's head,
With scraps and leavings to be fed?
    Then, Chloe, still go on to prate
Of thirty-six and thirty-eight;
Pursue your trade of scandal-picking,
Your hints that Stella is no chicken;
Your innuendoes, when you tell us,
That Stella loves to talk with fellows:
But let me warn you to believe
A truth, for which your soul should grieve;
That should you live to see the day,
When Stella's locks must all be gray,
When age must print a furrow'd trace
On every feature of her face;
Though you, and all your senseless tribe,
Could Art, or Time, or Nature bribe,
To make you look like Beauty's Queen,
And hold for ever at fifteen;
No bloom of youth can ever blind
The cracks and wrinkles of your mind:
All men of sense will pass your door,
And crowd to Stella's at four-score.

To Stella, who Collected and Transcribed his Poems 1720

As, when a lofty pile is raised,
We never hear the workmen praised,
Who bring the lime, or place the stones.
But all admire Inigo Jones:
So, if this pile of scatter'd rhymes
Should be approved in aftertimes;
If it both pleases and endures,
The merit and the praise are yours.
　　Thou, Stella, wert no longer young,
When first for thee my harp was strung,
Without one word of Cupid's darts,
Of killing eyes, or bleeding hearts;
With friendship and esteem possest,
I ne'er admitted Love a guest.
　　In all the habitudes of life,
The friend, the mistress, and the wife,
Variety we still pursue,
In pleasure seek for something new;
Or else, comparing with the rest,
Take comfort that our own is best;
The best we value by the worst,
As tradesmen show their trash at first;
But his pursuits are at an end,
Whom Stella chooses for a friend.
A poet starving in a garret,
Conning all topics like a parrot,
Invokes his mistress and his Muse,
And stays at home for want of shoes:
Should but his Muse descending drop
A slice of bread and mutton-chop;
Or kindly, when his credit's out,
Surprise him with a pint of stout;
Or patch his broken stocking soles;
Or send him in a peck of coals;

Exalted in his mighty mind,
He flies and leaves the stars behind;
Counts all his labours amply paid,
Adores her for the timely aid.
    Or, should a porter make inquiries
For Chloe, Sylvia, Phillis, Iris;
Be told the lodging, lane, and sign,
The bowers that hold those nymphs divine;
Fair Chloe would perhaps be found
With footmen tippling under ground;
The charming Sylvia beating flax,
Her shoulders mark'd with bloody tracks;
Bright Phillis mending ragged smocks:
And radiant Iris in the pox.
These are the goddesses enroll'd
In Curll's collection, new and old,
Whose scoundrel fathers would not know 'em,
If they should meet them in a poem.
    True poets can depress and raise,
Are lords of infamy and praise;
They are not scurrilous in satire,
Nor will in panegyric flatter.
Unjustly poets we asperse;
Truth shines the brighter clad in verse,
And all the fictions they pursue
Do but insinuate what is true.
    Now, should my praises owe their truth
To beauty, dress, or paint, or youth,
What stoics call without our power,
They could not be ensured an hour;
'Twere grafting on an annual stock,
That must our expectation mock,
And, making one luxuriant shoot,
Die the next year for want of root:
Before I could my verses bring,
Perhaps you're quite another thing.
    So Mævius, when he drain'd his skull
To celebrate some suburb trull,
His similes in order set,

And every crambo he could get;
Had gone through all the common-places
Worn out by wits, who rhyme on faces;
Before he could his poem close,
The lovely nymph had lost her nose.

Your virtues safely I commend;
They on no accidents depend:
Let malice look with all her eyes,
She dares not say the poet lies.

Stella, when you these lines transcribe,
Lest you should take them for a bribe,
Resolved to mortify your pride,
I'll here expose your weaker side.

Your spirits kindle to a flame,
Moved by the lightest touch of blame;
And when a friend in kindness tries
To show you where your error lies,
Conviction does but more incense;
Perverseness is your whole defence;
Truth, judgment, wit, give place to spite,
Regardless both of wrong and right;
Your virtues all suspended wait,
Till time has open'd reason's gate;
And, what is worse, your passion bends
Its force against your nearest friends,
Which manners, decency, and pride,
Have taught from you the world to hide;
In vain; for see, your friend has brought
To public light your only fault;
And yet a fault we often find
Mix'd in a noble, generous mind:
And may compare to Ætna's fire,
Which, though with trembling, all admire;
The heat that makes the summit glow,
Enriching all the vales below.
Those who, in warmer climes, complain
From Phoebus' rays they suffer pain,
Must own that pain is largely paid
By generous wines beneath a shade.

Yet, when I find your passions rise,
And anger sparkling in your eyes,
I grieve those spirits should be spent,
For nobler ends by nature meant.
One passion, with a different turn,
Makes wit inflame, or anger burn:
So the sun's heat, with different powers,
Ripens the grape, the liquor sours:
Thus Ajax, when with rage possest,
By Pallas breathed into his breast,
His valour would no more employ,
Which might alone have conquer'd Troy;
But, blinded by resentment, seeks
For vengeance on his friends the Greeks.
You think this turbulence of blood
From stagnating preserves the flood,
Which, thus fermenting by degrees,
Exalts the spirits, sinks the lees.
Stella, for once you reason wrong;
For, should this ferment last too long,
By time subsiding, you may find
Nothing but acid left behind;
From passion you may then be freed,
When peevishness and spleen succeed.
Say, Stella, when you copy next,
Will you keep strictly to the text?
Dare you let these reproaches stand,
And to your failing set your hand?
Or, if these lines your anger fire,
Shall they in baser flames expire?
Whene'er they burn, if burn they must,
They'll prove my accusation just.

To Stella Visiting me in my Sickness 1720

Pallas, observing Stella's wit
Was more than for her sex was fit,
And that her beauty, soon or late,
Might breed confusion in the state,
In high concern for human kind,
Fix'd honour in her infant mind.
    But (not in wrangling to engage
With such a stupid, vicious age)
If honour I would here define,
It answers faith in things divine.
As natural life the body warms,
And, scholars teach, the soul informs,
So honour animates the whole,
And is the spirit of the soul.
    Those numerous virtues which the tribe
Of tedious moralists describe,
And by such various titles call,
True honour comprehends them all.
Let melancholy rule supreme,
Choler preside, or blood, or phlegm,
It makes no difference in the case,
Nor is complexion honour's place.
    But, lest we should for honour take
The drunken quarrels of a rake:
Or think it seated in a scar,
Or on a proud triumphal car;
Or in the payment of a debt
We lose with sharpers at piquet;
Or when a whore, in her vocation,
Keeps punctual to an assignation;
Or that on which his lordship swears,
When vulgar knaves would lose their ears;
Let Stella's fair example preach
A lesson she alone can teach.
    In points of honour to be tried,

All passions must be laid aside:
Ask no advice, but think alone;
Suppose the question not your own.
How shall I act, is not the case;
But how would Brutus in my place?
In such a case would Cato bleed?
And how would Socrates proceed?
    Drive all objections from your mind,
Else you relapse to human kind:
Ambition, avarice, and lust,
A factious rage, and breach of trust,
And flattery tipt with nauseous fleer,
And guilty shame, and servile fear,
Envy, and cruelty, and pride,
Will in your tainted heart preside.
    Heroes and heroines of old,
By honour only were enroll'd
Among their brethren in the skies,
To which (though late) shall Stella rise.
Ten thousand oaths upon record
Are not so sacred as her word:
The world shall in its atoms end,
Ere Stella can deceive a friend.
By honour seated in her breast
She still determines what is best:
What indignation in her mind
Against enslavers of mankind!
Base kings, and ministers of state,
Eternal objects of her hate!
She thinks that nature ne'er design'd
Courage to man alone confined.
Can cowardice her sex adorn,
Which most exposes ours to scorn?
She wonders where the charm appears
In Florimel's affected fears;
For Stella never learn'd the art
At proper times to scream and start;
Nor calls up all the house at night,
And swears she saw a thing in white.

Doll never flies to cut her lace,
Or throw cold water in her face,
Because she heard a sudden drum,
Or found an earwig in a plum.
    Her hearers are amazed from whence
Proceeds that fund of wit and sense;
Which, though her modesty would shroud,
Breaks like the sun behind a cloud;
While gracefulness its art conceals,
And yet through every motion steals.
    Say, Stella, was Prometheus blind,
And, forming you, mistook your kind?
No; 'twas for you alone he stole
The fire that forms a manly soul;
Then, to complete it every way,
He moulded it with female clay:
To that you owe the nobler flame,
To this the beauty of your frame.
    How would Ingratitude delight,
And how would Censure glut her spite,
If I should Stella's kindness hide
In silence, or forget with pride!
When on my sickly couch I lay,
Impatient both of night and day,
Lamenting in unmanly strains,
Call'd every power to ease my pains;
Then Stella ran to my relief,
With cheerful face and inward grief;
And, though by Heaven's severe decree
She suffers hourly more than me,
No cruel master could require,
From slaves employ'd for daily hire,
What Stella, by her friendship warm'd
With vigour and delight perform'd:
My sinking spirits now supplies
With cordials in her hands and eyes:
Now with a soft and silent tread
Unheard she moves about my bed.
I see her taste each nauseous draught,

And so obligingly am caught;
I bless the hand from whence they came,
Nor dare distort my face for shame.
    Best pattern of true friends! beware;
You pay too dearly for your care,
If, while your tenderness secures
My life, it must endanger yours;
For such a fool was never found,
Who pull'd a palace to the ground,
Only to have the ruins made
Materials for a house decay'd.

Stella to Dr. Swift on his Birth-Day, Nov. 30, 1721

St. Patrick's Dean, your country's pride,
My early and my only guide,
Let me among the rest attend,
Your pupil and your humble friend,
To celebrate in female strains
The day that paid your mother's pains;
Descend to take that tribute due
In gratitude alone to you.
    When men began to call me fair,
You interposed your timely care:
You early taught me to despise
The ogling of a coxcomb's eyes;
Show'd where my judgment was misplaced;
Refined my fancy and my taste.
    Behold that beauty just decay'd,
Invoking art to nature's aid:
Forsook by her admiring train,
She spreads her tatter'd nets in vain;
Short was her part upon the stage;
Went smoothly on for half a page;
Her bloom was gone, she wanted art,
As the scene changed, to change her part;
She, whom no lover could resist,
Before the second act was hiss'd.
Such is the fate of female race
With no endowments but a face;
Before the thirtieth year of life,
A maid forlorn, or hated wife.
    Stella to you, her tutor, owes
That she has ne'er resembled those:
Nor was a burden to mankind
With half her course of years behind.
You taught how I might youth prolong,
By knowing what was right and wrong;
How from my heart to bring supplies

Of lustre to my fading eyes;
How soon a beauteous mind repairs
The loss of changed or falling hairs;
How wit and virtue from within
Send out a smoothness o'er the skin:
Your lectures could my fancy fix,
And I can please at thirty-six.
The sight of Chloe at fifteen,
Coquetting, gives not me the spleen;
The idol now of every fool
Till time shall make their passions cool;
Then tumbling down Time's steepy hill,
While Stella holds her station still.
O! turn your precepts into laws,
Redeem the women's ruin'd cause,
Retrieve lost empire to our sex,
That men may bow their rebel necks.
    Long be the day that gave you birth
Sacred to friendship, wit, and mirth;
Late dying may you cast a shred
Of your rich mantle o'er my head;
To bear with dignity my sorrow,
One day alone, then die to-morrow.

To Stella on her Birth-Day, 1721–2

While, Stella, to your lasting praise
The Muse her annual tribute pays,
While I assign myself a task
Which you expect, but scorn to ask;
If I perform this task with pain,
Let me of partial fate complain;
You every year the debt enlarge,
I grow less equal to the charge:
In you each virtue brighter shines,
But my poetic vein declines;
My harp will soon in vain be strung,
And all your virtues left unsung.
For none among the upstart race
Of poets dare assume my place;
Your worth will be to them unknown,
They must have Stellas of their own;
And thus, my stock of wit decay'd,
I dying leave the debt unpaid,
Unless Delany, as my heir,
Will answer for the whole arrear.

On the Great Buried Bottle
By Dr. Delany

Amphora, quae moestum linquis, laetumque revises
    Arentem dominum, sit tibi terra levis.
Tu quoque depositum serves, neve opprime, marmor;
    Amphora non meruit tam pretiosa mori.

Epitaph
By the Same

Hoc tumulata jacet proles Lenaea sepulchro,
Immortale genus, nee peritura jacet;
Quin oritura iterum, matris concreditur alvo:
Bis natum referunt te quoque, Bacche Pater.

Stella's Birth-Day: A Great Bottle of Wine, Long Buried, Being that Day Dug Up. 1722–3

Resolv'd my annual verse to pay,
By duty bound, on Stella's day,
Furnish'd with paper, pens, and ink,
I gravely sat me down to think:
I bit my nails, and scratch'd my head,
But found my wit and fancy fled:
Or if, with more than usual pain,
A thought came slowly from my brain,
It cost me Lord knows how much time
To shape it into sense and rhyme:
And, what was yet a greater curse,
Long thinking made my fancy worse.
    Forsaken by th'inspiring Nine,
I waited at Apollo's shrine:
I told him what the world would say,
If Stella were unsung to-day:
How I should hide my head for shame,
When both the Jacks and Robin came;
How Ford would frown, how Jim would leer,
How Sheridan the rogue would sneer,
And swear it does not always follow,
That *semel'n anno ridet Apollo*.
I have assur'd them twenty times,
That Phoebus help'd me in my rhymes;
Phoebus inspired me from above,
And he and I were hand and glove.
But, finding me so dull and dry since,
They'll call it all poetic license;
And when I brag of aid divine,
Think Eusden's right as good as mine.
    Nor do I ask for Stella's sake;
'Tis my own credit lies at stake:
And Stella will be sung, while I
Can only be a stander by.

Apollo, having thought a little,
Return'd this answer to a tittle.
Though you should live like old Methusalem,
I furnish hints and you shall use all 'em,
You yearly sing as she grows old,
You'd leave her virtues half untold.
But, to say truth, such dulness reigns,
Through the whole set of Irish deans,
I'm daily stunn'd with such a medley,
Dean White, Dean Daniel, and Dean Smedley,
That, let what dean soever come,
My orders are, I'm not at home;
And if your voice had not been loud,
You must have pass'd among the crowd.
But now, your danger to prevent,
You must apply to Mrs. Brent;
For she, as priestess, knows the rites
Wherein the god of earth delights.
First, nine ways looking, let her stand
With an old poker in her hand;
Let her describe a circle round
In Saunders' cellar on the ground:
A spade let prudent Archy hold,
And with discretion dig the mould.
Let Stella look with watchful eye,
Rebecca, Ford, and Grattans by.
Behold the bottle, where it lies
With neck elated toward the skies!
The god of winds and god of fire
Did to its wondrous birth conspire;
And Bacchus for the poet's use
Pour'd in a strong inspiring juice.
See! as you raise it from its tomb,
It drags behind a spacious womb,
And in the spacious womb contains
A sov'reign med'cine for the brains.
You'll find it soon, if fate consents;
If not, a thousand Mrs. Brents,
Ten thousand Archys, arm'd with spades,

May dig in vain to Pluto's shades.
    From thence a plenteous draught infuse,
And boldly then invoke the Muse;
But first let Robert on his knees
With caution drain it from the lees;
The Muse will at your call appear,
With Stella's praise to crown the year.

Stella at Wood Park
A House of Charles Ford, Esq., Near Dublin
1723

—cuicumque nocere volebat,
Vestimenta dabat pretiosa.

Don Carlos, in a merry spight,
Did Stella to his house invite:
He entertain'd her half a year
With generous wines and costly cheer.
Don Carlos made her chief director,
That she might o'er the servants hector.
In half a week the dame grew nice,
Got all things at the highest price:
Now at the table head she sits,
Presented with the nicest bits:
She look'd on partridges with scorn,
Except they tasted of the corn:
A haunch of ven'son made her sweat,
Unless it had the right *fumette*.
Don Carlos earnestly would beg,
"Dear Madam, try this pigeon's leg;"
Was happy, when he could prevail
To make her only touch a quail.
Through candle-light she view'd the wine,
To see that ev'ry glass was fine.
At last, grown prouder than the devil
With feeding high, and treatment civil,
Don Carlos now began to find
His malice work as he design'd.
The winter sky began to frown:
Poor Stella must pack off to town;
From purling streams and fountains bubbling,
To Liffey's stinking tide in Dublin:
From wholesome exercise and air

To sossing in an easy-chair:
From stomach sharp, and hearty feeding,
To piddle like a lady breeding:
From ruling there the household singly.
To be directed here by Dingley:
From every day a lordly banquet,
To half a joint, and God be thank it:
From every meal Pontac in plenty,
To half a pint one day in twenty:
From Ford attending at her call,
To visits of Archdeacon Wall:
From Ford, who thinks of nothing mean,
To the poor doings of the Dean:
From growing richer with good cheer,
To running out by starving here.
    But now arrives the dismal day;
She must return to Ormond Quay.
The coachman stopt; she look'd, and swore
The rascal had mistook the door:
At coming in, you saw her stoop;
The entry brush'd against her hoop:
Each moment rising in her airs,
She curst the narrow winding stairs:
Began a thousand faults to spy;
The ceiling hardly six feet high;
The smutty wainscot full of cracks:
And half the chairs with broken backs:
Her quarter's out at Lady-day;
She vows she will no longer stay
In lodgings like a poor Grisette,
While there are houses to be let.
    Howe'er, to keep her spirits up,
She sent for company to sup:
When all the while you might remark,
She strove in vain to ape Wood Park.
Two bottles call'd for, (half her store,
The cupboard could contain but four:)
A supper worthy of herself,
Five nothings in five plates of delf.

Thus for a week the farce went on;
When, all her country savings gone,
She fell into her former scene,
Small beer, a herring, and the Dean.
Thus far in jest: though now, I fear,
You think my jesting too severe;
But poets, when a hint is new,
Regard not whether false or true:
Yet raillery gives no offence,
Where truth has not the least pretence;
Nor can be more securely placed
Than on a nymph of Stella's taste.
I must confess your wine and vittle
I was too hard upon a little:
Your table neat, your linen fine;
And, though in miniature, you shine:
Yet, when you sigh to leave Wood Park,
The scene, the welcome, and the spark,
To languish in this odious town,
And pull your haughty stomach down,
We think you quite mistake the case,
The virtue lies not in the place:
For though my raillery were true,
A cottage is Wood Park with you.

A New Year's Gift for Bec
1723–4

Returning Janus now prepares,
For Bec, a new supply of cares,
Sent in a bag to Dr. Swift,
Who thus displays the new-year's gift.
    First, this large parcel brings you tidings
Of our good Dean's eternal chidings;
Of Nelly's pertness, Robin's leasings,
And Sheridan's perpetual teazings.
This box is cramm'd on every side
With Stella's magisterial pride.
Behold a cage with sparrows fill'd,
First to be fondled, then be kill'd.
Now to this hamper I invite you,
With six imagined cares to fright you.
Here in this bundle Janus sends
Concerns by thousands for your friends.
And here's a pair of leathern pokes,
To hold your cares for other folks.
Here from this barrel you may broach
A peck of troubles for a coach.
This ball of wax your ears will darken,
Still to be curious, never hearken.
Lest you the town may have less trouble in
Bring all your Quilca's cares to Dublin,
For which he sends this empty sack;
And so take all upon your back.

Dingley and Brent
A Song

To the tune of "Ye Commons and Peers."

Dingley and Brent,
Wherever they went,
Ne'er minded a word that was spoken;
Whatever was said,
They ne'er troubled their head,
But laugh'd at their own silly joking.

Should Solomon wise
In majesty rise,
And show them his wit and his learning;
They never would hear,
But turn the deaf ear,
As a matter they had no concern in.

You tell a good jest,
And please all the rest;
Comes Dingley, and asks you, what was it?
And, curious to know,
Away she will go
To seek an old rag in the closet.

To Stella

Written on the Day of her Birth, March 13, 1723–4, But not on the Subject, when I was Sick in Bed

Tormented with incessant pains,
Can I devise poetic strains?
Time was, when I could yearly pay
My verse to Stella's native day:
But now unable grown to write,
I grieve she ever saw the light.
Ungrateful! since to her I owe
That I these pains can undergo.
She tends me like an humble slave;
And, when indecently I rave,
When out my brutish passions break,
With gall in every word I speak,
She with soft speech my anguish cheers,
Or melts my passions down with tears;
Although 'tis easy to descry
She wants assistance more than I;
Yet seems to feel my pains alone,
And is a stoic in her own.
When, among scholars, can we find
So soft and yet so firm a mind?
All accidents of life conspire
To raise up Stella's virtue higher;
Or else to introduce the rest
Which had been latent in her breast.
Her firmness who could e'er have known,
Had she not evils of her own?
Her kindness who could ever guess,
Had not her friends been in distress?
Whatever base returns you find
From me, dear Stella, still be kind.
In your own heart you'll reap the fruit,
Though I continue still a brute.
But, when I once am out of pain,

I promise to be good again;
Meantime, your other juster friends
Shall for my follies make amends;
So may we long continue thus,
Admiring you, you pitying us.

Verses by Stella

If it be true, celestial powers,
That you have form'd me fair,
And yet, in all my vainest hours,
My mind has been my care:
Then, in return, I beg this grace,
As you were ever kind,
What envious Time takes from my face
Bestow upon my mind!

A Receipt to Restore Stella's Youth. 1724–5

The Scottish hinds, too poor to house
In frosty nights their starving cows,
While not a blade of grass or hay
Appears from Michaelmas to May,
Must let their cattle range in vain
For food along the barren plain:
Meagre and lank with fasting grown,
And nothing left but skin and bone;
Exposed to want, and wind, and weather,
They just keep life and soul together,
Till summer showers and evening's dew
Again the verdant glebe renew;
And, as the vegetables rise,
The famish'd cow her want supplies;
Without an ounce of last year's flesh;
Whate'er she gains is young and fresh;
Grows plump and round, and full of mettle,
As rising from Medea's kettle.
With youth and beauty to enchant
Europa's counterfeit gallant.
    Why, Stella, should you knit your brow,
If I compare you to a cow?
'Tis just the case; for you have fasted
So long, till all your flesh is wasted;
And must against the warmer days
Be sent to Quilca down to graze;
Where mirth, and exercise, and air,
Will soon your appetite repair:
The nutriment will from within,
Round all your body, plump your skin;
Will agitate the lazy flood,
And fill your veins with sprightly blood.
Nor flesh nor blood will be the same
Nor aught of Stella but the name:
For what was ever understood,

By human kind, but flesh and blood?
And if your flesh and blood be new,
You'll be no more the former you;
But for a blooming nymph will pass,
Just fifteen, coming summer's grass,
Your jetty locks with garlands crown'd:
While all the squires for nine miles round,
Attended by a brace of curs,
With jockey boots and silver spurs,
No less than justices o' quorum,
Their cow-boys bearing cloaks before 'em,
Shall leave deciding broken pates,
To kiss your steps at Quilca gates.
But, lest you should my skill disgrace,
Come back before you're out of case;
For if to Michaelmas you stay,
The new-born flesh will melt away;
The 'squires in scorn will fly the house
For better game, and look for grouse;
But here, before the frost can mar it,
We'll make it firm with beef and claret.

Stella's Birth-Day. 1724–5

As when a beauteous nymph decays,
We say she's past her dancing days;
So poets lose their feet by time,
And can no longer dance in rhyme.
Your annual bard had rather chose
To celebrate your birth in prose:
Yet merry folks, who want by chance
A pair to make a country dance,
Call the old housekeeper, and get her
To fill a place for want of better:
While Sheridan is off the hooks,
And friend Delany at his books,
That Stella may avoid disgrace,
Once more the Dean supplies their place.
    Beauty and wit, too sad a truth!
Have always been confined to youth;
The god of wit and beauty's queen,
He twenty-one and she fifteen,
No poet ever sweetly sung,
Unless he were, like Phoebus, young;
Nor ever nymph inspired to rhyme,
Unless, like Venus, in her prime.
At fifty-six, if this be true,
Am I a poet fit for you?
Or, at the age of forty-three,
Are you a subject fit for me?
Adieu! bright wit, and radiant eyes!
You must be grave and I be wise.
Our fate in vain we would oppose:
But I'll be still your friend in prose:
Esteem and friendship to express,
Will not require poetic dress;
And if the Muse deny her aid
To have them sung, they may be said.
    But, Stella, say, what evil tongue
Reports you are no longer young;

That Time sits with his scythe to mow
Where erst sat Cupid with his bow;
That half your locks are turn'd to gray?
I'll ne'er believe a word they say.
'Tis true, but let it not be known,
My eyes are somewhat dimmish grown;
For nature, always in the right,
To your decays adapts my sight;
And wrinkles undistinguished pass,
For I'm ashamed to use a glass:
And till I see them with these eyes,
Whoever says you have them, lies.
    No length of time can make you quit
Honour and virtue, sense and wit;
Thus you may still be young to me,
While I can better hear than see.
O ne'er may Fortune show her spite,
To make me deaf, and mend my sight!

Bec's Birth-Day
Nov. 8, 1726

This day, dear Bec, is thy nativity;
Had Fate a luckier one, she'd give it ye.
She chose a thread of greatest length,
And doubly twisted it for strength:
Nor will be able with her shears
To cut it off these forty years.
Then who says care will kill a cat?
Rebecca shows they're out in that.
For she, though overrun with care,
Continues healthy, fat, and fair.
    As, if the gout should seize the head,
Doctors pronounce the patient dead;
But, if they can, by all their arts,
Eject it to the extremest parts,
They give the sick man joy, and praise
The gout that will prolong his days.
Rebecca thus I gladly greet,
Who drives her cares to hands and feet:
For, though philosophers maintain
The limbs are guided by the brain,
Quite contrary Rebecca's led;
Her hands and feet conduct her head;
By arbitrary power convey her,
She ne'er considers why or where:
Her hands may meddle, feet may wander,
Her head is but a mere by-stander:
And all her bustling but supplies
The part of wholesome exercise.
Thus nature has resolved to pay her
The cat's nine lives, and eke the care.
    Long may she live, and help her friends
Whene'er it suits her private ends;
Domestic business never mind
Till coffee has her stomach lined;
But, when her breakfast gives her courage,

Then think on Stella's chicken porridge:
I mean when Tiger has been served,
Or else poor Stella may be starved.
    May Bec have many an evening nap,
With Tiger slabbering in her lap;
But always take a special care
She does not overset the chair;
Still be she curious, never hearken
To any speech but Tiger's barking!
    And when she's in another scene,
Stella long dead, but first the Dean,
May fortune and her coffee get her
Companions that will please her better!
Whole afternoons will sit beside her,
Nor for neglects or blunders chide her.
A goodly set as can be found
Of hearty gossips prating round;
Fresh from a wedding or a christening,
To teach her ears the art of listening,
And please her more to hear them tattle,
Than the Dean storm, or Stella rattle.
    Late be her death, one gentle nod,
When Hermes, waiting with his rod,
Shall to Elysian fields invite her,
Where there will be no cares to fright her!

On the Collar of Tiger

Mrs. Dingley's Lap-Dog

Pray steal me not; I'm Mrs. Dingley's,
Whose heart in this four-footed thing lies.

Stella's Birth-Day

March 13, 1726–7

This day, whate'er the Fates decree,
Shall still be kept with joy by me:
This day then let us not be told,
That you are sick, and I grown old;
Nor think on our approaching ills,
And talk of spectacles and pills;
To-morrow will be time enough
To hear such mortifying stuff.
Yet, since from reason may be brought
A better and more pleasing thought,
Which can, in spite of all decays,
Support a few remaining days;
From not the gravest of divines
Accept for once some serious lines.
    Although we now can form no more
Long schemes of life, as heretofore;
Yet you, while time is running fast,
Can look with joy on what is past.
    Were future happiness and pain
A mere contrivance of the brain;
As atheists argue, to entice
And fit their proselytes for vice;
(The only comfort they propose,
To have companions in their woes;)
Grant this the case; yet sure 'tis hard
That virtue, styled its own reward,
And by all sages understood
To be the chief of human good,
Should acting die; nor leave behind
Some lasting pleasure in the mind,
Which, by remembrance, will assuage
Grief, sickness, poverty, and age;
And strongly shoot a radiant dart
To shine through life's declining part.

Say, Stella, feel you no content,
Reflecting on a life well spent?
Your skilful hand employ'd to save
Despairing wretches from the grave;
And then supporting with your store
Those whom you dragg'd from death before?
So Providence on mortals waits,
Preserving what it first creates.
Your generous boldness to defend
An innocent and absent friend;
That courage which can make you just
To merit humbled in the dust;
The detestation you express
For vice in all its glittering dress;
That patience under torturing pain,
Where stubborn stoics would complain:
Must these like empty shadows pass,
Or forms reflected from a glass?
Or mere chimeras in the mind,
That fly, and leave no marks behind?
Does not the body thrive and grow
By food of twenty years ago?
And, had it not been still supplied,
It must a thousand times have died.
Then who with reason can maintain
That no effects of food remain?
And is not virtue in mankind
The nutriment that feeds the mind;
Upheld by each good action past,
And still continued by the last?
Then, who with reason can pretend
That all effects of virtue end?
Believe me, Stella, when you show
That true contempt for things below,
Nor prize your life for other ends,
Than merely to oblige your friends;
Your former actions claim their part,
And join to fortify your heart.
For Virtue, in her daily race,

Like Janus, bears a double face;
Looks back with joy where she has gone
And therefore goes with courage on:
She at your sickly couch will wait,
And guide you to a better state.
    O then, whatever Heaven intends,
Take pity on your pitying friends!
Nor let your ills affect your mind,
To fancy they can be unkind.
Me, surely me, you ought to spare,
Who gladly would your suffering share;
Or give my scrap of life to you,
And think it far beneath your due;
You, to whose care so oft I owe
That I'm alive to tell you so.

Death and Daphne

To an Agreeable Young Lady, but Extremely Lean. 1730

Lord Orrery gives us the following curious anecdote respecting this poem:

> "I have just now cast my eye over a poem called 'Death and Daphne,' which makes me recollect an odd incident, relating to that nymph. Swift, soon after our acquaintance, introduced me to her as to one of his female favourites. I had scarce been half an hour in her company, before she asked me if I had seen the Dean's poem upon 'Death and Daphne.' As I told her I had not, she immediately unlocked a cabinet, and, bringing out the manuscript, read it to me with a seeming satisfaction, of which, at that time, I doubted the sincerity. While she was reading, the Dean was perpetually correcting her for bad pronunciation, and for placing a wrong emphasis upon particular words. As soon as she had gone through the composition, she assured me, smilingly, that the portrait of Daphne was drawn for herself. I begged to be excused from believing it; and protested that I could not see one feature that had the least resemblance; but the Dean immediately burst into a fit of laughter. 'You fancy,' says he, 'that you are very polite, but you are much mistaken. That lady had rather be a Daphne drawn by me, than a Sacharissa by any other pencil.' She confirmed what he had said with great earnestness, so that I had no other method of retrieving my error, than by whispering in her ear, as I was conducting her down stairs to dinner, that indeed I found
>
> 'Her hand as dry and cold as lead!'"
>
> —*Remarks on the Life of Swift*, Lond., 1752, p. 126

Death went upon a solemn day
At Pluto's hall his court to pay;
The phantom having humbly kiss'd
His grisly monarch's sooty fist,
Presented him the weekly bills
Of doctors, fevers, plagues, and pills.

Pluto, observing since the peace
The burial article decrease,
And vex'd to see affairs miscarry,
Declared in council Death must marry;
Vow'd he no longer could support
Old bachelors about his court;
The interest of his realm had need
That Death should get a numerous breed;
Young deathlings, who, by practice made
Proficient in their father's trade,
With colonies might stock around
His large dominions under ground.
    A consult of coquettes below
Was call'd, to rig him out a beau;
From her own head Megaera takes
A periwig of twisted snakes:
Which in the nicest fashion curl'd,
(Like toupees of this upper world)
With flower of sulphur powder'd well,
That graceful on his shoulders fell;
An adder of the sable kind
In line direct hung down behind:
The owl, the raven, and the bat,
Clubb'd for a feather to his hat:
His coat, a usurer's velvet pall,
Bequeath'd to Pluto, corpse and all.
But, loath his person to expose
Bare, like a carcass pick'd by crows,
A lawyer, o'er his hands and face
Stuck artfully a parchment case.
No new flux'd rake show'd fairer skin;
Nor Phyllis after lying in.
With snuff was fill'd his ebon box,
Of shin-bones rotted by the pox.
Nine spirits of blaspheming fops,
With aconite anoint his chops;
And give him words of dreadful sounds,
G—d d—n his blood! and b—d and w—ds!'
    Thus furnish'd out, he sent his train

To take a house in Warwick-lane:
The faculty, his humble friends,
A complimental message sends:
Their president in scarlet gown
Harangued, and welcomed him to town.
    But Death had business to dispatch;
His mind was running on his match.
And hearing much of Daphne's fame,
His majesty of terrors came,
Fine as a colonel of the guards,
To visit where she sat at cards;
She, as he came into the room,
Thought him Adonis in his bloom.
And now her heart with pleasure jumps,
She scarce remembers what is trumps;
For such a shape of skin and bone
Was never seen except her own.
Charm'd with his eyes, and chin, and snout,
Her pocket-glass drew slily out;
And grew enamour'd with her phiz,
As just the counterpart of his.
She darted many a private glance,
And freely made the first advance;
Was of her beauty grown so vain,
She doubted not to win the swain;
Nothing she thought could sooner gain him,
Than with her wit to entertain him.
She ask'd about her friends below;
This meagre fop, that batter'd beau;
Whether some late departed toasts
Had got gallants among the ghosts?
If Chloe were a sharper still
As great as ever at quadrille?
(The ladies there must needs be rooks,
For cards, we know, are Pluto's books.)
If Florimel had found her love,
For whom she hang'd herself above?
How oft a-week was kept a ball
By Proserpine at Pluto's hall?

She fancied those Elysian shades
The sweetest place for masquerades;
How pleasant on the banks of Styx,
To troll it in a coach and six!
    What pride a female heart inflames?
How endless are ambition's aims:
Cease, haughty nymph; the Fates decree
Death must not be a spouse for thee;
For, when by chance the meagre shade
Upon thy hand his finger laid,
Thy hand as dry and cold as lead,
His matrimonial spirit fled;
He felt about his heart a damp,
That quite extinguished Cupid's lamp:
Away the frighted spectre scuds,
And leaves my lady in the suds.

Daphne

Daphne knows, with equal ease,
How to vex, and how to please;
But the folly of her sex
Makes her sole delight to vex.
Never woman more devised
Surer ways to be despised;
Paradoxes weakly wielding,
Always conquer'd, never yielding.
To dispute, her chief delight,
Without one opinion right:
Thick her arguments she lays on,
And with cavils combats reason;
Answers in decisive way,
Never hears what you can say;
Still her odd perverseness shows
Chiefly where she nothing knows;
And, where she is most familiar,
Always peevisher and sillier;
All her spirits in a flame
When she knows she's most to blame.
    Send me hence ten thousand miles,
From a face that always smiles:
None could ever act that part,
But a fury in her heart.
Ye who hate such inconsistence,
To be easy, keep your distance:
Or in folly still befriend her,
But have no concern to mend her;
Lose not time to contradict her,
Nor endeavour to convict her.
Never take it in your thought,
That she'll own, or cure a fault.
Into contradiction warm her,
Then, perhaps, you may reform her:
Only take this rule along,
Always to advise her wrong;

And reprove her when she's right;
She may then grow wise for spight.
No—that scheme will ne'er succeed,
She has better learnt her creed;
She's too cunning and too skilful,
When to yield, and when be wilful.
Nature holds her forth two mirrors,
One for truth, and one for errors:
That looks hideous, fierce, and frightful;
This is flattering and delightful:
That she throws away as foul;
Sits by this to dress her soul.
Thus you have the case in view,
Daphne, 'twixt the Dean and you:
Heaven forbid he should despise thee,
But he'll never more advise thee.

Riddles by Dr. Swift and his Friends. Written in or about the Year 1724

The following notice is subjoined to some of these riddles, in the Dublin edition: "About nine or ten years ago, (*i.e.* about 1724,) some ingenious gentlemen, friends to the author, used to entertain themselves with writing riddles, and send them to him and their other acquaintance; copies of which ran about, and some of them were printed, both here and in England. The author, at his leisure hours, fell into the same amusement; although it be said that he thought them of no great merit, entertainment, or use. However, by the advice of some persons, for whom the author hath a great esteem, and who were pleased to send us the copies, we have ventured to print the few following, as we have done two or three before, and which are allowed to be genuine; because we are informed that several good judges have a taste for such kind of compositions."

Pethox the Great. 1723

From Venus born, thy beauty shows;
But who thy father, no man knows:
Nor can the skilful herald trace
The founder of thy ancient race;
Whether thy temper, full of fire,
Discovers Vulcan for thy sire,
The god who made Scamander boil,
And round his margin singed the soil:
(From whence, philosophers agree,
An equal power descends to thee;)
Whether from dreadful Mars you claim
The high descent from whence you came,
And, as a proof, show numerous scars
By fierce encounters made in wars,
Those honourable wounds you bore
From head to foot, and all before,
And still the bloody field frequent,
Familiar in each leader's tent;
Or whether, as the learn'd contend,
You from the neighbouring Gaul descend;
Or from Parthenope the proud,
Where numberless thy votaries crowd;
Whether thy great forefathers came
From realms that bear Vespuccio's name,
For so conjectures would obtrude;
And from thy painted skin conclude;
Whether, as Epicurus shows,
The world from justling seeds arose,
Which, mingling with prolific strife
In chaos, kindled into life:
So your production was the same,
And from contending atoms came.
Thy fair indulgent mother crown'd
Thy head with sparkling rubies round:
Beneath thy decent steps the road
Is all with precious jewels strew'd,

The bird of Pallas, knows his post,
Thee to attend, where'er thou goest.
    Byzantians boast, that on the clod
Where once their Sultan's horse hath trod,
Grows neither grass, nor shrub, nor tree:
The same thy subjects boast of thee.
    The greatest lord, when you appear,
Will deign your livery to wear,
In all the various colours seen
Of red and yellow, blue and green.
    With half a word when you require,
The man of business must retire.
    The haughty minister of state,
With trembling must thy leisure wait;
And, while his fate is in thy hands,
The business of the nation stands.
    Thou darest the greatest prince attack,
Canst hourly set him on the rack;
And, as an instance of thy power,
Enclose him in a wooden tower,
With pungent pains on every side:
So Regulus in torments died.
    From thee our youth all virtues learn,
Dangers with prudence to discern;
And well thy scholars are endued
With temperance and with fortitude,
With patience, which all ills supports,
And secrecy, the art of courts.
    The glittering beau could hardly tell,
Without your aid, to read or spell;
But, having long conversed with you,
Knows how to scroll a billet-doux.
    With what delight, methinks, I trace
Your blood in every noble race!
In whom thy features, shape, and mien,
Are to the life distinctly seen!
The Britons, once a savage kind,
By you were brighten'd and refined,
Descendants to the barbarous Huns,

With limbs robust, and voice that stuns:
But you have moulded them afresh,
Removed the tough superfluous flesh,
Taught them to modulate their tongues,
And speak without the help of lungs.

Proteus on you bestow'd the boon
To change your visage like the moon;
You sometimes half a face produce,
Keep t'other half for private use.

How famed thy conduct in the fight
With Hermes, son of Pleias bright!
Outnumber'd, half encompass'd round,
You strove for every inch of ground;
Then, by a soldierly retreat,
Retired to your imperial seat.
The victor, when your steps he traced,
Found all the realms before him waste:
You, o'er the high triumphal arch
Pontific, made your glorious march:
The wondrous arch behind you fell,
And left a chasm profound as hell:
You, in your capitol secured,
A siege as long as Troy endured.

On a Pen. 1724

In youth exalted high in air,
Or bathing in the waters fair,
Nature to form me took delight,
And clad my body all in white.
My person tall, and slender waist,
On either side with fringes graced;
Till me that tyrant man espied,
And dragg'd me from my mother's side:
No wonder now I look so thin;
The tyrant stript me to the skin:
My skin he flay'd, my hair he cropt:
At head and foot my body lopt:
And then, with heart more hard than stone,
He pick'd my marrow from the bone.
To vex me more, he took a freak
To slit my tongue and make me speak:
But, that which wonderful appears,
I speak to eyes, and not to ears.
He oft employs me in disguise,
And makes me tell a thousand lies:
To me he chiefly gives in trust
To please his malice or his lust.
From me no secret he can hide;
I see his vanity and pride:
And my delight is to expose
His follies to his greatest foes.
All languages I can command,
Yet not a word I understand.
Without my aid, the best divine
In learning would not know a line:
The lawyer must forget his pleading;
The scholar could not show his reading.
    Nay; man my master is my slave;
I give command to kill or save,
Can grant ten thousand pounds a-year,
And make a beggar's brat a peer.

But, while I thus my life relate,
I only hasten on my fate.
My tongue is black, my mouth is furr'd,
I hardly now can force a word.
I die unpitied and forgot,
And on some dunghill left to rot.

On Gold

All-ruling tyrant of the earth,
To vilest slaves I owe my birth,
How is the greatest monarch blest,
When in my gaudy livery drest!
No haughty nymph has power to run
From me; or my embraces shun.
Stabb'd to the heart, condemn'd to flame,
My constancy is still the same.
The favourite messenger of Jove,
And Lemnian god, consulting strove
To make me glorious to the sight
Of mortals, and the gods' delight.
Soon would their altar's flame expire
If I refused to lend them fire.

    By fate exalted high in place,
    Lo, here I stand with double face:
    Superior none on earth I find;
    But see below me all mankind
    Yet, as it oft attends the great,
    I almost sink with my own weight.

At every motion undertook,
The vulgar all consult my look.
I sometimes give advice in writing,
But never of my own inditing.
    I am a courtier in my way;
For those who raised me, I betray;
And some give out that I entice
To lust, to luxury, and dice.
Who punishments on me inflict,
Because they find their pockets pickt.
    By riding post, I lose my health,
And only to get others wealth.

On the Posteriors

Because I am by nature blind,
I wisely choose to walk behind;
However, to avoid disgrace,
I let no creature see my face.
My words are few, but spoke with sense;
And yet my speaking gives offence:
Or, if to whisper I presume,
The company will fly the room.
By all the world I am opprest:
And my oppression gives them rest.
    Through me, though sore against my will,
Instructors every art instil.
By thousands I am sold and bought,
Who neither get nor lose a groat;
For none, alas! by me can gain,
But those who give me greatest pain.
Shall man presume to be my master,
Who's but my caterer and taster?
Yet, though I always have my will,
I'm but a mere depender still:
An humble hanger-on at best;
Of whom all people make a jest.
    In me detractors seek to find
Two vices of a different kind;
I'm too profuse, some censurers cry,
And all I get, I let it fly;
While others give me many a curse,
Because too close I hold my purse.
But this I know, in either case,
They dare not charge me to my face.
'Tis true, indeed, sometimes I save,
Sometimes run out of all I have;
But, when the year is at an end,
Computing what I get and spend,
My goings-out, and comings-in,
I cannot find I lose or win;

And therefore all that know me say,
I justly keep the middle way.
I'm always by my betters led;
I last get up, and first a-bed;
Though, if I rise before my time,
The learn'd in sciences sublime
Consult the stars, and thence foretell
Good luck to those with whom I dwell.

On a Horn

The joy of man, the pride of brutes,
Domestic subject for disputes,
Of plenty thou the emblem fair,
Adorn'd by nymphs with all their care!
I saw thee raised to high renown,
Supporting half the British crown;
And often have I seen thee grace
The chaste Diana's infant face;
And whensoe'er you please to shine,
Less useful is her light than thine:
Thy numerous fingers know their way,
And oft in Celia's tresses play.
    To place thee in another view,
I'll show the world strange things and true;
What lords and dames of high degree
May justly claim their birth from thee!
The soul of man with spleen you vex;
Of spleen you cure the female sex.
Thee for a gift the courtier sends
With pleasure to his special friends:
He gives, and with a generous pride,
Contrives all means the gift to hide:
Nor oft can the receiver know,
Whether he has the gift or no.
On airy wings you take your flight,
And fly unseen both day and night;
Conceal your form with various tricks;
And few know how or where you fix:
Yet some, who ne'er bestow'd thee, boast
That they to others give thee most.
Meantime, the wise a question start,
If thou a real being art;
Or but a creature of the brain,
That gives imaginary pain?
But the sly giver better knows thee;
Who feels true joys when he bestows thee.

On a Corkscrew

Though I, alas! a prisoner be,
My trade is prisoners to set free.
No slave his lord's commands obeys
With such insinuating ways.
My genius piercing, sharp, and bright,
Wherein the men of wit delight.
The clergy keep me for their ease,
And turn and wind me as they please.
A new and wondrous art I show
Of raising spirits from below;
In scarlet some, and some in white;
They rise, walk round, yet never fright.
In at each mouth the spirits pass,
Distinctly seen as through a glass:
O'er head and body make a rout,
And drive at last all secrets out;
And still, the more I show my art,
The more they open every heart.
    A greater chemist none than I
Who, from materials hard and dry,
Have taught men to extract with skill
More precious juice than from a still.
    Although I'm often out of case,
I'm not ashamed to show my face.
Though at the tables of the great
I near the sideboard take my seat;
Yet the plain 'squire, when dinner's done,
Is never pleased till I make one;
He kindly bids me near him stand,
And often takes me by the hand.
    I twice a-day a-hunting go;
Nor ever fail to seize my foe;
And when I have him by the poll,
I drag him upwards from his hole;
Though some are of so stubborn kind,

I'm forced to leave a limb behind.
    I hourly wait some fatal end;
For I can break, but scorn to bend.

The Gulf of all Human Possessions 1724

Come hither, and behold the fruits,
Vain man! of all thy vain pursuits.
Take wise advice, and look behind,
Bring all past actions to thy mind.
Here you may see, as in a glass,
How soon all human pleasures pass;
How will it mortify thy pride,
To turn the true impartial side!
How will your eyes contain their tears,
When all the sad reverse appears!
    This cave within its womb confines
The last result of all designs:
Here lie deposited the spoils
Of busy mortals' endless toils:
Here, with an easy search, we find
The foul corruptions of mankind.
The wretched purchase here behold
Of traitors, who their country sold.
    This gulf insatiate imbibes
The lawyer's fees, the statesman's bribes.
Here, in their proper shape and mien,
Fraud, perjury, and guilt are seen.
Necessity, the tyrant's law,
All human race must hither draw;
All prompted by the same desire,
The vigorous youth and aged sire.
Behold the coward and the brave,
The haughty prince, the humble slave,
Physician, lawyer, and divine,
All make oblations at this shrine.
Some enter boldly, some by stealth,
And leave behind their fruitless wealth.
For, while the bashful sylvan maid,
As half-ashamed and half-afraid,
Approaching finds it hard to part
With that which dwelt so near her heart;

The courtly dame, unmoved by fear,
Profusely pours her offering here.
    A treasure here of learning lurks,
Huge heaps of never-dying works;
Labours of many an ancient sage,
And millions of the present age.
    In at this gulf all offerings pass
And lie an undistinguish'd mass.
Deucalion, to restore mankind,
Was bid to throw the stones behind;
So those who here their gifts convey
Are forced to look another way;
For few, a chosen few, must know
The mysteries that lie below.
    Sad charnel-house! a dismal dome,
For which all mortals leave their home!
The young, the beautiful, and brave,
Here buried in one common grave!
Where each supply of dead renews
Unwholesome damps, offensive dews:
And lo! the writing on the walls
Points out where each new victim falls;
The food of worms and beasts obscene,
Who round the vault luxuriant reign.
    See where those mangled corpses lie,
Condemn'd by female hands to die;
A comely dame once clad in white,
Lies there consign'd to endless night;
By cruel hands her blood was spilt,
And yet her wealth was all her guilt.
    And here six virgins in a tomb,
All-beauteous offspring of one womb,
Oft in the train of Venus seen,
As fair and lovely as their queen;
In royal garments each was drest,
Each with a gold and purple vest;
I saw them of their garments stript,
Their throats were cut, their bellies ript,
Twice were they buried, twice were born,

Twice from their sepulchres were torn;
But now dismember'd here are cast,
And find a resting-place at last.
    Here oft the curious traveller finds
The combat of opposing winds;
And seeks to learn the secret cause,
Which alien seems from nature's laws;
Why at this cave's tremendous mouth,
He feels at once both north and south;
Whether the winds, in caverns pent,
Through clefts oppugnant force a vent;
Or whether, opening all his stores,
Fierce Æolus in tempest roars.
    Yet, from this mingled mass of things,
In time a new creation springs.
These crude materials once shall rise
To fill the earth, and air, and skies;
In various forms appear again,
Of vegetables, brutes, and men.
So Jove pronounced among the gods,
Olympus trembling as he nods.

Louisa to Strephon. 1724

Ah! Strephon, how can you despise
Her, who without thy pity dies!
To Strephon I have still been true,
And of as noble blood as you;
Fair issue of the genial bed,
A virgin in thy bosom bred:
Embraced thee closer than a wife;
When thee I leave, I leave my life.
Why should my shepherd take amiss,
That oft I wake thee with a kiss?
Yet you of every kiss complain;
Ah! is not love a pleasing pain?
A pain which every happy night
You cure with ease and with delight;
With pleasure, as the poet sings,
Too great for mortals less than kings.
    Chloe, when on thy breast I lie,
Observes me with revengeful eye:
If Chloe o'er thy heart prevails,
She'll tear me with her desperate nails;
And with relentless hands destroy
The tender pledges of our joy.
Nor have I bred a spurious race;
They all were born from thy embrace.
    Consider, Strephon, what you do;
For, should I die for love of you,
I'll haunt thy dreams, a bloodless ghost;
And all my kin, (a numerous host,)
Who down direct our lineage bring
From victors o'er the Memphian king;
Renown'd in sieges and campaigns,
Who never fled the bloody plains:
Who in tempestuous seas can sport,
And scorn the pleasures of a court;
From whom great Sylla found his doom,
Who scourged to death that scourge of Rome,

Shall on thee take a vengeance dire;
Thou like Alcides shalt expire,
When his envenom'd shirt he wore,
And skin and flesh in pieces tore.
Nor less that shirt, my rival's gift,
Cut from the piece that made her shift,
Shall in thy dearest blood be dyed,
And make thee tear thy tainted hide.

A Maypole. 1725

Deprived of root, and branch and rind,
Yet flowers I bear of every kind:
And such is my prolific power,
They bloom in less than half an hour;
Yet standers-by may plainly see
They get no nourishment from me.
My head with giddiness goes round,
And yet I firmly stand my ground:
All over naked I am seen,
And painted like an Indian queen.
No couple-beggar in the land
E'er join'd such numbers hand in hand.
I join'd them fairly with a ring;
Nor can our parson blame the thing.
And though no marriage words are spoke,
They part not till the ring is broke;
Yet hypocrite fanatics cry,
I'm but an idol raised on high;
And once a weaver in our town,
A damn'd Cromwellian, knock'd me down.
I lay a prisoner twenty years,
And then the jovial cavaliers
To their old post restored all three—
I mean the church, the king, and me.

On the Moon

I with borrow'd silver shine
What you see is none of mine.
First I show you but a quarter,
Like the bow that guards the Tartar:
Then the half, and then the whole,
Ever dancing round the pole.

What will raise your admiration,
I am not one of God's creation,
But sprung, (and I this truth maintain,)
Like Pallas, from my father's brain.
And after all, I chiefly owe
My beauty to the shades below.
Most wondrous forms you see me wear,
A man, a woman, lion, bear,
A fish, a fowl, a cloud, a field,
All figures Heaven or earth can yield;
Like Daphne sometimes in a tree;
Yet am not one of all you see.

On a Circle

I'm up and down, and round about,
Yet all the world can't find me out;
Though hundreds have employ'd their leisure,
They never yet could find my measure.
I'm found almost in every garden,
Nay, in the compass of a farthing.
There's neither chariot, coach, nor mill,
Can move an inch except I will.

On Ink

I am jet black, as you may see,
The son of pitch and gloomy night:
Yet all that know me will agree,
I'm dead except I live in light.

Sometimes in panegyric high,
Like lofty Pindar, I can soar;
And raise a virgin to the sky,
Or sink her to a pocky whore.

My blood this day is very sweet,
To-morrow of a bitter juice;
Like milk, 'tis cried about the street,
And so applied to different use.

Most wondrous is my magic power:
For with one colour I can paint;
I'll make the devil a saint this hour,
Next make a devil of a saint.

Through distant regions I can fly,
Provide me but with paper wings;
And fairly show a reason why
There should be quarrels among kings:

And, after all, you'll think it odd,
When learned doctors will dispute,
That I should point the word of God,
And show where they can best confute.

Let lawyers bawl and strain their throats:
'Tis I that must the lands convey,
And strip their clients to their coats;
Nay, give their very souls away.

On the Five Senses

All of us in one you'll find, Brethren of a wondrous kind;
Yet among us all no brother
Knows one tittle of the other;
We in frequent councils are,
And our marks of things declare,
Where, to us unknown, a clerk
Sits, and takes them in the dark.
He's the register of all
In our ken, both great and small;
By us forms his laws and rules,
He's our master, we his tools;
Yet we can with greatest ease
Turn and wind him where we please.
    One of us alone can sleep,
Yet no watch the rest will keep,
But the moment that he closes,
Every brother else reposes.
If wine's brought or victuals drest,
One enjoys them for the rest.
    Pierce us all with wounding steel,
One for all of us will feel.
    Though ten thousand cannons roar,
Add to them ten thousand more,
Yet but one of us is found
Who regards the dreadful sound.
    Do what is not fit to tell,
There's but one of us can smell.

Fontinella to Florinda

When on my bosom thy bright eyes,
    Florinda, dart their heavenly beams,
I feel not the least love surprise,
    Yet endless tears flow down in streams;
There's nought so beautiful in thee,
    But you may find the same in me.

The lilies of thy skin compare;
    In me you see them full as white:
The roses of your cheeks, I dare
    Affirm, can't glow to more delight.
Then, since I show as fine a face,
    Can you refuse a soft embrace?

Ah! lovely nymph, thou'rt in thy prime!
    And so am I, while thou art here;
But soon will come the fatal time,
    When all we see shall disappear.
'Tis mine to make a just reflection,
    And yours to follow my direction.

Then catch admirers while you may;
    Treat not your lovers with disdain;
For time with beauty flies away,
    And there is no return again.
To you the sad account I bring,
    Life's autumn has no second spring.

An Echo

Never sleeping, still awake,
Pleasing most when most I speak;
The delight of old and young,
Though I speak without a tongue.
Nought but one thing can confound me,
Many voices joining round me;
Then I fret, and rave, and gabble,
Like the labourers of Babel.
Now I am a dog, or cow,
I can bark, or I can low;
I can bleat, or I can sing,
Like the warblers of the spring.
Let the lovesick bard complain,
And I mourn the cruel pain;
Let the happy swain rejoice,
And I join my helping voice:
Both are welcome, grief or joy,
I with either sport and toy.
Though a lady, I am stout,
Drums and trumpets bring me out:
Then I clash, and roar, and rattle,
Join in all the din of battle.
Jove, with all his loudest thunder,
When I'm vext, can't keep me under;
Yet so tender is my ear,
That the lowest voice I fear;
Much I dread the courtier's fate,
When his merit's out of date,
For I hate a silent breath,
And a whisper is my death.

On a Shadow in a Glass

By something form'd, I nothing am,
Yet everything that you can name;
In no place have I ever been,
Yet everywhere I may be seen;
In all things false, yet always true,
I'm still the same—but ever new.
Lifeless, life's perfect form I wear,
Can show a nose, eye, tongue, or ear,
Yet neither smell, see, taste, or hear.
All shapes and features I can boast,
No flesh, no bones, no blood—no ghost:
All colours, without paint, put on,
And change like the cameleon.
Swiftly I come, and enter there,
Where not a chink lets in the air;
Like thought, I'm in a moment gone,
Nor can I ever be alone:
All things on earth I imitate
Faster than nature can create;
Sometimes imperial robes I wear,
Anon in beggar's rags appear;
A giant now, and straight an elf,
I'm every one, but ne'er myself;
Ne'er sad I mourn, ne'er glad rejoice,
I move my lips, but want a voice;
I ne'er was born, nor e'er can die,
Then, pr'ythee, tell me what am I?

Most things by me do rise and fall,
And, as I please, they're great and small;
Invading foes without resistance,
With ease I make to keep their distance:
Again, as I'm disposed, the foe
Will come, though not a foot they go.
Both mountains, woods, and hills, and rocks
And gamesome goats, and fleecy flocks,

And lowing herds, and piping swains,
Come dancing to me o'er the plains.
The greatest whale that swims the sea
Does instantly my power obey.
In vain from me the sailor flies,
The quickest ship I can surprise,
And turn it as I have a mind,
And move it against tide and wind.
Nay, bring me here the tallest man,
I'll squeeze him to a little span;
Or bring a tender child, and pliant,
You'll see me stretch him to a giant:
Nor shall they in the least complain,
Because my magic gives no pain.

On Time

Ever eating, never cloying,
All-devouring, all-destroying,
Never finding full repast,
Till I eat the world at last.

On the Gallows

There is a gate, we know full well,
That stands 'twixt Heaven, and Earth, and Hell,
Where many for a passage venture,
Yet very few are fond to enter:
Although 'tis open night and day,
They for that reason shun this way:
Both dukes and lords abhor its wood,
They can't come near it for their blood.
What other way they take to go,
Another time I'll let you know.
Yet commoners with greatest ease
Can find an entrance when they please.
The poorest hither march in state
(Or they can never pass the gate)
Like Roman generals triumphant,
And then they take a turn and jump on't,
If gravest parsons here advance,
They cannot pass before they dance;
There's not a soul that does resort here,
But strips himself to pay the porter.

On the Vowels

We are little airy creatures,
All of different voice and features;
One of us in glass is set,
One of us you'll find in jet.
T'other you may see in tin,
And the fourth a box within.
If the fifth you should pursue,
It can never fly from you.

On Snow

From Heaven I fall, though from earth I begin,
No lady alive can show such a skin.
I'm bright as an angel, and light as a feather,
But heavy and dark, when you squeeze me together.
Though candour and truth in my aspect I bear,
Yet many poor creatures I help to ensnare.
Though so much of Heaven appears in my make,
The foulest impressions I easily take.
My parent and I produce one another,
The mother the daughter, the daughter the mother.

On a Cannon

Begotten, and born, and dying with noise,
The terror of women, and pleasure of boys,
Like the fiction of poets concerning the wind,
I'm chiefly unruly when strongest confined.
For silver and gold I don't trouble my head,
But all I delight in is pieces of lead;
Except when I trade with a ship or a town,
Why then I make pieces of iron go down.
One property more I would have you remark,
No lady was ever more fond of a spark;
The moment I get one, my soul's all a-fire,
And I roar out my joy, and in transport expire.

On a Pair of Dice

We are little brethren twain,
Arbiters of loss and gain,
Many to our counters run,
Some are made, and some undone:
But men find it to their cost,
Few are made, but numbers lost.
Though we play them tricks for ever,
Yet they always hope our favour.

On a Candle

To Lady Carteret

Of all inhabitants on earth,
To man alone I owe my birth,
And yet the cow, the sheep, the bee,
Are all my parents more than he:
I, a virtue, strange and rare,
Make the fairest look more fair,
And myself, which yet is rarer,
Growing old, grow still the fairer.
Like sots, alone I'm dull enough,
When dosed with smoke, and smear'd with snuff;
But, in the midst of mirth and wine,
I with double lustre shine.
Emblem of the Fair am I,
Polish'd neck, and radiant eye;
In my eye my greatest grace,
Emblem of the Cyclops' race;
Metals I like them subdue,
Slave like them to Vulcan too;
Emblem of a monarch old,
Wise, and glorious to behold;
Wasted he appears, and pale,
Watching for the public weal:
Emblem of the bashful dame,
That in secret feeds her flame,
Often aiding to impart
All the secrets of her heart;
Various is my bulk and hue,
Big like Bess, and small like Sue:
Now brown and burnish'd like a nut,
At other times a very slut;
Often fair, and soft, and tender,
Taper, tall, and smooth, and slender:
Like Flora, deck'd with various flowers,
Like Phoebus, guardian of the hours:

But whatever be my dress,
Greater be my size or less,
Swelling be my shape or small,
Like thyself I shine in all.
Clouded if my face is seen,
My complexion wan and green,
Languid like a love-sick maid,
Steel affords me present aid.
Soon or late, my date is done,
As my thread of life is spun;
Yet to cut the fatal thread
Oft revives my drooping head;
Yet I perish in my prime,
Seldom by the death of time;
Die like lovers as they gaze,
Die for those I live to please;
Pine unpitied to my urn,
Nor warm the fair for whom I burn:
Unpitied, unlamented too,
Die like all that look on you.

To Lady Carteret

By Dr. Delany

I reach all things near me, and far off to boot,
Without stretching a finger, or stirring a foot;
I take them all in too, to add to your wonder,
Though many and various, and large and asunder,
Without jostling or crowding they pass side by side,
Through a wonderful wicket, not half an inch wide;
Then I lodge them at ease in a very large store,
Of no breadth or length, with a thousand things more.
All this I can do without witchcraft or charm,
Though sometimes they say, I bewitch and do harm;
Though cold, I inflame; and though quiet, invade:
And nothing can shield from my spell but a shade.
A thief that has robb'd you, or done you disgrace,
In magical mirror, I'll show you his face:
Nay, if you'll believe what the poets have said,
They'll tell you I kill, and can call back the dead.
Like conjurers safe in my circle I dwell;
I love to look black too, it heightens my spell;
Though my magic is mighty in every hue,
Who see all my power must see it in you.

Answered by Dr. Swift

WITH half an eye your riddle I spy,
I observe your wicket hemm'd in by a thicket,
And whatever passes is strain'd through glasses.
You say it is quiet: I flatly deny it.
It wanders about, without stirring out;
No passion so weak but gives it a tweak;
Love, joy, and devotion, set it always in motion.
And as for trie tragic effects of its magic,
Which you say it can kill, or revive at its will,
The dead are all sound, and they live above ground:
After all you have writ, it cannot be wit;
Which plainly does follow, since it flies from Apollo.
Its cowardice such it cries at a touch;
'Tis a perfect milksop, grows drunk with a drop,
Another great fault, it cannot bear salt:
And a hair can disarm it of every charm.

To Lady Carteret

By Dr. Swift

From India's burning clime I'm brought,
With cooling gales like zephyrs fraught.
Not Iris, when she paints the sky,
Can show more different hues than I;
Nor can she change her form so fast,
I'm now a sail, and now a mast.
I here am red, and there am green,
A beggar there, and here a queen.
I sometimes live in house of hair,
And oft in hand of lady fair.
I please the young, I grace the old,
And am at once both hot and cold.
Say what I am then, if you can,
And find the rhyme, and you're the man.

Answered by Dr. Sheridan

Your house of hair, and lady's hand,
At first did put me to a stand.
I have it now—'tis plain enough—
Your hairy business is a muff.
Your engine fraught with cooling gales,
At once so like your masts and sails;
Your thing of various shape and hue
Must be some painted toy, I knew;
And for the rhyme to you're the man,
What fits it better than a fan?

A Riddle

I'm wealthy and poor,
I'm empty and full,
I'm humble and proud,
I'm witty and dull.
I'm foul and yet fair:
I'm old, and yet young;
I lie with Moll Kerr,
And toast Mrs. Long.

Answer, by Mr. F——r

In rigging he's rich, though in pocket he's poor,
He cringes to courtiers, and cocks to the cits;
Like twenty he dresses, but looks like threescore;
He's a wit to the fools, and a fool to the wits.
Of wisdom he's empty, but full of conceit;
He paints and perfumes while he rots with the scab;
'Tis a beau you may swear by his sense and his gait;
He boasts of a beauty and lies with a drab.

A Letter to Dr. Helsham

Sir,

Pray discruciate what follows.

The dullest beast, and gentleman's liquor,
When young is often due to the vicar,

The dullest of beasts, and swine's delight,
Make up a bird very swift of flight.

The dullest beast, when high in stature,
And another of royal nature,
For breeding is a useful creature.

The dullest beast, and a party distress'd,
When too long, is bad at best.

The dullest beast, and the saddle it wears,
Is good for partridge, not for hares.

The dullest beast, and kind voice of a cat,
Will make a horse go, though he be not fat.

The dullest of beasts and of birds in the air,
Is that by which all Irishmen swear.

The dullest beast, and famed college for Teagues,
Is a person very unfit for intrigues.

The dullest beast, and a cobbler's tool,
With a boy that is only fit for school,
In summer is very pleasant and cool.

The dullest beast, and that which you kiss,
May break a limb of master or miss.

Of serpent kind, and what at distance kills,
Poor mistress Dingley oft hath felt its bills.

The dullest beast, and eggs unsound,
Without it I rather would walk on the ground.

The dullest beast, and what covers a house,
Without it a writer is not worth a louse.

The dullest beast, and scandalous vermin,
Of roast or boil'd, to the hungry is charming.

The dullest beast, and what's cover'd with crust,
There's nobody but a fool that would trust.

The dullest beast, and mending highways,
Is to a horse an evil disease.

The dullest beast, and a hole in the ground,
Will dress a dinner worth five pound.

The dullest beast, and what doctors pretend,
The cook-maid often has by the end.

The dullest beast, and fish for lent,
May give you a blow you'll for ever repent.

The dullest beast, and a shameful jeer,
Without it a lady should never appear.

Wednesday Night

I writ all these before I went to bed. Pray explain them for me, because I cannot do it.

Probatur Aliter

A long-ear'd beast, and a field-house for cattle,
Among the coals doth often rattle.

A long-ear'd beast, a bird that prates,
The bridegrooms' first gift to their mates,
Is by all pious Christians thought,
In clergymen the greatest fault.

A long-ear'd beast, and woman of Endor,
If your wife be a scold, that will mend her.

With a long-ear'd beast, and medicine's use,
Cooks make their fowl look tight and spruce.

A long-ear'd beast, and holy fable,
Strengthens the shoes of half the rabble.

A long-ear'd beast, and Rhenish wine,
Lies in the lap of ladies fine.

A long-ear'd beast, and Flanders College,
Is Dr. T——l, to my knowledge.

A long-ear'd beast, and building knight,
Censorious people do in spite.

A long-ear'd beast, and bird of night,
We sinners art too apt to slight.

A long-ear'd beast, and shameful vermin,
A judge will eat, though clad in ermine.

A long-ear'd beast, and Irish cart,
Can leave a mark, and give a smart.

A long-ear'd beast, in mud to lie,
No bird in air so swift can fly.

A long-ear'd beast, and a sputt'ring old Whig,
I wish he were in it, and dancing a jig.

A long-ear'd beast, and liquor to write,
Is a damnable smell both morning and night.

A long-ear'd beast, and the child of a sheep,
At Whist they will make a desperate sweep.

A beast long-ear'd, and till midnight you stay,
Will cover a house much better than clay.

A long-ear'd beast, and the drink you love best,
You call him a sloven in earnest for jest.

A long-ear'd beast, and the sixteenth letter,
I'd not look at all unless I look'd better.

A long-ear'd beast give me, and eggs unsound,
Or else I will not ride one inch of ground.

A long-ear'd beast, another name for jeer,
To ladies' skins there nothing comes so near.

A long-ear'd beast, and kind noise of a cat,
Is useful in journeys, take notice of that.

A long-ear'd beast, and what seasons your beef,
On such an occasion the law gives relief.

A long-ear'd beast, a thing that force must drive in,
Bears up his house, that's of his own contriving.

Poems Composed at Market Hill

On Cutting Down the Thorn at Market-Hill. 1727

At Market-Hill, as well appears
    By chronicle of ancient date,
There stood for many hundred years
    A spacious thorn before the gate.

Hither came every village maid,
    And on the boughs her garland hung,
And here, beneath the spreading shade,
    Secure from satyrs sat and sung.

Sir Archibald, that valorous knight.
    The lord of all the fruitful plain,
Would come to listen with delight,
    For he was fond of rural strain.

(Sir Archibald, whose favourite name
    Shall stand for ages on record,
By Scottish bards of highest fame,
    Wise Hawthornden and Stirling's lord.)

But time with iron teeth, I ween,
    Has canker'd all its branches round;
No fruit or blossom to be seen,
    Its head reclining toward the ground.

This aged, sickly, sapless thorn,
    Which must, alas! no longer stand,
Behold the cruel Dean in scorn
    Cuts down with sacrilegious hand.

Dame Nature, when she saw the blow,
    Astonish'd gave a dreadful shriek;
And mother Tellus trembled so,
    She scarce recover'd in a week.

The Sylvan powers, with fear perplex'd,
In prudence and compassion sent
(For none could tell whose turn was next)
Sad omens of the dire event.

The magpie, lighting on the stock,
Stood chattering with incessant din:
And with her beak gave many a knock,
To rouse and warn the nymph within.

The owl foresaw, in pensive mood,
The ruin of her ancient seat;
And fled in haste, with all her brood,
To seek a more secure retreat.

Last trotted forth the gentle swine,
To ease her itch against the stump,
And dismally was heard to whine,
All as she scrubb'd her meazly rump.

The nymph who dwells in every tree,
(If all be true that poets chant,)
Condemn'd by Fate's supreme decree,
Must die with her expiring plant.

Thus, when the gentle Spina found
The thorn committed to her care,
Received its last and deadly wound,
She fled, and vanish'd into air.

But from the root a dismal groan
First issuing struck the murderer's ears:
And, in a shrill revengeful tone,
This prophecy he trembling hears:

"Thou chief contriver of my fall,
Relentless Dean, to mischief born;
My kindred oft thine hide shall gall,
Thy gown and cassock oft be torn.

"And thy confederate dame, who brags
    That she condemn'd me to the fire,
Shall rend her petticoats to rags,
    And wound her legs with every brier.

"Nor thou, Lord Arthur, shall escape;
    To thee I often call'd in vain,
Against that assassin in crape;
    Yet thou couldst tamely see me slain:

"Nor, when I felt the dreadful blow,
    Or chid the Dean, or pinch'd thy spouse;
Since you could see me treated so,
    (An old retainer to your house:)

"May that fell Dean, by whose command
    Was form'd this Machiavelian plot,
Not leave a thistle on thy land;
    Then who will own thee for a Scot?

"Pigs and fanatics, cows and teagues,
    Through all my empire I foresee,
To tear thy hedges join in leagues,
    Sworn to revenge my thorn and me.

"And thou, the wretch ordain'd by fate,
    Neal Gahagan, Hibernian clown,
With hatchet blunter than thy pate,
To hack my hallow'd timber down;

"When thou, suspended high in air,
    Diest on a more ignoble tree,
(For thou shall steal thy landlord's mare,)
    Then, bloody caitiff! think on me."

To Dean Swift
By Sir Arthur Acheson. 1728

Good cause have I to sing and vapour,
For I am landlord to the Drapier:
He, that of every ear's the charmer,
Now condescends to be my farmer,
And grace my villa with his strains;
Lives such a bard on British plains?
No; not in all the British court;
For none but witlings there resort,
Whose names and works (though dead) are made
Immortal by the Dunciad;
And, sure as monument of brass,
Their fame to future times shall pass;
How, with a weakly warbling tongue,
Of brazen knight they vainly sung;
A subject for their genius fit;
He dares defy both sense and wit.
What dares he not? He can, we know it,
A laureat make that is no poet;
A judge, without the least pretence
To common law, or common sense;
A bishop that is no divine;
And coxcombs in red ribbons shine:
Nay, he can make, what's greater far,
A middle state 'twixt peace and war;
And say, there shall; for years together,
Be peace and war, and both, and neither.
Happy, O Market-Hill! at least,
That court and courtiers have no taste:
You never else had known the Dean,
But, as of old, obscurely lain;
All things gone on the same dull track,
And Drapier's-Hill been still Drumlack;
But now your name with Penshurst vies,
And wing'd with fame shall reach the skies.

Dean Swift at Sir Arthur Acheson's In the North of Ireland

The Dean would visit Market-Hill,
Our invitation was but slight;
I said—"Why let him, if he will:"
And so I bade Sir Arthur write.

His manners would not let him wait,
Lest we should think ourselves neglected,
And so we see him at our gate
Three days before he was expected,

After a week, a month, a quarter,
And day succeeding after day,
Says not a word of his departure,
Though not a soul would have him stay.

I've said enough to make him blush,
Methinks, or else the devil's in't;
But he cares not for it a rush,
Nor for my life will take the hint.

But you, my dear, may let him know,
In civil language, if he stays,
How deep and foul the roads may grow,
And that he may command the chaise.

Or you may say—"My wife intends,
Though I should be exceeding proud,
This winter to invite some friends,
And, sir, I know you hate a crowd."

Or, "Mr. Dean—I should with joy
Beg you would here continue still,
But we must go to Aghnecloy;
Or Mr. Moore will take it ill."

The house accounts are daily rising;
  So much his stay doth swell the bills:
My dearest life, it is surprising,
  How much he eats, how much he swills.

His brace of puppies how they stuff!
  And they must have three meals a-day,
Yet never think they get enough;
  His horses too eat all our hay.

O! if I could, how I would maul
  His tallow face and wainscot paws,
His beetle brows, and eyes of wall,
  And make him soon give up the cause!

Must I be every moment chid
  With *Skinnybonia, Snipe*, and *Lean?*
O! that I could but once be rid
  Of this insulting tyrant Dean!

On a very old Glass at Market-Hill

Frail glass! thou mortal art as well as I;
Though none can tell which of us first shall die.

Answered Extempore by Dr. Swift

We both are mortal; but thou, frailer creature,
    May'st die, like me, by chance, but not by nature.

Epitaph
In Berkeley Church-Yard, Gloucestershire

Here lies the Earl of Suffolk's fool,
    Men call'd him Dicky Pearce;
His folly served to make folks laugh,
    When wit and mirth were scarce.

Poor Dick, alas! is dead and gone,
    What signifies to cry?
Dickies enough are still behind,
    To laugh at by and by.

Buried, June 18, 1728, aged 63.

My Lady's Lamentation and Complaint Against the Dean

July 28, 1728

Sure never did man see
A wretch like poor Nancy,
So teazed day and night
By a Dean and a Knight.
To punish my sins,
Sir Arthur begins,
And gives me a wipe,
With Skinny and Snipe:,
His malice is plain,
Hallooing the Dean.

The Dean never stops,
When he opens his chops;
I'm quite overrun
With rebus and pun.
    Before he came here,
To spunge for good cheer,
I sat with delight,
From morning till night,
With two bony thumbs
Could rub my old gums,
Or scratching my nose
And jogging my toes;
But at present, forsooth,
I must not rub a tooth.
When my elbows he sees
Held up by my knees,
My arms, like two props,
Supporting my chops,
And just as I handle 'em
Moving all like a pendulum;
He trips up my props,
And down my chin drops

From my head to my heels,
Like a clock without wheels;
I sink in the spleen,
A useless machine.
    If he had his will,
I should never sit still:
He comes with his whims
I must move my limbs;
I cannot be sweet
Without using my feet;
To lengthen my breath,
He tires me to death.
By the worst of all squires,
Thro' bogs and thro' briers,
Where a cow would be startled,
I'm in spite of my heart led;
And, say what I will,
Haul'd up every hill;
Till, daggled and tatter'd,
My spirits quite shatter'd,
I return home at night,
And fast, out of spite:
For I'd rather be dead,
Than it e'er should be said,
I was better for him,
In stomach or limb.
    But now to my diet;
No eating in quiet,
He's still finding fault,
Too sour or too salt:
The wing of a chick
I hardly can pick:
But trash without measure
I swallow with pleasure.
    Next, for his diversion,
He rails at my person.
What court breeding this is!
He takes me to pieces:
From shoulder to flank

I'm lean and am lank;
My nose, long and thin,
Grows down to my chin;
My chin will not stay,
But meets it halfway;
My fingers, prolix,
Are ten crooked sticks:
He swears my el—bows
Are two iron crows,
Or sharp pointed rocks,
And wear out my smocks:
To 'scape them, Sir Arthur
Is forced to lie farther,
Or his sides they would gore
Like the tusks of a boar.
    Now changing the scene
But still to the Dean;
He loves to be bitter at
A lady illiterate;
If he sees her but once,
He'll swear she's a dunce;
Can tell by her looks
A hater of books;
Thro' each line of her face
Her folly can trace;
Which spoils every feature
Bestow'd her by nature;
But sense gives a grace
To the homeliest face:
Wise books and reflection
Will mend the complexion:
(A civil divine!
I suppose, meaning mine!)
No lady who wants them,
Can ever be handsome.
    I guess well enough
What he means by this stuff:
He haws and he hums,
At last out it comes:

What, madam? No walking,
No reading, nor talking?
You're now in your prime,
Make use of your time.
Consider, before
You come to threescore,
How the hussies will fleer
Where'er you appear;
"That silly old puss
Would fain be like us:
What a figure she made
In her tarnish'd brocade!"
    And then he grows mild:
Come, be a good child:
If you are inclined
To polish your mind,
Be adored by the men
Till threescore and ten,
And kill with the spleen
The jades of sixteen;
I'll show you the way;
Read six hours a-day.
The wits will frequent ye,
And think you but twenty.
(To make you learn faster,
I'll be your schoolmaster
And leave you to choose
The books you peruse.)
    Thus was I drawn in;
Forgive me my sin.
At breakfast he'll ask
An account of my task.
Put a word out of joint,
Or miss but a point,
He rages and frets,
His manners forgets;
And as I am serious,
Is very imperious.
No book for delight

Must come in my sight;
But, instead of new plays,
Dull Bacon's Essays,
And pore every day on
That nasty Pantheon.
If I be not a drudge,
Let all the world judge.
'Twere better be blind,
Than thus be confined.
    But while in an ill tone,
I murder poor Milton,
The Dean you will swear,
Is at study or prayer.
He's all the day sauntering,
With labourers bantering,
Among his colleagues,
A parcel of Teagues,
Whom he brings in among us
And bribes with mundungus.
(He little believes
How they laugh in their sleeves.)
Hail, fellow, well met,
All dirty and wet:
Find out, if you can,
Who's master, who's man;
Who makes the best figure,
The Dean or the digger;
And which is the best
At cracking a jest.
(Now see how he sits
Perplexing his wits
In search of a motto
To fix on his grotto.)
How proudly he talks
Of zigzags and walks,
And all the day raves
Of cradles and caves;
And boasts of his feats,
His grottos and seats;

Shows all his gewgaws,
And gapes for applause;
A fine occupation
For one in his station!
A hole where a rabbit
Would scorn to inhabit,
Dug out in an hour;
He calls it a bower.
    But, O! how we laugh,
To see a wild calf
Come, driven by heat,
And foul the green seat;
Or run helter-skelter,
To his arbour for shelter,
Where all goes to ruin
The Dean has been doing:
The girls of the village
Come flocking for pillage,
Pull down the fine briers
And thorns to make fires;
But yet are so kind
To leave something behind:
No more need be said on't,
I smell when I tread on't.
    Dear friend, Doctor Jinny.
If I could but win ye,
Or Walmsley or Whaley,
To come hither daily,
Since fortune, my foe,
Will needs have it so,
That I'm, by her frowns,
Condemn'd to black gowns;
No squire to be found
The neighbourhood round;
(For, under the rose,
I would rather choose those)
If your wives will permit ye,
Come here out of pity,
To ease a poor lady,

And beg her a play-day.
So may you be seen
No more in the spleen;
May Walmsley give wine
Like a hearty divine!
May Whaley disgrace
Dull Daniel's whey-face!
And may your three spouses
Let you lie at friends' houses!

A Pastoral Dialogue. 1728

Dermot, Sheelah: A Nymph and swain, Sheelah and Dermot hight;
Who wont to weed the court of Gosford knight;
While each with stubbed knife removed the roots,
That raised between the stones their daily shoots;
As at their work they sate in counterview,
With mutual beauty smit, their passion grew.
Sing, heavenly Muse, in sweetly flowing strain,
The soft endearments of the nymph and swain.
Dermot: My love to Sheelah is more firmly fixt,
Than strongest weeds that grow those stones betwixt;
My spud these nettles from the stones can part;
No knife so keen to weed thee from my heart.
Sheelah: My love for gentle Dermot faster grows,
Than yon tall dock that rises to thy nose.
Cut down the dock, 'twill sprout again; but, O!
Love rooted out, again will never grow.
Dermot: No more that brier thy tender leg shall rake:
(I spare the thistles for Sir Arthur's sake)
Sharp are the stones; take thou this rushy mat;
The hardest bum will bruise with sitting squat.
Sheelah: Thy breeches, torn behind, stand gaping wide;
This petticoat shall save thy dear backside;
Nor need I blush; although you feel it wet,
Dermot, I vow, 'tis nothing else but sweat.
Dermot: At an old stubborn root I chanced to tug,
When the Dean threw me this tobacco-plug;
A longer ha'p'orth never did I see;
This, dearest Sheelah, thou shall share with me.
Sheelah: In at the pantry door, this morn I slipt,
And from the shelf a charming crust I whipt:
Dennis was out, and I got hither safe;
And thou, my dear, shall have the bigger half.
Dermot: When you saw Tady at long bullets play,
You sate and loused him all a sunshine day:
How could you, Sheelah, listen to his tales,
Or crack such lice as his between your nails?

Sheelah: When you with Oonah stood behind a ditch,
I peep'd, and saw you kiss the dirty bitch;
Dermot, how could you touch these nasty sluts?
I almost wish'd this spud were in your guts.
Dermot: If Oonah once I kiss'd, forbear to chide;
Her aunt's my gossip by my father's side:
But, if I ever touch her lips again,
May I be doom'd for life to weed in rain!
Sheelah: Dermot, I swear, though Tady's locks could hold
Ten thousand lice, and every louse was gold;
Him on my lap you never more shall see;
Or may I lose my weeding knife—and thee!
Dermot: O, could I earn for thee, my lovely lass,
A pair of brogues to bear thee dry to mass!
But see, where Norah with the sowins comes—
Then let us rise, and rest our weary bums.

The Grand Question Debated

Whether Hamilton's Bawn should be Turned into a Barrack or Malt-House. 1729

The Preface to the English Edition

The author of the following poem is said to be Dr. J. S. D. S. P. D. who writ it, as well as several other copies of verses of the like kind, by way of amusement, in the family of an honourable gentleman in the north of Ireland, where he spent a summer, about two or three years ago. A certain very great person, then in that kingdom, having heard much of this poem, obtained a copy from the gentleman, or, as some say, the lady in whose house it was written, from whence I know not by what accident several other copies were transcribed full of errors. As I have a great respect for the supposed author, I have procured a true copy of the poem, the publication whereof can do him less injury than printing any of those incorrect ones which run about in manuscript, and would infallibly be soon in the press, if not thus prevented. Some expressions being peculiar to Ireland, I have prevailed on a gentleman of that kingdom to explain them, and I have put the several explanations in their proper places.

—*First Edition*

Thus spoke to my lady the knight full of care,
"Let me have your advice in a weighty affair.
This Hamilton's bawn, while it sticks in my hand
I lose by the house what I get by the land;
But how to dispose of it to the best bidder,
For a barrack or malt-house, we now must consider.
"First, let me suppose I make it a malt-house,
Here I have computed the profit will fall t'us:
There's nine hundred pounds for labour and grain,
I increase it to twelve, so three hundred remain;
A handsome addition for wine and good cheer,
Three dishes a-day, and three hogsheads a-year;

With a dozen large vessels my vault shall be stored;
No little scrub joint shall come on my board;
And you and the Dean no more shall combine
To stint me at night to one bottle of wine;
Nor shall I, for his humour, permit you to purloin
A stone and a quarter of beef from my sir-loin.
If I make it a barrack, the crown is my tenant;
My dear, I have ponder'd again and again on't:
In poundage and drawbacks I lose half my rent,
Whatever they give me, I must be content,
Or join with the court in every debate;
And rather than that, I would lose my estate."
 Thus ended the knight; thus began his meek wife:
"It must, and it shall be a barrack, my life.
I'm grown a mere *mopus*; no company comes
But a rabble of tenants, and rusty dull rums.
With parsons what lady can keep herself clean?
I'm all over daub'd when I sit by the Dean.
But if you will give us a barrack, my dear,
The captain I'm sure will always come here;
I then shall not value his deanship a straw,
For the captain, I warrant, will keep him in awe;
Or, should he pretend to be brisk and alert,
Will tell him that chaplains should not be so pert;
That men of his coat should be minding their prayers,
And not among ladies to give themselves airs."
 Thus argued my lady, but argued in vain;
The knight his opinion resolved to maintain.
 But Hannah, who listen'd to all that was past,
And could not endure so vulgar a taste,
As soon as her ladyship call'd to be dress'd,
Cried, "Madam, why surely my master's possess'd,
Sir Arthur the maltster! how fine it will sound!
I'd rather the bawn were sunk under ground.
But, madam, I guess'd there would never come good,
When I saw him so often with Darby and Wood.
And now my dream's out; for I was a-dream'd
That I saw a huge rat—O dear, how I scream'd!
And after, methought, I had lost my new shoes;

And Molly, she said, I should hear some ill news.
“Dear Madam, had you but the spirit to tease,
You might have a barrack whenever you please:
And, madam, I always believed you so stout,
That for twenty denials you would not give out.
If I had a husband like him, I *purtest,*
Till he gave me my will, I would give him no rest;
And, rather than come in the same pair of sheets
With such a cross man, I would lie in the streets:
But, madam, I beg you, contrive and invent,
And worry him out, till he gives his consent.
Dear madam, whene'er of a barrack I think,
An I were to be hang'd, I can't sleep a wink:
For if a new crotchet comes into my brain,
I can't get it out, though I'd never so fain.
I fancy already a barrack contrived
At Hamilton's bawn, and the troop is arrived;
Of this to be sure, Sir Arthur has warning,
And waits on the captain betimes the next morning.
“Now see, when they meet, how their honours behave;
‘Noble captain, your servant’—‘Sir Arthur, your slave;
You honour me much’—‘The honour is mine.’—
‘'Twas a sad rainy night’—‘But the morning is fine.’—
‘Pray, how does my lady?’—‘My wife's at your service.’—
‘I think I have seen her picture by Jervas.’—
‘Good-morrow, good captain’—‘I'll wait on you down’—
‘You shan't stir a foot’—‘You'll think me a clown.’—
‘For all the world, captain, not half an inch farther’—
‘You must be obey'd—Your servant, Sir Arthur!
My humble respects to my lady unknown.’—
‘I hope you will use my house as your own.’”
“Go bring me my smock, and leave off your prate,
Thou hast certainly gotten a cup in thy pate.”
“Pray, madam, be quiet: what was it I said?
You had like to have put it quite out of my head.
Next day to be sure, the captain will come,
At the head of his troop, with trumpet and drum.
Now, madam, observe how he marches in state:
The man with the kettle-drum enters the gate:

Dub, dub, adub, dub. The trumpeters follow.
Tantara, tantara; while all the boys holla.
See now comes the captain all daub'd with gold lace:
O la! the sweet gentleman! look in his face;
And see how he rides like a lord of the land,
With the fine flaming sword that he holds in his hand;
And his horse, the dear *creter*, it prances and rears;
With ribbons in knots at its tail and its ears:
At last comes the troop, by word of command,
Drawn up in our court; when the captain cries, STAND!
Your ladyship lifts up the sash to be seen,
For sure I had dizen'd you out like a queen.
The captain, to show he is proud of the favour,
Looks up to your window, and cocks up his beaver;
(His beaver is cock'd: pray, madam, mark that,
For a captain of horse never takes off his hat,
Because he has never a hand that is idle,
For the right holds the sword, and the left holds the bridle;)
Then flourishes thrice his sword in the air,
As a compliment due to a lady so fair;
(How I tremble to think of the blood it has spilt!)
Then he lowers down the point, and kisses the hilt.
Your ladyship smiles, and thus you begin:
'Pray, captain, be pleased to alight and walk in.'
The captain salutes you with congee profound,
And your ladyship curtseys half way to the ground.
'Kit, run to your master, and bid him come to us;
I'm sure he'll be proud of the honour you do us;
And, captain, you'll do us the favour to stay,
And take a short dinner here with us to-day:
You're heartily welcome; but as for good cheer,
You come in the very worst time of the year;
If I had expected so worthy a guest—'
'Lord, madam! your ladyship sure is in jest;
You banter me, madam; the kingdom must grant—'
'You officers, captain, are so complaisant!'"—
"Hist, hussey, I think I hear somebody coming"—
"No madam: 'tis only Sir Arthur a-humming.
To shorten my tale, (for I hate a long story,)

The captain at dinner appears in his glory;
The dean and the doctor have humbled their pride,
For the captain's entreated to sit by your side;
And, because he's their betters, you carve for him first;
The parsons for envy are ready to burst.
The servants, amazed, are scarce ever able
To keep off their eyes, as they wait at the table;
And Molly and I have thrust in our nose,
To peep at the captain in all his fine *clo'es.*
Dear madam, be sure he's a fine spoken man,
Do but hear on the clergy how glib his tongue ran;
And, 'madam,' says he, 'if such dinners you give,
You'll ne'er want for parsons as long as you live.
I ne'er knew a parson without a good nose;
But the devil's as welcome, wherever he goes:
G—d d—n me! they bid us reform and repent,
But, z—s! by their looks, they never keep Lent:
Mister curate, for all your grave looks, I'm afraid
You cast a sheep's eye on her ladyship's maid:
I wish she would lend you her pretty white hand
In mending your cassock, and smoothing your band:
(For the Dean was so shabby, and look'd like a ninny,
That the captain supposed he was curate to Jinny.)
'Whenever you see a cassock and gown,
A hundred to one but it covers a clown.
Observe how a parson comes into a room;
G—d d—n me, he hobbles as bad as my groom;
A *scholard*, when just from his college broke loose,
Can hardly tell how to cry bo to a goose;
Your Noveds, and Bluturks, and Omurs, and stuff
By G—, they don't signify this pinch of snuff.
To give a young gentleman right education,
The army's the only good school in the nation:
My schoolmaster call'd me a dunce and a fool,
But at cuffs I was always the cock of the school;
I never could take to my book for the blood o' me,
And the puppy confess'd he expected no good o' me.
He caught me one morning coquetting his wife,
But he maul'd me, I ne'er was so maul'd in my life:

So I took to the road, and, what's very odd,
The first man I robb'd was a parson, by G—.
Now, madam, you'll think it a strange thing to say,
But the sight of a book makes me sick to this day.
"Never since I was born did I hear so much wit,
And, madam, I laugh'd till I thought I should split.
So then you look'd scornful, and snift at the Dean,
As who should say, 'Now, am I skinny and lean?'
But he durst not so much as once open his lips,
And the doctor was plaguily down in the hips."
Thus merciless Hannah ran on in her talk,
Till she heard the Dean call, "Will your ladyship walk?"
Her ladyship answers, "I'm just coming down:"
Then, turning to Hannah, and forcing a frown,
Although it was plain in her heart she was glad,
Cried, "Hussey, why sure the wench is gone mad!
How could these chimeras get into your brains!—
Come hither and take this old gown for your pains.
But the Dean, if this secret should come to his ears,
Will never have done with his gibes and his jeers:
For your life, not a word of the matter I charge ye:
Give me but a barrack, a fig for the clergy."

Drapier's-Hill. 1730

We give the world to understand,
Our thriving Dean has purchased land;
A purchase which will bring him clear
Above his rent four pounds a-year;
Provided to improve the ground,
He will but add two hundred pound;
And from his endless hoarded store,
To build a house, five hundred more.
Sir Arthur, too, shall have his will,
And call the mansion Drapier's-Hill;
That, when a nation, long enslaved,
Forgets by whom it once was saved;
When none the Drapier's praise shall sing,
His signs aloft no longer swing,
His medals and his prints forgotten,
And all his handkerchiefs are rotten,
His famous letters made waste paper,
This hill may keep the name of Drapier;
In spite of envy, flourish still,
And Drapier's vie with Cooper's-Hill.

The Dean's Reasons

For not Building at Drapier's-Hill

I will not build on yonder mount;
And, should you call me to account,
Consulting with myself, I find
It was no levity of mind.
Whate'er I promised or intended,
No fault of mine, the scheme is ended;
Nor can you tax me as unsteady,
I have a hundred causes ready;
All risen since that flattering time,
When Drapier's-Hill appear'd in rhyme.
    I am, as now too late I find,
The greatest cully of mankind;
The lowest boy in Martin's school
May turn and wind me like a fool.
How could I form so wild a vision,
To seek, in deserts, Fields Elysian?
To live in fear, suspicion, variance,
With thieves, fanatics, and barbarians?
    But here my lady will object;
Your deanship ought to recollect,
That, near the knight of Gosford placed,
Whom you allow a man of taste,
Your intervals of time to spend
With so conversable a friend,
It would not signify a pin
Whatever climate you were in.
    'Tis true, but what advantage comes
To me from all a usurer's plums;
Though I should see him twice a-day,
And am his neighbour 'cross the way:
If all my rhetoric must fail
To strike him for a pot of ale?
    Thus, when the learned and the wise
Conceal their talents from our eyes,

And from deserving friends withhold
Their gifts, as misers do their gold;
Their knowledge to themselves confined
Is the same avarice of mind;
Nor makes their conversation better,
Than if they never knew a letter.
Such is the fate of Gosford's knight,
Who keeps his wisdom out of sight;
Whose uncommunicative heart
Will scarce one precious word impart:
Still rapt in speculations deep,
His outward senses fast asleep;
Who, while I talk, a song will hum,
Or with his fingers beat the drum;
Beyond the skies transports his mind,
And leaves a lifeless corpse behind.
　　But, as for me, who ne'er could clamber high,
To understand Malebranche or Cambray;
Who send my mind (as I believe) less
Than others do, on errands sleeveless;
Can listen to a tale humdrum,
And with attention read Tom Thumb;
My spirits with my body progging,
Both hand in hand together jogging;
Sunk over head and ears in matter.
Nor can of metaphysics smatter;
Am more diverted with a quibble
Than dream of words intelligible;
And think all notions too abstracted
Are like the ravings of a crackt head;
What intercourse of minds can be
Betwixt the knight sublime and me,
If when I talk, as talk I must,
It is but prating to a bust?
　　Where friendship is by Fate design'd,
It forms a union in the mind:
But here I differ from the knight
In every point, like black and white:

For none can say that ever yet
We both in one opinion met:
Not in philosophy, or ale;
In state affairs, or planting kale;
In rhetoric, or picking straws;
In roasting larks, or making laws;
In public schemes, or catching flies;
In parliaments, or pudding pies.
    The neighbours wonder why the knight
Should in a country life delight,
Who not one pleasure entertains
To cheer the solitary scenes:
His guests are few, his visits rare;
Nor uses time, nor time will spare;
Nor rides, nor walks, nor hunts, nor fowls,
Nor plays at cards, or dice, or bowls;
But seated in an easy-chair,
Despises exercise and air.
His rural walks he ne'er adorns;
Here poor Pomona sits on thorns:
And there neglected Flora settles
Her bum upon a bed of nettles.
Those thankless and officious cares
I used to take in friends' affairs,
From which I never could refrain,
And have been often chid in vain;
From these I am recover'd quite,
At least in what regards the knight.
Preserve his health, his store increase;
May nothing interrupt his peace!
But now let all his tenants round
First milk his cows, and after, pound;
Let every cottager conspire
To cut his hedges down for fire;
The naughty boys about the village
His crabs and sloes may freely pillage;
He still may keep a pack of knaves
To spoil his work, and work by halves;

His meadows may be dug by swine,
It shall be no concern of mine;
For why should I continue still
To serve a friend against his will?

The Revolution at Market-Hill
1730

From distant regions Fortune sends
An odd triumvirate of friends;
Where Phoebus pays a scanty stipend,
Where never yet a codling ripen'd:
Hither the frantic goddess draws
Three sufferers in a ruin'd cause:
By faction banish'd, here unite,
A Dean, a Spaniard, and a Knight;
Unite, but on conditions cruel;
The Dean and Spaniard find it too well,
Condemn'd to live in service hard;
On either side his honour's guard:
The Dean to guard his honour's back,
Must build a castle at Drumlack;
The Spaniard, sore against his will,
Must raise a fort at Market-Hill.
And thus the pair of humble gentry
At north and south are posted sentry;
While in his lordly castle fixt,
The knight triumphant reigns betwixt:
And, what the wretches most resent,
To be his slaves, must pay him rent;
Attend him daily as their chief,
Decant his wine, and carve his beef.
O Fortune! 'tis a scandal for thee
To smile on those who are least worthy:
Weigh but the merits of the three,
His slaves have ten times more than he.
    Proud baronet of Nova Scotia!
The Dean and Spaniard must reproach ye:
Of their two fames the world enough rings:
Where are thy services and sufferings?
What if for nothing once you kiss'd,
Against the grain, a monarch's fist?
What if, among the courtly tribe,

You lost a place and saved a bribe?
And then in surly mood came here,
To fifteen hundred pounds a-year,
And fierce against the Whigs harangu'd?
You never ventured to be hang'd.
How dare you treat your betters thus?
Are you to be compared with us?
    Come, Spaniard, let us from our farms
Call forth our cottagers to arms:
Our forces let us both unite,
Attack the foe at left and right;
From Market-Hill's exalted head,
Full northward let your troops be led;
While I from Drapier's-Mount descend,
And to the south my squadrons bend.
New-River Walk, with friendly shade,
Shall keep my host in ambuscade;
While you, from where the basin stands,
Shall scale the rampart with your bands.
Nor need we doubt the fort to win;
I hold intelligence within.
True, Lady Anne no danger fears,
Brave as the Upton fan she wears;
Then, lest upon our first attack
Her valiant arm should force us back,
And we of all our hopes deprived;
I have a stratagem contrived.
By these embroider'd high-heel shoes
She shall be caught as in a noose:
So well contriv'd her toes to pinch,
She'll not have power to stir an inch:
These gaudy shoes must Hannah place
Direct before her lady's face;
The shoes put on, our faithful portress
Admits us in, to storm the fortress,
While tortured madam bound remains,
Like Montezume, in golden chains;
Or like a cat with walnuts shod,
Stumbling at every step she trod.

Sly hunters thus, in Borneo's isle,
To catch a monkey by a wile,
The mimic animal amuse;
They place before him gloves and shoes;
Which, when the brute puts awkward on:
All his agility is gone;
In vain to frisk or climb he tries;
The huntsmen seize the grinning prize.
    But let us on our first assault
Secure the larder and the vault;
The valiant Dennis, you must fix on,
And I'll engage with Peggy Dixon:
Then, if we once can seize the key
And chest that keeps my lady's tea,
They must surrender at discretion!
And, soon as we have gain'd possession,
We'll act as other conquerors do,
Divide the realm between us two;
Then, (let me see,) we'll make the knight
Our clerk, for he can read and write.
But must not think, I tell him that,
Like Lorimer to wear his hat;
Yet, when we dine without a friend,
We'll place him at the lower end.
Madam, whose skill does all in dress lie,
May serve to wait on Mrs. Leslie;
But, lest it might not be so proper
That her own maid should over-top her,
To mortify the creature more,
We'll take her heels five inches lower.
    For Hannah, when we have no need of her,
'Twill be our interest to get rid of her;
And when we execute our plot,
'Tis best to hang her on the spot;
As all your politicians wise,
Dispatch the rogues by whom they rise.

Robin and Harry. 1730

Robin to beggars with a curse,
Throws the last shilling in his purse;
And when the coachman comes for pay,
The rogue must call another day.
    Grave Harry, when the poor are pressing
Gives them a penny and God's blessing;
But always careful of the main,
With twopence left, walks home in rain.
    Robin from noon to night will prate,
Run out in tongue, as in estate;
And, ere a twelvemonth and a day,
Will not have one new thing to say.
Much talking is not Harry's vice;
He need not tell a story twice:
And, if he always be so thrifty,
His fund may last to five-and-fifty.
    It so fell out that cautious Harry,
As soldiers use, for love must marry,
And, with his dame, the ocean cross'd;
(All for Love, or the World well Lost!)
Repairs a cabin gone to ruin,
Just big enough to shelter two in;
And in his house, if anybody come,
Will make them welcome to his modicum
Where Goody Julia milks the cows,
And boils potatoes for her spouse;
Or darns his hose, or mends his breeches,
While Harry's fencing up his ditches.
    Robin, who ne'er his mind could fix,
To live without a coach-and-six,
To patch his broken fortunes, found
A mistress worth five thousand pound;
Swears he could get her in an hour,
If gaffer Harry would endow her;
And sell, to pacify his wrath,
A birth-right for a mess of broth.

Young Harry, as all Europe knows,
Was long the quintessence of beaux;
But, when espoused, he ran the fate
That must attend the married state;
From gold brocade and shining armour,
Was metamorphosed to a farmer;
His grazier's coat with dirt besmear'd;
Nor twice a-week will shave his beard.
Old Robin, all his youth a sloven,
At fifty-two, when he grew loving,
Clad in a coat of paduasoy,
A flaxen wig, and waistcoat gay,
Powder'd from shoulder down to flank,
In courtly style addresses Frank;
Twice ten years older than his wife,
Is doom'd to be a beau for life;
Supplying those defects by dress,
Which I must leave the world to guess.

A Panegyric on the Dean

In the Person of a Lady in the North 1730

Resolved my gratitude to show,
Thrice reverend Dean, for all I owe,
Too long I have my thanks delay'd;
Your favours left too long unpaid;
But now, in all our sex's name,
My artless Muse shall sing your fame.
    Indulgent you to female kind,
To all their weaker sides are blind:
Nine more such champions as the Dean
Would soon restore our ancient reign;
How well to win the ladies' hearts,
You celebrate their wit and parts!
How have I felt my spirits raised,
By you so oft, so highly praised!
Transform'd by your convincing tongue
To witty, beautiful, and young,
I hope to quit that awkward shame,
Affected by each vulgar dame,
To modesty a weak pretence;
And soon grow pert on men of sense;
To show my face with scornful air;
Let others match it if they dare.
    Impatient to be out of debt,
O, may I never once forget
The bard who humbly deigns to chuse
Me for the subject of his Muse!
Behind my back, before my nose,
He sounds my praise in verse and prose.
    My heart with emulation burns,
To make you suitable returns;
My gratitude the world shall know;
And see, the printer's boy below;
Ye hawkers all, your voices lift;
"A Panegyric on Dean Swift!"

And then, to mend the matter still,
"By Lady Anne of Market-Hill!"
I thus begin: My grateful Muse
Salutes the Dean in different views;
Dean, butler, usher, jester, tutor;
Robert and Darby's coadjutor;
And, as you in commission sit,
To rule the dairy next to Kit;
In each capacity I mean
To sing your praise. And first as Dean:
Envy must own, you understand your
Precedence, and support your grandeur:
Nor of your rank will bate an ace,
Except to give Dean Daniel place.
In you such dignity appears,
So suited to your state and years!
With ladies what a strict decorum!
With what devotion you adore 'em!
Treat me with so much complaisance,
As fits a princess in romance!
By your example and assistance,
The fellows learn to know their distance.
Sir Arthur, since you set the pattern,
No longer calls me snipe and slattern,
Nor dares he, though he were a duke,
Offend me with the least rebuke.
Proceed we to your preaching next!
How nice you split the hardest text!
How your superior learning shines
Above our neighbouring dull divines!
At Beggar's Opera not so full pit
Is seen as when you mount our pulpit.
Consider now your conversation:
Regardful of your age and station,
You ne'er were known by passion stirr'd
To give the least offensive word:
But still, whene'er you silence break,
Watch every syllable you speak:
Your style so clear, and so concise,

We never ask to hear you twice.
But then a parson so genteel,
So nicely clad from head to heel;
So fine a gown, a band so clean,
As well become St. Patrick's Dean,
Such reverential awe express,
That cowboys know you by your dress!
Then, if our neighbouring friends come here
How proud are we when you appear,
With such address and graceful port,
As clearly shows you bred at court!
    Now raise your spirits, Mr. Dean,
I lead you to a nobler scene.
When to the vault you walk in state,
In quality of butler's mate;
You next to Dennis bear the sway:
To you we often trust the key:
Nor can he judge with all his art
So well, what bottle holds a quart:
What pints may best for bottles pass
Just to give every man his glass:
When proper to produce the best;
And what may serve a common guest.
With Dennis you did ne'er combine,
Not you, to steal your master's wine,
Except a bottle now and then,
To welcome brother serving-men;
But that is with a good design,
To drink Sir Arthur's health and mine,
Your master's honour to maintain:
And get the like returns again.
    Your usher's post must next be handled:
How blest am I by such a man led!
Under whose wise and careful guardship
I now despise fatigue and hardship,
Familiar grown to dirt and wet,
Though draggled round, I scorn to fret:
From you my chamber damsels learn
My broken hose to patch and darn.

Now as a jester I accost you;
Which never yet one friend has lost you.
You judge so nicely to a hair,
How far to go, and when to spare;
By long experience grown so wise,
Of every taste to know the size;
There's none so ignorant or weak
To take offence at what you speak.
Whene'er you joke, 'tis all a case
Whether with Dermot, or his grace;
With Teague O'Murphy, or an earl;
A duchess, or a kitchen girl.
With such dexterity you fit
Their several talents with your wit,
That Moll the chambermaid can smoke,
And Gahagan take every joke.
I now become your humble suitor
To let me praise you as my tutor.
Poor I, a savage bred and born,
By you instructed every morn,
Already have improved so well,
That I have almost learnt to spell:
The neighbours who come here to dine,
Admire to hear me speak so fine.
How enviously the ladies look,
When they surprise me at my book!
And sure as they're alive at night,
As soon as gone will show their spight:
Good lord! what can my lady mean,
Conversing with that rusty Dean!
She's grown so nice, and so penurious,
With Socrates and Epicurius!
How could she sit the livelong day,
Yet never ask us once to play?
But I admire your patience most;
That when I'm duller than a post,
Nor can the plainest word pronounce,
You neither fume, nor fret, nor flounce;
Are so indulgent, and so mild,

As if I were a darling child.
So gentle is your whole proceeding,
That I could spend my life in reading.
    You merit new employments daily:
Our thatcher, ditcher, gardener, baily.
And to a genius so extensive
No work is grievous or offensive:
Whether your fruitful fancy lies
To make for pigs convenient styes;
Or ponder long with anxious thought
To banish rats that haunt our vault:
Nor have you grumbled, reverend Dean,
To keep our poultry sweet and clean;
To sweep the mansion-house they dwell in,
And cure the rank unsavoury smelling.
    Now enter as the dairy handmaid:
Such charming butter never man made.
Let others with fanatic face
Talk of their milk for babes of grace;
From tubs their snuffling nonsense utter;
Thy milk shall make us tubs of butter.
The bishop with his foot may burn it,
But with his hand the Dean can churn it.
How are the servants overjoy'd
To see thy deanship thus employ'd!
Instead of poring on a book,
Providing butter for the cook!
Three morning hours you toss and shake
The bottle till your fingers ache;
Hard is the toil, nor small the art,
The butter from the whey to part:
Behold a frothy substance rise;
Be cautious or your bottle flies.
The butter comes, our fears are ceased;
And out you squeeze an ounce at least.
    Your reverence thus, with like success,
(Nor is your skill or labour less,)
When bent upon some smart lampoon,
Will toss and turn your brain till noon;

Which in its jumblings round the skull,
Dilates and makes the vessel full:
While nothing comes but froth at first,
You think your giddy head will burst;
But squeezing out four lines in rhyme,
Are largely paid for all your time.
    But you have raised your generous mind
To works of more exalted kind.
Palladio was not half so skill'd in
The grandeur or the art of building.
Two temples of magnific size
Attract the curious traveller's eyes,
That might be envied by the Greeks;
Raised up by you in twenty weeks:
Here gentle goddess Cloacine
Receives all offerings at her shrine.
In separate cells, the he's and she's,
Here pay their vows on bended knees:
For 'tis profane when sexes mingle,
And every nymph must enter single;
And when she feels an inward motion,
Come fill'd with reverence and devotion.
The bashful maid, to hide her blush,
Shall creep no more behind a bush;
Here unobserved she boldly goes,
As who should say, to pluck a rose,
    Ye, who frequent this hallow'd scene,
Be not ungrateful to the Dean;
But duly, ere you leave your station,
Offer to him a pure libation,
Or of his own or Smedley's lay,
Or billet-doux, or lock of hay:
And, O! may all who hither come,
Return with unpolluted thumb!
    Yet, when your lofty domes I praise
I sigh to think of ancient days.
Permit me then to raise my style,
And sweetly moralize a-while.
    Thee, bounteous goddess Cloacine,

To temples why do we confine?
Forbid in open air to breathe,
Why are thine altars fix'd beneath?
When Saturn ruled the skies alone,
(That golden age to gold unknown,)
This earthly globe, to thee assign'd,
Received the gifts of all mankind.
Ten thousand altars smoking round,
Were built to thee with offerings crown'd;
And here thy daily votaries placed
Their sacrifice with zeal and haste:
The margin of a purling stream
Sent up to thee a grateful steam;
Though sometimes thou wert pleased to wink,
If Naiads swept them from the brink:
Or where appointing lovers rove,
The shelter of a shady grove;
Or offer'd in some flowery vale,
Were wafted by a gentle gale,
There many a flower abstersive grew,
Thy favourite flowers of yellow hue;
The crocus and the daffodil,
The cowslip soft, and sweet jonquil.
    But when at last usurping Jove
Old Saturn from his empire drove,
Then gluttony, with greasy paws
Her napkin pinn'd up to her jaws,
With watery chops, and wagging chin,
Braced like a drum her oily skin;
Wedged in a spacious elbow-chair,
And on her plate a treble share,
As if she ne'er could have enough,
Taught harmless man to cram and stuff.
She sent her priests in wooden shoes
From haughty Gaul to make ragouts;
Instead of wholesome bread and cheese,
To dress their soups and fricassees;
And, for our home-bred British cheer,
Botargo, catsup, and caviare.

This bloated harpy, sprung from hell,
Confined thee, goddess, to a cell:
Sprung from her womb that impious line,
Contemners of thy rites divine.
First, lolling Sloth, in woollen cap,
Taking her after-dinner nap:
Pale Dropsy, with a sallow face,
Her belly burst, and slow her pace:
And lordly Gout, wrapt up in fur,
And wheezing Asthma, loth to stir:
Voluptuous Ease, the child of wealth,
Infecting thus our hearts by stealth.
None seek thee now in open air,
To thee no verdant altars rear;
But, in their cells and vaults obscene,
Present a sacrifice unclean;
From whence unsavoury vapours rose,
Offensive to thy nicer nose.
Ah! who, in our degenerate days,
As nature prompts, his offering pays?
Here nature never difference made
Between the sceptre and the spade.
Ye great ones, why will ye disdain
To pay your tribute on the plain?
Why will you place in lazy pride
Your altars near your couches' side:
When from the homeliest earthen ware
Are sent up offerings more sincere,
Than where the haughty duchess locks
Her silver vase in cedar box?
Yet some devotion still remains
Among our harmless northern swains,
Whose offerings, placed in golden ranks,
Adorn our crystal rivers' banks;
Nor seldom grace the flowery downs,
With spiral tops and copple crowns;
Or gilding in a sunny morn
The humble branches of a thorn.
So poets sing, with golden bough

The Trojan hero paid his vow.
    Hither, by luckless error led,
The crude consistence oft I tread;
Here when my shoes are out of case,
Unweeting gild the tarnish'd lace;
Here, by the sacred bramble tinged,
My petticoat is doubly fringed.
    Be witness for me, nymph divine,
I never robb'd thee with design;
Nor will the zealous Hannah pout
To wash thy injured offering out.
But stop, ambitious Muse, in time,
Nor dwell on subjects too sublime.
In vain on lofty heels I tread,
Aspiring to exalt my head;
With hoop expanded wide and light,
In vain I 'tempt too high a flight.
    Me Phoebus in a midnight dream
Accosting, said, "Go shake your cream
Be humbly-minded, know your post;
Sweeten your tea, and watch your toast.
Thee best befits a lowly style;
Teach Dennis how to stir the guile;
With Peggy Dixon thoughtful sit,
Contriving for the pot and spit.
Take down thy proudly swelling sails,
And rub thy teeth and pare thy nails;
At nicely carving show thy wit;
But ne'er presume to eat a bit:
Turn every way thy watchful eye,
And every guest be sure to ply:
Let never at your board be known
An empty plate, except your own.
Be these thy arts; nor higher aim
Than what befits a rural dame.
    "But Cloacina, goddess bright,
Sleek——claims her as his right;
And Smedley, flower of all divines,
Shall sing the Dean in Smedley's lines."

Twelve Articles

I

Lest it may more quarrels breed,
I will never hear you read.

II

By disputing, I will never,
To convince you once endeavour.

III

When a paradox you stick to,
I will never contradict you.

IV

When I talk and you are heedless,
I will show no anger needless.

V

When your speeches are absurd,
I will ne'er object a word.

VI

When you furious argue wrong,
I will grieve and hold my tongue.

VII

Not a jest or humorous story
Will I ever tell before ye:
To be chidden for explaining,
When you quite mistake the meaning.

VIII

Never more will I suppose,
You can taste my verse or prose.

IX

You no more at me shall fret,
While I teach and you forget.

X

You shall never hear me thunder,
When you blunder on, and blunder.

XI

Show your poverty of spirit,
And in dress place all your merit;
Give yourself ten thousand airs:
That with me shall break no squares.

XII

Never will I give advice,
Till you please to ask me thrice:
Which if you in scorn reject,
'Twill be just as I expect.

Thus we both shall have our ends,
And continue special friends.

Political Poetry

Parody

On the Recorder of Blessington's Address to Queen Anne

Mr. William Crowe, Recorder of Blessington's Address to her Majesty, as copied from the London Gazette.

To the Queen's most Excellent Majesty,

The humble Address of the Sovereign, Recorder, Burgesses, and Freemen, of the Borough of Blessington.

May it please your Majesty,

Though we stand almost last on the roll of boroughs of this your majesty's kingdom of Ireland, and therefore, in good manners to our elder brothers, press but late among the joyful crowd about your royal throne: yet we beg leave to assure your majesty, that we come behind none in our good affection to your sacred person and government; insomuch, that the late surprising accounts from Germany have filled us with a joy not inferior to any of our fellow-subjects.

We heard with transport that the English warmed the field to that degree, that thirty squadrons, part of the vanquished enemy, were forced to fly to water, not able to stand their fire, and drank their last draught in the Danube, for the waste they had before committed on its injured banks, thereby putting an end to their master's long-boasted victories: a glorious push indeed, and worthy a general of the Queen of England. And we are not a little pleased, to find several gentlemen in considerable posts of your majesty's army, who drew their first breath in this country, sharing in the good fortune of those who so effectually put in execution the command of your gallant, enterprizing general, whose twin-battles have, with his own title of Marlborough, given immortality to the otherwise perishing names of Schellenberg and Hogstete: actions that speak him born under stars as propitious to England as that he now wears, on both which he has so often reflected lustre, as to have now abundantly repaid the glory they once lent him. Nor can we but congratulate with a joy proportioned to the success of your majesty's fleet, our last campaign at sea, since by it we observe the French obliged to steer their wonted course for security, to their ports; and Gibraltar, the Spaniards' ancient defence, bravely stormed, possessed, and maintained by your majesty's subjects.

May the supplies for reducing the exorbitant power of France be such, as may soon turn your wreaths of laurel into branches of olive: that, after the toils of a just and honourable war, carried on by a confederacy of which your majesty is most truly, as of the faith, styled Defender, we may live to enjoy, under your majesty's auspicious government, the blessings of a profound and lasting peace; a peace beyond the power of him to violate, who, but for his own unreasonable conveniency, destructive always of his neighbours, never yet kept any. And, to complete our happiness, may your majesty again prove to *your own family*, what you have been so eminently to the true church, a nursing mother. So wish, and so pray, may it please your majesty, your majesty's most dutiful and loyal subjects, and devoted humble servants.

This Address was presented January 17, 1704–5.

Mr. William Crowe's Address to her Majesty, Turned into Metre

From a town that consists of a church and a steeple,
With three or four houses, and as many people,
There went an Address in great form and good order,
Composed, as 'tis said, by Will Crowe, their Recorder.
And thus it began to an excellent tune:
Forgive us, good madam, that we did not as soon
As the rest of the cities and towns of this nation
Wish your majesty joy on this glorious occasion.
Not that we're less hearty or loyal than others,
But having a great many sisters and brothers,
Our borough in riches and years far exceeding,
We let them speak first, to show our good breeding.
We have heard with much transport and great satisfaction
Of the victory obtain'd in the late famous action,
When the field was so warm'd, that it soon grew too hot
For the French and Bavarians, who had all gone to pot,
But that they thought best in great haste to retire,
And leap into the water for fear of the fire.
But says the good river, Ye fools, plague confound ye,
Do ye think to swim through me, and that I'll not drown ye?
Who have ravish'd, and murder'd, and play'd such damn'd pranks,
And trod down the grass on my much-injured banks?
Then, swelling with anger and rage to the brink,
He gave the poor Monsieur his last draught of drink.
So it plainly appears they were very well bang'd,
And that some may be drown'd, who deserved to be hang'd.
Great Marlbro' well push'd: 'twas well push'd indeed:
Oh, how we adore you, because you succeed!
And now I may say it, I hope without blushing,
That you have got twins, by your violent pushing;
Twin battles I mean, that will ne'er be forgotten,
But live and be talk'd of, when we're dead and rotten.
Let other nice lords sculk at home from the wars,
Prank'd up and adorn'd with garters and stars,
Which but twinkle like those in a cold frosty night;

While to yours you are adding such lustre and light,
That if you proceed, I'm sure very soon
'Twill be brighter and larger than the sun or the moon:
A blazing star, I foretell, 'twill prove to the Gaul,
That portends of his empire the ruin and fall.
    Now God bless your majesty, and our Lord Murrough,
And send him in safety and health to his borough.

Jack Frenchman's Lamentation

An Excellent New Song

To the Tune of "I tell thee, Dick, where I have been."

Ye Commons and Peers,
Pray lend me your ears,
I'll sing you a song, (if I can,)
How Lewis le Grand
Was put to a stand,
By the arms of our gracious Queen Anne.

How his army so great,
Had a total defeat,
And close by the river Dender:
Where his grandchildren twain,
For fear of being slain,
Gallop'd off with the Popish Pretender.

To a steeple on high,
The battle to spy,
Up mounted these clever young men;
But when from the spire,
They saw so much fire,
Most cleverly came down again.

Then on horseback they got
All on the same spot,
By advice of their cousin Vendosme,
O Lord! cried out he,
Unto young *Burgundy*,
Would your brother and you were at home!

While this he did say,
Without more delay,
Away the young gentry fled;
Whose heels for that work,

Were much lighter than cork,
Though their hearts were as heavy as lead.

Not so did behave
Young Hanover brave,
In this bloody field I assure ye:
When his war-horse was shot
He valued it not,
But fought it on foot like a fury.

Full firmly he stood,
As became his high blood,
Which runs in his veins so blue:
For this gallant young man,
Being a-kin to QUEEN ANNE,
Did as (were she a man) she would do.

What a racket was here,
(I think 'twas last year,)
For a little misfortune in Spain!
For by letting 'em win,
We have drawn the puts in,
To lose all they're worth this campaign.

Though *Bruges* and Ghent
To *Monsieur* we lent,
With interest they shall repay 'em;
While *Paris* may sing,
With her sorrowful king,
Nunc dimittis instead of *Te Deum*.

From this dream of success,
They'll awaken, we guess,
At the sound of great Marlborough's drums,
They may think, if they will,
Of Ahnanza still,
But 'tis Blenheim wherever he comes.

O *Lewis* perplex'd,

What general next!
Thou hast hitherto changed in vain;
He has beat 'em all round,
If no new one's found,
He shall beat 'em over again.

We'll let *Tallard* out,
If he'll take t'other bout;
And much he's improved, let me tell ye,
With *Nottingham* ale
At every meal,
And good beef and pudding in belly.

But as losers at play,
Their dice throw away,
While the winners do still win on;
Let who will command,
Thou hadst better disband,
For, old Bully, thy doctors are gone.

The Garden Plot

1709

When Naboth's vineyard look'd so fine,
The king cried out, "Would this were mine!"
And yet no reason could prevail
To bring the owner to a sale.
Jezebel saw, with haughty pride,
How Ahab grieved to be denied;
And thus accosted him with scorn:
"Shall Naboth make a monarch mourn?
A king, and weep! The ground's your own;
I'll vest the garden in the crown."
With that she hatch'd a plot, and made
Poor Naboth answer with his head;
And when his harmless blood was spilt,
The ground became his forfeit guilt.

Sid Hamet's Rod

Poor Hall, renown'd for comely hair,
Whose hands, perhaps, were not so fair,
Yet had a Jezebel as near;
Hall, of small scripture conversation,
Yet, howe'er Hungerford's quotation,
By some strange accident had got
The story of this garden-plot;—Wisely
foresaw he might have reason
To dread a modern bill of treason,
If Jezebel should please to want
His small addition to her grant:
Therefore resolved, in humble sort,
To begin first, and make his court;
And, seeing nothing else would do,
Gave a third part, to save the other two.

The Virtues of Sid Hamet The Magician's Rod. 1710

The rod was but a harmless wand,
While Moses held it in his hand;
But, soon as e'er he laid it down,
Twas a devouring serpent grown.
Our great magician, Hamet Sid,
Reverses what the prophet did:
His rod was honest English wood,
That senseless in a corner stood,
Till metamorphos'd by his grasp,
It grew an all-devouring asp;
Would hiss, and sting, and roll, and twist.
By the mere virtue of his fist:
But, when he laid it down, as quick
Resum'd the figure of a stick.
So, to her midnight feasts, the hag
Rides on a broomstick for a nag,
That, rais'd by magic of her breech,
O'er sea and land conveys the witch;
But with the morning dawn resumes
The peaceful state of common brooms.
They tell us something strange and odd,
About a certain magic rod,
That, bending down its top, divines
Whene'er the soil has golden mines;
Where there are none, it stands erect,
Scorning to show the least respect:
As ready was the wand of Sid
To bend where golden mines were hid:
In Scottish hills found precious ore,
Where none e'er look'd for it before;
And by a gentle bow divine
How well a cully's purse was lined;
To a forlorn and broken rake,
Stood without motion like a stake.
The rod of Hermes was renown'd

For charms above and under ground;
To sleep could mortal eyelids fix,
And drive departed souls to Styx.
That rod was a just type of Sid's,
Which o'er a British senate's lids
Could scatter opium full as well,
And drive as many souls to hell.
Sid's rod was slender, white, and tall,
Which oft he used to fish withal;
A PLACE was fasten'd to the hook,
And many score of *gudgeons* took;
Yet still so happy was his fate,
He caught his fish and sav'd his bait.
Sid's brethren of the conj'ring tribe,
A circle with their rod describe,
Which proves a magical redoubt,
To keep mischievous spirits out.
Sid's rod was of a larger stride,
And made a circle thrice as wide,
Where spirits throng'd with hideous din,
And he stood there to take them in;
But when th'enchanted rod was broke,
They vanish'd in a stinking smoke.
Achilles' sceptre was of wood,
Like Sid's, but nothing near so good;
Though down from ancestors divine
Transmitted to the heroes line;
Thence, thro' a long descent of kings,
Came an HEIRLOOM, as Homer sings.
Though this description looks so big,
That sceptre was a sapless twig,
Which, from the fatal day, when first
It left the forest where 'twas nurs'd,
As Homer tells us o'er and o'er,
Nor leaf, nor fruit, nor blossom bore.
Sid's sceptre, full of juice, did shoot
In golden boughs, and golden fruit;
And he, the dragon never sleeping,
Guarded each fair Hesperian Pippin.

No hobby-horse, with gorgeous top,
The dearest in Charles Mather's shop,
Or glittering tinsel of May Fair,
Could with this rod of Sid compare.
    Dear Sid, then why wert thou so mad
To break thy rod like naughty lad?
You should have kiss'd it in your distress,
And then return'd it to your mistress;
Or made it a Newmarket switch,
And not a rod for thine own breech.
But since old Sid has broken this,
His next may be a rod in piss.

The Famous Speech-Maker of England

Or Baron (Alias Barren) Lovel's Charge At the Assizes at Exon, April 5, 1710

Risum teneatis?

—Horat., *Ars Poetica*, 5.

From London to Exon,
By special direction,
Came down the world's wonder,
Sir Salathiel Blunder,
With a quoif on his head
As heavy as lead;
And thus opened and said:

Gentlemen of the Grand Inquest,

Her majesty, mark it,
Appointed this circuit
For me and my brother,
Before any other;
To execute laws,
As you may suppose,
Upon such as offenders have been.
So then, not to scatter
More words on the matter,
We're beginning just now to begin.
But hold—first and foremost, I must enter a clause,
As touching and concerning our excellent laws;
Which here I aver,
Are better by far
Than them all put together abroad and beyond sea;
For I ne'er read the like, nor e'er shall, I fancy
The laws of our land
Don't abet, but withstand,
Inquisition and thrall,

And whatever may gall,
And fire withal;
And sword that devours
Wherever it scowers:
They preserve liberty and property, for which men pull and haul so,
And they are made for the support of good government also.
Her majesty, knowing
The best way of going
To work for the weal of the nation,
Builds on that rock,
Which all storms will mock,
Since Religion is made the foundation.
And, I tell you to boot, she
Resolves resolutely,
No promotion to give
To the best man alive,
In church or in state,
(I'm an instance of that,)
But only to such of a good reputation
For temper, morality, and moderation.
Fire! fire! a wild-fire,
Which greatly disturbs the queen's peace
Lies running about;
And if you don't put it out,
(That's positive) will increase:
And any may spy,
With half of an eye,
That it comes from our priests and Papistical fry.
Ye have one of these fellows,
With fiery bellows,
Come hither to blow and to puff here;
Who having been toss'd
From pillar to post,
At last vents his rascally stuff here:
Which to such as are honest must sound very oddly,
When they ought to preach nothing but what's very godly;
As here from this place we charge you to do,
As ye'll answer to man, besides ye know who.
Ye have a Diocesan,—

But I don't know the man;—
The man's a good liver,
They tell me, however,
And fiery never!
Now, ye under-pullers,
That wear such black colours,
How well would it look,
If his measures ye took,
Thus for head and for rump
Together to jump;
For there's none deserve places,
I speak't to their faces,
But men of such graces,
And I hope he will never prefer any asses;
Especially when I'm so confident on't,
For reasons of state, that her majesty won't
Know, I myself I
Was present and by,
At the great trial, where there was a great company,
Of a turbulent preacher, who, cursedly hot,
Turn'd the fifth of November, even the gun-powder plot,
Into impudent railing, and the devil knows what:
Exclaiming like fury—it was at Paul's, London—
How church was in danger, and like to be undone,
And so gave the lie to gracious Queen Anne;
And, which is far worse, to our parliament-men:
And then printed a book,
Into which men did look:
True, he made a good text;
But what follow'd next
Was nought but a dunghill of sordid abuses,
Instead of sound doctrine, with proofs to't, and uses.
It was high time of day
That such inflammation
should be extinguish'd without more delay:
But there was no engine could possibly do't,
Till the commons play'd theirs, and so quite put it out.
So the man was tried for't,
Before highest court:

Now it's plain to be seen,
It's his principles I mean,
Where they suffer'd this noisy and his lawyers to bellow:
Which over, the blade
A poor punishment had
For that racket he made.
By which ye may know
They thought as I do,
That he is but at best an inconsiderable fellow.
Upon this I find here,
And everywhere,
That the country rides rusty, and is all out of gear:
And for what?
May I not
In opinion vary,
And think the contrary,
But it must create
Unfriendly debate,
And disunion straight;
When no reason in nature
Can be given of the matter,
Any more than for shapes or for different stature?
If you love your dear selves, your religion or queen,
Ye ought in good manners to be peaceable men:
For nothing disgusts her
Like making a bluster:
And your making this riot,
Is what she could cry at,
Since all her concern's for our welfare and quiet.
I would ask any man
Of them all that maintain
Their passive obedience
With such mighty vehemence,
That damn'd doctrine, I trow!
What he means by it, ho',
To trump it up now?
Or to tell me in short,
What need there is for't?
Ye may say, I am hot;

I say I am not;
Only warm, as the subject on which I am got.
There are those alive yet,
If they do not forget,
May remember what mischiefs it did church and state:
Or at least must have heard
The deplorable calamities
It drew upon families,
About sixty years ago and upward.
And now, do ye see,
Whoever they be,
That make such an oration
In our Protestant nation,
As though church was all on a fire,—
With whatever cloak
They may cover their talk,
And wheedle the folk,
That the oaths they have took,
As our governors strictly require;—
I say they are men—(and I'm a judge, ye all know,)
That would our most excellent laws overthrow;
For the greater part of them to church never go;
Or, what's much the same, it by very great chance is,
If e'er they partake of her wise ordinances.
Their aim is, no doubt,
Were they made to speak out,
To pluck down the queen, that they make all this rout;
And to set up, moreover,
A bastardly brother;
Or at least to prevent the House of Hanover.
Ye gentlemen of the jury,
What means all this fury,
Of which I'm inform'd by good hands, I assure ye;
This insulting of persons by blows and rude speeches,
And breaking of windows, which, you know, maketh breaches?
Ye ought to resent it,
And in duty present it,
For the law is against it;
Not only the actors engaged in this job,

But those that encourage and set on the mob:
The mob, a paw word, and which I ne'er mention,
But must in this place, for the sake of distinction.
I hear that some bailiffs and some justices
Have strove what they could, all this rage to suppress;
And I hope many more
Will exert the like power,
Since none will, depend on't,
Get a jot of preferment.
But men of this kidney, as I told you before.—
I'll tell you a story: Once upon a time,
Some hot-headed fellows must needs take a whim,
And so were so weak
(Twas a mighty mistake)
To pull down and abuse
Bawdy-houses and stews;
Who, tried by the laws of the realm for high-treason,
Were hang'd, drawn, and quarter'd for that very reason.
When the time came about
For us all to set out,
We went to take leave of the queen;
Where were great men of worth,
Great heads and so forth,
The greatest that ever were seen:
And she gave us a large
And particular charge;—
Good part on't indeed
Is quite out of my head;—
But I remember she said,
We should recommend peace and good neighbourhood,
wheresoever we came;
and so I do here;
For that every one, not only men and their wives,
Should do all that they can to lead peaceable lives;
And told us withal, that she fully expected
A special account how ye all stood affected;
When we've been at St. James's, you'll hear of the matter.
Again then I charge ye,
Ye men of the clergy,

That ye follow the track all
Of your own Bishop Blackall,
And preach, as ye should,
What's savoury and good;
And together all cling,
As it were, in a string;
Not falling out, quarrelling one with another,
Now we're treating with Monsieur,—that son of his mother.

Then proceeded on the common matters of the law; and concluded:

Once more, and no more, since few words are best,
I charge you all present, by way of request,
If ye honour, as I do,
Our dear royal widow,
Or have any compassion
For church or the nation;
And would live a long while
In continual smile,
And eat roast and boil,
And not be forgotten,
When ye are dead and rotten;
That ye would be quiet, and peaceably dwell,
And never fall out, but p—s all in a quill.

Parody on the Recorder's Speech

To his Grace the Duke of Ormond, 4th July, 1711

This city can omit no opportunity of expressing their hearty affection for her majesty's person and government; and their regard for your grace, who has the honour of representing her in this kingdom.

We retain, my lord, a grateful remembrance of the mild and just Administration of the government of this kingdom by your noble ancestors; and, when we consider the share your grace had in the happy Revolution, in 1688, and the many good laws you have procured us since, particularly that for preventing the farther growth of Popery, we are assured that that liberty and property, that happy constitution in church and state, to which we were restored by King William of glorious memory, will be inviolably preserved under your grace's administration. And we are persuaded that we cannot more effectually recommend ourselves to your grace's favour and protection, than by assuring you that we will, to the utmost of our power, contribute to the honour and safety of her majesty's government, the maintenance of the succession in the illustrious house of Hanover, and that we shall at all times oppose the secret and open attempts of the Pretender, and all his abettors.

The Recorder's Speech Explained by the Tories

An ancient metropolis, famous of late
For opposing the Church, and for nosing the State,
For protecting sedition and rejecting order,
Made the following speech by their mouth, the Recorder:
First, to tell you the name of this place of renown,
Some still call it Dublin, but most Forster's town.

The Speech

May it please your Grace,
We cannot omit this occasion to tell,
That we love the Queen's person and government well;
Then next, to your Grace we this compliment make,
That our worships regard you, but 'tis for her sake:
Though our mouth be a Whig, and our head a Dissenter,
Yet salute you we must, 'cause you represent her:
Nor can we forget, sir, that some of your line
Did with mildness and peace in this government shine.
But of all your exploits, we'll allow but one fact,
That your Grace has procured us a Popery Act.
By this you may see that the least of your actions
Does conduce still the most to our satisfactions.
And lastly, because in the year eighty-eight
You did early appear in defence of our right,
We give no other proof of your zeal to your Prince;
So we freely forget all your services since.
It's then only we hope, that whilst you rule o'er us,
You'll tread in the steps of King William the glorious,
Whom we're always adoring, tho' hand over head,
For we owe him allegiance, although he be dead;
Which shows that good zeal may be founded in spleen,
Since a dead Prince we worship, to lessen the Queen.
And as for her Majesty, we will defend her
Against our hobgoblin, the Popish Pretender.
Our valiant militia will stoutly stand by her,
Against the sly Jack, and the sturdy High-flier.
She is safe when thus guarded, if Providence bless her,
And Hanover's sure to be next her successor.
    Thus ended the speech, but what heart would not pity
His Grace, almost choked with the breath of the City!

Ballad

To the tune of "Commons and Peers."

A Wonderful age
Is now on the stage:
I'll sing you a song, if I can,
How modern Whigs,
Dance forty-one jigs,
But God bless our gracious Queen Anne.

The kirk with applause
Is established by laws
As the orthodox church of the nation.
The bishops do own
It's as good as their own.
And this, Sir, is call'd moderation.

It's no riddle now
To let you see how
A church by oppression may speed;
Nor is't banter or jest,
That the kirk faith is best
On the other side of the Tweed.

For no soil can suit
With every fruit,
Even so, Sir, it is with religion;
The best church by far
Is what grows where you are,
Were it Mahomet's ass or his pigeon.

Another strange story
That vexes the Tory,
But sure there's no mystery in it,
That a pension and place
Give communicants grace,
Who design to turn tail the next minute.

For if it be not strange,
That religion should change,
As often as climates and fashions;
Then sure there's no harm,
That one should conform.
To serve their own private occasions.

Another new dance,
Which of late they advance,
Is to cry up the birth of Pretender,
And those that dare own
The queen heir to the crown,
Are traitors, not fit to defend her.

The subject's most loyal
That hates the blood royal,
And they for employments have merit,
Who swear queen and steeple
Were made by the people,
And neither have right to inherit.

The monarchy's fixt,
By making on't mixt,
And by non-resistance o'erthrown;
And preaching obedience
Destroys our allegiance,
And thus the Whigs prop up the throne.

That viceroy is best,
That would take off the test,
And made a sham speech to attempt it;
But being true blue,
When he found 'twould not do,
Swore, damn him, if ever he meant it.

'Tis no news that Tom Double
The nation should bubble,
Nor is't any wonder or riddle,
That a parliament rump

Should play hop, step, and jump,
And dance any jig to his fiddle.

But now, sir, they tell,
How Sacheverell,
By bringing old doctrines in fashion,
Hath, like a damn'd rogue,
Brought religion in vogue,
And so open'd the eyes of the nation.

Then let's pray without spleen,
May God bless the queen,
And her fellow-monarchs the people;
May they prosper and thrive,
Whilst I am alive,
And so may the church with the steeple.

Atlas; or, the Minister of State

To the Lord Treasurer Oxford
1710

Atlas, we read in ancient song,
Was so exceeding tall and strong,
He bore the skies upon his back,
Just as the pedler does his pack;
But, as the pedler overpress'd
Unloads upon a stall to rest,
Or, when he can no longer stand
Desires a friend to lend a hand;
So Atlas, lest the ponderous spheres
Should sink, and fall about his ears,
Got Hercules to bear the pile,
That he might sit and rest awhile.
Yet Hercules was not so strong,
Nor could have borne it half so long.
Great statesmen are in this condition;
And Atlas is a politician,
A premier minister of state;
Alcides one of second rate.
Suppose then Atlas ne'er so wise;
Yet, when the weight of kingdoms lies
Too long upon his single shoulders,
Sink down he must, or find upholders.

Lines Written Extempore on Mr. Harley's being stabbed, And Addressed to his Physician, 1710–11

On Britain Europe's safety lies,
Britain is lost if Harley dies:
Harley depends upon your skill:
Think what you save, or what you kill.

An Excellent New Song

Being the Intended Speech of a Famous Orator Against Peace. 1711

An orator *dismal* of *Nottinghamshire,*
Who has forty years let out his conscience to hire,
Out of zeal for his country, and want of a place,
Is come up, *vi et armis*, to break the queen's peace.
He has vamp'd an old speech, and the court, to their sorrow,
Shall hear him harangue against Prior to-morrow.
When once he begins, he never will flinch,
But repeats the same note a whole day like a Finch.
I have heard all the speech repeated by Hoppy,'
And, "mistakes to prevent, I've obtained a copy."

The Speech

Whereas, notwithstanding I am in great pain,
To hear we are making a peace without Spain;
But, most noble senators, 'tis a great shame,
There should be a peace, while I'm *Not-in-game.*
The duke show'd me all his fine house; and the duchess
From her closet brought out a full purse in her clutches:
I talk'd of a peace, and they both gave a start,
His grace swore by G—d, and her grace let a f—t:
My long old-fashion'd pocket was presently cramm'd;
And sooner than vote for a peace I'll be damn'd.
    But some will cry turn-coat, and rip up old stories,
How I always pretended to be for the Tories:
I answer; the Tories were in my good graces,
Till all my relations were put into places.
But still I'm in principle ever the same,
And will quit my best friends, while I'm *Not-in-game.*
    When I and some others subscribed our names
To a plot for expelling my master King James,
I withdrew my subscription by help of a blot,
And so might discover or gain by the plot:
I had my advantage, and stood at defiance,
For Daniel was got from the den of the lions:
I came in without danger, and was I to blame?
For, rather than hang, I would be *Not-in-game.*
    I swore to the queen, that the Prince of Hanover
During her sacred life would never come over:
I made use of a trope; that "an heir to invite,
Was like keeping her monument always in sight."
But, when I thought proper, I alter'd my note;
And in her own hearing I boldly did vote,
That her Majesty stood in great need of a tutor,
And must have an old or a young coadjutor:
For why; I would fain have put all in a flame,
Because, for some reasons, I was *Not-in-game.*
    Now my new benefactors have brought me about,
And I'll vote against peace, with Spain or without:

Though the court gives my nephews, and brothers, and cousins,
And all my whole family, places by dozens;
Yet, since I know where a full purse may be found,
And hardly pay eighteen-pence tax in the pound:
Since the Tories have thus disappointed my hopes,
And will neither regard my figures nor tropes,
I'll speech against peace while *Dismal's* my name,
And be a true Whig, while I'm *Not-in-game.*

The Windsor Prophecy

"About three months ago, at Windsor, a poor knight's widow was buried in the cloisters. In digging the grave, the sexton struck against a small leaden coffer, about half a foot in length, and four inches wide. The poor man, expecting he had discovered a treasure, opened it with some difficulty; but found only a small parchment, rolled up very fast, put into a leather case; which case was tied at the top, and sealed with St. George, the impression on black wax, very rude and gothic. The parchment was carried to a gentleman of learning, who found in it the following lines, written in a black old English letter, and in the orthography of the age, which seems to be about two hundred years ago. I made a shift to obtain a copy of it; but the transcriber, I find, hath in many parts altered the spelling to the modern way. The original, as I am informed, is now in the hands of the ingenious Dr. Woodward, F. R. S. where, I suppose, the curious will not be refused the satisfaction of seeing it.

"The lines seem to be a sort of prophecy, and written in verse, as old prophecies usually are, but in a very hobbling kind of measure. Their meaning is very dark, if it be any at all; of which the learned reader can judge better than I: however it be, several persons were of opinion that they deserved to be published, both as they discover somewhat of the genius of a former age, and may be an amusement to the present."

—Swift

The subject of this virulent satire was Elizabeth, Baroness Percy, daughter and heiress of Josceline, Earl of Northumberland, who died in 1670. She was born in 1666. In 1679 she was married to Henry Cavendish, Earl of Ogle, who died in 1680. In 1681, she married Thomas Thynne, a man of great wealth, a friend of the Duke of Monmouth and the Issachar of Dryden's "Absalom and Achitophel." A few months afterwards, in February 1681–2, Thynne was assassinated in the Haymarket by foreigners, who were devoted friends of Count Konigsmark, and appear to have acted under his direction. The Count had been in London shortly before Lady Ogle's marriage to Thynne, and had then paid his addresses to her. He fled the day after the murder, but was brought back, and was tried with the principals as an accessory, but was acquitted. Four months after the murder of Thynne, his widow was married to Charles Seymour, Duke of Somerset, on 30th May, 1682, and ultimately became the favourite and friend of Queen Anne, and a zealous partisan of the Whig party. Hence Swift's "Prophecy." See "State Trials," vol. ix, and "Notes and Queries," 1st S., v. 269.

—W. E. B.

When a holy black Swede, the son of Bob,
With a saint at his chin and a seal at his fob,
Shall not see one New-Years-day in that year,
Then let old England make good cheer:
Windsor and Bristol then shall be
Joined together in the Low-countree.
Then shall the tall black Daventry Bird
Speak against peace right many a word;
And some shall admire his coneying wit,
For many good groats his tongue shall slit.
But spight of the Harpy that crawls on all four,
There shall be peace, pardie, and war no more
But England must cry alack and well-a-day,
If the stick be taken from the dead sea.
And, dear Englond, if ought I understond,
Beware of Carrots from Northumberlond.
Carrots sown Thynne a deep root may get,
If so be they are in Somer set:
Their Conyngs mark thou; for I have been told,
They assassine when younge, and poison when old.
Root out these Carrots, O thou, whose name
is backwards and forwards always the same;
And keep thee close to thee always that name
Which backwards and forwards is almost the same.
And, England, wouldst thou be happy still,
Burn those Carrots under a Hill.

Corinna, a Ballad
1711–12

This day (the year I dare not tell)
    Apollo play'd the midwife's part;
Into the world Corinna fell,
    And he endued her with his art.

But Cupid with a Satyr comes;
    Both softly to the cradle creep;
Both stroke her hands, and rub her gums,
    While the poor child lay fast asleep.

Then Cupid thus: "This little maid
    Of love shall always speak and write;"
"And I pronounce," the Satyr said,
    "The world shall feel her scratch and bite."

Her talent she display'd betimes;
    For in a few revolving moons,
She seem'd to laugh and squall in rhymes,
    And all her gestures were lampoons.

At six years old, the subtle jade
    Stole to the pantry-door, and found
The butler with my lady's maid:
    And you may swear the tale went round.

She made a song, how little miss
    Was kiss'd and slobber'd by a lad:
And how, when master went to p—,
    Miss came, and peep'd at all he had.

At twelve, a wit and a coquette;
    Marries for love, half whore, half wife;
Cuckolds, elopes, and runs in debt;
    Turns authoress, and is Curll's for life.

Her common-place book all gallant is,
    Of scandal now a cornucopia;
She pours it out in Atalantis
    Or memoirs of the New Utopia.

The Fable of Midas. 1711–12

Collated with Stella's copy.

—Forster

Midas, we are in story told,
Turn'd every thing he touch'd to gold:
He chipp'd his bread; the pieces round
Glitter'd like spangles on the ground:
A codling, ere it went his lip in,
Would straight become a golden pippin.
He call'd for drink; you saw him sup
Potable gold in golden cup:
His empty paunch that he might fill,
He suck'd his victuals thro' a quill.
Untouch'd it pass'd between his grinders,
Or't had been happy for gold-finders:
He cock'd his hat, you would have said
Mambrino's helm adorn'd his head;
Whene'er he chanced his hands to lay
On magazines of corn or hay,
Gold ready coin'd appear'd instead
Of paltry provender and bread;
Hence, we are by wise farmers told
Old hay is equal to old gold:
And hence a critic deep maintains
We learn'd to weigh our gold by grains.
    This fool had got a lucky hit;
And people fancied he had wit,
Two gods their skill in music tried
And both chose Midas to decide:
He against Ph(oelig)bus' harp decreed,
And gave it for Pan's oaten reed:
The god of wit, to show his grudge,
Clapt asses' ears upon the judge,
A goodly pair, erect and wide,
Which he could neither gild nor hide.

And now the virtue of his hands
Was lost among Pactolus' sands,
Against whose torrent while he swims
The golden scurf peels off his limbs:
Fame spreads the news, and people travel
From far, to gather golden gravel;
Midas, exposed to all their jeers,
Had lost his art, and kept his ears.
This tale inclines the gentle reader
To think upon a certain leader;
To whom, from Midas down, descends
That virtue in the fingers' ends.
What else by perquisites are meant,
By pensions, bribes, and three per cent.?
By places and commissions sold,
And turning dung itself to gold?
By starving in the midst of store,
As t'other Midas did before?
None e'er did modern Midas chuse
Subject or patron of his muse,
But found him thus their merit scan,
That Phoebus must give place to Pan:
He values not the poet's praise,
Nor will exchange his plums for bays.
To Pan alone rich misers call;
And there's the jest, for Pan is ALL.
Here English wits will be to seek,
Howe'er, 'tis all one in the Greek.
Besides, it plainly now appears
Our Midas, too, has ass's ears:
Where every fool his mouth applies,
And whispers in a thousand lies;
Such gross delusions could not pass
Thro' any ears but of an ass.
But gold defiles with frequent touch,
There's nothing fouls the hand so much;
And scholars give it for the cause
Of British Midas' dirty paws;
Which, while the senate strove to scour,

They wash'd away the chemic power.
While he his utmost strength applied,
To swim against this popular tide,
The golden spoils flew off apace,
Here fell a pension, there a place:
The torrent merciless imbibes
Commissions, perquisites, and bribes,
By their own weight sunk to the bottom;
Much good may't do 'em that have caught 'em!
And Midas now neglected stands,
With ass's ears, and dirty hands.

Toland's Invitation to Dismal to Dine with the Calves' Head Club

Written A.D. 1712. —*Stella*

Imitated from Horace, Lib. i, Epist. 5.

Toland, the Deist, distinguished himself as a party writer in behalf of the Whigs. He wrote a pamphlet on the demolition of Dunkirk, and another called "The Art of Reasoning," in which he directly charged Oxford with the purpose of bringing in the Pretender. The Earl of Nottingham, here, as elsewhere, called Dismal from his swarthy complexion, was bred a rigid High-Churchman, and was only induced to support the Whigs, in their resolutions against a peace, by their consenting to the bill against occasional conformity. He was so distinguished for regularity, as to be termed by Rowe

"The sober Earl of Nottingham,
Of sober sire descended."

—Hor., *Odes*, ii, 4.

From these points of his character, we may estimate the severity of the following satire, which represents this pillar of High-Church principles as invited by the republican Toland to solemnize the 30th January, by attending the Calves' Head Club.

—*Scott*

If, dearest Dismal, you for once can dine
Upon a single dish, and tavern wine,
Toland to you this invitation sends,
To eat the calfs head with your trusty friends.
Suspend awhile your vain ambitious hopes,
Leave hunting after bribes, forget your tropes.
To-morrow we our mystic feast prepare,
Where thou, our latest proselyte, shall share:
When we, by proper signs and symbols, tell,
How by brave hands the royal traitor fell;

The meat shall represent the tyrant's head,
The wine, his blood our predecessors shed;
Whilst an alluding hymn some artist sings,
We toast, Confusion to the race of kings!
At monarchy we nobly show our spight,
And talk, what fools call treason, all the night.
Who, by disgraces or ill fortune sunk,
Feels not his soul enliven'd when he's drunk?
Wine can clear up Godolphin's cloudy face,
And fill Jack Smith with hopes to keep his place:
By force of wine, ev'n Scarborough is brave,
Hal grows more pert, and Somers not so grave:
Wine can give Portland wit, and Cleaveland sense,
Montague learning, Bolton eloquence:
Cholmondeley, when drunk, can never lose his wand;
And Lincoln then imagines he has land.
My province is, to see that all be right,
Glasses and linen clean, and pewter bright;
From our mysterious club to keep out spies,
And Tories (dress'd like waiters) in disguise.
You shall be coupled as you best approve,
Seated at table next the man you love.
Sunderland, Orford, Boyle, and Richmond's grace
Will come; and Hampden shall have Walpole's place;
Wharton, unless prevented by a whore,
Will hardly fail; and there is room for more;
But I love elbow-room whene'er I drink;
And honest Harry is too apt to stink.
Let no pretence of bus'ness make you stay;
Yet take one word of counsel by the way.
If Guernsey calls, send word you're gone abroad;
He'll teaze you with King Charles, and Bishop Laud,
Or make you fast, and carry you to prayers;
But, if he will break in, and walk up stairs,
Steal by the back-door out, and leave him there;
Then order Squash to call a hackney chair.

Peace and Dunkirk

Being an Excellent New Song upon the Surrender
Of Dunkirk to General Hill
1712

To the tune of "The King shall enjoy his own again."

Spite of Dutch friends and English foes,
Poor Britain shall have peace at last:
Holland got towns, and we got blows;
But Dunkirk's ours, we'll hold it fast.
We have got it in a string,
And the Whigs may all go swing,
For among good friends I love to be plain;
All their false deluded hopes
Will, or ought to end in ropes;
"But the Queen shall enjoy her own again."

Sunderland's run out of his wits,
And Dismal double Dismal looks;
Wharton can only swear by fits,
And strutting Hal is off the hooks;
Old Godolphin, full of spleen,
Made false moves, and lost his Queen:
Harry look'd fierce, and shook his ragged mane:
But a Prince of high renown
Swore he'd rather lose a crown,
"Than the Queen should enjoy her own again."

Our merchant-ships may cut the line,
And not be snapt by privateers.
And commoners who love good wine
Will drink it now as well as peers:
Landed men shall have their rent,
Yet our stocks rise *cent, per cent.*
The Dutch from hence shall no more millions drain:
We'll bring on us no more debts,

Nor with bankrupts fill gazettes;
"And the Queen shall enjoy her own again."

The towns we took ne'er did us good:
What signified the French to beat?
We spent our money and our blood,
To make the Dutchmen proud and great:
But the Lord of Oxford swears,
Dunkirk never shall be theirs.
The Dutch-hearted Whigs may rail and complain;
But true Englishmen may fill
A good health to General Hill:
"For the Queen now enjoys her own again."

Horace, Epist. I, VII
Imitation of Horace
To Lord Oxford, a.d. 1713

Harley, the nation's great support,
Returning home one day from court,
His mind with public cares possest,
All Europe's business in his breast,
Observed a parson near Whitehall,
Cheap'ning old authors on a stall.
The priest was pretty well in case,
And show'd some humour in his face;
Look'd with an easy, careless mien,
A perfect stranger to the spleen;
Of size that might a pulpit fill,
But more inclining to sit still.
My lord, (who, if a man may say't,
Loves mischief better than his meat),
Was now disposed to crack a jest
And bid friend Lewis go in quest.
(This Lewis was a cunning shaver,
And very much in Harley's favour)—
In quest who might this parson be,
What was his name, of what degree;
If possible, to learn his story,
And whether he were Whig or Tory.
    Lewis his patron's humour knows;
Away upon his errand goes,
And quickly did the matter sift;
Found out that it was Doctor Swift,
A clergyman of special note
For shunning those of his own coat;
Which made his brethren of the gown
Take care betimes to run him down:
No libertine, nor over nice,
Addicted to no sort of vice;
Went where he pleas'd, said what he thought;
Not rich, but owed no man a groat;

In state opinions à la mode,
He hated Wharton like a toad;
Had given the faction many a wound,
And libell'd all the junto round;
Kept company with men of wit,
Who often father'd what he writ:
His works were hawk'd in ev'ry street,
But seldom rose above a sheet:
Of late, indeed, the paper-stamp
Did very much his genius cramp;
And, since he could not spend his fire,
He now intended to retire.
    Said Harley, "I desire to know
From his own mouth, if this be so:
Step to the doctor straight, and say,
I'd have him dine with me to-day."
Swift seem'd to wonder what he meant,
Nor could believe my lord had sent;
So never offer'd once to stir,
But coldly said, "Your servant, sir!"
"Does he refuse me?" Harley cry'd:
"He does; with insolence and pride."
    Some few days after, Harley spies
The doctor fasten'd by the eyes
At Charing-cross, among the rout,
Where painted monsters are hung out:
He pull'd the string, and stopt his coach,
Beck'ning the doctor to approach.
Swift, who could neither fly nor hide,
Came sneaking to the chariot side,
And offer'd many a lame excuse:
He never meant the least abuse—
"My lord—the honour you design'd—
Extremely proud—but I had dined—
I am sure I never should neglect—
No man alive has more respect"—
Well, I shall think of that no more,
If you'll be sure to come at four."
    The doctor now obeys the summons,

Likes both his company and commons;
Displays his talent, sits till ten;
Next day invited, comes again;
Soon grows domestic, seldom fails,
Either at morning or at meals;
Came early, and departed late;
In short, the gudgeon took the bait.
My lord would carry on the jest,
And down to Windsor takes his guest.
Swift much admires the place and air,
And longs to be a Canon there;
In summer round the Park to ride,
In winter—never to reside.
A Canon!—that's a place too mean:
No, doctor, you shall be a Dean;
Two dozen canons round your stall,
And you the tyrant o'er them all:
You need but cross the Irish seas,
To live in plenty, power, and ease.
Poor Swift departed, and, what's worse,
With borrow'd money in his purse,
Travels at least a hundred leagues,
And suffers numberless fatigues.

Suppose him now a dean complete,
Demurely lolling in his seat,
And silver verge, with decent pride,
Stuck underneath his cushion side.
Suppose him gone through all vexations,
Patents, instalments, abjurations,
First-fruits, and tenths, and chapter-treats;
Dues, payments, fees, demands, and cheats.
(The wicked laity's contriving
To hinder clergymen from thriving.)
Now all the doctor's money's spent,
His tenants wrong him in his rent,
The farmers spitefully combine,
Force him to take his tithes in kine,
And Parvisol discounts arrears
By bills, for taxes and repairs.

Poor Swift, with all his losses vex'd,
Not knowing where to turn him next,
Above a thousand pounds in debt,
Takes horse, and in a mighty fret
Rides day and night at such a rate,
He soon arrives at Harley's gate;
But was so dirty, pale, and thin,
Old Read would hardly let him in.
Said Harley, "Welcome, rev'rend dean!
What makes your worship look so lean?
Why, sure you won't appear in town
In that old wig and rusty gown?
I doubt your heart is set on pelf
So much that you neglect yourself.
What! I suppose, now stocks are high,
You've some good purchase in your eye?
Or is your money out at use?"—
"Truce, good my lord, I beg a truce!"
The doctor in a passion cry'd,
"Your raillery is misapply'd;
Experience I have dearly bought;
You know I am not worth a groat:
But you resolved to have your jest,
And 'twas a folly to contest;
Then, since you now have done your worst,
Pray leave me where you found me first."

The Author upon Himself

1713

A few of the first lines were wanting in the copy sent us by a friend of the Author's from London.

—Dublin Edition

* * * * *
* * * * *
* * By an old — pursued,
A crazy prelate, and a royal prude;
By dull divines, who look with envious eyes
On ev'ry genius that attempts to rise;
And pausing o'er a pipe, with doubtful nod,
Give hints, that poets ne'er believe in God.
So clowns on scholars as on wizards look,
And take a folio for a conj'ring book.
Swift had the sin of wit, no venial crime:
Nay, 'twas affirm'd, he sometimes dealt in rhyme;
Humour and mirth had place in all he writ;
He reconcil'd divinity and wit:
He moved and bow'd, and talk'd with too much grace;
Nor show'd the parson in his gait or face;
Despised luxurious wines and costly meat;
Yet still was at the tables of the great;
Frequented lords; saw those that saw the queen;
At Child's or Truby's, never once had been;
Where town and country vicars flock in tribes,
Secured by numbers from the laymen's gibes;
And deal in vices of the graver sort,
Tobacco, censure, coffee, pride, and port.
But, after sage monitions from his friends,
His talents to employ for nobler ends;
To better judgments willing to submit,
He turns to politics his dang'rous wit.
And now, the public Int'rest to support,

By Harley Swift invited, comes to court;
In favour grows with ministers of state;
Admitted private, when superiors wait:
And Harley, not ashamed his choice to own,
Takes him to Windsor in his coach alone.
At Windsor Swift no sooner can appear,
But St. John comes, and whispers in his ear:
The waiters stand in ranks: the yeomen cry,
Make room, as if a duke were passing by.
    Now Finch alarms the lords: he hears for certain
This dang'rous priest is got behind the curtain.
Finch, famed for tedious elocution, proves
That Swift oils many a spring which Harley moves.
Walpole and Aislaby, to clear the doubt,
Inform the Commons, that the secret's out:
"A certain doctor is observed of late
To haunt a certain minister of state:
From whence with half an eye we may discover
The peace is made, and Perkin must come over."
    York is from Lambeth sent, to show the queen
A dang'rous treatise writ against the spleen;
Which, by the style, the matter, and the drift,
'Tis thought could be the work of none but Swift.
Poor York! the harmless tool of others' hate;
He sues for pardon, and repents too late.
    Now angry Somerset her vengeance vows
On Swift's reproaches for her ******* spouse:
From her red locks her mouth with venom fills,
And thence into the royal ear instils.
The queen incensed, his services forgot,
Leaves him a victim to the vengeful Scot.
Now through the realm a proclamation spread,
To fix a price on his devoted head.
While innocent, he scorns ignoble flight;
His watchful friends preserve him by a sleight.
    By Harley's favour once again he shines;
Is now caress'd by candidate divines,
Who change opinions with the changing scene:
Lord! how were they mistaken in the dean!

Now Delawar again familiar grows;
And in Swift's ear thrusts half his powder'd nose.
The Scottish nation, whom he durst offend,
Again apply that Swift would be their friend.
    By faction tired, with grief he waits awhile,
His great contending friends to reconcile;
Performs what friendship, justice, truth require:
What could he more, but decently retire?

The Fagot

Written in the year 1713, when the Queen's ministers were quarrelling among themselves.

Observe the dying father speak:
Try, lads, can you this bundle break?
Then bids the youngest of the six
Take up a well-bound heap of sticks.
They thought it was an old man's maggot;
And strove, by turns, to break the fagot:
In vain: the complicated wands
Were much too strong for all their hands.
See, said the sire, how soon 'tis done:
Then took and broke them one by one.
So strong you'll be, in friendship ty'd;
So quickly broke, if you divide.
Keep close then, boys, and never quarrel:
Here ends the fable, and the moral.

This tale may be applied in few words,
To treasurers, comptrollers, stewards;
And others, who, in solemn sort,
Appear with slender wands at court;
Not firmly join'd to keep their ground,
But lashing one another round:
While wise men think they ought to fight
With quarterstaffs instead of white;
Or constable, with staff of peace,
Should come and make the clatt'ring cease;
Which now disturbs the queen and court,
And gives the Whigs and rabble sport.

In history we never found
The consul's fasces were unbound:
Those Romans were too wise to think on't,
Except to lash some grand delinquent,
How would they blush to hear it said,
The praetor broke the consul's head!
Or consul in his purple gown,

Came up and knock'd the praetor down!
Come, courtiers: every man his stick!
Lord treasurer, for once be quick:
And that they may the closer cling,
Take your blue ribbon for a string.
Come, trimming Harcourt, bring your mace;
And squeeze it in, or quit your place:
Dispatch, or else that rascal Northey
Will undertake to do it for thee:
And be assured, the court will find him
Prepared to leap o'er sticks, or bind them.
To make the bundle strong and safe,
Great Ormond, lend thy general's staff:
And, if the crosier could be cramm'd in
A fig for Lechmere, King, and Hambden!
You'll then defy the strongest Whig
With both his hands to bend a twig;
Though with united strength they all pull,
From Somers, down to Craggs and Walpole.

Imitation
Of Part of the Sixth Satire of the Second Book of Horace. 1714

I often wish'd that I had clear,
For life, six hundred pounds a-year,
A handsome house to lodge a friend,
A river at my garden's end,
A terrace walk, and half a rood
Of land, set out to plant a wood.
    Well, now I have all this and more,
I ask not to increase my store;
But should be perfectly content,
Could I but live on this side Trent;
Nor cross the channel twice a-year,
To spend six months with statesmen here.
    I must by all means come to town,
'Tis for the service of the crown.
"Lewis, the Dean will be of use;
Send for him up, take no excuse."
The toil, the danger of the seas,
Great ministers ne'er think of these;
Or let it cost a hundred pound,
No matter where the money's found,
It is but so much more in debt,
And that they ne'er consider'd yet.
    "Good Mr. Dean, go change your gown,
Let my lord know you're come to town."
I hurry me in haste away,
Not thinking it is levee-day;
And find his honour in a pound,
Hemm'd by a triple circle round,
Chequer'd with ribbons blue and green:
How should I thrust myself between?
Some wag observes me thus perplex'd,
And, smiling, whispers to the next,
"I thought the Dean had been too proud,

To justle here among a crowd!"
Another, in a surly fit,
Tells me I have more zeal than wit.
"So eager to express your love,
You ne'er consider whom you shove,
But rudely press before a duke."
I own I'm pleased with this rebuke,
And take it kindly meant, to show
What I desire the world should know.
    I get a whisper, and withdraw;
When twenty fools I never saw
Come with petitions fairly penn'd,
Desiring I would stand their friend.
    This humbly offers me his case;
That begs my interest for a place;
A hundred other men's affairs,
Like bees, are humming in my ears.
"To-morrow my appeal comes on;
Without your help, the cause is gone—"
"The duke expects my lord and you,
About some great affair, at two—"
"Put my Lord Bolingbroke in mind,
To get my warrant quickly sign'd:
Consider, 'tis my first request."—
Be satisfied I'll do my best:
Then presently he falls to tease,
"You may for certain, if you please;
I doubt not if his lordship knew—
And Mr. Dean, one word from you——"
    'Tis (let me see) three years and more,
(October next it will be four,)
Since Harley bid me first attend,
And chose me for an humble friend;
Would take me in his coach to chat,
And question me of this and that;
As "What's o'clock?" And, "How's the wind?"
"Whose chariot's that we left behind?"
Or gravely try to read the lines

Writ underneath the country signs;
And mark at Brentford how they spell
Hear is good Eal and Bear to cell.
Or, "Have you nothing new to-day
To shew from Parnell, Pope and Gay?"
Such tattle often entertains
My lord and me as far as Staines,
As once a-week we travel down
To Windsor, and again to town;
Where all that passes *inter nos*
Might be proclaim'd at Charing-cross.
Yet some I know with envy swell,
Because they see me used so well:
"How think you of our friend the Dean?
I wonder what some people mean!
My lord and he are grown so great,
Always together, *tête-à-tête*;
What! they admire him for his jokes?—
See but the fortune of some folks!"
There flies about a strange report
Of mighty news arrived at court:
I'm stopp'd by all the fools I meet,
And catechised in every street.
"You, Mr. Dean, frequent the great:
Inform us, will the emperor treat?
Or do the prints and papers lie?"
Faith, sir, you know as much as I.
"Ah, Doctor, how you love to jest!
'Tis now no secret"—I protest
It's one to me—"Then tell us, pray,
When are the troops to have their pay?"
And, though I solemnly declare
I know no more than my lord mayor,
They stand amazed, and think me grown
The closest mortal ever known.
Thus in a sea of folly toss'd,
My choicest hours of life are lost:
Yet always wishing to retreat,
O, could I see my country-seat!

There leaning near a gentle brook,
Sleep, or peruse some ancient book;
And there in sweet oblivion drown
Those cares that haunt the court and town.

Horace, Book II, Ode I, Paraphrased Addressed to Richard Steele, Esq. 1714

Dick, thou'rt resolved, as I am told,
Some strange arcana to unfold,
And with the help of Buckley's pen,
To vamp the good old cause again:
Which thou (such Burnet's shrewd advice is)
Must furbish up, and nickname Crisis.
Thou pompously wilt let us know
What all the world knew long ago,
(E'er since Sir William Gore was mayor,
And Harley fill'd the commons' chair,)
That we a German prince must own,
When Anne for Heaven resigns her throne.
But, more than that, thou'lt keep a rout,
With—who is in—and who is out;
Thou'lt rail devoutly at the peace,
And all its secret causes trace,
The bucket-play 'twixt Whigs and Tories,
Their ups and downs, with fifty stories
Of tricks the Lord of Oxford knows,
And errors of our plenipoes.
Thou'lt tell of leagues among the great,
Portending ruin to our state:
And of that dreadful *coup d'éclat*,
Which has afforded thee much chat.
The queen, forsooth! (despotic,) gave
Twelve coronets without thy leave!
A breach of liberty, 'tis own'd,
For which no heads have yet atoned!
Believe me, what thou'st undertaken
May bring in jeopardy thy bacon;
For madmen, children, wits, and fools,
Should never meddle with edged tools.
But, since thou'st got into the fire,
And canst not easily retire,
Thou must no longer deal in farce,

Nor pump to cobble wicked verse;
Until thou shall have eased thy conscience,
Of spleen, of politics, and nonsense;
And, when thou'st bid adieu to cares,
And settled Europe's grand affairs,
'Twill then, perhaps, be worth thy while
For Drury Lane to shape thy style:
"To make a pair of jolly fellows,
The son and father, join to tell us,
How sons may safely disobey,
And fathers never should say nay;
By which wise conduct they grow friends
At last—and so the story ends."
When first I knew thee, Dick, thou wert
Renown'd for skill in Faustus' art;
Which made thy closet much frequented
By buxom lasses—some repented
Their luckless choice of husbands—others
Impatient to be like their mothers,
Received from thee profound directions
How best to settle their affections.
Thus thou, a friend to the distress'd,
Didst in thy calling do thy best.

But now the senate (if things hit,
And thou at Stockbridge wert not bit)
Must feel thy eloquence and fire,
Approve thy schemes, thy wit admire,
Thee with immortal honours crown,
While, patriot-like, thou'lt strut and frown.

What though by enemies 'tis said,
The laurel, which adorns thy head,
Must one day come in competition,
By virtue of some sly petition:
Yet mum for that; hope still the best,
Nor let such cares disturb thy rest.

Methinks I hear thee loud as trumpet,
As bagpipe shrill or oyster-strumpet;
Methinks I see thee, spruce and fine,

With coat embroider'd richly shine,
And dazzle all the idol faces,
As through the hall thy worship paces;
(Though this I speak but at a venture,
Supposing thou hast tick with Hunter,)
Methinks I see a blackguard rout
Attend thy coach, and hear them shout
In approbation of thy tongue,
Which (in their style) is purely hung.
Now! now you carry all before you!
Nor dares one Jacobite or Tory
Pretend to answer one syl-lable,
Except the matchless hero Abel.
What though her highness and her spouse,
In Antwerp keep a frugal house,
Yet, not forgetful of a friend,
They'll soon enable thee to spend,
If to Macartney thou wilt toast,
And to his pious patron's ghost.
Now, manfully thou'lt run a tilt
"On popes, for all the blood they've spilt,
For massacres, and racks, and flames,
For lands enrich'd by crimson streams,
For inquisitions taught by Spain,
Of which the Christian world complain."
Dick, we agree—all's true thou'st said,
As that my Muse is yet a maid.
But, if I may with freedom talk,
All this is foreign to thy walk:
Thy genius has perhaps a knack
At trudging in a beaten track,
But is for state affairs as fit
As mine for politics and wit.
Then let us both in time grow wise,
Nor higher than our talents rise;
To some snug cellar let's repair,
From duns and debts, and drown our care;
Now quaff of honest ale a quart,

Now venture at a pint of port;
With which inspired, we'll club each night
Some tender sonnet to indite,
And with Tom D'Urfey, Phillips, Dennis,
Immortalize our Dolls and Jennys.

Dennis' Invitation to Steele

Horace, Book I, EP. V

John Dennis, the Sheltering Poet's Invitation to Richard Steele,
The Secluded Party-Writer and Member,
To come and live with him, in the Mint 1714

Fit to be bound up with "The Crisis"

If thou canst lay aside a spendthrift's air,
And condescend to feed on homely fare,
Such as we minters, with ragouts unstored,
Will, in defiance of the law, afford:
Quit thy patrols with Toby's Christmas box,
And come to me at The Two Fighting Cocks;
Since printing by subscription now is grown
The stalest, idlest cheat about the town;
And ev'n Charles Gildon, who, a Papist bred,
Has an alarm against that worship spread,
Is practising those beaten paths of cruising,
And for new levies on proposals musing.
    'Tis true, that Bloomsbury-square's a noble place:
But what are lofty buildings in thy case?
What's a fine house embellish'd to profusion,
Where shoulder dabbers are in execution?
Or whence its timorous tenant seldom sallies,
But apprehensive of insulting bailiffs?
This once be mindful of a friend's advice,
And cease to be improvidently nice;
Exchange the prospects that delude thy sight,
From Highgate's steep ascent and Hampstead's height,
With verdant scenes, that, from St. George's Field,
More durable and safe enjoyments yield.
    Here I, even I, that ne'er till now could find
Ease to my troubled and suspicious mind,
But ever was with jealousies possess'd,

Am in a state of indolence and rest;
Fearful no more of Frenchmen in disguise,
Nor looking upon strangers as on spies,
But quite divested of my former spleen,
Am unprovoked without, and calm within:
And here I'll wait thy coming, till the sun
Shall its diurnal course completely run.
Think not that thou of sturdy bub shalt fail,
My landlord's cellar stock'd with beer and ale,
With every sort of malt that is in use,
And every country's generous produce.
The ready (for here Christian faith is sick,
Which makes us seldom trespass upon tick)
Instantly brings the choicest liquors out,
Whether we ask for home-brew'd or for stout,
For mead or cider, or, with dainties fed,
Ring for a flask or two of white or red,
Such as the drawer will not fail to swear
Was drunk by Pilkington when third time mayor.
That name, methinks, so popularly known
For opposition to the church and crown,
Might make the Lusitanian grape to pass,
And almost give a sanction to the glass;
Especially with thee, whose hasty zeal
Against the late rejected commerce bill
Made thee rise up, like an audacious elf,
To do the speaker honour, not thyself.
    But if thou soar'st above the common prices,
By virtue of subscription to thy Crisis,
And nothing can go down with thee but wines
Press'd from Burgundian and Campanian vines,
Bid them be brought; for, though I hate the French,
I love their liquors, as thou lovest a wench;
Else thou must humble thy expensive taste,
And, with us, hold contentment for a feast.
    The fire's already lighted; and the maid
Has a clean cloth upon the table laid,
Who never on a Saturday had struck,
But for thy entertainment, up a buck.

Think of this act of grace, which by your leave
Susan would not have done on Easter Eve,
Had she not been inform'd over and over,
'Twas for th'ingenious author of The Lover.
    Cease, therefore, to beguile thyself with hopes,
Which is no more than making sandy ropes,
And quit the vain pursuit of loud applause,
That must bewilder thee in faction's cause.
Pr'ythee what is't to thee who guides the state?
Why Dunkirk's demolition is so late?
Or why her majesty thinks fit to cease
The din of war, and hush the world to peace?
The clergy too, without thy aid, can tell
What texts to choose, and on what topics dwell;
And, uninstructed by thy babbling, teach
Their flocks celestial happiness to reach.
Rather let such poor souls as you and I,
Say that the holidays are drawing nigh,
And that to-morrow's sun begins the week,
Which will abound with store of ale and cake,
With hams of bacon, and with powder'd beef,
Stuff d to give field-itinerants relief.
    Then I, who have within these precincts kept,
And ne'er beyond the chimney-sweeper's stept,
Will take a loose, and venture to be seen,
Since 'twill be Sunday, upon Shanks's green;
There, with erected looks and phrase sublime,
To talk of unity of place and time,
And with much malice, mix'd with little satire,
Explode the wits on t'other side o' th' water.
    Why has my Lord Godolphin's special grace
Invested me with a queen's waiter's place,
If I, debarr'd of festival delights,
Am not allow'd to spend the perquisites?
He's but a short remove from being mad,
Who at a time of jubilee is sad,
And, like a griping usurer, does spare
His money to be squander'd by his heir;
Flutter'd away in liveries and in coaches,

And washy sorts of feminine debauches.
As for my part, whate'er the world may think,
I'll bid adieu to gravity, and drink;
And, though I can't put off a woful mien,
Will be all mirth and cheerfulness within:
As, in despight of a censorious race,
I most incontinently suck my face.
What mighty projects does not he design,
Whose stomach flows, and brain turns round with wine?
Wine, powerful wine, can thaw the frozen cit,
And fashion him to humour and to wit;
Makes even Somers to disclose his art
By racking every secret from his heart,
As he flings off the statesman's sly disguise,
To name the cuckold's wife with whom he lies.
Ev'n Sarum, when he quaffs it'stead of tea,
Fancies himself in Canterbury's see,
And S****, when he carousing reels,
Imagines that he has regain'd the seals:
W****, by virtue of his juice, can fight,
And Stanhope of commissioners make light.
Wine gives Lord Wingham aptitude of parts,
And swells him with his family's deserts:
Whom can it not make eloquent of speech;
Whom in extremest poverty not rich?
Since, by the means of the prevailing grape,
Th***n can Lechmere's warmth not only ape,
But, half seas o'er, by its inspiring bounties,
Can qualify himself in several counties.
What I have promised, thou may'st rest assured
Shall faithfully and gladly be procured.
Nay, I'm already better than my word,
New plates and knives adorn the jovial board:
And, lest you at their sight shouldst make wry faces
The girl has scour'd the pots, and wash'd the glasses
Ta'en care so excellently well to clean 'em,
That thou may'st see thine own dear picture in 'em.
    Moreover, due provision has been made,
That conversation may not be betray'd;

I have no company but what is proper
To sit with the most flagrant Whig at supper.
There's not a man among them but must please,
Since they're as like each other as are pease.
Toland and Hare have jointly sent me word
They'll come; and Kennet thinks to make a third,
Provided he's no other invitation
From men of greater quality and station.
Room will for Oldmixon and J—s be left:
But their discourses smell so much of theft,
There would be no abiding in the room,
Should two such ignorant pretenders come.
However, by this trusty bearer write,
If I should any other scabs invite;
Though, if I may my serious judgment give,
I'm wholly for King Charles's number five:
That was the stint in which that monarch fix'd,
Who would not be with noisiness perplex'd:
And that, if thou'lt agree to think it best,
Shall be our tale of heads, without one other guest.
    I've nothing more, now this is said, to say,
But to request thou'lt instantly away,
And leave the duties of thy present post,
To some well-skill'd retainer in a host:
Doubtless he'll carefully thy place supply,
And o'er his grace's horses have an eye.
While thou, who slunk thro' postern more than once,
Dost by that means avoid a crowd of duns,
And, crossing o'er the Thames at Temple Stairs,
Leav'st Phillips with good words to cheat their ears.

In Sickness

Written in October, 1714

Soon after the author's coming to live in Ireland, upon the Queen's death.

—*Swift*

'Tis true—then why should I repine
To see my life so fast decline?
But why obscurely here alone,
Where I am neither loved nor known?
My state of health none care to learn;
My life is here no soul's concern:
And those with whom I now converse
Without a tear will tend my hearse.
Removed from kind Arbuthnot's aid,
Who knows his art, but not his trade,
Preferring his regard for me
Before his credit, or his fee.
Some formal visits, looks, and words,
What mere humanity affords,
I meet perhaps from three or four,
From whom I once expected more;
Which those who tend the sick for pay,
Can act as decently as they:
But no obliging, tender friend,
To help at my approaching end.
My life is now a burthen grown
To others, ere it be my own.
Ye formal weepers for the sick,
In your last offices be quick;
And spare my absent friends the grief
To hear, yet give me no relief;
Expired to-day, entomb'd to-morrow,
When known, will save a double sorrow.

The Fable of the Bitches

Written in the Year 1715, on an Attempt to Repeal the Test Act

A bitch, that was full pregnant grown
By all the dogs and curs in town,
Finding her ripen'd time was come,
Her litter teeming from her womb,
Went here, and there, and everywhere,
To find an easy place to lay her.
    At length to Music's house she came,
And begg'd like one both blind and lame;
"My only friend, my dear," said she,
"You see 'tis mere necessity
Hath sent me to your house to whelp:
I die if you refuse your help."
    With fawning whine, and rueful tone,
With artful sigh, and feigned groan,
With couchant cringe, and flattering tale,
Smooth Bawty did so far prevail,
That Music gave her leave to litter;
(But mark what follow'd—faith! she bit her;)
Whole baskets full of bits and scraps,
And broth enough to fill her paps;
For well she knew, her numerous brood,
For want of milk, would suck her blood.
    But when she thought her pains were done,
And now 'twas high time to be gone,
In civil terms, "My friend," said she,
"My house you've had on courtesy;
And now I earnestly desire,
That you would with your cubs retire;
For, should you stay but one week longer,
I shall be starved with cold and hunger."
The guest replied—"My friend, your leave
I must a little longer crave;
Stay till my tender cubs can find

Their way—for now, you see, they're blind;
But, when we've gather'd strength, I swear,
We'll to our barn again repair."
    The time pass'd on; and Music came
Her kennel once again to claim,
But Bawty, lost to shame and honour,
Set all her cubs at once upon her;
Made her retire, and quit her right,
And loudly cried—"A bite! bite!"

The Moral

Thus did the Grecian wooden horse
Conceal a fatal armed force:
No sooner brought within the walls,
But Ilium's lost, and Priam falls.

Horace, Book III, Ode II

To the Earl of Oxford, Late Lord Treasurer
Sent to him when in the Tower, 1716

These spirited verses, although they have not the affecting pathos of those addressed by Pope to the same great person, during his misfortunes, evince the firmness of Swift's political principles and personal attachment.

—Scott. *See Moral Essays, Epistle V, Pope's "Works," edit.*

Elwin and Courthope, iii, 191.

—W. E. B.

How blest is he who for his country dies,
Since death pursues the coward as he flies!
The youth in vain would fly from Fate's attack;
With trembling knees, and Terror at his back;
Though Fear should lend him pinions like the wind,
Yet swifter Fate will seize him from behind.
Virtue repulsed, yet knows not to repine;
But shall with unattainted honour shine;
Nor stoops to take the staff, nor lays it down,
Just as the rabble please to smile or frown.
Virtue, to crown her favourites, loves to try
Some new unbeaten passage to the sky;
Where Jove a seat among the gods will give
To those who die, for meriting to live.
Next faithful Silence hath a sure reward;
Within our breast be every secret barr'd!
He who betrays his friend, shall never be
Under one roof, or in one ship, with me:
For who with traitors would his safety trust,
Lest with the wicked, Heaven involve the just?
And though the villain'scape a while, he feels
Slow vengeance, like a bloodhound, at his heels.

On the Church's Danger

Good Halifax and pious Wharton cry,
The Church has vapours; there's no danger nigh.
In those we love not, we no danger see,
And were they hang'd, there would no danger be.
But we must silent be, amidst our fears,
And not believe our senses, but the Peers.
So ravishers, that know no sense of shame,
First stop her mouth, and then debauch the dame.

A Poem on High Church

High Church is undone,
As sure as a gun,
    For old Peter Patch is departed;
And Eyres and Delaune,
And the rest of that spawn,
    Are tacking about broken-hearted.

For strong Gill of Sarum,
That *decoctum amarum*,
    Has prescribed a dose of cant-fail;
Which will make them resign
Their flasks of French wine,
    And spice up their Nottingham ale.

It purges the spleen
Of dislike to the queen,
    And has one effect that is odder;
When easement they use,
They always will chuse
    The Conformity Bill for bumfodder.

A Poem Occasioned by the Hangings in the Castle of Dublin, In which the Story of Phaethon is Expressed

Not asking or expecting aught,
  One day I went to view the court,
Unbent and free from care or thought,
  Though thither fears and hopes resort.

A piece of tapestry took my eye,
  The faded colours spoke it old;
But wrought with curious imagery,
  The figures lively seem'd and bold.

Here you might see the youth prevail,
  (In vain are eloquence and wit,)
The boy persists, Apollo's frail;
  Wisdom to nature does submit.

There mounts the eager charioteer;
  Soon from his seat he's downward hurl'd;
Here Jove in anger doth appear,
  There all, beneath, the flaming world.

What does this idle fiction mean?
  Is truth at court in such disgrace,
It may not on the walls be seen,
  Nor e'en in picture show its face?

No, no, 'tis not a senseless tale,
  By sweet-tongued Ovid dress'd so fine;
It does important truths conceal,
  And here was placed by wise design.

A lesson deep with learning fraught,
Worthy the cabinet of kings;
Fit subject of their constant thought,
In matchless verse the poet sings.

Well should he weigh, who does aspire
To empire, whether truly great,
His head, his heart, his hand, conspire
To make him equal to that seat.

If only fond desire of sway,
By avarice or ambition fed,
Make him affect to guide the day,
Alas! what strange confusion's bred!

If, either void of princely care,
Remiss he holds the slacken'd rein;
If rising heats or mad career,
Unskill'd, he knows not to restrain:

Or if, perhaps, he gives a loose,
In wanton pride to show his skill,
How easily he can reduce
And curb the people's rage at will;

In wild uproar they hurry on;—
The great, the good, the just, the wise,
(Law and religion overthrown,)
Are first mark'd out for sacrifice.

When, to a height their fury grown,
Finding, too late, he can't retire,
He proves the real Phaethon,
And truly sets the world on fire.

A Tale of a Nettle

A man with expense and infinite toil,
By digging and dunging, ennobled his soil;
There fruits of the best your taste did invite,
And uniform order still courted the sight.
No degenerate weeds the rich ground did produce,
But all things afforded both beauty and use:
Till from dunghill transplanted, while yet but a seed,
A nettle rear'd up his inglorious head.
The gard'ner would wisely have rooted him up,
To stop the increase of a barbarous crop;
But the master forbid him, and after the fashion
Of foolish good nature, and blind moderation,
Forbore him through pity, and chose as much rather,
To ask him some questions first, how he came thither.
Kind sir, quoth the nettle, a stranger I come,
For conscience compell'd to relinquish my home,
'Cause I wouldn't subscribe to a mystery dark,
That the prince of all trees is the Jesuit's bark,
An erroneous tenet I know, sir, that you,
No more than myself, will allow to be true.
To you, I for refuge and sanctuary sue,
There's none so renown'd for compassion as you;
And, though in some things I may differ from these,
The rest of your fruitful and beautiful trees;
Though your digging and dunging, my nature much harms,
And I cannot comply with your garden in forms:
Yet I and my family, after our fashion,
Will peaceably stick to our own education.
Be pleased to allow them a place for to rest 'em,
For the rest of your trees we will never molest 'em;
A kind shelter to us and protection afford,
We'll do you no harm, sir, I'll give you my word.
The good man was soon won by this plausible tale,
So fraud on good-nature doth often prevail.
He welcomes his guest, gives him free toleration
In the midst of his garden to take up his station,

And into his breast doth his enemy bring,
He little suspected the nettle could sting.
'Till flush'd with success, and of strength to be fear'd,
Around him a numerous offspring he rear'd.
Then the master grew sensible what he had done,
And fain he would have his new guest to be gone;
But now 'twas too late to bid him turn out,
A well rooted possession already was got.
The old trees decay'd, and in their room grew
A stubborn, pestilent, poisonous crew.
The master, who first the young brood had admitted,
They stung like ingrates, and left him unpitied.
No help from manuring or planting was found,
The ill weeds had eat out the heart of the ground.
All weeds they let in, and none they refuse
That would join to oppose the good man of the house.
Thus one nettle uncropp'd, increased to such store,
That 'twas nothing but weeds what was garden before.

A Satirical Elegy
On the Death of a Late Famous General

His Grace! impossible! what, dead!
Of old age too, and in his bed!
And could that mighty warrior fall,
And so inglorious, after all?
Well, since he's gone, no matter how,
The last loud trump must wake him now;
And, trust me, as the noise grows stronger,
He'd wish to sleep a little longer.
And could he be indeed so old
As by the newspapers we're told?
Threescore, I think, is pretty high;
'Twas time in conscience he should die!
This world he cumber'd long enough;
He burnt his candle to the snuff;
And that's the reason, some folks think,
He left behind so great a stink.
Behold his funeral appears,
Nor widows' sighs, nor orphans' tears,
Wont at such times each heart to pierce,
Attend the progress of his hearse.
But what of that? his friends may say,
He had those honours in his day.
True to his profit and his pride,
He made them weep before he died.

Come hither, all ye empty things!
Ye bubbles raised by breath of kings!
Who float upon the tide of state;
Come hither, and behold your fate!
Let Pride be taught by this rebuke,
How very mean a thing's a duke;
From all his ill-got honours flung,
Turn'd to that dirt from whence he sprung.

Parody
On the Speech of Dr. Benjamin Pratt, Provost of Trinity College to the Prince of Wales

Illustrious prince, we're come before ye,
Who, more than in our founders, glory
To be by you protected;
Deign to descend and give us laws,
For we are converts to your cause,
From this day well-affected.

The noble view of your high merits
Has charm'd our thoughts and fix'd our spirits,
With zeal so warm and hearty;
That we resolved to be devoted,
At least until we be promoted,
By your just power and party.

Urged by a passionate desire
Of being raised a little higher,
From lazy cloister'd life;
We cannot flatter you nor fawn,
But fain would honour'd be with lawn,
And settled by a wife.

For this we have before resorted,
Paid levees punctually, and courted,
Our charge at home long quitting,
But now we're come just in the nick,
Upon a vacant bishopric,
This bait can't fail of hitting.

Thus, sir, you see how much affection,
Not interest, sways in this election,
But sense of loyal duty.

For you surpass all princes far,
As glow-worms do exceed a star,
                    In goodness, wit, and beauty.

To you our Irish Commons owe
That wisdom which their actions show,
                    Their principles from ours springs,
Taught, ere the deel himself could dream on't,
That of their illustrious house a stem on't,
                    Should rise the best of kings.

The glad presages with our eyes
Behold a king, chaste, vigilant, and wise,
                    In foreign fields victorious,
Who in his youth the Turks attacks,
And (made) them still to turn their backs;
                    Was ever king so glorious?

Since Ormond's like a traitor gone,
We scorn to do what some have done,
                    For learning much more famous;
Fools may pursue their adverse fate,
And stick to the unfortunate;
                    We laugh while they condemn us.

For, being of that gen'rous mind,
To success we are still inclined,
                    And quit the suffering side,
If on our friends cross planets frown,
We join the cry, and hunt them down,
                    And sail with wind and tide.

Hence 'twas this choice we long delay'd,
Till our rash foes the rebels fled,
                    Whilst fortune held the scale;
But (since) they're driven like mist before you,
Our rising sun, we now adore you,
                    Because you now prevail.

Descend then from your lofty seat,
Behold th' attending Muses wait
With us to sing your praises;
Calliope now strings up her lyre,
And Clio Phoebus does inspire,
The theme their fancy raises.

If then our nursery you will nourish,
We and our Muses too will flourish,
Encouraged by your favour;
We'll doctrines teach the times to serve,
And more five thousand pounds deserve,
By future good behaviour.

Now take our harp into your hand,
The joyful strings, at your command,
In doleful sounds no more shall mourn.
We, with sincerity of heart,
To all your tunes shall bear a part,
Unless we see the tables turn.

If so, great sir, you will excuse us,
For we and our attending Muses
May live to change our strain;
And turn, with merry hearts, our tune,
Upon some happy tenth of June,
To "the king enjoys his own again."

An Excellent New Song On a Seditious Pamphlet. 1720–21

To the tune of "Packington's Pound."

Brocades, and damasks, and tabbies, and gauzes,
Are, by Robert Ballantine, lately brought over,
With forty things more: now hear what the law says,
Whoe'er will not wear them is not the king's lover.
        Though a printer and Dean,
        Seditiously mean,
Our true Irish hearts from Old England to wean,
We'll buy English silks for our wives and our daughters,
In spite of his deanship and journeyman Waters.

In England the dead in woollen are clad,
    The Dean and his printer then let us cry fie on;
To be clothed like a carcass would make a Teague mad,
    Since a living dog better is than a dead lion.
        Our wives they grow sullen
        At wearing of woollen,
And all we poor shopkeepers must our horns pull in.
Then we'll buy English silks for our wives and our daughters,
In spite of his deanship and journeyman Waters.

Whoever our trading with England would hinder,
    To inflame both the nations do plainly conspire,
Because Irish linen will soon turn to tinder,
    And wool it is greasy, and quickly takes fire.
        Therefore, I assure ye,
        Our noble grand jury,
When they saw the Dean's book, they were in a great fury;
They would buy English silks for their wives and their daughters,
In spite of his deanship and journeyman Waters.

This wicked rogue Waters, who always is sinning,
    And before *coram nobis* so oft has been call'd,
Henceforward shall print neither pamphlets nor linen,

And if swearing can do't shall be swingingly maul'd:
And as for the Dean,
You know whom I mean,
If the printer will peach him, he'll scarce come off clean.
Then we'll buy English silks for our wives and our daughters,
In spite of his deanship and journeyman Waters.

The Run upon the Bankers

The bold encroachers on the deep
Gain by degrees huge tracts of land,
Till Neptune, with one general sweep,
Turns all again to barren strand.

The multitude's capricious pranks
Are said to represent the seas,
Breaking the bankers and the banks,
Resume their own whene'er they please.

Money, the life-blood of the nation,
Corrupts and stagnates in the veins,
Unless a proper circulation
Its motion and its heat maintains.

Because 'tis lordly not to pay,
Quakers and aldermen in state,
Like peers, have levees every day
Of duns attending at their gate.

We want our money on the nail;
The banker's ruin'd if he pays:
They seem to act an ancient tale;
The birds are met to strip the jays.

"Riches," the wisest monarch sings,
"Make pinions for themselves to fly;"
They fly like bats on parchment wings,
And geese their silver plumes supply.

No money left for squandering heirs!
Bills turn the lenders into debtors:
The wish of Nero now is theirs,
"That they had never known their letters."

Conceive the works of midnight hags,
    Tormenting fools behind their backs:
Thus bankers, o'er their bills and bags,
    Sit squeezing images of wax.

Conceive the whole enchantment broke;
    The witches left in open air,
With power no more than other folk,
    Exposed with all their magic ware.

So powerful are a banker's bills,
    Where creditors demand their due;
They break up counters, doors, and tills,
    And leave the empty chests in view.

Thus when an earthquake lets in light
    Upon the god of gold and hell,
Unable to endure the sight,
    He hides within his darkest cell.

As when a conjurer takes a lease
    From Satan for a term of years,
The tenant's in a dismal case,
    Whene'er the bloody bond appears.

A baited banker thus desponds,
    From his own hand foresees his fall,
They have his soul, who have his bonds;
    'Tis like the writing on the wall.

How will the caitiff wretch be scared,
    When first he finds himself awake
At the last trumpet, unprepared,
    And all his grand account to make!

For in that universal call,
    Few bankers will to heaven be mounters;
They'll cry, "Ye shops, upon us fall!
    Conceal and cover us, ye counters!"

When other hands the scales shall hold,
    And they, in men's and angels' sight
Produced with all their bills and gold,
    "Weigh'd in the balance and found light!"

Upon the Horrid Plot Discovered by Harlequin, the Bishop of Rochester's French Dog, In a Dialogue between a Whig and a Tory

I ask'd a Whig the other night,
How came this wicked plot to light?
He answer'd, that a dog of late
Inform'd a minister of state.
Said I, from thence I nothing know;
For are not all informers so?
A villain who his friend betrays,
We style him by no other phrase;
And so a perjured dog denotes
Porter, and Pendergast, and Oates,
And forty others I could name.
    Whig. But you must know this dog was lame.
    Tory. A weighty argument indeed!
Your evidence was lame:—proceed:
Come, help your lame dog o'er the stile.
    Whig. Sir, you mistake me all this while:
I mean a dog (without a joke)
Can howl, and bark, but never spoke.
    Tory. I'm still to seek, which dog you mean;
Whether cur Plunkett, or whelp Skean,
An English or an Irish hound;
Or t'other puppy, that was drown'd;
Or Mason, that abandon'd bitch:
Then pray be free, and tell me which:
For every stander-by was marking,
That all the noise they made was barking.
You pay them well, the dogs have got
Their dogs-head in a porridge-pot:
And 'twas but just; for wise men say,
That every dog must have his day.
Dog Walpole laid a quart of nog on't,
He'd either make a hog or dog on't;

And look'd, since he has got his wish,
As if he had thrown down a dish,
Yet this I dare foretell you from it,
He'll soon return to his own vomit.
WHIG. Besides, this horrid plot was found
By Neynoe, after he was drown'd.
TORY. Why then the proverb is not right,
Since you can teach dead dogs to bite.
WHIG. I proved my proposition full:
But Jacobites are strangely dull.
Now, let me tell you plainly, sir,
Our witness is a real cur,
A dog of spirit for his years;
Has twice two legs, two hanging ears;
His name is Harlequin, I wot,
And that's a name in every plot:
Resolved to save the British nation,
Though French by birth and education;
His correspondence plainly dated,
Was all decipher'd and translated:
His answers were exceeding pretty,
Before the secret wise committee;
Confest as plain as he could bark:
Then with his fore-foot set his mark.
TORY. Then all this while have I been bubbled,
I thought it was a dog in doublet:
The matter now no longer sticks:
For statesmen never want dog-tricks.
But since it was a real cur,
And not a dog in metaphor,
I give you joy of the report,
That he's to have a place at court.
WHIG. Yes, and a place he will grow rich in;
A turnspit in the royal kitchen.
Sir, to be plain, I tell you what,
We had occasion for a plot;
And when we found the dog begin it,
We guess'd the bishop's foot was in it.
TORY. I own it was a dangerous project,

And you have proved it by dog-logic.
Sure such intelligence between
A dog and bishop ne'er was seen,
Till you began to change the breed;
Your bishops are all dogs indeed!

A Quibbling Elegy on Judge Boat
1723

To mournful ditties, Clio, change thy note,
Since cruel fate has sunk our Justice Boat;
Why should he sink, where nothing seem'd to press
His lading little, and his ballast less?
Tost in the waves of this tempestuous world,
At length, his anchor fix'd and canvass furl'd,
To Lazy-hill retiring from his court,
At his Ring's end he founders in the port.
With water fill'd, he could no longer float,
The common death of many a stronger boat.
A post so fill'd on nature's laws entrenches:
Benches on boats are placed, not boats on benches.
And yet our Boat (how shall I reconcile it?)
Was both a Boat, and in one sense a pilot.
With every wind he sail'd, and well could tack:
Had many pendants, but abhorr'd a Jack.
He's gone, although his friends began to hope,
That he might yet be lifted by a rope.
Behold the awful bench, on which he sat!
He was as hard and ponderous wood as that:
Yet when his sand was out, we find at last,
That death has overset him with a blast.
Our Boat is now sail'd to the Stygian ferry,
There to supply old Charon's leaky wherry;
Charon in him will ferry souls to Hell;
A trade our Boat has practised here so well:
And Cerberus has ready in his paws
Both pitch and brimstone, to fill up his flaws.
Yet, spite of death and fate, I here maintain
We may place Boat in his old post again.
The way is thus: and well deserves your thanks:
Take the three strongest of his broken planks,

Fix them on high, conspicuous to be seen,
Form'd like the triple tree near Stephen's Green:
And, when we view it thus with thief at end on't,
We'll cry; look, here's our Boat, and there's the pendant.

The Epitaph

Here lies Judge Boat within a coffin:
Pray, gentlefolks, forbear your scoffing.
A Boat a judge! yes; where's the blunder?
A wooden judge is no such wonder.
And in his robes you must agree,
No boat was better deckt than he.
'Tis needless to describe him fuller;
In short, he was an able sculler.

Verses Occasioned by Whitshed's Motto on his Coach. 1724

Libertas *et natale solum:*
Fine words! I wonder where you stole 'em.
Could nothing but thy chief reproach
Serve for a motto on thy coach?
But let me now the words translate:
Natale solum, my estate;
My dear estate, how well I love it,
My tenants, if you doubt, will prove it,
They swear I am so kind and good,
I hug them till I squeeze their blood.
    Libertas bears a large import:
First, how to swagger in a court;
And, secondly, to show my fury
Against an uncomplying jury;
And, thirdly, 'tis a new invention,
To favour Wood, and keep my pension;
And, fourthly, 'tis to play an odd trick,
Get the great seal and turn out Broderick;
And, fifthly, (you know whom I mean,)
To humble that vexatious Dean:
And, sixthly, for my soul to barter it
For fifty times its worth to Carteret.
Now since your motto thus you construe,
I must confess you've spoken once true.
Libertas et natale solum:
You had good reason when you stole 'em.

Prometheus
On Wood the Patentee's Irish Halfpence
1724

When first the squire and tinker Wood
Gravely consulting Ireland's good,
Together mingled in a mass
Smith's dust, and copper, lead, and brass;
The mixture thus by chemic art
United close in ev'ry part,
In fillets roll'd, or cut in pieces,
Appear'd like one continued species;
And, by the forming engine struck,
On all the same impression took.
    So, to confound this hated coin,
All parties and religions join;
Whigs, Tories, Trimmers, Hanoverians,
Quakers, Conformists, Presbyterians,
Scotch, Irish, English, French, unite,
With equal interest, equal spite
Together mingled in a lump,
Do all in one opinion jump;
And ev'ry one begins to find
The same impression on his mind.
    A strange event! whom gold incites
To blood and quarrels, brass unites;
So goldsmiths say, the coarsest stuff
Will serve for solder well enough:
So by the kettle's loud alarms
The bees are gather'd into swarms,
So by the brazen trumpet's bluster
Troops of all tongues and nations muster;
And so the harp of Ireland brings
Whole crowds about its brazen strings.
    There is a chain let down from Jove,
But fasten'd to his throne above,
So strong that from the lower end,
They say all human things depend.

This chain, as ancient poets hold,
When Jove was young, was made of gold,
Prometheus once this chain purloin'd,
Dissolved, and into money coin'd;
Then whips me on a chain of brass;
(Venus was bribed to let it pass.)
    Now while this brazen chain prevail'd,
Jove saw that all devotion fail'd;
No temple to his godship raised;
No sacrifice on altars blazed;
In short, such dire confusion follow'd,
Earth must have been in chaos swallow'd.
Jove stood amazed; but looking round,
With much ado the cheat he found;
'Twas plain he could no longer hold
The world in any chain but gold;
And to the god of wealth, his brother,
Sent Mercury to get another.
    Prometheus on a rock is laid,
Tied with the chain himself had made,
On icy Caucasus to shiver,
While vultures eat his growing liver.

    Ye powers of Grub-Street, make me able
Discreetly to apply this fable;
Say, who is to be understood
By that old thief Prometheus?—Wood.
For Jove, it is not hard to guess him;
I mean his majesty, God bless him.
This thief and blacksmith was so bold,
He strove to steal that chain of gold,
Which links the subject to the king,
And change it for a brazen string.
But sure, if nothing else must pass
Betwixt the king and us but brass,
Although the chain will never crack,
Yet our devotion may grow slack.
    But Jove will soon convert, I hope,
This brazen chain into a rope;

With which Prometheus shall be tied,
And high in air for ever ride;
Where, if we find his liver grows,
For want of vultures, we have crows.

Verses on the Revival of the Order of the Bath, During Walpole's Administration, a.d. 1725

Quoth King Robin, our ribbons I see are too few
Of St. Andrew's the green, and St. George's the blue.
I must find out another of colour more gay,
That will teach all my subjects with pride to obey.
Though the exchequer be drain'd by prodigal donors,
Yet the king ne'er exhausted his fountain of honours.
Men of more wit than money our pensions will fit,
And this will fit men of more money than wit.
Thus my subjects with pleasure will obey my commands,
Though as empty as Younge, and as saucy as Sandes
And he who'll leap over a stick for the king,
Is qualified best for a dog in a string.

Epigram on Wood's Brass Money

Carteret was welcomed to the shore
First with the brazen cannon's roar;
To meet him next the soldier comes,
With brazen trumps and brazen drums;
Approaching near the town he hears
The brazen bells salute his ears:
But when Wood's brass began to sound,
Guns, trumpets, drums, and bells, were drown'd.

A Simile
On our want of Silver, and the only Way to Remedy it. 1725

As when of old some sorceress threw
O'er the moon's face a sable hue,
To drive unseen her magic chair,
At midnight, through the darken'd air;
Wise people, who believed with reason
That this eclipse was out of season,
Affirm'd the moon was sick, and fell
To cure her by a counter spell.
Ten thousand cymbals now begin,
To rend the skies with brazen din;
The cymbals' rattling sounds dispel
The cloud, and drive the hag to hell.
The moon, deliver'd from her pain,
Displays her silver face again.
Note here, that in the chemic style,
The moon is silver all this while.
    So (if my simile you minded,
Which I confess is too long-winded)
When late a feminine magician,
Join'd with a brazen politician,
Exposed, to blind the nation's eyes,
A parchment of prodigious size;
Conceal'd behind that ample screen,
There was no silver to be seen.
But to this parchment let the Drapier
Oppose his counter-charm of paper,
And ring Wood's copper in our ears
So loud till all the nation hears;
That sound will make the parchment shrivel
And drive the conjurors to the Devil;
And when the sky is grown serene,
Our silver will appear again.

Wood an Insect. 1725

By long observation I have understood,
That two little vermin are kin to Will Wood.
The first is an insect they call a wood-louse,
That folds up itself in itself for a house,
As round as a ball, without head, without tail,
Enclosed *cap à pie*, in a strong coat of mail.
And thus William Wood to my fancy appears
In fillets of brass roll'd up to his ears;
And over these fillets he wisely has thrown,
To keep out of danger, a doublet of stone.
The louse of the wood for a medicine is used
Or swallow'd alive, or skilfully bruised.
And, let but our mother Hibernia contrive
To swallow Will Wood, either bruised or alive,
She need be no more with the jaundice possest,
Or sick of obstructions, and pains in her chest.
The next is an insect we call a wood-worm,
That lies in old wood like a hare in her form;
With teeth or with claws it will bite or will scratch,
And chambermaids christen this worm a death-watch;
Because like a watch it always cries click;
Then woe be to those in the house who are sick:
For, as sure as a gun, they will give up the ghost,
If the maggot cries click when it scratches the post;
But a kettle of scalding hot-water injected
Infallibly cures the timber affected;
The omen is broken, the danger is over;
The maggot will die, and the sick will recover.
Such a worm was Will Wood, when he scratch'd at the door
Of a governing statesman or favourite whore;
The death of our nation he seem'd to foretell,
And the sound of his brass we took for our knell.
But now, since the Drapier has heartily maul'd him,
I think the best thing we can do is to scald him;
For which operation there's nothing more proper
Than the liquor he deals in, his own melted copper;

Unless, like the Dutch, you rather would boil
This coiner of raps in a caldron of oil.
Then choose which you please, and let each bring a fagot,
For our fear's at an end with the death of the maggot.

On Wood the Ironmonger. 1725

Salmoneus, as the Grecian tale is,
Was a mad coppersmith of Elis:
Up at his forge by morning peep,
No creature in the lane could sleep;
Among a crew of roystering fellows
Would sit whole evenings at the alehouse;
His wife and children wanted bread,
While he went always drunk to bed.
This vapouring scab must needs devise
To ape the thunder of the skies:
With brass two fiery steeds he shod,
To make a clattering as they trod,
Of polish'd brass his flaming car
Like lightning dazzled from afar;
And up he mounts into the box,
And he must thunder, with a pox.
Then furious he begins his march,
Drives rattling o'er a brazen arch;
With squibs and crackers arm'd to throw
Among the trembling crowd below.
All ran to prayers, both priests and laity,
To pacify this angry deity;
When Jove, in pity to the town,
With real thunder knock'd him down.
Then what a huge delight were all in,
To see the wicked varlet sprawling;
They search'd his pockets on the place,
And found his copper all was base;
They laugh'd at such an Irish blunder,
To take the noise of brass for thunder.
    The moral of this tale is proper,
Applied to Wood's adulterate copper:
Which, as he scatter'd, we, like dolts,
Mistook at first for thunderbolts,

Before the Drapier shot a letter,
(Nor Jove himself could do it better)
Which lighting on the impostor's crown,
Like real thunder knock'd him down.

Will Wood's Petition to the People of Ireland

Being an Excellent New Song,
Supposed to be made, and Sung in the Streets of Dublin,
By William Wood, Ironmonger and Halfpenny-Monger. 1725

My dear Irish folks,
Come leave off your jokes,
And buy up my halfpence so fine;
So fair and so bright
They'll give you delight;
Observe how they glisten and shine!

They'll sell to my grief
As cheap as neck-beef,
For counters at cards to your wife;
And every day
Your children may play
Span-farthing or toss on the knife.

Come hither and try,
I'll teach you to buy
A pot of good ale for a farthing;
Come, threepence a score,
I ask you no more,
And a fig for the Drapier and Harding.

When tradesmen have gold,
The thief will be bold,
By day and by night for to rob him:
My copper is such,
No robber will touch,
And so you may daintily bob him.

The little blackguard
Who gets very hard
His halfpence for cleaning your shoes:

When his pockets are cramm'd
With mine, and be d—d,
He may swear he has nothing to lose.

Here's halfpence in plenty,
For one you'll have twenty,
Though thousands are not worth a pudden.
Your neighbours will think,
When your pocket cries chink.
You are grown plaguy rich on a sudden.

You will be my thankers,
I'll make you my bankers,
As good as Ben Burton or Fade;
For nothing shall pass
But my pretty brass,
And then you'll be all of a trade.

I'm a son of a whore
If I have a word more
To say in this wretched condition.
If my coin will not pass,
I must die like an ass;
And so I conclude my petition.

A New Song on Wood's Halfpence

Ye people of Ireland, both country and city,
Come listen with patience, and hear out my ditty:
At this time I'll choose to be wiser than witty.
Which nobody can deny.

The halfpence are coming, the nation's undoing,
There's an end of your ploughing, and baking, and brewing;
In short, you must all go to wreck and to ruin.
Which, &c.

Both high men and low men, and thick men and tall men,
And rich men and poor men, and free men and thrall men,
Will suffer; and this man, and that man, and all men.
Which, &c.

The soldier is ruin'd, poor man! by his pay;
His fivepence will prove but a farthing a-day,
For meat, or for drink; or he must run away.
Which, &c.

When he pulls out his twopence, the tapster says not,
That ten times as much he must pay for his shot;
And thus the poor soldier must soon go to pot.
Which, &c.

If he goes to the baker, the baker will huff,
And twentypence have for a twopenny loaf,
Then dog, rogue, and rascal, and so kick and cuff.
Which, &c.

Again, to the market whenever he goes,
The butcher and soldier must be mortal foes,
One cuts off an ear, and the other a nose.
Which, &c.

The butcher is stout, and he values no swagger;
A cleaver's a match any time for a dagger,
And a blue sleeve may give such a cuff as may stagger.
Which, &c.

The beggars themselves will be broke in a trice,
When thus their poor farthings are sunk in their price;
When nothing is left they must live on their lice.
Which, &c.

The squire who has got him twelve thousand a-year,
O Lord! what a mountain his rents would appear!
Should he take them, he would not have house-room, I fear.
Which, &c.

Though at present he lives in a very large house,
There would then not be room in it left for a mouse;
But the squire is too wise, he will not take a souse.
Which, &c.

The farmer who comes with his rent in this cash,
For taking these counters and being so rash,
Will be kick'd out of doors, both himself and his trash.
Which, &c.

For, in all the leases that ever we hold,
We must pay our rent in good silver and gold,
And not in brass tokens of such a base mould.
Which, &c.

The wisest of lawyers all swear, they will warrant
No money but silver and gold can be current;
And, since they will swear it, we all may be sure on't.
Which, &c.

And I think, after all, it would be very strange,
To give current money for base in exchange,
Like a fine lady swapping her moles for the mange.
Which, &c.

But read the king's patent, and there you will find,
That no man need take them, but who has a mind,
For which we must say that his Majesty's kind.
Which, &c.

Now God bless the Drapier who open'd our eyes!
I'm sure, by his book, that the writer is wise:
He shows us the cheat, from the end to the rise.
Which, &c.

Nay, farther, he shows it a very hard case,
That this fellow Wood, of a very bad race,
Should of all the fine gentry of Ireland take place.
Which, &c.

That he and his halfpence should come to weigh down
Our subjects so loyal and true to the crown:
But I hope, after all, that they will be his own.
Which, &c.

This book, I do tell you, is writ for your goods,
And a very good book 'tis against Mr. Wood's,
If you stand true together, he's left in the suds.
Which, &c.

Ye shopmen, and tradesmen, and farmers, go read it,
For I think in my soul at this time that you need it;
Or, egad, if you don't, there's an end of your credit.
Which nobody can deny.

A Serious Poem Upon William Wood, Brazier, Tinker, Hard-Wareman, Coiner, Founder, and Esquire

When foes are o'ercome, we preserve them from slaughter,
To be hewers of wood, and drawers of water.
Now, although to draw water is not very good,
Yet we all should rejoice to be hewers of Wood.
I own it has often provoked me to mutter,
That a rogue so obscure should make such a clutter;
But ancient philosophers wisely remark,
That old rotten wood will shine in the dark.
The Heathens, we read, had gods made of wood,
Who could do them no harm, if they did them no good;
But this idol Wood may do us great evil,
Their gods were of wood, but our Wood is the devil.
To cut down fine wood is a very bad thing;
And yet we all know much gold it will bring:
Then, if cutting down wood brings money good store
Our money to keep, let us cut down one more.
    Now hear an old tale. There anciently stood
(I forget in what church) an image of wood;
Concerning this image, there went a prediction,
It would burn a whole forest; nor was it a fiction.
'Twas cut into fagots and put to the flame,
To burn an old friar, one Forest by name,
My tale is a wise one, if well understood:
Find you but the Friar; and I'll find the Wood.
    I hear, among scholars there is a great doubt,
From what kind of tree this Wood was hewn out,
Teague made a good pun by a brogue in his speech:
And said, "By my shoul, he's the son of a Beech."
Some call him a thorn, the curse of the nation,
As thorns were design'd to be from the creation.
Some think him cut out from the poisonous yew,
Beneath whose ill shade no plant ever grew.

Some say he's a birch, a thought very odd;
For none but a dunce would come under his rod.
But I'll tell the secret; and pray do not blab:
He is an old stump, cut out of a crab;
And England has put this crab to a hard use,
To cudgel our bones, and for drink give us ver-juice;
And therefore his witnesses justly may boast,
That none are more properly knights of the post,
    But here Mr. Wood complains that we mock,
Though he may be a blockhead, he's no real block.
He can eat, drink, and sleep; now and then for a friend
He'll not be too proud an old kettle to mend;
He can lie like a courtier, and think it no scorn,
When gold's to be got, to forswear and suborn.
He can rap his own raps and has the true sapience,
To turn a good penny to twenty bad halfpence.
Then in spite of your sophistry, honest Will Wood
Is a man of this world, all true flesh and blood;
So you are but in jest, and you will not, I hope,
Unman the poor knave for the sake of a trope.
'Tis a metaphor known to every plain thinker,
Just as when we say, the devil's a tinker,
Which cannot, in literal sense be made good,
Unless by the devil we mean Mr. Wood.
    But some will object that the devil oft spoke,
In heathenish times, from the trunk of an oak;
And since we must grant there never were known
More heathenish times, than those of our own;
Perhaps you will say, 'tis the devil that puts
The words in Wood's mouth, or speaks from his guts:
And then your old arguments still will return;
Howe'er, let us try him, and see how he'll burn:
You'll pardon me, sir, your cunning I smoke,
But Wood, I assure you, is no heart of oak;
And, instead of the devil, this son of perdition
Hath join'd with himself two hags in commission.
    I ne'er could endure my talent to smother:
I told you one tale, and I'll tell you another.
A joiner to fasten a saint in a niche,

Bored a large auger-hole in the image's breech;
But, finding the statue to make no complaint,
He would ne'er be convinced it was a true saint.
When the true Wood arrives, as he soon will, no doubt,
(For that's but a sham Wood they carry about;)
What stuff he is made of you quickly may find
If you make the same trial and bore him behind.
I'll hold you a groat, when you wimble his bum,
He'll bellow as loud as the de'il in a drum.
From me, I declare you shall have no denial;
And there can be no harm in making a trial:
And when to the joy of your hearts he has roar'd,
You may show him about for a new groaning board.

Now ask me a question. How came it to pass
Wood got so much copper? He got it by brass;
This brass was a dragon, (observe what I tell ye,)
This dragon had gotten two sows in his belly;
I know you will say this is all heathen Greek.
I own it, and therefore I leave you to seek.

I often have seen two plays very good,
Call'd Love in a Tub, and Love in a Wood;
These comedies twain friend Wood will contrive
On the scene of this land very soon to revive.
First, Love in a Tub: Squire Wood has in store
Strong tubs for his raps, two thousand and more;
These raps he will honestly dig out with shovels,
And sell them for gold, or he can't show his love else.
Wood swears he will do it for Ireland's good,
Then can you deny it is Love in a Wood?
However, if critics find fault with the phrase,
I hope you will own it is Love in a Maze:
For when to express a friend's love you are willing,
We never say more than your love is a million;
But with honest Wood's love there is no contending,
'Tis fifty round millions of love and a mending.
Then in his first love why should he be crost?
I hope he will find that no love is lost.

Hear one story more, and then I will stop.
I dreamt Wood was told he should die by a drop:

So methought he resolved no liquor to taste,
For fear the first drop might as well be his last.
But dreams are like oracles; 'tis hard to explain 'em;
For it proved that he died of a drop at Kilmainham.
I waked with delight; and not without hope,
Very soon to see Wood drop down from a rope.
How he, and how we at each other should grin!
'Tis kindness to hold a friend up by the chin.
But soft! says the herald, I cannot agree;
For metal on metal is false heraldry.
Why that may be true; yet Wood upon Wood,
I'll maintain with my life, is heraldry good.

An Excellent New Song, Upon the Declarations of the Several Corporations of the City of Dublin Against Wood's Halfpence

To the tune of "London is a fine town," &c.

O Dublin is a fine town
And a gallant city,
For Wood's trash is tumbled down,
Come listen to my ditty,
O Dublin is a fine town, &c.

In full assembly all did meet
Of every corporation,
From every lane and every street,
To save the sinking nation.
O Dublin, &c.

The bankers would not let it pass
For to be Wood's tellers,
Instead of gold to count his brass,
And fill their small-beer cellars.
O Dublin, &c.

And next to them, to take his coin
The Gild would not submit,
They all did go, and all did join,
And so their names they writ.
O Dublin, &c.

The brewers met within their hall,
And spoke in lofty strains,
These halfpence shall not pass at all,
They want so many grains.
O Dublin, &c.

The tailors came upon this pinch,
And wish'd the dog in hell,
Should we give this same Wood an inch,
We know he'd take an ell.
O Dublin, &c.

But now the noble clothiers
Of honour and renown,
If they take Wood's halfpence
They will be all cast down.
O Dublin, &c.

The shoemakers came on the next,
And said they would much rather,
Than be by Wood's copper vext,
Take money stampt on leather.
O Dublin, &c.

The chandlers next in order came,
And what they said was right,
They hoped the rogue that laid the scheme
Would soon be brought to light.
O Dublin, &c.

And that if Wood were now withstood,
To his eternal scandal,
That twenty of these halfpence should
Not buy a farthing candle.
O Dublin, &c.

The butchers then, those men so brave,
Spoke thus, and with a frown;
Should Wood, that cunning scoundrel knave,
Come here, we'd knock him down.
O Dublin, &c.

For any rogue that comes to truck
And trick away our trade,
Deserves not only to be stuck,

But also to be flay'd.
O Dublin, &c.

The bakers in a ferment were,
And wisely shook their head;
Should these brass tokens once come here
We'd all have lost our bread.
O Dublin, &c.

It set the very tinkers mad,
The baseness of the metal,
Because, they said, it was so bad
It would not mend a kettle.
O Dublin, &c.

The carpenters and joiners stood
Confounded in a maze,
They seem'd to be all in a wood,
And so they went their ways.
O Dublin, &c.

This coin how well could we employ it
In raising of a statue,
To those brave men that would destroy it,
And then, old Wood, have at you.
O Dublin, &c.

God prosper long our tradesmen then,
And so he will I hope,
May they be still such honest men,
When Wood has got a rope.
O Dublin is a fine town, &c.

Verses On the Upright Judge, who condemned the Drapier's Printer

The church I hate, and have good reason,
For there my grandsire cut his weasand:
He cut his weasand at the altar;
I keep my gullet for the halter.

On the Same

In church your grandsire cut his throat;
    To do the job too long he tarried:
He should have had my hearty vote
    To cut his throat before he married.

On the Same

The Judge Speaks

I'm not the grandson of that ass Quin;
Nor can you prove it, Mr. Pasquin.
My grandame had gallants by twenties,
And bore my mother by a 'prentice.
This when my grandsire knew, they tell us he
In Christ-Church cut his throat for jealousy.
And, since the alderman was mad you say,
Then I must be so too, *ex traduce*.

Epigram

In Answer to the Dean's verses
On his own Deafness

What though the Dean hears not the knell
Of the next church's passing bell;
What though the thunder from a cloud,
Or that from female tongue more loud,
Alarm not; At the Drapier's ear,
Chink but Wood's halfpence, and he'll hear.

Horace, Book I, Ode XIV Paraphrased and Inscribed to Ireland 1726

The Inscription

Poor floating isle, tost on ill fortune's waves,
Ordain'd by fate to be the land of slaves;
Shall moving Delos now deep-rooted stand;
Thou fix'd of old, be now the moving land!
Although the metaphor be worn and stale,
Betwixt a state, and vessel under sail;
Let me suppose thee for a ship a while,
And thus address thee in the sailor style.

Unhappy ship, thou art return'd in vain;
New waves shall drive thee to the deep again.
Look to thyself, and be no more the sport
Of giddy winds, but make some friendly port.
Lost are thy oars, that used thy course to guide,
Like faithful counsellors, on either side.
Thy mast, which like some aged patriot stood,
The single pillar for his country's good,
To lead thee, as a staff directs the blind,
Behold it cracks by yon rough eastern wind;
Your cables burst, and you must quickly feel
The waves impetuous enter at your keel;
Thus commonwealths receive a foreign yoke,
When the strong cords of union once are broke.
Tom by a sudden tempest is thy sail,
Expanded to invite a milder gale.
As when some writer in a public cause
His pen, to save a sinking nation, draws,
While all is calm, his arguments prevail;
The people's voice expands his paper sail;
Till power, discharging all her stormy bags,
Flutters the feeble pamphlet into rags,

The nation scared, the author doom'd to death,
Who fondly put his trust in poplar breath.
    A larger sacrifice in vain you vow;
There's not a power above will help you now;
A nation thus, who oft Heaven's call neglects,
In vain from injured Heaven relief expects.
    'Twill not avail, when thy strong sides are broke
That thy descent is from the British oak;
Or, when your name and family you boast,
From fleets triumphant o'er the Gallic coast.
Such was Ierne's claim, as just as thine,
Her sons descended from the British line;
Her matchless sons, whose valour still remains
On French records for twenty long campaigns;
Yet, from an empress now a captive grown,
She saved Britannia's rights, and lost her own.
    In ships decay'd no mariner confides,
Lured by the gilded stern and painted sides:
Yet at a ball unthinking fools delight
In the gay trappings of a birth-day night:
They on the gold brocades and satins raved,
And quite forgot their country was enslaved.
Dear vessel, still be to thy steerage just,
Nor change thy course with every sudden gust;
Like supple patriots of the modern sort,
Who turn with every gale that blows from court.
    Weary and sea-sick, when in thee confined,
Now for thy safety cares distract my mind;
As those who long have stood the storms of state
Retire, yet still bemoan their country's fate.
Beware, and when you hear the surges roar,
Avoid the rocks on Britain's angry shore.
They lie, alas! too easy to be found;
For thee alone they lie the island round.

Verses On the Sudden Drying up of St. Patrick's Well Near Trinity College, Dublin. 1726

By holy zeal inspired, and led by fame,
To thee, once favourite isle, with joy I came;
What time the Goth, the Vandal, and the Hun,
Had my own native Italy o'errun.
Ierne, to the world's remotest parts,
Renown'd for valour, policy, and arts.
    Hither from Colchos, with the fleecy ore,
Jason arrived two thousand years before.
Thee, happy island, Pallas call'd her own,
When haughty Britain was a land unknown:
From thee, with pride, the Caledonians trace
The glorious founder of their kingly race:
Thy martial sons, whom now they dare despise,
Did once their land subdue and civilize;
Their dress, their language, and the Scottish name,
Confess the soil from whence the victors came.
Well may they boast that ancient blood which runs
Within their veins, who are thy younger sons.
A conquest and a colony from thee,
The mother-kingdom left her children free;
From thee no mark of slavery they felt:
Not so with thee thy base invaders dealt;
Invited here to vengeful Morrough's aid,
Those whom they could not conquer they betray'd.
Britain, by thee we fell, ungrateful isle!
Not by thy valour, but superior guile:
Britain, with shame, confess this land of mine
First taught thee human knowledge and divine;
My prelates and my students, sent from hence,
Made your sons converts both to God and sense:
Not like the pastors of thy ravenous breed,
Who come to fleece the flocks, and not to feed.

Wretched Ierne! with what grief I see
The fatal changes time has made in thee!
The Christian rites I introduced in vain:
Lo! infidelity return'd again!
Freedom and virtue in thy sons I found,
Who now in vice and slavery are drown'd.
By faith and prayer, this crosier in my hand,
I drove the venom'd serpent from thy land:
The shepherd in his bower might sleep or sing,
Nor dread the adder's tooth, nor scorpion's sting.
With omens oft I strove to warn thy swains,
Omens, the types of thy impending chains.
I sent the magpie from the British soil,
With restless beak thy blooming fruit to spoil;
To din thine ears with unharmonious clack,
And haunt thy holy walls in white and black.
What else are those thou seest in bishop's gear,
Who crop the nurseries of learning here;
Aspiring, greedy, full of senseless prate,
Devour the church, and chatter to the state?
As you grew more degenerate and base,
I sent you millions of the croaking race;
Emblems of insects vile, who spread their spawn
Through all thy land, in armour, fur, and lawn;
A nauseous brood, that fills your senate walls,
And in the chambers of your viceroy crawls!
See, where that new devouring vermin runs,
Sent in my anger from the land of Huns!
With harpy-claws it undermines the ground,
And sudden spreads a numerous offspring round.
Th' amphibious tyrant, with his ravenous band,
Drains all thy lakes of fish, of fruits thy land.
Where is the holy well that bore my name?
Fled to the fountain back, from whence it came!
Fair Freedom's emblem once, which smoothly flows,
And blessings equally on all bestows.
Here, from the neighbouring nursery of arts,
The students, drinking, raised their wit and parts;
Here, for an age and more, improved their vein,

Their Phoebus I, my spring their Hippocrene.
Discouraged youths! now all their hopes must fail,
Condemn'd to country cottages and ale;
To foreign prelates make a slavish court,
And by their sweat procure a mean support;
Or, for the classics, read "The Attorney's Guide;"
Collect excise, or wait upon the tide.
Oh! had I been apostle to the Swiss,
Or hardy Scot, or any land but this;
Combined in arms, they had their foes defied,
And kept their liberty, or bravely died;
Thou still with tyrants in succession curst,
The last invaders trampling on the first;
Nor fondly hope for some reverse of fate,
Virtue herself would now return too late.
Not half thy course of misery is run,
Thy greatest evils yet are scarce begun.
Soon shall thy sons (the time is just at hand)
Be all made captives in their native land;
When for the use of no Hibernian born,
Shall rise one blade of grass, one ear of corn;
When shells and leather shall for money pass,
Nor thy oppressing lords afford thee brass,
But all turn leasers to that mongrel breed,
Who, from thee sprung, yet on thy vitals feed;
Who to yon ravenous isle thy treasures bear,
And waste in luxury thy harvest there;
For pride and ignorance a proverb grown,
The jest of wits, and to the court unknown.
I scorn thy spurious and degenerate line,
And from this hour my patronage resign.

On Reading Dr. Young's Satire, Called the Universal Passion
1726

If there be truth in what you sing,
Such godlike virtues in the king;
A minister so fill'd with zeal
And wisdom for the commonweal;
If he who in the chair presides,
So steadily the senate guides;
If others, whom you make your theme,
Are seconds in the glorious scheme;
If every peer whom you commend,
To worth and learning be a friend;
If this be truth, as you attest,
What land was ever half so blest!
No falsehood now among the great,
And tradesmen now no longer cheat:
Now on the bench fair Justice shines;
Her scale to neither side inclines:
Now Pride and Cruelty are flown,
And Mercy here exalts her throne;
For such is good example's power,
It does its office every hour,
Where governors are good and wise;
Or else the truest maxim lies:
For so we find all ancient sages
Decree, that, *ad exemplum regis*,
Through all the realm his virtues run,
Ripening and kindling like the sun.
If this be true, then how much more
When you have named at least a score
Of courtiers, each in their degree,
If possible, as good as he?
    Or take it in a different view.
I ask (if what you say be true)
If you affirm the present age
Deserves your satire's keenest rage;

If that same universal passion
With every vice has fill'd the nation:
If virtue dares not venture down
A single step beneath the crown:
If clergymen, to show their wit,
Praise classics more than holy writ:
If bankrupts, when they are undone,
Into the senate-house can run,
And sell their votes at such a rate,
As will retrieve a lost estate:
If law be such a partial whore,
To spare the rich, and plague the poor:
If these be of all crimes the worst,
What land was ever half so curst?

The Dog and Thief. 1726

Quoth the thief to the dog, let me into your door
  And I'll give you these delicate bits.
Quoth the dog, I shall then be more villain than you're,
  And besides must be out of my wits.

Your delicate bits will not serve me a meal,
  But my master each day gives me bread;
You'll fly, when you get what you came here to steal,
  And I must be hang'd in your stead.

The stockjobber thus from 'Change Alley goes down,
  And tips you the freeman a wink;
Let me have but your vote to serve for the town,
  And here is a guinea to drink.

Says the freeman, your guinea to-night would be spent!
  Your offers of bribery cease:
I'll vote for my landlord to whom I pay rent,
  Or else I may forfeit my lease.

From London they come, silly people to chouse,
  Their lands and their faces unknown:
Who'd vote a rogue into the parliament-house,
  That would turn a man out of his own?

A Dialogue between Mad Mullinix and Timothy
1728

M: I own, 'tis not my bread and butter,
But prithee, Tim, why all this clutter?
Why ever in these raging fits,
Damning to hell the Jacobites?
When if you search the kingdom round,
There's hardly twenty to be found;
No, not among the priests and friars——
T: 'Twixt you and me, G—d d—n the liars!
M: The Tories are gone every man over
To our illustrious house of Hanover;
From all their conduct this is plain;
And then——
T: G—d d—n the liars again!
Did not an earl but lately vote,
To bring in (I could cut his throat)
Our whole accounts of public debts?
M: Lord, how this frothy coxcomb frets! (*Aside*)
T: Did not an able statesman bishop
This dangerous horrid motion dish up
As Popish craft? did he not rail on't?
Show fire and fagot in the tail on't?
Proving the earl a grand offender;
And in a plot for the Pretender;
Whose fleet, 'tis all our friends' opinion,
Was then embarking at Avignon?
M: These wrangling jars of Whig and Tory,
Are stale and worn as Troy-town story:
The wrong, 'tis certain, you were both in,
And now you find you fought for nothing.
Your faction, when their game was new,
Might want such noisy fools as you;
But you, when all the show is past,
Resolve to stand it out the last;
Like Martin Marall, gaping on,

Not minding when the song is done.
When all the bees are gone to settle,
You clatter still your brazen kettle.
The leaders whom you listed under,
Have dropt their arms, and seized the plunder;
And when the war is past, you come
To rattle in their ears your drum:
And as that hateful hideous Grecian,
Thersites, (he was your relation,)
Was more abhorr'd and scorn'd by those
With whom he served, than by his foes;
So thou art grown the detestation
Of all thy party through the nation:
Thy peevish and perpetual teasing
With plots, and Jacobites, and treason,
Thy busy never-meaning face,
Thy screw'd-up front, thy state grimace,
Thy formal nods, important sneers,
Thy whisperings foisted in all ears,
(Which are, whatever you may think,
But nonsense wrapt up in a stink,)
Have made thy presence, in a true sense,
To thy own side, so d—n'd a nuisance,
That, when they have you in their eye,
As if the devil drove, they fly.
T: My good friend Mullinix, forbear;
I vow to G—, you're too severe:
If it could ever yet be known
I took advice, except my own,
It should be yours; but, d—n my blood!
I must pursue the public good:
The faction (is it not notorious?)
Keck at the memory of Glorious:
'Tis true; nor need I to be told,
My *quondam* friends are grown so cold,
That scarce a creature can be found
To prance with me his statue round.
The public safety, I foresee,
Henceforth depends alone on me;

And while this vital breath I blow,
Or from above or from below,
I'll sputter, swagger, curse, and rail,
The Tories' terror, scourge, and flail.
M: Tim, you mistake the matter quite;
The Tories! you are their delight;
And should you act a different part,
Be grave and wise, 'twould break their heart.
Why, Tim, you have a taste you know,
And often see a puppet-show:
Observe the audience is in pain,
While Punch is hid behind the scene:
But, when they hear his rusty voice,
With what impatience they rejoice!
And then they value not two straws,
How Solomon decides the cause,
Which the true mother, which pretender
Nor listen to the witch of Endor.
Should Faustus with the devil behind him
Enter the stage, they never mind him:
If Punch, to stir their fancy, shows
In at the door his monstrous nose,
Then sudden draws it back again;
O what a pleasure mixt with pain!
You every moment think an age,
Till he appears upon the stage:
And first his bum you see him clap
Upon the Queen of Sheba's lap:
The Duke of Lorraine drew his sword;
Punch roaring ran, and running roar'd,
Reviled all people in his jargon,
And sold the King of Spain a bargain;
St. George himself he plays the wag on,
And mounts astride upon the dragon;
He gets a thousand thumps and kicks,
Yet cannot leave his roguish tricks;
In every action thrusts his nose;
The reason why, no mortal knows:
In doleful scenes that break our heart,

Punch comes like you, and lets a fart.
There's not a puppet made of wood,
But what would hang him if they could;
While, teasing all, by all he's teased,
How well are the spectators pleased!
Who in the motion have no share,
But purely come to hear and stare;
Have no concern for Sabra's sake,
Which gets the better, saint or snake,
Provided Punch (for there's the jest)
Be soundly maul'd, and plague the rest.
    Thus, Tim, philosophers suppose,
The world consists of puppet-shows;
Where petulant conceited fellows
Perform the part of Punchinelloes:
So at this booth which we call Dublin,
Tim, thou'rt the Punch to stir up trouble in:
You wriggle, fidge, and make a rout,
Put all your brother puppets out,
Run on in a perpetual round,
To tease, perplex, disturb, confound:
Intrude with monkey grin and clatter
To interrupt all serious matter;
Are grown the nuisance of your clan,
Who hate and scorn you to a man:
But then the lookers-on, the Tories,
You still divert with merry stories,
They would consent that all the crew
Were hang'd before they'd part with you.
    But tell me, Tim, upon the spot,
By all this toil what hast thou got?
If Tories must have all the sport,
I fear you'll be disgraced at court.
T: Got? D—n my blood! I frank my letters,
Walk to my place before my betters;
And, simple as I now stand here,
Expect in time to be a peer—
Got? D—n me! why I got my will!
Ne'er hold my peace, and ne'er stand still:

I fart with twenty ladies by;
They call me beast; and what care I?
I bravely call the Tories Jacks,
And sons of whores—behind their backs.
But could you bring me once to think,
That when I strut, and stare, and stink,
Revile and slander, fume and storm,
Betray, make oath, impeach, inform,
With such a constant loyal zeal
To serve myself and commonweal,
And fret the Tories' souls to death,
I did but lose my precious breath;
And, when I damn my soul to plague 'em,
Am, as you tell me, but their May-game;
Consume my vitals! they shall know,
I am not to be treated so;
I'd rather hang myself by half,
Than give those rascals cause to laugh.
    But how, my friend, can I endure,
Once so renown'd, to live obscure?
No little boys and girls to cry,
"There's nimble Tim a-passing by!"
No more my dear delightful way tread
Of keeping up a party hatred?
Will none the Tory dogs pursue,
When through the streets I cry halloo?
Must all my d—n me's! bloods and wounds!
Pass only now for empty sounds?
Shall Tory rascals be elected,
Although I swear them disaffected?
And when I roar, "a plot, a plot!"
Will our own party mind me not?
So qualified to swear and lie,
Will they not trust me for a spy?
    Dear Mullinix, your good advice
I beg; you see the case is nice:
O! were I equal in renown,
Like thee to please this thankless town!
Or blest with such engaging parts

To win the truant schoolboys' hearts!
Thy virtues meet their just reward,
Attended by the sable guard.
Charm'd by thy voice, the 'prentice drops
The snow-ball destined at thy chops;
Thy graceful steps, and colonel's air,
Allure the cinder-picking fair.
M: No more—in mark of true affection,
I take thee under my protection;
Your parts are good, 'tis not denied;
I wish they had been well applied.
But now observe my counsel, *(viz.)*
Adapt your habit to your phiz;
You must no longer thus equip ye,
As Horace says *optat ephippia;*
(There's Latin, too, that you may see
How much improved by Dr.—)
I have a coat at home, that you may try:
'Tis just like this, which hangs by geometry;
My hat has much the nicer air;
Your block will fit it to a hair;
That wig, I would not for the world
Have it so formal, and so curl'd;
'Twill be so oily and so sleek,
When I have lain in it a week,
You'll find it well prepared to take
The figure of toupee and snake.
Thus dress'd alike from top to toe,
That which is which 'tis hard to know,
When first in public we appear,
I'll lead the van, keep you the rear:
Be careful, as you walk behind;
Use all the talents of your mind;
Be studious well to imitate
My portly motion, mien, and gait;
Mark my address, and learn my style,
When to look scornful, when to smile;
Nor sputter out your oaths so fast,
But keep your swearing to the last.

Then at our leisure we'll be witty,
And in the streets divert the city;
The ladies from the windows gaping,
The children all our motions aping.
Your conversation to refine,
I'll take you to some friends of mine,
Choice spirits, who employ their parts
To mend the world by useful arts;
Some cleansing hollow tubes, to spy
Direct the zenith of the sky;
Some have the city in their care,
From noxious steams to purge the air;
Some teach us in these dangerous days
How to walk upright in our ways;
Some whose reforming hands engage
To lash the lewdness of the age;
Some for the public service go
Perpetual envoys to and fro:
Whose able heads support the weight
Of twenty ministers of state.
We scorn, for want of talk, to jabber
Of parties o'er our bonnyclabber;
Nor are we studious to inquire,
Who votes for manors, who for hire:
Our care is, to improve the mind
With what concerns all human kind;
The various scenes of mortal life;
Who beats her husband, who his wife;
Or how the bully at a stroke
Knock'd down the boy, the lantern broke.
One tells the rise of cheese and oatmeal;
Another when he got a hot-meal;
One gives advice in proverbs old,
Instructs us how to tame a scold;
One shows how bravely Audouin died,
And at the gallows all denied;
How by the almanack 'tis clear,
That herrings will be cheap this year.
T: Dear Mullinix, I now lament

My precious time so long mispent,
By nature meant for nobler ends:
O, introduce me to your friends!
For whom by birth I was design'd,
Till politics debased my mind;
I give myself entire to you;
G—d d—n the Whigs and Tories too!

Tim and the Fables

My meaning will be best unravell'd,
When I premise that Tim has travell'd.
In Lucas's by chance there lay
The Fables writ by Mr. Gay.
Tim set the volume on a table,
Read over here and there a fable:
And found, as he the pages twirl'd,
The monkey who had seen the world;
(For Tonson had, to help the sale,
Prefix'd a cut to every tale.)
The monkey was completely drest,
The beau in all his airs exprest.
Tim, with surprise and pleasure staring,
Ran to the glass, and then comparing
His own sweet figure with the print,
Distinguish'd every feature in't,
The twist, the squeeze, the rump, the fidge in all,
Just as they look'd in the original.
"By —," says Tim, and let a f—t,
"This graver understood his art.
'Tis a true copy, I'll say that for't;
I well remember when I sat for't.
My very face, at first I knew it;
Just in this dress the painter drew it."
Tim, with his likeness deeply smitten,
Would read what underneath was written,
The merry tale, with moral grave;
He now began to storm and rave:
"The cursed villain! now I see
This was a libel meant at me:
These scribblers grow so bold of late
Against us ministers of state!
Such Jacobites as he deserve—
D—n me! I say they ought to starve."

Tom and Dick

Tim and Dick had equal fame,
    And both had equal knowledge;
Tom could write and spell his name,
    But Dick had seen the college.

Dick a coxcomb, Tom was mad,
    And both alike diverting;
Tom was held the merrier lad,
    But Dick the best at farting.

Dick would cock his nose in scorn,
    But Tom was kind and loving;
Tom a footboy bred and born,
    But Dick was from an oven.

Dick could neatly dance a jig,
    But Tom was best at borees;
Tom would pray for every Whig,
    And Dick curse all the Tories.

Dick would make a woful noise,
    And scold at an election;
Tom huzza'd the blackguard boys,
    And held them in subjection.

Tom could move with lordly grace,
    Dick nimbly skipt the gutter;
Tom could talk with solemn face,
    But Dick could better sputter.

Dick was come to high renown
    Since he commenced physician;
Tom was held by all the town
    The deeper politician.

Tom had the genteeler swing,
    His hat could nicely put on;
Dick knew better how to swing
    His cane upon a button.

Dick for repartee was fit,
    And Tom for deep discerning;
Dick was thought the brighter wit,
    But Tom had better learning.

Dick with zealous noes and ayes
    Could roar as loud as Stentor,
In the house 'tis all he says;
    But Tom is eloquenter.

Dick, a Maggot

As when, from rooting in a bin,
All powder'd o'er from tail to chin,
A lively maggot sallies out,
You know him by his hazel snout:
So when the grandson of his grandsire
Forth issues wriggling, Dick Drawcansir,
With powder'd rump and back and side,
You cannot blanch his tawny hide;
For 'tis beyond the power of meal
The gipsy visage to conceal;
For as he shakes his wainscot chops,
Down every mealy atom drops,
And leaves the tartar phiz in show,
Like a fresh t—d just dropp'd on snow.

Clad all in Brown

To Dick

Foulest brute that stinks below,
Why in this brown dost thou appear?
For wouldst thou make a fouler show,
Thou must go naked all the year.
Fresh from the mud, a wallowing sow
Would then be not so brown as thou.

'Tis not the coat that looks so dun,
His hide emits a foulness out;
Not one jot better looks the sun
Seen from behind a dirty clout.
So t—ds within a glass enclose,
The glass will seem as brown as those.

Thou now one heap of foulness art,
All outward and within is foul;
Condensed filth in every part,
Thy body's clothed like thy soul:
Thy soul, which through thy hide of buff
Scarce glimmers like a dying snuff.

Old carted bawds such garments wear,
When pelted all with dirt they shine;
Such their exalted bodies are,
As shrivell'd and as black as thine.
If thou wert in a cart, I fear
Thou wouldst be pelted worse than they're.

Yet, when we see thee thus array'd,
The neighbours think it is but just,
That thou shouldst take an honest trade,
And weekly carry out the dust.
Of cleanly houses who will doubt,
When Dick cries "Dust to carry out!"

Dick's Variety

Dull uniformity in fools
I hate, who gape and sneer by rules;
You, Mullinix, and slobbering C——
Who every day and hour the same are
That vulgar talent I despise
Of pissing in the rabble's eyes.
And when I listen to the noise
Of idiots roaring to the boys;
To better judgment still submitting,
I own I see but little wit in:
Such pastimes, when our taste is nice,
Can please at most but once or twice.
    But then consider Dick, you'll find
His genius of superior kind;
He never muddles in the dirt,
Nor scours the streets without a shirt;
Though Dick, I dare presume to say,
Could do such feats as well as they.
Dick I could venture everywhere,
Let the boys pelt him if they dare,
He'd have them tried at the assizes
For priests and jesuits in disguises;
Swear they were with the Swedes at Bender,
And listing troops for the Pretender.
    But Dick can f—t, and dance, and frisk,
No other monkey half so brisk;
Now has the speaker by his ears,
Next moment in the House of Peers;
Now scolding at my Lady Eustace,
Or thrashing Baby in her new stays.
Presto! begone; with t'other hop
He's powdering in a barber's shop;
Now at the antichamber thrusting
His nose, to get the circle just in;
And damns his blood that in the rear

He sees a single Tory there:
Then woe be to my lord-lieutenant,
Again he'll tell him, and again on't

Traulus. Part I

A Dialogue between Tom and Robin
1730

Tom: Say, Robin, what can Traulus mean
By bellowing thus against the Dean?
Why does he call him paltry scribbler,
Papist, and Jacobite, and libeller,
Yet cannot prove a single fact?
Robin: Forgive him, Tom: his head is crackt.
T: What mischief can the Dean have done him,
That Traulus calls for vengeance on him?
Why must he sputter, spawl, and slaver it
In vain against the people's favourite?
Revile that nation-saving paper,
Which gave the Dean the name of Drapier?
R: Why, Tom, I think the case is plain;
Party and spleen have turn'd his brain.
T: Such friendship never man profess'd,
The Dean was never so caress'd;
For Traulus long his rancour nursed,
Till, God knows why, at last it burst.
That clumsy outside of a porter,
How could it thus conceal a courtier?
R: I own, appearances are bad;
Yet still insist the man is mad.
T: Yet many a wretch in Bedlam knows
How to distinguish friends from foes;
And though perhaps among the rout
He wildly flings his filth about,
He still has gratitude and sap'ence,
To spare the folks that give him ha'pence;
Nor in their eyes at random pisses,
But turns aside, like mad Ulysses;
While Traulus all his ordure scatters
To foul the man he chiefly flatters.
Whence comes these inconsistent fits?

R: Why, Tom, the man has lost his wits.
T: Agreed: and yet, when Towzer snaps
At people's heels, with frothy chaps,
Hangs down his head, and drops his tail,
To say he's mad will not avail;
The neighbours all cry, "Shoot him dead,
Hang, drown, or knock him on the head."
So Traulus, when he first harangued,
I wonder why he was not hang'd;
For of the two, without dispute,
Towzer's the less offensive brute.
R: Tom, you mistake the matter quite;
Your barking curs will seldom bite
And though you hear him stut-tut-tut-ter,
He barks as fast as he can utter.
He prates in spite of all impediment,
While none believes that what he said he meant;
Puts in his finger and his thumb
To grope for words, and out they come.
He calls you rogue; there's nothing in it,
He fawns upon you in a minute:
"Begs leave to rail, but, d—n his blood!
He only meant it for your good:
His friendship was exactly timed,
He shot before your foes were primed:
By this contrivance, Mr. Dean,
By G—! I'll bring you off as clean—"
Then let him use you e'er so rough,
"'Twas all for love," and that's enough.
But, though he sputter through a session,
It never makes the least impression:
Whate'er he speaks for madness goes,
With no effect on friends or foes.
T: The scrubbiest cur in all the pack
Can set the mastiff on your back.
I own, his madness is a jest,
If that were all. But he's possest
Incarnate with a thousand imps,
To work whose ends his madness pimps;

Who o'er each string and wire preside,
Fill every pipe, each motion guide;
Directing every vice we find
In Scripture to the devil assign'd;
Sent from the dark infernal region,
In him they lodge, and make him legion.
Of brethren he's a false accuser;
A slanderer, traitor, and seducer;
A fawning, base, trepanning liar;
The marks peculiar of his sire.
Or, grant him but a drone at best;
A drone can raise a hornet's nest.
The Dean had felt their stings before;
And must their malice ne'er give o'er?
Still swarm and buzz about his nose?
But Ireland's friends ne'er wanted foes.
A patriot is a dangerous post,
When wanted by his country most;
Perversely comes in evil times,
Where virtues are imputed crimes.
His guilt is clear, the proofs are pregnant;
A traitor to the vices regnant.
    What spirit, since the world began,
Could always bear to strive with man?
Which God pronounced he never would,
And soon convinced them by a flood.
Yet still the Dean on freedom raves;
His spirit always strives with slaves.
'Tis time at last to spare his ink,
And let them rot, or hang, or sink.

Traulus. Part II

Traulus, of amphibious breed,
Motley fruit of mongrel seed;
By the dam from lordlings sprung.
By the sire exhaled from dung:
Think on every vice in both,
Look on him, and see their growth.
    View him on the mother's side,
Fill'd with falsehood, spleen, and pride;
Positive and overbearing,
Changing still, and still adhering;
Spiteful, peevish, rude, untoward,
Fierce in tongue, in heart a coward;
When his friends he most is hard on,
Cringing comes to beg their pardon;
Reputation ever tearing,
Ever dearest friendship swearing;
Judgment weak, and passion strong,
Always various, always wrong;
Provocation never waits,
Where he loves, or where he hates;
Talks whate'er comes in his head;
Wishes it were all unsaid.
    Let me now the vices trace,
From the father's scoundrel race.
Who could give the looby such airs?
Were they masons, were they butchers?
Herald, lend the Muse an answer
From his *atavus* and grandsire:
This was dexterous at his trowel,
That was bred to kill a cow well:
Hence the greasy clumsy mien
In his dress and figure seen;
Hence the mean and sordid soul,
Like his body, rank and foul;
Hence that wild suspicious peep,
Like a rogue that steals a sheep;

Hence he learnt the butcher's guile,
How to cut your throat and smile;
Like a butcher, doom'd for life
In his mouth to wear a knife:
Hence he draws his daily food
From his tenants' vital blood.
Lastly, let his gifts be tried,
Borrow'd from the mason's side:
Some perhaps may think him able
In the state to build a Babel;
Could we place him in a station
To destroy the old foundation.
True indeed I should be gladder
Could he learn to mount a ladder:
May he at his latter end
Mount alive and dead descend!
In him tell me which prevail,
Female vices most, or male?
What produced him, can you tell?
Human race, or imps of Hell?

A Fable of the Lion And other Beasts

One time a mighty plague did pester
All beasts domestic and sylvester,
The doctors all in concert join'd,
To see if they the cause could find;
And tried a world of remedies,
But none could conquer the disease.
The lion in this consternation.
Sends out his royal proclamation,
To all his loving subjects greeting,
Appointing them a solemn meeting:
And when they're gather'd round his den,
He spoke,—My lords and gentlemen,
I hope you're met full of the sense
Of this devouring pestilence;
For sure such heavy punishment,
On common crimes is rarely sent;
It must be some important cause,
Some great infraction of the laws.
Then let us search our consciences,
And every one his faults confess:
Let's judge from biggest to the least
That he that is the foulest beast,
May for a sacrifice be given
To stop the wrath of angry Heaven.
And since no one is free from sin,
I with myself will first begin.
I have done many a thing that's ill
From a propensity to kill,
Slain many an ox, and, what is worse,
Have murder'd many a gallant horse;
Robb'd woods and fens, and, like a glutton,
Devour'd whole flocks of lamb and mutton;
Nay sometimes, for I dare not lie,
The shepherd went for company.—
He had gone on, but Chancellor Fox

Stands up——What signifies an ox?
What signifies a horse? Such things
Are honour'd when made sport for kings.
Then for the sheep, those foolish cattle,
Not fit for courage, or for battle;
And being tolerable meat,
They're good for nothing but to eat.
The shepherd too, young enemy,
Deserves no better destiny.
Sir, sir, your conscience is too nice,
Hunting's a princely exercise:
And those being all your subjects born,
Just when you please are to be torn.
And, sir, if this will not content ye,
We'll vote it nemine contradicente.
Thus after him they all confess,
They had been rogues, some more some less;
And yet by little slight excuses,
They all get clear of great abuses.
The Bear, the Tiger, beasts of flight,
And all that could but scratch and bite,
Nay e'en the Cat, of wicked nature,
That kills in sport her fellow-creature,
Went scot-free; but his gravity,
An ass of stupid memory,
Confess'd, as he went to a fair,
His back half broke with wooden-ware,
Chancing unluckily to pass
By a church-yard full of good grass,
Finding they'd open left the gate,
He ventured in, stoop'd down and ate
Hold, says Judge Wolf, such are the crimes
Have brought upon us these sad times,
'Twas sacrilege, and this vile ass
Shall die for eating holy grass.

On the Irish Bishops. 1731

Old Latimer preaching did fairly describe
A bishop, who ruled all the rest of his tribe;
And who is this bishop? and where does he dwell?
Why truly 'tis Satan, Archbishop of Hell.
And He was a primate, and He wore a mitre,
Surrounded with jewels of sulphur and nitre.
How nearly this bishop our bishops resembles!
But he has the odds, who believes and who trembles,
Could you see his grim grace, for a pound to a penny,
You'd swear it must be the baboon of Kilkenny:
Poor Satan will think the comparison odious,
I wish I could find him out one more commodious;
But, this I am sure, the most reverend old dragon
Has got on the bench many bishops suffragan;
And all men believe he resides there incog,
To give them by turns an invisible jog.
Our bishops, puft up with wealth and with pride,
To hell on the backs of the clergy would ride.
They mounted and labour'd with whip and with spur
In vain—for the devil a parson would stir.
So the commons unhors'd them; and this was their doom,
On their crosiers to ride like a witch on a broom.
Though they gallop'd so fast, on the road you may find 'em,
And have left us but three out of twenty behind 'em.
Lord Bolton's good grace, Lord Carr and Lord Howard,
In spite of the devil would still be untoward:
They came of good kindred, and could not endure
Their former companions should beg at their door.
    When Christ was betray'd to Pilate the pretor
Of a dozen apostles but one proved a traitor:
One traitor alone, and faithful eleven;
But we can afford you six traitors in seven.
    What a clutter with clippings, dividings, and cleavings!
And the clergy forsooth must take up with their leavings;
If making divisions was all their intent,
They've done it, we thank them, but not as they meant;

And so may such bishops for ever divide,
That no honest heathen would be on their side.
How should we rejoice, if, like Judas the first,
Those splitters of parsons in sunder should burst!
Now hear an allusion:—A mitre, you know,
Is divided above, but united below.
If this you consider our emblem is right;
The bishops divide, but the clergy unite.
Should the bottom be split, our bishops would dread
That the mitre would never stick fast on their head:
And yet they have learnt the chief art of a sovereign,
As Machiavel taught them, "divide and ye govern."
But courage, my lords, though it cannot be said
That one cloven tongue ever sat on your head;
I'll hold you a groat (and I wish I could see't)
If your stockings were off, you could show cloven feet.
But hold, cry the bishops, and give us fair play;
Before you condemn us, hear what we can say.
What truer affections could ever be shown,
Than saving your souls by damning our own?
And have we not practised all methods to gain you;
With the tithe of the tithe of the tithe to maintain you;
Provided a fund for building you spittals!
You are only to live four years without victuals.
Content, my good lords; but let us change hands;
First take you our tithes, and give us your lands.
So God bless the Church and three of our mitres;
And God bless the Commons, for biting the biters.

Horace, Book IV, Ode IX

Addressed to Humphry French, Esq.
Late Lord Mayor of Dublin

Patron of the tuneful throng,
O! too nice, and too severe!
Think not, that my country song
Shall displease thy honest ear.
Chosen strains I proudly bring,
Which the Muses' sacred choir,
When they gods and heroes sing,
Dictate to th' harmonious lyre.
Ancient Homer, princely bard!
Just precedence still maintains,
With sacred rapture still are heard
Theban Pindar's lofty strains.
Still the old triumphant song,
Which, when hated tyrants fell,
Great Alcæus boldly sung,
Warns, instructs, and pleases well.
Nor has Time's all-darkening shade
In obscure oblivion press'd
What Anacreon laugh'd and play'd;
Gay Anacreon, drunken priest!
Gentle Sappho, love-sick muse,
Warms the heart with amorous fire;
Still her tenderest notes infuse
Melting rapture, soft desire.
Beauteous Helen, young and gay,
By a painted fopling won,
Went not first, fair nymph, astray,
Fondly pleased to be undone.
Nor young Teucer's slaughtering bow,
Nor bold Hector's dreadful sword,
Alone the terrors of the foe,
Sow'd the field with hostile blood.
Many valiant chiefs of old

Greatly lived and died before
Agamemnon, Grecian bold,
Waged the ten years' famous war.
But their names, unsung, unwept,
Unrecorded, lost and gone,
Long in endless night have slept,
And shall now no more be known.
Virtue, which the poet's care
Has not well consign'd to fame,
Lies, as in the sepulchre
Some old king, without a name.
But, O Humphry, great and free,
While my tuneful songs are read,
Old forgetful Time on thee
Dark oblivion ne'er shall spread.
When the deep cut notes shall fade
On the mouldering Parian stone,
On the brass no more be read
The perishing inscription;
Forgotten all the enemies,
Envious G——n's cursed spite,
And P——l's derogating lies,
Lost and sunk in Stygian night;
Still thy labour and thy care,
What for Dublin thou hast done,
In full lustre shall appear,
And outshine th' unclouded sun.
Large thy mind, and not untried,
For Hibernia now doth stand,
Through the calm, or raging tide,
Safe conducts the ship to land.
Falsely we call the rich man great,
He is only so that knows
His plentiful or small estate
Wisely to enjoy and use.
He in wealth or poverty,
Fortune's power alike defies;
And falsehood and dishonesty
More than death abhors and flies:

Flies from death!—no, meets it brave,
    When the suffering so severe
May from dreadful bondage save
    Clients, friends, or country dear.
This the sovereign man, complete;
    Hero; patriot; glorious; free;
Rich and wise; and good and great;
    Generous Humphry, thou art he.

On Mr. Pulteney's being put out of the Council. 1731

Sir Robert, wearied by Will Pulteney's teasings,
Who interrupted him in all his leasings,
Resolved that Will and he should meet no more,
Full in his face Bob shuts the council door;
Nor lets him sit as justice on the bench,
To punish thieves, or lash a suburb wench.
Yet still St. Stephen's chapel open lies
For Will to enter—What shall I advise?
Ev'n quit the house, for thou too long hast sat in't,
Produce at last thy dormant ducal patent;
There near thy master's throne in shelter placed,
Let Will, unheard by thee, his thunder waste;
Yet still I fear your work is done but half,
For while he keeps his pen you are not safe.
Hear an old fable, and a dull one too;
It bears a moral when applied to you.

A hare had long escaped pursuing hounds,
By often shifting into distant grounds;
Till, finding all his artifices vain,
To save his life he leap'd into the main.
But there, alas! he could no safety find,
A pack of dogfish had him in the wind.
He scours away; and, to avoid the foe,
Descends for shelter to the shades below:
There Cerberus lay watching in his den,
(He had not seen a hare the lord knows when.)
Out bounced the mastiff of the triple head;
Away the hare with double swiftness fled;
Hunted from earth, and sea, and hell, he flies
(Fear lent him wings) for safety to the skies.
How was the fearful animal distrest!
Behold a foe more fierce than all the rest:
Sirius, the swiftest of the heavenly pack,
Fail'd but an inch to seize him by the back.

He fled to earth, but first it cost him dear;
He left his scut behind, and half an ear.
    Thus was the hare pursued, though free from guilt;
Thus, Bob, shall thou be maul'd, fly where thou wilt.
Then, honest Robin, of thy corpse beware;
Thou art not half so nimble as a hare:
Too ponderous is thy bulk to mount the sky;
Nor can you go to Hell before you die.
So keen thy hunters, and thy scent so strong,
Thy turns and doublings cannot save thee long.

On the Words Brother Protestants and Fellow Christians, So Familiarly used By the Advocates for the Repeal of the Test-Act in Ireland 1733

An inundation, says the fable,
Overflow'd a farmer's barn and stable;
Whole ricks of hay and stacks of corn
Were down the sudden current borne;
While things of heterogeneous kind
Together float with tide and wind.
The generous wheat forgot its pride,
And sail'd with litter side by side;
Uniting all, to show their amity,
As in a general calamity.
A ball of new-dropp'd horse's dung,
Mingling with apples in the throng,
Said to the pippin plump and prim,
"See, brother, how we apples swim."
    Thus Lamb, renown'd for cutting corns,
An offer'd fee from Radcliff scorns,
"Not for the world—we doctors, brother,
Must take no fees of one another."
Thus to a dean some curate sloven
Subscribes, "Dear sir, your brother loving."
Thus all the footmen, shoeboys, porters,
About St. James's, cry, "We courtiers."
Thus Horace in the house will prate,
"Sir, we, the ministers of state."
Thus at the bar the booby Bettesworth,
Though half a crown o'erpays his sweat's worth;
Who knows in law nor text nor margent,
Calls Singleton his brother sergeant.
And thus fanatic saints, though neither in
Doctrine nor discipline our brethren,

Are brother Protestants and Christians,
As much as Hebrews and Philistines:
But in no other sense, than nature
Has made a rat our fellow-creature.
Lice from your body suck their food;
But is a louse your flesh and blood?
Though born of human filth and sweat, it
As well may say man did beget it.
And maggots in your nose and chin
As well may claim you for their kin.
    Yet critics may object, why not?
Since lice are brethren to a Scot:
Which made our swarm of sects determine
Employments for their brother vermin.
But be they English, Irish, Scottish,
What Protestant can be so sottish,
While o'er the church these clouds are gathering
To call a swarm of lice his brethren?
    As Moses, by divine advice,
In Egypt turn'd the dust to lice;
And as our sects, by all descriptions,
Have hearts more harden'd than Egyptians
As from the trodden dust they spring,
And, turn'd to lice, infest the king:
For pity's sake, it would be just,
A rod should turn them back to dust.
    Let folks in high or holy stations
Be proud of owning such relations;
Let courtiers hug them in their bosom,
As if they were afraid to lose 'em:
While I, with humble Job, had rather
Say to corruption—"Thou'rt my father."
For he that has so little wit
To nourish vermin, may be bit.

Bettesworth's Exultation

Upon Hearing that his Name would be Transmitted to Posterity In Dr. Swift's Works. By William Dunkin

Well! now, since the heat of my passion's abated,
That the Dean hath lampoon'd me, my mind is elated:—
Lampoon'd did I call it?—No—what was it then?
What was it?—'Twas fame to be lash'd by his pen:
For had he not pointed me out, I had slept till
E'en doomsday, a poor insignificant reptile;
Half lawyer, half actor, pert, dull, and inglorious,
Obscure, and unheard of—but now I'm notorious:
Fame has but two gates, a white and a black one;
The worst they can say is, I got in at the back one:
If the end be obtain'd 'tis equal what portal
I enter, since I'm to be render'd immortal:
So clysters applied to the anus, 'tis said,
By skilful physicians, give ease to the head—
Though my title be spurious, why should I be dastard,
A man is a man, though he should be a bastard.
Why sure 'tis some comfort that heroes should slay us,
If I fall, I would fall by the hand of Æneas;
And who by the Drapier would not rather damn'd be,
Than demigoddized by madrigal Namby?
    A man is no more who has once lost his breath;
But poets convince us there's life after death.
They call from their graves the king, or the peasant;
Re-act our old deeds, and make what's past present:
And when they would study to set forth alike,
So the lines be well drawn, and the colours but strike,
Whatever the subject be, coward or hero,
A tyrant or patriot, a Titus or Nero;
To a judge 'tis all one which he fixes his eye on,
And a well-painted monkey's as good as a lion.

An Epigram

The scriptures affirm (as I heard in my youth,
For indeed I ne'er read them, to speak for once truth)
That death is the wages of sin, but the just
Shall die not, although they be laid in the dust.
They say so; so be it, I care not a straw,
Although I be dead both in gospel and law;
In verse I shall live, and be read in each climate;
What more can be said of prime sergeant or primate?
While Carter and Prendergast both may be rotten,
And damn'd to the bargain, and yet be forgotten.

An Epigram
Inscribed to the Honourable
Sergeant Kite

In your indignation what mercy appears,
While Jonathan's threaten'd with loss of his ears;
For who would not think it a much better choice,
By your knife to be mangled than rack'd with your voice.
If truly you (would) be revenged on the parson,
Command his attendance while you act your farce on;
Instead of your maiming, your shooting, or banging,
Bid Povey secure him while you are haranguing.
Had this been your method to torture him, long since,
He had cut his own ears to be deaf to your nonsense.

The Yahoo's Overthrow, or, the Kevan Bayl's New Ballad, Upon Sergeant Kite's Insulting the Dean

To the Tune of "Derry Down."

Jolly boys of St. Kevan's, St. Patrick's, Donore
And Smithfield, I'll tell you, if not told before,
How Bettesworth, that booby, and scoundrel in grain,
Has insulted us all by insulting the Dean.
Knock him down, down, down, knock him down.

The Dean and his merits we every one know,
But this skip of a lawyer, where the de'il did he grow?
How greater his merit at Four Courts or House,
Than the barking of Towzer, or leap of a louse!
Knock him down, etc.

That he came from the Temple, his morals do show;
But where his deep law is, few mortals yet know:
His rhetoric, bombast, silly jests, are by far
More like to lampooning, than pleading at bar.
Knock him down, etc.

This pedler, at speaking and making of laws,
Has met with returns of all sorts but applause;
Has, with noise and odd gestures, been prating some years,
What honester folk never durst for their ears.
Knock him down, etc.

Of all sizes and sorts, the fanatical crew
Are his brother Protestants, good men and true;
Red hat, and blue bonnet, and turban's the same,
What the de'il is't to him whence the devil they came.
Knock him down, etc.

Hobbes, Tindal, and Woolston, and Collins, and Nayler,
And Muggleton, Toland, and Bradley the tailor,

Are Christians alike; and it may be averr'd,
He's a Christian as good as the rest of the herd.
        Knock him down, etc.

    He only the rights of the clergy debates;
Their rights! their importance! We'll set on new rates
On their tithes at half-nothing, their priesthood at less;
What's next to be voted with ease you may guess.
        Knock him down, etc.

    At length his old master, (I need not him name,)
To this damnable speaker had long owed a shame;
When his speech came abroad, he paid him off clean,
By leaving him under the pen of the Dean.
        Knock him down, etc.

    He kindled, as if the whole satire had been
The oppression of virtue, not wages of sin:
He began, as he bragg'd, with a rant and a roar;
He bragg'd how he bounced, and he swore how he swore.
        Knock him down, etc.

    Though he cringed to his deanship in very low strains,
To others he boasted of knocking out brains,
And slitting of noses, and cropping of ears,
While his own ass's zags were more fit for the shears.
        Knock him down, etc.

    On this worrier of deans whene'er we can hit,
We'll show him the way how to crop and to slit;
We'll teach him some better address to afford
To the dean of all deans, though he wears not a sword.
        Knock him down, etc.

    We'll colt him through Kevan, St. Patrick's, Donore,
And Smithfield, as rap was ne'er colted before;
We'll oil him with kennel, and powder him with grains,
A modus right fit for insulters of deans.
        Knock him down, etc.

And, when this is over, we'll make him amends,
To the Dean he shall go; they shall kiss and be friends:
But how? Why, the Dean shall to him disclose
A face for to kiss, without eyes, ears, or nose.
Knock him down, etc.

If you say this is hard on a man that is reckon'd
That sergeant-at-law whom we call Kite the Second,
You mistake; for a slave, who will coax his superiors,
May be proud to be licking a great man's posteriors.
Knock him down, etc.

What care we how high runs his passion or pride?
Though his soul he despises, he values his hide;
Then fear not his tongue, or his sword, or his knife;
He'll take his revenge on his innocent wife.
Knock him down, down, down, keep him down.

On the Archbishop of Cashel, and Bettesworth

Dear Dick, pr'ythee tell by what passion you move?
The world is in doubt whether hatred or love;
And, while at good Cashel you rail with such spite,
They shrewdly suspect it is all but a bite.
You certainly know, though so loudly you vapour,
His spite cannot wound who attempted the Drapier.
Then, pr'ythee, reflect, take a word of advice;
And, as your old wont is, change sides in a trice:
On his virtues hold forth; 'tis the very best way;
And say of the man what all honest men say.
But if, still obdurate, your anger remains,
If still your foul bosom more rancour contains,
Say then more than they, nay, lavishly flatter;
Tis your gross panegyrics alone can bespatter;
For thine, my dear Dick, give me leave to speak plain,
Like very foul mops, dirty more than they clean.

On the Irish Club. 1733

Ye paltry underlings of state,
Ye senators who love to prate;
Ye rascals of inferior note,
Who, for a dinner, sell a vote;
Ye pack of pensionary peers,
Whose fingers itch for poets' ears;
Ye bishops, far removed from saints,
Why all this rage? Why these complaints?
Why against printers all this noise?
This summoning of blackguard boys?
Why so sagacious in your guesses?
Your *effs*, and *tees*, and *arrs*, and *esses*!
Take my advice; to make you safe,
I know a shorter way by half.
The point is plain; remove the cause;
Defend your liberties and laws.
Be sometimes to your country true,
Have once the public good in view:
Bravely despise champagne at court,
And choose to dine at home with port:
Let prelates, by their good behaviour,
Convince us they believe a Saviour;
Nor sell what they so dearly bought,
This country, now their own, for nought.
Ne'er did a true satiric muse
Virtue or innocence abuse;
And 'tis against poetic rules
To rail at men by nature fools:
But * * *
* * * *

On Noisy Tom

Horace, Part of Book I, Sat. VI, Paraphrased
1733

If Noisy Tom should in the senate prate,
"That he would answer both for church and state;
And, farther, to demonstrate his affection,
Would take the kingdom into his protection;"
All mortals must be curious to inquire,
Who could this coxcomb be, and who his sire?
"What! thou, the spawn of him who shamed our isle,
Traitor, assassin, and informer vile!
Though by the female side, you proudly bring,
To mend your breed, the murderer of a king:
What was thy grandsire, but a mountaineer,
Who held a cabin for ten groats a-year:
Whose master Moore preserved him from the halter,
For stealing cows! nor could he read the Psalter!
Durst thou, ungrateful, from the senate chase
Thy founder's grandson, and usurp his place?
Just Heaven! to see the dunghill bastard brood
Survive in thee, and make the proverb good?
Then vote a worthy citizen to jail,
In spite of justice, and refuse his bail!"

On Dr. Rundle, Bishop of Derry
1734–5

Make Rundle bishop! fie for shame!
An Arian to usurp the name!
A bishop in the isle of saints!
How will his brethren make complaints!
Dare any of the mitred host
Confer on him the Holy Ghost:
In mother church to breed a variance,
By coupling orthodox with Arians?
    Yet, were he Heathen, Turk, or Jew:
What is there in it strange or new?
For, let us hear the weak pretence,
His brethren find to take offence;
Of whom there are but four at most,
Who know there is a Holy Ghost;
The rest, who boast they have conferr'd it,
Like Paul's Ephesians, never-heard it;
And, when they gave it, well 'tis known
They gave what never was their own.
    Rundle a bishop! well he may;
He's still a Christian more than they.
    We know the subject of their quarrels;
The man has learning, sense, and morals.
    There is a reason still more weighty;
'Tis granted he believes a Deity.
Has every circumstance to please us,
Though fools may doubt his faith in Jesus.
But why should he with that be loaded,
Now twenty years from court exploded?
And is not this objection odd
From rogues who ne'er believed a God?
For liberty a champion stout,
Though not so Gospel-ward devout.
While others, hither sent to save us
Come but to plunder and enslave us;
Nor ever own'd a power divine,

But Mammon, and the German line.
    Say, how did Rundle undermine 'em?
Who shew'd a better *jus divinum*?
From ancient canons would not vary,
But thrice refused *episcopari*.
    Our bishop's predecessor, Magus,
Would offer all the sands of Tagus;
Or sell his children, house, and lands,
For that one gift, to lay on hands:
But all his gold could not avail
To have the spirit set to sale.
Said surly Peter, "Magus, prithee,
Be gone: thy money perish with thee."
Were Peter now alive, perhaps,
He might have found a score of chaps,
Could he but make his gift appear
In rents three thousand pounds a-year.
    Some fancy this promotion odd,
As not the handiwork of God;
Though e'en the bishops disappointed
Must own it made by God's anointed,
And well we know, the *congé* regal
Is more secure as well as legal;
Because our lawyers all agree,
That bishoprics are held in fee.
    Dear Baldwin chaste, and witty Crosse,
How sorely I lament your loss!
That such a pair of wealthy ninnies
Should slip your time of dropping guineas;
For, had you made the king your debtor,
Your title had been so much better.

Epigram

Friend Rundle fell, with grievous bump,
Upon his reverential rump.
Poor rump! thou hadst been better sped,
Hadst thou been join'd to Boulter's head;
A head, so weighty and profound,
Would needs have kept thee from the ground.

A Character, Panegyric, and Description of the Legion Club

1736

The immediate provocation to this fierce satire upon the Irish Parliament was the introduction of a Bill to put an end to the tithe on pasturage, called *agistment*, and thus to free the landlords from a legal payment, with severe loss to the Church.

As I stroll the city, oft I
See a building large and lofty,
Not a bow-shot from the college;
Half the globe from sense and knowledge
By the prudent architect,
Placed against the church direct,
Making good my grandam's jest,
"Near the church"—you know the rest.
Tell us what the pile contains?
Many a head that has no brains.
These demoniacs let me dub
With the name of Legion Club.
Such assemblies, you might swear,
Meet when butchers bait a bear:
Such a noise, and such haranguing,
When a brother thief's a hanging:
Such a rout and such a rabble
Run to hear Jackpudding gabble:
Such a crowd their ordure throws
On a far less villain's nose.
Could I from the building's top
Hear the rattling thunder drop,
While the devil upon the roof
(If the devil be thunder proof)
Should with poker fiery red
Crack the stones, and melt the lead;
Drive them down on every skull,
When the den of thieves is full;

Quite destroy that harpies' nest;
How might then our isle be blest!
For divines allow, that God
Sometimes makes the devil his rod;
And the gospel will inform us,
He can punish sins enormous.
Yet should Swift endow the schools,
For his lunatics and fools,
With a rood or two of land,
I allow the pile may stand.
You perhaps will ask me, Why so?
But it is with this proviso:
Since the house is like to last,
Let the royal grant be pass'd,
That the club have right to dwell
Each within his proper cell,
With a passage left to creep in
And a hole above for peeping.
Let them, when they once get in,
Sell the nation for a pin;
While they sit a-picking straws,
Let them rave of making laws;
While they never hold their tongue,
Let them dabble in their dung:
Let them form a grand committee,
How to plague and starve the city;
Let them stare, and storm, and frown,
When they see a clergy gown;
Let them, ere they crack a louse,
Call for th'orders of the house;
Let them, with their gosling quills,
Scribble senseless heads of bills;
We may, while they strain their throats,
Wipe our a—s with their votes.
Let Sir Tom, that rampant ass,
Stuff his guts with flax and grass;
But before the priest he fleeces,
Tear the Bible all to pieces:
At the parsons, Tom, halloo, boy,

Worthy offspring of a shoeboy,
Footman, traitor, vile seducer,
Perjured rebel, bribed accuser,
Lay thy privilege aside,
From Papist sprung, and regicide;
Fall a-working like a mole,
Raise the dirt about thy hole.
    Come, assist me, Muse obedient!
Let us try some new expedient;
Shift the scene for half an hour,
Time and place are in thy power.
Thither, gentle Muse, conduct me;
I shall ask, and you instruct me.
    See, the Muse unbars the gate;
Hark, the monkeys, how they prate!
    All ye gods who rule the soul:
Styx, through Hell whose waters roll!
Let me be allow'd to tell
What I heard in yonder Hell.
    Near the door an entrance gapes,
Crowded round with antic shapes,
Poverty, and Grief, and Care,
Causeless Joy, and true Despair;
Discord periwigg'd with snakes,'
See the dreadful strides she takes!
    By this odious crew beset,
I began to rage and fret,
And resolved to break their pates,
Ere we enter'd at the gates;
Had not Clio in the nick
Whisper'd me, "Lay down your stick."
What! said I, is this a mad-house?
These, she answer'd, are but shadows,
Phantoms bodiless and vain,
Empty visions of the brain.
    In the porch Briareus stands,
Shows a bribe in all his hands;
Briareus the secretary,
But we mortals call him Carey.

When the rogues their country fleece,
They may hope for pence a-piece.
    Clio, who had been so wise
To put on a fool's disguise,
To bespeak some approbation,
And be thought a near relation,
When she saw three hundred brutes
All involved in wild disputes,
Roaring till their lungs were spent,
PRIVILEGE OF PARLIAMENT,
Now a new misfortune feels,
Dreading to be laid by th' heels.
Never durst a Muse before
Enter that infernal door;
Clio, stifled with the smell,
Into spleen and vapours fell,
By the Stygian steams that flew
From the dire infectious crew.
Not the stench of Lake Avernus
Could have more offended her nose;
Had she flown but o'er the top,
She had felt her pinions drop.
And by exhalations dire,
Though a goddess, must expire.
In a fright she crept away,
Bravely I resolved to stay.
When I saw the keeper frown,
Tipping him with half-a-crown,
Now, said I, we are alone,
Name your heroes one by one.
    Who is that hell-featured brawler?
Is it Satan? No; 'tis Waller.
In what figure can a bard dress
Jack the grandson of Sir Hardress?
Honest keeper, drive him further,
In his looks are Hell and murther;
See the scowling visage drop,
Just as when he murder'd Throp.
    Keeper, show me where to fix

On the puppy pair of Dicks:
By their lantern jaws and leathern,
You might swear they both are brethren:
Dick Fitzbaker, Dick the player,
Old acquaintance, are you there?
Dear companions, hug and kiss,
Toast Old Glorious in your piss;
Tie them, keeper, in a tether,
Let them starve and stink together;
Both are apt to be unruly,
Lash them daily, lash them duly;
Though 'tis hopeless to reclaim them,
Scorpion's rods, perhaps, may tame them.
    Keeper, yon old dotard smoke,
Sweetly snoring in his cloak:
Who is he? 'Tis humdrum Wynne,
Half encompass'd by his kin:
There observe the tribe of Bingham,
For he never fails to bring 'em;
And that base apostate Vesey
With Bishop's scraps grown fat and greasy,
While Wynne sleeps the whole debate,
They submissive round him wait;
(Yet would gladly see the hunks,
In his grave, and search his trunks,)
See, they gently twitch his coat,
Just to yawn and give his vote,
Always firm in his vocation,
For the court against the nation.
    Those are Allens Jack and Bob,
First in every wicked job,
Son and brother to a queer
Brain-sick brute, they call a peer.
We must give them better quarter,
For their ancestor trod mortar,
And at Hoath, to boast his fame,
On a chimney cut his name.
    There sit Clements, Dilks, and Carter;
Who for Hell would die a martyr.

Such a triplet could you tell
Where to find on this side Hell?
Gallows Carter, Dilks, and Clements,
Souse them in their own excrements.
Every mischief's in their hearts;
If they fail, 'tis want of parts.
    Bless us! Morgan, art thou there, man?
Bless mine eyes! art thou the chairman?
Chairman to yon damn'd committee!
Yet I look on thee with pity.
Dreadful sight! what, learned Morgan
Metamorphosed to a Gorgon!
For thy horrid looks, I own,
Half convert me to a stone.
Hast thou been so long at school,
Now to turn a factious tool?
Alma Mater was thy mother,
Every young divine thy brother.
Thou, a disobedient varlet,
Treat thy mother like a harlot!
Thou ungrateful to thy teachers,
Who are all grown reverend preachers!
Morgan, would it not surprise one!
To turn thy nourishment to poison!
When you walk among your books,
They reproach you with their looks;
Bind them fast, or from their shelves
They'll come down to right themselves:
Homer, Plutarch, Virgil, Flaccus,
All in arms, prepare to back us:
Soon repent, or put to slaughter
Every Greek and Roman author.
Will you, in your faction's phrase,
Send the clergy all to graze;
And to make your project pass,
Leave them not a blade of grass?
How I want thee, humorous Hogarth!
Thou, I hear, a pleasant rogue art.
Were but you and I acquainted,

Every monster should be painted:
You should try your graving tools
On this odious group of fools;
Draw the beasts as I describe them:
Form their features while I gibe them;
Draw them like; for I assure you,
You will need no *car'catura;*
Draw them so that we may trace
All the soul in every face.
  Keeper, I must now retire,
You have done what I desire:
But I feel my spirits spent
With the noise, the sight, the scent.
"Pray, be patient; you shall find
Half the best are still behind!
You have hardly seen a score;
I can show two hundred more."
Keeper, I have seen enough.
Taking then a pinch of snuff,
I concluded, looking round them,
"May their god, the devil, confound them!"

On a Printer's being sent to Newgate

Better we all were in our graves,
Than live in slavery to slaves;
Worse than the anarchy at sea,
Where fishes on each other prey;
Where every trout can make as high rants
O'er his inferiors, as our tyrants;
And swagger while the coast is clear:
But should a lordly pike appear,
Away you see the varlet scud,
Or hide his coward snout in mud.
Thus, if a gudgeon meet a roach,
He dares not venture to approach;
Yet still has impudence to rise,
And, like Domitian, leap at flies.

A Vindication of the Libel; Or, a New Ballad, Written by a Shoe-Boy, on an Attorney Who was Formerly a Shoe-Boy

"Qui color ater erat, nunc est contrarius atro."

With singing of ballads, and crying of news,
With whitening of buckles, and blacking of shoes,
Did Hartley set out, both shoeless and shirtless,
And moneyless too, but not very dirtless;
Two pence he had gotten by begging, that's all;
One bought him a brush, and one a black ball;
For clouts at a loss he could not be much,
The clothes on his back as being but such;
Thus vamp'd and accoutred, with clouts, ball, and brush,
He gallantly ventured his fortune to push:
Vespasian thus, being bespatter'd with dirt,
Was omen'd to be Rome's emperor for't.
But as a wise fiddler is noted, you know,
To have a good couple of strings to one bow;
So Hartley judiciously thought it too little,
To live by the sweat of his hands and his spittle:
He finds out another profession as fit,
And straight he becomes a retailer of wit.
One day he cried—"Murders, and songs, and great news!"
Another as loudly—"Here blacken your shoes!"
At Domvile's full often he fed upon bits,
For winding of jacks up, and turning of spits;
Lick'd all the plates round, had many a grubbing,
And now and then got from the cook-maid a drubbing;
Such bastings effect upon him could have none:
The dog will be patient that's struck with a bone.
Sir Thomas, observing this Hartley withal
So expert and so active at brushes and ball,
Was moved with compassion, and thought it a pity
A youth should be lost, that had been so witty:

Without more ado, he vamps up my spark,
And now we'll suppose him an eminent clerk!
Suppose him an adept in all the degrees
Of scribbling *cum dasho*, and hooking of fees;
Suppose him a miser, attorney, *per* bill,
Suppose him a courtier—suppose what you will—
Yet, would you believe, though I swore by the Bible,
That he took up two news-boys for crying the libel?

A Friendly Apology for a Certain Justice of Peace By way of Defence of Hartley Hutcheson, Esq. By James Black-Well, Operator for the Feet

But he by bawling news about,
And aptly using brush and clout,
A justice of the peace became,
To punish rogues who do the same.

I sing the man of courage tried,
O'errun with ignorance and pride,
Who boldly hunted out disgrace
With canker'd mind, and hideous face;
The first who made (let none deny it)
The libel-vending rogues be quiet.
The fact was glorious, we must own,
For Hartley was before unknown,
Contemn'd I mean;—for who would chuse
So vile a subject for the Muse?
'Twas once the noblest of his wishes
To fill his paunch with scraps from dishes,
For which he'd parch before the grate,
Or wind the jack's slow-rising weight,
(Such toils as best his talents fit,)
Or polish shoes, or turn the spit;
But, unexpectedly grown rich in
Squire Domvile's family and kitchen,
He pants to eternize his name,
And takes the dirty road to fame;
Believes that persecuting wit
Will prove the surest way to it;
So with a colonel at his back,
The Libel feels his first attack;
He calls it a seditious paper,

Writ by another patriot Drapier;
Then raves and blunders nonsense thicker
Than alderman o'ercharged with liquor:
And all this with design, no doubt,
To hear his praises hawk'd about;
To send his name through every street,
Which erst he roam'd with dirty feet;
Well pleased to live in future times,
Though but in keen satiric rhymes.
So, Ajax, who, for aught we know,
Was justice many years ago,
And minding then no earthly things,
But killing libellers of kings;
Or if he wanted work to do,
To run a bawling news-boy through;
Yet he, when wrapp'd up in a cloud,
Entreated father Jove aloud,
Only in light to show his face,
Though it might tend to his disgrace.
And so the Ephesian villain fired
The temple which the world admired,
Contemning death, despising shame,
To gain an ever-odious name.

Ay and No

A Tale from Dublin. Written in 1737

At Dublin's high feast sat Primate and Dean,
Both dress'd like divines, with band and face clean:
Quoth Hugh of Armagh, "The mob is grown bold."
"Ay, ay," quoth the Dean, "the cause is old gold."
"No, no," quoth the Primate, "if causes we sift,
This mischief arises from witty Dean Swift."
The smart one replied, "There's no wit in the case;
And nothing of that ever troubled your grace.
Though with your state sieve your own notions you split,
A Boulter by name is no bolter of wit.
It's matter of weight, and a mere money job;
But the lower the coin the higher the mob.
Go tell your friend Bob and the other great folk,
That sinking the coin is a dangerous joke.
The Irish dear joys have enough common sense,
To treat gold reduced like Wood's copper pence.
It is a pity a prelate should die without law;
But if I say the word—take care of Armagh!"

A Ballad

Patrick astore, what news upon the town?
By my soul there's bad news, for the gold she was pull'd down,
The gold she was pull'd down, of that I'm very sure,
For I saw'd them reading upon the towlsel *doore*.
Sing, och, och, hoh, hoh.

Arrah! who was him reading? 'twas *jauntleman* in ruffles,
And Patrick's bell she was ringing all in muffles;
She was ringing very sorry, her tongue tied up with rag,
Lorsha! and out of her shteeple there was hung a black flag.
Sing, och, &c.

Patrick astore, who was him made this law?
Some they do say, 'twas the big man of straw;
But others they do say, that it was Jug-Joulter,
The devil he may take her into hell and *Boult-her!*
Sing, och, &c.

Musha! Why Parliament wouldn't you maul,
Those *carters*, and paviours, and footmen, and all;
Those rascally paviours who did us undermine,
Och ma ceade millia molighart on the feeders of swine!
Sing, och, &c.

A Wicked Treasonable Libel

While the king and his ministers keep such a pother,
And all about changing one whore for another,
Think I to myself, what need all this strife,
His majesty first had a whore of a wife,
And surely the difference mounts to no more
Than, now he has gotten a wife of a whore.
Now give me your judgment a very nice case on;
Each queen has a son, say which is the base one?
Say which of the two is the right Prince of Wales,
To succeed, when, (God bless him,) his majesty fails;
Perhaps it may puzzle our loyal divines
To unite these two Protestant parallel lines,
From a left-handed wife, and one turn'd out of doors,
Two reputed king's sons, both true sons of whores;
No law can determine it, which is first oars.
But, alas! poor old England, how wilt thou be master'd;
For, take which you please, it must needs be a bastard.

Epigrams against Carthy By Swift and Others

Charles Carthy, a schoolmaster in the city of Dublin, was publisher of a translation of Horace, in which the Latin was printed on the one side, and the English on the other, whence he acquired the name of Mezentius, alluding to the practice of that tyrant, who chained the dead to the living.

Carthy was almost continually involved in satirical skirmishes with Dunkin, for whom Swift had a particular friendship, and there is no doubt that the Dean himself engaged in the warfare.

—*Scott*

On Carthy's Translation of Horace

Containing, on one side, the original Latin, on the other, his own version.

This I may boast, which few e'er could,
Half of my book at least is good.

On Carthy Minotaurus

How monstrous Carthy looks with Flaccus braced,
For here we see the man and there the beast.

On the Same

Once Horace fancied from a man,
He was transformed to a swan;
But Carthy, as from him thou learnest,
Has made the man a goose in earnest.

On the Same

Talis erat quondam Tithoni splendida conjux,
Effulsit misero sic Dea juncta viro;

Hunc tandem imminuit sensim longaeva senectus,
    Te vero extinxit, Carole, prima dies.

Imitated

So blush'd Aurora with celestial charms,
So bloom'd the goddess in a mortal's arms;
He sunk at length to wasting age a prey,
But thy book perish'd on its natal day.

Ad Horatium Cum Carthio Constrictum

Lectores ridere jubes dum Carthius astat?
Iste procul depellit olens tibi Maevius omnes:
Sic triviis veneranda diu, Jovis inclyta proles
Terruit, assumpto, mortales, Gorgonis ore.

Imitated

Could Horace give so sad a monster birth?
Why then in vain he would excite our mirth;
His humour well our laughter might command,
But who can bear the death's head in his hand?

An Irish Epigram on the Same

While with the fustian of thy book,
    The witty ancient you enrobe,
You make the graceful Horace look
    As pitiful as Tom M'Lobe.
Ye Muses, guard your sacred mount,
    And Helicon, for if this log
Should stumble once into the fount,
    He'll make it muddy as a bog.

On Carthy's Translation of Longinus

High as Longinus to the stars ascends,
So deeply Carthy to the centre tends.

Ratio Inter Longinum Et Carthium Computata

Aethereas quantum Longinus surgit in auras,
Carthius en tantum ad Tartara tendit iter.

On the Same

What Midas touch'd became true gold, but then,
Gold becomes lead touch'd lightly by thy pen.

Carthy Knocked out some Teeth from his News-Boy

For saying he could not live by the profits of Carthy's works, as they did not sell.

I must confess that I was somewhat warm,
I broke his teeth, but where's the mighty harm?
My work he said could ne'er afford him meat,
And teeth are useless where there's nought to eat!

To Carthy

On his sending about specimens to force people to subscribe to his Longinus.

Thus vagrant beggars, to extort
By charity a mean support,
Their sores and putrid ulcers show,
And shock our sense till we bestow.

To Carthy

On his accusing Mr. Dunkin for not publishing his book of Poems.

How different from thine is Dunkin's lot!
Thou'rt curst for publishing, and he for not.

On Carthy's Publishing Several Lampoons, under the Names of Infamous Poetasters

So witches bent on bad pursuits,
Assume the shapes of filthy brutes.

To Carthy

Thy labours, Carthy, long conceal'd from light,
Piled in a garret, charm'd the author's sight,
But forced from their retirement into day,
The tender embryos half unknown decay;
Thus lamps which burn'd in tombs with silent glare,
Expire when first exposed to open air.

To Carthy, Attributing some Performances to Mr. Dunkin

From the Gentleman's London Magazine for January.

My lines to him you give; to speak your due,
'Tis what no man alive will say of you.
Your works are like old Jacob's speckled goats,
Known by the verse, yet better by the notes.
Pope's essays upon some for Young's may pass,
But all distinguish thy dull leaden mass;
So green in different lights may pass for blue,
But what's dyed black will take no other hue.

Upon Carthy's Threatening to Translate Pindar

You have undone Horace,—what should hinder
Thy Muse from falling upon Pindar?
But ere you mount his fiery steed,
Beware, O Bard, how you proceed:—
For should you give him once the reins,
High up in air he'll turn your brains;
And if you should his fury check,
'Tis ten to one he breaks your neck.

Dr. Swift Wrote the Following Epigram

On one Delacourt's complimenting Carthy on his Poetry

Carthy, you say, writes well—his genius true,
You pawn your word for him—he'll vouch for you.
So two poor knaves, who find their credit fail,
To cheat the world, become each other's bail.

Poetical Epistle to Dr. Sheridan

Some ancient authors wisely write,
That he who drinks will wake at night,
Will never fail to lose his rest,
And feel a streightness in his chest;
A streightness in a double sense,
A streightness both of breath and pence:
Physicians say, it is but reasonable,
He that comes home at hour unseasonable,
(Besides a fall and broken shins,
Those smaller judgments for his sins;)
If, when he goes to bed, he meets
A teasing wife between the sheets,
'Tis six to five he'll never sleep,
But rave and toss till morning peep.
Yet harmless Betty must be blamed
Because you feel your lungs inflamed
But if you would not get a fever,
You never must one moment leave her.
This comes of all your drunken tricks,
Your Parry's and your brace of Dicks;
Your hunting Helsham in his laboratory
Too, was the time you saw that Drab lac a Pery
But like the prelate who lives yonder-a,
And always cries he is like Cassandra;
I always told you, Mr. Sheridan,
If once this company you were rid on,
Frequented honest folk, and very few,
You'd live till all your friends were weary of you.
But if rack punch you still would swallow,
I then forewarn'd you what would follow.
Are the Deanery sober hours?
Be witness for me all ye powers.
The cloth is laid at eight, and then
We sit till half an hour past ten;
One bottle well might serve for three
If Mrs. Robinson drank like me.

Ask how I fret when she has beckon'd
To Robert to bring up a second;
I hate to have it in my sight,
And drink my share in perfect spite.
If Robin brings the ladies word,
The coach is come, I 'scape a third;
If not, why then I fall a-talking
How sweet a night it is for walking;
For in all conscience, were my treasure able,
I'd think a quart a-piece unreasonable;
It strikes eleven,—get out of doors.—
This is my constant farewell
    Yours,
    J. S.

October 18, 1724, nine in the morning.

You had best hap yourself up in a chair, and dine with me than with the provost.

Lines written on a Window in the Episcopal Palace at Kilmore

Resolve me this, ye happy dead,
Who've lain some hundred years in bed,
From every persecution free
That in this wretched life we see;
Would ye resume a second birth,
And choose once more to live on earth?

Dr. Sheridan wrote underneath the Following Lines

Thus spoke great Bedel from his tomb:
"Mortal, I would not change my doom,
To live in such a restless state,
To be unfortunately great;
To flatter fools, and spurn at knaves,
To shine amidst a race of slaves;
To learn from wise men to complain
And only rise to fall again:
No! let my dusty relics rest,
Until I rise among the blest."

The Upstart

The following lines occur in the Swiftiana, and are by Mr. Wilson, the editor, ascribed to Swift.

—Scott

"— The rascal! that's too mild a name;
Does he forget from whence he came?
Has he forgot from whence he sprung?
A mushroom in a bed of dung;
A maggot in a cake of fat,
The offspring of a beggar's brat;
As eels delight to creep in mud,
To eels we may compare his blood;
His blood delights in mud to run,
Witness his lazy, lousy son!
Puff'd up with pride and insolence,
Without a grain of common sense.
See with what consequence he stalks!
With what pomposity he talks!
See how the gaping crowd admire
The stupid blockhead and the liar!
How long shall vice triumphant reign?
How long shall mortals bend to gain?
How long shall virtue hide her face,
And leave her votaries in disgrace?
—Let indignation fire my strains,
Another villain yet remains—
Let purse-proud C——n next approach;
With what an air he mounts his coach!
A cart would best become the knave,
A dirty parasite and slave!
His heart in poison deeply dipt,
His tongue with oily accents tipt,
A smile still ready at command,
The pliant bow, the forehead bland—"

* * * * *

* * * * *

On the Arms of the Town of Waterford

—URBS Intacta Manet—semper intacta manebit,
  Tangere crabrones quis bene sanus amat?

Translation

A thistle is the Scottish arms,
Which to the toucher threatens harms,
What are the arms of Waterford,
That no man touches—but a ——?

Verses on Blenheim

Atria longa patent. Sed nec cenantibus usquam
Nec somno locus est. Quam bene non habitas!

—Mart., lib. xii, Ep. 50.

See, here's the grand approach,
That way is for his grace's coach;
There lies the bridge, and there the clock,
Observe the lion and the cock;
The spacious court, the colonnade,
And mind how wide the hall is made;
The chimneys are so well design'd,
They never smoke in any wind:
The galleries contrived for walking,
The windows to retire and talk in;
The council-chamber to debate,
And all the rest are rooms of state.
Thanks, sir, cried I, 'tis very fine,
But where d'ye sleep, or where d'ye dine?
I find, by all you have been telling,
That 'tis a house, but not a dwelling.

An Excellent New Song upon the Late Grand Jury

Poor Monsieur his conscience preserved for a year,
Yet in one hour he lost it, 'tis known far and near;
To whom did he lose it?—A judge or a peer.
Which nobody can deny.

This very same conscience was sold in a closet,
Nor for a baked loaf, or a loaf in a losset,
But a sweet sugar-plum, which you put in a posset.
Which nobody can deny.

O Monsieur, to sell it for nothing was nonsense,
For, if you would sell it, it should have been long since,
But now you have lost both your cake and your conscience.
Which nobody can deny.

So Nell of the Dairy, before she was wed,
Refused ten good guineas for her maidenhead,
Yet gave it for nothing to smooth-spoken Ned.
Which nobody can deny.

But, Monsieur, no vonder dat you vere collogue,
Since selling de contre be now all de vogue,
You be but von fool after seventeen rogue.
Which nobody can deny.

Some sell it for profit, 'tis very well known,
And some but for sitting in sight of the throne,
And other some sell what is none of their own.
Which nobody can deny.

But Philpot, and Corker, and Burrus, and Hayze,
And Rayner, and Nicholson, challenge our praise,
With six other worthies as glorious as these.
Which nobody can deny.

There's Donevan, Hart, and Archer, and Blood,
And Gibson, and Gerard, all true men and good,
All lovers of Ireland, and haters of Wood.
        Which nobody can deny.

But the slaves that would sell us shall hear on't in time,
Their names shall be branded in prose and in rhyme,
We'll paint 'em in colours as black as their crime.
        Which nobody can deny.

But P——r and copper L——h we'll excuse,
The commands of your betters you dare not refuse,
Obey was the word when you wore wooden shoes.
        Which nobody can deny.

An Excellent New Song Upon his Grace our Good Lord Archbishop of Dublin

Dr. King, Archbishop of Dublin, stood high in Swift's estimation by his opposition to Wood's coinage.

By Honest Jo. One of his Grace's Farmers in Fingal

I sing not of the Drapier's praise, nor yet of William Wood,
But I sing of a famous lord, who seeks his country's good;
Lord William's grace of Dublin town, 'tis he that first appears,
Whose wisdom and whose piety do far exceed his years.
In ev'ry council and debate he stands for what is right,
And still the truth he will maintain, whate'er he loses by't.
And though some think him in the wrong, yet still there comes a season
When every one turns round about, and owns his grace had reason.
His firmness to the public good, as one that knows it swore,
Has lost his grace for ten years past ten thousand pounds and more.
Then come the poor and strip him so, they leave him not a cross,
For he regards ten thousand pounds no more than Wood's dross.
To beg his favour is the way new favours still to win,
He makes no more to give ten pounds than I to give a pin.
Why, there's my landlord now, the squire, who all in money wallows,
He would not give a groat to save his father from the gallows.
"A bishop," says the noble squire, "I hate the very name,
To have two thousand pounds a-year—O 'tis a burning shame!
Two thousand pounds a-year! good lord! And I to have but five!"
And under him no tenant yet was ever known to thrive:
Now from his lordship's grace I hold a little piece of ground,
And all the rent I pay is scarce five shillings in the pound.
Then master steward takes my rent, and tells me, "Honest Jo,
Come, you must take a cup of sack or two before you go."
He bids me then to hold my tongue, and up the money locks,
For fear my lord should send it all into the poor man's box.
And once I was so bold to beg that I might see his grace,

Good lord! I wonder how I dared to look him in the face:
Then down I went upon my knees, his blessing to obtain;
He gave it me, and ever since I find I thrive amain.
"Then," said my lord, "I'm very glad to see thee, honest friend,
I know the times are something hard, but hope they soon will
mend,
Pray never press yourself for rent, but pay me when you can;
I find you bear a good report, and are an honest man."
Then said his lordship with a smile, "I must have lawful cash,
I hope you will not pay my rent in that same Wood's trash!"
"God bless your Grace," I then replied, "I'd see him hanging higher,
Before I'd touch his filthy dross, than is Clandalkin spire."
To every farmer twice a-week all round about the Yoke,
Our parsons read the Drapier's books, and make us honest folk.
And then I went to pay the squire, and in the way I found,
His bailie driving all my cows into the parish pound;
"Why, sirrah," said the noble squire, "how dare you see my face,
Your rent is due almost a week, beside the days of grace."
And yet the land I from him hold is set so on the rack,
That only for the bishop's lease 'twould quickly break my back.
Then God preserve his lordship's grace, and make him live as long
As did Methusalem of old, and so I end my song.

To his Grace the Archbishop of Dublin

A Poem

Serus in coelum redeas, diuque
Laetus intersis populo.

—Hor., *Carm.* I, ii, 45.

Great, good, and just, was once applied
To one who for his country died;
To one who lives in its defence,
We speak it in a happier sense.
O may the fates thy life prolong!
Our country then can dread no wrong:
In thy great care we place our trust,
Because thou'rt great, and good, and just:
Thy breast unshaken can oppose
Our private and our public foes:
The latent wiles, and tricks of state,
Your wisdom can with ease defeat.
When power in all its pomp appears,
It falls before thy rev'rend years,
And willingly resigns its place
To something nobler in thy face.
When once the fierce pursuing Gaul
Had drawn his sword for Marius' fall,
The godlike hero with a frown
Struck all his rage and malice down;
Then how can we dread William Wood,
If by thy presence he's withstood?
Where wisdom stands to keep the field,
In vain he brings his brazen shield;
Though like the sibyl's priest he comes,
With furious din of brazen drums
The force of thy superior voice
Shall strike him dumb, and quell their noise.

To the Citizens

And shall the Patriot who maintain'd your cause,
From future ages only meet applause?
Shall he, who timely rose t'his country's aid,
By her own sons, her guardians, be betray'd?
Did heathen virtues in your hearts reside,
These wretches had been damn'd for parricide.
Should you behold, whilst dreadful armies threat
The sure destruction of an injured state,
Some hero, with superior virtue bless'd,
Avert their rage, and succour the distress'd;
Inspired with love of glorious liberty,
Do wonders to preserve his country free;
He like the guardian shepherd stands, and they
Like lions spoil'd of their expected prey,
Each urging in his rage the deadly dart,
Resolved to pierce the generous hero's heart;
Struck with the sight, your souls would swell with grief,
And dare ten thousand deaths to his relief,
But, if the people he preserved should cry,
He went too far, and he deserved to—die,
Would not your soul such treachery detest,
And indignation boil within your breast,
Would not you wish that wretched state preserved,
To feel the tenfold ruin they deserved?
If, then, oppression has not quite subdued
At once your prudence and your gratitude,
If you yourselves conspire not your undoing,
And don't deserve, and won't draw down your ruin,
If yet to virtue you have some pretence,
If yet ye are not lost to common sense,
Assist your patriot in your own defence;
That stupid cant, "he went too far," despise,
And know that to be brave is to be wise:
Think how he struggled for your liberty,
And give him freedom, whilst yourselves are free.
M. B.

Punch's Petition to the Ladies

——Quid non mortalia pectora cogis,
Auri sacra fames!——

—Virg., *Aen.*, iii

This poem partly relates to Wood's halfpence, but resembles the style of Sheridan rather than of Swift. Hoppy, or Hopkins, here mentioned, seems to be the master of the revels, and secretary to the Duke of Grafton, when Lord-Lieutenant. See also Verses on the Puppet-Show.

—*Scott.* See vol. i, p. 169.—W. E. B.

Fair ones who do all hearts command,
And gently sway with fan in hand
Your favourite—Punch a suppliant falls,
And humbly for assistance calls;
He humbly calls and begs you'll stop
The gothic rage of Vander Hop,
Wh'invades without pretence and right,
Or any law but that of might,
Our Pigmy land—and treats our kings
Like paltry idle wooden things;
Has beat our dancers out of doors,
And call'd our chastest virgins whores;
He has not left our Queen a rag on,
Has forced away our George and Dragon,
Has broke our wires, nor was he civil
To Doctor Faustus nor the devil;
E'en us he hurried with full rage,
Most hoarsely squalling off the stage;
And faith our fright was very great
To see a minister of state,
Arm'd with power and fury come
To force us from our little home—
We fear'd, as I am sure we had reason,
An accusation of high-treason;
Till, starting up, says Banamiere,

"Treason, my friends, we need not fear,
For 'gainst the Brass we used no power,
Nor strove to save the chancellor.
Nor did we show the least affection
To Rochford or the Meath election;
Nor did we sing,—'Machugh he means.'"
"You villain, I'll dash out your brains,
'Tis no affair of state which brings
Me here—or business of the King's;
I'm come to seize you all as debtors,
And bind you fast in iron fetters,
From sight of every friend in town,
Till fifty pound's to me paid down."
—"Fifty!" quoth I, "a devilish sum;
But stay till the brass farthings come,
Then we shall all be rich as Jews,
From Castle down to lowest stews;
That sum shall to you then be told,
Though now we cannot furnish gold."
Quoth he, "thou vile mis-shapen beast,
Thou knave, am I become thy jest;
And dost thou think that I am come
To carry nought but farthings home!
Thou fool, I ne'er do things by halves,
Farthings are made for Irish slaves;
No brass for me, it must be gold,
Or fifty pounds in silver told,
That can by any means obtain
Freedom for thee and for thy train."
"Votre très humble serviteur,
I'm not in jest," said I, "I'm sure,
But from the bottom of my belly,
I do in sober sadness tell you,
I thought it was good reasoning,
For us fictitious men to bring
Brass counters made by William Wood
Intrinsic as we flesh and blood;
Then since we are but mimic men,
Pray let us pay in mimic coin."

Quoth he, "Thou lovest, Punch, to prate,
And couldst for ever hold debate;
But think'st thou I have nought to do
But to stand prating thus with you?
Therefore to stop your noisy parly,
I do at once assure you fairly,
That not a puppet of you all
Shall stir a step without this wall,
Nor merry Andrew beat thy drum,
Until you pay the foresaid sum."
Then marching off with swiftest race
To write dispatches for his grace,
The revel-master left the room,
And us condemn'd to fatal doom.
Now, fair ones, if e'er I found grace,
Or if my jokes did ever please,
Use all your interest with your sec,
(They say he's at the ladies' beck,)
And though he thinks as much of gold
As ever Midas did of old:
Your charms I'm sure can never fail,
Your eyes must influence, must prevail;
At your command he'll set us free,
Let us to you owe liberty.
Get us a license now to play,
And we'll in duty ever pray.

Epigram

Great folks are of a finer mould;
Lord! how politely they can scold!
While a coarse English tongue will itch,
For whore and rogue, and dog and bitch.

Epigram on Josiah Hort

Archbishop of Tuam, who, on One Occasion, Left his Church During Service In Order to Wait on the Duke of Dorset

Lord Pam in the church (you'd you think it) kneel'd down;
When told that the Duke was just come to Town—
His station despising, unawed by the place,
He flies from his God to attend to his Grace.
To the Court it was better to pay his devotion,
Since God had no hand in his Lordship's promotion.

Epigram

Behold! a proof of *Irish* sense;
    Here *Irish* wit is seen!
When nothing's left that's worth defence,
    We build a magazine.

Trifles
George Rochfort's verses For the Rev. Dr. Swift, Dean of St. Patrick's, At Laracor, near Trim

Musa Clonshoghiana

That Downpatrick's Dean, or Patrick's down went,
Like two arrand Deans, two Deans errant I meant;
So that Christmas appears at Bellcampe like a Lent,
Gives the gamesters of both houses great discontent.
  Our parsons agree here, as those did at Trent,
Dan's forehead has got a most damnable dent,
Besides a large hole in his Michaelmas rent.
  But your fancy on rhyming so cursedly bent,
With your bloody ouns in one stanza pent;
Does Jack's utter ruin at picket prevent,
For an answer in specie to yours must be sent;
So this moment at crambo (not shuffling) is spent,
And I lose by this crotchet quaterze, point, and quint,
Which you know to a gamester is great bitterment;
But whisk shall revenge me on you, Batt, and Brent.
Bellcampe, January 1, 1717.

A Left-Handed Letter

To Dr. Sheridan, 1718

Delany reports it, and he has a shrewd tongue,
That we both act the part of the clown and cow-dung;
We lie cramming ourselves, and are ready to burst,
Yet still are no wiser than we were at first.

Pudet haec opprobria, I freely must tell ye,
Et dici potuisse, et non potuisse refelli.
Though Delany advised you to plague me no longer,
You reply and rejoin like Hoadly of Bangor;
I must now, at one sitting, pay off my old score;
How many to answer? One, two, three, or four,
But, because the three former are long ago past,
I shall, for method-sake, begin with the last.
You treat me like a boy that knocks down his foe,
Who, ere t'other gets up, demands the rising blow.
Yet I know a young rogue, that, thrown flat on the field,
Would, as he lay under, cry out, Sirrah! yield.
So the French, when our generals soundly did pay them,
Went triumphant to church, and sang stoutly, *Te Deum.*
So the famous Tom Leigh, when quite run a-ground,
Comes off by out-laughing the company round:
In every vile pamphlet you'll read the same fancies,
Having thus overthrown all our farther advances.
My offers of peace you ill understood;
Friend Sheridan, when will you know your own good?
'Twas to teach you in modester language your duty;
For, were you a dog, I could not be rude t'ye;
As a good quiet soul, who no mischief intends
To a quarrelsome fellow, cries, Let us be friends.
But we like Antæus and Hercules fight,
The oftener you fall, the oftener you write:
And I'll use you as he did that overgrown clown,
I'll first take you up, and then take you down;

And, 'tis your own case, for you never can wound
The worst dunce in your school, till he's heaved from the ground.

I beg your pardon for using my left hand, but I was in great haste, and the other hand was employed at the same time in writing some letters of business. September 20, 1718.—I will send you the rest when I have leisure: but pray come to dinner with the company you met here last.

To the Dean of St. Patrick's in Answer to his Left-Handed Letter

Since your poetic prancer is turn'd into Cancer,
I'll tell you at once, sir, I'm now not your man, sir;
For pray, sir, what pleasure in fighting is found
With a coward, who studies to traverse his ground?
When I drew forth my pen, with your pen you ran back;
But I found out the way to your den by its track:
From thence the black monster I drew, o' my conscience,
And so brought to light what before was stark nonsense.
When I with my right hand did stoutly pursue,
You turn'd to your left, and you writ like a Jew;
Which, good Mister Dean, I can't think so fair,
Therefore turn about to the right, as you were;
Then if with true courage your ground you maintain,
My fame is immortal, when Jonathan's slain:
Who's greater by far than great Alexander,
As much as a teal surpasses a gander;
As much as a game-cock's excell'd by a sparrow;
As much as a coach is below a wheelbarrow:
As much and much more as the most handsome man
Of all the whole world is exceeded by Dan.

T. Sheridan

This was written with that hand which in others is commonly called the left hand.

Oft have I been by poets told,
That, poor Jonathan, thou grow'st old.
Alas, thy numbers failing all,
Poor Jonathan, how they do fall!
Thy rhymes, which whilom made thy pride swell,
Now jingle like a rusty bridle:
Thy verse, which ran both smooth and sweet,
Now limp upon their gouty feet:
Thy thoughts, which were the true sublime,

Are humbled by the tyrant, Time:
Alas! what cannot Time subdue?
Time has reduced my wine and you;
Emptied my casks, and clipp'd your wings,
Disabled both in our main springs;
So that of late we two are grown
The jest and scorn of all the town.
But yet, if my advice be ta'en,
We two may be as great again;
I'll send you wings, you send me wine;
Then you will fly, and I shall shine.

This was written with my right hand, at the same time with the other.

How does Melpy like this? I think I have vex'd her;
Little did she know, I was *ambidexter*.

T. Sheridan

To Mr. Thomas Sheridan

Reverend and Learned Sir,

I am teacher of English, for want of a better, to a poor charity-school, in the lower end of St. Thomas's Street; but in my time I have been a Virgilian, though I am now forced to teach English, which I understood less than my own native language, or even than Latin itself: therefore I made bold to send you the enclosed, the fruit of my Muse, in hopes it may qualify me for the honour of being one of your most inferior Ushers: if you will vouchsafe to send me an answer, direct to me next door but one to the Harrow, on the left hand in Crocker's Lane.

I am yours,

Reverend Sir, to command,
Pat. Reyly

Scribimus indocti doctique poemata passim.
Hor., *Epist.* II, i, 117

Ad Amicum Eruditum Thomam Sheridan

Deliciæ, Sheridan, Musarum, dulcis amice,
Sic tibi propitius Permessi ad flumen Apollo
Occurrat, seu te mimum convivia rident,
Aequivocosque sales spargis, seu ludere versu
Malles; dic, Sheridan, quisnam fuit ille deorum,
Quae melior natura orto tibi tradidit artem
Rimandi genium puerorum, atque ima cerebri
Scrutandi? Tibi nascenti ad cunabula Pallas
Astitit; et dixit, mentis praesaga futurae,
Heu, puer infelix! nostro sub sidere natus;
Nam tu pectus eris sine corpore, corporis umbra;
Sed levitate umbram superabis, voce cicadam:
Musca femur, palmas tibi mus dedit, ardea crura.
Corpore sed tenui tibi quod natura negavit,
Hoc animi dotes supplebunt; teque docente,
Nec longum tempus, surget tibi docta juventus,
Artibus egregiis animas instructa novellas.
Grex hinc Paeonius venit, ecce, salutifer orbi;
Ast, illi causas orant: his insula visa est
Divinam capiti nodo constringere mitram.
    Natalis te horae non fallunt signa, sed usque
Conscius, expedias puero seu laetus Apollo
Nascenti arrisit; sive ilium frigidus horror
Saturni premit, aut septem inflavere triones.
    Quin tu altè penitusque latentia semina cernis
Quaeque diu obtundendo olim sub luminis auras
Erumpent, promis; quo ritu saepè puella
Sub cinere hesterno sopitos suscitat ignes.
    Te dominum agnoscit quocunque sub aëre natus:
Quos indulgentis nimium custodia matris
Pessundat: nam saepè vides in stipite matrem.
    Aureus at ramus, venerandae dona Sibyllae,
Aeneae sedes tantùm patefecit Avernas;
Saepè puer, tua quem tetigit semel aurea virga,
Et coelum, terrasque videt, noctemque profundam.

Ad te, doctissime Delany,
Pulsus à foribus Decani,
Confugiens edo querelam,
Pauper petens clientelam.
Petebam Swift doctum patronum,
Sed ille dedit nullum donum,
Neque cibum neque bonum.
Quaeris quàm malè sit stomacho num?
Iratus valdè valdè latrat,
Crumenicidam fermè patrat:
Quin ergo releves aegrotum,
Dato cibum, dato potum.
Ita in utrumvis oculum,
Dormiam bibens vestrum poculum.

Quaeso, Reverende Vir, digneris hanc epistolam inclusam cum versiculis perlegere, quam cum fastidio abjecit et respuebat Decanus ille (inquam) lepidissimus et Musarum et Apollinis comes.

Reverende Vir,

De vestrâ benignitate et clementiâ in frigore et fame exanimatos, nisi persuasum esset nobis, hanc epistolam reverentiae vestrae non scripsissem; quam profectò, quoniam eo es ingenio, in optimam accipere partem nullus dubito. Saevit Boreas, mugiunt procellae, dentibus invitis maxillae bellum gerunt. Nec minus, intestino depraeliantibus tumult visceribus, classicum sonat venter. Ea nostra est conditio, haec nostra querela. Proh Deûm atque hominum fidem! quare illi, cui ne libella nummi est, dentes, stomachum, viscera concessit natura? mehercule, nostro ludibrium debens corpori, frustra laboravit a patre voluntario exilio, qui macrum ligone macriorem reddit agellum. Huc usque evasi, ad te, quasi ad asylum, confugiens, quem nisi bene nôssem succurrere potuisse, mehercule, neque fores vestras pultûssem, neque limina tetigissem. Quàm longum iter famelicus peregi! nudus, egenus, esuriens, perhorrescens, despectus, mendicans; sunt lacrymae rerum et mentem carnaria tangunt. In viâ nullum fuit solatium praeterquam quod Horatium, ubi macros in igne turdos versat, perlegi. Catii dapes, Maecenatis convivium, ita me picture pascens inani, saepius volvebam. Quid non mortalium pectora cogit Musarum sacra fames? Haec omnia, quae nostra fuit necessitas, curavi ut scires; nunc re experiar quid dabis, quid negabis. Vale.

Vivitur parvo malè, sed canebat
Flaccus ut parvo benè: quod negamus:
Pinguis et lautè saturatus ille
Ridet inanes.

Pace sic dicam liceat poetae
Nobilis laeti salibus faceti
Usque jocundi, lepidè jocantis
Non sine curâ.

Quis potest versus (meditans merendam,
Prandium, coenam) numerare? quis non
Quot panes pistor locat in fenestrâ
Dicere mallet?

Ecce jejunus tibi venit unus;
Latrat ingenti stomachus furore;
Quaeso digneris renovare fauces,
Docte Patrone.

Vestiant lanae tenues libellos,
Vestiant panni dominum trementem,
Aedibus vestris trepidante pennâ
Musa propinquat.

Nuda ne fiat, renovare vestes
Urget, et nunquam tibi sic molestam
Esse promittit, nisi sit coacta
Frigore iniquo.

Si modo possem! Vetat heu pudor me
Plura, sed praestat rogitare plura,
An dabis binos digitos crumenae im-
ponere vestrae?

To the Dean of St. Patrick's

Dear Sir, Since you in humble wise
    Have made a recantation,
From your low bended knees arise;
    I hate such poor prostration.

'Tis bravery that moves the brave,
    As one nail drives another;
If you from me would mercy have,
    Pray, Sir, be such another.

You that so long maintain'd the field
    With true poetic vigour;
Now you lay down your pen and yield,
    You make a wretched figure.

Submit, but do't with sword in hand,
    And write a panegyric
Upon the man you cannot stand;
    I'll have it done in lyric:

That all the boys I teach may sing
    The achievements of their Chiron;
What conquests my stern looks can bring
    Without the help of iron.

A small goose-quill, yclep'd a pen,
    From magazine of standish
Drawn forth, 's more dreadful to the Dean,
    Than any sword we brandish.

My ink's my flash, my pen's my bolt;
    Whene'er I please to thunder,
I'll make you tremble like a colt,
    And thus I'll keep you under.

—Thomas Sheridan

To the Dean of St. Patrick's

Dear Dean, I'm in a sad condition,
  I cannot see to read or write;
Pity the darkness of thy Priscian,
  Whose days are all transform'd to night.

My head, though light, 's a dungeon grown,
  The windows of my soul are closed;
Therefore to sleep I lay me down,
  My verse and I are both composed.

Sleep, did I say? that cannot be;
  For who can sleep, that wants his eyes?
My bed is useless then to me,
  Therefore I lay me down to rise.

Unnumber'd thoughts pass to and fro
  Upon the surface of my brain;
In various maze they come and go,
  And come and go again.

So have you seen in sheet burnt black,
  The fiery sparks at random run;
Now here, now there, some turning back
  Some ending where they just begun.

—Thomas Sheridan

An Answer, by Delany, to Thomas Sheridan

Dear Sherry, I'm sorry for your bloodsheded sore eye,
And the more I consider your case, still the more I
Regret it, for see how the pain on't has wore ye.
Besides, the good Whigs, who strangely adore ye,
In pity cry out, "He's a poor blinded Tory."
But listen to me, and I'll soon lay before ye
A sovereign cure well attested in Gory.
First wash it with *ros*, that makes dative *rori*,
Then send for three leeches, and let them all gore ye;
Then take a cordial dram to restore ye,
Then take Lady Judith, and walk a fine boree,
Then take a glass of good claret *ex more*,
Then stay as long as you can *ab uxore*;
And then if friend Dick will but ope your back-door, he
Will quickly dispel the black clouds that hang o'er ye,
And make you so bright, that you'll sing tory rory,
And make a new ballad worth ten of John Dory:
(Though I work your cure, yet he'll get the glory.)
I'm now in the back school-house, high up one story,
Quite weary with teaching, and ready to *mori*.
My candle's just out too, no longer I'll pore ye,
But away to Clem Barry's,—there's an end of my story.

A Reply, by Sheridan, to Delany

I like your collyrium,
Take my eyes, sir, and clear ye 'um,
  'Twill gain you a great reputation;
By this you may rise,
Like the doctor so wise,
  Who open'd the eyes of the nation.

And these, I must tell ye,
Are bigger than its belly;—
  You know, there's in Livy a story
Of the hands and the feet
Denying of meat,—
  Don't I write in the dark like a Tory?

Your water so far goes,
'Twould serve for an Argus,
  Were all his whole hundred sore;
So many we read
He had in his head,
  Or Ovid's a son of a whore.

For your recipe, sir,
May my lids never stir,
  If ever I think once to fee you;
For I'd have you to know,
When abroad I can go,
  That it's honour enough, if I see you.

Another Reply, by Sheridan

My pedagogue dear, I read with surprise
Your long sorry rhymes, which you made on my eyes;
As the Dean of St. Patrick's says, earth, seas, and skies!
I cannot lie down, but immediately rise,
To answer your stuff and the Doctor's likewise.
Like a horse with a gall, I'm pester'd with flies,
But his head and his tail new succour supplies,
To beat off the vermin from back, rump, and thighs.
The wing of a goose before me now lies,
Which is both shield and sword for such weak enemies.
Whoever opposes me, certainly dies,
Though he were as valiant as Condé or Guise.
The women disturb me a-crying of pies,
With a voice twice as loud as a horse when he neighs.
By this, Sir, you find, should we rhyme for a prize,
That I'd gain cloth of gold, when you'd scarce merit frize.

To Thomas Sheridan

Dear Tom, I'm surprised that your verse did not jingle;
But your rhyme was not double, 'cause your sight was but single.
For, as Helsham observes, there's nothing can chime,
Or fit more exact than one eye and one rhyme.
If you had not took physic, I'd pay off your bacon,
But now I'll write short, for fear you're short-taken.
Besides, Dick forbid me, and call'd me a fool;
For he says, short as 'tis, it will give you a stool.
In libris bellis, tu parum parcis ocellis;
Dum nimium scribis, vel talpâ caecior ibis,
Aut ad vina redis, nam sic tua lumina laedis:
Sed tibi coenanti sunt collyria tanti?
Nunquid eges visu, dum comples omnia risu?
Heu Sheridan caecus, heu eris nunc cercopithecus.
Nunc benè nasutus mittet tibi carmina tutus:
Nunc ope Burgundi, malus Helsham ridet abundà,
Nec Phoebe fili versum quîs mittere Ryly.
    Quid tibi cum libris? relavet tua lumina Tybris
Mixtus Saturno; penso sed parcè diurno
Observes hoc tu, nec scriptis utere noctu.
Nonnulli mingunt et palpebras sibi tingunt.
Quidam purgantes, libros in stercore nantes
Lingunt; sic vinces videndo, mî bone, lynces.
Culum oculum tergis, dum scripta hoc flumine mergis;
Tunc oculi et nates, ni fallor, agent tibi grates.
Vim fuge Decani, nec sit tibi cura Delani:
Heu tibi si scribant, aut si tibi fercula libant,
Pone loco mortis, rapis fera pocula fortis
Haec tibi pauca dedi, sed consule Betty my Lady,
Huic te des solae, nec egebis pharmacopolae.
        Haec somnians cecini,

—Jon. Swift

Oct. 23, 1718.

Swift to Sheridan, in Reply

Tom, for a goose you keep but base quills,
They're fit for nothing else but pasquils.
I've often heard it from the wise,
That inflammations in the eyes
Will quickly fall upon the tongue,
And thence, as famed John Bunyan sung,
From out the pen will presently
On paper dribble daintily.
Suppose I call'd you goose, it is hard
One word should stick thus in your gizzard.
You're my goose, and no other man's;
And you know, all my geese are swans:
Only one scurvy thing I find,
Swans sing when dying, geese when blind.
But now I smoke where lies the slander,—
I call'd you goose instead of gander;
For that, dear Tom, ne'er fret and vex,
I'm sure you cackle like the sex.
I know the gander always goes
With a quill stuck across his nose:
So your eternal pen is still
Or in your claw, or in your bill.
But whether you can tread or hatch,
I've something else to do than watch.
As for your writing I am dead,
I leave it for the second head.

Deanery-House, Oct. 27, 1718.

An Answer by Sheridan

Perlegi versus versos, Jonathan bone, tersos;
Perlepidos quidèm; scribendo semper es idem.
Laudibus extollo te, tu mihi magnus Apollo;
Tu frater Phoebus, oculis collyria praebes,
Ne minus insanae reparas quoque damna Dianae,
Quae me percussit radiis (nec dixeris ussit)
Frigore collecto; medicus moderamine tecto
Lodicem binum premit, atque negat mihi vinum.
O terra et coelum! quàm redit pectus anhelum.
Os mihi jam siccum, liceat mihi bibere dic cum?
Ex vestro grato poculo, tam saepe prolato,
Vina crepant: sales ostendet quis mihi tales?
Lumina, vos sperno, dum cuppae gaudia cerno:
Perdere etenim pellem nostram, quoque crura mavellem.
    Amphora, quàm dulces risus queis pectora mulces,
Pangitur a Flacco, cum pectus turget Iaccho:
Clarius evohe ingeminans geminatur et ohe;
Nempe jocosa propago, haesit sic vocis imago.

To Dr. Sheridan. 1718

Whate'er your predecessors taught us,
I have a great esteem for Plautus;
And think your boys may gather there-hence
More wit and humour than from Terence;
But as to comic Aristophanes,
The rogue too vicious and too profane is.
I went in vain to look for Eupolis
Down in the Strand, just where the New Pole is;
For I can tell you one thing, that I can,
You will not find it in the Vatican.
He and Cratinus used, as Horace says,
To take his greatest grandees for asses.
Poets, in those days, used to venture high;
But these are lost full many a century.
Thus you may see, dear friend, *ex pede* hence,
My judgment of the old comedians.
    Proceed to tragics: first Euripides
(An author where I sometimes dip a-days)
Is rightly censured by the Stagirite,
Who says, his numbers do not fadge aright.
A friend of mine that author despises
So much he swears the very best piece is,
For aught he knows, as bad as Thespis's;
And that a woman in these tragedies,
Commonly speaking, but a sad jade is.
At least I'm well assured, that no folk lays
The weight on him they do on Sophocles.
But, above all, I prefer Eschylus,
Whose moving touches, when they please, kill us.
    And now I find my Muse but ill able,
To hold out longer in trissyllable.
I chose those rhymes out for their difficulty;
Will you return as hard ones if I call t'ye?

The Answer, by Dr. Sheridan

Sir,

I thank you for your comedies.
I'll stay and read 'em now at home a-days,
Because Parcus wrote but sorrily
Thy notes, I'll read Lambinus thoroughly;
And then I shall be stoutly set a-gog
To challenge every Irish Pedagogue.
I like your nice epistle critical,
Which does in threefold rhymes so witty fall;
Upon the comic dram' and tragedy
Your notion's right, but verses maggotty;
'Tis but an hour since I heard a man swear it,
The Devil himself could hardly answer it.
As for your friend the sage Euripides,
I believe you give him now the slip o' days;
But mum for that—pray come a Saturday
And dine with me, you can't a better day:
I'll give you nothing but a mutton chop,
Some nappy mellow'd ale with rotten hop,
A pint of wine as good as Falern',
Which we poor masters, God knows, all earn;
We'll have a friend or two, sir, at table,
Right honest men, for few're comeatable;
Then when our liquor makes us talkative,
We'll to the fields, and take a walk at eve.
    Because I'm troubled much with laziness,
    These rhymes I've chosen for their easiness.

Dr. Sheridan to Dr. Swift
1718

Dear Dean, since in *cruxes* and *puns* you and I deal,
Pray why is a woman a sieve and a riddle?
'Tis a thought that came into my noddle this morning,
In bed as I lay, sir, a-tossing and turning.
You'll find if you read but a few of your histories,
All women, as Eve, all women are mysteries.
To find out this riddle I know you'll be eager,
And make every one of the sex a Belphegor.
But that will not do, for I mean to commend them;
I swear without jest I an honour intend them.
In a sieve, sir, their ancient extraction I quite tell,
In a riddle I give you their power and their title.
This I told you before; do you know what I mean, sir?
"Not I, by my troth, sir."—Then read it again, sir.
The reason I send you these lines of rhymes double,
Is purely through pity, to save you the trouble
Of thinking two hours for a rhyme as you did last,
When your Pegasus canter'd in triple, and rid fast.
As for my little nag, which I keep at Parnassus,
With Phoebus's leave, to run with his asses,
He goes slow and sure, and he never is jaded,
While your fiery steed is whipp'd, spurr'd, bastinaded.

The Dean's Answer

In reading your letter alone in my hackney,
Your damnable riddle my poor brains did rack nigh.
And when with much labour the matter I crack'd,
I found you mistaken in matter of fact.
A woman's no sieve, (for with that you begin,)
Because she lets out more than e'er she takes in.
And that she's a riddle can never be right,
For a riddle is dark, but a woman is light.
But grant her a sieve, I can say something archer;
Pray what is a man? he's a fine linen searcher.
Now tell me a thing that wants interpretation,
What name for a maid, was the first man's damnation?
If your worship will please to explain me this rebus,
I swear from henceforward you shall be my Phoebus.

From my hackney-coach, Sept. 11, 1718, past 12 at noon.

Dr. Sheridan's Reply to the Dean

Don't think these few lines which I send, a reproach,
From my Muse in a car, to your Muse in a coach.
The great god of poems delights in a car,
Which makes him so bright that we see him from far;
For, were he mew'd up in a coach, 'tis allow'd
We'd see him no more than we see through a cloud.
    You know to apply this—I do not disparage
Your lines, but I say they're the worse for the carriage.
    Now first you deny that a woman's a sieve;
I say that she is: What reason d'ye give?
Because she lets out more than she takes in.
Is't that you advance for't? you are still to begin.
Your major and minor I both can refute,
I'll teach you hereafter with whom to dispute.
A sieve keeps in half, deny't if you can.
D. "Adzucks, I mistook it, who thought of the bran?"
I tell you in short, sir, you should have a pair o' stocks
For thinking to palm on your friend such a paradox.
Indeed, I confess, at the close you grew better,
But you light from your coach when you finish'd your letter.
Your thing which you say wants interpretation,
What's name for a maiden—the first man's damnation?
A damsel—Adam's hell—ay, there I have hit it,
Just as you conceived it, just so have I writ it.
Since this I've discover'd, I'll make you to know it,
That now I'm your Phoebus, and you are my poet.
But if you interpret the two lines that follow,
I'll again be your poet, and you my Apollo.
Why a noble lord's dog, and my school-house this weather,
Make up the best catch when they're coupled together?

From my Ringsend car, Sept. 12, 1718, past 5 in the morning, on a repetition day.

To the Same. By Dr. Sheridan

12 o'Clock at Noon
Sept. 12, 1718

Sir,
Perhaps you may wonder, I send you so soon
Another epistle; consider 'tis noon.
For all his acquaintance well know that friend Tom is,
Whenever he makes one, as good as his promise.
Now Phoebus exalted, sits high on his throne,
Dividing the heav'ns, dividing my crown,
Into poems and business, my skull's split in two,
One side for the lawyers, and t'other for you.
With my left eye, I see you sit snug in your stall,
With my right I'm attending the lawyers that scrawl
With my left I behold your bellower a cur chase;
With my right I'm a-reading my deeds for a purchase.
My left ear's attending the hymns of the choir,
My right ear is stunn'd with the noise of the crier.
My right hand's inditing these lines to your reverence,
My left is indenting for me and heirs ever-hence.
Although in myself I'm divided in two,
Dear Dean, I shall ne'er be divided from you.

The Dean of St. Patrick's

To Thomas Sheridan

Sir,
I cannot but think that we live in a bad age,
O tempora, O mores! as 'tis in the adage.
My foot was but just set out from my cathedral,
When into my hands comes a letter from the droll.
I can't pray in quiet for you and your verses;
But now let us hear what the Muse from your car says.
    Hum—excellent good—your anger was stirr'd;
Well, punners and rhymers must have the last word.
But let me advise you, when next I hear from you,
To leave off this passion which does not become you;
For we who debate on a subject important,
Must argue with calmness, or else will come short on't.
For myself, I protest, I care not a fiddle,
For a riddle and sieve, or a sieve and a riddle;
And think of the sex as you please, I'd as lieve
You call them a riddle, as call them a sieve.
Yet still you are out, (though to vex you I'm loth,)
For I'll prove it impossible they can be both;
A school-boy knows this, for it plainly appears
That a sieve dissolves riddles by help of the shears;
For you can't but have heard of a trick among wizards,
To break open riddles with shears or with scissars.
    Think again of the sieve, and I'll hold you a wager,
You'll dare not to question my minor or major.
A sieve keeps half in, and therefore, no doubt,
Like a woman, keeps in less than it lets out.
Why sure, Mr. Poet, your head got a-jar,
By riding this morning too long in your car:
And I wish your few friends, when they next see your cargo,
For the sake of your senses would lay an embargo.
You threaten the stocks; I say you are scurrilous
And you durst not talk thus, if I saw you at our ale-house.
But as for your threats, you may do what you can

I despise any poet that truckled to Dan
But keep a good tongue, or you'll find to your smart
From rhyming in cars, you may swing in a cart.
You found out my rebus with very much modesty;
But thanks to the lady; I'm sure she's too good to ye:
Till she lent you her help, you were in a fine twitter;
You hit it, you say;—you're a delicate hitter.
How could you forget so ungratefully a lass,
And if you be my Phoebus, pray who was your Pallas?
    As for your new rebus, or riddle, or crux,
I will either explain, or repay it by trucks;
Though your lords, and your dogs, and your catches, methinks,
Are harder than ever were put by the Sphinx.
And thus I am fully revenged for your late tricks,
Which is all at present from the

—Dean of St. Patrick's

From my closet, Sept, 12, 1718, just 12 at noon.

To the Dean of St. Patrick's

Sir,
Your Billingsgate Muse methinks does begin
With much greater noise than a conjugal din.
A pox of her bawling, her *tempora et mores!*
What are times now to me; a'nt I one of the Tories?
You tell me my verses disturb you at prayers;
Oh, oh, Mr. Dean, are you there with your bears?
You pray, I suppose, like a Heathen, to Phoebus,
To give his assistance to make out my rebus:
Which I don't think so fair; leave it off for the future;
When the combat is equal, this God should be neuter.
I'm now at the tavern, where I drink all I can,
To write with more spirit; I'll drink no more Helicon;
For Helicon is water, and water is weak;
'Tis wine on the gross lee, that makes your Muse speak.
This I know by her spirit and life; but I think
She's much in the wrong to scold in her drink.
Her damn'd pointed tongue pierced almost to my heart;
Tell me of a cart,—tell me of a ——,
I'd have you to tell on both sides her ears,
If she comes to my house, that I'll kick her down stairs:
Then home she shall limping go, squalling out, O my knee;
You shall soon have a crutch to buy for your Melpomene.
You may come as her bully, to bluster and swagger;
But my ink is my poison, my pen is my dagger:
Stand off, I desire, and mark what I say to you,
If you come I will make your Apollo shine through you.
Don't think, sir, I fear a Dean, as I would fear a dun;
Which is all at present from yours,

Thomas Sheridan

The Dean to Thomas Sheridan

Sir,
When I saw you to-day, as I went with Lord Anglesey,
Lord, said I, who's that parson, how awkwardly dangles he!
When whip you trot up, without minding your betters,
To the very coach side, and threaten your letters.
Is the poison (and dagger) you boast in your jaws, trow?
Are you still in your cart with *convitia ex plaustro*?
But to scold is your trade, which I soon should be foil'd in,
For scolding is just *quasi diceres*—school-din:
And I think I may say, you could many good shillings get,
Were you drest like a bawd, and sold oysters at Billingsgate;
But coach it or cart it, I'd have you know, sirrah,
I'll write, though I'm forced to write in a wheelbarrow;
Nay, hector and swagger, you'll still find me stanch,
And you and your cart shall give me *carte blanche*.
Since you write in a cart, keep it *tecta et sarta*,
'Tis all you have for it; 'tis your best Magna Carta;
And I love you so well, as I told you long ago,
That I'll ne'er give my vote for *Delenda Cart-ago*.
Now you write from your cellar, I find out your art,
You rhyme as folks fence, in *tierce* and in *cart*:
Your ink is your poison, your pen is what not;
Your ink is your drink, your pen is your pot.
To my goddess Melpomene, pride of her sex,
I gave, as you beg, your most humble respects:
The rest of your compliment I dare not tell her,
For she never descends so low as the cellar;
But before you can put yourself under her banners,
She declares from her throne you must learn better manners.
If once in your cellar my Phoebus should shine,
I tell you I'd not give a fig for your wine;
So I'll leave him behind, for I certainly know it,
What he ripens above ground, he sours below it.
But why should we fight thus, my partner so dear
With three hundred and sixty-five poems a-year?
Let's quarrel no longer, since Dan and George Rochfort

Will laugh in their sleeves: I can tell you they watch for't.
Then George will rejoice, and Dan will sing highday:
Hoc Ithacus velit, et magni mercentur Atridae.

JON. SWIFT

Written, signed, and sealed, five minutes and eleven seconds after the receipt of yours, allowing seven seconds for sealing and superscribing, from my bed-side, just eleven minutes after eleven, Sept. 15, 1718.

Erratum in your last, 1. antepenult, pro "fear a *Dun*" lege "fear a *Dan*:" ita omnes MSS. quos ego legi, et ita magis congruum tam sensui quam veritati.

To Dr. Sheridan

Dec. 14, 1719, Nine at night

Sir,

It is impossible to know by your letter whether the wine is to be bottled to-morrow, or no.

If it be, or be not, why did not you in plain English tell us so?

For my part, it was by mere chance I came to sit with the ladies this night.

And if they had not told me there was a letter from you; and your man Alexander had not gone, and come back from the deanery; and the boy here had not been sent, to let Alexander know I was here, I should have missed the letter outright.

Truly I don't know who's bound to be sending for corks to stop your bottles, with a vengeance.

Make a page of your own age, and send your man Alexander to buy corks; for Saunders already has gone above ten jaunts.

Mrs. Dingley and Mrs. Johnson say, truly they don't care for your wife's company, though they like your wine; but they had rather have it at their own house to drink in quiet.

However, they own it is very civil in Mrs. Sheridan to make the offer; and they cannot deny it.

I wish Alexander safe at St. Catherine's to-night, with all my heart and soul, upon my word and honour:

But I think it base in you to send a poor fellow out so late at this time of year, when one would not turn out a dog that one valued; I appeal to your friend Mr. Connor.

I would present my humble service to my Lady Mountcashel; but truly I thought she would have made advances to have been acquainted with me, as she pretended.

But now I can write no more, for you see plainly my paper is ended.

1 P.S.

I wish, when you prated, your letter you'd dated:
Much plague it created. I scolded and rated;
My soul is much grated; for your man I long waited.
I think you are fated, like a bear to be baited:
Your man is belated: the case I have stated;
And me you have cheated. My stable's unslated.
Come back t'us well freighted.
I remember my late head; and wish you translated,
For teasing me.

2 P.S.

Mrs. Dingley desires me singly
Her service to present you; hopes that will content you;
But Johnson madam is grown a sad dame,
For want of your converse, and cannot send one verse.

3 P.S.

You keep such a twattling with you and your bottling;
But I see the sum total, we shall ne'er have a bottle;
The long and the short, we shall not have a quart,
I wish you would sign't, that we have a pint.
For all your colloguing, I'd be glad for a knoggin:
But I doubt 'tis a sham; you won't give us a dram.
'Tis of shine a mouth moon-ful, you won't part with a spoonful,
And I must be nimble, if I can fill my thimble,
You see I won't stop, till I come to a drop;
But I doubt the oraculum, is a poor supernaculum;
Though perhaps you may tell it, for a grace if we smell it.

STELLA

Dr. Sheridan's Answer

I'd have you to know, as sure as you're Dean,
On Thursday my cask of Obrien I'll drain;
If my wife is not willing, I say she's a quean;
And my right to the cellar, egad, I'll maintain
As bravely as any that fought at Dunblain:
Go tell her it over and over again.
I hope, as I ride to the town, it won't rain;
For, should it, I fear it will cool my hot brain,
Entirely extinguish my poetic vein;
And then I should be as stupid as Kain,
Who preach'd on three heads, though he mention'd but twain.
Now Wardel's in haste, and begins to complain;
Your most humble servant, dear Sir, I remain,

T. S.—N.

Get Helsham, Walmsley, Delany,
And some Grattans, if there be any:
Take care you do not bid too many.

Dr. Swift's Reply

The verses you sent on the bottling your wine
Were, in every one's judgment, exceedingly fine;
And I must confess, as a dean and divine,
I think you inspired by the Muses all nine.
I nicely examined them every line,
And the worst of them all like a barn-door did shine;
O, that Jove would give me such a talent as thine!
With Delany or Dan I would scorn to combine.
I know they have many a wicked design;
And, give Satan his due, Dan begins to refine.
However, I wish, honest comrade of mine,
You would really on Thursday leave St. Catharine,
Where I hear you are cramm'd every day like a swine;
With me you'll no more have a stomach to dine,
Nor after your victuals lie sleeping supine;
So I wish you were toothless, like Lord Masserine.
But were you as wicked as lewd Aretine,
I wish you would tell me which way you incline.
If when you return your road you don't line,
On Thursday I'll pay my respects at your shrine,
Wherever you bend, wherever you twine,
In square, or in opposite, circle, or trine.
Your beef will on Thursday be salter than brine;
I hope you have swill'd with new milk from the kine,
As much as the Liffee's outdone by the Rhine;
And Dan shall be with us with nose aquiline.
If you do not come back we shall weep out our eyne;
Or may your gown never be good Lutherine.
The beef you have got I hear is a chine;
But if too many come, your madam will whine;
And then you may kiss the low end of her spine.
But enough of this poetry Alexandrine;
I hope you will not think this a pasquine.

A Copy of a Copy of Verses From Thomas Sheridan, Clerk, to George-Nim-Dan-Dean, Esq.

Written July 15, 1721, at night

I'd have you t' know, George, Dan, Dean, and Nim,
That I've learned how verse t' compose trim,
Much better b'half th'n you, n'r you, n'r him,
And that I'd rid'cule their'nd your flam-flim.
Ay b't then, p'rhaps, says you, t's a merry whim,
With 'bundance of mark'd notes i' th' rim,
So th't I ought n't for t' be morose 'nd t' look grim,
Think n't your 'p'stle put m' in a megrim;
Though 'n rep't't'on day, I 'ppear ver' slim,
Th' last bowl't Helsham's did m' head t' swim,
So th't I h'd man' aches 'n v'ry scrubb'd limb,
Cause th' top of th' bowl I h'd oft us'd t' skim;
And b'sides D'lan' swears th't I h'd swall'w'd s'v'r'l brim-
Mers, 'nd that my vis'ge's cov'r'd o'er with r'd pim-
Ples: m'r'o'er though m' scull were ('s 'tis n't) 's strong's tim-
Ber, 't must have ach'd. Th' clans of th' c'llege Sanh'drim,
Pres'nt the'r humbl' and 'fect'nate respects; that's t' say,
    D'ln', 'chlin, P. Ludl', Dic' St'wart, H'lsham, Capt'n
    P'rr' Walmsl', 'nd Long sh'nks Timm.

George-Nim-Dan-Dean's Answer

Dear Sheridan! a gentle pair
Of Gaulstown lads (for such they are)
Besides a brace of grave divines,
Adore the smoothness of thy lines:
Smooth as our basin's silver flood,
Ere George had robb'd it of its mud;
Smoother than Pegasus' old shoe,
Ere Vulcan comes to make him new.
The board on which we set our a—s,
Is not so smooth as are thy verses;
Compared with which (and that's enough)
A smoothing-iron itself is rough.
    Nor praise I less that circumcision,
By modern poets call'd elision,
With which, in proper station placed,
Thy polish'd lines are firmly braced.
Thus a wise tailor is not pinching,
But turns at every seam an inch in:
Or else, be sure, your broad-cloth breeches
Will ne'er be smooth, nor hold their stitches.
Thy verse, like bricks, defy the weather,
When smooth'd by rubbing them together;
Thy words so closely wedged and short are,
Like walls, more lasting without mortar;
By leaving out the needless vowels,
You save the charge of lime and trowels.
One letter still another locks,
Each grooved and dovetail'd like a box;
Thy muse is tuckt up and succinct;
In chains thy syllables are linkt;
Thy words together tied in small hanks,
Close as the Macedonian phalanx;
Or like the *umbo* of the Romans,
Which fiercest foes could break by no means.
The critic, to his grief will find,
How firmly these indentures bind.

So, in the kindred painter's art,
The shortening is the nicest part.
    Philologers of future ages,
How will they pore upon thy pages!
Nor will they dare to break the joints,
But help thee to be read with points:
Or else, to show their learned labour, you
May backward be perused like Hebrew,
In which they need not lose a bit
Or of thy harmony or wit.
To make a work completely fine,
Number and weight and measure join;
Then all must grant your lines are weighty
Where thirty weigh as much as eighty;
All must allow your numbers more,
Where twenty lines exceed fourscore;
Nor can we think your measure short,
Where less than forty fill a quart,
With Alexandrian in the close,
Long, long, long, long, like Dan's long nose.

George-Nim-Dan-Dean's Invitation To Thomas Sheridan

Gaulstown, Aug. 2, 1721

Dear Tom, this verse, which however the beginning may appear, yet in the end's good metre,

Is sent to desire that, when your August vacation comes, your friends you'd meet here.

For why should you stay in that filthy hole, I mean the city so smoky,

When you have not one friend left in town, or at least not one that's witty, to joke w' ye?

For as for honest John, though I'm not sure on't, yet I'll be hang'd, lest he

Be gone down to the county of Wexford with that great peer the Lord Anglesey.

O! but I forgot; perhaps, by this time, you may have one come to town, but I don't know whether he be friend or foe, Delany:

But, however, if he be come, bring him down, and you shall go back in a fortnight, for I know there's no delaying ye.

O! I forgot too: I believe there may be one more, I mean that great fat joker, friend Helsham, he

That wrote the prologue, and if you stay with him, depend on't, in the end, he'll sham ye.

Bring down Longshanks Jim too; but, now I think on't, he's not yet come from Courtown, I fancy;

For I heard, a month ago, that he was down there a-courting sly Nancy.

However, bring down yourself, and you bring down all; for, to say it we may venture,

In thee Delany's spleen, John's mirth, Helsham's jokes, and the soft soul of amorous Jemmy, centre.

Postscript

I had forgot to desire you to bring down what I say you have, and you'll believe me as sure as a gun, and own it;

I mean, what no other mortal in the universe can boast of, your own spirit of pun, and own wit.

And now I hope you'll excuse this rhyming, which I must say is (though written somewhat at large) trim and clean;

And so I conclude, with humble respects as usual

Your most dutiful and obedient

George-Nim-Dan-Dean

To George-Nim-Dan-Dean, Esq.

Upon his Incomparable Verses. By Dr. Delany in Sheridan's Name

Hail, human compound quadrifarious,
Invincible as wight Briareus!
Hail! doubly-doubled mighty merry one,
Stronger than triple-bodied Geryon!
O may your vastness deign t' excuse
The praises of a puny Muse,
Unable, in her utmost flight,
To reach thy huge colossian height!
T' attempt to write like thee were frantic,
Whose lines are, like thyself, gigantic.
Yet let me bless, in humbler strain,
Thy vast, thy bold Cambysian vein,
Pour'd out t' enrich thy native isle,
As Egypt wont to be with Nile.
O, how I joy to see thee wander,
In many a winding loose meander,
In circling mazes, smooth and supple,
And ending in a clink quadruple;
Loud, yet agreeable withal,
Like rivers rattling in their fall!
Thine, sure, is poetry divine,
Where wit and majesty combine;
Where every line, as huge as seven,
If stretch'd in length, would reach to Heaven:
Here all comparing would be slandering,
The least is more than Alexandrine.
Against thy verse Time sees with pain,
He whets his envious scythe in vain;
For though from thee he much may pare,
Yet much thou still wilt have to spare.
Thou hast alone the skill to feast
With Roman elegance of taste,
Who hast of rhymes as vast resources

As Pompey's caterer of courses.
O thou, of all the Nine inspired!
My languid soul, with teaching tired,
How is it raptured, when it thinks
Of thy harmonious set of chinks;
Each answering each in various rhymes,
Like echo to St. Patrick's chimes!
Thy Muse, majestic in her rage,
Moves like Statira on the stage;
And scarcely can one page sustain
The length of such a flowing train:
Her train of variegated dye
Shows like Thaumantia's in the sky;
Alike they glow, alike they please,
Alike imprest by Phoebus' rays.
Thy verse—(Ye Gods! I cannot bear it)
To what, to what shall I compare it?
'Tis like, what I have oft heard spoke on,
The famous statue of Laocoon.
'Tis like,—O yes, 'tis very like it,
The long, long string, with which you fly kite.
'Tis like what you, and one or two more,
Roar to your Echo in good humour;
And every couplet thou hast writ
Concludes with Rhattah-whittah-whit.

To Mr. Thomas Sheridan upon his verses Written in Circles By Dr. Swift

It never was known that circular letters,
By humble companions were sent to their betters,
And, as to the subject, our judgment, *meherc'le*,
Is this, that you argue like fools in a circle.
But now for your verses; we tell you, *imprimis*,
The segment so large 'twixt your reason and rhyme is,
That we walk all about, like a horse in a pound,
And, before we find either, our noddles turn round.
Sufficient it were, one would think, in your mad rant,
To give us your measures of line by a quadrant.
But we took our dividers, and found your d—n'd metre,
In each single verse, took up a diameter.
But how, Mr. Sheridan, came you to venture
George, Dan, Dean, and Nim, to place in the centre?
'Twill appear to your cost, you are fairly trepann'd,
For the chord of your circle is now in their hand.
The chord, or the radius, it matters not whether,
By which your jade Pegasus, fix'd in a tether,
As his betters are used, shall be lash'd round the ring,
Three fellows with whips, and the Dean holds the string.
Will Hancock declares, you are out of your compass,
To encroach on his art by writing of bombast;
And has taken just now a firm resolution
To answer your style without circumlocution.
    Lady Betty presents you her service most humble,
And is not afraid your worship will grumble,
That she make of your verses a hoop for Miss Tam.
Which is all at present; and so I remain—

On Dr. Sheridan's Circular Verses By Mr. George Rochfort

With music and poetry equally blest,
A bard thus Apollo most humbly addrest:
"Great author of harmony, verses, and light!
Assisted by thee, I both fiddle and write.
Yet unheeded I scrape, or I scribble all day,
My verse is neglected, my tunes thrown away.
Thy substitute here, Vice Apollo, disdains
To vouch for my numbers, or list to my strains;
Thy manual signet refuses to put
To the airs I produce from the pen or the gut.
Be thou then propitious, great Phoebus! and grant
Relief, or reward, to my merit, or want.
Though the Dean and Delany transcendently shine,
O brighten one solo or sonnet of mine!
With them I'm content thou shouldst make thy abode;
But visit thy servant in jig or in ode;
Make one work immortal: 'tis all I request."
    Apollo look'd pleased; and, resolving to jest,
Replied, "Honest friend, I've consider'd thy case;
Nor dislike thy well-meaning and humorous face.
Thy petition I grant: the boon is not great;
Thy works shall continue; and here's the receipt.
On rondeaus hereafter thy fiddle-strings spend:
Write verses in circles: they never shall end."

On Dan Jackson's Picture, Cut in Silk and Paper

To fair Lady Betty Dan sat for his picture,
And defied her to draw him so oft as he piqued her,
He knew she'd no pencil or colouring by her,
And therefore he thought he might safely defy her.
Come sit, says my lady; then whips up her scissar,
And cuts out his coxcomb in silk in a trice, sir.
Dan sat with attention, and saw with surprise
How she lengthen'd his chin, how she hollow'd his eyes;
But flatter'd himself with a secret conceit,
That his thin lantern jaws all her art would defeat.
Lady Betty observed it, then pulls out a pin,
And varies the grain of the stuff to his grin:
And, to make roasted silk to resemble his raw-bone,
She raised up a thread to the jet of his jaw-bone;
Till at length in exactest proportion he rose,
From the crown of his head to the arch of his nose;
And if Lady Betty had drawn him with wig and all,
'Tis certain the copy had outdone the original.
    Well, that's but my outside, says Dan, with a vapour;
Say you so? says my lady; I've lined it with paper.

—Patr. Delany *sculpsit*

On the Same Picture

Clarissa draws her scissars from the case
To draw the lines of poor Dan Jackson's face;
One sloping cut made forehead, nose, and chin,
A nick produced a mouth, and made him grin,
Such as in tailor's measure you have seen.
But still were wanting his grimalkin eyes,
For which gray worsted stocking paint supplies.
Th' unravell'd thread through needle's eye convey'd,
Transferr'd itself into his pasteboard head.
How came the scissars to be thus outdone?
The needle had an eye, and they had none.
O wondrous force of art! now look at Dan—
You'll swear the pasteboard was the better man.
"The devil!" says he, "the head is not so full!"
Indeed it is—behold the paper skull.

—Tho. Sheridan *sculp*

On the Same

If you say this was made for friend Dan, you belie it,
I'll swear he's so like it that he was made by it.

—Tho. Sheridan *sculp*

On the Same Picture

Dan's evil genius in a trice
Had stripp'd him of his coin at dice.
Chloe, observing this disgrace,
On Pam cut out his rueful face.
By G—, says Dan, 'tis very hard,
Cut out at dice, cut out at card!

G. Rochfort *sculp*

On the Same Picture

Whilst you three merry poets traffic
To give us a description graphic
Of Dan's large nose in modern sapphic;

I spend my time in making sermons,
Or writing libels on the Germans,
Or murmuring at Whigs' preferments.

But when I would find rhyme for Rochfort,
And look in English, French, and Scotch for't,
At last I'm fairly forced to botch for't.

Bid Lady Betty recollect her,
And tell, who was it could direct her
To draw the face of such a spectre?

I must confess, that as to me, sirs,
Though I ne'er saw her hold the scissars,
I now could safely swear it is hers.

'Tis true, no nose could come in better;
'Tis a vast subject stuff'd with matter,
Which all may handle, none can flatter.

Take courage, Dan; this plainly shows,
That not the wisest mortal knows
What fortune may befall his nose.

Show me the brightest Irish toast,
Who from her lover e'er could boast
Above a song or two at most:

For thee three poets now are drudging all,
To praise the cheeks, chin, nose, the bridge and all,
Both of the picture and original.

Thy nose's length and fame extend
So far, dear Dan, that every friend
Tries who shall have it by the end.

And future poets, as they rise,
Shall read with envy and surprise
Thy nose outshining Celia's eyes.

Jon. Swift

Dan Jackson's Defence

My verse little better you'll find than my face is;
A word to the wise

—ut pictura poesis

Three merry lads, with envy stung,
Because Dan's face is better hung,
Combined in verse to rhyme it down,
And in its place set up their own;
As if they'd run it down much better
By number of their feet in metre.
Or that its red did cause their spite,
Which made them draw in black and white.
Be that as 'twill, this is most true,
They were inspired by what they drew.
Let then such critics know, my face
Gives them their comeliness and grace:
While every line of face does bring
A line of grace to what they sing.
But yet, methinks, though with disgrace
Both to the picture and the face,
I should name them who do rehearse
The story of the picture farce;
The squire, in French as hard as stone,
Or strong as rock, that's all as one,
On face on cards is very brisk, sirs,
Because on them you play at whisk, sirs.
But much I wonder, why my crany
Should envied be by De-el-any:
And yet much more, that half-namesake
Should join a party in the freak.
For sure I am it was not safe
Thus to abuse his better half,
As I shall prove you, Dan, to be,
Divisim and conjunctively.
For if Dan love not Sherry, can

Sherry be anything to Dan?
This is the case whene'er you see
Dan makes nothing of Sherry;
Or should Dan be by Sherry o'erta'en
Then Dan would be poor Sherridane
'Tis hard then he should be decried
By Dan, with Sherry by his side.
But, if the case must be so hard,
That faces suffer by a card,
Let critics censure, what care I?
Backbiters only we defy,
Faces are free from injury.

Mr. Rochfort's Reply

You say your face is better hung
Than ours—by what? by nose or tongue?
In not explaining you are wrong
to us, sir.

Because we thus must state the case,
That you have got a hanging face,
Th' untimely end's a damn'd disgrace
of noose, sir.

But yet be not cast down: I see
A weaver will your hangman be:
You'll only hang in tapestry
with many;

And then the ladies, I suppose,
Will praise your longitude of nose,
For latent charms within your clothes,
dear Danny.

Thus will the fair of every age
From all parts make their pilgrimage,
Worship thy nose with pious rage
of love, sir:

All their religion will be spent
About thy woven monument,
And not one orison be sent
to Jove, sir.

You the famed idol will become,
As gardens graced in ancient Rome,
By matrons worshipp'd in the gloom
of night.

O happy Dan! thrice happy sure!
Thy fame for ever shall endure,
Who after death can love secure
at sight.

So far I thought it was my duty
To dwell upon thy boasted beauty;
Now I'll proceed: a word or two t' ye
in answer

To that part where you carry on
This paradox, that rock and stone
In your opinion, are all one:
How can, sir,

A man of reasoning so profound
So stupidly be run a-ground,
As things so different to confound
t'our senses?

Except you judged them by the knock
Of near an equal hardy block;
Such an experimental stroke
convinces.

Then might you be, by dint of reason,
A proper judge on this occasion;
'Gainst feeling there's no disputation,
is granted:

Therefore to thy superior wit,
Who made the trial, we submit;
Thy head to prove the truth of it
we wanted.

In one assertion you're to blame,
Where Dan and Sherry's made the same,
Endeavouring to have your name
refined, sir:

You'll see most grossly you mistook,
If you consult your spelling-book,
(The better half you say you took,)
you'll find, sir,

S, H, E, she—and R, I, ri,
Both put together make Sherry;
D, A, N, Dan—makes up the three
syllables;

Dan is but one, and Sherry two,
Then, sir, your choice will never do;
Therefore I've turn'd, my friend, on you
the tables.

Dr. Delany's Reply

Assist me, my Muse, while I labour to limn him.
Credite, Pisones, isti tabulae persimilem.
You look and you write with so different a grace,
That I envy your verse, though I did not your face.
And to him that thinks rightly, there's reason enough,
'Cause one is as smooth as the other is rough.
 But much I'm amazed you should think my design
Was to rhyme down your nose, or your harlequin grin,
Which you yourself wonder the de'el should malign.
And if 'tis so strange, that your monstership's crany
Should be envied by him, much less by Delany;
Though I own to you, when I consider it stricter,
I envy the painter, although not the picture.
And justly she's envied, since a fiend of Hell
Was never drawn right but by her and Raphael.
 Next, as to the charge, which you tell us is true,
That we were inspired by the subject we drew.
Inspired we were, and well, sir, you knew it;
Yet not by your nose, but the fair one that drew it;
Had your nose been the Muse, we had ne'er been inspired,
Though perhaps it might justly 've been said we were fired,
 As to the division of words in your staves,
Like my countryman's horn-comb, into three halves,
I meddle not with 't, but presume to make merry,
You call'd Dan one half, and t'other half Sherry:
Now if Dan's a half, as you call't o'er and o'er,
Then it can't be denied that Sherry's two more.
For pray give me leave to say, sir, for all you,
That Sherry's at least of double the value.
But perhaps, sir, you did it to fill up the verse;
So crowds in a concert (like actors in farce)
Play two parts in one, when scrapers are scarce.
But be that as 'twill, you'll know more anon, sir,
When Sheridan sends to merry Dan answer.

Sheridan's Reply

Three merry lads you own we are;
'Tis very true, and free from care:
But envious we cannot bear,
believe, sir:

For, were all forms of beauty thine,
Were you like Nereus soft and fine,
We should not in the least repine,
or grieve, sir.

Then know from us, most beauteous Dan,
That roughness best becomes a man;
'Tis women should be pale, and wan,
and taper;

And all your trifling beaux and fops,
Who comb their brows, and sleek their chops,
Are but the offspring of toy-shops,
mere vapour.

We know your morning hours you pass
To cull and gather out a face;
Is this the way you take your glass?
Forbear it:

Those loads of paint upon your toilet
Will never mend your face, but spoil it,
It looks as if you did parboil it:
Drink claret.

Your cheeks, by sleeking, are so lean,
That they're like Cynthia in the wane,
Or breast of goose when 'tis pick'd clean,
or pullet:

See what by drinking you have done:
You've made your phiz a skeleton,
From the long distance of your crown,
t' your gullet.

A Rejoinder by the Dean in Jackson's Name

Wearied with saying grace and prayer,
I hasten'd down to country air,
To read your answer, and prepare
reply to't:

But your fair lines so grossly flatter,
Pray do they praise me or bespatter?
I must suspect you mean the latter—
Ah! slyboot!

It must be so! what else, alas!
Can mean by culling of a face,
And all that stuff of toilet, glass,
and box-comb?

But be't as 'twill, this you must grant,
That you're a daub, whilst I but paint;
Then which of us two is the quaint-
er coxcomb?

I value not your jokes of noose,
Your gibes and all your foul abuse,
More than the dirt beneath my shoes,
nor fear it.

Yet one thing vexes me, I own,
Thou sorry scarecrow of skin and bone;
To be called lean by a skeleton,
who'd bear it?

'Tis true, indeed, to curry friends,
You seem to praise, to make amends,
And yet, before your stanza ends,
you flout me,

'Bout latent charms beneath my clothes,
For every one that knows me, knows
That I have nothing like my nose
about me:

I pass now where you fleer and laugh,
'Cause I call Dan my better half!
O there you think you have me safe!
But hold, sir;

Is not a penny often found
To be much greater than a pound!
By your good leave, my most profound
and bold sir,

Dan's noble metal, Sherry base;
So Dan's the better, though the less,
An ounce of gold's worth ten of brass,
dull pedant!

As to your spelling, let me see,
If SHE makes sher, and RI makes ry,
Good spelling-master: your crany
has lead in't.

Another Rejoinder by the Dean, in Jackson's Name

Three days for answer I have waited,
I thought an ace you'd ne'er have bated
And art thou forced to yield, ill-fated
poetaster?

Henceforth acknowledge, that a nose
Of thy dimension's fit for prose;
But every one that knows Dan, knows
thy master.

Blush for ill spelling, for ill lines,
And fly with hurry to Rathmines;
Thy fame, thy genius, now declines,
proud boaster.

I hear with some concern your roar
And flying think to quit the score,
By clapping billets on your door
and posts, sir.

Thy ruin, Tom, I never meant,
I'm grieved to hear your banishment,
But pleased to find you do relent
and cry on.

I maul'd you, when you look'd so bluff,
But now I'll secret keep your stuff;
For know, prostration is enough
to th' lion.

Sheridan's Submission
By the Dean

Miserae cognosce prooemia rixae,
Si rixa est ubi tu pulsas, ego vapulo tantum.

Poor Sherry, inglorious,
To Dan the victorious,
Presents, as 'tis fitting,
Petition and greeting.

To you, victorious and brave,
Your now subdued and suppliant slave
Most humbly sues for pardon;
Who when I fought still cut me down,
And when I vanquish'd, fled the town
Pursued and laid me hard on.

Now lowly crouch'd, I cry *peccavi*,
And prostrate, supplicate *pour ma vie*;
Your mercy I rely on;
For you my conqueror and my king,
In pardoning, as in punishing,
Will show yourself a lion.

Alas! sir, I had no design,
But was unwarily drawn in;
For spite I ne'er had any;
'Twas the damn'd squire with the hard name;
The de'il too that owed me a shame,
The devil and Delany;

They tempted me t' attack your highness,
And then, with wonted wile and slyness,
They left me in the lurch:
Unhappy wretch! for now, I ween,
I've nothing left to vent my spleen
But ferula and birch:

And they, alas! yield small relief,
Seem rather to renew my grief,
    My wounds bleed all anew:
For every stroke goes to my heart
And at each lash I feel the smart
    Of lash laid on by you.

The Pardon

The suit which humbly you have made
Is fully and maturely weigh'd;
    And as 'tis your petition,
I do forgive, for well I know,
Since you're so bruised, another blow
    Would break the head of Priscian.

'Tis not my purpose or intent
That you should suffer banishment;
    I pardon, now you've courted;
And yet I fear this clemency
Will come too late to profit thee,
    For you're with grief transported.

However, this I do command,
That you your birch do take in hand,
    Read concord and syntax on;
The bays, your own, are only mine,
Do you then still your nouns decline,
    Since you've declined Dan Jackson.

The Last Speech and Dying Words of Daniel Jackson

My Dear Countrymen,

—mediocribus esse poetis
Non funes, non gryps, non concessere columnae.

To give you a short translation of these two lines from Horace's Art of Poetry, which I have chosen for my neck-verse, before I proceed to my speech, you will find they fall naturally into this sense:

For poets who can't tell (high) rocks from stones,
The rope, the hangman, and the gallows groans.

I was born in a fen near the foot of Mount Parnassus, commonly called the Logwood Bog. My mother, whose name was Stanza, conceived me in a dream, and was delivered of me in her sleep. Her dream was, that Apollo, in the shape of a gander, with a prodigious long bill, had embraced her; upon which she consulted the Oracle of Delphos, and the following answer was made:

You'll have a gosling, call it Dan,
And do not make your goose a swan.
'Tis true, because the God of Wit
To get him in that shape thought fit,
He'll have some glowworm sparks of it.
Venture you may to turn him loose,
But let it be to another goose.
The time will come, the fatal time,
When he shall dare a swan to rhyme;
The tow'ring swan comes sousing down,
And breaks his pinions, cracks his crown.
From that sad time, and sad disaster,
He'll be a lame, crack'd poetaster.
At length for stealing rhymes and triplets,
He'll be content to hang in giblets.

You see now, Gentlemen, this is fatally and literally come to pass; for it was my misfortune to engage with that Pindar of the times, Tom Sheridan, who did so confound me by sousing on my crown, and did so batter my pinions, that I was forced to make use of borrowed wings, though my false accusers have deposed that I stole my feathers from Hopkins, Sternhold, Silvester, Ogilby, Durfey, etc., for which I now forgive them and all the world. I die a poet; and this ladder shall be my Gradus ad Parnassum; and I hope the critics will have mercy on my works.

Then lo, I mount as slowly as I sung,
And then I'll make a line for every rung;
There's nine, I see,—the Muses, too, are nine.
Who would refuse to die a death like mine!

1. Thou first rung, Clio, celebrate my name;
2. Euterp, in tragic numbers do the same.
3. This rung, I see, Terpsichore's thy flute;
4. Erato, sing me to the Gods; ah, do't:
5. Thalia, don't make me a comedy;
6. Urania, raise me tow'rds the starry sky:
7. Calliope, to ballad-strains descend,
8. And Polyhymnia, tune them for your friend;
9. So shall Melpomene mourn my fatal end.

—Poor Dan Jackson

To the Rev. Daniel Jackson To be Humbly Presented by Mr. Sheridan in Person, With Respect, Care, and Speed. To be Delivered by and with Mr. Sheridan

Dear Dan,

Here I return my trust, nor ask
    One penny for remittance;
If I have well perform'd my task,
    Pray send me an acquittance.

Too long I bore this weighty pack,
    As Hercules the sky;
Now take him you, Dan Atlas, back,
    Let me be stander-by.

Not all the witty things you speak
    In compass of a day,
Not half the puns you make a-week,
    Should bribe his longer stay.

With me you left him out at nurse,
    Yet are you not my debtor;
For, as he hardly can be worse,
    I ne'er could make him better.

He rhymes and puns, and puns and rhymes,
    Just as he did before;
And, when he's lash'd a hundred times,
    He rhymes and puns the more.

When rods are laid on school-boys' bums,
    The more they frisk and skip:
The school-boys' top but louder hums
    The more they use the whip.

Thus, a lean beast beneath a load
    (A beast of Irish breed)
Will, in a tedious dirty road,
    Outgo the prancing steed.

You knock him down and down in vain,
    And lay him flat before ye,
For soon as he gets up again,
    He'll strut, and cry, Victoria!

At every stroke of mine, he fell,
    'Tis true he roar'd and cried;
But his impenetrable shell
    Could feel no harm beside.

The tortoise thus, with motion slow,
    Will clamber up a wall;
Yet, senseless to the hardest blow,
    Gets nothing but a fall.

Dear Dan, then, why should you, or I,
    Attack his pericrany?
And, since it is in vain to try,
    We'll send him to Delany.

Postscript

Lean Tom, when I saw him last week on his horse awry,
Threaten'd loudly to turn me to stone with his sorcery,
But, I think, little Dan, that in spite of what our foe says,
He will find I read Ovid and his Metamorphoses,
For omitting the first (where I make a comparison,
With a sort of allusion to Putland or Harrison)
Yet, by my description, you'll find he in short is
A pack and a garran, a top and a tortoise.
So I hope from henceforward you ne'er will ask, can I maul
This teasing, conceited, rude, insolent animal?
And, if this rebuke might turn to his benefit,
(For I pity the man) I should be glad then of it.

Sheridan to Swift

A Highlander once fought a Frenchman at Margate,
The weapons a rapier, a backsword, and target;
Brisk Monsieur advanced as fast as he could,
But all his fine pushes were caught in the wood;
While Sawney with backsword did slash him and nick him,
While t'other, enraged that he could not once prick him,
Cried, "Sirrah, you rascal, you son of a whore,
Me'll fight you, begar, if you'll come from your door!"
    Our case is the same; if you'll fight like a man,
Don't fly from my weapon, and skulk behind Dan;
For he's not to be pierced; his leather's so tough,
The devil himself can't get through his buff.
Besides, I cannot but say that it is hard,
Not only to make him your shield, but your vizard;
And like a tragedian, you rant and you roar,
Through the horrible grin of your larva's wide bore.
Nay, farther, which makes me complain much, and frump it,
You make his long nose your loud speaking-trumpet;
With the din of which tube my head you so bother,
That I scarce can distinguish my right ear from t'other.

You made me in your last a goose;
    I lay my life on't you are wrong,
To raise me by such foul abuse;
    My quill you'll find's a woman's tongue;

And slit, just like a bird will chatter,
    And like a bird do something more;
When I let fly, 'twill so bespatter,
    I'll change you to a black-a-moor.

I'll write while I have half an eye in my head;
I'll write while I live, and I'll write when you're dead.
Though you call me a goose, you pitiful slave,
I'll feed on the grass that grows on your grave.

Sheridan to Swift

I can't but wonder, Mr. Dean,
To see you live, so often slain.
My arrows fly and fly in vain,
But still I try and try again.
I'm now, Sir, in a writing vein;
Don't think, like you, I squeeze and strain,
Perhaps you'll ask me what I mean;
I will not tell, because it's plain.
Your Muse, I am told, is in the wane;
If so, from pen and ink refrain.
Indeed, believe me, I'm in pain
For her and you; your life's a scene
Of verse, and rhymes, and hurricane,
Enough to crack the strongest brain.
Now to conclude, I do remain,
Your honest friend,

—Tom Sheridan

Swift to Sheridan

Poor Tom, wilt thou never accept a defiance,
Though I dare you to more than quadruple alliance.
You're so retrograde, sure you were born under Cancer;
Must I make myself hoarse with demanding an answer?
If this be your practice, mean scrub, I assure ye,
And swear by each Fate, and your new friends, each Fury,
I'll drive you to Cavan, from Cavan to Dundalk;
I'll tear all your rules, and demolish your pun-talk:
Nay, further, the moment you're free from your scalding,
I'll chew you to bullets, and puff you at Baldwin.

Mary the Cook-Maid's Letter to Dr. Sheridan. 1723

Well, if ever I saw such another man since my mother bound up my head!
You a gentleman! Marry come up! I wonder where you were bred.
I'm sure such words does not become a man of your cloth;
I would not give such language to a dog, faith and troth.
Yes, you call'd my master a knave; fie, Mr. Sheridan! 'tis a shame
For a parson who should know better things, to come out with such a name.
Knave in your teeth, Mr. Sheridan! 'tis both a shame and a sin;
And the Dean, my master, is an honester man than you and all your kin:
He has more goodness in his little finger than you have in your whole body:
My master is a personable man, and not a spindle-shank hoddy doddy.
And now, whereby I find you would fain make an excuse,
Because my master, one day, in anger, call'd you a goose:
Which, and I am sure I have been his servant four years since October,
And he never call'd me worse than sweet-heart, drunk or sober:
Not that I know his reverence was ever concern'd to my knowledge,
Though you and your come-rogues keep him out so late in your wicked college.
You say you will eat grass on his grave: a Christian eat grass!
Whereby you now confess yourself to be a goose or an ass:
But that's as much as to say, that my master should die before ye;
Well, well, that's as God pleases; and I don't believe that's a true story:
And so say I told you so, and you may go tell my master; what care I?
And I don't care who knows it; 'tis all one to Mary.
Everybody knows that I love to tell truth, and shame the devil:
I am but a poor servant; but I think gentlefolks should be civil.
Besides, you found fault with our victuals one day that you was here;
I remember it was on a Tuesday, of all days in the year.
And Saunders, the man, says you are always jesting and mocking:

Mary, said he, (one day as I was mending my master's stocking;)
My master is so fond of that minister that keeps the school—
I thought my master a wise man, but that man makes him a fool.
Saunders, said I, I would rather than a quart of ale
He would come into our kitchen, and I would pin a dish-clout to his tail.
And now I must go, and get Saunders to direct this letter;
For I write but a sad scrawl; but my sister Marget she writes better.
Well, but I must run and make the bed, before my master comes from prayers:
And see now, it strikes ten, and I hear him coming up stairs;
Whereof I could say more to your verses, if I could write written hand;
And so I remain, in a civil way, your servant to 'command,

Mary

A Portrait from the Life

Come sit by my side, while this picture I draw:
In chattering a magpie, in pride a jackdaw;
A temper the devil himself could not bridle;
Impertinent mixture of busy and idle;
As rude as a bear, no mule half so crabbed;
She swills like a sow, and she breeds like a rabbit;
A housewife in bed, at table a slattern;
For all an example, for no one a pattern.
Now tell me, friend Thomas, Ford, Grattan, and Merry Dan,
Has this any likeness to good Madam Sheridan?

On Stealing a Crown, When the Dean was Asleep

Dear Dean, since you in sleepy wise
Have oped your mouth, and closed your eyes,
Like ghost I glide along your floor,
And softly shut the parlour door:
For, should I break your sweet repose,
Who knows what money you might lose:
Since oftentimes it has been found,
A dream has given ten thousand pound?
Then sleep, my friend; dear Dean, sleep on,
And all you get shall be your own;
Provided you to this agree,
That all you lose belongs to me.

The Dean's Answer

So, about twelve at night, the punk
Steals from the cully when he's drunk:
Nor is contented with a treat,
Without her privilege to cheat:
Nor can I the least difference find,
But that you left no clap behind.
But, jest apart, restore, you capon ye,
My twelve thirteens and sixpence-ha'penny
To eat my meat and drink my medlicot,
And then to give me such a deadly cut—
But 'tis observed, that men in gowns
Are most inclined to plunder crowns.
Could you but change a crown as easy
As you can steal one, how 'twould please ye!
I thought the lady at St. Catherine's
Knew how to set you better patterns;
For this I will not dine with Agmondisham,
And for his victuals, let a ragman dish 'em.

Saturday night.

A Prologue to a Play Performed at Mr. Sheridan's School. Spoken by One of the Scholars

As in a silent night a lonely swain,
'Tending his flocks on the Pharsalian plain,
To Heaven around directs his wandering eyes,
And every look finds out a new surprise;
So great's our wonder, ladies, when we view
Our lower sphere made more serene by you.
O! could such light in my dark bosom shine,
What life, what vigour, should adorn each line!
Beauty and virtue should be all my theme,
And Venus brighten my poetic flame.
The advent'rous painter's fate and mine are one
Who fain would draw the bright meridian sun;
Majestic light his feeble art defies,
And for presuming, robs him of his eyes.
Then blame your power, that my inferior lays
Sink far below your too exalted praise:
Don't think we flatter, your applause to gain;
No, we're sincere,—to flatter you were vain.
You spurn at fine encomiums misapplied,
And all perfections but your beauties hide.
Then as you're fair, we hope you will be kind,
Nor frown on those you see so well inclined
To please you most. Grant us your smiles, and then
Those sweet rewards will make us act like men.

The Epilogue

Now all is done, ye learn'd spectators, tell
Have we not play'd our parts extremely well?
We think we did, but if you do complain,
We're all content to act the play again:
'Tis but three hours or thereabouts, at most,
And time well spent in school cannot be lost.
But what makes you frown, you gentlemen above?
We guess'd long since you all desired to move:
But that's in vain, for we'll not let a man stir,
Who does not take up Plautus first, and conster,
Him we'll dismiss, that understands the play;
He who does not, i'faith, he's like to stay.
Though this new method may provoke your laughter,
To act plays first, and understand them after;
We do not care, for we will have our humour,
And will try you, and you, and you, sir, and one or two more.
Why don't you stir? there's not a man will budge;
How much they've read, I leave you all to judge.

The Song

A parody on the popular song beginning,
"My time, O ye Muses, was happily spent."

My time, O ye Grattans, was happily spent,
When Bacchus went with me, wherever I went;
For then I did nothing but sing, laugh, and jest;
Was ever a toper so merrily blest?
But now I so cross, and so peevish am grown,
Because I must go to my wife back to town;
To the fondling and toying of "honey," and "dear,"
And the conjugal comforts of horrid small beer.
    My daughter I ever was pleased to see
Come fawning and begging to ride on my knee:
My wife, too, was pleased, and to the child said,
Come, hold in your belly, and hold up your head:
But now out of humour, I with a sour look,
Cry, hussy, and give her a souse with my book;
And I'll give her another; for why should she play,
Since my Bacchus, and glasses, and friends, are away?
    Wine, what of thy delicate hue is become,
That tinged our glasses with blue, like a plum?
Those bottles, those bumpers, why do they not smile,
While we sit carousing and drinking the while?
Ah, bumpers, I see that our wine is all done,
Our mirth falls of course, when our Bacchus is gone.
Then since it is so, bring me here a supply;
Begone, froward wife, for I'll drink till I die.

A New Year's Gift for the Dean of St. Patrick's Given him at Quilca. By Sheridan 1723

How few can be of grandeur sure!
The high may fall, the rich be poor.
The only favourite at court,
To-morrow may be Fortune's sport;
For all her pleasure and her aim
Is to destroy both power and fame.
Of this the Dean is an example,
No instance is more plain and ample.
The world did never yet produce,
For courts a man of greater use.
Nor has the world supplied as yet,
With more vivacity and wit;
Merry alternately and wise,
To please the statesman, and advise.
Through all the last and glorious reign,
Was nothing done without the Dean;
The courtier's prop, the nation's pride;
But now, alas! he's thrown aside;
He's quite forgot, and so's the queen,
As if they both had never been.
To see him now a mountaineer!
Oh! what a mighty fall is here!
From settling governments and thrones,
To splitting rocks, and piling stones.
Instead of Bolingbroke and Anna,
Shane Tunnally, and Bryan Granna,
Oxford and Ormond he supplies,
In every Irish Teague he spies:
So far forgetting his old station,
He seems to like their conversation,
Conforming to the tatter'd rabble,

He learns their Irish tongue to gabble;
And, what our anger more provokes,
He's pleased with their insipid jokes;
Then turns and asks them who do lack a
Good plug, or pipefull of tobacco.
All cry they want, to every man
He gives, extravagant, a span.
Thus are they grown more fond than ever,
And he is highly in their favour.
Bright Stella, Quilca's greatest pride,
For them he scorns and lays aside;
And Sheridan is left alone
All day, to gape, and stretch, and groan;
While grumbling, poor, complaining Dingley,
Is left to care and trouble singly.
All o'er the mountains spreads the rumour,
Both of his bounty and good humour;
So that each shepherdess and swain
Comes flocking here to see the Dean.
All spread around the land, you'd swear
That every day we kept a fair.
My fields are brought to such a pass,
I have not left a blade of grass;
That all my wethers and my beeves
Are slighted by the very thieves.
At night right loath to quit the park,
His work just ended by the dark,
With all his pioneers he comes,
To make more work for whisk and brooms.
Then seated in an elbow-chair,
To take a nap he does prepare;
While two fair damsels from the lawns,
Lull him asleep with soft cronawns.
Thus are his days in delving spent,
His nights in music and content;
He seems to gain by his distress,
His friends are more, his honours less.

To Quilca
A Country-House of Dr. Sheridan, in no very good Repair. 1725

Let me thy properties explain:
A rotten cabin, dropping rain:
Chimneys, with scorn rejecting smoke;
Stools, tables, chairs, and bedsteads broke.
Here elements have lost their uses,
Air ripens not, nor earth produces:
In vain we make poor Sheelah toil,
Fire will not roast, nor water boil.
Through all the valleys, hills, and plains,
The goddess Want, in triumph reigns;
And her chief officers of state,
Sloth, Dirt, and Theft, around her wait.

The Blessings of a Country Life
1725

Far from our debtors; no Dublin letters;
Not seen by our betters.

The Plagues of a Country Life

A companion with news; a great want of shoes;
Eat lean meat or choose; a church without pews;
Our horses away; no straw, oats, or hay;
December in May; our boys run away; all servants at play.

A Faithful Inventory Of the Furniture Belonging to—— Room in T. C. D. In Imitation of Dr. Swift's Manner. Written in the Year 1725

——quaeque ipse miserrima vidi.

This description of a scholar's room in Trinity College, Dublin, was found among Mr. Smith's papers. It is not in the Dean's hand, but seems to have been the production of Sheridan.

Imprimis, there's a table blotted,
A tatter'd hanging all bespotted.
A bed of flocks, as I may rank it,
Reduced to rug and half a blanket.
A tinder box without a flint,
An oaken desk with nothing in't;
A pair of tongs bought from a broker,
A fender and a rusty poker;
A penny pot and basin, this
Design'd for water, that for piss;
A broken-winded pair of bellows,
Two knives and forks, but neither fellows.
Item, a surplice, not unmeeting,
Either for table-cloth, or sheeting;
There is likewise a pair of breeches,
But patch'd, and fallen in the stitches,
Hung up in study very little,
Plaster'd with cobweb and spittle,
An airy prospect all so pleasing,
From my light window without glazing,
A trencher and a College bottle,
Piled up on Locke and Aristotle.
A prayer-book, which he seldom handles
A save-all and two farthing candles.
A smutty ballad, musty libel,

A Burgersdicius and a Bible.
The C**** Seasons and the Senses
By Overton, to save expenses.
Item, (if I am not much mistaken,)
A mouse-trap with a bit of bacon.
A candlestick without a snuffer,
Whereby his fingers often suffer.
Two odd old shoes I should not skip here,
Each strapless serves instead of slippers,
And chairs a couple, I forgot 'em,
But each of them without a bottom.
Thus I in rhyme have comprehended
His goods, and so my schedule's ended.

Palinodia

Horace, Book I, Ode XVI

Great Sir, than Phoebus more divine,
Whose verses far his rays outshine,
    Look down upon your quondam foe;
O! let me never write again,
If e'er I disoblige you, Dean,
    Should you compassion show.

Take those iambics which I wrote,
When anger made me piping hot,
    And give them to your cook,
To singe your fowl, or save your paste
The next time when you have a feast;
    They'll save you many a book.

To burn them, you are not content;
I give you then my free consent,
    To sink them in the harbour;
If not, they'll serve to set off blocks,
To roll on pipes, and twist in locks;
    So give them to your barber.

Or, when you next your physic take,
I must entreat you then to make
    A proper application;
'Tis what I've done myself before,
With Dan's fine thoughts and many more,
    Who gave me provocation.

What cannot mighty anger do?
It makes the weak the strong pursue,
    A goose attack a swan;
It makes a woman, tooth and nail,
Her husband's hands and face assail,
    While he's no longer man.

Though some, we find, are more discreet,
Before the world are wondrous sweet,
    And let their husbands hector:
But when the world's asleep, they wake,
That is the time they choose to speak:
    Witness the curtain lecture.

Such was the case with you, I find:
All day you could conceal your mind;
    But when St. Patrick's chimes
Awaked your muse, (my midnight curse,
When I engaged for better for worse,)
    You scolded with your rhymes.

Have done! have done! I quit the field,
To you as to my wife, I yield:
    As she must wear the breeches:
So shall you wear the laurel crown,
Win it and wear it, 'tis your own;
    The poet's only riches.

A Letter to the Dean When in England. 1726. By Dr. Sheridan

You will excuse me, I suppose,
For sending rhyme instead of prose.
Because hot weather makes me lazy,
To write in metre is more easy.
    While you are trudging London town,
I'm strolling Dublin up and down;
While you converse with lords and dukes,
I have their betters here, my books:
Fix'd in an elbow-chair at ease,
I choose companions as I please.
I'd rather have one single shelf
Than all my friends, except yourself;
For, after all that can be said,
Our best acquaintance are the dead.
While you're in raptures with Faustina;
I'm charm'd at home with our Sheelina.
While you are starving there in state,
I'm cramming here with butchers' meat.
You say, when with those lords you dine,
They treat you with the best of wine,
Burgundy, Cyprus, and Tokay;
Why, so can we, as well as they.
No reason then, my dear good Dean,
But you should travel home again.
What though you mayn't in Ireland hope
To find such folk as Gay and Pope;
If you with rhymers here would share
But half the wit that you can spare,
I'd lay twelve eggs, that in twelve days,
You'd make a dozen of Popes and Gays.
    Our weather's good, our sky is clear;
We've every joy, if you were here;
So lofty and so bright a sky
Was never seen by Ireland's eye!
I think it fit to let you know,

This week I shall to Quilca go;
To see M'Faden's horny brothers
First suck, and after bull their mothers;
To see, alas! my wither'd trees!
To see what all the country sees!
My stunted quicks, my famish'd beeves,
My servants such a pack of thieves;
My shatter'd firs, my blasted oaks,
My house in common to all folks,
No cabbage for a single snail,
My turnips, carrots, parsneps, fail;
My no green peas, my few green sprouts;
My mother always in the pouts;
My horses rid, or gone astray;
My fish all stolen or run away;
My mutton lean, my pullets old,
My poultry starved, the corn all sold.
A man come now from Quilca says,
"*They*'ve stolen the locks from all your keys;"
But, what must fret and vex me more,
He says, "*They* stole the keys before.
They've stol'n the knives from all the forks;
And half the cows from half the sturks."
Nay more, the fellow swears and vows,
"*They*'ve stol'n the sturks from half the cows:"
With many more accounts of woe,
Yet, though the devil be there, I'll go:
'Twixt you and me, the reason's clear,
Because I've more vexation here.

An Invitation to Dinner
From Doctor Sheridan to Doctor Swift
1727

I've sent to the ladies this morning to warn 'em,
To order their chaise, and repair to Rathfarnam;
Where you shall be welcome to dine, if your deanship
Can take up with me, and my friend Stella's leanship.
I've got you some soles, and a fresh bleeding bret,
That's just disengaged from the toils of a net:
An excellent loin of fat veal to be roasted,
With lemons, and butter, and sippets well toasted:
Some larks that descended, mistaking the skies,
Which Stella brought down by the light of her eyes;
And there, like Narcissus, they gazed till they died,
And now they're to lie in some crumbs that are fried.
My wine will inspire you with joy and delight,
'Tis mellow, and old, and sparkling, and bright;
An emblem of one that you love, I suppose,
Who gathers more lovers the older she grows.
Let me be your Gay, and let Stella be Pope,
We'll wean you from sighing for England I hope;
When we are together there's nothing that is dull,
There's nothing like Durfey, or Smedley, or Tisdall.
We've sworn to make out an agreeable feast,
Our dinner, our wine, and our wit to your taste.

Your answer in half-an-hour, though you are at prayers;
you have a pencil in your pocket.

On the Five Ladies at Sot's Hole With the Doctor at their Head

N.B. The Ladies treated the Doctor.
Sent as from an Officer in the Army. 1728

Fair ladies, number five,
Who in your merry freaks,
With little Tom contrive
To feast on ale and steaks;

While he sits by a-grinning,
To see you safe in Sot's Hole,
Set up with greasy linen,
And neither mugs nor pots whole;

Alas! I never thought
A priest would please your palate;
Besides, I'll hold a groat
He'll put you in a ballad;

Where I shall see your faces,
On paper daub'd so foul,
They'll be no more like graces,
Than Venus like an owl.

And we shall take you rather
To be a midnight pack
Of witches met together,
With Beelzebub in black.

It fills my heart with woe,
To think such ladies fine
Should be reduced so low,
To treat a dull divine.

Be by a parson cheated!
Had you been cunning stagers,

You might yourselves be treated
    By captains and by majors.

See how corruption grows,
    While mothers, daughters, aunts,
Instead of powder'd beaux,
    From pulpits choose gallants.

If we, who wear our wigs
    With fantail and with snake,
Are bubbled thus by prigs;
    Z——ds! who would be a rake?

Had I a heart to fight,
    I'd knock the Doctor down;
Or could I read or write,
    Egad! I'd wear a gown.

Then leave him to his birch;
    And at the Rose on Sunday,
The parson safe at church,
    I'll treat you with burgundy.

The Five Ladies' Answer to the Beau

With the Wig and Wings at his Head
By Dr. Sheridan

You little scribbling beau,
  What demon made you write?
Because to write you know
  As much as you can fight.

For compliment so scurvy,
  I wish we had you here;
We'd turn you topsy-turvy
  Into a mug of beer.

You thought to make a farce on
  The man and place we chose;
We're sure a single parson
  Is worth a hundred beaux.

And you would make us vassals,
  Good Mr. Wig and Wings,
To silver clocks and tassels;
  You would, you Thing of Things!

Because around your cane
  A ring of diamonds is set;
And you, in some by-lane,
  Have gain'd a paltry grisette;

Shall we, of sense refined,
  Your trifling nonsense bear,
As noisy as the wind,
  As empty as the air?

We hate your empty prattle;
    And vow and swear 'tis true,
There's more in one child's rattle,
    Than twenty fops like you.

The Beau's Reply to the Five Ladies' Answer

Why, how now, dapper black!
    I smell your gown and cassock,
As strong upon your back,
    As Tisdall smells of a sock.

To write such scurvy stuff!
    Fine ladies never do't;
I know you well enough,
    And eke your cloven foot.

Fine ladies, when they write,
    Nor scold, nor keep a splutter:
Their verses give delight,
    As soft and sweet as butter.

But Satan never saw
    Such haggard lines as these:
They stick athwart my maw,
    As bad as Suffolk cheese.

Dr. Sheridan's Ballad on Bally-Spellin. 1728

All you that would refine your blood,
As pure as famed Llewellyn,
By waters clear, come every year
To drink at Ballyspellin.

Though pox or itch your skins enrich
With rubies past the telling,
'Twill clear your skin before you've been
A month at Ballyspellin.

If lady's cheek be green as leek
When she comes from her dwelling,
The kindling rose within it glows
When she's at Ballyspellin.

The sooty brown, who comes from town,
Grows here as fair as Helen;
Then back she goes, to kill the beaux,
By dint of Ballyspellin.

Our ladies are as fresh and fair
As Rose, or bright Dunkelling:
And Mars might make a fair mistake,
Were he at Ballyspellin.

We men submit as they think fit,
And here is no rebelling:
The reason's plain; the ladies reign,
They're queens at Ballyspellin.

By matchless charms, unconquer'd arms,
They have the way of quelling
Such desperate foes as dare oppose
Their power at Ballyspellin.

Cold water turns to fire, and burns
    I know, because I fell in
A stream, which came from one bright dame
    Who drank at Ballyspellin.

Fine beaux advance, equipt for dance,
    To bring their Anne or Nell in,
With so much grace, I'm sure no place
    Can vie with Ballyspellin.

No politics, no subtle tricks,
    No man his country selling:
We eat, we drink; we never think
    Of these at Ballyspellin.

The troubled mind, the puff'd with wind,
    Do all come here pell-mell in;
And they are sure to work their cure
    By drinking Ballyspellin.

Though dropsy fills you to the gills,
    From chin to toe though swelling,
Pour in, pour out, you cannot doubt
    A cure at Ballyspellin.

Death throws no darts through all these parts,
    No sextons here are knelling;
Come, judge and try, you'll never die,
    But live at Ballyspellin.

Except you feel darts tipp'd with steel,
    Which here are every belle in:
When from their eyes sweet ruin flies,
    We die at Ballyspellin.

Good cheer, sweet air, much joy, no care,
    Your sight, your taste, your smelling,
Your ears, your touch, transported much
    Each day at Ballyspellin.

Within this ground we all sleep sound,
    No noisy dogs a-yelling;
Except you wake, for Celia's sake,
    All night at Ballyspellin.

There all you see, both he and she,
    No lady keeps her cell in;
But all partake the mirth we make,
    Who drink at Ballyspellin.

My rhymes are gone; I think I've none,
    Unless I should bring Hell in;
But, since I'm here to Heaven so near,
    I can't at Ballyspellin!

Answer. By Dr. Swift

Dare you dispute, you saucy brute,
And think there's no refelling
Your scurvy lays, and senseless praise
You give to Ballyspellin?

Howe'er you flounce, I here pronounce,
Your medicine is repelling;
Your water's mud, and sours the blood
When drunk at Ballyspellin.

Those pocky drabs, to cure their scabs,
You thither are compelling,
Will back be sent worse than they went,
From nasty Ballyspellin.

Llewellyn why? As well may I
Name honest Doctor Pellin;
So hard sometimes you tug for rhymes,
To bring in Ballyspellin.

No subject fit to try your wit,
When you went colonelling:
But dull intrigues 'twixt jades and teagues,
You met at Ballyspellin.

Our lasses fair, say what you dare,
Who sowins make with shelling,
At Market-hill more beaux can kill,
Than yours at Ballyspellin.

Would I was whipt, when Sheelah stript,
To wash herself our well in,
A bum so white ne'er came in sight
At paltry Ballyspellin.

Your mawkins there smocks hempen wear;
    Of Holland not an ell in,
No, not a rag, whate'er your brag,
    Is found at Ballyspellin.

But Tom will prate at any rate,
    All other nymphs expelling:
Because he gets a few grisettes
    At lousy Ballyspellin.

There's bonny Jane, in yonder lane,
    Just o'er against the Bell inn;
Where can you meet a lass so sweet,
    Round all your Ballyspellin?

We have a girl deserves an earl;
    She came from Enniskellin;
So fair, so young, no such among
    The belles of Ballyspellin.

How would you stare, to see her there,
    The foggy mists dispelling,
That cloud the brows of every blowse
    Who lives at Ballyspellin!

Now, as I live, I would not give
    A stiver or a skellin,
To towse and kiss the fairest miss
    That leaks at Ballyspellin.

Whoe'er will raise such lies as these
    Deserves a good cudgelling:
Who falsely boasts of belles and toasts
    At dirty Ballyspellin.

My rhymes are gone to all but one,
    Which is, our trees are felling;
As proper quite as those you write,
    To force in Ballyspellin.

An Epistle to two Friends

To Dr. Helsham

Nov. 23, at night, 1731

Sir,
When I left you, I found myself of the grape's juice sick;
I'm so full of pity I never abuse sick;
And the patientest patient ever you knew sick;
Both when I am purge-sick, and when I am spew-sick.
I pitied my cat, whom I knew by her mew sick:
She mended at first, but now she's anew sick.
Captain Butler made some in the church black and blue sick.
Dean Cross, had he preach'd, would have made us all pew-sick.
Are not you, in a crowd when you sweat and you stew, sick?
Lady Santry got out of the church when she grew sick,
And as fast as she could, to the deanery flew sick.
Miss Morice was (I can assure you 'tis true) sick:
For, who would not be in that numerous crew sick?
Such music would make a fanatic or Jew sick,
Yet, ladies are seldom at ombre or loo sick.
Nor is old Nanny Shales, whene'er she does brew, sick.
My footman came home from the church of a bruise sick,
And look'd like a rake, who was made in the stews sick:
But you learned doctors can make whom you choose sick:
And poor I myself was, when I withdrew, sick:
For the smell of them made me like garlic and rue sick,
And I got through the crowd, though not led by a clew, sick.
Yet hoped to find many (for that was your cue) sick;
But there was not a dozen (to give them their due) sick,
And those, to be sure, stuck together like glue sick.
So are ladies in crowds, when they squeeze and they screw, sick;
You may find they are all, by their yellow pale hue, sick;
So am I, when tobacco, like Robin, I chew, sick.

To Dr. Sheridan

Nov. 23, at night

If I write any more, it will make my poor Muse sick.
This night I came home with a very cold dew sick,
And I wish I may soon be not of an ague sick;
But I hope I shall ne'er be like you, of a shrew sick,
Who often has made me, by looking askew, sick.

Dr. Helsham's Answer

The Doctor's first rhyme would make any Jew sick:
I know it has made a fine lady in blue sick,
For which she is gone in a coach to Killbrew sick,
Like a hen I once had, from a fox when she flew sick:
Last Monday a lady at St. Patrick's did spew sick:
And made all the rest of the folks in the pew sick,
The surgeon who bled her his lancet out drew sick,
And stopp'd the distemper, as being but new sick.
The yacht, the last storm, had all her whole crew sick;
Had we two been there, it would have made me and you sick:
A lady that long'd, is by eating of glue sick;
Did you ever know one in a very good Q sick?
I'm told that my wife is by winding a clew sick;
The doctors have made her by rhyme and by rue sick.
    There's a gamester in town, for a throw that he threw sick,
And yet the whole trade of his dice he'll pursue sick;
I've known an old miser for paying his due sick;
At present I'm grown by a pinch of my shoe sick,
And what would you have me with verses to do sick?
Send rhymes, and I'll send you some others in lieu sick.

Of rhymes I have plenty,
And therefore send twenty.

Answered the same day when sent, Nov. 23.

I desire you will carry both these to the Doctor together with his own; and let him know we are not persons to be insulted.

I was at Howth to-day, and staid abroad a-visiting till just now.

Tuesday Evening, Nov. 23, 1731.

"Can you match with me,
Who send thirty-three?
You must get fourteen more,

To make up thirty-four:
But, if me you can conquer,
I'll own you a strong cur."

This morning I'm growing, by smelling of yew, sick;
My brother's come over with gold from Peru sick;
Last night I came home in a storm that then blew sick;
This moment my dog at a cat I halloo sick;
I hear from good hands, that my poor cousin Hugh's sick;
By quaffing a bottle, and pulling a screw sick:
And now there's no more I can write (you'll excuse) sick;
You see that I scorn to mention word music.

I'll do my best,
To send the rest;
Without a jest,
I'll stand the test.

These lines that I send you, I hope you'll peruse sick;
I'll make you with writing a little more news sick;
Last night I came home with drinking of booze sick;
My carpenter swears that he'll hack and he'll hew sick.
An officer's lady, I'm told, is tattoo sick;
I'm afraid that the line thirty-four you will view sick.
Lord! I could write a dozen more;
You see I've mounted thirty-four.

A True and Faithful Inventory Of the Goods Belonging to Dr. Swift, Vicar of Laracor. Upon Lending his House to the Bishop of Meath, Until His Own was Built

An oaken broken elbow-chair;
A caudle cup without an ear;
A batter'd, shatter'd ash bedstead;
A box of deal, without a lid;
A pair of tongs, but out of joint;
A back-sword poker, without point;
A pot that's crack'd across, around,
With an old knotted garter bound;
An iron lock, without a key;
A wig, with hanging, grown quite grey;
A curtain, worn to half a stripe;
A pair of bellows, without pipe;
A dish, which might good meat afford once;
An Ovid, and an old Concordance;
A bottle-bottom, wooden-platter
One is for meal, and one for water;
There likewise is a copper skillet,
Which runs as fast out as you fill it;
A candlestick, snuff-dish, and save-all,
And thus his household goods you have all.
These, to your lordship, as a friend,
'Till you have built, I freely lend:
They'll serve your lordship for a shift;
Why not as well as Doctor Swift?

A New Simile for the Ladies With Useful Annotations, by Dr. Sheridan 1733

To make a writer miss his end,
You've nothing else to do but mend.

I often tried in vain to find
A simile for womankind,
A simile, I mean, to fit 'em,
In every circumstance to hit 'em.
Through every beast and bird I went,
I ransack'd every element;
And, after peeping through all nature,
To find so whimsical a creature,
A cloud presented to my view,
And straight this parallel I drew:
Clouds turn with every wind about,
They keep us in suspense and doubt,
Yet, oft perverse, like womankind,
Are seen to scud against the wind:
And are not women just the same?
For who can tell at what they aim?
Clouds keep the stoutest mortals under,
When, bellowing, they discharge their thunder:
So, when the alarum-bell is rung,
Of Xanti's everlasting tongue,
The husband dreads its loudness more
Than lightning's flash, or thunder's roar.
Clouds weep, as they do, without pain;
And what are tears but women's rain?
The clouds about the welkin roam:
And ladies never stay at home.
The clouds build castles in the air,
A thing peculiar to the fair:
For all the schemes of their forecasting,

Are not more solid nor more lasting.
A cloud is light by turns, and dark,
Such is a lady with her spark;
Now with a sudden pouting gloom
She seems to darken all the room;
Again she's pleased, his fear's beguiled,
And all is clear when she has smiled.
In this they're wondrously alike,
(I hope the simile will strike,)
Though in the darkest dumps you view them,
Stay but a moment, you'll see through them.
The clouds are apt to make reflection,
And frequently produce infection;
So Celia, with small provocation,
Blasts every neighbour's reputation.
The clouds delight in gaudy show,
(For they, like ladies, have their bow;)
The gravest matron will confess,
That she herself is fond of dress.
Observe the clouds in pomp array'd,
What various colours are display'd;
The pink, the rose, the violet's dye,
In that great drawing-room the sky;
How do these differ from our Graces,
In garden-silks, brocades, and laces?
Are they not such another sight,
When met upon a birth-day night?
The clouds delight to change their fashion:
(Dear ladies, be not in a passion!)
Nor let this whim to you seem strange,
Who every hour delight in change.
In them and you alike are seen
The sullen symptoms of the spleen;
The moment that your vapours rise,
We see them dropping from your eyes.
In evening fair you may behold
The clouds are fringed with borrow'd gold;
And this is many a lady's case,
Who flaunts about in borrow'd lace.

Grave matrons are like clouds of snow,
Their words fall thick, and soft, and slow;
While brisk coquettes, like rattling hail,
Our ears on every side assail.
Clouds, when they intercept our sight,
Deprive us of celestial light:
So when my Chloe I pursue,
No heaven besides I have in view.
Thus, on comparison, you see,
In every instance they agree;
So like, so very much the same,
That one may go by t'other's name.
Let me proclaim it then aloud,
That every woman is a cloud.

An Answer to a Scandalous Poem

Wherein the Author most audaciously presumes to cast an indignity upon their highnesses the Clouds, by comparing them to a woman. Written by Dermot O'Nephely, Chief Cape of Howth.

By Dr. Swift

Advertisement from the Clouds

N.B. The following answer to that scurrilous libel against us, should have been published long ago in our own justification: But it was advised, that, considering the high importance of the subject, it should be deferred until the meeting of the General Assembly of the Nation.

(Two passages within crotchets are added to this poem, from a copy found amongst Swift's papers. It is indorsed, "Quære, should it go." And a little lower, "More, but of no use.")

Presumptuous bard! how could you dare
A woman with a cloud compare?
Strange pride and insolence you show
Inferior mortals there below.
And is our thunder in your ears
So frequent or so loud as theirs?
Alas! our thunder soon goes out;
And only makes you more devout.
Then is not female clatter worse,
That drives you not to pray, but curse?
We hardly thunder thrice a-year;
The bolt discharged, the sky grows clear;
But every sublunary dowdy,
The more she scolds, the more she's cloudy.
(How useful were a woman's thunder,
If she, like us, would burst asunder!
Yet, though her stays hath often cursed her,
And, whisp'ring, wish'd the devil burst her:
For hourly thund'ring in his face,

She ne'er was known to burst a lace.)
Some critic may object, perhaps,
That clouds are blamed for giving claps;
But what, alas! are claps ethereal,
Compared for mischief to venereal?
Can clouds give buboes, ulcers, blotches,
Or from your noses dig out notches?
We leave the body sweet and sound;
We kill, 'tis true, but never wound.
You know a cloudy sky bespeaks
Fair weather when the morning breaks;
But women in a cloudy plight,
Foretell a storm to last till night.
A cloud in proper season pours
His blessings down in fruitful showers;
But woman was by fate design'd
To pour down curses on mankind.
When Sirius o'er the welkin rages,
Our kindly help his fire assuages;
But woman is a cursed inflamer,
No parish ducking-stool can tame her:
To kindle strife, dame Nature taught her;
Like fireworks, she can burn in water.
For fickleness how durst you blame us,
Who for our constancy are famous?
You'll see a cloud in gentle weather
Keep the same face an hour together;
While women, if it could be reckon'd,
Change every feature every second.
Observe our figure in a morning,
Of foul or fair we give you warning;
But can you guess from women's air
One minute, whether foul or fair?
Go read in ancient books enroll'd
What honours we possess'd of old.
To disappoint Ixion's rape
Jove dress'd a cloud in Juno's shape;
Which when he had enjoy'd, he swore,
No goddess could have pleased him more;

No difference could he find between
His cloud and Jove's imperial queen;
His cloud produced a race of Centaurs,
Famed for a thousand bold adventures;
From us descended *ab origine*,
By learned authors, called *nubigenae*;
But say, what earthly nymph do you know,
So beautiful to pass for Juno?
    Before Æneas durst aspire
To court her majesty of Tyre,
His mother begg'd of us to dress him,
That Dido might the more caress him:
A coat we gave him, dyed in grain,
A flaxen wig, and clouded cane,
(The wig was powder'd round with sleet,
Which fell in clouds beneath his feet)
With which he made a tearing show;
And Dido quickly smoked the beau.
    Among your females make inquiries,
What nymph on earth so fair as Iris?
With heavenly beauty so endow'd?
And yet her father is a cloud.
We dress'd her in a gold brocade,
Befitting Juno's favourite maid.
    'Tis known that Socrates the wise
Adored us clouds as deities:
To us he made his daily prayers,
As Aristophanes declares;
From Jupiter took all dominion,
And died defending his opinion.
By his authority 'tis plain
You worship other gods in vain;
And from your own experience know
We govern all things there below.
You follow where we please to guide;
O'er all your passions we preside,
Can raise them up, or sink them down,
As we think fit to smile or frown:
And, just as we dispose your brain,

Are witty, dull, rejoice, complain.
Compare us then to female race!
We, to whom all the gods give place!
Who better challenge your allegiance
Because we dwell in higher regions.
You find the gods in Homer dwell
In seas and streams, or low as Hell:
Ev'n Jove, and Mercury his pimp,
No higher climb than mount Olymp.
Who makes you think the clouds he pierces?
He pierce the clouds! he kiss their a—es;
While we, o'er Teneriffa placed,
Are loftier by a mile at least:
And, when Apollo struts on Pindus,
We see him from our kitchen windows;
Or, to Parnassus looking down,
Can piss upon his laurel crown.
Fate never form'd the gods to fly;
In vehicles they mount the sky:
When Jove would some fair nymph inveigle,
He comes full gallop on his eagle;
Though Venus be as light as air,
She must have doves to draw her chair;
Apollo stirs not out of door,
Without his lacquer'd coach and four;
And jealous Juno, ever snarling,
Is drawn by peacocks in her berlin:
But we can fly where'er we please,
O'er cities, rivers, hills, and seas:
From east to west the world we roam,
And in all climates are at home;
With care provide you as we go
With sunshine, rain, and hail, or snow.
You, when it rains, like fools, believe
Jove pisses on you through a sieve:
An idle tale, 'tis no such matter;
We only dip a sponge in water,
Then squeeze it close between our thumbs,
And shake it well, and down it comes;

As you shall to your sorrow know;
We'll watch your steps where'er you go;
And, since we find you walk a-foot,
We'll soundly souse your frieze surtout.
'Tis but by our peculiar grace,
That Phoebus ever shows his face;
For, when we please, we open wide
Our curtains blue from side to side;
And then how saucily he shows
His brazen face and fiery nose;
And gives himself a haughty air,
As if he made the weather fair!
'Tis sung, wherever Celia treads,
The violets ope their purple heads;
The roses blow, the cowslip springs;
'Tis sung; but we know better things.
'Tis true, a woman on her mettle
Will often piss upon a nettle;
But though we own she makes it wetter,
The nettle never thrives the better;
While we, by soft prolific showers,
Can every spring produce you flowers.
Your poets, Chloe's beauty height'ning,
Compare her radiant eyes to lightning;
And yet I hope 'twill be allow'd,
That lightning comes but from a cloud.
But gods like us have too much sense
At poets' flights to take offence;
Nor can hyperboles demean us;
Each drab has been compared to Venus.
We own your verses are melodious;
But such comparisons are odious.
(Observe the case—I state it thus:
Though you compare your trull to us,
But think how damnably you err
When you compare us clouds to her;
From whence you draw such bold conclusions;
But poets love profuse allusions.
And, if you now so little spare us,

Who knows how soon you may compare us
To Chartres, Walpole, or a king,
If once we let you have your swing.
Such wicked insolence appears
Offensive to all pious ears.
To flatter women by a metaphor!
What profit could you hope to get of her?
And, for her sake, turn base detractor
Against your greatest benefactor.
    But we shall keep revenge in store
If ever you provoke us more:
For, since we know you walk a-foot,
We'll soundly drench your frieze surtout;
Or may we never thunder throw,
Nor souse to death a birth-day beau.
    We own your verses are melodious;
But such comparisons are odious.)

Peg Radcliffe the Hostess's Invitation

To the Reverend Dr. Swift, D.S.P.D. written with a design to be spoken by her on his arrival at Glassnevin, Dr. Delany having complimented him with a house there. From the London and Dublin Magazine for June, 1735. The lines are probably by Delany or Sheridan.

Though the name of this place may make you to frown,
Your Deanship is welcome to *Glassnevin* town;
A glass and no wine, to a man of your taste,
Alas! is enough, sir, to break it in haste;
Be that as it will, your presence can't fail
To yield great delight in drinking our ale;
Would you but vouchsafe a mug to partake,
And as we can brew, believe we can bake.
The life and the pleasure we now from you hope,
The famed Violante can't show on the rope;
Your genius and talents outdo even Pope.
Then while, sir, you live at Glassnevin, and find
The benefit wish'd you, by friends who are kind;
One night in the week, sir, your favour bestow,
To drink with Delany and others your know:
They constantly meet at Peg Radcliffe's together,
Talk over the news of the town and the weather;
Reflect on mishaps in church and in state,
Digest many things as well as good meat;
And club each alike that no one may treat.
This if you will grant without coach or chair,
You may, in a trice, cross the way and be there;
For Peg is your neighbour, as well as Delany,
A housewifely woman full pleasing to any.

Verses by Sheridan

When to my house you come, dear Dean,
Your humble friend to entertain,
Through dirt and mire along the street,
You find no scraper for your feet;
At which you stamp and storm and swell,
Which serves to clean your feet as well.
By steps ascending to the hall,
All torn to rags by boys and ball,
With scatter'd fragments on the floor;
A sad, uneasy parlour door,
Besmear'd with chalk, and carved with knives,
(A plague upon all careless wives,)
Are the next sights you must expect,
But do not think they are my neglect.
Ah that these evils were the worst!
The parlour still is farther curst.
To enter there if you advance,
If in you get, it is by chance.
How oft by turns have you and I
Said thus—"Let me—no—let me try—
This turn will open it, I'll engage"—
You push me from it in a rage.
Turning, twisting, forcing, fumbling,
Stamping, staring, fuming, grumbling,
At length it opens—in we go—
How glad are we to find it so!
Conquests through pains and dangers please,
Much more than those attain'd with ease.
Are you disposed to take a seat;
The instant that it feels your weight,
Out goes its legs, and down you come
Upon your reverend deanship's bum.
Betwixt two stools, 'tis often said,
The sitter on the ground is laid;
What praise then to my chairs is due,
Where one performs the feat of two!

Now to the fire, if such there be,
At present nought but smoke we see.
"Come, stir it up!"—"Ho, Mr. Joker,
How can I stir it without a poker?"
"The bellows take, their batter'd nose
Will serve for poker, I suppose."
Now you begin to rake—alack
The grate has tumbled from its back—
The coals all on the hearth are laid—
"Stay, sir—I'll run and call the maid;
She'll make the fire again complete—
She knows the humour of the grate."
"Pox take your maid and you together—
This is cold comfort in cold weather."
Now all is right again—the blaze
Suddenly raised as soon decays.
Once more apply the bellows—"So—
These bellows were not made to blow—
Their leathern lungs are in decay,
They can't even puff the smoke away."
"And is your reverence vext at that,
Get up, in God's name, take your hat;
Hang them, say I, that have no shift;
Come blow the fire, good Doctor Swift.
If trifles such as these can tease you,
Plague take those fools that strive to please you.
Therefore no longer be a quarrel'r
Either with me, sir, or my parlour.
If you can relish ought of mine,
A bit of meat, a glass of wine,
You're welcome to it, and you shall fare
As well as dining with the mayor."
"You saucy scab—you tell me so!
Why, booby-face, I'd have you know
I'd rather see your things in order,
Than dine in state with the recorder.
For water I must keep a clutter,
Or chide your wife for stinking butter;
Or getting such a deal of meat

As if you'd half the town to eat.
That wife of yours, the devil's in her,
I've told her of this way of dinner
Five hundred times, but all in vain—
Here comes a rump of beef again:
O that that wife of yours would burst—
Get out, and serve the boarders first.
Pox take 'em all for me—I fret
So much, I shall not eat my meat—
You know I'd rather have a slice."
"I know, dear sir, you are not nice;
You'll have your dinner in a minute,
Here comes the plate and slices in it—
Therefore no more, but take your place—
Do you fall to, and I'll say grace."

Verses Addressed to Swift and to his Memory

To Dr. Swift on His Birth-Day

While I the godlike men of old,
In admiration wrapt, behold;
Revered antiquity explore,
And turn the long-lived volumes o'er;
Where Cato, Plutarch, Flaccus, shine
In every excellence divine;
I grieve that our degenerate days
Produce no mighty soul like these:
Patriot, philosopher, and bard,
Are names unknown, and seldom heard.
"Spare your reflection," Phoebus cries;
"'Tis as ungrateful as unwise:
Can you complain, this sacred day,
That virtues or that arts decay?
Behold, in Swift revived appears:
The virtues of unnumber'd years;
Behold in him, with new delight,
The patriot, bard, and sage unite;
And know, Iërne in that name
Shall rival Greece and Rome in fame."

On Dr. Swift
1733

No pedant Bentley proud, uncouth,
Nor sweetening dedicator smooth,
In one attempt has ever dared
To sap, or storm, this mighty bard,
Nor Envy does, nor ignorance,
Make on his works the least advance.
For *this*, behold! still flies afar
Where'er his genius does appear;
Nor has *that* aught to do above,
So meddles not with Swift and Jove.
A faithful, universal fame
In glory spreads abroad his name;
Pronounces Swift, with loudest breath,
Immortal grown before his death.

To the Rev. Dr. Swift, Dean of St. Patrick's A Birth-Day Poem. Nov. 30, 1736

To you, my true and faithful friend,
These tributary lines I send,
Which every year, thou best of deans,
I'll pay as long as life remains;
But did you know one half the pain
What work, what racking of the brain,
It costs me for a single clause,
How long I'm forced to think and pause;
How long I dwell upon a proem,
To introduce your birth-day poem,
How many blotted lines; I know it,
You'd have compassion for the poet.
    Now, to describe the way I think,
I take in hand my pen and ink;
I rub my forehead, scratch my head,
Revolving all the rhymes I read.
Each complimental thought sublime,
Reduced by favourite Pope to rhyme,
And those by you to Oxford writ,
With true simplicity and wit.
Yet after all I cannot find
One panegyric to my mind.
Now I begin to fret and blot,
Something I schemed, but quite forgot;
My fancy turns a thousand ways,
Through all the several forms of praise,
What eulogy may best become
The greatest dean in Christendom.
At last I've hit upon a thought——
Sure this will do—— 'tis good for nought——
This line I peevishly erase,
And choose another in its place;
Again I try, again commence,
But cannot well express the sense;
The line's too short to hold my meaning:

I'm cramp'd, and cannot bring the Dean in.
O for a rhyme to glorious birth!
I've hit upon't——The rhyme is earth——
But how to bring it in, or fit it,
I know not, so I'm forced to quit it.
    Again I try—I'll sing the man—
Ay do, says Phoebus, if you can;
I wish with all my heart you would not;
Were Horace now alive he could not:
And will you venture to pursue,
What none alive or dead could do?
Pray see, did ever Pope or Gay
Presume to write on his birth-day;
Though both were fav'rite bards of mine,
The task they wisely both decline.
    With grief I felt his admonition,
And much lamented my condition:
Because I could not be content
Without some grateful compliment,
If not the poet, sure the friend
Must something on your birth-day send.
    I scratch'd, and rubb'd my head once more:
"Let every patriot him adore."
Alack-a-day, there's nothing in't—
Such stuff will never do in print.
    Pray, reader, ponder well the sequel;
I hope this epigram will take well.
    In others, life is deem'd a vapour,
In Swift it is a lasting taper,
Whose blaze continually refines,
The more it burns the more it shines.
    I read this epigram again,
'Tis much too flat to fit the Dean.
    Then down I lay some scheme to dream on
Assisted by some friendly demon.
I slept, and dream'd that I should meet
A birth-day poem in the street;
So, after all my care and rout,
You see, dear Dean, my dream is out.

Epigrams Occasioned by Dr. Swift's Intended Hospital for Idiots and Lunatics

I

The Dean must die—our idiots to maintain!
Perish, ye idiots! and long live the Dean!

II

O Genius of Hibernia's state,
Sublimely good, severely great,
How doth this latest act excel
All you have done or wrote so well!
Satire may be the child of spite,
And fame might bid the Drapier write:
But to relieve, and to endow,
Creatures that know not whence or how
Argues a soul both good and wise,
Resembling Him who rules the skies,
He to the thoughtful mind displays
Immortal skill ten thousand ways;
And, to complete his glorious task,
Gives what we have not sense to ask!

III

Lo! Swift to idiots bequeaths his store:
Be wise, ye rich!—consider thus the poor!

IV

Great wits to madness nearly are allied,
This makes the Dean for kindred *thus* provide.

On the Dean of St. Patrick's Birth-Day Being Nov. 30, St. Andrew's Day

Between the hours of twelve and one,
When half the world to rest were gone,
Entranced in softest sleep I lay,
Forgetful of an anxious day;
From every care and labour free,
My soul as calm as it could be.
The queen of dreams, well pleased to find
An undisturb'd and vacant mind,
With magic pencil traced my brain,
And there she drew St. Patrick's Dean:
I straight beheld on either hand
Two saints, like guardian angels, stand,
And either claim'd him for their son,
And thus the high dispute begun:
St. Andrew, first, with reason strong,
Maintain'd to him he did belong.
"Swift is my own, by right divine,
All born upon this day are mine."
St. Patrick said, "I own this true
So far he does belong to you:
But in my church he's born again,
My son adopted, and my Dean.
When first the Christian truth I spread,
The poor within this isle I fed,
And darkest errors banish'd hence,
Made knowledge in their place commence:
Nay more, at my divine command,
All noxious creatures fled the land.
I made both peace and plenty smile,
Hibernia was my favourite isle;
Now his—for he succeeds to me,
Two angels cannot more agree.
His joy is, to relieve the poor;
Behold them weekly at his door!
His knowledge too, in brightest rays,

He like the sun to all conveys,
Shows wisdom in a single page,
And in one hour instructs an age
When ruin lately stood around
Th'enclosures of my sacred ground,
He gloriously did interpose,
And saved it from invading foes;
For this I claim immortal Swift
As my own son, and Heaven's best gift.
The Caledonian saint, enraged,
Now closer in dispute engaged.
Essays to prove, by transmigration,
The Dean is of the Scottish nation;
And, to confirm the truth, he chose
The loyal soul of great Montrose;
"Montrose and he are both the same,
They only differ in the name:
Both heroes in a righteous cause,
Assert their liberties and laws;
He's now the same Montrose was then,
But that the sword is turn'd a pen,
A pen of so great power, each word
Defends beyond the hero's sword."
Now words grew high—we can't suppose
Immortals ever come to blows,
But lest unruly passion should
Degrade them into flesh and blood,
An angel quick from Heaven descends,
And he at once the contest ends:
"Ye reverend pair, from discord cease,
Ye both mistake the present case;
One kingdom cannot have pretence
To so much virtue! so much sense!
Search Heaven's record; and there you'll find
That he was born for all mankind."

An Epistle to Robert Nugent, Esq.

With a Picture of Dr. Swift. By William Dunkin, D.D.

To gratify thy long desire,
(So love and piety require,)
From Bindon's colours you may trace
The patriot's venerable face.
The last, O Nugent! which his art
Shall ever to the world impart;
For know, the prime of mortal men,
That matchless monarch of the pen,
(Whose labours, like the genial sun,
Shall through revolving ages run,
Yet never, like the sun, decline,
But in their full meridian shine,)
That ever honour'd, envied sage,
So long the wonder of the age,
Who charm'd us with his golden strain,
Is not the shadow of the Dean:
He only breathes Boeotian air—
"O! what a falling off was there!"
Hibernia's Helicon is dry,
Invention, Wit, and Humour die;
And what remains against the storm
Of Malice but an empty form?
The nodding ruins of a pile,
That stood the bulwark of this isle?
In which the sisterhood was fix'd
Of candid Honour, Truth unmix'd,
Imperial Reason, Thought profound,
And Charity, diffusing round
In cheerful rivulets to flow
Of Fortune to the sons of woe?
Such one, my Nugent, was thy Swift,
Endued with each exalted gift,
But lo! the pure ethereal flame
Is darken'd by a misty steam:

The balm exhausted breathes no smell,
The rose is wither'd ere it fell.
That godlike supplement of law,
Which held the wicked world in awe
And could the tide of faction stem,
Is but a shell without the gem.
    Ye sons of genius, who would aim
To build an everlasting fame,
And in the field of letter'd arts,
Display the trophies of your parts,
To yonder mansion turn aside,
And mortify your growing pride.
Behold the brightest of the race,
And Nature's honour, in disgrace:
With humble resignation own,
That all your talents are a loan;
By Providence advanced for use,
Which you should study to produce
Reflect, the mental stock, alas!
However current now it pass,
May haply be recall'd from you
Before the grave demands his due,
Then, while your morning star proceeds,
Direct your course to worthy deeds,
In fuller day discharge your debts;
For, when your sun of reason sets,
The night succeeds; and all your schemes
Of glory vanish with your dreams.
    Ah! where is now the supple train,
That danced attendance on the Dean?
Say, where are those facetious folks,
Who shook with laughter at his jokes,
And with attentive rapture hung,
On wisdom, dropping from his tongue;
Who look'd with high disdainful pride
On all the busy world beside,
And rated his productions more
Than treasures of Peruvian ore?
    Good Christians! they with bended knees

Ingulf'd the wine, but loathe the lees,
Averting, (so the text commands,)
With ardent eyes and upcast hands,
The cup of sorrow from their lips,
And fly, like rats, from sinking ships.
While some, who by his friendship rose
To wealth, in concert with his foes
Run counter to their former track,
Like old Actæon's horrid pack
Of yelling mongrels, in requitals
To riot on their master's vitals;
And, where they cannot blast his laurels,
Attempt to stigmatize his morals;
Through Scandal's magnifying glass
His foibles view, but virtues pass,
And on the ruins of his fame
Erect an ignominious name.
So vermin foul, of vile extraction,
The spawn of dirt and putrefaction,
The sounder members traverse o'er,
But fix and fatten on a sore.
Hence! peace, ye wretches, who revile
His wit, his humour, and his style;
Since all the monsters which he drew
Were only meant to copy you;
And, if the colours be not fainter,
Arraign yourselves, and not the painter.
    But, O! that He, who gave him breath,
Dread arbiter of life and death:
That He, the moving soul of all,
The sleeping spirit would recall,
And crown him with triumphant meeds,
For all his past heroic deeds,
In mansions of unbroken rest,
The bright republic of the bless'd!
Irradiate his benighted mind
With living light of light refined;
And there the blank of thought employ
With objects of immortal joy!

Yet, while he drags the sad remains
Of life, slow-creeping through his veins,
Above the views of private ends,
The tributary Muse attends,
To prop his feeble steps, or shed
The pious tear around his bed.
So pilgrims, with devout complaints,
Frequent the graves of martyr'd saints,
Inscribe their worth in artless lines,
And, in their stead, embrace their shrines.

On the Drapier. By Dr. Dunkin

Undone by fools at home, abroad by knaves,
The isle of saints became the land of slaves,
Trembling beneath her proud oppressor's hand;
But, when thy reason thunder'd through the land,
Then all the public spirit breathed in thee,
And all, except the sons of guilt, were free.
Blest isle, blest patriot, ever glorious strife!
You gave her freedom, as she gave you life!
Thus Cato fought, whom Brutus copied well,
And with those rights for which you stand, he fell.

Epitaph Proposed for Dr. Swift. 1745

Hic Jacet
Democritvs Ille Neotericvs, Rabelaesivs Noster,
Ionathan Swift, S.T.P. Hvivs Cathedralis Nvper
Decanvs;
Momi, Mvsarvm, Minervae, Alvmnvs Perqvam Dilectvs;
Insvlsis, Hypocritis, Theomachis, Ivxta Exosvs;
Qvos Tribvtim Svmmo Cvm Lepore
Derisit, Denvdavit, Debellavit.
Patriae Infelicis Patronvs Impiger, Et Propvgnator
Primores Arripvit, Popvlvmqve Interritvs,
Vni Scilicet Aeqvvs Virtvti.
Hanc Favillam
Si Qvis Ades, Nec Penitvs Excors Videtvr,
Debita Sparges Lacryma.

Epigram on Two Great Men. 1754

Two geniuses one age and nation grace!
Pride of our isles, and boast of human race!
Great sage! great bard! supreme in knowledge born!
The world to mend, enlighten, and adorn.
Truth on Cimmerian darkness pours the day!
Wit drives in smiles the gloom of minds away!
Ye kindred suns on high, ye glorious spheres,
Whom have ye seen, in twice three thousand years,
Whom have ye seen, like these, of mortal birth;
Though Archimede and Horace blest the earth?
Barbarians, from th' Equator to the Poles,
Hark! reason calls! wisdom awakes your souls!
Ye regions, ignorant of Walpole's name;
Ye climes, where kings shall ne'er extend their fame;
Where men, miscall'd, God's image have defaced,
Their form belied, and human shape disgraced!
Ye two-legg'd wolves! slaves! superstition's sons!
Lords! soldiers! holy Vandals! modern Huns!
Boors, mufties, monks; in Russia, Turkey, Spain!
Who does not know Sir Isaac, and The Dean?

To the Memory of Doctor Swift

When wasteful death has closed the Poet's eyes,
And low in earth his mortal essence lies;
When the bright flame, that once his breast inspired,
Has to its first, its noblest seat retired;
All worthy minds, whom love of merit sways,
Should shade from slander his respected bays;
And bid that fame, his useful labours won,
Pure and untainted through all ages run.
  Envy's a fiend all excellence pursues,
But mostly poets favour'd by the Muse;
Who wins the laurel, sacred verse bestows,
Makes all, who fail in like attempts, his foes;
No puny wit of malice can complain,
The thorn is theirs, who most applauses gain.
  Whatever gifts or graces Heaven design'd
To raise man's genius, or enrich his mind,
Were Swift's to boast—alike his merits claim
The statesman's knowledge, and the poet's flame;
The patriot's honour, zealous to defend
His country's rights—and *faithful to the end*;
The sound divine, whose charities display'd
He more by virtue than by forms was sway'd;
Temperate at board, and frugal of his store,
Which he but spared, to make his bounties more:
The generous friend, whose heart alike caress'd,
The friend triumphant, or the friend distress'd;
Who could, unpain'd, another's merit spy,
Nor view a rival's fame with jaundiced eye;
Humane to all, his love was unconfined,
And in its scope embraced all human kind;
Sharp, not malicious, was his charming wit,
And less to anger than reform he writ;
Whatever rancour his productions show'd,
From scorn of vice and folly only flow'd;
He thought that fools were an invidious race,
And held no measures with the vain or base.

Virtue so clear! who labours to destroy,
Shall find the charge can but himself annoy:
The slanderous theft to his own breast recoils,
Who seeks renown from injured merit's spoils;
All hearts unite, and Heaven with man conspires
To guard those virtues she herself admires.
O sacred bard!—once ours!—but now no more,
Whose loss, for ever, Ireland must deplore,
No earthly laurels needs thy happy brow,
Above the poet's are thy honours now:
Above the patriot's, (though a greater name
No temporal monarch for his crown can claim.)
From noble breasts if envy might ensue,
Thy death is all the brave can envy you.
You died, when merit (to its fate resign'd)
Saw scarce one friend to genius left behind,
When shining parts did jealous hatred breed,
And 'twas a crime in science to succeed,
When ignorance spread her hateful mist around,
And dunces only an acceptance found.
What could such scenes in noble minds beget,
But life with pain, and talents with regret?
Add that thy spirit from the world retired,
Ere hidden foes its further grief conspired;
No treacherous friend did stories yet contrive,
To blast the Muse he flatter'd when alive,
Or sordid printer (by his influence led)
Abused the fame that first bestow'd him bread.
Slanders so mean, had he whose nicer ear
Abhorr'd all scandal, but survived to hear,
The fraudful tale had stronger scorn supplied,
And he (at length) with more disdain had died,
But since detraction is the portion here
Of all who virtuous durst, or great, appear,
And the free soul no true existence gains,
While earthly particles its flight restrains,
The greatest favour grimful Death can show,
Is with swift dart to expedite the blow.
So thought the Dean, who, anxious for his fate,

Sigh'd for release, and deem'd the blessing late.
And sure if virtuous souls (life's travail past)
Enjoy (as churchmen teach) repose at last,
There's cause to think, a mind so firmly good,
Who vice so long, and lawless power, withstood,
Has reach'd the limits of that peaceful shore,
Where knaves molest, and tyrants awe, no more;
These blissful seats the pious but attain,
Where incorrupt, immortal spirits reign.
There his own Parnell strikes the living lyre.
And Pope, harmonius, joins the tuneful choir;
His Stella too, (no more to forms confined,
For heavenly beings all are of a kind,)
Unites with his the treasures of her mind,
With warmer friendships bids their bosoms glow,
Nor dreads the rage of vulgar tongues below.
Such pleasing hope the tranquil breast enjoys,
Whose inward peace no conscious crime annoys;
While guilty minds irresolute appear,
And doubt a state their vices needs must fear.

R——T B——N.

Dublin, Nov. 4, 1755.

A Schoolboy's Theme

The following lines were enclosed in a letter from Mr. Pulteney, (afterwards Earl of Bath,) to Swift, in which he says—"You must give me leave to add to my letter a copy of verses at the end of a declamation made by a boy at Westminster school on this theme,—*Ridentem dicere verum quid vetat?*"

Dulce, Decane, decus, flos optime gentis Hibernae
  Nomine quique audis, ingenioque celer:
Dum lepido indulges risu, et mutaris in horas,
  Quò nova vis animi, materiesque rapit?
Nunc gravis astrologus, coelo dominaris et astris,
  Filaque pro libitu Partrigiana secas.
Nunc populo speciosa hospes miracula promis,
  Gentesque aequoreas, aëriasque creas.
Seu plausum captat queruli persona Draperi,
  Seu levis a vacuo tabula sumpta cado.
Mores egregius mira exprimis arte magister,
  Et vitam atque homines pagina quaeque sapit;
Socraticae minor est vis et sapientia chartae,
  Nec tantum potuit grande Platonis opus.

Verses on the Battle of the Books

By Mr. James Sterling, of the County of Meath

While the Dean with more wit than man ever wanted,
Or than Heaven to any man else ever granted,
Endeavours to prove, how the ancients in knowledge
Have excell'd our adepts of each modern college;
How by heroes of old our chiefs are surpass'd
In each useful science, true learning, and taste.
While thus he behaves, with more courage than manners,
And fights for the foe, deserting our banners;
While Bentley and Wotton, our champions, he foils,
And wants neither Temple's assistance, nor Boyle's;
In spite of his learning, fine reasons, and style,
—Would you think it?—he favours our cause all the while:
We raise by his conquest our glory the higher,
And from our defeat to a triumph aspire;
Our great brother-modern, the boast of our days,
Unconscious, has gain'd for our party the bays:
St. James's old authors, so famed on each shelf,
Are vanquish'd by what he has written himself.

On Dr. Swift's Leaving his Estate to Idiots

Swift, wondrous genius, bright intelligence,
Pities the orphan's, idiot's want of sense;
And rich in supernumerary pelf,
Adopts posterity unlike himself.
To one great individual wit's confined!
Such eunuchs never propagate their kind.
Thus nature's prodigies bestow the gifts
Of fortune, their descendants are no Swifts.
When did prime statesman, for a sceptre fit
His ministerial successor beget?
No age, no state, no world, can hope to see
Two Swifts or Walpoles in one family.

On Several Petty Pieces

Lately published against Dean Swift, now Deaf and Infirm

Thy mortal part, ingenious Swift! must die,
Thy fame shall reach beyond mortality!
How puny whirlings joy at thy decline,
Thou darling offspring of the tuneful nine!
The noble *lion* thus, as vigour passes,
The fable tells us, is abused by *asses*.

On Faulkner's Edition of Swift

Ornamented with an Engraving of the Dean, by Vertue.

In a little dark room at the back of his shop,
Where poets and scribes have dined on a chop,
Poor Faulkner sate musing alone thus of late,
"Two volumes are done—it is time for the plate;
Yes, time to be sure;—but on whom shall I call
To express the great Swift in a compass so small?
Faith, *Vertue* shall do it, I'm pleased at the thought,
Be the cost what it will—the copper is bought."
Apollo o'erheard, (who as some people guess,
Had a hand in the work, and corrected the press;)
And pleased, he replied, "Honest George, you are right,
The thought was my own, howsoe'er you came by't.
For though both the wit and the style is my gift,
'Tis Vertue alone can design us a Swift."

Epigram
On Lord Orrery's Remarks on Swift's Life and Writings

A sore disease this scribbling itch is!
    His Lordship, in his Pliny seen,
Turns Madam Pilkington in breeches,
    And now attacks our Patriot Dean.

What! libel his friend when laid in ground:
    Nay, good sir, you may spare your hints,
His parallel at last is found,
    For what he writes George Faulkner prints.

Had Swift provoked to this behaviour,
    Yet after death resentment cools,
Sure his last act bespoke his favour,
    He built an hospital—for fools.

To Doctor Delany

On his Book entitled "Observations on Lord Orrery's Remarks"

Delany, to escape your friend the Dean,
    And prove all false that Orrery had writ,
You kindly own his Gulliver profane,
    Yet make his puns and riddles sterling wit.

But if for wrongs to Swift you would atone,
    And please the world, one way you may succeed,
Collect Boyle's writings and your own,
    And serve them as you served The Deed.

Epigram

On Faulkner's displaying in his shop the Dean's bust in marble, (now placed in the great aisle of St. Patrick's church), while he was publishing Lord Orrery's Remarks.

Faulkner! for once you have some judgment shown,
By representing Swift transform'd to stone;
For could he thy ingratitude have known,
Astonishment itself the work had done!

An Inscription

Intended for a compartment in Dr. Swift's monument, designed by Cunningham, on College Green, Dublin.

Say, to the Drapier's vast unbounded fame,
    What added honours can the sculptor give?
None.—'Tis a sanction from the Drapier's name
    Must bid the sculptor and his marble live.

June 4, 1765.

An Epigram Occasioned by the above Inscription

Which gave the Drapier birth two realms contend;
And each asserts her poet, patriot, friend:
Her mitre jealous Britain may deny;
That loss Iërne's laurel shall supply;
Through life's low vale, she, grateful, gave him bread;
Her vocal stones shall vindicate him dead.

W. B. J. N.

1766.

A Note About the Author

Jonathan Swift (1667–1745) was an Irish poet and satirical writer. When the spread of Catholicism in Ireland became prevalent, Swift moved to England, where he lived and worked as a writer. Due to the controversial nature of his work, Swift often wrote under pseudonyms. In addition to his poetry and satirical prose, Swift also wrote for political pamphlets and since many of his works provided political commentary this was a fitting career stop for Swift. When he returned to Ireland, he was ordained as a priest in the Anglican church. Despite this, his writings stirred controversy about religion and prevented him from advancing in the clergy.

A Note from the Publisher

www.ingramcontent.com/pod-product-compliance
Lightning Source LLC
LaVergne TN
LVHW090428230725
816804LV00022B/758
* 9 7 8 1 5 1 3 2 7 0 2 8 9 *